Healthy Highways
The Traveler's Guide to Healthy Eating

Nikki & David Goldbeck

CERES PRESS
WOODSTOCK, NY

About the Cover: On the left is David Lewis biking. At this writing, David is in the Peace Corps in Ecuador. We think of him as the future. Representing our history is hiker Beatrice Trum Hunter, a courageous food activist whom we consider our mentor. After more than four decades of alerting the public, she continues to write on food and environmental issues. In the car, your guides for this adventure, Nikki and David Goldbeck.

Cover Concept: David Goldbeck
Cover Design: Naomi Schmidt www.naomigraphics.com
Cover Illustrations: Jeff Mandel www. http://caricature.com/
Interior Layout: Nikki Goldbeck, Teal Hutton, Naomi Schmidt
"Eat It or Not" Illustrations: Durga Bernhard www.durgabernhard.com

CERES PRESS
PO Box 87
Woodstock, NY 12498
Ceres Press Catalog: www.CeresPress.com
Healthy Highways website: www.HealthyHighways.com
Phone/Fax 845-679-5573 Email Cem620@aol.com
Copyright © 2004 Nikki & David Goldbeck
Printed in Canada on recycled paper with vegetable oil-based ink

Library of Congress Control Number (LCCNS) 2004090025
Library of Congress CIP Data by Amy Booth Raff
Goldbeck, Nikki and David.
    Healthy highways : the traveler's guide to healthy eating /
Nikki & David Goldbeck.
275 p. : maps, 21 cm.
ISBN 1-886101-10-8
1. Natural food restaurants—United States—Guidebooks. 2.
Vegetarian restaurants-United States-Directories. I. Title.
"1900 Eateries & Natural Food Stores with Directions." –Cover
641.302
TX907.2 G64 2004

Other Books by Nikki & David Goldbeck

*Cooking What Comes Naturally**
The Supermarket Handbook
The Dieters' Companion
Nikki & David Goldbeck's American Wholefoods Cuisine
Goldbecks' Guide to Good Food
*The Smart Kitchen***
The Good Breakfast Book
Choose to Reuse
The Healthiest Diet in the World
Eat Well the YoChee Way

* Nikki Goldbeck, sole author ** David Goldbeck, sole author

CONTENTS

Introduction v

The Real Price of Fast Food vii

Symbols & Descriptions viii

Alabama 1
Alaska 4
Arizona 7
Arkansas 14
California 16
Colorado 68
Connecticut 78
Delaware 85
District of Colombia 87
Florida 90
Georgia 114
Hawaii 122
Idaho 127
Illinois 130
Indiana 140
Iowa 146
Kansas 150
Kentucky 154
Louisiana 157
Maine 160
Maryland 166
Massachusetts 174
Michigan 188
Minnesota 198
Mississippi 208
Missouri 210

Montana 216
Nebraska 220
Nevada 223
New Hampshire 225
New Jersey 230
New Mexico 243
New York 248
North Carolina 284
North Dakota 294
Ohio 296
Oklahoma 308
Oregon 310
Pennsylvania 226
Rhode Island 341
South Carolina 344
South Dakota 348
Tennessee 350
Texas 354
Utah 366
Vermont 371
Virginia 378
Washington 390
West Virginia 402
Wisconsin 406
Wyoming 413

Eating On and Off the Healthy Highway 415
Resources 421

Acknowledgements

Many thanks to these folks for their contributions or inspiration. Scott Anderson, Tina Bromberg, Evan Cohen, Jonathan Delson, Bill Hicks, Cathy Lewis, Deborah McMenemy, Barry Samuels, Richard Segalman, Rudy Schur, Dar Williams, Elizabeth Zippern. And above and beyond, Susan Goldman and Sandy King,

Healthy Highways Tripsters

These wonderful volunteers provided comments for some of the venues. The initials that appear below following their names are used in the listings to indicate their contributions. If you would like to be a "HH Tripster," visit www.HealthyHighways.com or send a letter or fax with your two- or three-line comment, experience or observation to the address or fax number on the copyright page. For new listings, please follow the format in the book. Make sure you include email and/or phone number and the initials you would like used.

- •Lee Alexander (LA)
- •Jeremy Black (JB)
- •Lenore & Joe Baum (L&JB)
- •Mark & Barbara Cane (M&BC)
- •Peter Desberg (PD)
- •Mark Edmiston (ME)
- •Carolyn Felton (CF)
- •Jeffrey Fulvimari (JF)
- •Richard Goldman (RG)
- •Susan & Dick Goldman (S&DG)
- •David Madison (DLM)
- •Julie Mathis (JM)
- •Leslie Pardue (LP)
- •Barbara Rothberg (BR)
- •Nancy Rumbel (NR)
- •Rudy Shur (RS)
- •Gary Stern (GS)
- •Roberta Wall (RW)
- •Ruth Wilf (RTW)

Call Ahead.

We suggest you call first if possible before visiting a location. Stores and restaurants have a habit of moving (and closing), and hours, services, etc. change more often than you might expect.

INTRODUCTION

Welcome to *Healthy Highways*, a unique guide for anyone who wants to eat healthfully, particularly while away from home. With this resource, you aren't restricted to chance roadside eateries and highway rest stops, but instead can make informed, planned choices as to where to find a nourishing meal or snack, or restock your cooler. *Healthy Highways* offers real alternatives to the stock fare of supersized, fatty, calorie-laden, repetitious, fast food and restaurant meals. Moreover, it provides an opportunity to explore new territory, as you take the healthy highway rather than the fast food lane.

Healthy Highways features more than 1,900 health food stores, food co-ops and health-oriented restaurants throughout the U.S.A. Each entry includes address, phone number and hours of operation, and is keyed to such details as organic produce, freshly prepared food, salad or juice bar, deli, bakery, vegetarian and vegan friendly, organic focus, kosher, alcohol, handicap access, chain, co-op, and type of service.

Most important, with *Healthy Highways* you can easily find upcoming locations and plan refreshment stops by using the keyed maps found at the beginning of every state chapter. Once you have selected your stop, the local directions, included with each listing, guide you from the nearest highway or main road.

This guide is designed with motorists, bikers and hikers in mind. It will, of course, be useful to everyone who is concerned about their health, weight, is a vegetarian or vegan—even if they aren't venturing far from home.

Types of Listings

Natural food stores. In order to qualify for a listing, natural food stores must have a good selection of groceries. We have also noted when stores offer freshly prepared food and a place to sit and enjoy it.

Eateries. All of the eating places listed provide a reasonable selection of vegetarian options and serve freshly prepared food using a minimum of processed ingredients. We also highlight those that emphasize wholefoods cooking, pay attention to organic or locally grown ingredients, or cater to vegans. Restaurants noted as vegan are done so according to their own description. Some dishes in these restaurants may not meet strict vegan standards, since they may contain whey, casein, honey or sugar. This is often the case with some soy cheeses and baked items or where imitation meat is served.

You will also notice some listings described as "Certified Green Restaurants." These establishments meet the Green Restaurant Association's standards for an ecologically sustainable restaurant industry (see Resources).

In general, restaurants serving ethnic cuisines that traditionally include vegetarian options (Indian, Mexican, Middle Eastern, Asian, etc.) are not listed. There are simply too many of them. However, we do list those that are exclusively vegetarian, surpass the usual expectations in terms of meat-free or wholefoods choices, or have an organic focus.

Road Maps & Driving Directions Guide You to Local Options

We have done our best to provide concise and accurate directions. However, there are often different ways to arrive at the same place, as well as various possible points of origin. Many of the directions were furnished by the establishments themselves; others were culled from online and telephone research. If you have ever asked for (or given) a driving route, you know that furnishing good directions is almost an art. Likewise, online routing is not always the most direct or reliable. Hopefully, you won't encounter any errors, but if you think you may be lost (or even confused), we suggest you call.

The maps that appear at the beginning of each state chapter orient you in relation to cities and towns that have *Healthy Highways* listings. We have attempted to place the arrows as accurately as possible, but these are not designed to be road maps.

More than Food

Thanks to the owners and staff of many establishments who answered our questionnaire, *Healthy Highways* occasionally mentions local attractions you might otherwise miss. They include lesser known natural phenomena, campsites, museums, hiking and biking areas, local shopping opportunities, and assorted quirky entertainment options.

Become a "HH Tripster" and Help *Healthy Highways* Grow

We invite you to become a "HH Tripster" and help make *Healthy Highways* grow. It is our intention to keep this guide up to date and to see it expand. You can lend a hand via our website at www.HealthyHighways.com or by writing or faxing us (see details on the copyright page). Join our merry band of HH Tripsters and you will be listed in each new edition.

Bon Appetit!

We have been fortunate, to borrow from Napoleon, to have "traveled on our stomachs." We have ventured throughout the U.S. and many other parts of the world in search of healthful and interesting cuisines. And we have returned to share our culinary experiences in our cookbooks and other writings. While there are many important health, social and environmental problems relating to diet, our search for solutions has always included the delight food gives, along with the sustenance. Although we have not visited all the establishments listed in *Healthy Highways* (yet!), it gives us great joy knowing that you will.

Happy Trails,

Nikki & David Goldbeck

THE REAL PRICE OF FAST FOOD

- Americans are eating out more than ever. Approximately 30 percent of the population eats at least one meal away from home daily—an increase of more than two-thirds over the past two decades.
- Approximately 22 percent of snacking takes place outside the home.
- The U.S. Centers for Disease Control and Prevention (CDC) estimates that about six out of ten Americans are either overweight or obese. Furthermore, the prevalence of obesity has almost doubled, going from about 15 percent in 1980 to 27 percent in 1999.
- A Rand Corp. study found that from 1986 to 2000, the number of severely obese Americans quadrupled, going from one in 200 to one in 50.
- The 1999-2000 CDC data claims 15 percent of 6- to 19-year-olds are overweight, almost triple the number from 1980.
- Children's fast food consumption has increased five-fold since 1970.
- One in every three children in the U.S. eats a fast food meal every day. This includes boys and girls from all regions of the country and different socio-economic levels.
- Not surprisingly, young fast food lovers consumed more fats, sugars and carbohydrates, and fewer fruits and non-starchy vegetables than youngsters who didn't eat fast food. These children consume, on average, an additional 187 calories daily. This translates into an additional six pounds a year in excess body weight.
- Type II diabetes, once dubbed adult-onset because it was only adults who got it, is now afflicting youngsters.

According to Dr. J. Michael McGinnis, senior vice president of The Robert Wood Johnson Foundation's health group:

The sheer availability of food has led people to graze throughout the day on foods that are largely nutrient-poor and calorie-rich.

People are also less likely to cook for themselves these days. Now roughly half of [all] meals are consumed outside the home and a substantial share of those are from fast foods.

...fast food marketing often portrays big portions as a bargain. But a supersize soft drink can contain as many as 800 calories, which is about a third of the daily caloric requirement of a large man.

We may be raising the first generation of children that is sicker and dies younger than their parents.

Stephen H. Webb, professor of religion and philosophy at Wabash College doesn't mince words:

"Fast food, in fact, is slow murder. Nobody has proved that doughnuts are addictive, but our fast-food culture is as dangerous as an under-age driver with a six-pack or a middle-aged man with a carton of smokes. Of course, food does not really kill. Only people do. But the abundance of unhealthy food in our nation makes healthy eating almost impossible."

SYMBOLS & DESCRIPTIONS

The symbols and standard list of features we used are explained below. Because not all establishments responded in full to our questionnaire, some details will inevitably be missing.

🐑 natural food store

✗ restaurant

✗ 🐑 natural food store with an eating area

♿ handicap accessible restrooms

🚫 no credit cards accepted

alcohol indicates beer, wine and/or hard liquor is served.

bakery denotes baked goods made on site.

café signifies an eating area. Most often used in natural food store listings or combination juice bar/cafés.

chain and **co-op** refer to ownership.

counter and **tables** refer to seating options.

deli implies a display case with freshly made food.

freshly prepared foods is reserved for natural food stores that make food on the premises. This attribute is implied for restaurants.

juice bar signifies that fresh juice is made on the premises.

kosher is for kitchens that have been so certified.

organic focus means a significant portion of the menu incorporates organic ingredients.

organic produce is noted where we have been able to verify a reasonable selection. These stores may also sell conventional produce. Other stores may sell organic produce but haven't made us aware of it.

salad bar is just what it says.

self-service includes buffets, cafeterias, salad bars, and venues where orders are placed at the counter (even if the food is brought to your table).

take-out is available in many restaurants. It is noted when we know it to be a significant feature.

vegan means no animal products at all are served.

vegan-friendly signifies attention to providing animal-free choices.

vegetarian means no animal flesh is served.

vegetarian-friendly signifies fish, poultry or meat may also be served.

wait staff denotes full table service. When both **self-service** and **wait staff** appear, orders are taken at the table and there is also either a buffet or salad bar option.

Editorial note regarding the use of periods. Fussy readers please note that to save space we did not use periods in the following abbreviations, except in addresses: Days of the week, Ave, Blvd, Bus (business route), Ctr, Dr, Ln, Pkwy, Rd, Rt, St, and NESW.

ALABAMA

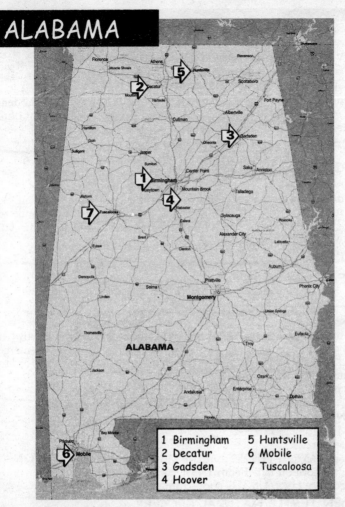

1 Birmingham
2 Decatur
3 Gadsden
4 Hoover
5 Huntsville
6 Mobile
7 Tuscaloosa

BIRMINGHAM

B & C NUTRITION 🥩
1615 Montgomery Hwy. ℰ 205-979-8307 ⊘ M-F 10-6:30, Sat 10-5
· organic produce · bakery

📅 **From I-35**, take exit 252 onto Hwy 31S about 1 mile to store on left in Hoover Commons strip mall (between Books-A-Million and music store).

GOLDEN TEMPLE NATURAL GROCERY & CAFE 🍴🥩   ♿
1901 11th Ave. S. ℰ 205-933-8933 ⊘ Store M-F 11:30-6:15, Sat 9:30-5:30,
Sun 12-5:30, Cafe M-F 11:30-6:15, Sat 12-2:30
The food is vegetarian and lunch is free the last Saturday of every month.
· organic produce · freshly prepared food · juice bar · café · vegetarian · counter · tables
· self-service · take-out

📅 **From I-65N**, take exit 259 right onto University Ave about 1 mile to 19th St. Turn right onto 19th 3 blocks to store on corner 19th & 11th Ave. **From I-65S**, take exit 259B onto 4th Ave about ¾ mile to 19th.

Turn right onto 19th 7 blocks to store at 19th & 11th.

THE GREEN DOOR 🍏
2843 Culver Rd. © 205-871-2651 ⊘ M-F 9:30-5:30, Sat 10-5

🍎 **From I-59**, take exit 126A onto US 31E/280E toward Zoo-Gardens about ½ mile. Take ramp toward Mountain Brook and turn right onto Culver Rd less than ¼ mile to store.

DECATUR_____

GLORIA'S GOOD HEALTH 🍏
1820 6th Ave. S.E. © 256-355-2439 ⊘ M-F 10-6, Sat 10-5

🍎 **From I-65N**, take exit 334 toward Decatur onto AL 67N about 4½ miles to 6th Ave (US 31N). Turn right onto 6th more than 1 mile to store. **From I-65S** exit 340A or **I-565W**, take AL 20 W (becomes 6th Ave) over 7 miles to store.

GADSDEN_____

APPLE-A-DAY 🍏
280 N. 3rd St. © 256-546-8458 ⊘ M-Th 9-6, F-Sat 9-8, Sun 12:30-6
A natural food store in a conventional grocery.
· organic produce

🍎 **From I-59**, take exit 182 onto I-759E about 5 miles to exit 4B (Rt 411N) toward Gasden. Take 411N about 2 miles and turn left to merge onto US 278W/W Meighan Blvd ¼ mile to 3rd St. Turn left onto 3rd to store in Midtown Plaza (inside Foodmax).

HOOVER_____

B&C NUTRITION 🍏
1615 Montgomery Hwy. © 205-979-8307 ⊘ M-F 10-6:30, Sat 10-5
· organic produce

🍎 **From I-65**, take exit 252 south on Montgomery Hwy (US 31S) about 1 mile to store on left. **From I-459**, take exit 13 toward Hoover onto Montgomery Hwy/US 31N about 1 mile to store on right.

GOLDEN TEMPLE NATURAL GROCERY 🍏
3309 Lorna Rd. © 205-823-7002 ⊘ M-F 10-6:30, Sat 10-6
· organic produce

🍎 **From I-65S**, take exit 252 onto Montgomery Hwy (US 31S) about 1¼ miles to Patton Chapel Rd. Turn left onto Patton Chapel about ½ mile to Lorna Rd. Turn right onto Lorna to store on left. **From I-65N**, take exit 250 onto I-459S toward Hoover about 1½ miles to exit 13 (Montgomery Hwy/ US 31). **From I-459 exit 13**, take US 31N about 1 mile to Patton Chapel. Turn right onto Patton Chapel about ½ mile to Lorna. Turn right onto Lorna to store on left.

HUNTSVILLE_____

EDEN'S DELICACIES ✗
2413 Jordan Lane N.W. © 256-721-9491 ⊘ M-Th 11-6, F 11-3
The daily menu features a selection of vegan entrees and side dishes with a West Indian/Soul Food character, plus a salad bar. Run by members of the Seventh-day Adventist Church.

· juice bar · salad bar · vegan · tables · self-service · wait staff

From I-565E, take exit 17A left onto Jordan Ln about 2²/₃ miles to restaurant on left (between Oakwood Ave & Sparkman Dr). **From I-565W**, take exit 19A toward Downtown right onto Washington St 1 block to Pratt Ave. Turn left onto Pratt (becomes University Dr) about 1¼ miles to Jordan. Turn right onto Jordan about 1½ miles to restaurant on left.

GARDEN COVE PRODUCE CENTER

628 Meridian St. © 256-534-2683 ⊙ M-Tues 10-7, W 10-6, Th 9-7, F 9-3, Sun 12-5

· organic produce · juice bar

From I-565E, take exit 19C (Washington St/Jefferson St) toward Downtown. Merge onto Washington St NW to Pratt Ave NW. Turn right onto Pratt about ¼ mile to Meridian St. Turn right onto Meridian to store just off corner. **From I-565W**, take exit 19B toward Washington St N and make sharp left onto Pratt less than ¼ mile to Meridian. Turn right onto Meridian to store just off corner.

PEARLY GATES NATURAL FOODS, INC.

2308 Memorial Pkwy. S. © 256-534-6233 ⊙ M-Sat 10-6:30

· freshly prepared food · deli · vegetarian friendly · tables · self-service · take-out

From I-565E, take exit 19A onto Memorial Pkwy/Hwy 231S almost 1½ miles to store on right. **From I-565W**, take exit 19B onto Memorial Pkwy/Hwy 231S almost 2²/₃ miles to store on right.

VEGGIE FACTORY

3620 Governor's Dr. © 256-534-0109 ⊙ M-Th 11-6, F 11-3
Southern-style cooking done vegan (mock fried chicken, mashed potatoes, collard greens, corn bread). Take-out only.

· freshly prepared food · vegan · take-out

From I-565E, take exit 17B onto Governor's Dr about ¾ mile to store. **From I-565W**, take exit 17 left onto Jordan Ln and follow ramp on left onto Governor's ¾ mile to store.

MOBILE

ORGANIC FOODS INC.

444B Azalea Rd. © 251-342-9554 ⊙ M-F 10-6

From I-65, take exit 3B and follow ramp right onto Airport Blvd (CR 56W) about 1 mile to Azalea Rd/McGregor Rd intersection. Turn left onto Azalea to store on right. **From I-65N**, take exit 3A left onto Airport Blvd about 1¹/₃ miles and follow directions above.

TUSCALOOSA

MANNA GROCERY NATURAL GOURMET & ETHNIC FOODS

2300 McFarland Blvd. #12 © 205-752-9955 ⊙ Daily 9-7

· organic produce · freshly prepared food · deli · vegetarian friendly · tables · self-service · take-out

From I-20/59, take exit 73 onto US 82W/McFarland Blvd E (right from 20W/59S, left from 20E/59N) about 1 mile to store on left in Meadowbrook Shopping Center (across from Snow Hinton Park).

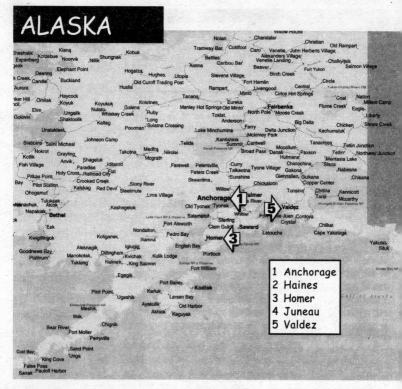

ALASKA

1 Anchorage
2 Haines
3 Homer
4 Juneau
5 Valdez

ANCHORAGE

JENS' RESTAURANT ✕
701 W. 36th Ave. ✆ 907-561-5367 ☺ Tues-Sat 6-10
The menu is mostly meat and fish, but there is a raw menu daily at dinner.
· vegetarian friendly · alcohol · tables · wait staff
🍎 **From Seward Hwy** (Rt 1), go west on Tudor Rd about ¼ mile to Old Seward Hwy. Turn right onto Old Seward Hwy ½ mile to 36th Ave. Turn left onto 36th about 1 mile to Olympic Center. Turn right into Olympic Center to restaurant at end (next to Scanhome).

MIDDLEWAY CAFE ✕
1200 W. Northern Lights Blvd. ✆ 907-272-6433 ☺ Daily Coffee/Baked goods 7-6:30, Juice bar 8:30-4:30, Kitchen 10:30-4:30
The emphasis is on healthy food, including whole grains and some organic ingredients. Good choices for vegetarians and vegans, but also poultry and fish.
· juice bar · vegetarian friendly · vegan friendly · tables · self-service
🍎 **From Seward Hwy** (Rt 1), take Northern Lights Blvd exit west about 1¼ miles to restaurant.

NATURAL PANTRY 🛒
3801 Old Seward Hwy. ✆ 907-770-1444 ☺ M-Sat 9-9
· organic produce · freshly prepared food · café · vegetarian friendly · tables · self-service · take-out
🍎 **From Seward Hwy** (Rt 1), take E Tudor Rd exit west about ¼ mile to Old Seward Hwy. Turn right onto Old Seward less than ½ mile to store at Telephone Ave.

ORGANIC OASIS RESTAURANT & JUICE BAR ✕

2610 Spenard Rd. © 907-277-7882 ⊙ M 11:30-7, Tues 11:30-10:30, W-Th 11:30-9, F-Sat 11:30-10

Free-range meat, homemade organic pizza dough and always a vegan soup .

· vegetarian friendly · organic focus · alcohol · tables · wait staff

▢ **From Seward Hwy** (Rt 1), take Northern Lights Blvd exit west about 1¼ miles to Spenard Rd. Turn right onto Spenard to restaurant at 26th Ave.

SNOW CITY CAFE ✕

1034 W. 4th Ave. © 907-272-2489 ⊙ Daily 7-4

Not a natural foods restaurant, but ample vegetarian and vegan offerings (homemade soup, all-day breakfast with homemade granola, real oatmeal and tofu scramble) to feed health-conscious travelers. No dinner, but Wednesday and Sunday evenings there's free live music at 7 and light fare is available.

· vegetarian friendly · vegan friendly · alcohol · counter · tables · wait staff · take-out

▢ **From south of Anchorage**, take Seward Hwy (Rt 1N) to 5th Ave. Turn left onto 5th about 1 mile to K St. Turn right onto K and left onto 4th Ave to restaurant on left between K & L St. **From north of Anchorage**, take Glenn Hwy west (becomes 5th Ave) to K St and follow directions above.

HAINES

Haines sits at the base of 2 huge mountain ranges and overlooks the Lynn Canal.

MOUNTAIN MARKET & CAFE ✕ 🍎

151 3rd Ave. S. © 907-766-3340 ⊙ M-F 7-7, Sat-Sun 7-6

Fresh vegetarian soups and hot specials, along with a few nonvegetarian selections.

· organic produce · freshly prepared food · café · deli · bakery · vegetarian friendly · counter · tables · self-service · take-out

▢ Haines Hwy is the only road to town from the Canadian Border. Store is at corner 3rd Ave & Haines, 1 block off Main St.

HOMER

Come see brown bears, whales, glaciers or for world class halibut and salmon fishing.

FRESH SOURDOUGH EXPRESS BAKERY & CAFE ✕   ♿

1316 Ocean Drive © 907-235-7571 ⊙ Daily Summer 7-9, Off-season 8-3

Alaskan seafood predominates, but there's also tofu, black beans, reindeer sausage, and buffalo burgers, along with more conventional fare. Breakfast includes homemade granola and hot mush. Baked goods are made with organic grains ground on site, and the cocoa, chocolate and coffee are organic. Box lunches available for charters. (If you need a place to stay, ask about their B&B, which includes a complementary meal at the cafe for Healthy Highway travelers.)

· bakery · vegetarian friendly · organic focus · alcohol · tables · wait staff · take-out

▢ The Seward Hwy from Anchorage becomes the Sterling Hwy on the lower penninsula and runs into Homer, where it becomes the Bypass and then Ocean Dr. Restaurant is on Ocean (look for kelly green van, flower gardens and sandbox full of toys for the kids).

SMOKY BAY NATURAL FOODS 🛒
248 W. Pioneer Ave. © 907-235-7252 ⊙ M-F 9-7, Sat 10-6
· organic produce · freshly prepared food · deli · take-out

📖 **From Sterling Hwy (AK 1)**, go north (inland) on Pioneer Ave about ¼ mile to store (in bright yellow bldg).

JUNEAU

FIDDLEHEAD RESTAURANT & BAKERY ✖
429 W. Willoughby Ave. © 907-586-3150 ⊙ Summer Daily 7-10, Off-season M-F 7-9, Sat-Sun 8-9

From tofu, brown rice, granola pancakes, vegetarian French Onion Soup, bean burgers, and Alaskan seafood, to bacon and eggs, ribeye steak, Italian sausage, and meatloaf with cheese. NR: Friendly spot with great food, and up in Alaska that isn't always the easiest thing to find!

· bakery · vegetarian friendly · tables · wait staff

📖 **From ferry terminal**, take Glacier Hwy (AK 7) east about 12½ miles to Glacier Ave. Turn left (inland) onto Glacier and take 1st right onto W Willoughby Ave to restaurant.

RAINBOW FOODS ✖🛒
224 4th St. © 907-586-6476 ⊙ M-F 9-7, Sat 10-6, Sun 12-6

All-organic deli serves soups, salads, sandwiches, and 2 hot items daily.

· organic produce · freshly prepared food · deli · vegetarian friendly · organic focus
· tables · self-service · take-out

📖 **From Glacier Hwy (AK 7)**, go inland on Main St 4 blocks to 4th St. Turn right onto 4th 2 blocks to store at corner 4th & Franklin Ave.

VALDEZ

Majestic mountains on three sides, Prince William Sound on the fourth. Back country skiing, snowshoeing, sea kayaking, wilderness camping, bird-viewing (look for bald eagles), fresh and saltwater fly fishing, and much more. Welcome to Alaska!

A ROGUES GARDEN 🛒
354 Fairbanks Drive © 907-835-5880 ⊙ M-F 10-6:30, Sat 11-5

· organic produce · juice bar · take-out

📖 At the southern tip of Richardson Hwy turn right onto Hazelet Ave. Take next right onto Fairbanks Dr to store.

Goldbeck's **"EAT IT OR NOT"**

FASCINATING & FAR-OUT FACTS ABOUT FOOD

TRUE OR FALSE?

Saltwater fish have more than twice the sodium content of freshwater fish.

False The sodium content is the same.

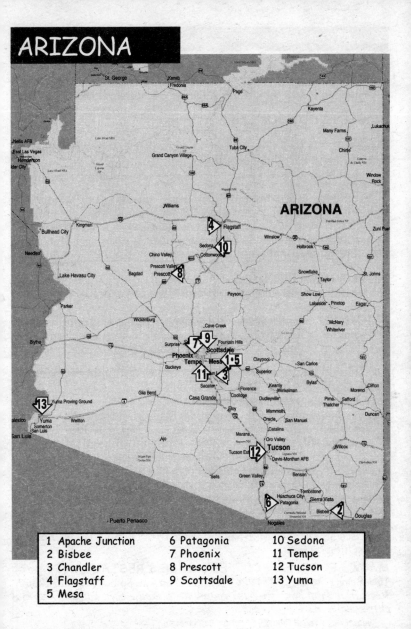

ARIZONA

1	Apache Junction	6	Patagonia
2	Bisbee	7	Phoenix
3	Chandler	8	Prescott
4	Flagstaff	9	Scottsdale
5	Mesa		

10	Sedona
11	Tempe
12	Tucson
13	Yuma

APACHE JUNCTION

THE GOOD APPLE NATURAL MARKET
100 N. Plaza Drive ✆ 480-982-2239 ☺ M-Sat 8-8, Sun 11-5

· organic produce

🍽 **From Hwy 60**, take exit 195 north on Ironwood Drive (left from 60E, right from 60W) about 2½ miles to 3rd traffic light at Apache Trail. Turn right onto Apache Trail (aka Main St). Stay left and turn left at 1st light to continue on Apache Trail to store in plaza on left (with Basha's Grocery).

BISBEE

An old mining town just 5 miles from the Mexican border and a hub for local arts and crafts. Bird watchers come for the hummingbirds.

BISBEE FOOD COOP ✂ 🍴   &

72 Erie St. © 520-432-4011 ⊙ M-Sat 9-7, Sun 10-5
Restaurant/deli features vegetarian and vegan soups, sandwiches, salads, and more. Strives to use organic ingredients.

· organic produce · freshly prepared food · café · deli · vegetarian · vegan friendly
· organic focus · co-op · tables · self-service · take-out

👜 **From Hwy 80**, go through Old Bisbee to end of copper pit. Store is on right in Lowell Plaza. **From Hwy 92** (from Sierra Vista), go through traffic circle, turn left at Chevron Station and go under overpass to store in Lowell Plaza.

COTTONWOOD

MOUNT HOPE FOODS 🍴

853 S. Main St. © 928-634-8251 ⊙ M-Sat 9-7, Sun 10-5

· organic produce

👜 **From I-17**, take exit 287 toward AZ 89A/Cottonwood north onto 260 (left from 1-17N, right from I-17S) about 11 miles to intersection with 89A. Turn left and continue on 260 (aka S Main St) about 1½ miles to store on right.

FLAGSTAFF

CAFE ESPRESS ✂

16 N. San Francisco St. © 928-774-0541 ⊙ Daily 7-5
A large selection of vegetarian choices, but plenty of meat as well.

· vegetarian friendly · alcohol · counter · tables · wait staff · take-out

👜 **From I-17N**, merge onto AZ 89A (Milton Rd) about 1¾ miles and continue right on 40Bus about ¼ mile to San Francisco St. Turn left onto San Francisco to restaurant ½ block north of train station on right. **From I-40E**, take exit 195 toward AZ 89A/Flagstaff onto I-17N and follow directions above. **From I-40W**, take exit 198 toward Flagstaff right onto Butler Ave ¼ mile to Enterprise Rd. Turn right onto Enterprise about ¼ mile to S Santa Fe Ave (40Bus). Turn left onto Santa Fe about 1¼ miles to San Francisco St. Turn left onto San Francisco to restaurant ½ block north of train station on right.

MACY'S EUROPEAN COFFEE HOUSE & RESTAURANT ✂   🥖

14 S. Beaver St. © 928-774-2243 ⊙ M-Th, Sun 6am-8pm, F-Sat 6am-10pm
Vegetarian (and largely vegan) soups, salads, sandwiches, and 4 to 6 special entrees daily. Also, vegan baked goods.

· vegetarian · vegan friendly · tables · self-service

👜 **From I-17N**, merge onto AZ 89A (Milton Rd) about 1¾ miles and continue right on I-40Bus less than ¼ mile to Beaver St. Turn right onto Beaver ½ block to restaurant. **From I-40E**, take exit 195 toward AZ 89A/Flagstaff onto I-17N and follow directions above. **From I-40W**, take exit 198 toward Flagstaff right onto Butler Ave ¼ mile to Enterprise Rd. Turn right onto Enterprise about ¼ mile to S Santa Fe Ave (40Bus). Turn left onto Santa Fe about 1¼ miles to Beaver. Turn left onto Beaver ½ block to restaurant.

MOUNTAIN HARVEST ✕ 🍎

6 W. Phoenix Ave. ℰ 928-779-9456 ⏰ M-F 8-8, Sat-Sun 8-7

· organic produce · freshly prepared food · juice bar · deli · vegetarian friendly · tables
· self-service · take-out

🍎 **From I-17N**, merge onto AZ 89A (Milton Rd) about 1⅔ miles to W Phoenix Ave. Turn right onto Phoenix less than ¼ mile to store between Beaver & San Francisco St. **From I-40E**, take exit 195 toward AZ 89A/Flagstaff onto I-17N and follow directions above. **From I-40W**, take exit 198 toward Flagstaff right onto Butler Ave ¼ mile to Enterprise Rd. Turn right onto Enterprise about ¼ mile to S Santa Fe Ave (40Bus). Turn left onto Santa Fe about 1¼ miles to Beaver. Turn left onto Beaver across tracks to Phoenix. Turn left onto Phoenix to store.

NEW FRONTIERS NATURAL MARKETPLACE ✕ 🍎   ♿

1000 S. Milton Rd. ℰ 928-774-5747 ⏰ M-Sat 8-8, Sun 10-8

· organic produce · freshly prepared food · deli · bakery · vegetarian friendly · chain
· tables · self-service · take-out

🍎 **From I-40**, take exit 195 toward AZ 89A/Flagstaff and merge onto I-17N. **From I-17N**, merge onto AZ 89A (Milton Rd) about 1 mile to store.

MESA

C'S & J'S HEALTH SHOPPE 🍎

2665 E. Broadway #107 ℰ 480-649-6145 ⏰ M-F 9-7, Sat 9-6

🍎 **From I-10**, take Superstition Fwy (Hwy 60) east to exit 182. Go north on Gilbert Rd (left from 60E, right from 60W) about 1½ miles to Broadway. Turn right onto Broadway about 1 mile (over canal) to store on SW corner Lindsey Rd & Broadway (in middle of strip mall).

PATAGONIA

RED MOUNTAIN FOODS 🍎

376 Naugle Ave. ℰ 520-394-2786 ⏰ W-Sat 9-6 (Closed July & August)

· organic produce

🍎 Take Hwy 82 to Patagonia. Store is near corner Naugle Ave (82) & 4th Ave.

TREE OF LIFE CAFE ✕   ♿

771 Harshaw Rd. ℰ 520-394-2520 ⏰ M-F 8am-9am, 1pm-2pm, dinner hours vary, Sat-Sun 10:30-noon

Part of the Tree of Life Foundation eco-retreat and holistic health center, set on 166 acres where you can hike, meditate, take classes, or simply "be." Come stay or just to enjoy the raw, organic, vegan food. Reservations required for the cafe.

· vegan · kosher · alcohol · tables · self-service

🍎 Take Hwy 82 into Patagonia. Once there, turn onto 3rd Ave (2nd left past high school) 1 block to stop sign at McKeown. Turn left onto McKeown (bends right and becomes Harshaw Rd) just under 1 mile to Tree of Life Center on right (short, pink stucco walls and sign mark entrance). Turn right onto center grounds and continue up hill to dark pink stucco cafe.

PHOENIX

SUPREME MASTER CHING HAI VEGETARIAN HOUSE ✕
3239 E. Indian School Rd. © 602-264-3480 ⊙ Tues-Sat 11-2:30, 5-9
Chinese Buddhist vegetarian cooking.

· vegetarian · vegan friendly · tables · wait staff · take-out

🗇 **From I-10**, take exit 147 (147B from 10E) onto AZ 51N less than 2½ miles to exit 3 (Indian School Rd). Turn right onto Indian School about 1¾ miles to restaurant at 32nd St. **From I-17**, take exit 202 toward Indian School onto Black Canyon Hwy to Indian School. Turn east onto Indian School (left from 17S, right from 17N) less than 6 miles to restaurant.

WHOLE FOODS MARKET ✕ 🍲   ♿
10810 N. Tatum Blvd. © 602-569-7600 ⊙ Daily 8-10

· organic produce · freshly prepared food · salad bar · café · deli · bakery · vegetarian friendly · chain · counter · tables · self-service · take-out

🗇 **From north of Phoenix on I-17S**, take exit 215 on left onto AZ 101 Loop E about 7¼ miles to exit 31. Merge right onto N Tatum Blvd about 6½ miles to store. **From 101 Loop N**, take exit 41 west on Shea Blvd 5 miles to N Tatum. Turn right onto N Tatum to store.

WILD OATS MARKET ✕ 🍲   ♿
13823 N. Tatum Blvd. © 602-953-7546 ⊙ Daily 7-11

· organic produce · freshly prepared food · juice bar · salad bar · café · deli · bakery · vegetarian friendly · chain · tables · self-service · take-out

🗇 **From I-17S**, take exit 215 on left onto AZ 101 Loop E about 7¼ miles to exit 31. Merge right onto N Tatum Blvd about 4 miles to store. **From I-10**, take exit 147 onto AZ 51N about 10 miles to exit 10. Take Cactus Rd E ramp right onto Cactus ⅔ miles to Tatum. Turn left onto Tatum 1 mile to store.

WILD OATS MARKET ✕ 🍲   ♿
3933 E. Camelback Rd. © 602-954-0584 ⊙ Daily 7-10

· organic produce · freshly prepared food · juice bar · salad bar · café · deli · bakery · vegetarian friendly · chain · tables · self-service · take-out

🗇 **From I-17**, take exit 203 east on Camelback Rd about 10 miles to store on SW corner Camelback & 40th.

PRESCOTT

NEW FRONTIERS NATURAL MARKETPLACE ✕ 🍲   ♿
1112 Iron Springs Rd. © 928-445-7370 ⊙ M-Sat 8-8, Sun 10-6
Store features live music in the deli on Wednesday evenings.

· organic produce · freshly prepared food · juice bar · salad bar · café · deli · vegetarian friendly · chain · counter · tables · self-service · take-out

🗇 Take Hwy 69 (via I-17) or Hwy 89 (via I-40) to Prescott. Go west on Sheldon St or Gurley St (aka Hwy 69) to Montezuma St. Turn right onto Montezuma (becomes Whipple, then Iron Springs Rd) about 1¼-1½ miles to store on right 1 block past Yavapai Regional Medical Hospital.

PRESCOTT NATURAL FOODS ✕ 🍲
330 W. Gurley St. © 928-778-5875 ⊙ M-Sat 8-8, Sun 8-7

· organic produce · freshly prepared food · deli · bakery · vegetarian friendly · chain · tables · self-service · take-out

🗇 Take Hwy 69 (via I-17) or Hwy 89 (via I-40) to Prescott. Store is on Hwy 69 (aka W Gurley St) just west of intersection with Hwy 89 (Montezuma St) on east side (1 block past town square).

SCOTTSDALE

WILD OATS MARKET ✕ ● &

7129 E. Shea Blvd. ✆ 480-905-1141 ☉ Daily 7-10

· organic produce · freshly prepared food · juice bar · salad bar · café · deli · vegetarian friendly · chain · counter · tables · self-service · take-out

From I-10, take exit 147 north on Squaw Peak Fwy/AZ 51N over 9 miles to exit 9 (Shea Blvd). Turn right (east) onto Shea 4²⁄₃ miles to store at SW corner Shea & Scottsdale Blvd. **From AZ 101 Loop**, take exit 41 west on Shea (right from 101E, left from 101N) 2 miles to store at SW corner Shea & Scottsdale.

SEDONA

The drive to Sedona from any direction is spectacular.

NEW FRONTIERS NATURAL FOODS ✕ ●

1420 W. Hwy. 89A ✆ 928-282-6311 ☉ M-Sat 8-9, Sun 8-8

· organic produce · freshly prepared food · deli · vegetarian friendly · chain · tables · self-service · take-out

Hwy 89A runs through Sedona. Store is west of the center between Soldier's Pass Rd & Oak Creek Blvd on west side.

TEMPE

GENTLE STRENGTH COOPERATIVE ✕ ●

234 W. University Drive ✆ 480-968-4831 ☉ Daily 9-9, Cafe M-F 7-2:30, Sat 9-7, Sun 10-2

Store houses the Desert Greens Cafe and the Rawsome! Cafe (see below).

· organic produce · freshly prepared food · café · co-op

From I-17, merge onto I-10 E toward Tucson. **From 10E**, take exit 151 left onto 32nd St (becomes University Dr) about 4 miles to store on left just after railroad tracks at University & Ash Ave. **From I-10W**, take exit 153B north on 52nd St about 1 mile to University. Turn right onto University 1½ miles to store on left just after railroad tracks at University & Ash.

RAWSOME! CAFE ✕

234 W. University Drive ✆ 480-496-5959 ☉ M, Tues, Th, F 4-8

Cafe (inside Gentle Strength Co-op) features raw, organic, vegan cuisine.

· vegan · organic focus · counter · tables · self-service

See directions above for Gentle Strength Co-op.

WHOLE FOODS MARKET ✕ ● &

5120 S. Rural Rd. ✆ 480-456-1400 ☉ Daily 8-10

· organic produce · freshly prepared food · salad bar · café · deli · bakery · vegetarian friendly · chain · tables · self-service · take-out

From Hwy 60, take exit 174 toward Scottsdale south on Rural Rd (right from 60E, left from 60W) about ½ mile to store at Rural & Baseline Rd.

Please tell these businesses that you found them in Healthy Highways.

TUCSON

Tucsaon is home to the Arizona-Sonora Desert Museum, where you can stroll the outdoor trails and see typical Sonoran desert plants and animals.

AQUA VITA 🍎

2801 N. Country Club ☏ 520-293-7770 ⏰ M-Sat 8-8, Sun 10-6

· organic produce

🍎 From I-10, take exit 255 straight onto N Freeway Rd to Miracle Mile. Turn east on Miracle Mile (left from 10E, right from 10W) 1¾ miles to W Oracle Rd. Turn left onto Oracle 2 blocks to E Ft Lowell Rd. Turn right onto Ft Lowell 2 miles to N Country Club Rd. Turn right onto Country Club ½ mile to store.

CASBAH TEA HOUSE ✕

628 N. 4th Ave. ☏ 520-740-0393 ⏰ M-Th, Sun 9:30-10, F-Sat 9:30-11

· juice bar · café · bakery · vegetarian · vegan friendly · organic focus · tables

🍎 From I-10W, take exit 257A right onto St Mary's Rd (becomes W 6th St) 1 mile to 4th Ave. Turn left onto 4th to restaurant on right. From I-10E, take exit 257 (Speedway Blvd) but continue past Speedway along N Freeway Rd to St Mary's/6th St. Turn left onto St Mary's and follow directions above.

FOOD CONSPIRACY CO-OP 🍎   &

412 N. 4th Ave. ☏ 520-624-4821 ⏰ Daily 9-8
Check the bulletin board for community happenings.

· organic produce · freshly prepared food · café · co-op · take-out

🍎 From I-10W, take exit 257A right onto St Mary's Rd (becomes W 6th St) 1 mile to 4th Ave. Turn right onto 4th to store on left between 6th & 7th (blue building with pink & turquoise highlights). From I-10E, take exit 257 (Speedway Blvd) but continue past Speedway along N Freeway Rd to St Mary's/6th St. Turn left onto St Mary's and follow directions above.

GOVINDA'S NATURAL FOODS BUFFET ✕   &

711 E. Blacklidge Drive ☏ 520-792-0630 ⏰ Lunch W-Sun 11:30-2:30, Dinner Tues-Sat 5-9
All-you-can-eat, mostly-vegan buffet, including salad bar, pastas, rice dishes, hot entrees, homemade bread, natural desserts. Eat inside or outdoors among the landscaped gardens, waterfall, fountains, koi pond, and bird aviaries.

· salad bar · vegetarian · vegan friendly · organic focus · tables · self-service

🍎 From I-10, take exit 256 straight onto N Freeway Rd to Grant Rd. Turn east onto Grant (left from 10E, right from 10W) 5 traffic lights (almost 2 miles) to 1st Ave. Turn left onto 1st less than 1 mile (past light at Glenn St) to 2nd light at Blacklidge Dr. Turn right onto Blacklidge to restaurant in the Chaitanya Cultural Center (behind Jack Farrers Tires).

OASIS VEGETARIAN EATERY ✕

375 S. Stone Ave. ☏ 520-884-1616 ⏰ M-Sat 11:30-3, 5-9 ("bar" menu after 9)
The emphasis is on vegan and the menu is extensive. Indoor and outdoor dining, live entertainment.

· juice bar · café · vegetarian · vegan friendly · counter · tables · wait staff

🍎 From I-10, take exit 258 toward Congress St/Broadway straight onto N Freeway Rd to Congress. Turn east onto Congress (left from 10E, right from 10W) less than ½ mile to W Broadway (where Congress becomes one-way in the opposite direction). Turn right onto W Broadway 2 blocks to S Stone Ave. Turn right onto Stone ⅓ mile to restaurant.

THE GARLAND ✂

119 E. Speedway Blvd. ℂ 520-792-4221 ⊙ M-Th 8am-2pm, F-Sat 8am-10pm, Sun 8am-9pm

Although mostly a vegetarian and natural foods orientation, they do serve tuna and chicken. HH Tripsters L&JB: 70s-style vegetarian restaurant with a friendly, funky atmosphere.

· vegetarian friendly · alcohol · tables · wait staff

🚪 **From I-10,** take exit 257 straight onto N Freeway Rd to Speedway Blvd. Turn east onto Speedway (left from 10E, right from 10W) less than 1 mile to restaurant.

WILD OATS MARKET ✂ 🍎

7133 N. Oracle Rd. ℂ 520-297-5394 ⊙ Daily 7-11

· organic produce · freshly prepared food · juice bar · salad bar · café · deli · bakery
· vegetarian friendly · chain · tables · self-service · take-out

🚪 **From I-10,** take exit 248 east on Ina Rd (left from 10E, right from 10W) about 5¼ miles to N Oracle Rd. Turn right onto N Oracle to store on west side of intersection.

WILD OATS MARKET ✂ 🍎

3360 E. Speedway Blvd. ℂ 520-795-9844 ⊙ Daily 7-11

· organic produce · freshly prepared food · juice bar · salad bar · café · deli · bakery
· vegetarian friendly · chain · tables · self-service · take-out

🚪 **From I-10,** take exit 257 straight onto N Freeway Rd to Speedway Blvd. Turn east onto Speedway (left from 10E, right from 10W) about 6 miles to store a block or so past Tucson Blvd on right in strip mall .

WILD OATS MARKET ✂ 🍎

4751 E. Sunrise Drive ℂ 520-299-8858 ⊙ Daily 7-11

· organic produce · freshly prepared food · salad bar · café · deli · bakery · vegetarian friendly · chain · tables · self-service · take-out

🚪 **From I-10,** take exit 248 east on Ina Rd (left from 10E, right from 10W) almost 11¼ miles (becomes Skyline Dr, then Sunrise Dr) to store on right.

YUMA

FULL CIRCLE HEALTH FOODS 🍎

2099 S. 4th Ave. ℂ 928-783-8080 ⊙ Tues-F 9:30-6, Sat 9:30-5

🚪 **From I-8,** take exit 2 toward San Luis west on 16th St (left from 8W, right from 8E) about 1 mile to 4th Ave (8Bus). Turn left onto 4th about ¾ mile to store at 24th St & 4th.

Goldbeck's "EAT IT OR NOT"

FASCINATING & FAR-OUT FACTS ABOUT FOOD

TRUE or FALSE?

At one time Americans sold potatoes for an equal weight in gold.

True When scurvy was rampant during the gold rush of 1898, potatoes were exchanged for an equal weight of gold. (Scurvy is a deficiency disease caused by lack of vitamin C.)

ARKANSAS

ARKANSAS

1 Fayetteville
2 Fort Smith
3 Harrison
4 Hot Springs
5 Little Rock
6 Pine Bluff
7 Sherwood
8 Van Buren

FAYETTEVILLE

OZARK NATURAL FOODS CO-OP ✕ 🍴
1554 N. College Ave. ✆ 479-521-7558 ⏰ M-Sat 9-8, Sun 10-6
· organic produce · freshly prepared food · juice bar · deli · vegetarian friendly · co-op
· tables · self-service · take-out

🛏 From I-540, take exit 66 right onto AR 112 (Garland Ave) to AR 180.
Veer left onto 180 (W Drake St, becomes W Township St) 1¾ miles to US
71Bus. Turn right onto 71Bus (aka N College Ave) less than 1 mile to store
between E Sycamore & E North St.

FORT SMITH

OLDE FASHIONED FOODS 🍴
123 N. 18th St. ✆ 479-782-6183 ⏰ M-Sat 9-6
· organic produce

🛏 From I-540, take exit 8 (8A from 540E) onto AR 22W/Rogers Ave
(right from 540W, left from 50E) 3¼ mile to N 18th St. Turn right onto 18th
to store on left.

OLDE FASHIONED FOODS 🍴
4600 Towson Ave. ✆ 501-649-8200 ⏰ M-Sat 9-6
· organic produce

🛏 From I-540, take exit 10 west on AR 255 (right from 540W, left from
540E) about 1⅓ miles to 71Bus (Towson Ave). Turn right onto Towson 1
mile to store.

HARRISON

ALMOND TREE, INC. 🐀
126 N. Willow St. © 870-741-8980 ☺ M-F 9-5:30, Sat 9:30-3

📖 **From US 65**, take 65Bus west about 1½ miles to W Stephenson Ave. Turn left onto W Stephenson 1½ blocks to store at N Willow St.

HOT SPRINGS

Hot Springs is a national park, with several lakes in the area.

THE OLD COUNTRY STORE ✗🐀
455 Broadway © 501-624-1172 ☺ M-F 9-5:30 (winter 9-4), Deli M-Th 9-4:30, F 9-2
A good selection of vegetarian sandwiches, plus soup from October to April.
- · organic produce · freshly prepared food · juice bar · deli · bakery · vegetarian · vegan friendly · tables · self-service · take-out

📖 Hot Springs is about 30 miles west of I-30 exit 111 (Benton) on Hwy 70W. Store is on corner Hwy 70E & Broadway.

LITTLE ROCK

WILD OATS MARKET ✗🐀   ♿
10700 N. Rodney Parham Drive © 501-312-2326 ☺ Daily 8-9
- · organic produce · freshly prepared food · juice bar · salad bar · café · deli · bakery · vegetarian friendly · chain · counter · tables · self-service · take-out

📖 **From I-40**, take exit 147 onto I-430S about 5 miles (across Arkansas River) to exit 8. Turn right onto Rodney Parham Dr to store at 1st intersection on right in shopping mall (behind Chile's restaurant).

PINE BLUFF

SWEET CLOVER HEALTH FOODS 🐀
2624 W. 28th Ave. © 870-536-0107 ☺ M-F 10-5, Sat 10-4

📖 **From I-530**, take exit 39 (US 79/79Bus) north on Camden Rd (left from 530S, right from 530N) about 1 mile to W 28th Ave. Turn right onto W 28th about 1 mile to store in Oak Park Village.

SHERWOOD

ANN'S HEALTH FOOD STORE 🐀
9800 Hwy. 107 © 501-835-6415 ☺ M-F 8:30-6
- · organic produce

📖 From I-40, take exit 153A onto Hwy 107N about 5½ miles to store.

VAN BUREN

SQUASH BLOSSOM 🐀
5005 Dora Rd. © 501-474-1147 ☺ M-F 9-6, Sat 9-5
- · organic produce

📖 **From I-40W**, take exit 1 toward Fort Smith onto Dora Rd about ⅔ mile to store on left (in 100 year-old restored general store). **From I-40E**, take exit 330 toward Dora/Fort Smith left onto Greenwood Rd to Dora Rd. Turn left onto Dora about ¼ mile to store.

CALIFORNIA

NORTHERN CALIFORNIA

1   Alameeda
2   Alamo
3   Altadena
4   Anaheim
5   Angwin
6   Aptos
7   Arcata
8   Auburn
9   Bakersfield
10 Belmont
11 Berkeley
12 Beverly Hills
13 Bolinas
14 Brentwood
15 Burlingame
16 Camarillo
17 Campbell
18 Canoga Park
19 Capitola
20 Cardiff
21 Carmel
22 Cerritos
23 Chico
24 Chula Vista
25 Citrus Heights
26 Concord
27 Costa Mesa
28 Culver City
29 Cupertino
30 Davis
31 El Cajon
32 El Cerrito
33 Encinitas
34 Escondido
35 Eureka
36 Fair Oaks
37 Fairfax
38 Fountain Valley
39 Fresno
40 Fullerton
41 Garberville
42 Glendale
43 Goleta
44 Granada Hills
45 Grass Valley
46 Guerneville
47 Half Moon Bay
48 Hemet
49 Hermosa Beach
50 Hollywood
51 Huntington Beach
52 Irvine
53 Jackson

54 La Jolla	85 Oxnard	116 Santa Rosa
55 La Mesa	86 Pacifica	117 Santee
56 Laguna Beach	87 Palm Desert	118 Sebastopol
57 Laguna Niguel	88 Palm Springs	119 Sherman Oaks
58 Laguna Woods	89 Palo Alto	120 Simi Valley
59 Lake Elsinore	90 Paradise	121 South El Monte
60 Lancaster	91 Pasadena	122 Stanford
61 Larkspur	92 Petaluma	123 Studio City
62 Lemon Grove	93 Porter Ranch	124 Sunnyvale
63 Loma Linda	94 Poway	125 Tahoe City
64 Lomita	95 Quincy	126 Thousand Oaks
65 Long Beach	96 Rancho Palos Verdes	127 Topanga
66 Los Angeles	97 Redondo Beach	128 Torrance
67 Los Gatos	98 Richmond	129 Truckee
68 Mendocino	99 Rowland Heights	130 Tustin
69 Menlo Park	100 Sacramento	131 Ukiah
70 Mill Valley	101 San Diego	132 Upland
71 Monterey	102 San Dimas	133 Valley Springs
72 Monterey Park	103 San Francisco	134 Venice
73 Mountain View	104 San Gabriel	135 Ventura
74 Mt. Shasta	105 San Jose	136 Vista
75 Napa	106 San Luis Obispo	137 Walnut Creek
76 Nevada City	107 San Mateo	138 Watsonville
77 North Hollywood	108 San Rafael	139 West Hollywood
78 Northridge	109 San Ramon	140 Westwood
79 Norwalk	110 Santa Barbara	141 Whittier
80 Oakland	111 Santa Clara	142 Willits
81 Ocean Beach	112 Santa Clarita	143 Woodland Hills
82 Ojai	113 Santa Cruz	144 Yorba Linda
83 Olympic Valley	114 Santa Maria	145 Yountville
84 Orange	115 Santa Monica	146 Yuba City

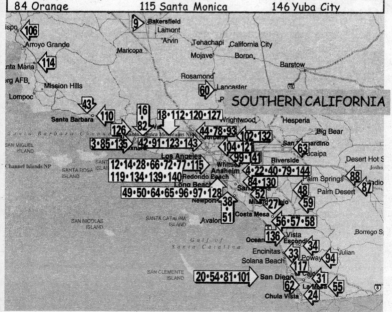

ALAMEDA

ALAMEDA NATURAL GROCERY 🥬
1650 Park St. ☏ 510-864-7190 ⏰ Daily 9-8
Situated in the Alameda Marketplace, which also houses a bakery, juice bar, fish market, natural meat market, and organic take-out/eat-in deli.
 · organic produce
🚗 **From I-880S**, take 23rd Ave exit toward Alameda. Follow 23rd (becomes 29th Ave) across bridge onto Park St 4 blocks to store on left. **From I-880N**, take 29th Ave exit toward Fruitvale Rd. Turn right onto 29th 1 block then U-turn back onto 29th about ¼ mile to Ford Ave. Turn right onto Ford, left onto 23rd and merge back onto 29th. Cross bridge onto Park 4 blocks to store on left.

ALAMO

NATURAL TEMPTATIONS 🥬
19A Alamo Plaza ☏ 925-820-0606 ⏰ M-F 10-6, Sat 9:30-5
🚗 **From I-680**, take Stone Valley Rd W exit right onto Stone Valley Rd about ¼ mile (just past Danville Blvd) to store in shopping plaza on right (next to Safeway).

ALTADENA

O HAPPY DAYS 🍴🥬
2283 Lake Ave. ☏ 626-797-0383 ⏰ M-F 11-6:30, Sat 11-6
The only cafe item that isn't vegan is the lasagna, with casein in the soy cheese.
 · organic produce · freshly prepared food · deli · vegan · tables · self-service · take-out
🚗 **From I-210**, take Lake Ave exit north on Lake (straight onto Corson St then left from 210E, right from 210W) about 2¼ miles to restaurant.

ANAHEIM

YOGIRAJ VEGETARIAN RESTAURANT 🍴
3107 W. Lincoln Ave. ☏ 714-995-5900 ⏰ Tues-Sun 11-8:30
Vegetarian Gujarati Indian food.
 · vegetarian · vegan friendly · tables · wait staff · take-out
🚗 **From I-5 or Rt 91**, take Beach Blvd exit south on Beach about 2½ miles to Lincoln Ave. Turn right onto Lincoln to restaurant.

ANGWIN

COLLEGE MARKET 🥬
15 Angwin Plaza ☏ 707-965-6321 ⏰ M-Th, Sun 7:30-7:30, F 7:30-3:30 (5:30 in summer)
On the campus of Pacific Union College
 · organic produce · salad bar · deli · vegetarian friendly · take-out
🚗 **From Rt 29** about 6 miles north of St Helena, head northeast on Deer Park Rd toward Pacific Union College (becomes Howell Mt Rd) about 1⅔ miles to store at top of hill on college campus.

APTOS

APTOS NATURAL FOODS 🥬
506 Soquel Drive ☏ 831-685-3334 ⏰ Daily 8-8

From Rt 1, take Park Ave exit north on Park (left from 1S, right from 1N) about ⅓ mile to Soquel Dr. Turn right onto Soquel to store on right in Aptos Shopping Center.

ARCATA

ARCATA FOOD CO-OP 🥬
811 I St. © 707-822-5947 ⊙ Daily 6-10
 · organic produce · freshly prepared food · juice bar · deli · bakery · vegetarian friendly
 · co-op · take-out

From Hwy 101, take Samoa Blvd west about ½ mile to I St. Turn right onto I about ¼ mile (4 blocks) to store on left (1 block west of town plaza).

DAYBREAK CAFE ✗
758 18th St. © 707-826-7543 ⊙ M-Tues, F-Sun 7am-4pm
According to cafe co-owners, their standard is "locally grown, organic, vegetarian fare." However, there are a few "token" meat dishes.
 · vegetarian friendly · organic focus · counter · tables · wait staff

From Hwy 101, take Sunset Ave/Humboldt State U exit. From 101N, turn left at stop sign, go over bridge, and turn left immediately onto H St to restaurant at H & 18th St. From 101S, go straight onto H 2 blocks to restaurant at 18th.

AUBURN

SUNRISE NATURAL FOODS 🥬
2160 Grass Valley Hwy. © 530-888-8973 ⊙ M-F 9:30-6:30, Sat 9:30-5, Sun 12-5

From I-80, take Hwy 49 exit north toward Grass Valley about 2 miles to store on right.

BAKERSFIELD

CONE'S HEALTH FOODS 🥬
1002 Wible Rd. © 661-832-5669 ⊙ M-F 9-8, Sat 10-6, Sun 11-6

From CA 99N, take Ming Ave exit right onto Ming 1 block to Wible Rd. Turn right onto Wible about ⅓ mile to store. From CA 99S, take CA 58E exit onto Stockdale Hwy toward Brundage Ln ⅓ mile to Wible. Turn right onto Wible about ⅖ mile to store.

BELMONT

HOBEE'S ✗
1101 Shoreway Rd. © 650-596-0400 ⊙ M-F 7-2:30, Sat-Sun 8-3
Although the menu may vary by location, see the description at the Mountain View site (the 1st Hobee's) for the basics.
 · salad bar · vegetarian friendly · alcohol · chain · tables · wait staff · take-out

From Hwy 101, take Ralston Ave exit and take ramp toward Marine World Pkwy onto Ralston. Restaurant is at intersection next to Motel 6.

BERKELEY

ASHKENAZ MUSIC & DANCE COMMUNITY CENTER ✗ &
1317 San Pablo Ave. © 510-525-5099 ⊙ Open during performances: Call 510-525-5054 for show times.
See world music and dance performances, take a class or just enjoy the vegetarian food in this a warehouse transformed to look like an old wooden synagogue.

Cafe hours vary with show schedule, but something happens most evenings.

· vegetarian · organic focus · alcohol · tables · self-service

From I-80, take Gillman St east about ⅔ mile to San Pablo Ave. Turn right onto San Pablo to center on left (across from shopping center & REI).

BERKELEY NATURAL GROCERY COMPANY

1336 Gilman St. © 510-526-2456 ⊙ Daily 9-8

· organic produce

From I-80, take Gilman St east 1 mile to store on right.

CHA-YA RESTAURANT ✕

1686 Shattuck Ave. © 510-981-1213 ⊙ Tues-Sun 5-9:30

Vegan Japanese, with tofu dishes, sushi, noodles, even vegan desserts.

· vegan · alcohol · tables · wait staff · take-out

From I-80, take University Ave east 2 miles to Shattuck Ave. Turn left onto Shattuck 4 blocks to Virginia. Restaurant is 3rd store from corner.

RAW ENERGY ORGANIC JUICE CAFÉ

2050 Addison Street © 510-665-9464 ⊙ Daily 8-7

Raw vegan take-out.

· juice bar · vegan · organic focus · take-out

From I-80, take University Ave east about 1¾ miles to Milvia St. Turn right onto Milvia 1 bock to Addison St. Turn left onto Addison to restaurant.

RAZAN'S ORGANIC KITCHEN ✕

2119 Kittredge St. © 510-486-0449 ⊙ M-Sat 10-9

Claiming "100% organic," the fare includes vegetarian, fish, chicken, and meat.

· juice bar · vegetarian friendly · organic focus · tables · self-service · take-out

From I-80, take University Ave east 2 miles to Shattuck Ave. Turn right onto Shattuck 4 blocks to restaurant at Kittredge St.

SMART ALEC'S ✕

2355 Telegraph Ave. © 510-704-4000 ⊙ Daily 11-9

Described as "healthy fast food," the menu features vegan soups, salads, veggie or chicken burgers, and vegetarian, poultry or dolphin-safe tuna sandwiches, all on whole grain breads. A great perch to view the Berkeley scene.

· vegetarian friendly · counter · wait staff · take-out

From I-80, take Ashby Ave east 2 miles to Telegraph Ave. Turn left onto Telegraph less than 1 mile to restaurant 1 block south of UC Berkeley.

SMOKEY JOE'S CAFE ✕

1620 Shattuck Ave. © none ⊙ Daily 9-2

Healthy basic vegetarian breakfast and lunch. Vegan accommodations.

· vegetarian · vegan friendly · organic focus · tables · self-service · take-out

From I-80, take University Ave east 2 miles to Shattuck Ave. Turn left onto Shattuck 5 blocks to restaurant.

WHOLE FOODS MARKET ✕

3000 Telegraph Ave. © 510-649-1333 ⊙ Daily 8-10

· organic produce · freshly prepared food · juice bar · salad bar · café · deli · bakery
· vegetarian friendly · chain · tables · self-service · take-out

From I-80, take Ashby Ave east 2 miles to Telegraph Ave. Store is on corner Ashby & Telegraph.

BEVERLY HILLS

WHOLE FOODS MARKET ✕ 🍎
239 N. Crescent Drive ✆ 310-274-3360 ⊙ Daily 8-9
  · organic produce · freshly prepared food · juice bar · salad bar · café · deli · bakery
  · vegetarian friendly · chain · counter · tables · self-service · take-out

🍎 **From I-405** (San Diego Fwy), take Santa Monica Blvd exit east (right from 405N, left from 405S) onto Santa Monica about 3 miles to Crescent Blvd. Turn right onto Crescent about 2 blocks to store on right between Santa Monica & Wilshire Blvd.

BOLINAS

BOLINAS PEOPLE'S STORE 🍎
14 Wharf Rd. ✆ 415-868-1433 ⊙ Daily 8:30-6:30
There are tables outside in the courtyard where you can enjoy the store's home-made sandwiches, soups and vegetarian tamales.
  · organic produce · freshly prepared food · vegetarian friendly · co-op · take-out

🍎 **From Hwy 1**, take Olema Bolinas Rd (left from 1N, slight right from 1S) about 2 miles to store (where road becomes Wharf Rd).

BRENTWOOD

A VOTRE SANTE ✕
13016 San Vicente Blvd. ✆ 310-451-1813 ⊙ M-Sat 8am-10pm, Sun 8-9
A natural foods restaurant with vegetarian dishes, organic poultry and salmon.
  · vegetarian friendly · alcohol · tables · wait staff

🍎 **From I-405N**, take Wilshire Blvd exit toward Westwood and take Wilshire Blvd W ramp onto Wilshire about ⅔ mile to San Vicente Blvd. Turn right onto San Vicente to restaurant on left just before 26th St. **From I-405S**, take Wilshire Blvd W exit onto Wilshire less than ½ mile to San Vicente and follow directions above.

BURLINGAME

EARTHBEAM NATURAL FOODS 🍎
1399 Broadway ✆ 650-347-2058 ⊙ M-Sat 9-7, Sun 10-6
  · organic produce

🍎 **From Hwy 101** (Bayshore Fwy), take Broadway exit west (right) 5 blocks to store on corner Broadway & Carpuchino Ave.

CAMARILLO

LASSEN'S NATURAL FOODS 🍎
2207 Pickwick Drive ✆ 805-482-3287 ⊙ M-Sat 9-8
  · chain

🍎 **From Hwy 101S** (Ventura Fwy), take Carmen Dr exit left onto Ventura Blvd about ¾ mile to traffic light at Arneill Rd. Turn left onto Arneill less than ½ mile to light at Pickwick Dr. Turn left onto Pickwick and right into Ponderosa Shopping Center to store (next to Napa Auto Parts). **From Hwy 101N**, take Lewis Rd exit left onto Daily Dr about ¼ mile to light at Arneill. Turn right onto Arneill about ⅓ mile to light at Pickwick. Turn left onto Pickwick and right into Ponderosa Shopping Center to store.

CAMPBELL

HOBEE'S ✗
1875 S. Bascom Ave., Unit 190 © 408-369-0575 ⊙ M-F 7-9, Sat-Sun 8-9
Although the menu may vary by location, see the description of the Mountain View locale (the 1st Hobee's) for the basics.
· salad bar · vegetarian friendly · alcohol · chain · tables · wait staff · take-out
🍎 **From I-280 or I-880**, merge onto Rt 17S to Campbell Ave. Turn left onto Campbell (right from 17N) to 1st big intersection at S Bascom Ave. Turn right onto Bascom restaurant in back of The Prunyard (next to Camera Cinemas).

WHOLE FOODS MARKET ✗🥩 &
1690 S. Bascom Ave. © 408-371-5000 ⊙ Daily 8-10, Bakery/Juice bar from 7:30
· organic produce · freshly prepared food · juice bar · salad bar · café · deli · bakery · vegetarian friendly · chain · tables · self-service · take-out
🍎 **From I-280 or I-880**, merge onto Rt 17S to Hamilton Ave exit. Turn left onto Hamilton (right from 17N) 2 blocks to store in shopping center at corner Hamilton & S Bascom Ave.

CANOGA PARK

FOLLOW YOUR HEART NATURAL FOODS ✗🥩
21825 Sherman Way © 818-348-3240 ⊙ Daily 8-9
Extensive cafe menu of vegetarian and vegan offerings.
· organic produce · freshly prepared food · café · vegetarian · vegan friendly · counter · tables · self-service · take-out
🍎 **From Hwy 101 (Ventura Fwy)**, take Topanga Canyon Blvd exit north (right from 101N, left from 101S) about 2 miles to Sherman Way. Turn right onto Sherman to store.

CAPITOLA

DHARMA'S NATURAL FOODS RESTAURANT ✗
4250 Capitola Rd. © 831-462-1717 ⊙ Daily 7:30am-9pm
· vegetarian · vegan friendly · tables · self-service · take-out
🍎 **From north on Hwy 17S**, take Hwy 1S toward Monterey. **From Hwy 1**, take 41st Ave exit toward the ocean onto 41st (right from 1S, left from 1N) ½ mile to Capitola Rd. Turn left onto Capitola to restaurant at corner 42nd Ave.

NEW LEAF COMMUNITY MARKET ✗🥩 &
1210 41st Ave. © 831-479-7987 ⊙ Daily 8-9
· organic produce · freshly prepared food · juice bar · café · deli · vegetarian friendly · chain · counter · tables · self-service · take-out
🍎 **From north on Hwy 17S**, take Hwy 1S toward Monterey. **From Hwy 1**, take 41st Ave exit toward the ocean onto 41st (right from 1S, left from 1N) less than 1 mile to store on left in Begonia Plaza (just past Jade & Brommer St, near Spa Fitness).

CARDIFF

KI'S RESTAURANT ✗ &
2591 South Coast Hwy 101 © 760-346-3181 ⊙ M-Th, Sun 8-9, F-Sat 8-9:30
Health-oriented vegetarian, fish and poultry dishes, including soups, salads and sandwiches. Hot entrees at dinner, many with tofu or chicken. Upstairs dining room opens at 5 for full-service dinner, while breakfast and lunch are self-serve.

· vegetarian friendly· organic focus · tables · self-service · wait staff

🏠 **From I-5,** take Lomas Santa Fe Dr west about 2 miles to Hwy 101. Turn right (north) onto 101 about 1½ miles to restaurant on "restaurant row."

CARMEL

CORNUCOPIA COMMUNITY MARKET 🍎
26135 Carmel Rancho Blvd. © 831-625-1454 ☺ M-Sat 9-7, Sun 10-7
Pre-made sandwiches available.

🏠 **From Hwy 1,** take Carmel Valley Rd east to Carmel Rancho Blvd. Turn right on Carmel Rancho to store on left in Carmel Rancho Shopping Ctr.

CERRITOS

VEGI WOKERY 🍴
11329 183rd St. © 562-809-3928 ☺ M-Sat 11:30-2:30, 4:30-9
Chinese vegetarian. No meat, no eggs, no dairy, no msg. Brown "rice" is actually a mix of 7 grains, including barley, oats and buckwheat.
· vegetarian · vegan friendly · tables · wait staff · take-out

🏠 **From I-605,** take South St exit west (right from 605S, left from 605N) 1 block to Studebaker Rd. Turn right on Studebaker ½ mile to 183rd St. Turn right onto 183rd about ½ mile to restaurant.

CHICO

CHICO NATURAL FOODS 🍴🍎
818 Main St. © 530-891-1713 ☺ Daily 11-10
Self-serve soup and outdoor seating.
· freshly prepared food · vegetarian friendly · tables · self-service · take-out

🏠 **From I-5,** take Hwy 32 east (becomes 8th St in Chico) about ⅔ mile to store on corner 8th & Main St.

CHULA VISTA

CILANTRO LIVE! 🍴 ♿
315½ 3rd Ave. © 619-827-7401 ☺ M-Th 11:30-8, F-Sun 12-9
Entirely organic and vegan "live" food, with nothing heated to above 112^0.
· juice bar · salad bar · vegan · organic focus · tables · wait staff

🏠 **From I-5,** take E St east about 1¼ miles to 3rd Ave. Turn right onto 3rd about ¼ mile to restaurant on left.

CITRUS HEIGHTS

ELLIOTT'S NATURAL FOODS 🍎 ♿
8063 Greenback Lane © 916-726-3033 ☺ M-Sat 9:30-6, Sun 11-5
· organic produce · freshly prepared food · take-out

🏠 **From I-80,** take Greenback Lane east about 4 miles (past Arcadia Dr) to store on left in Greenback Square Shopping Center.

CONCORD

HARVEST HOUSE 🍎
2395 Monument Blvd. © 925-676-2305 ☺ M-F 9-8, Sat 9-7, Sun 10-7

🏠 **From I-680N,** take Monument Blvd exit right onto Monument about 1½ miles to Detroit Ave. Make U-turn at Detroit and go 1 block to store (across from Costco). **From I-680S,** take Concord Ave (becomes Galindo, then Monument) almost 3 miles (through town) to store (1 block past Detroit).

COSTA MESA

MOTHER'S MARKET & KITCHEN ✗🍽 &

225 E. 17th St. © 949-631-4741 ⊙ Daily 9-10, Restaurant & Deli 9-9

An extensive menu of wholesome vegetarian and vegan fare for breakfast, lunch and dinner. Whole-grain breads, brown rice, fresh juices, and smoothies.

· organic produce · freshly prepared food · juice bar · salad bar · deli · bakery
· vegetarian · vegan friendly · alcohol · counter · tables · wait staff · take-out

🍱 **From I-405** (San Diego Fwy), take CA 55S (becomes Newport Blvd) toward Newport Beach about 5 miles to 17th St. Turn left onto 17th 1 block to store on right (just past Orange Ave).

CULVER CITY

RAINBOW ACRES ✗🍽

13208 Washington Blvd. © 310-306-8330 ⊙ M-F 8:30-9, Sat-Sun 9-8

· freshly prepared food · deli · vegetarian friendly · tables · self-service · take-out

🍱 **From I-405S** (San Diego Fwy), take Washington Blvd exit right onto Sawtelle Blvd to Washington. Turn left onto Washington to store on right. **From I-405N**, take Culver Blvd exit left onto Sawtelle ½ mile to Washington. Turn left onto Washington to store on right.

CUPERTINO

HOBEE'S ✗ &

21267 Stevens Creek Blvd. © 408-255-6010 ⊙ M-F 6:30-10, Sat-Sun 7:30-10

Although the menu may vary by location, see the description of the Mountain View locale (the 1st Hobee's) for the basics.

· salad bar · vegetarian friendly · alcohol · chain · tables · wait staff · take-out

🍱 **From I-280 or Hwy 101**, take Hwy 85 south to Stevens Creek Blvd exit. Turn left (east) onto Stevens Creek 1 block to restaurant in The Oaks Shopping Center (across from De Anza College).

WHOLE FOODS MARKET ✗🍽 &

20830 Stevens Creek Blvd. © 408-257-7000 ⊙ Daily 8-10

· organic produce · freshly prepared food · juice bar · salad bar · café · deli · bakery
· vegetarian friendly · chain · tables · self-service · take-out

🍱 **From I-280 or Hwy 101**, take Hwy 85 south to Stevens Creek Blvd exit. Take Stevens Creek east (left) 1 mile to store between Stelling Rd & DeAnza Blvd (near Mervyns).

DAVIS

Home of UC Davis and the Mondavi Center, with top music and dance performances.

DAVIS FOOD CO-OP 🍽

620 G St. © 530-758-2667 ⊙ Daily 8-10

· organic produce · freshly prepared food · deli · vegetarian friendly · co-op · take-out

🍱 **From I-80**, take Richards Blvd exit toward Downtown right onto Richards less than ½ mile (Richards becomes E St). Veer right onto E about ⅓ mile to 6th St. Turn right onto 6th 2 blocks to store on right corner 6th & G St.

DELTA OF VENUS CAFE & PUB ✗ &

122 B St. © 530-753-8639 ⊙ M-Sat 8am-midnight, Sun 8am-2pm

Breakfast is vegetarian, while meat appears later in the day on the Caribbean-style menu. Outdoor patio, fireplace, sofas, local art, and music.

· vegetarian friendly · alcohol · counter · tables · wait staff

🍎 **From I-80**, take Richards Blvd exit toward Downtown right onto Richards less than ½ mile to 1st St. Turn left onto 1st 3 blocks to B St. Turn right onto B ½ block to restaurant on right.

EL CAJON

NATURE'S FIRST LAW 🍎 &

1567 N. Cuyamaca St. © 619-596-7979 ⊘ M-F 10-4

Owned by raw foodists selling only products compatible with a raw foods diet.

· organic produce

🍎 **From I-8**, take Hwy 125 north about 1¾ miles to Navajo Rd. Turn right onto Navajo about ¼ mile to 2nd traffic light at Fletcher Pkwy. Turn left onto Fletcher about 1⅓ miles to Cuyamaca St. Turn left onto Cuyamaca about ⅔ mile to store on right.

EL CERRITO

EL CERRITO NATURAL GROCERY 🍎

10367 San Pablo Ave. © 510-526-1155 ⊘ Daily 9-8

· organic produce

🍎 **From I-80E**, take Central Ave exit toward El Cerrito right on Central less than ½ mile to San Pablo Ave. Turn left onto San Pablo about ⅓ mile to store just before Stockton Ave. **From I-80W**, take Carlson Blvd exit left onto Carlson about ½ mile to Sutter Ave. Turn left onto Sutter 1 block to San Pablo. Turn right onto San Pablo less than ¼ mile to store just past Stockton.

ENCINITAS

HENRY'S MARKETPLACE 🍎

1327 Encinitas Blvd. © 760-633-4747 ⊘ Daily 8-9

· organic produce · freshly prepared food · deli · vegetarian friendly · chain · take-out

🍎 **From I-5**, take Encinitas Blvd exit east toward Encinitas (left from 5S, right from 5N) about 1¾ miles to store.

SWAMI'S CAFE ✖

1163 S. Coast Hwy 101 © 760-944-0612 ⊘ Daily 7-5

Casual whole foods breakfast and lunch place on the highway. "California cuisine" with vegetarian and vegan specialties.

· juice bar · café · vegetarian friendly · vegan friendly · counter · tables · self-service

🍎 **On Hwy 101** in Encinitas (between San Diego & Oceanside).

ESCONDIDO

HENRY'S MARKETPLACE 🍎

510 W. 13th Ave. © 760-745-2141 ⊘ Daily 8-9

· organic produce · freshly prepared food · deli · vegetarian friendly · chain · take-out

🍎 **From I-15N**, take Centre City Pkwy exit 1 mile. Merge onto S Centre City Pkwy about 1⅖ miles to W 13th Ave. Turn left onto W 13th to store. **From I-15S (or I-5)**, take CA 78E less than 1 mile (about 17 miles from 5) to Centre City Pkwy S ramp. Merge onto N Centre City Pkwy about 1⅔ miles to W 13th. Turn right onto W 13th to store.

Please tell these businesses that you found them in Healthy Highways.

JIMBO'S NATURALLY ✖️🐑 &

1633 S. Centre City Pkwy. © 760-489-7755 ⊘ Daily 8-9

· organic produce · freshly prepared food · juice bar · deli · vegetarian friendly · tables · self-service · take-out

🍎 From I-15N, take Centre City Pwky exit 1 mile on pkwy. Merge onto S Centre City Pkwy about 2½ miles to store on left (behind Sav-on). **From I-15S**, merge onto CA 78E toward Ramona almost 1 mile to Centre City Pkwy S exit. Merge onto N Centre City Pkwy (becomes S Centre City Pkwy) almost 2 miles to store on right (behind Sav-on).

EUREKA

EUREKA CO-OP 🐑

1036 5th St. © 707-443-6027 ⊘ Daily 6-9

On-site bakery emphasizes whole grains and organic ingredients. Specialty breads, homemade cereals, even the cakes are made with organic whole wheat pastry flour and unrefined sweeteners.

· organic produce · freshly prepared food · deli · bakery · vegetarian friendly · co-op · take-out

🍎 At corner 5th St (Hwy 101N) & L (huge fruit & vegetable mural on bldg).

EUREKA NATURAL FOODS 🐑 &

1626 Broadway © 707-442-6325 ⊘ M-F 8-8, Deli 8-7, Sat-Sun 9-7, Deli 9-5

· organic produce · freshly prepared food · juice bar · deli · vegetarian friendly · take-out

🍎 On Hwy 101 (aka Broadway) between Wabash Ave & 15th St (behind Jack in the Box).

FAIR OAKS

SUNFLOWER DRIVE-IN ✖️

10344 Fair Oaks Blvd. © 916-967-4331 ⊘ M 10:30-4, Tues-Sat 10:30-9 (8 in winter), Sun 11-5

Homemade nutburgers and millet burgers, burritos and sandwiches, all served on whole grain wrappers. Plus, seasonal soups and chili, salad, fresh juice, smoothies, and "fountain delights". Indoor and outdoor tables.

· juice bar · vegetarian · vegan friendly · tables · self-service · take-out

🍎 From US 50, take Sunrise Blvd north (right from 50W, loop around right from 50E) 2-3 miles to California Ave. Turn right onto California to 2nd left at Fair Oaks Blvd. Turn left onto Fair Oaks 2 blocks and turn right to continue on Fair Oaks less than 1 block to restaurant.

FAIRFAX

GOOD EARTH NATURAL & ORGANIC FOODS ✖️🐑 &

1966 Sir Francis Drake Blvd. © 415-454-0123 ⊘ Daily 9-8

For over 30 years, Good Earth has promoted organic foods and claims their vegetarian deli is "the most elaborate, eclectic and ethnically diverse in all of CA." Shares profits with employees.

· organic produce · freshly prepared food · juice bar · salad bar · deli · bakery · vegetarian · vegan friendly · organic focus · counter · tables · self-service · take-out

🍎 From Hwy 101, take Central San Rafael exit west on 3rd St about 5 miles. Merge right onto Sir Francis Drake Blvd about 3 miles to store at traffic light at Claus Dr on NW corner.

FOUNTAIN VALLEY

AU LAC ✖   &

16563 Brookhurst St. © 714-418-0658 ⊘ Tues-Sun 10:30-9
Meatless Chinese and Vietnamese dining, plus a daily selection of raw foods.
· vegan · tables · wait staff

🍎 **From I-405S** (San Diego Fwy), take Warner Ave E exit right onto Warner ¾ mile to Brookhurst St. Turn left onto Brookhurst about ⅓ mile to restaurant at Heil Ave. **From I-405N**, take exit 14 onto Brookhurst St N ramp. Merge onto Brookhurst about 1 mile to restaurant.

FRESNO

WHOLE FOODS MARKET ✖ 🍟   &

650 W. Shaw Ave. © 559-241-0300 ⊘ Daily 8-9
· organic produce · freshly prepared food · juice bar · salad bar · café · deli · bakery
· vegetarian friendly · chain · tables · self-service · take-out

🍎 **From Hwy 99**, take exit 140 east on Shaw Ave (loop around and right from 99S, loop around and left from 99N) over 4½ miles to store on left in Fig Garden Shopping Center.

FULLERTON

RUTABEGORZ ✖   &

211 N. Pomona Ave. © 714-738-9339 ⊘ M-Sat 11-10, Sun 4-9
Self-described as "hippie home cooking." The clientele 30 years ago was largely college students, but now it's a varied crowd. Not primarily vegetarian, but a daily vegetarian soup, vegetarian Mexican option, wraps (with whole wheat tortillas), all-vegetable stews, sandwiches, salads, smoothies, compose-your-own ice cream or frozen yogurt sundae, and more.
· vegetarian friendly · alcohol · tables · wait staff · take-out

🍎 **From CA 91**, take Harbor Blvd exit north (left from 99E, right from 99W) about 1 mile (past several traffic lights and under railroad crossing) to light at Commonwealth Ave. Turn right onto Commonwealth 1 block to light at Pomona Ave. Turn left onto Pomona 1½ blocks to restaurant on right.

GARBERVILLE

CHAUTAUQUA NATURAL FOODS 🍟

436 Church St. © 707-923-2452 ⊘ M-Sat 10-6

🍎 **From Hwy 101**, take Garberville exit onto Redwood Rd about ¼ mile to Church St. Turn onto Church (begins at Redwood) to store ½ block on right.

WOOD ROSE CAFE ✖   🍟

911 Redwood Dr. © 707-923-3191 ⊘ M-F 8-2:30, Sat-Sun 8-1
Healthy breakfasts with whole grain breads, organic home fries, fresh organic OJ, organic oatmeal, creative egg and tofu dishes, and more. Lunch time soups, salads, burritos, and sandwiches feature many vegetarian choices, some vegan, plus tuna, shrimp, turkey, and nitrite-free (Niman Ranch) bacon.
· vegetarian friendly · vegan friendly · organic focus · alcohol · counter · tables · wait staff

🍎 **From Hwy 101**, take Garberville exit onto Redwood Rd to restaurant on east side.

GLENDALE

GLENDALE ADVENTIST MEDICAL CENTER ✗ &

1509 Wilson Terrace © 818-409-8095 ⊘ Daily 6am-7:30pm
An all-vegetarian cafeteria in the Seventh-day Adventist tradition.

· vegetarian · tables · self-service

From **Ventura Fwy** (CA 134), take Harvey Dr exit north (right from 134W, left from 134E) to 1st left (Wilson Terrace). Turn left onto Wilson and follow signs to hospital parking. Cafeteria is on ground floor.

WHOLE FOODS MARKET 🍃

826 N. Glendale Ave. © 818-240-9350 ⊘ Daily 8-9
The current store has some outdoor tables, but they are planning to move to a bigger space sometime in 2003/2004 and expand their offerings.

· organic produce · freshly prepared food · deli · bakery · vegetarian friendly · chain · take-out

From **Ventura Fwy** (CA 134W), take Glendale Ave exit right onto Monterey Rd 2 blocks to Glendale. Turn left onto Glendale to store on right. **From 134E**, turn left directly onto Glendale ¼ mile to store on right.

GOLETA

GOOD EARTH RESTAURANT & BAKERY ✗ &

5955 Calle Real © 805-683-6101 ⊘ Daily 7:30-9:30
A "natural food" restaurant with poultry, fish and vegetarian choices. Soups, salads, sandwiches, burgers, hot entrees, whole grains, fresh juices, and shakes.

· juice bar · bakery · vegetarian friendly · alcohol · chain · tables · wait staff

From **Hwy 101**, take Fairview Ave exit inland (left from 101S, right from 101N) about ¼ mile to Calle Real. Turn right onto Calle Real to restaurant.

LASSEN'S NATURAL FOODS 🍃

5154 Hollister Ave. © 805-683-7696 ⊘ M-Sat 8-8

· chain

From **Hwy 101**, take Rt 217 (Ward Memorial Blvd) south (right from 101S, left from 101N) about ½ mile to Hollister Ave. Turn right onto Hollister to store.

GRANADA HILLS

VEGETABLE DELIGHT ✗

17823 Chatsworth St. © 818-360-3997 ⊘ M-F 11:30-9:30, Sat-Sun 4-9:30
Chinese vegan menu with many faux meat items.

· organic produce · alcohol · tables · wait staff · take-out

From **I-5**, take CA 118W about 3¾ miles to Bilboa St exit. Turn left onto Bilboa about 1 mile to Chatsworth St. Turn right onto Chatsworth over 1 mile to restaurant between White Oak & Zelzah Ave.

GRASS VALLEY

BRIAR PATCH COMMUNITY MARKET 🍃

10061 Joerschke Drive © 530-272-5333 ⊘ M-Sat 8:30-8, Sun 10-7
Sandwiches to go and tables outside.

From **CA 49 or CA 20**, take Brunswick Rd ramp west on Brunswick (left and across hwy from 49N/20E, straight from 49S/20W) to 1st left at Maltman Dr. Turn left onto Maltman about ¼ mile to Joerschke Dr. Turn right onto Joerschke to store on left.

NATURAL VALLEY HEALTH FOODS
562 Sutton Way © 530-273-6525 ⊙ M-F 10-6, Sat 9:30-5:30

From CA 49 or CA 20, take Brunswick Rd ramp east on Brunswick (right from from 49N/20E, left and across hwy from 49S/20W) to store at corner Brunswick & Sutton Way.

GUERNEVILLE

Lovely, small northern California town with Redwood State Park, Armstrong Woods and camping on the Russian River.

FOOD FOR HUMANS
16385 First St. © 707-869-3612 ⊙ Daily 10-8
· organic produce · freshly prepared food · vegetarian friendly · take-out

From Hwy 101 just north of Santa Rosa, take River Rd/Mark West Springs exit west on River Rd about 12 miles (through Forestville) to Guerneville where River Rd merges with Hwy 116. Turn left onto Mill St (right coming from coast) to store straight ahead at 1st St.

SPARKS RESTAURANT
16248 Main St. © 707-869-8206 ⊙ Dinner F-Sat 5:30-9:30, Sun 5:30-9, Brunch Sat-Sun 10-3
Entirely vegan organic fare (including the beer and wine).
· vegan · organic focus · alcohol · counter · tables · wait staff

From Hwy 101 just north of Santa Rosa, take River Rd/Mark West Springs exit west on River Rd about 12 miles to Armstrong Woods Rd in Guerneville (traffic light at intersection). Continue straight (River becomes Main St) 1 block to restaurant on right near intersection at Church St.

HALF MOON BAY

OASIS NATURAL FOODS
523 Main St. © 650-726-7881 ⊙ Daily 10-6
Almost completely organic focus, serving vegan soups, sandwiches and tea in the herb garden behind the store.
· organic produce · freshly prepared food · vegan · organic focus · tables · self-service · take-out

From Hwy 1, take Kelly Ave exit east 3 blocks to Main St. Turn right onto Main to store on left. From I-280, take Hwy 92 east about 8 miles to Half Moon Bay. Turn left at 1st traffic light onto Main. Pass 3 stop signs to store on left (½ block past Kelly).

HEMET

HENRY'S MARKETPLACE
1295 S. State St. © 909-766-6746 ⊙ Daily 8-9
· organic produce · freshly prepared food · deli · vegetarian friendly · chain · take-out

Hemet is about 13 miles east of I-215 on CA 74E. From CA 74, turn south onto S State St (right from 74E, left from 74W) about 1½ miles to store.

HERMOSA BEACH

THE SPOT
110 2nd St. © 310-376-2355 ⊙ Daily 11-10
Organic whole grains, beans and seasonal produce form the mainstay of this vegetarian, vegan-friendly casual beach restaurant.

· vegetarian · vegan friendly · organic focus · alcohol · tables · wait staff · take-out

⛶ **From Hwy 101**, turn west onto 190th St to end (the ocean). Turn right onto Hermosa Ave 3 blocks to 2nd St. Turn right onto 2nd to restaurant on right. **From I-405S** (San Diego Fwy), take Hawthorne exit south (right) on Hawthorne about 2 miles to 190th St. Turn right into 190th about 2½ miles and follow directions above. **From I-405N**, take Normandie exit left (across hwy) about ¼ mile to 190th St. Turn right onto 190th more than 5 miles and follow directions above.

HOLLYWOOD

PARU'S ✕
5140 W. Sunset Blvd. ℂ 323-661-7600 🕐 M-F 12-3, 6-10, Sat-Sun 1-10
Southern Indian vegetarian menu.
· vegetarian · vegan friendly · alcohol · tables · wait staff

⛶ **From Hwy 101** (Hollywood Fwy), take Sunset Blvd exit east to restaurant on south side between Western & Normandie.

HUNTINGTON BEACH

GOOD MOOD FOOD CAFE ✕
5930 Warner Ave. ℂ 714-377-2028 🕐 M-Th 11-7, F-Sat 11-9
All raw, organic, vegan menu.
· vegan · organic focus · tables · wait staff

⛶ **From Hwy 1** (Pacific Coast Hwy), go east on Warner Ave about 2⅓ miles to restaurant (before Springdale St). **From I-405S**, take Springdale exit toward Westminster Ave W, right onto Springdale 3 miles to Warner. Turn right onto Warner to restaurant. **From I-405N**, take Warner W exit toward Magnolia St S. Go west on Warner 3⅓ miles to restaurant (past Springdale).

HAPPY VEGGIE ✕
7251 Warner Ave ℂ 714-375-9505 🕐 M-Th 11-3, 5-9, F-Sat 11-9
Vegetarian Asian cuisine, featuring tofu, soy meat and no msg.
· vegetarian · vegan friendly · tables · wait staff · take-out

⛶ **From Hwy 1** (Pacific Coast Hwy), go east on Warner Ave about 3⅔ miles to restaurant in Ross & Stater Bros Shopping Ctr (just past Goldenwest St). **From I-405S**, take Bolsa Ave W exit toward Goldenwest St right onto Goldenwest about 2 miles to Warner. Turn left onto Warner to restaurant in Ross & Stater Bros Shopping Ctr. **From I-405N**, take Warner Ave W exit 2 miles to restaurant in Ross & Stater Bros Shopping Ctr.

MOTHER'S MARKET & KITCHEN ✕🍽   ♿
19770 Beach Blvd. ℂ 714-963-6667 🕐 Daily 9-10, Restaurant & Deli 9-9
An extensive menu of wholesome vegetarian and vegan fare for breakfast, lunch and dinner. Whole-grain breads, brown rice, fresh juices, and smoothies.
· organic produce · freshly prepared food · juice bar · salad bar · deli · bakery
· vegetarian · vegan friendly · alcohol · counter · tables · wait staff · take-out

⛶ **From Hwy 1N** (Pacific Coast Hwy), take Beach Blvd north about 2 miles to store just before E Utica. **From 1S**, turn left onto Seapoint Ave about 1 mile to Garfield Ave. Turn right onto Garfield 1¾ miles to Beach. Turn right onto Beach about ¾ mile to store (just past Utica). **From I-405S**, take Beach Blvd exit and follow Center St ramp toward Huntington Beach. Merge onto Beach almost 4 miles to store (just past Utica). **From I-405N**, take Harbor Blvd exit left onto Harbor about 1 mile to Adams Ave. Turn right onto Adams 4 miles to Beach. Turn left onto Beach ¼ mile to store (before Utica).

IRVINE

MOTHER'S MARKET & KITCHEN ✕🍴 &

2963 Michelson Drive © 949-752-6667 ☉ Daily 9-10, Restaurant & Deli 9-9
An extensive menu of wholesome vegetarian and vegan fare for breakfast,
lunch and dinner. Whole-grain breads, brown rice, fresh juices and smoothies.
· organic produce · freshly prepared food · juice bar · salad bar · deli · bakery
· vegetarian · vegan friendly · alcohol · tables · self-service · wait staff · take-out
🍎 **From I-405** (San Diego Fwy), take Jamboree Rd south (right from
405S, left from 405N) 1 block to Michelson Dr. Turn left onto Michelson
to store in Park Place Center.

VEGGIE & TEA HOUSE ✕ &

14988 Sand Canyon, Studio #1 © 949-559-0577 ☉ Daily 11-9
Asian vegetarian, with three locales. Focus is "healthy cuisine," with many of
the vegetables grown on their 400-acre organic farm. Brown rice available.
· vegetarian · vegan friendly · organic focus · tables · wait staff · take-out
🍎 **From I-405** (San Diego Fwy), take Jeffrey Rd/University Dr exit onto
Jeffrey Rd (left from 405S, right from 405N) about ⅔ mile to Alton Pkwy.
Turn left onto Alton 1 block to E Yale Loop. Turn left onto Yale almost ½
mile to Fallingstar. Turn right onto Fallingstar, left onto Pebble and left
onto Sand to restaurant.

WILD OATS MARKET ✕🍴

18040 Culver Drive © 949-651-8880 ☉ Daily 7-10
· organic produce · freshly prepared food · juice bar · salad bar · café · deli · bakery
· vegetarian friendly · chain · tables · self-service · take-out
🍎 **From I-405** (San Diego Fwy), take Culver Dr exit south (right from 405S,
left from 405N) about ½ mile to Michelson Dr. Turn left onto Michelson
to store on right.

JACKSON

GOLD TRAIL NATURAL FOODS ✕🍴

625 S. Hwy. 49 © 209-223-1896 ☉ M-F 10-6, Sat-Sun 10-5, Juice bar M-F 10:30-
4, Sat 10:30-3
· organic produce · juice bar · tables · self-service · take-out
🍎 In the Central Sierra Nevada foothills on Hwy 49 (about 50 miles south
of I-80 at Auburn). Store is on east side of Hwy 49 in Mother Lode Plaza.

LA JOLLA

CHE CAFE COLLECTIVE ✕🍴 &

9500 Gillman Drive, Student Center B-0323C © 858-534-1233 ☉ M-W, F-
Sun 7pm-2am, Th 5:30-7 (call as hours vary with staffing and school calendar)
Volunteer, student-run, cooperative serving vegan fare along with live enter-
tainment and progressive politics. Thursday night is all-you-can-eat dinner.
· vegan · organic focus · co-op · tables · self-service
🍎 On the UC San Diego Campus. **From I-5**, take La Jolla Village Dr exit
west just past Villa La Jolla Dr (and gas station) to ramp on right onto
Gillman Dr. Turn right at stop sign off ramp onto Gillman and left at 1st
stop sign onto Scholar's Dr (info booth on right.) Cafe is in mural-covered
building on left. (Continue up hill for parking.)

WHOLE FOODS MARKET ✂️🍽️   ♿

8825 Villa La Jolla Drive ✆ 858-642-6700 ⏰ Daily 8-10

· organic produce · freshly prepared food · juice bar · salad bar · deli · bakery
· vegetarian friendly · chain · take-out

🍎 **From I-5S**, take La Jolla Village Dr exit to the right, then get in left lane. Turn left at traffic light onto Villa La Jolla past next light to store in shopping plaza on left at La Jolla & Nobel Dr. **From I-5N**, take Nobel Dr exit. Turn left at light and cross back over interstate. Store is in shopping plaza on right at La Jolla & Nobel.

LA MESA

HENRY'S MARKETPLACE 🍽️

4630 Palm Ave. ✆ 619-460-7722 ⏰ Daily 8-9

· organic produce · freshly prepared food · deli · vegetarian friendly · chain · take-out

🍎 **From I-8E**, take Spring St exit toward Downtown right onto Spring about 1/3 mile to La Mesa Blvd. Turn left onto La Mesa 1 block to Palm Ave. Turn right onto Palm 2 blocks to store. **From I-8W**, take El Cajon Blvd exit toward Spring. Pass Spring, turn left onto Baltimore Dr and follow onto University Ave about 1/4 mile to Spring. Turn right onto Spring 2 blocks to La Mesa and follow directions above from La Mesa.

LAGUNA BEACH

THE STAND ✂️   ♿

238 Thalia St. ✆ 949-494-8101 ⏰ Daily 7-7

Thirty years on the beach serving healthy, vegan whole wheat burritos, tamales, sandwiches, salads, and beans-brown rice-and-vegetables in a variety of ways.

· vegan · organic focus · counter · self-service · take-out

🍎 **From I-405 or I-5**, take Rt 133 (Laguna Canyon Rd) south (toward beach) 8-10 miles to Pacific Coast Hwy (Hwy 1). Turn left (south) onto 1 about 2/3 mile to Thalia St. Turn left (inland) onto Thalia to restaurant on right.

WILD OATS MARKET ✂️🍽️   ♿

283 Broadway ✆ 949-376-7888 ⏰ Daily 7-10

· organic produce · freshly prepared food · juice bar · salad bar · café · deli · bakery
· vegetarian friendly · chain · tables · self-service · take-out

🍎 **From I-405 or I-5**, take Rt 133 (Laguna Canyon Rd) south (toward beach) 8-10 miles to store on left 1 block before ocean.

LAGUNA NIGUEL

HENRY'S MARKETPLACE 🍽️

27271 La Paz Rd. ✆ 949-349-1994 ⏰ Daily 8-9

· organic produce · freshly prepared food · deli · vegetarian friendly · chain · take-out

🍎 **From I-5S**, take Alicia Pkwy exit right onto Alicia Pkwy about 1 2/3 miles to Moulton Pkwy. Turn left onto Moulton about 1/2 mile to La Paz Rd. Turn right onto La Paz about 3/4 mile to store. **From I-5N**, merge onto CA 73N toward Long Beach almost 3 miles to La Paz Rd exit. Follow exit 3/4 mile to La Paz. Turn left onto La Paz about 1/2 mile to store.

LAGUNA WOODS

MOTHER'S MARKET & KITCHEN ✂️🍽️   ♿

24165 Paseo de Valencia ✆ 949-768-6667 ⏰ Daily 9-10, Restaurant & Deli 9-9

An extensive menu of wholesome vegetarian and vegan fare for breakfast, lunch and dinner. Whole-grain breads, brown rice, fresh juices and smoothies.
· organic produce · freshly prepared food · juice bar · salad bar · café · deli · bakery
· vegetarian · vegetarian friendly · alcohol · tables · wait service · take-out

From I-5S, take El Toro Rd exit right onto Paseo de Valencia about ⅓ mile to store. **From I-5N,** take El Toro Rd exit left onto El Toro about ½ mile to Paseo de Valencia. Turn left onto Paseo de Valencia to store.

LAKE ELSINORE

Visitors come for the lake, hang gliding and the Cleveland National Forest.

EARTH IS ENOUGH
31712 Casino Drive, #1C © 909-245-0288 ⊙ M-F 10-6, Sat 10-4
· organic produce

From I-15, take Railroad Canyon Rd exit west on Railroad Canyon/Diamond Dr (left from 15N, right from 15S) 1 block to store.

LANCASTER

THE WHOLE WHEATERY
44264 10th St. W. © 661-945-0773 ⊙ M-F 9-7, Sat 9-6, Sun 11-5, Cafe M-Sat 10:30-4, Sun 11-4
Free lectures and after-hours monthly live jazz from 6-9 in Natcheryl's Cafe.
· organic produce · freshly prepared food · juice bar · café · deli · bakery · vegetarian
friendly · alcohol · tables · wait staff · take-out

Lancaster is about 40 miles north of I-5 (Golden Gate Fwy) on CA 14 (Antelope Vally Fwy) or 40 miles east of I-5 on CA 138. **From 14N,** take Ave K exit right on K about ½ mile to 10th St. Turn left onto 10th less than 1 mile store on right in bright orange strip mall (at north end). **From 14S,** take W Ave J exit left about 1¼ miles to 10th. Turn right onto 10th to store on left. **From 138E,** take Ave I exit left onto W Ave I about ¼ mile to 20th St W. Turn right onto 20th 1 mile to W Ave J. Turn left onto J 1 mile to 10th St. Turn right onto 10th to store on left.

LARKSPUR

ROXANNE'S
320 Magnolia Ave. © 415-924-5004 ⊙ M-Sat 5:30-10
Upscale "living food" menu and many home grown ingredients. A la carte or price-fixed, 10-course tasting menu paired with wine. Reservations suggested.
· vegan · organic focus · alcohol · tables · wait staff

From Hwy 101, take Tamalpais Dr exit west toward Paradise Dr (right from 101S, left from 101N)less than 1 mile. Bear left when Tamalpais becomes Redwood Ave. Turn right onto Corte Madera Ave (becomes Magnolia Ave) over ½ mile to restaurant at corner Magnolia & King St.

LEMON GROVE

HENRY'S MARKETPLACE
3205 Lemon Grove Ave. © 619-667-8686 ⊙ Daily 8-9
· organic produce · freshly prepared food · deli · vegetarian friendly · chain · take-out

From I-805, take CA 94E about 5¼ miles to Lemon Grove Ave. Turn right onto Lemon Grove about ¼ mile to store.

LOMA LINDA

LOMA LINDA MARKET 🍎
11161 Anderson St. © 909-558-4565 ☺ M-Th 7-7, F 7-3, Sun 8-6
A completely vegetarian market.

🍎 **From I-10**, take Anderson St exit and follow Anderson south (right from 10E, left from 10W) about 1 mile (past Loma Linda University Medical Center) to store at Prospect St (behind bank & post office).

LOMITA

HOUSE OF VEGE ✗
2439 Pacific Coast Hwy. © 310-530-1180 ☺ M-Th 11-3, 5-9, F 11-3, 5-9:30, Sat 11-9:30, Sun 11-9
Chinese vegetarian, featuring faux meat and offering brown rice.
· vegan friendly · tables · wait staff · take-out

🍎 **From I-110**, take CA 1/Pacific Coast Hwy exit west (right from 110S, left from 110N) 2½ miles to restaurant between Pennsylvania Ave & Airport Dr.

LONG BEACH

Take a look at the Queen Mary while you're here or passing through.

PAPA JON'S MARKETING, INC. ✗🍎
5000 E. 2nd St. © 562-439-3444 ☺ Daily 8-9
· freshly prepared food · café · vegetarian · vegan friendly · tables · wait staff · take-out

🍎 **From I-605S or I-405N**, take CA 22W towards Long Beach about 1 mile to Studebaker Rd exit. Turn right onto Studebaker 1⅓ miles to Westminster Ave. Turn right onto Westminster (becomes 2nd St) about 1 mile to store on left. **From I-405S**, merge onto N Lakewood Blvd (CA 19S) almost 1½ miles to roundabout. Take E Pacific Coast Hwy (Hwy 1S) exit about ⅓ mile to Ximeno Ave. Turn right onto Ximeno less than ½ mile to E Anaheim St. Turn left onto Anaheim and next right onto Park Ave 1½ miles to 2nd St. Turn left onto 2nd to store on right.

WILD OATS MARKET ✗🍎   ♿
6550 E. Pacific Coast Hwy. © 562-598-8687 ☺ Daily 7-10
Conveniently located in the Long Beach Marina for boaters and beach-goers.
· organic produce · freshly prepared food · juice bar · salad bar · café · deli · bakery · vegetarian friendly · chain · tables · self-service · take-out

🍎 **From I-605S or I-405**, take CA 22W towards Long Beach about 1 mile to Studebaker Rd exit. Turn right onto Studebaker 1⅓ miles to Westminster Ave. Turn right onto Westminster (becomes 2nd St) about ½ mile to Hwy 1 (Pacific Coast Hwy). Turn left onto PCH to store (next to PetCo).

LOS ANGELES

Los Angeles is a very vegetarian-friendly town. It would take a whole book to list all the possibilities, so we acknowledge that there will be omissions.

DR. J.'S RESTAURANT ✗   ♿
1303 Westwood Blvd. © 310-477-2721 ☺ M-Sat 11-7
Asian vegetarian (mostly vegan and organic) fast food sold by the pound.
· vegetarian · vegan friendly · organic focus · tables · self-service · take-out

🍎 **From I-405** (San Diego Fwy), take Wilshire Blvd toward UCLA/Westwood east on Wilshire about ⅔ mile to Westwood Blvd. Turn right onto Westwood to restaurant.

EREWHON NATURAL FOODS MARKET ✗ 🍴 ♿

7660 Beverly Blvd. ✆ 323-937-0777 ⏰ M-Sat 8-10, Sun 9-9

· organic produce · freshly prepared food · juice bar · salad bar · deli · vegetarian friendly · tables · self-service · take-out

🍎 **From Hwy 101** (Hollywood Fwy), take Highland Ave/Hollywood Bowl exit south on Cahuenga Blvd (becomes Highland) about 2½ miles to Beverly Blvd. Turn right onto Beverly 1 mile to store on right.

FATTY'S ✗ ♿

1627 Colorado Blvd. ✆ 323-254-8804 ⏰ M, Sun 8-3, W-Sat 8-10

Vegetarian breakfast/lunch/dinner. Soups, salads, sandwiches, and daily specials.

· vegetarian · vegan friendly · tables · self-service

🍎 **From I-5**, take CA 2N toward Glendale about 3¼ miles to Broadway/ Colorado Blvd exit. Turn right onto Colorado about 1½ miles to restaurant between Vincent & Townsend Ave. **From CA 134W**, merge onto Colorado Blvd toward Eagle Rock less than 1½ miles to restaurant. **From CA 134E**, take Harvey Dr exit right onto Harvey and left onto E Wilson (becomes W Broadway, then Colorado) about 1¾ miles to restaurant.

GOVINDA'S ✗

3764 Watseka Ave. ✆ 310-836-1269 ⏰ M-Sat 11-3, 5-8:30

All-you-can-eat vegetarian hot and cold lunch and dinner buffets at very affordable prices. Run by the Hari Krishna temple.

· salad bar · vegetarian · vegan friendly · tables · self-service

🍎 **From I-10E**, take exit 4 toward Overland Ave left onto National Blvd about ¼ mile and turn left to stay on National ½ mile to Exposition Blvd. Merge straight onto Exposition about ¼ mile to Watseka Ave. Turn right onto Watseka about ¼ mile to restaurant. **From I-10W**, take exit 6 onto Roberston Blvd 1 block to National. Turn left onto National 1 block to Venice Blvd. Turn left onto Venice over ½ mile to Watseka. Turn right onto Watseka to restaurant.

LUNA TIERRA SOL CAFE ✗

2501 W. 6th St. ✆ 213-380-4754 ⏰ M-F 7-10, Sat 10-10, Sun 9-10

Mexican vegetarian with many vegan choices for breakfast, lunch and dinner. Worker-owned and a venue for local talent, including music, poetry, open mike, forums, art, and more.

· vegetarian · vegan friendly · alcohol · co-op · tables · wait staff · take-out

🍎 **From Hwy 101S** (Hollywood Fwy), take Benton Way exit right onto N Rampart Blvd 1 mile to 6th St. Turn left onto 6th 2 blocks to restaurant on left. **From 101N**, take Alvarado St exit left onto Alvardo 1 mile to 6th. Turn right onto 6th 4 blocks to restaurant on right.

NATURE MART 🍴

2080 Hillhurst Ave. ✆ 323-660-0052 ⏰ Daily 8-10

🍎 **From I-5** (Santa Ana Fwy), take Los Feliz Blvd W exit toward Hollywood (merge right from 5S, turn left from 5N) over 1 mile to Hillhurst Ave. Turn left onto Hillhurst 2 blocks to store on east side (left).

SANTE LA BREA ✗ ♿

345 N. La Brea Ave. ✆ 323-857-0412 ⏰ Daily 8-10

Self-described as an "all natural, mostly organic, healthy restaurant that caters to all intolerances." Will alter dishes to make vegan, or add fish or free-range chicken on request.

· café · bakery · vegetarian friendly · vegan friendly · organic focus · alcohol · tables
· wait staff · take-out

From downtown LA, take I-10 west to LaBrea Ave. Turn right onto La Brea to restaurant ½ block north of Beverly Blvd. **From San Fernando Valley**, take Hwy 101S (Hollywood Fwy) to Highland Ave/Hollywood Bowl exit. Go south on Cahuenga Blvd (becomes Highland) about 1¼ miles to Melrose Ave. Turn right onto Melrose 5 blocks to La Brea. Turn left onto La Brea 3½ blocks to restaurant.

VEGAN EXPRESS ✖

3217 Cahuenga Blvd. W. ℂ 323-851-8837 ⊙ M-Th, Sun 11-9, F-Sat 10-10
Another California vegan fast-food option. An Asian orientation, but with interesting deviations, such as vege meat dinners mimicking old-fashioned American fare, as well as sandwiches and wraps. For breakfast, there are unusual burritos and wheat-free pancakes. The all-vegan desserts feature several raw selections. PD: Hard-core vegan. Funky but delicious.

· vegan · tables · self-service · take-out

From Hwy 101N (Hollywood Fwy), take exit toward Barham Blvd/Burbank onto Cahuenga Blvd about ½ mile to Barham. Turn left onto Barham and right onto Cahuenga to restaurant. **From 101S**, take exit toward Barham left onto Cahuenga to restaurant just off fwy.

VEGETARIAN AFFAIR ✖

3715 Santa Rosalia Drive ℂ 323-292-8664 ⊙ M-Th 10:30-8:30, F 10:30-3:30 (5 in summer), Sun 11-8:30
Vegetarian fast food, including drive-through window service.

· vegetarian · vegan friendly · tables · self-service · take-out

From I-10 (Santa Monica Fwy), take exit 8 south on Crenshaw Blvd (right from 10E, left from 10W) about 2 miles to Stocker St. Turn right onto Stocker and after Baldwin Hills Crenshaw Shopping Plaza turn right onto Santa Rosalia Dr to restaurant.

WHOLE FOODS MARKET ✖

11737 San Vincente Blvd. ℂ 310-826-4433 ⊙ Daily 8-10
Dining is outside on the patio.

· organic produce · freshly prepared food · salad bar · deli · bakery · vegetarian friendly
· chain · tables · self-service · take-out

Located in the Brentwood section of LA. **From I-405** (San Diego Fwy), take Wilshire Blvd west about ½ mile to San Vincente Blvd. Turn right onto San Vincente about ½ mile to store.

WHOLE FOODS MARKET ✖

6350 W. 3rd St. ℂ 323-964-6800 ⊙ Daily 8-10

· organic produce · freshly prepared food · salad bar · café · deli · bakery · vegetarian
friendly · chain · tables · self-service · take-out

From Hwy 101 (Hollywood Fwy), take Highland Ave/Hollywood Bowl exit south on Cahuenga Blvd (becomes Highland) about 1 mile to Hollywood Blvd. Turn right onto Hollywood about 1⅓ miles to Fairfax Ave. Turn left onto Fairfax 2 miles to E 3rd St. Turn left onto 3rd to store.

WHOLE FOODS MARKET ✖

11666 National Blvd. ℂ 310-996-8840 ⊙ Daily 8-10, Cafe & Juice bar 7-8:30

· organic produce · freshly prepared food · juice bar · salad bar · café · deli · bakery
· vegetarian friendly · chain · tables · self-service · take-out

From I-10E (Santa Monica Fwy), take exit 2A left onto Pico Blvd about ½ mile to S Barrington Ave. Turn right onto Barrington ¾ mile to store at corner Barrington & National Blvd. **From I-10W**, take exit 4 (Overland Ave) straight onto National 1⅓ miles to store at corner Barrington & National.

WILD OATS MARKET ✕ 🍂   &

3476 S. Centinela Ave. © 310-636-1300 ⊙ Daily 7-10
  · organic produce · freshly prepared food · juice bar · café · deli · bakery · vegetarian friendly · chain · tables · self-service · take-out

🍎 **From I-10E** (Santa Monica Fwy), take exit 2A onto Pico Blvd and turn right onto S Bundy Dr (becomes S Centinela Ave) about 1 mile to store. **From I-10W**, take exit 2B south on S Bundy and follow directions above. **From I-405** (San Diego Fwy), take Washington Blvd/Venice Blvd exit west on Venice over 1 mile to S Centinela. Turn right onto Centinela about ½ mile to store.

LOS GATOS

WHOLE FOODS MARKET ✕ 🍂   &

15980 Los Gatos Blvd. © 408-358-4434 ⊙ Daily 8-9, Bakery & Cafe from 7
  · organic produce · freshly prepared food · juice bar · salad bar · café · deli · bakery · vegetarian friendly · chain · tables · self-service · take-out

🍎 **From Hwy 85**, take Bascom Ave exit toward Los Gatos Blvd south on Bascom (becomes Los Gatos) about 1½ miles to store in Cornerstone Plaza (near Blossom Hill Rd). **From I-880**, merge onto CA 17S about 5¼ miles to Lark Ave exit. Turn left onto Lark ⅓ mile to Los Gatos. Turn right onto Los Gatos almost 1 mile to store in Cornerstone Plaza.

MENDOCINO

CORNERS OF THE MOUTH 🍂

45015 Ukiah St. © 707-937-5345 ⊙ Daily 9-7
  · organic produce · co-op · chain · counter · tables · self-service · wait staff · take-out

🍎 **From Hwy 1**, take Main St west about ⅓ mile to Lansing St. Turn right onto Lansing 2 blocks to Ukiah St. Turn left onto Ukiah to store on left.

MENLO PARK

If you're in downtown Menlo Park on Sunday, visit the organic farmers' market.

FLEA STREET CAFE ✕

3607 Alameda de las Pulgas © 650-854-1226 ⊙ Tues-Sat 5:30-9, Sun 10-2, 5:30-8
The original of three organic restaurants in the area under the same ownership. The upscale, gourmet dinner fare has choices for vegetarians, fish- and meat-eaters. Committed to local organic food producers and the environment, to the extent that all compostable restaurant waste is saved for the farmers.

  · vegetarian friendly · organic focus · alcohol · tables · wait staff

🍎 **From Hwy 101** (Bayshore Fwy), take Woodside Rd exit west on Woodside (past El Camino) almost 3 miles to Alameda de las Pulagas. Turn left onto Alameda 2 miles to restaurant on left (between Valparaiso Ave & Sand Hill Rd). **From I-280**, take Sand Hill Rd exit east on Sand Hill about 1¾ miles to Santa Cruz Ave. Turn left onto Santa Cruz about ¼ mile. Stay in left lane onto Alameda de las Pulgas about ⅓ mile to restaurant.

THE JZ COOL EATERY ✕

827 Santa Cruz Ave. © 650-325-3665 ⊙ M 9-3, Tues-Sat 11-8, Sun 9-2
Same owners as the Flea Street Cafe. Similar organic focus, but more casual menu of soups, salads, sandwiches, organic burgers and hot dogs. Weekend brunch.

  · vegetarian friendly · organic focus · alcohol · tables · self-service

🛏 From Hwy 101 (Bayshore Fwy), take Willow Rd toward Menlo Park about 1¼ miles to Middlefield Rd. Turn right onto Middlefield ¾ mile to Ravenswood Ave. Turn left onto Ravenswood (becomes Menlo Ave) less than 1 mile to Crane St. Turn right onto Crane 1 block to Santa Cruz Ave. Turn left onto Santa Cruz to restaurant on left. **From I-280**, take Sand Hill Rd exit east on Sand Hill about 1 mile to Santa Cruz. Turn left onto Santa Cruz over 2 miles to restaurant on right.

MILL VALLEY

WHOLE FOODS MARKET ✗ 🍽   ♿
414 Miller Ave. © 415-381-1200 ⊘ Daily 8-8
   · organic produce · freshly prepared food · juice bar · salad bar · deli · bakery
   · vegetarian friendly · chain · tables · self-service · take-out
🛏 From Hwy 101N, take Stinson Beach/Mill Valley exit onto Hwy 1N about ¾ mile to Altamonte Blvd. Merge straight onto Altamonte (becomes Miller Ave) about 1⅓ miles to store on left. **From 101S**, take E Blithedale Ave exit right onto Blithedale ¾ mile to Camino Alto. Turn left onto Camino Alto ½ mile to Miller. Turn right onto Miller less than ½ mile to store on left.

MONTEREY

Don't miss the Monterey Aquarium.

WHOLE FOODS MARKET ✗ 🍽   ♿
800 Del Monte Center © 831-333-1660 ⊘ Daily 8-9
   · organic produce · freshly prepared food · juice bar · salad bar · deli · bakery
   · vegetarian friendly · chain · tables · self-service · take-out
🛏 From Hwy 1N, take Monterey exit onto Monrus Ave less than ¼ mile to store on right in Del Monte Shopping Center. **From 1S**, take Soledad Dr toward Monrus Ave about ⅓ mile to Monrus. Turn right onto Monrus to store on right in Del Monte Shopping Center.

MONTEREY PARK

HAPPY FAMILY 3 ✗
608 N. Atlantic Blvd. © 626-282-8986 ⊘ M-Th 11:30-2:45, 5-8:45, F 11:30-2:45, 5-9:15, Sat 11:30-9:15, Sun 11:30-8:45
Chinese vegetarian menu.
   · vegetarian · vegan friendly · tables · wait staff · take-out
🛏 From I-10, take Atlantic Blvd exit toward Monterey Park south on Atlantic (right from 10E, ramp on left from 10W) to restaurant just off fwy.

MOUNTAIN VIEW

DEEDEE'S ✗ 🍽
2551 W. Middlefield Rd. © 650-967-9333 ⊘ Grocery M-Sat 9-9, Sun 9-3, Restaurant M-Sat 11:30-2:30, Sun 12-3
Vegetarian Indian lunch. A la carte, one-price daily buffet, or special lunch-to-go. Regional menus on Sunday. Indian groceries and video rental on premises.
   · vegetarian · vegan friendly · tables · self-service · take-out
🛏 From Hwy 101 (Bayshore Fwy), take San Antonio Rd exit south about 1 mile to Middlefield Rd. Turn left onto Middlefield to restaurant.

GARDEN FRESH VEGETARIAN RESTAURANT ✗
1245 W. El Camino Real © 650-961-7795 ⊘ M-Th, Sun 11-9:30, F-Sat 11-10
Asian vegetarian. Brown rice served.

· vegetarian · vegan friendly · tables · wait staff · take-out

From Hwy 101 (Bayshore Fwy), take Shoreline Blvd exit toward Mtn View south on N Shoreline about 1¾ miles to El Camino Real. Turn right onto El Camino to restaurant on left. **From I-280**, take El Monte Rd exit toward Mtn View right onto El Monte Rd (becomes El Monte Ave) less than 3 miles to El Camino Real. Turn right onto El Camino about ½ mile to restaurant on right just before Shoreline.

HOBEE'S ✕

2312 Central Expwy. © 650-968-6050 ⊙ M-F 6:30am-2:30pm, Sat-Sun 7:30am-2:30pm
This California chain caters to just about every taste, from "bacon and fries" to "tofu and brown rice." Big breakfast selection (includes whole wheat pancakes), homemade soups (most vegetarian), burgers (ground chuck, veggie-grain or turkey) on whole wheat bun, whole wheat quesadillas, choice of chicken, salmon, tofu or veggie-grain patty on most entrees, even soymilk for a nondairy option.

· salad bar · café · vegetarian friendly · chain · tables · wait staff · take-out

From Hwy 101 (Bayshore Fwy), take Rengstorff Ave south (left from 101S, loop around right from 101N) about 1 mile to Central Expwy. Turn right onto Central to restaurant on right. **From I-280**, take Page Mill Rd/G3N (left from 280S, right from 280N) about 1⅓ miles to Foothills Expwy. Turn right onto Foothills 1⅓ miles to Arastradero Rd. Turn left onto Arastradero (becomes W Charleston) about 1½ miles to Alma. Turn right onto Alma (becomes Central Expwy) about 1½ miles to restaurant on left.

MT. SHASTA

BERRYVALE GROCERY ✕ 🍽

305 S. Mt. Shasta Blvd. © 530-926-1576 ⊙ M-Sat 8:30-7:30, Sun 10-6:30
· organic produce · freshly prepared food · juice bar · café · deli · vegetarian friendly
· tables · self-service · take-out

From I-5, take Central Mt Shasta exit east about ¼ mile (across railroad tracks) to traffic light at Mt Shasta Blvd. Turn right onto Mt Shasta 2 blocks to store on right.

NAPA

THE GOLDEN CARROT 🍽

1621 W. Imola Ave. © 707-224-3177 ⊙ M-F 10-6, Sat 10-5, Sun 10-4

From Hwy 29, take Imola Ave/CA 121N exit east about ¾ mile to store on right in River Park Shopping Center.

NEVADA CITY

Nevada City is where gold was first discovered.

EARTH SONG MARKET & CAFE ✕ 🍽

135 Argall Way © Store 530-265-9392 Restaurant 530-265-8025 ⊙ Daily 8-9
The predominantly organic menu (including wine and beer) includes vegan, vegetarian (both clearly noted), wild fish, organic poultry, and grain-fed bison. In-house organic bakery. Live music on weekends. Eat outside on the patio, in the formal dining room, or pick up a picnic for the road.

· organic produce · freshly prepared food · juice bar · salad bar · café · deli · bakery
· vegetarian friendly · organic focus · alcohol · tables · wait staff · take-out

From Hwy 49, take Gold Flat Rd east to Searls Ave (1st corner). Turn right onto Seals about ¼ mile to Argall Way. Turn left onto Argall ¾ block to store on left.

NORTH HOLLYWOOD

LEONOR'S MEXICAN RESTAURANT ✕
11403 Victory Blvd. ✆ 818-980-9011 ⊙ M-Th, Sun 10-10, F-Sat 10-11
Meatless Mexican cuisine featuring soy-based meats and cheese.
· vegan · tables · wait staff

🍎 **From Hwy 101N** (Hollywood Fwy), take CA 170N toward Sacramento about 1½ miles to Burbank Blvd. Turn right onto Burbank about ½ mile to Tujunga Ave. Turn right onto Tujunga 1 mile to Victory Bvd. Turn left onto Victory to restaurant. **From 101S** (Ventura Fwy), take Tujunga Ave exit toward N·Hollywood. Turn right onto Tujunga, merge onto CA 170N over ¾ mile to Burbank Blvd and follow directions above.

NORTHRIDGE

GOOD EARTH RESTAURANT & BAKERY ✕   ♿
19510 Nordhoff St. ✆ 818-993-7306 ⊙ Daily 8-9
A "natural food" restaurant with poultry, fish and vegetarian choices. Soups, salads, sandwiches, burgers, hot entrees, whole grains, fresh juices, and shakes.
· juice bar · bakery · vegetarian friendly · alcohol · chain · tables · wait staff

🍎 **From Hwy 101** (Ventura Fwy), take Tampa Ave north (left from 101S, right from 101N) about 4⅓ miles to Nordhoff St. Turn left onto Nordhoff ¼ mile to restaurant (across from Northridge Mall). **From I-210, I-5 or I-405**, take CA 118 west to Tampa Ave exit. Turn left onto Tampa about 2⅔ miles to Nordhoff. Turn left onto Nordhoff ¼ mile to restaurant .

SAAM'S A-1 PRODUCE ✕ 🍖   ♿
9043 Reseda Blvd. ✆ 818-998-6900 ⊙ Tues-Sun 9-8
The "deli" inside this grocery/produce market serves all-vegetarian Indian fare.
· freshly prepared food · vegetarian · vegan friendly · tables · self-service · take-out

🍎 **From Hwy 101** (Ventura Fwy), take Reseda Blvd exit north (left from 101S, right from 101N) about 4¼ miles to store.

NORWALK

OUR DAILY BREAD ✕ 🍖
12201 Firestone Blvd. ✆ 562-863-6897 ⊙ M, W, Th 10-4:30, Tues 10-7, F 10-2
A Seventh-day Adventist-run bookstore, grocery and vegan lunch counter.
· freshly prepared food · vegan · tables · self-service · take-out

🍎 **From I-5S** (Santa Ana Fwy), take San Antonio Dr/Norwalk Blvd exit left onto Union St and right onto San Antonio less than ¼ mile to Firestone Blvd. Turn left onto Firestone to store. **From I-5N**, take Firestone Blvd exit on left toward CA 42 about ¾ mile to store.

OAKLAND

FOOD MILL 🍖
3033 MacArthur Blvd. ✆ 510-482-3848 ⊙ M-Sat 8:30-6:30, Sun 9-5:30

🍎 **From I-580E**, take 35th St exit left onto 35th about ¼ mile to MacArthur Blvd. Turn left onto MacArthur 2½ blocks to store on left. **From I-580W**, take Coolidge Ave exit left onto Montana St and right onto Coolidge 3 blocks to MacArthur. Turn right onto MacArthur 1½ blocks to store on right.

ITAL KALABASH ✕

1405 Franklin S. © 510-836-4825 ⊙ M-F 8-7
Vegan food, Jamaican style. Special raw meals on select days.
  · vegan · counter · wait staff · take-out

▭ **From I-880N**, take Broadway exit toward Downtown and follow ramp to Alameda onto Broadway about ½ mile to 14th St. Turn right onto 14th 1 block to Franklin. Turn left onto Franklin to restaurant (2nd store on left). **From I-80E** (San Francisco), merge onto I-880S. Take W Grand Ave exit toward Maritime St about ½ mile and merge onto W Grand about 1⅓ miles to Market St. Turn right onto Market about ½ mile to 14th. Turn left onto 14th ⅔ mile to Franklin. Turn left onto Franklin to restaurant. **From I-980W**, take 18th St exit toward 14th onto Brush St about ¼ mile to 14th. Turn left onto 14th ½ mile to Franklin St. Turn left onto Franklin to restaurant.

MACROBIOTIC GROCERY & ORGANIC CAFE ✕

1050 40th St. © 510-653-6510 ⊙ Daily 9-9
Macrobiotic, organic, vegan meals, baked goods, groceries, and books.
  · organic produce · freshly prepared food · café · bakery · vegan · organic focus · tables · wait staff · take-out

▭ **From I-580E**, take MacArthur Blvd exit toward San Pablo Ave. Follow MacArthur to Adeline St. Turn left onto Adeline 3 blocks to store at 40th St. **From I-580W**, take West St/San Pablo exit left onto 36th St about ½ mile. Merge onto San Pablo about ⅓ mile to 40th. Turn right onto 40th 1 block to store at Adeline.

OCEAN BEACH

RANCHOS COCINA ✕

1830 Sunset Cliffs Blvd. © 619-226-7619 ⊙ Daily 8am-10pm
Mexican cuisine with an emphasis on "natural cooking," and more interesting vegetarian options than typically found. All-day breakfast, whole wheat tortillas and brown rice available. A Certified Green Restaurant.
  · vegetarian friendly · alcohol · tables · wait staff · take-out

▭ **From I-8W**, follow to end and merge onto Sunset Cliffs Blvd about 1 mile to restaurant on Sunset Cliffs at Narragansett Ave (3 blocks from ocean). **From I-5**, exit onto I-8W and follow directions above.

RANCHOS MERCADO ✕

4705 Point Loma Ave. © 619-224-9815 ⊙ Daily 8am-10pm
Same menu as Ranchos Cocina (above). Also a Certified Green Restaurant.
  · vegetarian friendly · alcohol · tables · wait staff

▭ **From I-8W**, follow to end and merge onto Sunset Cliffs Blvd about 1¼ miles to Point Loma Ave. Turn left onto Point Loma 1 block to restaurant on Point Loma at Ebers St (2 blocks from ocean). **From I-5**, exit onto I-8W and follow directions above.

OJAI

Ojai is an "intentionally peaceful" village, where chain stores are "forbidden." Local shops, galleries and day hikes in the Los Padres Forest.

THE FARMER AND THE COOK ✕

339 W. El Roblar Drive © 805-640-9608 ⊙ M-Sat 8-8, Sun 11-5
All organic, vegetarian store and eatery, with a vegan emphasis. The proprietors organic farm furnishes the vegetables and herbs sold at the store and used in cooking. Fresh bakery items made from spelt, rather than wheat.

· organic produce · freshly prepared food · juice bar · salad bar · café · deli · bakery
· vegetarian · vegan friendly · organic focus · tables · self-service · take-out

From **Hwy 101** in Ventura, take CA33N (becomes 33/150) almost 11½ miles where 33 & 150 split. Turn left onto Baldwin Rd and right onto S Luna Ave 1½ miles to El Roblar Dr. Turn right onto El Roblar about ¼ mile to store on right corner El Roblar & Encinal Ave.

OLYMPIC VALLEY

SQUAW VALLEY COMMUNITY MARKET & VIDEO
1600 Squaw Valley Rd. © 530-581-2014 ⊙ M-Sat 10-8, Sun 11-5

From **I-80,** take Truckee exit onto Rt 89 south about 10 miles to Squaw Valley entrance. Turn right onto Squaw Valley Rd 2 miles to store on right in strip mall next to post office (just before the mountain).

ORANGE

RUTABEGORZ
264 N. Glassell St. © 714-633-3260 ⊙ M-Tues 11-4, W-Sat 11-9
See Fullerton location for description. Note, no alcohol at this locale.
· vegetarian friendly · tables · wait staff

From **I-5** (Santa Ana Fwy), take State College Ave/CA 57N to Chapman Ave exit. Turn right (east) onto Chapman about 1½ miles to traffic circle at S Glassell St. Turn left onto Glassell 1½ blocks to restaurant on left.

OXNARD

LASSEN'S NATURAL FOODS
3471 Saviors Rd. © 805-486-8266 ⊙ Daily 9-8

· chain

From **Hwy 101N** (Ventura Fwy), take Vineyard Ave exit toward Oxnard left onto Vineyard and left again onto Oxnard Rd. Take Oxnard south (becomes Saviers Rd) 4 miles to store on right. **From 101S,** take Oxnard Ave exit right (south) 4 miles to store on right.

PACIFICA

GOOD HEALTH NATURAL FOODS
80 W. Manor Drive © 650-355-5936 ⊙ M-Th 9:30-8, F 9:30-7, Sat 9:30-6, Sun 12-6

From **Hwy 1,** take Manor Dr exit west about 1 block to store on left.

PALM DESERT

NATIVE FOODS
73-890 El Paseo © 760-836-9396 ⊙ M-Sat 11-9:30
Vegan wraps, sandwiches, pizza (the "cheese" is cashews and sunflower seeds), and international entrees featuring tofu, tempeh, seitan, and soy chicken. L&JB. Leave room for "Rockin' Moroccan," made with couscous, for dessert.
· vegan · organic focus · chain · tables · wait staff

From **I-10,** take exit 131 south onto Monterey Ave (right from 10E, left from 10W) about 6 miles to Hwy 111. Turn left (east) onto 111 about 1 mile to Portola Ave. Turn right onto Portola to first right at El Paseo. Turn right onto El Paseo ½ block to restaurant on right.

VEGGIE & TEA HOUSE ✕

72281 Hwy. 111 © 760-674-9579 ☺ Daily 11-8

Asian vegetarian, with three locales. Focus is on "healthy cuisine," with many of the vegetables grown on their 400-acre organic farm. Brown rice available.

· vegetarian · vegan friendly · organic focus · tables · wait staff · take-out

🚗 **From I-10**, take exit 130 toward Bob Hope Dr west onto Ramon Rd (right from 10E, left from 10 W) to Bob Hope. Turn left (south) onto Bob Hope 5½ miles to Hwy 111. Turn left onto 111 about ⅔ mile to restaurant.

PALM SPRINGS

NATIVE FOODS ✕

1775 E. Palm Canyon Drive © 760-416-0070 ☺ M-Sat 11:30-9:30

See Palm Desert branch above for description.

· vegan · organic focus · alcohol · chain · tables · wait staff

🚗 **From I-10**, take Palm Dr exit toward Desert Hot Springs south on N Gene Autry Trail (right from 10E, left from 10W) 6 miles to E Palm Canyon Dr. Turn right onto Palm Canyon 2 miles to restaurant on left in Smoke Tree Village.

PALO ALTO

Home of Stanford University.

COUNTRY SUN NATURAL FOODS ✕ 🍴

440 S. California Ave. © 650-324-9190 ☺ M-F 9-8, Sat 9-7, Sun 10-6, Deli M-F 8-4, Sat 8-3

· organic produce · freshly prepared food · juice bar · deli · vegetarian friendly
· counter · self-service · take-out

🚗 **From Hwy 101** (Bayshore Fwy), take Oregon Expwy exit and follow ramp onto Oregon about 2 miles to El Camino Real. Turn right onto El Camino ¼ mile to traffic light at California Ave. Turn right onto California to store on left (next to Bank of the West). **From I-280**, take Page Mill Rd exit toward Arastradero Rd (away from hills, left from 280S, right from 280N) about 3 miles to El Camino Real. Turn left onto El Camino ¼ mile to light at California. Turn right onto California to store on left.

HOBEE'S ✕

4224 El Camino Real © 650-856-6124 ☺ M 7-2:30, Tues-F 7-9, Sat 7:30-9, Sun 8-2:30

Although the menu may vary by location, see the description of the Mountain View site (the 1st Hobee's) for the basics.

· salad bar · vegetarian friendly · alcohol · chain · tables · wait staff · take-out

🚗 **From Hwy 101S** (Bayshore Fwy), take San Antonio Rd S exit straight onto San Antonio about ⅓ mile to E Charleston Rd. Turn right onto E Charleston (becomes W Charleston) about 1½ miles to El Camino Real. Turn left onto El Camino to restaurant. **From 101N**, take Rengstorff Rd exit and follow ramp around and right onto Rengstorff to Charleston. Turn left onto Charleston and follow directions above. **From I-280**, take Page Mill Rd exit toward Arastradero Rd/Palo Alto (away from hills, left from 280S, right from 280N) about 3 miles to El Camino Real. Turn right onto El Camino about 1½ miles to restaurant (just past W Charleston).

HOBEE'S ✄

67 Town & Country Village ℭ 650-327-4111 ☺ M-F 7-9, Sat-Sun 8-9
Near Stanford U. See the description of the Mountain View site for the basics.
  · salad bar · vegetarian friendly · alcohol · tables · wait staff · take-out

🕮 **From Hwy 101** (Bayshore Fwy), take Embarcadero Rd west (right from 101S, loop around right from 101N) about 2¼ miles to El Camino Real. Turn right onto El Camino to restaurant in Town & Country Village (just north of Stanford stadium). **From I-280**, take Sand Hill Rd exit toward Palo Alto and follow Sand Hill Rd E ramp onto Sand Hill about 3½ miles to El Camino Real. Turn right on El Camino less than 1 mile to restaurant.

STOA ✄

3750 Fabian Way ℭ 650-424-3900 ☺ M-F 11:30-11, Sat-Sun 2-11 (Bar to 1am)
Natural foods meet wine bar. An upscale vegetarian fusion of European, Mediterranean, Spanish, and Asian cuisines, emphasizing fresh local produce.
  · vegetarian · vegan friendly · alcohol · tables · wait staff

🕮 **From Hwy 101S** (Bayshore Fwy), take San Antonio Rd S exit straight onto San Antonio about ⅓ mile to 1st traffic light at Charleston Rd. Turn right onto Charleston 1 block to Fabian Way. Turn right onto Fabian about ½ mile (past 1st intersection) to restaurant. **From 101N**, take Rengstorff Rd exit and follow ramp around and right onto Rengstorff to Charleston. Turn left onto Charleston ½ mile and follow directions above. **From I-280S**, take Page Mill Rd exit ramp onto Arastradero Rd (becomes Charleston) about 4½ miles (go under 280, past Foothills Expwy, El Camino Real and railroad tracks) to Fabian Way. Turn left onto Fabian about ½ mile (past 1st intersection) to restaurant.

WHOLE FOODS MARKET ✄ 🍃   ♿

774 Emerson St. ℭ 650-326-8676 ☺ Daily 8-10
  · organic produce · freshly prepared food · juice bar · salad bar · deli · bakery
  · vegetarian friendly · chain · tables · self-service · take-out

🕮 From Hwy 101 (Bayshore Fwy), take University Ave exit toward Stanford (right from 101S, loop around right from 101N) under 2 miles to Emerson St. Turn left onto Emerson 3 blocks to Homer Ave. Turn right onto Homer to store on right. **From I-280**, take Page Mill Rd exit toward Arastradero Rd/Palo Alto (away from hills, left from 280S, right from 280N) about 3 miles to El Camino Real. Turn left on El Camino about 1½ miles to University Ave exit. Turn right onto University 2 blocks to Emerson. Turn right onto Emerson 3 blocks to Homer. Turn right onto Homer to store on right.

PARADISE

NATURE'S PANTRY 🍃

6008D Clark Rd. ℭ 530-872-0549 ☺ M-F 9-6, Sun 11-4

🕮 From Hwy 99S, take Skyway Ave east about 11 miles to Elliot Rd. Turn right onto Elliot about 1 mile to Clark Rd. Turn left onto Clark, then right into Safeway Plaza to store. **From Hwy 70N**, turn left onto CA 191 (Clark Rd) about 12 miles (past Elliot) to store on right in Safeway Plaza.

PARADISE NATURAL FOODS 🍃

5729 Almond St. ℭ 530-877-5164 ☺ M-Th 9-6, F 9-4, Sun 10-3

🕮 From Hwy 99N, take Skyway Ave east about 10½ miles to Pearson Rd. Turn right onto Pearson 2 blocks to Almond St. Turn left onto Almond to store on left. **From Hwy 70N,** turn left onto CA 171 (Clark Rd) almost 11½ miles to Pearson Rd. Turn left onto Pearson 1 mile (past 2 stop signs) to Almond St. Turn right onto Almond to store on left.

PASADENA

Museum-goers, stop by the Norton Simon Museum.

GOOD EARTH RESTAURANT & BAKERY ✕ &

257 North Rosemead © 626-351-5488 ☺ Daily 8-10
A "natural food" restaurant with poultry, fish and vegetarian choices. Soups, salads, sandwiches, burgers, hot entrees, whole grains, fresh juices, and shakes.
· juice bar · bakery · vegetarian friendly · alcohol · chain · tables · wait staff
⌂ From I-210, take Rosemead Blvd N exit onto Rosemead (loop around right from 210E, right from 210W) about ⅓ mile to restaurant just past Foothills Blvd.

OREAN'S: THE HEALTH EXPRESS ✕

817 N. Lake Ave. © 626-794-0861 ☺ Daily 9:30-9
Vegan fast food. There is even a drive-through window. Outdoor tables only.
· vegan · tables · self-service · take-out
⌂ From I-210, take Lake Ave exit north on Lake (straight onto Corson St then left from 210E, right from 210W) about ½ mile to restaurant.

WHOLE FOODS MARKET ✕ 🍖 &

3751 E. Foothills Blvd. © 626-351-5994 ☺ Daily 8-10
· organic produce · freshly prepared food · salad bar · deli · bakery · vegetarian friendly
· chain · tables · self-service · take-out
⌂ From I-210, take Rosemead Blvd N exit onto Rosemead (loop around right from 210E, right from 210W) about ⅓ mile to store on NE corner Rosemead & Foothills Blvd.

WILD OATS MARKET ✕ 🍖 &

603 S. Lake St. © 626-792-1788 ☺ Daily 7-10
· organic produce · freshly prepared food · juice bar · salad bar · deli · bakery
· vegetarian friendly · chain · tables · self-service · take-out
⌂ From I-210, take Lake Ave exit south on Lake (straight onto Corson St then right from 210E, left from 210W) about 1 mile to store on right.

PETALUMA

WHOLE FOODS MARKET ✕ 🍖 &

621 E. Washington St. © 707-762-9352 ☺ M-F 8-9, Sat-Sun 9-9
· organic produce · freshly prepared food · juice bar · salad bar · deli · bakery
· vegetarian friendly · chain · tables · self-service · take-out
⌂ From Hwy 101, take E Washington St exit toward Central Petaluma (left from 101S, right from 101N) 4 blocks to store.

PORTER RANCH

WHOLE FOODS MARKET ✕ 🍖 &

19340 Rinaldi St. © 818-363-3933 ☺ Daily 8-10
· organic produce · freshly prepared food · salad bar · deli · bakery · vegetarian friendly
· chain · tables · self-service · take-out
⌂ From CA 118, take Tampa Ave exit north (right from 118W, left from 118E) 1 block to store in shopping center on right before Rinaldi St. **From I-5** (Golden State Fwy) **or I-405** (San Diego Fwy), take CA 118W 5-7 miles and follow directions above.

POWAY

HENRY'S MARKETPLACE 🍎
13536 Poway Rd. ℂ 858-486-7851 ⊘ Daily 8-9
· organic produce · freshly prepared food · deli · vegetarian friendly · chain · take-out
🛒 **From I-15,** take Rancho Pensaquitos Blvd/Poway Rd exit east on Poway Rd (merge right from 15N, left from 15S) about 4¼ miles to store on left. (U-turn to other side at Midland Rd.)

QUINCY

Rural mountain community in the Northern Sierras. A place to camp, hike and fish.

QUINCY NATURAL FOODS CO-OP 🍎
269 Main St. ℂ 530-283-3528 ⊘ M-F 9-7, Sat 9-6, Sun 9-5
· organic produce · freshly prepared food · bakery · co-op · take-out
🛒 CA 70 & 89 meet in Quincy. Store is on 70/89 (Main St) next to post office.

RANCHO PALOS VERDES

VEGAN TERRA CAFE ✕   ♿
28901 S. Western Ave. #123 ℂ 310-833-7977 ⊘ M-Sat 11-9
All vegan cafe menu. Fresh wheat grass and carrot juice available.
· juice bar · vegan · tables · self-service · take-out
🛒 **From I-110S,** take exit toward Chanel St/Pacific Ave right onto Gaffey St about ½ mile to W Capitol Dr. Turn left onto W Capitol about 1 mile (turns right after about ¼ mile) to S Western Ave. Turn right onto S Western about ¼ mile to restaurant in The Terraces Shopping Center.

REDONDO BEACH

THE GREEN TEMPLE ✕
1700 S. Catalina Ave. ℂ 310-944-4525 ⊘ Tues-Th, Sun 11-9, F-Sat 11-10
Vegan (except the soy cheese has casein). An eclectic "funky" decor.
· juice bar · vegan · organic focus · tables · wait staff
🛒 **From I-405S** (San Diego Fwy), take Rt 107S (Hawthorne Blvd) about 3½ miles to Torrance Blvd. Turn right onto Torrance 2 miles to S Catalina Ave. Turn left onto Catalina about 1⅓ miles to restaurant. **From I-405N,** take Artesia Blvd/CA 91W exit right about ⅔ mile to Hawthorne. Turn left onto Hawthorne about 2½ miles to Torrance and follow directions above. **From I-110S,** take I-405/190th St exit right (west) on 190th 6 miles to Hwy 1 (Pacific Coast Hwy). Turn left onto PCH. Make next right onto N Catalina about 2½ miles to restaurant. **From Hwy 1,** take Ave H west 1 block to S Catalina. Turn left onto Catalina 1 block to restaurant.

WHOLE FOODS MARKET ✕🍎   ♿
405 N. Pacific Coast Hwy. ℂ 310-376-6931 ⊘ Daily 8-9
· organic produce · freshly prepared food · salad bar · café · deli · bakery · vegetarian friendly · chain · tables · self-service · take-out
🛒From I-405S (San Diego Fwy), take Rt 107S (Hawthorne Blvd) about 2 miles to 190th St. Turn right onto 190th about 2 miles to Hwy 1 (PCH). Turn left onto PCH ½ mile to store on right. **From I-405N,** take Western Ave exit left onto Western and right onto 190th about 4 miles to PCH. Turn left onto PCH ½ mile to store on right.

RICHMOND

WILLIAMS NATURAL FOODS ✿
12249 San Pablo Ave. © 510-232-1911 ⊙ M-F 9:30-7, Sat 9:30-6, Sun 11-6

🚗 **From I-80**, take San Pablo Ave exit south on San Pablo (sharp right from 80N, from 80S left onto Barrett Ave and 2nd right onto San Pablo) to store between Barrett & McDonald Ave. **From I-580E**, take Marina Bay Pkwy exit left onto Marina Bay (becomes 23rd St) about ⅓ mile to Cutting Blvd. Turn right onto Cutting about 1½ miles to San Pablo. Turn left onto San Pablo about ⅔ mile to store.

ROWLAND HEIGHTS

HAPPY FAMILY RESTAURANT ✕
18425 E. Colima Rd. © 626-965-9923 ⊙ M-F 11:30-2:45, 5-9:20, Sat-Sun 11:30-9:20
Chinese vegetarian menu.
· vegetarian · vegan friendly · tables · wait staff · take-out

🚗 **From US 60E**, take Fullerton Rd exit and take ramp for Fullerton Rd S onto Fullerton about ¼ mile to Colima Rd. Turn left onto Colima past 1st block to restaurant. **From US 60W**, take Fullerton Rd exit left onto Fullerton ½ mile to Colima and follow directions above.

SACRAMENTO

ELLIOTT'S NATURAL FOODS ✿   ♿
3347 El Camino Ave. © 916-481-3173 ⊙ M-F 9-6, Sat 9-5, Sun 11-4
· organic produce · freshly prepared food · take-out

🚗 **From I-80**, take Watt Ave south (right from 80E, left from 80W) about 2½ miles to El Camino Ave. Turn right onto El Camino to store at Yorktown Ave. **From US 50**, take Watt north about 3½ miles to El Camino. Turn left onto El Camino to store at Yorktown.

JULIANA'S KITCHEN ✕
1401 G St. © 916-444-0866 ⊙ M-Th 10-7, F-Sat 10-3
Vegetarian Middl Eastern food and internet cafe. Poetry readings and live music.
· vegetarian · tables · self-service · take-out

🚗 **From I-5**, take J St exit toward Downtown east on J (right from 5N, left from 5S) about 1 mile to 14th St. Turn left onto 14th 3 blocks to G St. Turn left onto G to restaurant at corner. **From I-80E**, merge onto Capital City Fwy (US 50E/I-80Bus) about 3⅓ miles to I-5N and follow directions above. **From US 50W**, turn right onto 16th St/CA 160N about 1¼ miles to G. Turn left onto G 2 blocks to restaurant.

SACRAMENTO NATURAL FOODS CO-OP ✕ ✿   ♿
1900 Alhambra Blvd. © 916-455-2667 ⊙ Daily 8-10, Deli & Juice bar 7:30-9
· organic produce · freshly prepared food · juice bar · salad bar · café · deli · vegetarian friendly · co-op · chain · counter · tables · self-service · wait staff · take-out

🚗 **From US 50W**, take Stockton Blvd exit right onto Stockton 1 block to 34th St. Turn sharp left onto 34th 1 block to S St. Turn right onto S 2 blocks to store parking lot on left. **From US 50E**, take 34th St exit left onto 34th 3 blocks to S. Turn left onto S 2 blocks to store parking on left. **From I 80E**, merge onto 50E and follow directions above. **From I-80 BusW**, take P St exit and veer left onto 29th St about ¼ mile to S. Turn left onto S 2 blocks to store parking on right.

SAN DIEGO

EATOPIA EPRESS ✗
5001-A Newport Ave. © 619-224-3237 ⊙ Daily 10-8
Vegan wraps, fresh juices and smoothies, plus daily raw foods specials. Located right on Ocean Beach.
· juice bar · vegan · counter · self-service · take-out
🍎 **From I-5**, merge onto I-8W about 3⅓ miles to end where it becomes Sunset Cliffs Blvd. Continue on Sunset Cliffs about 1 mile to Newport Ave. Turn right onto Newport about 2 blocks to restaurant.

HENRY'S MARKETPLACE 🍴
1260 Garnet Ave. © 858-270-8200 ⊙ Daily 8-9
· organic produce · freshly prepared food · deli · vegetarian friendly · chain · take-out
🍎 **From I-5S**, take Balboa Ave/Garnet Ave exit onto Mission Bay Dr ¼ mile to Garnet. Turn right onto Garnet (becomes Balboa, then Grand Ave) about 1¾ miles to Faneul St. Turn right onto Faneul 2 blocks back to Garnet. Turn left onto Garnet to store. **From I-5N**, take Grand Ave/Garnet Ave exit onto Mission Bay to Grand. Turn left onto Grand to Faneul and follow directions above.

HENRY'S MARKETPLACE 🍴
4175 Park Blvd. © 619-291-8287 ⊙ M-F 8-10, Sat-Sun 8-9
· organic produce · freshly prepared food · deli · vegetarian friendly · chain · take-out
🍎 **From I-805**, take El Cajon Blvd exit west on El Cajon (right from 805S, left from 805N) about 1¼ miles to Park Blvd. Turn left onto Park to store.

HENRY'S MARKETPLACE 🍴
3315 Rosecrans St. © 619-523-3640 ⊙ Daily 8-9
· organic produce · freshly prepared food · deli · vegetarian friendly · chain · take-out
🍎 **From I-5S**, merge onto CA 209S toward Rosencrans St about 1 mile to store on left (209N/aka Rosencrans). **From I-5N**, exit onto Pacific Coast Hwy 1⅓ miles to exit on left onto Barnett Ave. Take Barnett about ¾ mile to Lytton St. Veer right onto Lytton less than ¼ mile to Rosencrans. Turn right onto Rosencrans almost ½ mile to store on right.

HENRY'S MARKETPLACE 🍴
4439 Genesee Ave. © 858-268-2400 ⊙ Daily 8-9
· organic produce · freshly prepared food · deli · vegetarian friendly · chain · take-out
🍎 **From I-805**, take Balboa Ave W/CA 274W about 1 mile to Genessee Ave. Turn right onto Genessee about ⅓ mile to store.

HENRY'S MARKETPLACE 🍴
3358 Governor Drive © 858-457-5006 ⊙ Daily 8-9
· organic produce · freshly prepared food · deli · vegetarian friendly · chain · take-out
🍎 **From I-805**, merge onto CA 52W about 1⅔ miles to Genessee Ave exit. Follow Genessee Ave N ramp onto Genessee about ½ mile to Governor Dr. Turn left onto Governor about ½ mile to store. **From I-5S**, take Genessee Ave exit and follow Genessee Ave E ramp onto Genessee about 3 miles to Governor. Turn right onto Governor about ½ mile to store. **From I-5N**, merge onto CA 52E toward San Clemente almost 1 mile to Regents Rd exit. Take left fork off ramp onto Regents about ¾ mile to Governor. Turn right onto Governor about ¼ mile to store.

JIMBO'S NATURALLY ✕ 🍽   ♿

12853 El Camino Real ✆ 858-793-7755 ☺ Daily 8-9

· organic produce · freshly prepared food · juice bar · salad bar · deli · bakery
· vegetarian friendly · tables · self-service · take-out

📖 **From I-5**, take Del Mar Heights Rd exit east on Del Mar (left from 5S, right from 5N) about ¾ mile to El Camino Real. Turn right onto El Camino to store on left in Del Mar Highlands Town Center.

JYOTI BIHANGA RESTAURANT ✕   ♿

3351 Adams Ave. ✆ 619-282-4116 ☺ M-Tues, Th-Sat 11-9, Wed 11-3, Sun (sporadically) 9-1

Run by disciples of Sri Chinmoy. The health-oriented, vegetarian menu features salads, sandwiches, wraps, and internationally-inspired hot entrees.

· vegetarian · vegan friendly · tables · wait staff

📖 **From I-805N**, take El Cajon Blvd exit right onto El Cajon about ½ mile to 35th St. Turn left onto 35th to 2nd traffic light at Adams Ave. Turn left onto Adams ¼ mile to restaurant at Adams & Felton St. **From I-805S**, take Adams Ave exit (first exit past Fwy 8) and turn right at stop sign onto Ohio St to light at Adams. Turn right onto Adams about ½ mile to restaurant at Adams & Felton. **From I-15**, go west on I-8 to 805S and follow directions above. **From I-8**, take 805S and follow directions above.

OCEAN BEACH PEOPLE'S ORGANIC FOOD CO-OP 🍽   ♿

4765 Voltaire St. ✆ 619-224-1387 ☺ Daily 8-9

Completely vegetarian market and deli, emphasizing organic ingredients.

· organic produce · freshly prepared food · salad bar · café · deli · bakery · vegetarian
· vegan friendly · organic focus · co-op · counter · tables · self-service · take-out

📖 **From I-5**, merge onto I-8W about 3⅓ miles to end where it becomes Sunset Cliffs Blvd. Continue on Sunset Cliffs about ⅔ mile to Voltaire St. Turn left onto Voltaire to store on right.

RANCHOS NORTH PARK ✕   ♿

3910 30th St. ✆ 619-574-1288 ☺ Daily 8-10

Mexican cuisine with an emphasis on "natural cooking," and more interesting vegetarian options than typically found. All-day breakfast, whole wheat tortillas and brown rice available. A Certified Green Restaurant.

· vegetarian friendly · alcohol · tables · wait staff · take-out

📖 **From I-805S**, take North Park Way exit toward University Ave right onto Boundary Ave and left onto University about ⅓ mile to restaurant at 30th St. **From I-805N**, take University Ave exit and veer left onto Wabash Ave and left onto University about ½ mile to restaurant at 30th St.

WHOLE FOODS MARKET ✕ 🍽   ♿

711 University Ave. ✆ 619-294-2800 ☺ Daily 8-10

· organic produce · freshly prepared food · juice bar · salad bar · café · deli · bakery
· vegetarian friendly · chain · tables · self-service · take-out

📖 **From I-805S**, merge onto CA 163S (Cabrillo Fwy) toward Downtown about 4 miles to University Ave exit. Take 6th Ave south about ½ mile to University. Turn left onto University 1 block to store. **From I-8**, merge onto CA 163S and follow directions above. **From I-5N**, merge onto CA 163N toward Escondido about 1¾ miles to Robinson Ave. Turn left onto Robinson 2 blocks to 7th Ave. Turn right onto 7th 1 block to store at University.

SAN DIMAS

VEGGIE & TEA HOUSE ✕
641 Arrow Hwy. © 909-592-6323 ⊙ Daily 11-9
Asian vegetarian, with three locales. Focus is "healthy cuisine," with many of the vegetables grown on their 400-acre organic farm. Brown rice available.
  · vegetarian · vegan friendly · organic focus · tables · wait staff · take-out
🍴 From I-210, take CA 57S about 1¼ miles to Arrow Hwy. Turn left onto Arrow Hwy about ⅓ mile to restaurant.

SAN FRANCISCO

22 02 OXYGEN BAR ✕
795 Valencia St. © 415-255-2102 ⊙ M 12-6, Tues-Th, Sun 12-12, F-Sat noon-2am, Dinner Tues & Th from 7
Primarily an oxygen bar serving herbal elixers, but on Tuesday and Thursday evenings visiting chefs prepare a raw foods menu.
  · juice bar · vegan · organic focus · counter · tables · wait staff · take-out
🍴 In the Mission District. **From US 101S** (across Golden Gate Bridge), follow 101S east on Lombard St to Van Ness. Turn right onto Van Ness about 2⅔ miles to 18th St. Turn right onto 18th ¼ mile to Valencia. Turn left onto Valencia to restaurant. **From 101N**, take Duboce Ave/Mission St exit and follow ramp onto Duboce about 3 blocks to Valencia St. Turn left onto Valencia about ⅔ mile to restaurant.

ANANDA FUARA ✕
1298 Market St © 415-621-1994 ⊙ M-Tues, Th-Sat 8-8, Wed. 8-3
Multicultural vegetarian entrees, wraps, sandwiches, burgers, and pizza. Open for breakfast, lunch and dinner.
  · vegetarian · vegetarian friendly · tables · wait staff · take-out
🍴 **From US 101N**, take 9th St exit left onto 9th over ½ mile to Market St. Turn left onto Market to restaurant just past corner. **From I-80W**, take 9th St exit and follow split in road right to Harrison St. Turn left onto Harrison to 1st right onto 9th. Turn right onto 9th and follow directions above.

BUFFALO WHOLE FOOD & GRAIN CO. 🍃
598 Castro St. © 415-626-7038 ⊙ M-Sat 9-8, Sun 10-8
🍴 **From US 101S**, turn right onto Divisadero St (becomes Castro St) about 2¼ miles to store on right at 19th St. **From US 101N**, merge onto Central Skyway to Fell St. Turn left onto Fell 7 blocks to Divisadero. Turn left onto Divisadero (becomes Castro) about 1 mile to store on right at 19th St.

FIREFLY ✕
4288 24th St. © 415-821-7652 ⊙ Daily from 5:30
Upscale menu featuring local, organic foods. Appetizers are mostly vegetarian, entrees are a mix of vegetarian, fish, free-range chicken, and "drug-free" beef.
  · vegetarian friendly · organic focus · alcohol · tables · wait staff
🍴 **From US 101**, take Cesar Chavez exit west on Chavez to end at Noe St. Turn right onto Noe 5 blocks to 24th St. Turn left onto 24th 3 blocks to restaurant between Diamond & Douglass St. **From Golden Gate Bridge**, follow 101S east on Lombard St to Divisadero St. Turn right onto Divisadero 2 miles to Castro. Merge left onto Castro 1⅓ miles to 24th. Turn right onto 24th 2 blocks to restaurant.

GOLDEN ERA VEGETARIAN RESTAURANT ✕
572 O'Farrell St. ✆ 415- 673-3136 ⊙ M, W-Sun 11-9
Vietnamese vegetarian cuisine. Brown rice available. DLM: Best pot stikkers I've ever had, veggie or not.

· vegan · tables · wait staff · take-out

📇 **From I-80**, take 7th St exit toward US 101N/Downtown left on 7th (becomes Leavenworth St) about 1 mile to restaurant on right at O'Farrell St.

GOOD LIFE GROCERY 🍎
448 Cortland Ave. ✆ 415-648-3221 ⊙ M-Sat 8-8, Sun 8-7

📇 **From 101S**, take C Chavez St exit and follow ramp onto Bay Shore Blvd ²/₃ mile to Cortland. Turn right (west) onto Cortland ½ mile to store between Andover & Wool St. **From US 101N**, take Alemany Blvd exit toward Bay Shore. Follow exit right onto Alemany to Bay Shore and left onto Bay Shore to Cortland Ave. Turn left (west) onto Cortland ½ mile to store between Andover & Wool.

GOOD LIFE GROCERY 🍎
1524 20th St. ✆ 415-282-9204 ⊙ M-Sat 8:30-8, Sun 8:30-7

📇 **From I-280S**, take Mariposa St exit toward 18th St. Follow 18th St ramp and turn left onto Pennsylvania Ave 2 blocks to 20th St. Turn right onto 20th about 3 blocks to store between Missouri & Connecticut St. **From I-280N**, take Army St exit about ½ mile and merge north onto Pennsylvania ²/₃ mile to 20th. Turn left onto 20th about 3 blocks to store between Missouri & Connecticut.

GREENS RESTAURANT ✕
204 Bay St. ✆ 415-771-6222 ⊙ Lunch Tues-Sat 12-2:30, Afternoon Tea Tues-F 2:30-4:30, Dinner M-F 5:30-9:30, Sat (Prix Fixe Only) 5:30-9, Evening Dessert M-Sat 9:30-11, Brunch Sun 10:30-2
Creative vegetarian cooking with Mediterranean, Mexican and Southwest influences. Features local organic produce and a new menu daily. On the water overlooking the Golden Gate Bridge, in the Fort Mason Center—home to 50 nonprofit arts, cultural and environmental groups. DLM: The view is incredible, the atmosphere wonderful, the food excellent, and the prices match it.

· vegetarian · vegan friendly · organic focus · tables · wait staff · take-out

📇 From US 101S (across Golden Gate Bridge), take Marina Blvd exit and follow Marina 1½ miles to Buchanan St. Turn left into Fort Mason Center to restaurant. **From 101N**, merge onto I-280N toward Port of SF. Go 3⅓ miles and merge onto King St (becomes The Embarcadero) 2¾ miles to Bay St. Turn left onto Bay to Buchanan. Turn right onto Buchanan, cross Marina Blvd and make sharp right into Fort Mason Center.

HERBIVORE ✕
531 Divisadero St. ✆ 415-885-7133 ⊙ M-Th 11-10, F 11-11, Sat 9-11, Sun 9-10
Vegan soups, salads, sandwiches, and noodles.

· vegan · alcohol · tables · wait staff

📇 **From US 101S**, turn right onto Divisadero St 1¾ miles to restaurant at Fell St. **From US 101N**, merge onto Central Skyway to Fell. Turn left onto Fell 7 blocks restaurant at Divisadero.

HERBIVORE ✕
983 Valencia St. ✆ 415-826-5657 ⊙ M-Th, Sun 11-10, F-Sat 11-11
Vegan soups, salads, sandwiches, and noodles.

· vegan · alcohol · tables · wait staff

🍎 **From US 101S** (aka Van Ness Ave), go west on 21st St 5 blocks to Valencia St. Turn right onto Valencia to restaurant between 21st & 20th St. **From 101N**, take C Chavez/Protrero Ave exit left onto Protrero and right onto Chavez less than 1 mile to Valencia. Turn right onto Valencia about ⅔ mile to restaurant between 21st & 20th.

HULA HOUSE VEGETARIAN RESTAURANT ✕
754 Kirkham St. ✆ 415-682-0826 ⊘ M, W-Sun 11-9
DLM: A Buddhist-style menu with mock meats. Really great food! Brown rice.
· vegetarian · vegan friendly · tables · wait staff

🍎 **From Golden Gate Bridge**, take Hwy 1S (Park Presidio Blvd) almost 5½ miles (through park) to Irving St. Turn right onto Irving 1 block to 20th St. Turn left onto 20th 1 block to Judah St. Turn left onto Judah 7 blocks (less than ½ mile) to Funston Ave. Turn right onto Funston 1 block to Kirkham St. Turn left onto Kirkham 1 block to restaurant at Kirkham & 12th Ave.

JUICEY LUCY'S JUICE BAR & RESTAURANT ✕
703 Columbus Ave. ✆ 415-786-1285 ⊘ Daily 11-6
Fresh juices, salads and sandwiches, featuring all organic seasonal produce.
· juice bar · vegetarian · vegan friendly · organic focus · tables · self-service · take-out

🍎 In North Beach. **From The Embarcadero**, go inland on either Broadway St or Bay St to Columbus Ave. From Broadway, turn right onto Columbus about 4 blocks to restaurant at Filbert St. From Bay, turn left onto Columbus about 5 blocks to restaurant at Filbert.

LUCKY CREATION ✕
854 Washington St. ✆ 415-989-0818 ⊘ M-Tues, Th-Sun 11-9:30
One among many vegetarian Chinese restaurants in Chinatown. Has been described as "downscale."
· vegetarian · vegetarian friendly · tables · wait staff · take-out

🍎 In Chinatown on Washington St 1 block west of Grant St.

MILLENNIUM ✕
580 Geary St. ✆ 415-345-3900 ⊘ M-Th, Sun 5-10, F-Sat 5-11
Upscale vegan gourmet menu, largely organic (incuding beer and wine), no genetically modified foods, and supporting environmental principles, including composting and recycling. PD: If I'm in SF three nights, I eat there three times.
· vegan · organic focus · alcohol · tables · wait staff

🍎 **From US 101S** (across Golden Gate Bridge), follow 101S east on Lombard St to Van Ness Ave. Turn right onto Van Ness about 1 mile to Bush St. Turn left onto Bush 7 blocks (about ½ mile) to Mason St. Turn right onto Mason 3 blocks to Geary St. Turn right onto Geary 3 blocks to restaurant on right at Geary & Jones St (in the Savoy Hotel). **From Bay Bridge**, take I-80W to 5th St exit. Turn right onto 5th about ½ mile to Ellis St ((2 blocks past Market St). Turn left onto Ellis 2 blocks to Taylor St. Turn right onto Taylor 2 blocks to Geary. Turn left onto Geary 2 blocks to restaurant on right at Geary & Jones (in the Savoy Hotel).

MINAKO ✕
2154 Mission St. ✆ 415-864-1888 ⊘ M, W-Sun 5:30-9:15
Organic Japanese food. Small place with a big selection of vegan items, as well as fish and free-range chicken.
· vegetarian friendly · vegan friendly · organic focus · alcohol · tables · wait staff

🍴 **From Bay Bridge or US 101N**, take Mission St exit toward Van Ness Ave right onto Mission and right (south) onto Van Ness about ⅔ mile to 17th St. Turn left onto 17th 2 blocks to Mission. Turn left onto Mission to restaurant between 17th & 18th St.

NEW GANGES ✕
775 Frederick St. ℂ 415-681-4355 ☺ Daily 11-2, 5-10
Vegetarian Indian cuisine.

· vegetarian · vegan friendly · tables · wait staff

🍴 **From Bay Bridge or US 101N**, take Fell St exit west to Golden Gate Park. When road enters park, take left fork onto Kezar Dr to Lincoln Way. Turn left onto Lincoln 2 blocks to Arguello Blvd. Turn right onto Arguello 1 block to Frederick St. Turn left onto Frederick to restaurant.

OTHER AVENUES FOOD STORE 🍆
3930 Judah St. ℂ 415-661-7475 ☺ Daily 10-8

· organic produce · co-op

🍴 **From Golden Gate Bridge**, take 19th Ave exit about 5½ miles (through park) to Judah St. Turn right onto Judah about 1½ miles to store between 44th & 45th Ave. **From Bay Bridge**, take Fell St exit west to Golden Gate Park. When road enters park, take left fork onto Kezar Dr to Lincoln Way. Merge right onto Lincoln about 2½ miles to 44th Ave. Turn left onto 44th 2 blocks to Judah. Turn right onto Judah to store. **From I-280N**, take 1N/ 19th Ave about 4 miles to Irving St. Turn right onto Irving 1 block to 18th Ave. Turn right onto 18th 1 block to Judah. Turn right onto Judah about 1½ miles to store between 44th & 45th.

RAINBOW GROCERY COOPERATIVE 🍆   ♿
1745 Folsom St. ℂ 415-863-0620 ☺ Daily 9-9

· organic produce · freshly prepared food · bakery · vegetarian friendly · co-op · take-out

🍴 **From I-80W**, take 9th St exit and follow split in road right to Harrison St. Turn left onto Harrison about ¼ mile to 14th St (1 block past fwy overpass). Turn right onto 14th 2 blocks to Folsom St. Turn right on Folsom to store on right. (Parking lot is 1 block further on 13th St.) **From US 101N**, take 9th St exit 1 block to Harrison. Turn left onto Harrison and follow directions above. **From 101S** (across Golden Gate Bridge), follow 101S east on Lombard St to Van Ness Ave. Turn right onto Van Ness about 2¼ miles to 14th (1 block past fwy overpass). Turn left onto 14th 2 blocks to Folsom. Turn left onto Folsom to store on right.

REAL FOOD CO. 🍆
3060 Fillmore St ℂ 415-567-6900 ☺ Daily 8-9

· organic produce

🍴 **From US 101S** (across Golden Gate Bridge), follow 101S east on Lombard St to Fillmore St (4 blocks past Divisadero St). Turn right onto Fillmore 4 blocks to store at Filbert St (1 block north of Union St).

REAL FOOD CO 🍆
2140 Polk St. ℂ 415-673-7420 ☺ Daily 9-9

· organic produce

🍴 **From US 101S** (across Golden Gate Bridge), follow 101S east on Lombard St to Van Ness Ave. Turn right onto Van Ness 2 blocks to Filbert St. Turn left onto Filbert 1 block to Polk St. Turn right onto Polk about 4 blocks to store (just north of Broadway St).

REGGAE RUNNINS VILLAGE STORE & EMPRESS SARAH'S VEGETARIAN CAFE & KITCHEN ✕🍖
505 Divisadero St. ℂ 415-922-2442 ☺ Daily 11-7
African-Caribbean market and menu featuring mostly vegan dishes (some baked goods contain dairy) made with organic ingredients.
· freshly prepared food · juice bar · vegetarian · vegan friendly · organic focus · counter · tables · wait staff · take-out
🍎 **From US 101S**, turn right onto Divisadero St 1¾ miles to store at Fell St. **From US 101N**, merge onto Central Skyway to Fell. Turn left onto Fell 7 blocks to store at Divisadero.

SHANGRI-LA VEGETARIAN RESTAURANT ✕
2026 Irving St. ℂ 415-731-2548 ☺ Daily 11:30-9
Chinese vegan menu.
· vegan · organic focus · kosher · alcohol · tables · wait staff · take-out
🍎 **From Golden Gate Bridge**, take Hwy 1S (Park Presidio Blvd/19th Ave) 5½ miles (through park) to Irving St. Turn right onto Irving about 2 blocks to restaurant at 21st Ave. **From I-280N**, take 1N/19th Ave about 4 miles to Irving St. Turn left onto Irving to restaurant at 21st.

THE NATURE STOP 🍖
1336 Grant Ave. ℂ 415-398-3810 ☺ Daily 9-9
· deli · vegetarian friendly · take-out
🍎 On Grant Ave between Vallejo St & Green St. **From The Embarcadero**, go west on Broadway St ½ mile to Columbus Ave. Turn right onto Columbus and right onto Grant Ave 2 blocks to store.

THOM'S NATURAL FOODS 🍖
5843 Geary Blvd. ℂ 415-387-6367 ☺ Daily 10-8
🍎 **From Golden Gate Bridge**, take Hwy 1S (Park Presidio Blvd) 4 miles to Geary Blvd. Turn right (west) onto Geary ½ mile to store between 22nd & 23 Ave.

URBAN FORAGE ✕   ♿
254 Fillmore St. ℂ 415-255-6701 ☺ M-F 8-9, Sat-Sun 10-9
Organic raw foods restaurant. Adjacent studio offers yoga, tai chi, reiki, and other forms of energy work. Local artworks on exhibit in dining room.
· vegan · organic focus · counter · tables · self-service · take-out
🍎 **From US 101S** (across Golden Gate Bridge), follow 101S east on Lombard St to Divisadero St. Turn right onto Divisadero about 2 miles to Haight St. Turn left onto Haight 4 blocks to Fillmore St. Turn right onto Fillmore to restaurant. **From US 101N**, follow Skyline Hwy to Haight St exit. Turn left onto Haight less than ½ mile to Fillmore. Turn left onto Fillmore to restaurant.

WHOLE FOODS MARKET ✕🍖   ♿
1765 California St. ℂ 415-674-0500 ☺ Daily 8-10
· organic produce · freshly prepared food · juice bar · salad bar · café · deli · bakery · vegetarian friendly · chain · tables · self-service · take-out
🍎 **From Hwy 101S** (across Golden Gate Bridge), follow 101S east on Lombard St to Van Ness Ave. Turn right onto Van Ness ¾ mile to California St. Turn right onto California 1 block to store on corner California & Franklin St. **From US 101N**, take Mission St exit toward Van Ness onto 101N (becomes Van Ness) 1⅓ miles to Pine St. Turn left onto Pine 1 block to Franklin. Turn right onto Franklin 1 block to store on corner Franklin & California.

SAN GABRIEL

TEA SHAKER RESTAURANT ✕
7258 N. Rosemead Blvd. © 626-287-5850 ⊙ Daily 11-9
Vegan foods with an eclectic Asian influence.
· vegan · tables · wait staff

From I-10, take CA 19N/Rosemead Blvd exit toward Pasadena north on Rosemead about 4 miles to restaurant. **From I-210,** take Rosemead exit south on Rosemead about 1¼ miles to restaurant.

SAN JOSE

DI LAC CUISINE ✕
1644 E. Capitol Expwy. © 408-238-8686 ⊙ Daily 9-9
"Vegetarian & Tofu" with Asian orientation. No eggs, no msg.
· vegetarian · vegan friendly · tables · wait staff

From Hwy 101 (Bayshore Fwy), take Capitol Expwy exit and ramp onto Capitol Expwy E about ⅓ mile (less from 101N) to restaurant on right behind Hollywood Video (before Silver Creek/King Rd intersection).

HOBEE'S ✕
680 River Oaks Plaza © 408-232-0190 ⊙ M-F 6:30am-2:30pm, Sat-Sun 8am-2:30pm
Although the menu may vary by location, see the description of the Mountain View site (the 1st Hobee's) for the basics.
· salad bar · vegetarian friendly · chain · tables · wait staff · take-out

From I-880, take Montague Expwy exit and Montague Expwy W ramp west on Montague about 1⅓ miles to restaurant in River Oaks Plaza. **From Hwy 101 (Bayshore Fwy),** take Montague Expwy exit and Montague Expwy ramp east less than 3 miles to restaurant in River Oaks Plaza.

SAN LUIS OBISPO

HOBEE'S ✕
1443 Calle Joaquin © 805-549-9186 ⊙ M-F 7am-2:30pm, Sat-Sun 7:30am-3pm
The southernmost Hobees (for the time being, at least), midway between San Francisco and LA. Although the menu may vary by location, see the description of the Mountain View site for the basics.
· salad bar · vegetarian friendly · alcohol · chain· tables · wait staff · take-out

On Hwy 101 at Los Osos Valley Rd.

NATURAL FOODS CO-OP OF SAN LUIS OBISPO 🌿
745 Francis St. © 805-544-7928 ⊙ Daily 8-8
· organic produce · co-op

From Hwy 101, take Marsh St exit east ½ mile to Broad St. Turn right onto Broad about ¾ mile to Francis St (Mazda dealer on left). Turn left onto Francis to store at corner Broad & Francis (behind Z&Z Market).

SAN MATEO

WHOLE FOODS MARKET ✕🌿   ♿
1010 Park Place © 650-358-6900 ⊙ Daily 8-10
· organic produce · freshly prepared food · juice bar · salad bar · deli · bakery
· vegetarian friendly · chain · tables · self-service · take-out

From Hwy 101, take E Hillsdale exit west 1 block to Park Place. Turn right onto Park to store.

SAN RAFAEL

WHOLE FOODS MARKET ✂🍴 &
340 Third St. © 415-451-6333 ☺ Daily 9-9, Bakery & Food bar from 8am
- · organic produce · freshly prepared food · juice bar · salad bar · deli · bakery
- · vegetarian friendly · chain · tables · self-service · take-out

🍎 **From Hwy 101**, take Central San Rafael exit onto 2nd St (right from 101N, left from 101S). Get into left lane (2nd merges onto 3rd St) about ¼ mile (past Montecito Shopping Center) to Union St. Turn left onto Union to store on corner Union & 3rd.

SAN RAMON

WHOLE FOODS MARKET ✂🍴 &
100 Sunset Drive © 925-355-9000 ☺ Daily 9-9
- · organic produce · freshly prepared food · juice bar · salad bar · deli · bakery
- · vegetarian friendly · chain · tables · self-service · take-out

🍎 **From I-680**, take Bollinger Canyon Rd exit west on Bollinger Canyon (left over fwy from 680S, right from 680N) about ⅓ mile to Sunset Dr. Turn left onto Sunset to store.

SANTA BARBARA

LAZY ACRES ✂🍴
302 Meigs Rd. © 805-564-4410 ☺ Daily 7-10
- · organic produce · freshly prepared food · café · vegetarian friendly · tables · self-service · take-out

🍎 **From Hwy 101**, take Carrillo St west (becomes Meigs Rd) about 2 miles to store on left.

SOJOURNER CAFE ✂
134 E. Canon Perdido © 805-965-7922 ☺ M-Sat 11-11, Sun 10-10
Gourmet vegetarian, vegan and seafood.
- · vegetarian friendly · vegan friendly · alcohol · tables · wait staff

🍎 **From Hwy 101N**, take Garden St toward Downtown (right) about ½ mile to E Canon Perdido. Turn left onto E Canon Perdido less than 2 blocks to restaurant. **From Hwy 101S**, take W Carillo St toward Downtown (left) about ½ mile to Anacapa St. Turn right onto Anacapa 1 block and left onto E Canon Perdido to restaurant.

SANTA CLARA

DASAPRAKASH ✂
2636 Homestead Rd. © 408-246-8292 ☺ Lunch M-F 11:30-2:30, Dinner M-Th 5:30-9:30, F 5:30-10, Sat-Sun 11:30-10
South Indian vegetarian menu.
- · vegetarian · vegan friendly · tables · wait staff

🍎 **From Hwy 101** (Bayshore Fwy), take San Tomas Expwy south (right from 101S, loop around right from 101N) about 3 miles to Homestead Rd. Turn right onto Homestead to restaurant. **From I-280**, take Saratoga Ave N exit toward Santa Clara (right from 280N, left from 280S) about 1 mile to San Tomas. Turn left onto San Tomas about 1 mile to Homestead. Turn left onto Homestead to restaurant.

SANTA CLARITA

LASSEN'S NATURAL FOODS 🍎
26861 Bouquet Canyon Rd. © 661-263-6935 ☺ M-Sat 9-8

· chain

🍎 **From I-5** (Golden State Pkwy), take Magic Mt Pkwy east (sharp left from 5S, right from 5N) about 2 miles to Valencia Blvd. Turn left onto Valencia about 1 mile and bear left onto Bouquet Canyon Rd about 1½ miles to store.

SANTA CRUZ

Surf City, USA. When you tire of the beach, ride the wooden roller coaster at the boardwalk or take the Big Trees train up into the Santa Cruz Mountains.

ASIAN ROSE ✗
1547B Pacific Ave. © 831-458-3023 ☺ Daily 11-4:30
Asian vegetarian "deli." Eat-in or take-out lunches.

· vegan · tables · self-service · take-out

🍎 **From Hwy 17**, take Hwy 1 north (right) toward Half Moon Bay about 1 mile to Chestnut St. Merge onto Chestnut ½ mile to Laurel St. Turn left onto Laurel 1 block to Washington Ave. Turn right onto Washington ⅓ mile to Pacific Ave. Turn left onto Pacific to restaurant .

ASIAN ROSE ✗
1116 Soquel Ave. © 831-423-7906 ☺ Daily 5:30-9:30
Asian vegetarian dinners.

· vegan · tables · wait staff · take-out

🍎 **From Hwy 17**, take Hwy 1 south (left) toward Monterey. **From Hwy 1**, take Morrisey Blvd exit south on Morrisey (left onto Fairmont and right from 1S, left at fork in ramp and left from 1N) about ½ mile to Water St. Turn right onto Water 1 block to Soquel Ave. Turn left onto Soquel to restaurant.

FOOD BIN & HERB ROOM 🍎
1130 Mission St. © 831-423-5526 ☺ Daily 9am-midnight

· organic produce

🍎 **From Hwy 17**, take Hwy 1 north (right) toward Half Moon Bay. **From Hwy 1** (Mission St in town) store is on north corner Mission & Laurel St.

NEW LEAF COMMUNITY MARKET ✗🍎
2351 Mission St. © 831-426-1306 ☺ Daily 8-9
Sarah at New Leaf describes Santa Cruz as "an organic farming mecca," and the New Leaf Community Markets feature local farm produce.

· organic produce · freshly prepared food · deli · vegetarian friendly · tables · self-service · take-out

🍎 **From Hwy 17**, take Hwy 1 north (right) toward Half Moon Bay. **From Hwy 1** (Mission St in town) go south (toward ocean) on Swift St and immediately left onto MacPherson St to store about ½ block on left in Mission Plaza Center.

NEW LEAF COMMUNITY MARKET ✗🍎
1134 Pacific Ave. © 831-425-1793 ☺ Daily 9-9

· organic produce · freshly prepared food · deli · vegetarian friendly · tables · self-service · take-out

🍎 **From Hwy 17 or Hwy 1**, take Ocean St south about ¾ mile to Soquel Ave. Turn right onto Soquel over bridge and past traffic light at Front St to store on left corner Pacific Ave & Soquel (in old Bank of America bldg).

SATURN CAFE ✕ &

145 Laurel St. © 831-429-8505 ⊙ M-Th, Sun 11:30am-3am, F-Sat 11:30-4am
Vegetarian, except for the tuna. A variety of meat-free burgers, sandwiches, soups, salads, and standard entrees, including steamed veggies and brown rice, nachos, a Middle Eastern plate, and pasta. Weekdays from 11:30am-5pm there's a "Cheap Eats" menu. Note: this place goes until the wee hours of the morning.
· vegetarian friendly · vegan friendly · alcohol · tables · wait staff

🛏 **From Hwy 17**, take Hwy 1 north (right) toward Half Moon Bay about 1 mile to Chestnut St. Merge onto Chestnut ½ mile to Laurel St. Turn left onto Laurel 1 block to restaurant .

STAFF OF LIFE NATURAL FOODS MARKET ✕🍖 &

1305 Water St. © 831-423-8632 ⊙ Daily 8-9
Deli offers vegetarian and vegan choices, fish, poultry, and a sushi bar.
· organic produce · freshly prepared food · juice bar · salad bar · deli · bakery
· vegetarian friendly · tables · self-service · take-out

🛏 **From Hwy 17**, take Hwy 1 south (left) toward Monterey. **From Hwy 1**, take Morrisey Blvd exit south on Morrisey (left onto Fairmont and right from 1S, left at fork in ramp and left from 1N) about ½ mile to Water St. Turn right onto Water 1 block to Poplar for store parking lot.

THE 418 ORGANIC CAFE ✕ ⊜&

418 Front St. © 831-425-5483 ⊙ M-F 11-3, 5-10
All raw, organic, vegan menu.
· juice bar · salad bar · café · vegan · organic focus · tables · wait staff

🛏 **From Hwy 17 or Hwy 1**, take Ocean St south about ¾ mile to Soquel Ave. Turn right onto Soquel over bridge to traffic light at Front St. Turn left onto Front 1½ blocks to restaurant.

SANTA MARIA

FOODS FOR THE FAMILY ✕🍖

1790 S Broadway © 805-925-3432 ⊙ M-F 8:30-8, Sat 9-6, Sun 10-5
· organic produce · freshly prepared food · juice bar · café · deli · tables · self-service
· take-out

🛏 **From Hwy 101**, take Bettaravia Rd exit west toward Sisquoc (left from 101N, right from 101S) about 1 mile to Broadway. Turn right onto Broadway about ½ mile to store on right just past Jiffy Lube.

SANTA MONICA

CHANDI ✕

1909 Wilshire Blvd. © 310-828-7060 ⊙ Daily 11:30-2:30, 5-10
Vegetarian Indian cuisine.
· vegetarian · vegan friendly · alcohol · tables · wait staff

🛏 **From I-10W** (Santa Monica Fwy), take exit 2 right (north) on Cloverfield Blvd about ¼ mile to Olympic Blvd. Turn left onto Olympic about ¼ mile to 20th St. Turn right onto 20th ²/₃ mile to Wilshire. Turn left onto Wilshire to restaurant. **From Ocean Ave**, go inland on Wilshire about 1¹/₃ miles to restaurant.

CO-OPPORTUNITY 🍖

1525 Broadway © 310-451-8902 ⊙ Daily 8-10
· organic produce · freshly prepared food · juice bar · deli · vegetarian friendly · co-op
· take-out

From I-10W (Santa Monica Fwy), take exit 2 north (right) on Cloverfield Blvd ½ mile to Broadway. Turn left onto Broadway just over ½ mile to store at corner Broadway & 16th St. **From Santa Monica Pier**, go inland on Colorado Blvd about 1 mile to 14th St. Turn left onto 14th 1 block to Broadway. Turn right onto Broadway 2 blocks to store at 16th.

JULIANO'S RAW ✕

609 Broadway ✆ 310-587-1552 ☺ M-Th, Sun 11:30-10, F-Sat 11:30-11
An intriguing menu based entirely on raw "living" foods. A certified organic restaurant—including the paint on the walls.

· vegan · organic focus · alcohol · counter · tables · wait staff

From I-10W (Santa Monica Fwy), take exit 1A (4th/5th St) right at fork in ramp and bear left (north) onto 5th 2 blocks to Broadway. Turn right onto Broadway to restaurant. **From Santa Monica Pier**, take Colorado Blvd less than ½ mile to 6th St. Turn left onto 6th 1 block to restaurant at Broadway.

ONE LIFE NATURAL FOODS ✕ 🍴

3001 Main St. ✆ 310-392-4501 ☺ Daily 9-9

· organic produce · freshly prepared food · deli · vegetarian friendly · tables · self-service · take-out

From I-10W (Santa Monica Fwy), take exit 1A (4th/5th St) left at fork in ramp and left (south) onto 4th St less than 1 mile to Ocean Park Blvd. Turn right onto ramp and merge onto Ocean Park 3 blocks to Main St. Turn left onto Main about ⅓ mile to store on left at Main & Pier Ave. **From Hwy 1** (Pacific Coast Hwy), turn inland at Pier Ave 1 block to store at Main.

REAL FOOD DAILY ✕

514 Santa Monica Blvd. ✆ 310-451-7544 ☺ Daily 11:30-10
Based on the macrobiotic principles of "five elements." Fresh, seasonal, locally grown and certified organic ingredients in creative, globally-inspired dishes. PD: Trendy decor, excellent vegan food, very inventive.

· vegan · organic focus · tables · wait staff · take-out

From I-10W (Santa Monica Fwy), take exit 1A (4th/5th St) right at fork in ramp and bear left (north) onto 5th 3 blocks to Santa Monica Blvd. Turn right onto Santa Monica to restaurant. **From Ocean Ave**, go inland on Santa Monica about 3 blocks to restaurant.

WILD OATS MARKET ✕ 🍴

500 Wilshire Blvd. ✆ 310-395-4510 ☺ Daily 7-10

· organic produce · freshly prepared food · juice bar · salad bar · café · deli · bakery · vegetarian friendly · chain · tables · self-service · take-out

From I-10W (Santa Monica Fwy), take exit 1A (4th/5th St) right at fork in ramp and bear left (north) onto 5th about ⅔ mile to Wilshire Blvd. Turn right onto Wilshire to store. **From Ocean Ave**, go inland on Wilshire about 4 blocks to store.

WILD OATS MARKET ✕ 🍴

1425 Montana Ave. ✆ 310-576-4707 ☺ Daily 7-10

· organic produce · freshly prepared food · juice bar · salad bar · café · deli · bakery · vegetarian friendly · chain · tables · self-service · take-out

From I-10W (Santa Monica Fwy), take exit 2 north (right) on Cloverfield Blvd about ¼ mile to Olympic Blvd. Turn left onto Olympic almost ¾ mile to 14th St. Turn right onto 14th 1¼ miles to Montana Ave. Turn right onto Montana to store. **From Ocean Ave**, go inland on Montana about 1 mile to store.

SANTA ROSA

Suggested cultural stops include the Jr. College Indigenous Peoples' and Art Museums, the Charles Schultz Museum (for Peanuts' fans), and the Rural Cemetery.

EAST WEST CAFE ✕

2323 Sonoma Ave. © 707-546-6142 ⊘ M, Sun 8-8, Tues-Sat 8-9
· juice bar · café · vegetarian friendly · alcohol · tables · wait staff · take-out

From Hwy 101, take Hwy 12E about 1¾ miles to Farmer's Ln. Turn left onto Farmer's about ⅔ mile to restaurant at Sonoma Ave intersection.

SANTA ROSA COMMUNITY MARKET & CAFE ✕

1899 Mendocino Ave. © 707-546-1806 ⊘ Store daily 9-9, Cafe call 707-525-8125
Vegetarian cafe, nearly all organic, with an espresso bar. Worker run for 25 years.
· organic produce · freshly prepared food · café · deli · vegetarian · organic focus
· alcohol · co-op · tables · self-service · take-out

From Hwy 101, take Steele Lane exit east (right from 101N, left from 101S) about ½ mile to Mendocino Ave. Turn right onto Mendocino to 1st right onto Clement St. Store is on left corner (parking in back).

WHOLE FOODS MARKET ✕

1181 Yulupa Ave. © 707-575-9915 ⊘ M-Sat 8-9, Sun 9-9
Store will be moving in 2004 to Hwy 12& Streamside Lane, so call to confirm.
· organic produce · freshly prepared food · juice bar · salad bar · deli · bakery
· vegetarian friendly · chain · tables · self-service · take-out

From Hwy 101, take Hwy 12E about 1¾ miles to Hoen Frontage Rd. Stay right on Hoen Frontage (becomes Hoen Ave) almost 1 mile to Yulupa Ave. Turn left onto Yulupa to store.

SANTEE

HENRY'S MARKETPLACE

9751 Mission Gorge Rd. © 619-258-4060 ⊘ Daily 8-9
· organic produce · freshly prepared food · deli · vegetarian friendly · chain · take-out

From I-15 (or I-805), take CA 52E about 7¾ miles (11 miles) to Mission Gorge Rd exit. Turn left onto Mission Gorge about 1⅓ miles to store.

SEBASTOPOL

Hundreds of wineries in the surrounding area.

EAST WEST CAFÉ ✕

128 N. Main St. © 707-829-2822 ⊘ M-Th, Sun 8-8, F-Sat 8-9
More than half the menu is vegetarian, plus tofu can be substituted for chicken in many entrees. Also fish, turkey and free-range beef burgers.
· vegetarian friendly · alcohol · tables · wait staff

From Hwy 101 just south of Santa Rosa, take Hwy 12W about 8 miles into town to Hwy 116 (Petaluma Ave). Turn right onto 116W and left onto McKinley St 2 blocks to end at Main St. Turn left onto Main to restaurant.

SLICE OF LIFE ✕

6970 McKinley St. © 707-829-6627 ⊘ Tues-Th 11:30-9, F 11:30-10, Sat 11-10, Sun 11-9
Mostly vegan, Italian and Mexican focus, all-day breakfasts, organic salads, organic crust pizza (available by the slice), fresh juices, homemade desserts.
· juice bar · vegetarian · vegan friendly · organic focus · alcohol · tables · wait staff · take-out

From Hwy 101 south of Santa Rosa, take Hwy 12W about 8 miles into town to Hwy 116 (Petaluma Ave). Turn right onto 116W and left onto

McKinley St to restaurant (across from Town Plaza).

WHOLE FOODS MARKET ✂️🍴 ♿
6910 McKinley St. © 707-829-9801 ⊙ M-Sat 8-9, Sun 9-8

· organic produce · freshly prepared food · juice bar · salad bar · café · deli · bakery
· vegetarian friendly · chain · tables · self-service · take-out

📮 **From Hwy 101** just south of Santa Rosa, take Hwy 12W about 8 miles into town to Hwy 116 (Petaluma Ave). Turn right onto 116W and left onto McKinley St to store.

SHERMAN OAKS

WHOLE FOODS ✂️🍴 ♿
4520 Sepulveda Blvd. © 818-382-3700 ⊙ M-F 7-10, Sat-Sun 8-10
Seating is outdoors at this location.

· organic produce · freshly prepared food · salad bar · café · deli · bakery · vegetarian
friendly · chain · tables · self-service · take-out

📮 **From I-405N**, take Ventura Blvd/Sherman Oaks exit to Sepulveda Blvd. Merge left onto Sepulveda to store. **From I-405S**, take Valley Vista Blvd/Sepulveda Blvd exit. Merge left onto Sepulveda to store. **From Hwy 101** (Hollywood Fwy), take Sepulveda exit south about ½ mile (past Sherman Oaks Galleria & Ventura Blvd) to store.

WHOLE FOODS MARKET ✂️🍴 ♿
12905 Riverside Drive © 818-762-5548 ⊙ Daily 8-10, Juice bar from 7am
Seating is outdoors only at this location.

· organic produce · freshly prepared food · juice bar · salad bar · café · deli · bakery
· vegetarian friendly · chain · tables · self-service · take-out

📮 **From Hwy 101** (Hollywood Fwy/Ventura Fwy), take Coldwater Canyon Ave north 1 block to store on left at Riverside Dr.

SIMI VALLEY

LASSEN'S NATURAL FOODS ✂️
2955-A4 Cochran St. © 805-526-9287 ⊙ M-F 9-8, Sat 9-6

· chain

📮 **From I-405**, take Rt 118 west (left from 405N, right from 405S) almost 17 miles to Sycamore Dr. Turn left onto Sycamore about ⅓ mile to Cochran St. Turn left onto Cochran to store.

SOUTH EL MONTE

VEGGIE-LIFE RESTAURANT ✂️
9324 E. Garvey Ave. #8 © 626-443-8687 ⊙ Tues-Sun 9-9
Vegetarian Vietnamese menu.

· vegan · tables · wait staff

📮 **From I-10**, take CA 19/Rosemead Blvd exit south on Rosemead about ⅔ mile to Garvey Ave. Turn left onto Garvey about ¼ mile to restaurant.

STANFORD

THE COOL CAFE ✂️ ♿
328 Lomalita Drive © 650-725-4758 ⊙ W, F-Sun 11-5, Th 11-8
One of three "sister" restaurants in the Menlo Park area. In the Cantor Center for Visual Arts at Stanford U, overlooking the Rodin sculpture garden. Gourmet sandwiches, soups and salads at lunch, and full-service dinner Thursdays. Ingredients are 85% organic, including meat, poultry and vegetarian choices.

· vegetarian friendly · organic focus · alcohol · tables · self-service · wait staff

🍽 From Hwy 101 (Bayshore Fwy), take Embarcadero Rd exit west on Embarcadero (becomes Galvez Dr) over 2 miles (past El Camino Real & Stanford U Hospital) to Campus Dr. Turn left onto Campus to Palm Dr. Turn left onto Palm into campus to Museum Way. Turn right onto Museum to restaurant straight ahead in Canter Arts Center. **From I-280**, take Sand Hill Rd exit toward Menlo Park east on Sand Hill about 1¾ miles to Santa Cruz Ave. Turn right onto Santa Cruz and make next left onto Junipero Serra about ½ mile (past golf course) to Campus Dr. Turn left onto Campus past Hospital to Palm. Turn right onto Palm to Museum Way. Turn right onto Museum to restaurant in Canter Arts Center.

STUDIO CITY

GOOD EARTH RESTAURANT & BAKERY ✕   ♿
12345 Ventura Blvd. © 818-506-7400 ☺ Daily 8:30-10
A "natural food" restaurant with poultry, fish and vegetarian choices. Soups, salads, sandwiches, burgers, hot entrees, whole grains, fresh juices, and shakes.

· juice bar · bakery · vegetarian friendly · alcohol · chain · tables · wait staff

🍽 From Hwy 101 (Ventura Fwy), take Laurel Canyon Blvd exit toward Studio City south on Laurel Canyon (left from 101N, right from 101S) about ¾ mile to Ventura Blvd. Turn left onto Ventura 3 blocks (about ⅓ mile) to restaurant.

LEONOR'S MEXICAN RESTAURANT ✕
12445 Moorpark St. © 818-762-0660 ☺ Daily 10-10
Meatless Mexican cuisine featuring soy-based meats and cheese.

· vegan · tables · wait staff

🍽 From Hwy 101(Ventura Fwy), take Laurel Canyon Blvd south (left from 101N, right from 101S) about ¼ mile to Moorpark St. Turn right onto Moorpark about ½ mile to restaurant.

SUNNYVALE

HOBEE'S ✕
800 Ahwanee Ave. © 408-524-3580 ☺ M 7-2:30, Tues-F 7-9, Sat 8-9, Sun 8-3
Although the menu may vary by location, see the description of the Mountain View site (the 1st Hobee's) for the basics.

· salad bar · vegetarian friendly · alcohol · chain · tables · wait staff · take-out

🍽 From Hwy 101 (Bayshore Fwy), take N Matilda Ave exit toward Sunnyvale south (right) about 1/3 mile to restaurant at Ahwanee Ave.

KOMALA VILAS ✕
1020 E. El Camino Real © 408-733-7400 ☺ M, W-Sun, Lunch 11:30-2:30, Dinner 5-10:30
South Indian vegetarian. Table service at lunch, pick-up counter orders at night.

· vegetarian · vegan friendly · tables · self-service · wait staff

🍽 From Hwy 101 (Bayshore Fwy), take Lawrence Expwy exit south about 2¼ miles to El Camino Real ramp. Turn right onto El Camino about ½ mile to restaurant at Henderson Ave Intersection. **From I-280**, take Lawrence Expwy north about 1¾ miles to El Camino Real. Turn left onto El Camino ½ mile to restaurant at Henderson.

TAHOE CITY

NEW MOON NATURAL FOODS 🌱 ♿

505 W. Lake Blvd ☎ 530-583-7426 ⏰ M-Sat 10-7, Sun 10-6

· organic produce · freshly prepared food · take-out

🍎 **From I-80**, take exit 185 onto Hwy 89S 13 miles to Tahoe City. Turn right at (only) traffic light (Albertson's on left) onto W Lake Blvd (no street sign) 1 mile to Granlibakken Rd. Turn right onto Granlibakken to store parking immediately on left (across from Tahoe Tree Nursery).

THOUSAND OAKS

LASSEN'S NATURAL FOODS 🌱

2857 E. Thousand Oaks Blvd. ☎ 805-495-2609 ⏰ M-Sat 8-9

· chain

🍎 **From Hwy 101** (Ventura Fwy), take Hampshire St exit north (right from 101N, left from 101S) about ¼ mile to Thousand Oaks Blvd. Turn left onto Thousand Oaks, right onto Skyline Dr and left into Skyline Plaza to store.

WHOLE FOODS MARKET ✖🌱 ♿

451 Avenida de los Arboles ☎ 805-492-5340 ⏰ Daily 8-9

· organic produce · freshly prepared food · salad bar · café · deli · bakery · vegetarian friendly · chain · tables · self-service · take-out

🍎 **From Hwy 101** (Ventura Fwy), take Moorpark Rd north (right from 101N, left from 101S) almost 3 miles to E Avenida de los Arboles. Turn left onto los Arboles to store on right.

TOPANGA

Walk up an appetite on the hiking trails in the nearby Santa Monica Mountains.

INN OF THE SEVENTH RAY ✖ ♿

128 Old Topanga Canyon Rd. ☎ 310-455-1311 ⏰ Lunch M-F 11:30-3, Brunch Sat-Sun 10:30-3, Dinner Daily 5:30-10

Menu includes vegetarian, vegan, hormone-free poultry, wild fish, and many organic ingredients. Separate raw foods menu.

· vegetarian friendly · vegan friendly · organic focus · alcohol · tables · wait staff

🍎 **From Hwy 101** (Ventura Fwy), take Topanga Canyon Blvd (south about 8 miles (past traffic light at Topanga School Rd, restaurant sign on right). Turn right onto Old Topanga Canyon Rd across bridge to restaurant on right. **From I-10**, go west to end and turn right onto Pacific Coast Hwy almost 6 miles to Topanga Canyon Blvd. Turn right onto Topanga Canyon 4¼ miles. Turn left after post office onto Old Topanga Canyon to restaurant on right.

TORRANCE

WHOLE FOODS MARKET ✖🌱 ♿

2655 Pacific Coast Hwy. ☎ 310-257-8700 ⏰ Daily 8-10

· organic produce · freshly prepared food · salad bar · café · deli · bakery · vegetarian friendly · chain · tables · self-service · take-out

🍎 **From I-110** (Harbor Fwy), take Hwy 1/Pacific Coast Hwy exit west on PCH almost 3 miles to store just before Crenshaw Blvd. **From I-405N** (San Diego Fwy), take Carson St W exit left onto E Carson almost 2 miles to I-110S. Take 110S about 2¾ miles to PCH and follow directions above. **From I-405S**, turn right onto Hawthorne Blvd (CA 107S) about 5½ miles to PCH. Turn left onto PCH almost 1½ miles to store just past Crenshaw.

TRUCKEE

NEW MOON NATURAL FOODS 🍎
11357C Donner Pass Rd. © 530-587-7426 ⊙ M-Sat 9-7, Sun 10-7

🍎 **From I-80E**, take exit 186 toward Central Truckee. Turn right onto Donner Pass Rd about ½ mile to store in Donner Plaza. **From I-80W**, take exit 188 (CA 267/89) toward Lake Tahoe. Turn right onto 89 (Truckee Byp) less than ¼ mile to Donner Pass. Turn left onto Donner Pass over 1 mile to store in Donner Plaza.

TUSTIN

RUTABEGORZ ✕   ♿
158 W. Main St. © 714-731-9807 ⊙ Daily 11-9
See Fullerton location for menu description. Friendly, informal setting in a turn-of-the-century historic building.

· vegetarian friendly · tables · wait staff · take-out

🍎 **From I-5S**, take Newport Ave exit left onto Newport, left at 1st traffic light onto El Camino Real and left at 2nd light onto Main St. Go 1 block to restaurant on left. **From I-5N**, take Red Hill Ave exit right onto Red Hill and immediately left onto El Camino Real almost 1 mile (past several lights) to Main. Turn left onto Main 1 block to restaurant on left.

WHOLE FOODS MARKET ✕🍎   ♿
14945 Holt Ave. © 714-731-3400 ⊙ Daily 9-9

· organic produce · freshly prepared food · juice bar · salad bar · deli · bakery
· vegetarian friendly · chain · tables · self-service · take-out

🍎 **From I-5S**, take 4th St exit left onto 4th (becomes Irvine Blvd) about 1²⁄₃ miles to Holt Ave. Turn right onto Holt to store on right in Tustin Courtyard (next to Meryn's). **From I-5N**, take Red Hill Ave exit right onto Red Hill about ²⁄₃ mile to E 1st St. Turn left onto E 1st ½ mile to Newport Ave. Turn right onto Newport and next left onto Holt to store on left in Tustin Courtyard.

UKIAH

UKIAH NATURAL FOODS ✕🍎
721 S. State St. © 707-462-4778 ⊙ M-F 9-7, Sat 9-6, Sun 10-5

· organic produce · co-op

🍎 **From Hwy 101**, take Gobbi St exit west (left from 101S, loop around right from 101N) about ½ mile to S State St. Turn left onto State to store on (left) SW corner.

UPLAND

Skiing just 20 minutes away at Baldy Mountain.

VEGGIE PANDA WOK ✕
903-B W. Foothill Blvd. © 909-982-3882 ⊙ M, Sun 4-9, Tues-Sat 11-9
Chinese-Indonesian vegan menu.

· vegan · tables · self-service · wait staff · take-out

🍎 **From I-10**, take Mountain Ave exit north (left from 10E, right from 10W) about 1¹⁄₃ miles to Foothill Blvd. Turn right onto Foothill less than ½ mile (past traffic light) to restaurant on left in Upland Square.

VALLEY SPRINGS

Valley Springs is a small spot on the map, about 60 miles southeast of Sacramento and 30 miles northeast of Stockton. In the area are five lakes for boating and fishing, along with hiking in the Sierra Nevada hills.

HEALTH HABIT 🍎   ♿
200 Hwy. 12, #8C © 209-772-3000 ⊘ M-Sat 10-6, Sun 11-5
· organic produce
🍎 Store is in shopping center at Hwy 12 & 26 in downtown Valley Springs.

VENICE

VENICE OCEAN PARK FOOD CO-OP 🍎
839 Lincoln Blvd. © 310-399-5623 ⊘ Daily 9-9
· organic produce · freshly prepared food · deli · vegetarian friendly · co-op · take-out
🍎 **From I-405N**, take CA 90W toward Marina Del Rey about 3 miles to Lincoln Blvd. Turn right onto Lincoln 1½ miles to store on left corner Lincoln & Brooks Ave. **From I-10W** (Santa Monica Fwy), take exit 1B onto Olympic Blvd and turn left (south) onto Lincoln about 1¾ miles to store on right corner Lincoln & Brooks. **From the beach**, take Rose Ave or Venice Blvd inland to Lincoln. Store is south of Rose & north of Venice.

VENTURA

LASSEN NATURAL FOODS 🍎
4071 E. Main St. © 805-644-6990 ⊘ M-Sat 9-8
· chain
🍎 **From Hwy101N** (Ventura Fwy), take Telephone Rd exit left onto Telephone and turn right onto Main St less than ½ mile to store on right. **From 101S**, take Main St exit right onto Main about ⅓ mile to store on left.

VISTA

HENRY'S MARKETPLACE 🍎
705 E. Vista Way © 760-758-7175 ⊘ M-Sat 8-8, Sun 9-7
· organic produce · freshly prepared food · deli · bakery · vegetarian friendly · chain · take-out
🍎 **From Hwy 78**, take Escondido Ave north about 1¼ miles to E Vista Way. Turn right onto E Vista ½ block to store on right.

WALNUT CREEK

WHOLE FOODS MARKET 🍴🍎   ♿
13333 E. Newell Ave. © 925-274-9700 ⊘ Daily 8-10
· organic produce · freshly prepared food · juice bar · salad bar · deli · bakery
· vegetarian friendly · chain · tables · self-service · take-out
🍎 **From I-680**, take S Main St exit north toward Walnut Creek to Newell Ave. Turn right (east) onto Newell a few blocks to store.

Please tell these businesses that you found them in Healthy Highways.

WATSONVILLE

NINA'S KITCHEN ✕
924 E. Lake Ave. ℂ 831-724-6176 ⊙ M, W-Sat 7-4
Russian vegetarian fare, including borscht, piroshki, blintzes.
· vegetarian · tables · wait staff

⌂ **From Hwy 1**, take CA 152/Main St toward Watsonville/Gilroy (inland) about 2⅓ miles to E Beach St (aka CA 152). Turn left onto Beach and follow CA 152 (turn left onto Lincoln St and right onto E Lake Ave) over 1 mile to restaurant.

WEST HOLLYWOOD

REAL FOOD DAILY ✕
414 N. La Cienega Blvd. ℂ 310-289-9910 ⊙ Daily 11:30-11
See Santa Monica location for description. A bonus is the valet parking at night.
· vegan · organic focus · alcohol · counter · tables · wait staff · take-out

⌂ **From I-10** (Santa Monica Fwy), take La Cienega Blvd north about 3 miles to restaurant 1½ blocks past the Beverly Center between Beverly Blvd & Melrose Ave.

WHOLE FOODS MARKET ✕ 🍴   ♿
7871 Santa Monica Blvd. ℂ 323-848-4200 ⊙ Daily 8-10
· organic produce · freshly prepared food · juice bar · salad bar · café · deli · bakery · vegetarian friendly · chain · counter · self-service · take-out

⌂ **From I-10** (Santa Monica Fwy), take exit 7B north on Fairfax Ave (left from 10E, right from 10W) almost 4 miles to store on NE corner Fairfax & Santa Monica Blvd. **From Hwy 101N** (Hollywood Fwy), take Santa Monica Blvd left (toward Western Ave) about 3 miles to store on right at Fairfax. **From 101S**, take Highland Ave/Hollywood Bowl exit onto Cahuenga Ave (becomes N Highland) about 1 mile to Hollywood Blvd. Turn right onto Hollywood about 1⅓ miles to Fairfax. Turn left onto Fairfax about ¾ mile to store on left at Santa Monica.

WESTWOOD

NATIVE FOODS ✕
1110½ Gayley Ave. ℂ 310-209-1055 ⊙ Daily 11-10
See Palm Dessert location for description.
· vegan · organic focus · chain · counter · tables · self-service

⌂ **From I-405** (San Diego Fwy), take Wilshire Blvd exit toward UCLA east on Wilshire about ½ mile to Gayley Ave. Turn left onto Gayley to restaurant on right in Westwood Village.

WHOLE FOODS MARKET ✕ 🍴   ♿
1050 S. Gayley Ave. ℂ 310-824-0858 ⊙ Daily 8-10
· organic produce · freshly prepared food · juice bar · salad bar · café · deli · bakery · vegetarian friendly · chain · tables · self-service · take-out

⌂ **From I-405** (San Diego Fwy), take Wilshire Blvd exit toward UCLA east on Wilshire about ½ mile to Gayley Ave. Turn left onto Gayley about ¼ mile to store.

WHITTIER

VEGGIE BISTRO ✕
6557 Comstock Ave. ℂ 562-907-7898 ⊙ Tues-Sun 11-9
Chinese vegetarian menu.

· vegetarian · vegan friendly · tables · wait staff

From I-605, take Beverly Blvd East exit east on Beverly almost 2 miles to Pickering Ave. Turn right onto Pickering ⅓ mile to Hadley St. Turn left onto Hadley about ¼ mile to Comstock Ave. Turn right onto Comstock to restaurant.

WILLITS

MARIPOSA MARKET

600 S. Main St. © 707-459-9630 ⊙ M-F 9:30-6:30, Sat 10-6, Sun 11-4

· organic produce · freshly prepared food · take-out

Store is on Hwy 101 as you go through town..

WOODLAND HILLS

WHOLE FOODS MARKET

21347 Ventura Blvd. © 818-610-0000 ⊙ Daily 8-10

Seating is outdoors.

· organic produce · freshly prepared food · salad bar · café · deli · bakery · vegetarian friendly · chain · tables · self-service · take-out

From Hwy 101N (Ventura Fwy), take Canoga Ave exit left to Ventura Blvd. Turn left onto Ventura to store. **From 101S**, take Ventura Blvd exit and bear right onto Ventura less than 1 mile to store.

YORBA LINDA

HENRY'S MARKETPLACE

17482 Yorba Linda Blvd. © 714-572-3535 ⊙ Daily 8-9

· organic produce · freshly prepared food · deli · vegetarian friendly · chain · take-out

From CA 91, take N Tustin Ave exit north (right from 91W, left from 91E) about ⅓ mile to E La Palma Ave. Turn right onto E La Palma ¾ mile to N Richfield Rd. Turn left onto N Richfield 2 miles to Yorba Linda Blvd. Turn left onto Yorba Linda to store.

YOUNTVILLE

FRENCH LAUNDRY

6640 Washington St. © 707-944-2380 ⊙ Lunch F-Sun 11-1, Dinner daily 5:30-9:30

What makes this restaurant noteworthy for vegetarians is the 5-course prix fixe tasting menu at dinner. Reserve 2 months ahead, if you don't want to miss it.

· vegetarian friendly · alcohol · tables · wait staff

Take Hwy 29 (St Helena Hwy) to Yountville. Turn east onto Madison St (right from 29N, left from 29S) 1 block to Washington St. Turn right onto Washington about 3 blocks to restaurant.

YUBA CITY

SUNFLOWER NATURAL FOODS MARKET

726 Sutter St. © 530-671-9511 ⊙ M-Sat 10-6, Deli M-F 10-2:30

· freshly prepared food· deli · vegetarian friendly · tables · self-service · take-out

From CA 20E, take Colusa Ave right about ¼ mile to Sutter St. Turn right onto Sutter to store on right. **From CA 20W**, take Sutter St ramp toward Garden Hwy left onto Sutter ¼ mile to store on right.

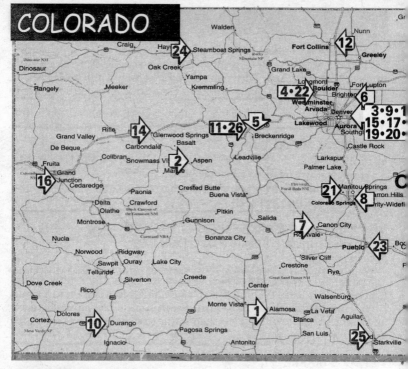

ALAMOSA

Home of Great Sand Dune National Monument.

VALLEY FOOD CO-OP ✗

3211 Main St., Suite G ℂ 719-589-5727 ⊘ M-Sat 9-6

· organic produce · co-op

⬭ Located on Hwy 160 on west side of town in Villa Mall.

ASPEN

EXPLORE BOOKSELLERS & BISTRO ✗

221 E. Main St. ℂ 970-925-5338 ⊘ Daily 10-9

Vegetarian, mostly vegan and organic food, plus books, periodicals and music.

· vegetarian · vegan friendly · organic focus · alcohol · tables · wait staff

⬭ Take Hwy 82 into Aspen, where it become Main St. Store is 1 block past park in Victorian house with small sign in front yard.

MOUNTAIN NATURAL'S ✗ 🍞

316B Aspen Airport Business Center ℂ 970-925-5502 ⊘ M-Sat 7:30-6

· freshly prepared food · deli · vegetarian friendly · counter · self-service · take-out

⬭ **From Hwy 82**, store is across from Aspen airport.

AURORA

WILD OATS MARKET 🍞

12131 Iliff Ave. ℂ 303-695-8801 ⊘ M-Sat 8-9, Sun 8-8

· organic produce · freshly prepared food · juice bar · deli · bakery · vegetarian friendly · chain · take-out

⬭ **From I-225**, take exit 5 west on Iliff Ave (left from 225N, right from 225S) 1 mile to store on NE corner Iliff & Peoria St.

1 Alamosa
2 Aspen
3 Aurora
4 Boulder
5 Breckenridge

28

6 Brighton
7 Canon City
8 Colorado Springs
9 Denver
10 Durango
11 Frisco
12 Ft. Collins
13 Glendale
14 Glenwood Springs
15 Golden
16 Grand Junction
17 Highlands Ranch
18 Idaho Springs
19 Lakewood
20 Littleton
21 Manitou Springs
22 Nederland
23 Pueblo
24 Steamboat Springs
25 Trinidad
26 Vail
27 Westminster
28 Wray

BOULDER

There are a lot of opportunities to eat well in Boulder, since a number of restaurants include a good selection of vegetarian and vegan items.

BOULDER CO-OP MARKET ✗ 🛒

1904 Pearl St. ✆ 303-447-2667 ☺ Daily 8-9, Cafe 11-8
All vegetarian community-owned store and cafe. Emphasis is on locally made and organic foods. Live acoustic music on Friday nights in the cafe.

· organic produce · freshly prepared food · juice bar · salad bar · café · deli · vegetarian · vegan friendly · organic focus · co-op · tables · self-service · take-out

🍎 **From Hwy 36**, take Canyon Blvd/CO 7N west about ¾ mile to 18th St. Turn right onto 18th 2 blocks to Pearl St. Turn right onto Pearl to store at 19th St & Pearl (4 blocks east of Pearl St Mall). **From Foothills Pkwy**, take Pearl St ramp west onto Pearl Pkwy (becomes Pearl St) about 1⅓ miles to store at 19th.

RUDI'S ✗

4720 Table Mesa Dr. ✆ 303-494-5858 ☺ M-Th 10:30-9:30, F 10:30-10:30, Sat 5-10:30, Sun 10:30-10
This upscale eatery began as a vegetarian health food restaurant in the 1970s. There are still many vegetarian dishes, but they also serve fish, natural, hormone-free meat and poultry. Local and organic produce when available, homemade bread.

· vegetarian friendly · organic focus · alcohol · tables · wait staff

🍎 **From Hwy 36**, take Foothills Pkwy exit toward Stadium and follow S Boulder Dr ramp toward Table Mesa Dr. Go west on Table Mesa about ⅓ mile to restaurant on left at Moorhead Ave in South Creek Shopping Center.

SUNFLOWER ✗   ♿

1701 Pearl St. ✆ 303-440-0220 ☺ Tues-Sat 10-10, Sun 10-9
Upscale dining, with an organic emphasis. Vegetarian/vegan dishes featuring tofu, tempeh and seitan, fish, free-range poultry, and exotic meats (elk, buffalo).

· juice bar · vegetarian friendly · vegan friendly · organic focus · alcohol · tables · wait staff

🍎 **From Hwy 36W**, turn left onto Canyon Blvd ¾ mile to 17th St. Turn right onto 17th 2 blocks to restaurant. From Foothills Pkwy, take Pearl St ramp west onto Pearl Pkwy (becomes Pearl St) about ⅓ mile to 28th St. Turn left onto 28th ⅓ mile to Canyon. Turn right onto Canyon ¾ mile to 17th. Turn right onto 17th, 2 blocks to restaurant.

TURLEY'S ✗

2350 Arapahoe Ave. ✆ 303-442-2800 ☺ M-Sat 6:30am-9pm, Sun 7-9
A casual place where vegetarians, meat-eaters, the health-conscious, and the not so health-conscious, all have ample options. Breads are locally made, eggs are from naturally raised hens, and Niman Ranch steers provide the natural beef. All-day breakfast (with whole grain pancakes and homemade granola). The kids menu is less original, with bacon, macaroni and cheese, burgers, and fries.

· vegetarian friendly · counter · tables · wait staff · take-out

🍎 **From Hwy 36**, take Arapahoe Ave west (left from 36W, right from 36E) about ⅓ mile to restaurant at north end of UCO Boulder campus.

WALNUT CAFE ✕   ♿
3073 Walnut St. © 303-447-2315 ⊙ M-Sun 7-4
*Menu includes tofu and tempeh dishes for breakfast and lunch. Soy cheese is
available to those who want dairy-free.*
  · vegetarian friendly · vegan friendly · tables · wait staff
From Hwy 36, take Arapahoe Ave exit east (right from 36W, left from
36E) ¼ mile to 30th St. Turn right onto 30th ⅓ mile to Walnut St. Turn right
onto Walnut to store (west of Crossroads Mall). **From Foothills Pkwy**,
take Pearl St ramp west onto Pearl Pkwy (becomes Pearl St) about ⅓ mile
to 30th. Turn left onto 30th ¼ mile to Walnut. Turn left onto Walnut to store.

WHOLE FOODS MARKET ✕🍴   ♿
2905 Pearl St. © 303-545-6611 ⊙ Daily 8-10
  · organic produce · freshly prepared food · juice bar · salad bar · café · deli · bakery
  · vegetarian friendly · chain · tables · self-service · take-out
From Hwy 36 (28th St in town), turn east onto Pearl St to store on left
between 28th & 30th St (across from Crossroads Mall). **From Foothills
Pkwy**, take Pearl St ramp west onto Pearl Pkwy (becomes Pearl St) about
½ mile to store on right.

WILD OATS MARKET ✕🍴   ♿
2584 Baseline Rd. © 303-499-7636 ⊙ Daily 7-10
The first store in the Wild Oats chain.
  · organic produce · freshly prepared food · juice bar · salad bar · café · deli · bakery
  · vegetarian friendly · chain · counter · tables · self-service · take-out
From Hwy 36, take Baseline Rd west (right from 36E, left under overpass
from 36W). Turn left just before Broadway into Basemar Center to store.

WILD OATS MARKET ✕🍴   ♿
1651 Broadway © 303-442-0909 ⊙ Daily 7-10
  · organic produce · freshly prepared food · juice bar · salad bar · café · deli · bakery
  · vegetarian friendly · chain · counter · self-service · take-out
From Hwy 36, take Arapahoe Ave west about 10 blocks (1 mile) to
store on SW corner Arapahoe & Broadway. **From Hwy 93 heading north**,
93 becomes Broadway in city limits. Go about 4 miles to store on SW
corner Broadway & Arapahoe.

BRECKENRIDGE

AMAZING GRACE NATURAL FOODS 🍴
213 Lincoln Ave. © 970-453-1445 ⊙ M-Sat 9-7, Sun 12-6
  · organic produce · freshly prepared food · deli · take-out
From I-70, take Hwy 9S about 10 miles to Breckenridge. Turn left at 3rd
traffic light onto French St 2 blocks to store at corner Lincoln Ave & French.

BRIGHTON

HIS PANTRY 🍴
115 Strong St. © 303-655-3752 ⊙ Tues, W, F 10-6, Th 10-7, Sat 10-5
Discount health foods.
  · co-op
From I-76W, take exit 25 toward CO 7W/Brighton right onto E 168th
St and immediately left onto N Frontage Rd about 1½ miles to Bridge St.
Turn left onto Bridge almost 4½ miles to traffic light at Main St. Turn
right onto Main 1 block to Strong St. Turn right onto Strong to store on left

in middle of block. **From 1-76E**, take exit 12 onto Hwy 85N. **From Hwy 85**, take Brighton exit for Bridge St east (right from 85N, left from 85S) to 1st light at Main. Turn left onto Main 1 block to Strong. Turn right onto Strong to store on left in middle of block.

CANON CITY

The Arkansas River, Royal Gorge Bridge, rafting, and hiking trails.

MOTHER NATURE'S HEALTH FOODS

915 Main St. © 719-275-9367 ⊙ M-F 9-6, Sat 9-5:30
  · organic produce

▢ Canon City is 36 miles west of I-25 exit 101 (Pueblo) on Hwy 50. **From Hwy 50**, go north on 9th St 1 block to store at Main St intersection.

COLORADO SPRINGS

CAMICE'S NATURAL FOODS

1837 N. Circle Drive © 719-630-1793 ⊙ M-F 10-6, Sat 10-3
  · organic produce · co-op

▢ **From I-25**, take exit 145 east on Fillmore St (right from 25N, left from 25S) about 4 miles (through residential area, becomes N Circle Dr) to Constitution Ave. Turn left at Constitution into store lot.

MOUNTAIN MAMA NATURAL FOODS

1625-A W. Uintah St. © 719-633-4139 ⊙ M-Sat 9-7, Sun 11-5
  · freshly prepared food · deli · take-out

▢ **From I-25**, take exit 143 west on Uintah St (right from 25S, left from 25N) about ½ mile to store on left.

THE VITAMIN COTTAGE NATURAL GROCERY

1780 E. Woodmen Rd. © 719-536-9606 ⊙ M-F 9-8, Sat 9-7, Sun 10-6
  · organic produce

▢ **From I-25**, take exit 149 east on Woodmen Rd (left from 25S, right from 25N) about 1 mile to store on right (behind Lenscrafters).

WILD OATS MARKET

5075 N. Academy Blvd.. © 719-548-1667 ⊙ Daily 8-9
  · organic produce · freshly prepared food · juice bar · salad bar · café · deli · bakery.
  vegetarian friendly · chain · counter · self-service · take-out

▢ **From I-25**, take exit 149 east on Woodmen Rd (left from 25S, right from 25N) about 1 mile to Academy Blvd. Turn right onto Academy about 2½ miles to Union Blvd. Turn left onto Union to store in 1st shopping center on right (next to Big Lots).

WILD SAGE AT COLORADO COLLEGE

1090 N. Cascade St. "Q"-McHugh Commons © 719-389-7000 ⊙ Daily 11am-midnight

Self-described as "clean cuisine," the food at this "planet-friendly" campus site is over 80% organic and additive-free. Serving "casual" veg and nonveg items, such as soups, wraps, burgers, chili, and smoothies. Menu includes nutritional analysis, with items keyed for organic, non-dairy, wheat-free, and vegan.

  · vegetarian friendly · vegan friendly · organic focus · counter · tables · self-service

▢ **From I-25**, take exit 143 east on Uintah St (left from 25S, right from 25N) about ½ mile to N Cascade Ave. Turn right onto N Cascade to Colorado College campus. Restaurant is in the "Q"-McHugh Commons (across from soccer field).

DENVER

GOVINDA'S BUFFET ✕
1390 Cherry St. © 303-333-5461 ⊘ M-F 11:30-2:30, 5-8, Sat 5-8
Vegetarian Indian lunch and dinner buffet. Bhakti yoga center next door.
· vegetarian · vegan friendly · organic focus · tables · self-service · take-out
From I-25, take exit 204 north on Colorado Blvd (right from 25N, left
from 25S) ⅓ mile to 14th St. Turn right onto 14th, 6 blocks to restaurant on
corner 14th & Cherry St. **From I-70**, take exit 276B south on Colorado
(right from 70E, left from 70W) about 3 miles to 14th. Turn left onto 14th
6 blocks to restaurant on corner 14th & Cherry.

MERCURY CAFE ✕
2199 California St. © 303-294-9281 ⊘ Lunch Sat-Sun 9-3, Dinner M-Tues,
Th -Sun 5:30-11, Desserts & drinks until 1:30am
*"Tofu Rancheros" to bacon-and-egg breakfast, tofu "chops" to steak as the day
goes on. Homemade whole-grain, naturally-sweetened baked goods, late night
desserts. Plus, dancing (come for a free class), tai chi, poetry readings, and more.*
· vegetarian friendly · vegan friendly · tables · wait staff
From I-25S, take exit 213 (38th St/Park Ave) south on Park about 1
mile where it becomes 22nd St. Follow 22nd ¾ mile to restaurant on right
at California St. **From I-25N**, take exit 210A east on W Colfax Ave 1 mile
to Stout St. Turn left onto Stout about 1 mile to 22nd. Turn right onto 22nd
1 block to restaurant on right at California. **From I-70W**, take exit 275B
left onto Brighton Blvd (becomes Broadway) about 2⅓ miles to 22nd.
Turn left onto 22nd, 3 blocks to restaurant on right at California.

PORTER MEMORIAL HOSPITAL CAFETERIA ✕
2525 S. Downing St. © 303-778-5881 ⊘ Daily 6:45am-7pm
An all-vegetarian cafeteria.
· vegetarian · tables · self-service
From I-25S, take exit 206B toward Washington St/Emerson St left onto
Bechtel Blvd about ½ mile to Downing St. Turn right onto Downing 1¼ miles
to Porter Hospital on right. Cafeteria is 2nd door on right from main entrance.
From I-25N, take exit 206A left onto Downing and follow directions above.

WATERCOURSE FOODS ✕
206 E. 13th Ave. © 303-832-7313 ⊘ Tues-Sun 8-10
*A broad selection of vegetarian and vegan choices for breakfast, lunch and
dinner. Including "biscuits & gravy," "Seitan Philly," a portobello Reuben,
and many other interesting seitan, tempeh and tofu variations.*
· vegetarian · vegan friendly · tables · wait staff
From I-25, take exit 210A east on W Colfax Ave (right from 25N, left
from 25S) about 2 miles (past Civic Center Park) to Grant St. Turn right
onto Grant 2 blocks to 13th Ave. Turn right onto 13th to restaurant between Grant & Sherman St.

WHOLE FOODS MARKET ✕
2375 E. 1st Ave. © 720-941-4100 ⊘ Daily 8-10
· organic produce · freshly prepared food · juice bar · salad bar · café · deli · bakery
· vegetarian friendly · chain · counter · tables · self-service · take-out
From I-25S, take exit 212A south on Speer Blvd (becomes 1st Ave)
about 4 miles to store at University Blvd. **From I-25N**, take exit 205A
north on University Blvd about 2 miles to store on corner University & 1st.

WILD OATS MARKET ✕🛒 &

900 E.11th Ave. © 303-832-7701 ⊙ Daily 7-10

· organic produce · freshly prepared food · juice bar · salad bar · café · deli · bakery
· vegetarian friendly · chain · counter · tables · self-service · take-out

From I-25, take take exit 210A east on W Colfax Ave (right from 25N, left from 25S) about 2½ miles to Emerson St. Turn right onto Emerson 4 blocks to store on SE corner Emerson & 11th.

WILD OATS MARKET ✕🛒 &

1111 S. Washington St. © 303-733-6201 ⊙ Daily 7-11

· organic produce · freshly prepared food · juice bar · salad bar · café · deli · bakery
· vegetarian friendly · chain · tables · self-service · take-out

From I-25S, take exit 206B toward Washington St and follow ramp along Buchtel Blvd ½ mile to E Mississippi. Turn right onto Mississippi to store 2 blocks east of interstate at S Washington. From I-25N, take exit 207A (Lincoln St) toward Broadway right onto E Ohio Ave ⅓ mile to Washington. Turn right onto Washington about ⅓ mile (past 3rd intersection) to store.

DURANGO

DURANGO NATURAL FOODS 🛒

575 E. 8th Ave. © 970-247-8129 ⊙ M-Sat 8-8, Sun 9-7

· organic produce · freshly prepared food · deli · take-out

From US 550, turn east onto 6th St (right from 550N, left from 550S) ⅔ mile to store on right corner 6th & 8th Ave. From US 160E, merge onto US 550N less than ¼ mile to 6th St (aka College Dr) and follow directions above. From east of Durango on US 160W, turn right (north) onto Rt 3 (becomes 8th Ave) about 2½ miles to store on left at 1st traffic light (6th St).

LOCAL WILD LIFE ✕ &

845 E. 3rd Ave. © 970-247-8395 ⊙ Tues, F 11:11-2:22

The twice-a-week "educational" lunch, under the auspices of Turtle Lake Refuge, is a 4-course raw foods meal incorporating freshly harvested local produce.

· organic produce · vegan · tables · wait staff

From US 550 (Main Ave in town), turn east onto 9th St 2 blocks to E 3rd Ave. Turn right onto E 3rd to restaurant in the Rocky Mt Retreat Building (at the back).

NATURE'S OASIS ✕🛒

1123 Camino del Rio © 970-247-1988 ⊙ M-Sat 8-8:30, Sun 8-7

· organic produce · freshly prepared food · juice bar · deli · vegetarian friendly · tables
· self-service · take-out

On US 550 at about 11th St.

FRISCO

ALPINE NATURAL FOODS ✕🛒 &

310 W. Main St. © 970-668-5535 ⊙ M-Sat 8-8, Sun 9-7

· organic produce · freshly prepared food · salad bar · deli · vegetarian friendly · tables
· self-service · take-out

From I-70, take exit 201 toward Frisco east on Main St (left from 70W, right from 70E) about ⅓ mile to store at Creekside Dr.

Please tell these businesses that you found them in Healthy Highways.

FT. COLLINS

FORT COLLINS FOOD CO-OP 🍎
250 E. Mountain Ave. ℂ 970-484-7448 ⊙ M-F 8:30-7:30, Sat 8:30-7, Sun 11-6
· organic produce · freshly prepared food · deli · co-op · take-out

🍎 From I-25, take exit 269B west on Mulberry St about 3½ miles to College Ave. Turn right onto College 4 blocks to Mountain Ave. Turn right onto Mountain 1 block to store on left.

WILD OATS MARKET 🍴🍎
200 W. Foothills Pkwy. ℂ 970-225-1400 ⊙ Daily 7:30-10
· organic produce · freshly prepared food · juice bar · salad bar · café · deli · bakery
· vegetarian friendly · chain · counter · self-service · take-out

🍎 From 1-25, take exit 265 west on Harmony Rd (right from 25S, left from 25N) about 4½ miles to College Ave. Turn right onto College about 1⅓ miles (past Horsetooth Rd) to Foothills Pkwy (get in left lane). Turn left onto Foothills to store just ahead.

GLENDALE

WILD OATS MARKET 🍴🍎
870 S. Colorado Blvd. ℂ 303-691-0101 ⊙ Daily 7-10
· organic produce · freshly prepared food · juice bar · salad bar · café · deli · bakery
· vegetarian friendly · chain · tables · self-service · take-out

🍎 From I-25, take exit 204 north on Colorado Blvd about 15 blocks to store on east side between Kentucky & Ohio Ave (in lot with Home Depot & Eastern Mt Sports).

GLENWOOD SPRINGS

GOOD HEALTH GROCERY 🍎
772 Cooper Ave. ℂ 970-945-0235 ⊙ M-Sat 9-7, Sun 9-6
· organic produce · freshly prepared food · deli · take-out

🍎 From I-70, take exit 116 toward Glenwood Springs south on CA 82 (Grand Ave) about ¼ mile to 8th Ave. Turn left onto 8th to store on right corner Cooper Ave & 8th.

GOLDEN

WILD OATS MARKET 🍴🍎
14357 W. Colfax Ave. ℂ 303-277-1339 ⊙ Daily 7-10
According to Wild Oats, this is your last health food store before heading into the mountains. Just one minute from the highway.
· organic produce · freshly prepared food · juice bar · salad bar · café · deli · bakery
· vegetarian friendly · chain · tables · self-service · take-out

🍎 From I-70, take exit 263 onto Denver West Marriott Blvd (left from 70W, right from 70E) about ¼ mile to Cole Blvd. Turn right onto Cole to store (under Mission style tower).

GRAND JUNCTION

The Colorado National Monument, Grand Mesa, whitewater rafting, mountain biking, fishing, skiing, dinosaur digs — all right here.

APPLESEED HEALTH FOODS 🍎
2830 North Ave. ℂ 970-243-5541 ⊙ M-Sat 9-6

🍎 From I-70E, take exit 26 toward Grand Junction onto US 6E about 7 miles to store between 28¼ & 28½ Rd. **From I-70W**, take exit 37 toward Clifton/Grand Junction onto 70Bus W about 3½ miles. Continue on US 6W over 1½ miles to store.

SUNDROP GROCERY & GARDEN DELI ✕ 🍽   ♿

321 Rood Ave. ☎ 970-243-1175 ⊙ M-Sat 9-7
All vegetarian "world cuisine" at the deli.

· organic produce · freshly prepared food · juice bar · café · deli · bakery · vegetarian · vegan friendly · tables · self-service · take-out

⬜ **From I-70E**, take exit 26 onto 70Bus E (River Rd) about 5 miles to Rood Ave. Turn left onto Rood 2½ blocks to store on right between 3rd & 4th St (yellow building). **From I-70W**, take exit 31 south on Horizon Dr about 1½ miles to 7th St. Turn left onto 7th (into downtown) about 2 miles to Rood. Turn left onto Rood 3½ blocks to store on left between 3rd & 4th.

HIGHLANDS RANCH

WHOLE FOODS MARKET ✕ 🍽   ♿

9366 S Colorado Blvd. ☎ 303-470-6003 ⊙ Daily 8-9

· organic produce · freshly prepared food · juice bar · salad bar · café · deli · bakery · vegetarian friendly · chain · tables · self-service · take-out

⬜ **From I-25**, take exit 193 west on Lincoln Ave (left from 25N, right from 25S) almost 2½ miles (becomes University Blvd) to store on NE corner University & Colorado Blvd.

IDAHO SPRINGS

Hot springs three blocks from Whispering Weeds and a micro-brew across the street.

WHISPERING WEEDS ORGANIC BAKERY & CAFE ✕

1446 Miner St. ☎ 303-567-0140 ⊙ M-Sat 10-6, Sun 11-5
Organic juice bar and bakery, serving vegetarian sandwiches on organic bread.

· juice bar · café · deli · bakery · vegetarian · organic focus · counter · tables · wait staff · take-out

⬜ **From I-70**, take exit 240 toward Mt Evans north on 13th Ave (left from 70E, right from 70W) 2 blocks to stop sign at Miner St. Turn right onto Miner 2 blocks to store on left corner Miner & 15th Ave (big yellow sign on top of building).

LAKEWOOD

MISSION TRACE VITAMIN COTTAGE 🍽

3333 S. Wadsworth Blvd. ☎ 303-989-4866 ⊙ M-F 9-8:00, Sat 9-7:00, Sun 11-6:00

· freshly prepared food · deli · take-out

⬜ **From I-70**, take exit 261 onto US 6E about 3½ miles to Wadsworth Blvd. Turn right onto Wadsworth about 1¼ miles to store on west side in Mission Trace Shopping Center (2 blocks north of US 285).

LITTLETON

WILD OATS MARKET ✕ 🍽   ♿

5910 S. University Blvd. ☎ 303-798-9699 ⊙ M-Sat 7-9, Sun 8-9

· organic produce · freshly prepared food · juice bar · salad bar · café · deli · bakery · vegetarian friendly · chain · tables · self-service · take-out

⬜ **From I-25**, take exit 199 west (towards mountains) on Bellview Ave (right from 25S, left from 25N) about 2½ miles to University Blvd. Turn left onto University 1 mile to Orchard Dr (2nd traffic light). Turn left onto Orchard to store on SE corner University & Orchard.

MANITOU SPRINGS

At the base of Pikes Peak, with hiking trails, mineral springs and an arty community.

MANITOU NATURAL ✗🥗 &

56 Park Ave. © 719-685-5434 ⊙ Daily 9-7
Enjoy your food on the outdoor creekside patio.

· organic produce · freshly prepared food · juice bar · salad bar · café · deli · bakery
· vegetarian friendly · counter · tables · self-service · take-out

📋 **From I-25**, take exit 141 toward Cimarron St and and follow onto Cimarron/US 24W (left from 25N, ramp from 25S) about 5 miles to Bypass. Turn left onto Bypass and veer right onto Washington Ave (merge onto Canon Ave, then left onto Park Ave) ½ mile to store across from Soda Springs Park.

ORGANIC EARTH CAFE ✗ &

1124 Manitou Ave. © 719-685-0986 ⊙ M, Th 11-10, F-Sun 9-midnight Note: hours & days may vary seasonally
All vegan and organic menu. Dine indoors or out in the garden.

· juice bar · café · vegan · organic focus · alcohol · tables · wait staff

📋 **From I-25**, take exit 141 toward Cimarron St and follow onto Cimarron/US 24W (left from 25N, ramp from 25S) about 4 miles to 24 Bus/Manitou Ave ramp. Take right fork and turn right onto Manitou about 1½ miles to restaurant.

NEDERLAND

MOUNTAIN PEOPLE'S CO-OP 🥗 &

30 E. First St. © 303-258-7500 ⊙ Daily 8-8

· organic produce · freshly prepared food · deli · bakery · co-op · take-out

📋 Nederland is about 17 miles west of Boulder on Hwy 119S (which ends in Nederland). **From 119**, take roundabout onto S Bridge St 1 block to 1st St. Turn left onto 1st to store (along Boulder Creek).

PUEBLO

AMBROSIA NATURAL FOODS 🥗

112 Colorado Ave. © 719-545-2958 ⊙ M-Sat 8-8, Sun 9-5

· organic produce · co-op

📋 From **I-25**, take exit 97B toward Abriendo Ave onto W El Dorado Ave (becomes Abriendo) about ⅔ mile to Colorado Ave. Turn left onto Colorado ½ block to store on left.

STEAMBOAT SPRINGS

BAMBO MARKET ✗🥗

116 9th St. © 970-879-9992 ⊙ M-F 8-7, Sat 10-6, Sun 10-5, Deli daily until 5

· organic produce · freshly prepared food · juice bar · deli · vegetarian friendly · tables
· self-service · take-out

📋 From US 40, turn north (away from river) onto 9th St to store.

HEALTHY SOLUTIONS 🥗

335 Lincoln Ave. © 970-849-4747 ⊙ M-Sat 9-7, Sun 12-7

· organic produce · bakery

📋 On US 40 at 3rd St.

TRINIDAD

Camping available at Trinidad Lake State Park.

THE NATURAL FOOD STORE 🐑

316 Prospect St. © 719-846-7577 ⊙ M-F 10-5:30, Sat 10-5

· organic produce

🌰 **From I-25,** take exit 14A toward Cuchera-LaVeta (from 25S) or Trinidad State College (from 25N). Turn left onto Hwy 12/Scenic Highway of Legends. Follow 12 left (becomes Prospect St) to store around corner.

VAIL

CLARK'S ✕🐑

141 E. Meadow Drive © 970-476-1199 ⊙ Daily 7:30-10

· freshly prepared food · deli · vegetarian friendly · tables · self-service · take-out

🌰 From I-70, take exit 176 toward Vail. From roundabout, take S Frontage Rd E to E Meadow Dr. Turn right onto E Meadow and follow around to right to store.

WESTMINSTER

WILD OATS MARKET ✕🐑

9229 N. Sheridan Blvd. © 303-650-2333 ⊙ M-Sat 7:30-9, Sun 8-9

· organic produce · freshly prepared food · juice bar · salad bar · café · deli · bakery
· vegetarian friendly · chain · tables · self-service · take-out

🌰 **From US 36,** take Sheridan Blvd exit north on Sheridan (right coming from Denver, left coming from Boulder) 1/3-1/2 mile to 2nd traffic light at 93rd Ave. Turn left onto 93rd to store in shopping center.

WRAY

The Wray Rehabilitation and Activities Center (WRAC) offers nautilus equipment, basketball, racquetball, a track area, free weights, ping pong, aerobic exercises, water therapy, physical therapy, hot tub, sauna, steam room, and more.

STRAWBERRY PATCH 🐑

421 Main St. © 970-332-4064 ⊙ M-F 9:30-5:30, Sat 10-noon

Fresh smoothies, and while there are no freshly prepared foods, there is a microwave to heat packaged meals.

· organic produce · juice bar · take-out

🌰 **From Hwy 34,** turn south onto Main St about 1½ blocks to store on west side (across from theater).

Goldbeck's "EAT IT OR NOT"

FASCINATING & FAR-OUT FACTS ABOUT FOOD

DISTRIBUTION OF ANIMALS IN A BOX OF ANIMAL CRACKERS

6 gorillas, 5 bears, 4 camels, 3 rhinos, 2 tigers, 2 monkeys,
2 sheep, 1 buffalo, 1 lion

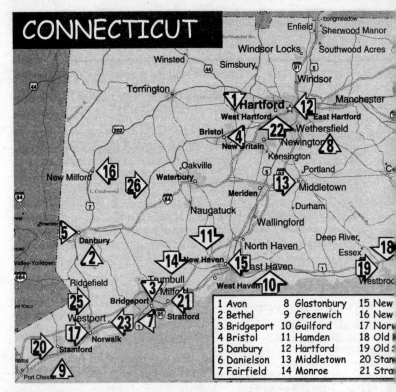

CONNECTICUT

1 Avon
2 Bethel
3 Bridgeport
4 Bristol
5 Danbury
6 Danielson
7 Fairfield
8 Glastonbury
9 Greenwich
10 Guilford
11 Hamden
12 Hartford
13 Middletown
14 Monroe
15 New
16 New
17 Nor
18 Old
19 Old
20 Stan
21 Stra

AVON

GARDEN OF LIGHT PURE FOODS MARKET ✕ 🛒
395 W. Main St. ✆ 860-409-2196 ⊙ M-F 9-8, Sat 9-6:30, Sun 11-5
· freshly prepared food · deli · vegetarian friendly · tables · self-service · take-out
⬠ Avon is 11 miles west of Hartford on Rt 44. Store is on 44 (aka Main St) just east of Rt 167 & Framington Valley Mall.

BETHEL

The town of Bethel is home to an art house cinema, a cooperative gallery for local artists, many antique and consignment shops, and quaint cobblestone sidewalks.

SAGE CAFÉ ✕
153 Greenwood Ave. ✆ 203-794-9394 ⊙ Tues-Sat 11-7, Sun seasonal
Vegetarian soups, salads, wraps, sandwiches, and homemade baked goods.
· juice bar · café · vegetarian · vegan friendly · tables · self-service · take-out
⬠ From I-84, take exit 5 toward Downtown Danbury/Bethel onto Rt 53S about 3 miles (through downtown Danbury) to Rt 302. Turn left onto Rt 302 (Greenwood Ave) about ¾ mile to restaurant on left.

BRIDGEPORT

BLOODROOT ✕
85 Ferris St. ✆ 203-576-9168 ⊙ Lunch Tues, Th-Sun 11:30-2:30, Dinner Tues-Th 6-9, F-Sat 6-10
All vegetarian, mostly vegan and organic menu is posted on the chalkboard and changes every few weeks. Standards include marinated tofu salad, Bloodroot Burgers, homemade bread, and at brunch, soysage patties, scrambled tofu and soudough

pancakes. Collectively run with a feminist bookstore on site.

· vegetarian · vegan friendly · organic focus · alcohol · co-op · tables · self-service · take-out

🛏 **From NY**, take I-95 to exit 24. Go straight through intersection and turn right onto Black Rock Tpke/Brewster St. At 4th traffic light turn left onto Fairfield Ave. At next light turn right onto Ellsworth St 2 blocks to Thurston St. Turn left onto Thurston and right onto Harbor Ave 3 blocks to Ferris St. Turn left onto Ferris to restaurant. **From New Haven**, take I-95 to exit 25. Turn left onto Fairfield Ave. At 3rd light turn left onto Ellsworth and follow directions above from Ellsworth.

BRISTOL

SUPER NATURAL MARKET & DELI ✕🛒 &
430 N. Main St. ✆ 860-582-1663 ⏱ M-F 8-6, Sat 9-5

· freshly prepared food · deli · vegetarian friendly · tables · self-service · take-out

🛏 **From I-84**, take exit 33 toward Bristol onto Rt 72W (becomes Memorial Blvd, then School Rd) about 3 miles to Main St. Turn right onto Main about ¾ mile to store.

DANBURY

CHAMOMILE NATURAL FOODS 🛒
58-60 Newtown Rd. (Rte. 6) ✆ 203-792-8952 ⏱ M-W, F 9:30-6:30, Th 9:30-7:30, Sat 10-5:30

· organic produce

🛏 **From I-84**, take exit 8 onto US 6E (Newtown Rd) about ¾ mile to store on right in Rt 6 Plaza.

DANIELSON

SUNFLOWERS NATURAL FOOD & CAFE ✕🛒 &
630 N. Main St. ✆ 860-779-7555 ⏱ Tues-F 9-5:30, Sat 9-5, Cafe Tues-F 11-3, Sat 9-3
Vegetarian soups, salads, burgers, and sandwiches, plus a bit of turkey and fish.

· organic produce · freshly prepared food · café · vegetarian friendly · tables · self-service · take-out

🛏 **From I-395**, take exit 92 toward S Killington west on Westcott Rd (left from 395N, right from 395S) about ⅓ mile to Main St (CT 12). Turn right onto Main ½ mile to store.

FAIRFIELD

MRS. GREEN'S NATURAL MARKET ✕🛒
1916 Post Rd. ✆ 203-255-4333 ⏱ M-Sat 9-7, Sun 10-6

· organic produce · freshly prepared food · vegetarian friendly · chain · tables · self-service · take-out

🛏 **From I-95**, take exit 21 south on Mill Plain Rd (right from 95N, left from 95S) about ¼ mile to Post Rd (aka US 1). Turn right onto Post less than ¼ mile to store on right.

FAIRFIELD DINER ✕ &
90 Kings Hwy. Cutoff ✆ 203-335-4090 ⏱ Daily 6am-midnight
A traditional diner with a surprising repertoire of vegetarian entrees beyond the typical salads and veggie burger. Menu offers tofu, tempeh, soy cheese, and more. There's even a (highly touted) vegan chocolate cake.

· vegetarian friendly · alcohol · counter · tables · wait staff · take-out

🍎 **From I-95**, take exit 24 toward Black Rock Tpke onto Kings Hwy Cutoff (right from 95N, right onto Chambers St and left from 95S) about ¼ mile to restaurant.

GLASTONBURY

GARDEN OF LIGHT PURE FOODS MARKET ✗🍲

2836 Main St. © 860-657-9131 ⊙ M-F 9-8, Sat 9-7, Sun 11-5

· organic produce · freshly prepared food · deli · vegetarian friendly · tables · self-service · take-out

🍎 **From I-91**, take exit 25 toward Glastonbury onto Rt 3N across bridge almost 2 miles to Main St Glastonbury exit. Turn left onto Glastonbury Blvd and right onto Main to store in plaza on left at traffic light.

GREENWICH

WHOLE FOODS MARKET ✗🍲   &

90 E. Putnam Ave. © 203-661-0631 ⊙ Daily 8-9

· organic produce · freshly prepared food · deli · bakery · vegetarian friendly · chain · take-out

🍎 **From I-95**, take exit 4 toward Cos Cob north on Indian Field Rd about ²/₃ mile to end. Turn left onto Rt 1 (E Putnam Ave) 1 mile to store on left.

GUILFORD

FOODWORKS ✗🍲

1055 Boston Post Rd. © 203-458-9778 ⊙ M, W, F 9:30-7, Tues, Th 9:30-7:30, Sat 11-7, Sun 12-6

· organic produce · freshly prepared food · juice bar · deli · vegetarian friendly · tables · self-service · take-out

🍎 **From I-95**, take exit 58 toward Guilford south on Rt 77 (right from 95N, left from 95S) ½ mile to store on right at intersection 77 & Boston Post Rd.

SHORELINE DINER ✗   &

35 Boston Post Rd. © 203-458-7380 ⊙ M-Th, Sun 7am-midnight, F-Sat 7am-1am
See Fairfield Diner on previous page for description.

· vegetarian friendly · alcohol · counter · tables · self-service · wait staff · take-out

🍎 **From I-95**, take exit 59 south on Soundview Rd (right from 95N, loop around right onto Goose Ln and across hwy from 95S) to Boston Post Rd (US 1). Turn left onto Boston Post less than 1 mile to restaurant.

HAMDEN

THYME & SEASON 🍲

3040 Whitney Ave. © 203-407-8128 ⊙ M-F 9-7:30, Sat 9-7, Sun 9-5

· organic produce · freshly prepared food · deli · take-out

🍎 **From I-91**, take exit 10 onto Rt 40N about 3 miles to Rt 10N. Take 10N (aka Whitney Ave) about ¼ mile to store on left.

HARTFORD

FRESH CITY ✗

280 Trumbull St. © 860-249-2489 ⊙ M-F 6:30am-4pm
A fast-food alternative featuring fresh food prepared in customer viewing area. Wraps, stir-fries, noodles, soups, salads, smoothies, and such. Vegetarian possibilities noted and the option to add tofu, poultry, steak or shrimp to most dishes.

· juice bar · vegetarian friendly · chain · tables · self-service · take-out

🍪 **From I-84**, take exit 50 toward Main St and follow exit to Trumbull St. Turn south onto Trumbull (right from I-84E, left from I-84W) to restaurant in lobby of 280.

LION'S DEN VEGETARIAN RESTAURANT ✕   ⓢ

403½ Woodland St. © 860-241-0512 ⊙ M-Th 8:30am-10pm, F-Sat 8:30am-11pm

A small place with a small seating area, offering a daily plate of homemade vegetarian West Indian food.

· vegetarian · vegan friendly · tables · self-service · take-out

🍪 **From I-84**, take exit 50 toward Main St onto Rt 44W (left from 84E, right from 84W) about 1½ miles to Woodland St. Turn left onto Woodland to restaurant.

MIDDLETOWN

IT'S ONLY NATURAL MARKET 🥬   &

386 Main St. © 860-346-1786 ⊙ M-W, Sat 9-6, Th-F 9-8, Sun 11-4

· organic produce · freshly prepared food · juice bar · vegetarian friendly · take-out

🍪 **From I-91**, take exit 22S toward Middletown/Old Saybrook onto Rt 9S about 5½ miles to Washington St (exit 15). Turn right onto Washington 2 blocks to Main St. Turn left onto Main 1 block to store on left.

IT'S ONLY NATURAL RESTAURANT ✕   &

386 Main St. © 860-346-9210 ⊙ M-Th 11:30-9, F-Sat 11:30-10, Sun 11:30-3

An extensive vegetarian, mostly vegan menu except for the tuna melt. Vegan soups, salads, sandwiches, whole wheat pizza, and creative entrees featuring tofu, tempeh, fresh vegetables and brown rice.

· juice bar · café · vegetarian friendly · vegan friendly · alcohol · tables · wait staff

🍪 **From I-91**, take exit 22S toward Middletown/Old Saybrook onto Rt 9S about 5½ miles to Washington St (exit 15). Turn right onto Washington and left into Mellilli Plaza (before Main St) to restaurant in back of Main St Market.

MONROE

SUNWHEEL HEALTH FOODS 🥬

444 Main St. © 203-268-2688 ⊙ M-F 10-6, Sat 1-05

🍪 Monroe is about 13 miles north of Bridgeport (I-95 exit 27A) on Rt 25. From Rt 25 (Main St), store is at juncture Rt 59 (Easton Rd) in back of big yellow house.

NEW HAVEN

CLAIRE'S CORNER COPIA ✕   &

1000 Chapel St. © 203-562-3888 ⊙ M-Th 8am-9pm, Sat-Sun 8am-10pm

Kosher vegetarian (except for the tuna fish). Eclectic menu with a Mexican/ Middle Eastern slant. Locally grown produce in summer.

· vegetarian friendly · vegan friendly · kosher · tables · self-service · take-out

🍪 **From I-95**, take exit 47 toward Downtown New Haven onto CT 34W about ²/₃ mile to exit 1. Follow exit to traffic light at Church St. Turn right onto Church to 3rd light (Chapel St). Turn left onto Chapel 2 lights to store on left corner Chapel & College St. **From I-91S**, take exit 3 onto Trumbull St about 4 blocks to Temple St. Turn left onto Temple ½ mile to Chapel. Turn right onto Chapel 1 block to store on left corner Chapel & College.

EDGE OF THE WOODS MARKET ✂🛒 ♿
379 Whalley Ave. ℗ 203-787-1055 ⊗ M-F 8:30-7:30, Sat 8:30-6:30, Sun 9-6
 · organic produce · freshly prepared food · juice bar · café · deli · bakery · vegetarian
 · vegan friendly · tables · self-service · take-out

🛒 **From I-95**, take exit 47 toward Downtown New Haven onto CA 34W (Frontage Rd) past Yale New Haven Medical Center to Howe St (2nd traffic light). Turn right onto Howe 5 blocks to Whalley Ave. Turn left onto Whalley to store in Market Square Shopping Ctr. **From I-91S**, take exit 3 onto Trumbull St about 4 blocks to Temple St. Turn left onto Temple 2 blocks to Grove St. Turn right onto Grove (becomes Tower Pkwy, then Whalley Ave) about 1¼ miles to store in Main Square Shopping Ctr.

NEW MILFORD

BANK STREET NATURAL FOODS 🛒
10 Bank St. ℗ 860-355-1515 ⊗ M-F 9:30-6, Sat 9:30-5:30, Sun 11-4
 · juice bar · take-out

🛒 **From I-84**, take exit 7 onto Rt 202E (becomes 7N) over 11 miles. Where road splits veers right to continue on 202/Bridge St over bridge into town. Turn left onto Main St and left onto Bank St to store on right.

NORWALK

FOOD FOR THOUGHT ✂🛒 ♿
596 Westport Ave. ℗ 203-847-5233 ⊗ M-Sat 8-9, Sun 9-7
On-site bakery specializes in wheat-free, vegan and dairy-free pastries.
 · organic produce · freshly prepared food · juice bar · salad bar · café · deli · bakery
 · vegetarian friendly · tables · self-service · take-out

🛒 **From I-95**, take exit 17 toward Wesport/Saugatuck. Turn left off ramp onto Saugatuck Rd, left onto Sunrise Rd, right onto Indian Hill Rd, left onto Treadwell Ave, right onto Kings Hwy, and left onto Renzulli Rd (1 mile total) to Rt 1 (Westport Ave). Turn left onto Westport about 2 miles to store on left.

THE LIME RESTAURANT ✂🛒
168 Main Ave. ℗ 203-846-9240 ⊗ M-Sat 11-4, 5-10, Sun 4:30-9:30
Meatless soups and sauces, brown rice and ample vegetarian choices.
 · juice bar · vegetarian friendly · alcohol · tables · wait staff

🛒 **From I-95**, take exit 15 onto Rt 7N about 1½ miles to exit 2. Turn left onto Rt 123 ⅓ mile to Main St. Turn right onto Main 2 blocks to restaurant on left.

OLD LYME

THE GRIST MILL ✂🛒
19 Halls Rd. ℗ 860-434-2990 ⊗ M-Sat 9-6, Sun 11-5

🛒 **From I-95N**, take exit 70 left onto US 1/Neck Rd less than ¼ mile to Halls Rd. Turn right onto Halls about ½ mile to store in Old Lyme Shopping Center. **From I-95S**, take exit 70 straight off ramp onto US 1/Halls Rd to store just off hwy in Old Lyme Shopping Center.

OLD SAYBROOK

FOODWORKS II 🛒
17 Main St. ℗ 860-395-0770 ⊗ M-F 9:30-6, Sat 11-6, Sun 11-5
 · organic produce

🛒 **From I-95N**, take exit 67 right onto Middlesex Tpke about ½ mile to Main St (Boston Post Rd is ahead). Veer left onto Main to store on right.

From I-95S, take exit 68 left onto US 1 (Springbrook Rd, becomes Boston Post) over 1 mile to Main. Veer left onto Main store on right.

STAMFORD

MRS. GREEN'S NATURAL MARKET ✗ 🍎
950 High Ridge Rd. © 203-329-1313 ☺ M, W, F 9-8, Tues, Th 9-9, Sat 9-7, Sun 10-6
 • organic produce • freshly prepared food • vegetarian friendly • chain • tables • self-service • take-out
🍎 From Merritt Pkwy, take exit 35 toward Stamford/Bus District right (south) onto High Ridge Rd/CT 137 about ½ mile to store.

STRATFORD

NATURE'S WAY NATURAL FOODS 🍎
922 Barnum Ave. Cutoff © 203-377-3652 ☺ M-Sat 9-9, Sun 9-5
 • organic produce
🍎 From I-95, take exit 32 (W Broad St) toward Stafford. From 95N, enter roundabout and take 1st exit onto Broad to Main St. Turn left onto Main about ⅔ mile to Barnum Ave Cutoff. Turn right onto Barnum to store on left. From 95S, turn right off exit onto Linden Ave about ¼ mile to Main. Turn left onto Main about ⅓ mile to Barnum. Turn right onto Barnum to store on left.

WEST HARTFORD

WILD OATS MARKET ✗ 🍎   ♿
340 N. Main St. © 860-523-7174 ☺ Daily 8-9
 • organic produce • freshly prepared food • salad bar • café • deli • bakery • vegetarian friendly • chain • tables • self-service • take-out
🍎 From I-84E, take exit 43 (on left) toward W Hartford Center and follow exit more than ¾ mile to Park Rd. Turn left onto Park about ⅓ mile to S Main St. Turn right onto S Main about 2 miles to store. From I-84W, take exit 50 onto US 44W (becomes Morgan St, then Main) about 4 miles to N Main. Turn left onto N Main to store. From I-91S, take exit 32B onto Trumbull St to US 44/Main St. Turn right onto 44 and follow directions above. From I-91N, take I-8W exit onto Trumbull St and follow directions above.

WESTPORT

FOUNTAIN OF YOUTH ✗ 🍎
1789 Post Rd. E. © 203-259-9378 ☺ M-Sat 9-7, Sun 10-5
 • organic produce • freshly prepared food • juice bar • salad bar • vegetarian friendly • tables • self-service • take-out
🍎 From I-95S, take exit 19 onto Pease Ave. Merge west on Rt 1 (Boston Post Rd) about ½ mile to store on right (across from Stop & Shop). From I-95N, take exit 19 left onto Center St, left onto Rt 1 and follow directions above.

ORGANIC MARKET ✗ 🍎
285 Post Rd. E. © 203-227-9007 ☺ M-Sat 9-6, Sun 10-5
 • organic produce • freshly prepared food • vegetarian friendly • counter • tables • self-service • take-out
🍎 From I-95N, take exit 17 toward Westport/Saugatuck left onto 136/Saugatuck Ave (becomes Riverside Ave) about 1⅔ miles to US 1/Post Rd. Turn right onto Post about ½ mile to store. From I-95S, take exit 18 toward Sherwood IS State Park and follow ramp toward US 1/Westport. Merge onto Sherwood IS Connector/CT 476N 1 mile to Post Rd/1S. Turn left onto Post about 1 mile to store.

WILD OATS MARKET ✗🍴   ♿

399 Post Rd. E. © 203-227-6858 ☺ M-Sat 8-9, Sun 8-8

• organic produce • freshly prepared food • juice bar • salad bar • café • deli • bakery
• vegetarian friendly • chain • tables • self-service • take-out

📖 **From I-95N**, take exit 17 toward Westport/Saugatuck left onto 136/Saugatuck Ave (becomes Riverside Ave) about 1⅖ miles to US 1/Post Rd. Turn right onto Post about ¾ mile to store. **From I-95S**, take exit 18 toward Sherwood IS State Park and follow ramp toward US 1/Westport. Merge onto Sherwood IS Connector/CT 476N 1 mile to Post Rd/1S. Turn left onto Post almost 1 mile to store.

WILLIMANTIC_____

WILLIMANTIC FOOD CO-OP 🍴

27 Meadow St. © 860-456-3611 ☺ M-F 9-8, Sat 9-6, Sun 10-5

• co-op

📖 **From Rt 44**, take Rt 6 or Rt 32 to Willimantic (becomes Rt 66). **From Rt 66** (Main St in town) turn left onto Bank St and right onto Meadow St ½ block to store on left.

WILTON_____

WILTON ORGANIC GOURMET ✗🍴

33 Danbury Rd. © 203-762-9711 ☺ M-Sat 7:30-6:30, Sun 11-3

• organic produce • freshly prepared food • juice bar • salad bar • vegetarian friendly
• counter • self-service • take-out

📖 **From I-95**, take exit 15 onto Rt 7N (becomes Main Ave, then Danbury Rd) almost 5 miles to store on left. **From Merritt Pkwy**, take exit 40B (Main Ave N/Rt 7N) right (north) onto Main (becomes Danbury Rd) about 1½ miles to store on left.

WOODBURY_____

GOOD NEW CAFE ✗

694 Main St. S. © 203-266-4663 ☺ M, W-Sat 11:30-10, Sun 12-10

Although the majority of the upscale, gourmet dishes here aren't vegetarian, there is always a vegetarian soup, appetizers, salads, and a couple of suitable entrees beyond pasta. Menu reflects seasonal fare, incorporating local organic foods as much as possible.

• vegetarian friendly • organic focus • alcohol • tables • wait staff • take-out

📖 **From I-84E**, take exit 15 toward Southbury left onto Rt 6/Main St N almost 4 miles to restaurant. **From I-84W**, take exit 17 toward Waterbury/Middlebury onto Rt 64 7½ miles to Main. Turn left onto Main to restaurant.

NEW MORNING COUNTRY STORE ✗🍴

738 Main St. S. © 203-263-4868 ☺ M-W, Sat 8-6, Th-F 8-8, Sun 11-5

• organic produce • freshly prepared food • juice bar • deli • vegetarian friendly • tables
• self-service • take-out

📖 **From I-84E**, take exit 15 toward Southbury left onto Rt 6/Main St N 3½-4 miles to store on left in strip mall. **From I-84W**, take exit 17 toward Waterbury/Middlebury onto Rt 64 7½ miles to Main. Turn left onto Main to store on right in strip mall.

DELAWARE

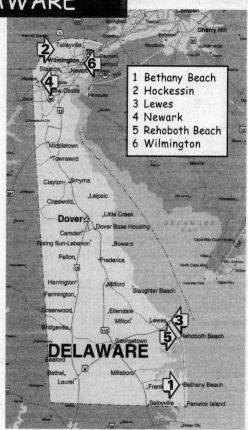

1 Bethany Beach
2 Hockessin
3 Lewes
4 Newark
5 Rehoboth Beach
6 Wilmington

BETHANY BEACH

WHOLESOME HABITS 🥜
Route 1, Beach Plaza ☏ 302-537-0567 ⊙ Daily 9-6
🍎 On Rt 1 in Bethany Beach (about 12 miles south of Rehoboth Beach and about 14 miles north of Ocean City, MD).

HOCKESSIN

HARVEST MARKET 🥜   ♿
1252 Old Lancaster Pike ☏ 302-234-6779 ⊙ M-F 9-7, Sat 10-7
· organic produce · freshly prepared food · vegetarian friendly · take-out
🍎 **From I-95S**, take exit 5A-B toward Newport onto DE 141N about 2⅓ miles to exit 6 (Rt 2/Kirkwood Hwy toward Newport). Merge onto 2W about ⅔ mile to 41N. Take 41N about 5 miles into Hockessin to Yorklyn Rd. Turn left onto Yorklyn 1 block to store at Old Lancaster Pike. **From I-95N**, take the I-295 exit (5A) toward NJ/NY. Merge onto 141N toward Newport and follow directions above.

LEWES

GARDEN MARKET 🛒
119 2nd St. © 302-645-8052 ⊘ M-Sat 10-5:30, Sun 11-4
· organic produce

🍎 **From Rt 1**, take Rt 9 east about ½ mile to Gills Neck Rd. Turn left onto Gills Neck 3 blocks to 9Bus. Turn left onto 9Bus and right onto 2nd St to store.

NEWARK

The UDE campus is here, and Janey at the Co-op says Main St has "cool, non-mainstream gift shops, record stores," and more.

NEWARK NATURAL FOODS COOPERATIVE 🛒   ♿
280 E. Main St. © 302-368-5894 ⊘ M-Sat 9-8, Sun 10-4
Pre-made vegetarian deli sandwiches. Juice bar next door.
· organic produce · deli · vegetarian friendly · coop · take-out

🍎 **From I-95**, take exit 3 (3B from 95N) onto Rt 273W toward Newark 4¼ miles (4-lane hwy becomes 2-lane past Rt 2, then one-way street which is Main St). At 2nd traffic light (Tyre Ave) turn right into Market East Plaza to store on right.

REHOBOTH BEACH

PLANET X CAFE 🍴
35 Wilmington Ave. © 302-226-1928 ⊘ Call for hours (vary with season)
Predominantly an upscale fish and poultry menu with a few meat choices, plus two creative gourmet vegan and three vegetarian entrees—so everyone should be happy. Eat inside or out on the veranda of this restored Victorian house, just 1 block from the ocean.
· vegetarian friendly · vegan friendly · alcohol · tables · wait staff

🍎 Take Rt 1 to Rehoboth Beach. Exit onto Rehoboth Ave/1 AltE over 1 mile to just past boardwalk. Turn right onto 1st St, 1 block to Wilmington Ave. Turn right onto Wilmington to restaurant on right.

RAINBOW EARTH FOODS 🛒
220 Rehoboth Ave. © 302-227-3177 ⊘ Daily 10:30-6
· organic produce

🍎 Take Rt 1 to Rehoboth Beach. Exit onto Rehoboth Ave/1 Alt E about 1 mile to town. Store is across from fire station (2½ blocks west of ocean).

WILMINGTON

COUNTRY HEALTH FOOD STORE 🍴🛒
2199 Kirkwood Hwy. © 302-995-6620 ⊘ M-Sat 9-9:30, Sun 9-7
A small selection of organic produce. Note, opening time tends to be a bit loose.
· organic produce

🍎 **From I-95S**, take exit 5A-B toward Newport onto DE 141N about 2⅔ miles to exit 6 (Kirkwood Hwy). Follow exit 6A toward Elsmere onto Kirkwood about ⅔ mile to store (next to Value City, near Elsmere border). **From I-95N**, merge onto I-295N toward NJ Tpke. Merge directly onto 141N about 3¼ miles to exit 6 and follow directions above.

DISTRICT OF COLUMBIA

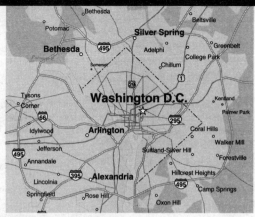

AMMA VEGETARIAN KITCHEN ✕
3291-A M St. N.W. ✆ 202-625-6625 ⏰ M-F 11:30-2:30, 5:30-10, Sat-Sun 11:30-3:15, 5:30-10:30
Traditional vegetarian South Indian fare.
· vegetarian · vegan friendly · alcohol · tables · wait staff · take-out

⬒ In Georgetown on M St between 33rd & Potomac St NW. **From downtown DC**, go west on NY Ave (becomes E St NW, then E St Expwy) onto Potomac River Fwy N to Whitehurst Fwy exit. Follow ramp toward Canal Rd onto fwy (aka US 29S) about ⅔ mile to M St. Turn right onto M ¼ mile (4-5 blocks) to restaurant. Coming **from VA on I-66**, take Potomac River Fwy N and follow directions above. **From VA across Francis Scott Key Bridge** (US 29), turn right onto M 4-5 blocks to restaurant.

ASIA NORA ✕
2213 M St. N.W. ✆ 202-797-4860 ⏰ M-Th 5:30-10 (last seating), F-Sat 5:30-10:30 (last seating)
While there is always a vegetarian entree, fish and poultry are the focus of this mostly organic venue. Reservations required.
· organic focus · alcohol · tables · wait staff

⬒ **From downtown DC**, go NW on Massachusetts Ave to 17th St. Turn left onto 17th 3 blocks to M St. Turn right onto M to restaurant on right between 22nd & 23rd St. **From Sheridan Circle**, turn right at 1st traffic light onto 23rd 5 blocks to M. Restaurant is ½ block on left. (M goes the wrong way, so drivers continue to L St, turn left onto L, left onto 22nd and left onto M to restaurant on right.)

EVERLASTING LIFE ✕🍴
2928 Georgia Ave. ✆ 202-232-1700 ⏰ M-Sat 9-9, Sun 11-9
Source of Life Juice Bar & Deli serves healthy, vegan, southern-style food from the Soul Vegetarian chain.
· organic produce · freshly prepared food · juice bar · vegan · coop · tables · self-service · take-out

⬒ **From downtown DC**, take Georgia Ave north through town about 2 miles to store on left at Georgia & Columbia Rd in Everlasting Life Health Complex. **From I-495**, take exit 30 (Colesville Rd/US 29) onto 29S (becomes Georgia Ave) about 4 miles to store on right at Columbia Rd in Everlasting Life Health Complex.

GOOD HEALTH NATURAL FOODS ✗✦
325 Pennsylvania Ave. © 202-543-2266 ⊙ M-F 9:30-7:30, Sat 11-7
· freshly prepared food · deli · vegetarian friendly · tables · self-service · take-out
🍎 On Pennsylvania Ave across from Library of Congress & Capitol.

HONEST TO GOODNESS BURRITOS ✗
15th & K St. N.W. © ⊙ M-F 11-2
On-the-street lunch wagon serving made-to-order meatless bean burritos with all the trimmings. Side by side with cappuccino and espresso cart.
· vegetarian · vegan friendly · take-out
🍎 Just off SW corner K St (which runs between Washington Circle & Mt Vernon Place) at 15th St.

NORA ✗
2132 Florida Ave. N.W. © 202-462-5143 ⊙ M-Th 5:30-10 (last seating), F-Sat 5:30-10:30 (last seating)
The food is mostly organic, and there's always a vegetarian entree on the daily menu, plus a 4-course vegetarian tasting menu. Reservations needed.
· vegetarian friendly · organic focus · alcohol · tables · wait staff
🍎 **From downtown DC**, go NW on Massachusetts Ave to Florida Ave (3rd traffic light past Dupont Circle). Turn right onto Florida 1 block to restaurant on right corner Florida & R St NW. **From Sheridan Circle**, go SE on Mass Ave to 1st light. Turn left onto Florida 1 block to restaurant.

PASTA A LA CART ✗
2121 H St. © ⊙ M-Th 11:30-4
On-the-street lunch wagon serving pasta with fresh pesto or marinara sauce.
· vegetarian friendly · vegan friendly · take-out
🍎 At H & 21st St on the GW Campus (across from Gellman Library).

SOUL VEGETARIAN CAFÉ ✗
2606 Georgia Ave. N.W. © 202-328-7685 ⊙ M-Sat 11-9, Sun 11-3
Healthy, vegan, southern-style soul food. Soups, sandwiches and steam table with rice, beans, cooked fresh vegetables and rotating entrees. Fruit smoothies, soy shakes, desserts. Homemade vegan soy cheese and "ice-kream."
· vegan · chain · tables · self-service · take-out
🍎 **From downtown DC**, take Georgia Ave north through town about 1½ miles to restaurant on left just past Euclid St (across from Howard U). **From I-495**, take exit 30 (Colesville Rd) onto 29S (becomes Georgia Ave) about 5 miles to restaurant on right 1 block past Fairmont St (across from Howard U).

THE PEOPLE GARDEN ✗✦
3155 Mount Pleasant St. N.W. © 202-232-4753 ⊙ M-Th 9-9, F-Sat 9-8, Sun 10-8
Mostly macrobiotic, vegan foods, with one free-range egg or chicken offering daily. For locals, there is a year-round Community Supported Agriculture (CSA) program featuring all organic produce. Note: Mount Pleasant is an historic neighborhood adjacent to Rock Creek Park and the National Zoo.
· organic produce · freshly prepared food · juice bar · café · deli · bakery · vegetarian friendly · vegan friendly · coop · chain · tables · wait staff
🍎 **From downtown DC** (White House), go north on 15th St about 1 mile to U St. Turn left onto U 1 block to 16th St. Turn right onto 16th almost ¾ mile to intersection at Columbia Rd (Mt Pleasant St joins 16th at a diagonal at Columbia). Continue on Mt Pleasant about ¼ mile to store.

WHOLE FOODS MARKET 🍴🛒 ♿
1440 P St. N.W. © 202-332-4300 ⊘ Daily 8-10
· organic produce · freshly prepared food · juice bar · salad bar · café · deli · bakery · vegetarian friendly · chain · counter · tables · self-service · take-out

🍎 **From downtown DC** (White House), take 15th St north (becomes VT Ave) less than ¾ mile to 14th St intersection. Take 14th 3 blocks to P St. Turn left onto P to store on left (a few blocks west of Logan Circle). **From I-395**, take 14th St Bridge and follow 14th 1¼ miles to P. Turn left onto P to store on left.

WHOLE FOODS MARKET 🍴🛒 ♿
4530 40th St. N.W. (Tenley Circle) © 202-237-5800 ⊘ M-Sat 8-10, Sun 8-9
· organic produce · freshly prepared food · salad bar · café · deli · bakery · vegetarian friendly · chain · tables · self-service · take-out

🍎 **From I-495** (Capitol Beltway), take exit 39 (MD 190E) toward Washington onto River Rd NW about 4¾ miles to Chesapeake St. Turn left onto Chesapeake 2 blocks to Wisconsin Ave. Turn right onto Wisconsin 1 block to Brandywine St. Turn left onto Brandywine 1 block to 40th St. Turn right onto 40th to store. **From downtown DC**, go NW on Wisconsin to Brandywine(about 3 miles starting at M St in Georgetown). Turn right onto Brandywine and right onto 40th to store.

WHOLE FOODS MARKET 🍴🛒 ♿
2323 Wisconsin Ave. N.W. © 202-333-5393 ⊘ Daily 8-10
· organic produce · freshly prepared food · juice bar · salad bar · café · deli · bakery · vegetarian friendly · chain · counter · tables · self-service · take-out

🍎 **From I-495** (Capitol Beltway), take exit 39 (MD-190E) toward Washington onto River Rd NW about 5 miles to Wisconsin Ave NW. Turn right onto Wisconsin about 2 miles to store on left just past intersection Wisconsin & Calvert St NW (2 blocks south of National Cathedral).

YES NATURAL GOURMET 🛒
1825 Columbia Rd. N.W. © 202-462-5150 ⊘ M-F 9-8, Sat 9-7, Sun 11-6
· freshly prepared food · deli · vegetarian friendly · take-out

🍎 **From I-495** (Capitol Beltway), take exit 33 south on Connecticut Ave about 6 miles to Calvert St. Turn left onto Calvert to Columbia Rd. Turn right onto Columbia to store on right. **From downtown DC**, take Connecticut north 1 mile to fork at Columbia Rd. Veer right onto Columbia almost ½ mile to store on left.

YES NATURAL GOURMET 🛒
3425 Connecticut Ave. N.W. © 202-363-1559 ⊘ M-Sat 8-9, Sun 10-7

🍎 **From I-495** (Capitol Beltway), take exit 33 south on Connecticut Ave about 5 miles to store on left (2½ miles south of Western Ave, near National Zoo). **From downtown DC**, head north on Connecticut Ave almost 2½ miles to store on right.

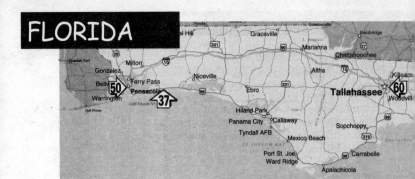

FLORIDA

1	Altamonte Springs	34	Miami Beach
2	Aventura	35	Miramar
3	Big Pine Key	36	Naples
4	Boca Raton	37	Navarre
5	Bonita Springs	38	New Smyrna Beach
6	Bradenton	39	North Miami
7	Brandon	40	North Miami Beach
8	Brooksville	41	North Palm Beach
9	Cape Canaveral	42	Ocala
10	Cape Coral	43	Orange Park
11	Clearwater	44	Orlando
12	Cocoa	45	Ormond Beach
13	Cocoa Beach	46	Osprey
14	Coconut Grove	47	Oviedo
15	Coral Springs	48	Palm Beach
16	Crystal River	49	Palm Harbor
17	Daytona Beach	50	Pensacola
18	Delray Beach	51	Pinecrest
19	Englewood	52	Plantation
20	Fort Lauderdale	53	Port Charlotte
21	Fort Myers	54	Port Orange
22	Gainesville	55	Sarasota
23	Holiday	56	South Miami
24	Holmes Beach	57	St. Augustine
25	Inverness	58	St. Petersburg
26	Jacksonville	59	Stuart
27	Key Largo	60	Tallahassee
28	Key West	61	Tampa
29	Kissimmee	62	Venice
30	Lakeland	63	West Palm Beach
31	Largo	64	Winter Haven
32	Melbourne	65	Winter Park
33	Miami		

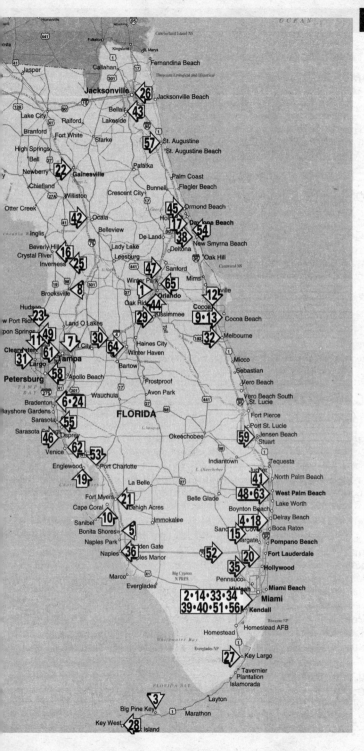

ALTAMONTE SPRINGS

CHAMBERLIN'S MARKET & CAFE ✗ 🍠 &
1086 Montgomery Rd. © 407-774-8866 ⊙ M-Sat 9-8:30, Sun 11-5:30
· organic produce · freshly prepared food · juice bar · bakery · vegetarian friendly · chain · tables · self-service · take-out

From I-4, take exit 94 toward Longwood/Winter Spr onto SR 434W (left from 4E, right from 4W) about 1 mile to Montgomery Rd. Turn left onto Montgomery to store on right in Winn-Dixie Plaza.

AVENTURA

WHOLE FOODS MARKET ✗ 🍠 &
21105 Biscayne Blvd. © 305-933-1543 ⊙ Daily 8-11
· organic produce · freshly prepared food · juice bar · salad bar · café · deli · bakery · vegetarian friendly · chain · tables · self-service · take-out

From I-95, take exit 18 east on Hallandale Beach Blvd 2 miles to US1/ Biscayne Blvd. Turn right (south) onto Biscayne 1½ miles to store on left in shopping center with Target.

BIG PINE KEY

GOOD FOOD CONSPIRACY ✗ 🍠
U.S. Hwy MM 30.2 © 305-872-3945 ⊙ M-Sat 9:30-7, Sun 11-5
Homegrown produce.
· organic produce · freshly prepared food · juice bar · café · vegetarian friendly · tables · self-service · take-out

On US 1 traveling through the FL keys at mile marker 30.2

BOCA RATON

BOMBAY CAFE ✗ &
628 Glades Rd. © 561-750-5299 ⊙ M-Sat 11:30-8
Fresh, homemade vegetarian Indian food in a friendly, no-frills setting.
· vegetarian · vegan friendly · tables · self-service · take-out

From I-95, take exit 45 east on Glades Rd about 1⅓ miles to Oaks Plaza on right (across from Florida Atlantic University). Restaurant is in back of shopping center behind Eckerd drugs.

EILAT CAFE ✗ &
6853 S.W. 18th St. © 561-368-6880 ⊙ M-Th 11-9, F 11-2, Sat after sundown to 11, Sun 12-9
The kosher menu is a mix of Middle Eastern vegetarian, pasta, pizza, and fish. Portions are ample, the staff friendly, and the clientele includes many obser- vant Jews. Dine inside or on the outdoor lakefront boardwalk.
· vegetarian friendly · kosher · alcohol · tables · wait staff

From I-95, take exit 44 west on Palmetto Park Rd 2 miles to Powerline Rd. Turn left onto Powerline 1 mile to SW 18th St (3rd traffic light). Turn left onto 18th to 1st left into Wharfside at Boca Pointe. Turn right in plaza to restaurant on left (go around back to enter on boardwalk side).

HEALTHY BITES ✗ &
21300 St. Andrews Blvd. © 561-338-6294 ⊙ M-Sat 10-9, Sun 11-9
A model for healthy fast food, including a drive-through window. Menu in- cludes vegetarian, vegan, chicken, turkey, fish, buffalo burgers and hot dogs,

baked fries, salads, fresh juices, smoothies. Sandwiches, pizzas and stuffed pockets all made with multigrain breads. A comfortable dining area. Even picky eaters and kids will like this place.

· juice bar · vegetarian friendly · counter · tables · self-service · take-out

From I-95, take exit 45 west on Glades Rd 1 mile to St Andrews Blvd. Turn left (south) onto St Andrews ½ mile to reataurant on left in Town Square strip mall (just past Shell station).

ORGANICALLY FRESH ✕ 🍎
21338 St. Andrews Blvd. ℂ 561-362-0770 ⊘ M-F 8:30-6, Sat 11-5

· organic produce · freshly prepared food · deli · vegetarian friendly · tables · self-service · take-out

From I-95, take exit 45 west on Glades Rd 1 mile to St Andrews. Turn south (left) onto St Andrews ½ mile to store in Town Square strip mall.

STIR CRAZY ✕   ♿
6000 Glades Rd. ℂ 561-338-7500 ⊘ Sun-Th 11:30-10, F-Sat 11:30-11

Although neither vegetarian nor wholefoods oriented, this emerging restaurant chain features a create-your-own stir-fry bar. Choose from a selection of 20 fresh vegetables (including tofu), 12 sauces, 5 noodles or rice (including brown), add an animal protein if desired, and watch it being woked. Or, order from a menu of prepared dishes. Portions are ample and prices reasonable.

· vegetarian friendly · alcohol · chain · counter · tables · self-service · wait staff

From I-95, take exit 45 west on Glades Road ¾ mile. Turn left into Town Center Mall to restaurant straight ahead next to mall entrance.

WHOLE FOODS MARKET ✕ 🍎   ♿
1400 Glades Rd. ℂ 561-447-0000 ⊘ Daily 8-11

· organic produce · freshly prepared food · juice bar · salad bar · café · deli · bakery · vegetarian friendly · chain · tables · self-service · take-out

From I-95, take exit 45 east on Glades Rd about ½ mile to store on right in University Commons Shopping Center (near Barnes & Noble).

BONITA SPRINGS

FOR GOODNESS SAKE ✕ 🍎
9118 Bonita Beach Rd. ℂ 239-992-5838 ⊘ M-Sat 10-6, Deli M-F 10-4

· freshly prepared food · juice bar · deli · vegetarian friendly · tables · self-service · take-out

From I-75, take exit 116 toward Bonita Springs/Gulf Beaches west on Bonita Beach Rd 3 miles to store on right in Sunshine Plaza.

BRADENTON

GOOD EARTH NATURAL FOODS 🍎
6717 Manatee Ave. W. ℂ 941-795-0478 ⊘ M-F 9-6, Sat 9-5:30

· organic produce

From I-75 exit 220 or US 41, take SR 64W (becomes Manatee Ave) to store on left in Northwest Promenade (10 miles from I-75, 1½ miles past 41).

GOOD EARTH NATURAL FOODS 🍎
3110 53rd Ave. E. ℂ 941-756-4372 ⊘ M-F 9-7, Sat 9-5:30

· organic produce · deli · vegetarian friendly · take-out

From I-75, take exit 217 onto SR 70W about 4 miles to store on left in Cedar Plaza. **From US 41 or US 301**, take 70E to store on right just past 301 in Cedar Plaza.

GOOD EARTH NATURAL FOODS

5153 14th St. W. © 941-753-8902 ☺ M-F 9-6, Sat 9-5:30

· organic produce

On US 41 (14th St) north of SR 70 on left in Plaza South.

RICHARD'S WHOLE FOODS

2601-B Manatee Ave. © 941-749-0829 ☺ M-Sat 9-7

Large selection of bulk foods.

· co-op

From I-75 exit 220, US 41 or US 301, take FL 64W (Manatee Ave) to store (about 1½ miles west of 301).

BRANDON

CHUCK'S NATURAL MARKETPLACE & PURPLE PLATE CAFE

114 N. Kings Ave. © 813-657-2555 ☺ M-F 9-8, Sat 9-6, Sun 12-6, Cafe M-F 9-5, Sat-Sun 9-3

· organic produce · freshly prepared food · juice bar · deli · vegetarian friendly · tables · self-service · take-out

From I-75, take exit 257 toward Brandon onto FL 60E about 2¾ miles to N Kings Ave. Turn left onto N Kings to store.

BROOKSVILLE

GO TO HEALTH

13007 Cortez Blvd. © 352-592-0717 ☺ M-Th 9-7, F-Sat 9-8, Sun 12-5

· organic produce · juice bar · take-out

From I-75, take exit 301 onto FL 50W (Cortez Blvd) over 18 miles to store at Mariner Blvd.

CAPE CANAVERAL

Lots to do in this area, including beaches, the Kennedy Space Center and Cocoa Beach Surf Museum.

SUNSEED FOOD CO-OP INC.

6615 N. Atlantic Ave., Ste. B © 407-784-0930 ☺ M-Sat 10-6

This not-for-profit co-op boasts great prices and an extensive selection of organic produce, beer and wine.

· organic produce · freshly prepared food · vegetarian friendly · co-op · take-out

From I-95, take exit 205 (Cape Canaveral) east on SR 528E (Beeline Expressway) about 12½ miles (across intercoastal). When road becomes A1A continue south about 2½ miles (becomes N Atlantic Ave) to store on west side. **From 528E** (from Orlando), follow directions above.

CAPE CORAL

BACK TO NATURE

1217 SE 47th Terrace © 239-549-7667 ☺ M-F 9-6, Sat 9-5

From I-75, take exit 131 toward Cape Coral west on Daniels Pkwy (becomes Cypress Lake Dr) about 6 miles to Summerlin Rd. Turn right onto Summerlin ¾ mile to College Pkwy. Turn left (west) onto College 1 mile (over bridge) to Vincennes Blvd. Turn right onto Vincennes and right onto 47th Terrace to store in strip mall on right.

MOTHER EARTH NATURAL FOODS 🍎

1631 Del Prado Blvd. ✆ 239-574-6333 ⊙ M-F 9-6, Sat 9-5:30

· chain

📷 **From I-75**, take exit 136 (884W) toward Ft Myers west on Colonial Blvd (becomes Veteran's Memorial Pkwy/884W) about 9 miles (across Mid-Point Bridge). Take 1st exit off bridge right (north) onto Del Prado Blvd less than 1 mile to store on right in Publix shopping center (after Coralwood Mall). From US Hwy 41, take Colonial Blvd west and follow directions above.

CLEARWATER

ANSLEY'S NATURAL MARKETPLACE 🍎

2481 McMullen Booth Rd. ✆ 727-723-1619 ⊙ M-F 9-7, Sat 10-6, Sun 11-5

· organic produce · juice bar · take-out

📷 **From 1-275 exit 39**, take Rt 60 west about 10 miles to McMullen Booth Rd. Turn right (north) onto McMullen about 3½ miles to store.

NATURE'S FOOD PATCH NATURAL MARKET & CAFE ✗🍎 ♿

1225 Cleveland St. ✆ 727-443-6703 ⊙ M-Sat 9-9, Sun 10-7 Cafe M-F 11-3

The Bunny Hop Cafe offers vegetarian, macrobiotic and free-range, additive-free meat choices. Or, try a "Build Your Own" sandwich.

· organic produce · freshly prepared food · juice bar · salad bar · café · deli · bakery
· vegetarian friendly · counter · tables · self-service · take-out

📷 **From I-275 exit 39 or I-4**, take Rt 60W (Gulf-to-Bay Blvd) about 14 miles (across water) to traffic light at Highland Ave. Take right fork toward Downtown/Beaches and continue on 60W (becomes Cleveland St) less than 1 mile to store on left corner Cleveland & Missouri Ave in Cleveland Shopping Plaza.

COCOA

GARDNER'S COTTAGE ✗🍎   ♿

902 Florida Ave. ✆ 321-631-2030 ⊙ M-F 8:30-2:30

Enjoy vegetarian and vegan soups, salads, sandwiches and more outside in the herb and flower garden, or at one of the vintage tables inside the 1925 cottage.

· organic produce · freshly prepared food · juice bar · café · vegetarian friendly · vegan
friendly · tables · wait staff · take-out

📷 **From I-95**, take exit 201 toward Cocoa Beach east on US 520 almost 4 miles to traffic light at US 1. Turn right (south) onto 1 to 1st light at Rosa L Jones Dr. Turn left onto Rosa Jones to next light at Florida Ave. Turn right onto Florida to store on left (little yellow cottage just before corner).

COCOA BEACH

THE NEW HABIT ✗

3 N. Atlantic Ave. ✆ 321-784-6646 ⊙ Daily 11-6

Vegetarian and healthier choices, along with conventional chips and soda.

· vegetarian friendly · tables · self-service · take-out

📷 **From I-95**, take exit 201 toward Cocoa Beach east on SR 520 almost 11½ miles (over intercoastal) to A1A (aka Atlantic Ave). Turn right onto Atlantic 2¾ miles to restaurant on NE corner Atlantic & Minuteman Cswy (1 block from ocean).

COCONUT GROVE

OAK FEED NATURAL FOODS ✗🍎
2830 Oak Ave. © 305-448-7595 ⊙ Daily 9-10
- · organic produce · freshly prepared food · café · deli · vegetarian friendly · tables
- · self-service · take-out

🍎 **From S Dixie Hwy (US 1)**, take 27th Ave toward Coconut Grove (left from 1S, right from 1N) ½ mile to Tigertail Ave. Turn right onto Tigertail (becomes Oak Ave) to store.

CORAL SPRINGS

WHOLE FOODS MARKET ✗🍎   ♿
810 University Drive © 954-753-8000 ⊙ Daily 8-9
- · organic produce · freshly prepared food · juice bar · salad bar · café · deli · bakery
- · vegetarian friendly · chain · tables · self-service · take-out

🍎 **From I-95**, take exit 36 west on Atlantic Blvd/Rt 814W about 7⅔ miles to University Dr. Turn right (north) onto University (Rt 817N). At 1st traffic light turn left into Atlantic Crossings Shopping Center (look for Home Depot) to store. **From FL Tpke**, take Atlantic Blvd west about 3 miles to University and follow directions above.

CRYSTAL RIVER

HUFFMAN'S HERITAGE WHOLE FOODS, INC. 🍎   ♿
430 S.E. Kings Bay Dr. © 352-795-2233 ⊙ M-F 9-6, Sat 9-4
- · organic produce · freshly prepared food · juice bar · salad bar · deli · vegetarian
- friendly · take-out

🍎 Crystal River is almost 33 miles west of I-75 and Fl Tpke exit 309 on Rt 44W. **From Rt 44**, take US 19S less than ½ mile to Kings Bay Dr. Turn right onto Kings Bay to store on left corner Kings Bay & Cutler Spur Blvd.

DAYTONA BEACH

DANCING AVOCADO KITCHEN ✗
110 S. Beach Street © 386-947-2022 ⊙ M-Sat 8-4
Among the nachos, sandwiches, quesadillas, burritos, and salads, there are ample choices for vegetarians and meateaters. Attention to unrefined ingredients and waste recycling. No smoking, even on the outdoor deck (with a view of the intercoastal).
- · juice bar · café · vegetarian friendly · alcohol · tables · wait staff · take-out

🍎 **From I-95**, take exit 261A toward Daytona Beach east on W International Speedway/US 92E about 5⅓ miles to Beach St (just before bridge across intercoastal). Turn right onto Beach to restaurant a few doors down on right.

NATURE'S TABLE ✗   ♿
1700 W. International Speedway Blvd. © 386-252-2424 ⊙ M-Sat 11-8, Sun 11-4:30
Healthier "fast food" in mall food court. Vegetarian and meat options.
- · vegetarian friendly · tables · self-service · take-out

🍎 **From I-95**, take exit 261A toward Daytona Beach east on W International Speedway/US 92E about 2½ miles to Volusia Mall on left. Enter mall, take first right and food court is on left just before Sears Auto Center.

DELRAY BEACH

KEF ROOM MEDITERRANEAN & VEGETARIAN GRILL ✗ ♿
1676 S. Federal Hwy. © 561-279-4020 ☺ Lunch Tues-F 11:30-2, Dinner Tues-Sun 5-10
Middleastern cuisine generally offers vegetarians a pretty good meal and Kef goes a step further, offering more than the usual repertoire.

· vegetarian friendly · tables · wait staff

🍴 **From I-95**, take exit 51 east on Linton Blvd about ¾ mile to Federal Hwy. Turn north (left) and enter Plaza at Delray on west side (sign says Regal 18). Restaurant is straight ahead (just left of movie theater).

NUTRITION COTTAGE ✗🍂
411 E. Atlantic Ave. © 561-276-9853 ☺ M-Th 9-6, F-Sat 9-11, Sun 12-6

· organic produce · freshly prepared food · juice bar · vegetarian · counter · self-service · take-out

🍴 **From I-95**, take exit 52 east on Atlantic Ave about 1½ miles to store on north side just past 4th Ave.

ENGLEWOOD

RICHARD'S WHOLE FOODS 🍂
471 S. Indiana Ave. © 941-473-0278 ☺ M-Sat 9:30-5:30
Large selection of bulk foods.

· chain

🍴 **From US 41**, go south on River Rd almost 9 miles to S Indiana Ave. Turn left onto S Indiana about ½ mile to store. **From I-75N**, take exit 161 toward Punta Gorda left onto Jones Loop Rd/Rt 768 W about ⅔ mile to Taylor Rd. Veer right onto Taylor about 3⅓ mile to US 41/Tamiami Trail. Turn right onto 41N 18½ miles to S River and follow directions above. **From I-75S**, take exit 191 toward US 41/Englewood/Gulf Beaches onto N River Rd about 12⅓ miles until River Rd becomes E Dearborn St. Continue on E Dearborn 1 mile to S Indiana Ave (FL 776). Turn left onto S Indiana about ½ mile to store.

FORT LAUDERDALE

SUBLIME ✗   ♿
1431 N Federal Hwy. © 954-615-1431 ☺ Lunch M-F 11:30-2, Dinner M-Th, Sun 5-9:30, F-Sat 5-10
Indoor and outdoor creative dining on vegan wholefoods. Started by animal rights advocates, along with a Lifestyle Emporium offering cruelty-free cosmetics, world music, cards, and gifts. Profits go to organizations that support animal welfare and vegan lifestyles. Future plans include a take-out cafe.

· juice bar · vegan · organic focus · alcohol · tables · wait staff

🍴 **From I-95S**, take exit 31A east (left) on Oakland Park Blvd about 2½ miles to US 1/North Federal Hwy. Turn right onto Federal 1½ miles to restaurant on right. **From I-95N**, take exit 29A east (right) on Sunrise Blvd almost 3 miles to Federal. Turn left onto Federal 6 blocks to restaurant on left.

WHOLE FOODS MARKET ✗🍴 &

2000 N. Federal Hwy. © 954-565-5655 ⊙ Daily 8-10

· organic produce · freshly prepared food · juice bar · salad bar · café · deli · bakery · vegetarian friendly · chain · tables · self-service · take-out

🍎 **From I-95,** take exit 31 east on Oakland Park Blvd about 2½ miles to US 1/North Federal Hwy. Turn right onto Federal 1 mile to store on left (east side) across from Barnes & Noble.

WILD OATS MARKET ✗🍴 &

2501 E. Sunrise Blvd. © 954-566-9333 ⊙ Daily 8-10

· organic produce · freshly prepared food · juice bar · salad bar · café · deli · bakery · vegetarian friendly · chain · counter · tables · self-service · take-out

🍎 **From I-95,** take exit 29 (29A from 95N) east on Sunrise Blvd about 3½ miles (pass US 1, follow signs "to beaches") to store on left across from Galleria Mall.

FORT MYERS

ADA'S NATURAL FOOD MARKET ✗🍴

11705 S. Cleveland Ave. © 239-939-9600 ⊙ M-Sat 9-7, Sun 10-5

· organic produce · freshly prepared food · deli · vegetarian friendly · tables · self-service · take-out

🍎 **From I-75,** take exit 136 (884W) toward Ft Myers west on Colonial Blvd 4¼ miles to Fowler St. Turn left onto Fowler 1⅓ miles to S Cleveland Ave (aka Tamiami Trail). Turn left (south) onto S Cleveland almost 1 mile to store on east side. (U-turn at Palm Dr to go north on S Cleveland).

MOTHER EARTH NATURAL FOODS 🍴

4600 Summerlin Rd. © 239-939-0990 ⊙ M, W, F 9-6, Tues, Th 9-6:30, Sat 9-5-30

· organic produce · chain

🍎 **From I-75,** take exit 136 (884W) toward Ft Myers west on Colonial Blvd 5¼ miles to Summerlin Rd. Turn left (south) onto Summerlin to store on right in Colonial Crossing Shopping Center.

MOTHER EARTH NATURAL FOODS 🍴 &

15271-7 McGregor Blvd. © 239-489-3377 ⊙ M, W, F 9-6, Tues, Th 9-6:30, Sat 9-5:30

· organic produce · chain

🍎 **From I-75,** take exit 131 west on Daniels Pkwy about 7½ miles (past US 41 becomes Cypress Lake Dr) to McGregor Blvd. Turn left (south) onto McGregor about 4 miles to store on left in McGregor Point (with K-mart).

MOTHER EARTH NATURAL MARKETS 🍴

16520 S. Tamiami Trail © 239-454-8009 ⊙ M, W, F 9-6, Tues, Th 9-6:30, Sat 9-5:30

· organic produce · chain

🍎 **From I-75,** take exit 131 west on Daniels Pkwy almost 5 miles to US 41 (Tamiami Trail). Turn left (south) onto Tamiami about 1½ miles to Island Park Rd. Turn right onto Island Park and left to store in Island Park Shopping Center.

GAINESVILLE

BOOK LOVER'S CAFE ✗ &

505 N.W. 13th St. © 352-374-4241 ⊙ Daily 10-9

Located in Books, Inc. The vegetarian menu is posted daily, with a rotating cycle of international themes, including Asian, Greek, Ethiopian, Italian, and more.

· juice bar · café · vegetarian · vegan friendly · tables · wait staff
⭕ **From I-75**, take exit 384 toward Gainesville onto FL 24E (Archer Rd) about 3¼ miles to 13th St (FL 25N/US 441N). Turn left onto 13th about 1 mile to store on left at 5th Ave.

MOTHER EARTH MARKET EAST 🌿
521 N.W. 13th St. © 352-378-5224 ⊙ M-Sat 8-8, Sun 10-6
· organic produce
⭕ **From I-75**, take exit 384 toward Gainesville onto FL 24E (Archer Rd) about 3¼ miles to 13th St (FL 25N/US 441N). Turn left onto 13th about 1 mile to store on right.

MOTHER EARTH MARKET WEST 🌿
1237 N.W. 76th Blvd. © 352-331-5224 ⊙ M-Sat 8-8, Sun 10-6
· organic produce
⭕ **From I-75**, take exit 387 toward Newberry onto SR 26W/Newberry Rd about ¼ mile to 76th Blvd. Turn right onto 76th about ¼ mile to end. Store is on right in strip mall.

TOP RESTAURANT ✗   ♿
30 N. Main St. © 352-337-1188 ⊙ Lunch Tues-F 11:30-2:30, Dinner M-F 5-1:45am, Sat 6-1:45am
About half the menu is vegetarian, and there is an interesting selection of tempeh and tofu creations.
· vegetarian friendly · alcohol · tables · wait staff
⭕ **From I-75**, take exit 384 toward Gainesville onto FL 24E (Archer Rd) about 3¼ miles to 13th St (FL 25N/US 441N). Turn left onto 13th about ¾ mile to University Dr. Turn right onto University less than 1 mile to Main St. Turn left onto Main 1 block to restaurant on left.

HOLIDAY

JUDY'S NATURAL FOODS ✗ 🌿
1922 US 19N © 727-943-0020 ⊙ M-F 7-5, Sat 9-5, Sun 10-4, Cafe M-F 11-3
Sandwiches, salads, and always vegetarian soup and chili.
· organic produce · freshly prepared food · juice bar · vegetarian friendly · tables · wait staff · take-out
⭕ Holiday is about 16 miles north of Clearwater on US 19. Store is at intersection 19 & Mile Stretch Rd.

HOLMES BEACH

ANSLEY'S NATURAL MARKETPLACE 🌿
5344 Gulf Drive © 941-778-4322 ⊙ M-F 9:30-6, Sat 9:30-5, Sun 11-5
· organic produce · freshly prepared food · juice bar · vegetarian friendly · take-out
⭕ **From I-75N**, take exit 220B onto FL 64W 15 miles (through Bradenton, across water to Anna Maria Island) to Gulf Dr. Turn right onto Gulf less than 1 mile to store at 52nd St. **From I-75S**, take exit 224 onto US 301S (across water) about 5⅔ miles to FL 64 (Manatee Ave). Turn right onto FL 64W 9 miles (to Anna Maria Island) and follow directions above.

INVERNESS

See the manatees and swim with them in winter in the Homasassa Wildlife Park.

RUTABAGA'S ETC. ✗🍎
299 S. Croft Ave. ☎ 352-344-0096 C M-W 9-6, Th-F 9-7, Sat 10-6
Deli is entirely vegan.

· organic produce · freshly prepared food · juice bar · deli · vegan · tables · self-service · take-out

📷 **From I-75**, take exit 329 onto Rt 44W 20 miles (through Inverness) to traffic light at Croft Ave (3rd Shell station, before Walmart). Turn right onto Croft to store on left.

JACKSONVILLE

GOOD EARTH MARKET 🍎
10950 San Jose Blvd. ☎ 904-260-9547 ⊘ M-Sat 9-7, Sun 10-6

📷 **From I-295**, take exit 5B onto San Jose Blvd/FL 13S 1 block to store (across from Walmart).

SOUTHERN NUTRITION CENTER 🍎
4345 University Blvd. S. ☎ 904-737-3312 ⊘ M-Sat 9-6

📷 From I-95S, take exit 346B (University Blvd E/SR 109) toward Bowden Rd straight onto University 4 blocks (about ¾ mile) to store on right in shopping center (just past Citgo gas). **From I-95N**, take exit 345 (Bowden Rd) toward University Blvd/SR 109 right onto Bowden to traffic light at Spring Park Rd. Turn left onto Spring Park less than ½ mile to next light at University. Turn right onto University 4 blocks to store on right.

KEY LARGO

REMEDY'S 🍎
US 1, MM 100.6 ☎ 305-451-2160 ⊘ M-Sat 9:30-6
A small selection of packaged food, drinks and snacks.

📷 On US 1 traveling through the FL keys at mile marker 100.6.

KEY WEST

BLUE HEAVEN 🍎
729 Thomas St. ☎ 305-296-8666 ⊘ M-Sat 8-11:30, 12-3, 6-10:30, Sun 8-2, 6-10:30
Tropical food in a great outdoor setting, with a rope swing and chickens in the yard. Not vegetarian, but plenty of choices and always a meatless dinner special.

· vegetarian friendly · alcohol · tables · wait staff

📷 Follow US 1 south to where it becomes Truman Ave. Turn right onto Thomas St about 2 blocks to restaurant on right (across from Truman Annex).

SUGAR APPLE VEGGIE DELI & JUICE BAR ✗🍎
917 Simonton St. ☎ 305-292-0043 ⊘ M-Sat 10-6 Cafe M-Sat 11-4
Kitchen serves up a selection of completely vegan dishes.

· freshly prepared food · juice bar · deli · vegan · tables · self-service · take-out

📷 Follow US 1 south to where it becomes Truman Ave. Turn right onto Center St 1 block to Olivia St. Turn right onto Olivia 1 block to Simonton St. Turn right onto Simonton to store.

KISSIMMEE

CHAMBERLIN'S MARKET & CAFE ✕🍎 ♿
1114 N. John Young Pkwy. ✆ 407-846-7454 ⏰ M-Sat 9-8:30, Sun 11-5:30
• organic produce • freshly prepared food • juice bar • café • bakery • vegan friendly • chain • tables • self-service • take-out

🍎 **From I-4W**, take exit 79 onto N John Young Pkwy/FL 423S about 10 miles to US 192 (Vine St). Store is on SW corner in Albertson's Town Corral Center. **From I-4E**, take exit 64B toward Kissimmee right onto US 192E about 9½ miles to N John Young Pkwy. Turn right onto John Young to store in Albertson's Town Corral Center. **From FL TpkeS**, take exit 249 right onto Osceola Pkwy 2½ miles to N John Young. Turn left onto N John Young almost 3 miles to store. **From FL TpkeN**, take exit 242 left onto US 192W 6⅓ miles to N John Young. Turn left onto N John Young to store.

LAKELAND

Close to Disney attractions.

ANTHONY'S HEALTH HUT ✕🍎
5329 S. Florida Ave. ✆ 863-644-5330 ⏰ M-F 9-6, Sat 9-5
Food service begins ½ hour after opening and stops ½ hour before closing.
• freshly prepared food • juice bar • vegetarian friendly • tables • self-service • take-out

🍎 **From I-4**, take exit 27 toward Lakeland onto FL 570 E (loop around right from 4E, onto Frontage Rd and right from 4W) about 6½ miles to exit 7. Turn right onto S Florida Ave almost 2 miles to store.

CHAMBERLIN'S MARKET & CAFE ✕🍎 ♿
1531 US Hwy. 98S. ✆ 863-687-8413 ⏰ M-Sat 9-8:30, Sun 11-5:30
• organic produce • freshly prepared food • juice bar • café • bakery • vegetarian friendly • chain • tables • self-service • take-out

🍎 **From I-4E**, take exit 28 toward US 92/Lakeland onto Rt 546E about 4½ miles (becomes 92E/98E) until 98 heads south. Continue south on 98 2½ miles to store between N & S Crystal Lake Dr. **From I-4W**, take exit 38 and follow US 98E onto 92E then back onto 98E for 9 miles to store between N & S Crystal Lake Dr.

LARGO

PIONEER NATURAL FOODS 🍎
12788 Indian Rocks Rd. ✆ 727-596-6600 ⏰ M-Sat 9-7

🍎 **From I-275**, take exit 31 (Indian Rocks Beach/FL 688) toward Largo onto FL 688W about 12 miles to Indian Rocks Rd. Turn right (north) onto Indian Rocks about ½ mile to store on left in King's Row Plaza.

MELBOURNE

COMMUNITY HARVEST MARKET & CAFE ✕🍎
1405 Highland Ave. ✆ 321-254-4966 ⏰ M-F 9-8, Sat 9-6
• organic produce • freshly prepared food • juice bar • deli • vegetarian friendly • counter • tables • self-service • take-out

🍎 **From I-95**, take exit 183 toward Melbourne onto SR 518E 5 miles to Highland Ave (1st traffic light after US 1). Turn left onto Highland to store on east side.

NATURE'S MARKET 🌿
461 N. Harbor City Blvd. ✆ 321-254-8688 ⊙ M-Th 9-8, F-Sat 9-7
Juice bar serves sandwiches and smoothies.
· organic produce · juice bar · take-out

🍎 **From I-95**, take exit 183 toward Melbourne onto SR 518E almost 5 miles to N Harbor City Blvd (US 1). Turn right onto Harbor City about 1 mile to store (about 1 mile north of airport).

WILD OATS MARKET 🍴🌿
1135 W. New Haven Ave. ✆ 321-674-5002 ⊙ M-Sat 9-8, Sun 10-7
· organic produce · freshly prepared food · juice bar · salad bar · café · deli · bakery
· vegetarian friendly · chain · tables · self-service · take-out

🍎 **From I-95**, take exit 180 toward Melbourne onto US 192E (New Haven Ave) about 4 miles (past Melbourne Square Mall) to store on right 3 buildings past Toys R Us (under Office Depot Sign). **From 192W**, store is at intersection New Haven & Dairy Rd (just past Eckerd's).

MIAMI_____

BEEHIVE NATURAL FOODS & DELI 🍴🌿   ♿
5750 S.W. 40th St. ✆ 305-666-3360 ⊙ M-Sat 9-7
· freshly prepared food · juice bar · deli · vegetarian · counter · self-service · take-out

🍎 **From S Dixie Hwy/US 1**, go west on Bird Rd (aka SW 40th St) about 2⅓ miles to store on left at SW 58th Ave. **From 826** (Palmetto Expwy), go east on Bird Rd 2 miles to store on right.

HALE'S HEALTH FOODS 🌿
109 W. Plaza Northside Shopping Center ✆ 305-696-2115 ⊙ M-Sat 10-6

🍎 **From I-95**, take 79th St west to 27th Ave to store in W Plaza Northside Shopping Center.

HALE'S HEALTH FOODS 🌿
16427 N.W. 67th Ave. ✆ 305-821-5331 ⊙ M-F 9:30-6:30, Sat 10-6

🍎 **From Palmetto Expwy** (826), take NW 67th Ave south 2 blocks to store on east side.

THE HONEY TREE 🍴🌿   ♿
5138 Biscayne Blvd. ✆ 305-759-1696 ⊙ M-Th 8-8, F 8-7, Sat 11-6
Deli features vegetarian and vegan entrees, soups, salads, and empanadas.
· freshly prepared food · juice bar · deli · vegetarian · vegan friendly · counter · tables
· self-service · take-out

🍎 **From I-95**, take exit 4 onto I-195E toward Miami Beach to Biscayne Blvd (exit 2B). Loop around right onto NE 36th St and right onto Biscayne (US 1N) almost 1 mile to store at 51st St on west side. **From I-195W** (across intercoastal), take exit 2B onto NE 38th St to Biscayne. Turn right onto Biscayne and follow directions above.

MIAMI BEACH_____

APPLE A DAY NATURAL FOOD 🍴🌿
1534 Alton Rd. ✆ 305-538-4569 ⊙ M-Sat 8-11, Sun 8-9
· organic produce · freshly prepared food · juice bar · café · vegetarian · vegan friendly
· counter · self-service · take-out

🍎 **From I-95 exit 4** (4A from 95N), take I-195E toward Miami Beach across Julia Tuttle Causeway to Miami Beach. Bear right (towards Convention Center) onto Alton Rd over 1½ miles to 15th St (1 block past Lincoln Rd). Turn right onto 15th to store on left just past corner in small shopping plaza.

FOOD WITHOUT FIRE ✕
747 4th St. © 305-674-9960 ☺ M-Sat 11-10, Sun 11:30-6
Organic, raw, vegan cuisine.
  • vegan • organic focus • tables • self-service
⬒ **From 836E, I-95S exit 5 or I-95N exit 2D** toward Miami Beach, take I-395E across MacArthur Causeway to Miami Beach. Merge onto 5th St 4 blocks to Meridian Ave. Turn right onto Meridian 1 block to 4th St. Turn left onto 4th to restaurant between Meridian & Euclid Ave.

FRONT PORCH CAFE ✕
1420 Ocean Drive © 304-531-8300 ☺ 8am-10:30pm
All-day breakfast (including whole grain pancakes), and an ample selection of vegetarian choices at lunch and dinner. Plus, a prime South Beach location across from the ocean, where you can sit outside and watch the scene.
  • vegetarian friendly • alcohol • tables • wait staff
⬒ **From 836E, I-95S exit 5 or I-95N exit 2D** toward Miami Beach, take I-395E across MacArthur Causeway to MB. Merge onto 5th St to end at Ocean Dr. Turn left onto Ocean to restaurant on left between 15th & 14th St.

WILD OATS MARKET ✕🍴   ♿
1020 Alton Rd. © 305-532-1707 ☺ Daily 7-11
  • organic produce • freshly prepared food • juice bar • salad bar • café • deli • bakery
  • vegetarian friendly • chain • tables • self-service • take-out
⬒ **From 836E, I-95S exit 5 or I-95N** exit 2D toward Miami Beach, take I-395E across MacArthur Causeway to MB. Stay in left lane after causeway and take Alton Rd exit onto Alton 4 blocks to store at NW corner 10th St & Alton.

MIRAMAR

THINGS VEGETARIAN ✕   ⬚
6060 Miramar Parkway, #4 © 954-965-3672 ☺ Tues-Sat 12-8
Daily plate of homemade West Indian vegetarian food. Not much room, but there is a small table and a couple of stools at the counter.
  • juice bar • vegan • counter • tables • self-service • take-out
⬒ **From I-95**, take exit 18 onto FL 858W (Hallandale Beach Blvd, becomes Miramar Pkwy) about 2½ miles to store on left. **From FL Tpke**, take exit 49 towards Hollywood onto FL 820E (Hollywood Blvd) about ⅓ mile to US 441/FL 7. Turn right onto 441S/7S 1¾ miles to Miramar Pkwy. Turn right onto Miramar to store on left.

NAPLES

SUNSPLASH MARKET ✕🍴
850 Neapolitan Way © 941-434-7221 ☺ M-F 9-8, Sat 9-8, Sun 10-6
  • freshly prepared food • café • vegetarian friendly • tables • self-service • take-out
⬒ **From I-75**, take exit 107 west on Pine Ridge Rd (896W) about 4 miles to 9th St/Tamiami Trail. Turn left (south) onto 9th ½ mile to Neapolitan Way. Turn right onto Neapolitan to store on left in Neapolitan Way Shopping Ctr.

NAVARRE

EMERALD COAST HEALTH & NUTRITION 🍃
1927 Ortega St. ℂ 850-939-0351 ⊘ M-F 9-6, Sat 10-4
🗐 On the western end of the FL panhandle on US 98 at Rt 87 (½ mile east of Navarre Beach Bridge) in Crown Point Plaza (behind bank).

NEW SMYRNA BEACH

HEATH'S NATURAL FOODS 🍃
1323 Saxon Drive ℂ 386-423-5126 ⊘ M-Sat 9-6
· organic produce · juice bar · bakery · take-out
🗐 **From I-95**, take exit 249 toward Deland/New Smyrna beach onto SR 44E almost 4 miles over intercoastal where 44E becomes A1A. Continue on A1A almost 2 miles to store 1 block after traffic light at Peninsula Ave on north corner 3rd Ave & Cooper St.

NORTH MIAMI

ABUNDANT ENERGY SOURCES, INC. 🍃
14248 N.W. 7th Ave. ℂ 305-685-0517 ⊘ M-Sat 10-6
🗐 **From I-95**, take exit 10B onto NW 6th Ave to Opa Locka Blvd. Turn west onto Opa Locka (left from 95N, right from 95S) 1 block to NW 7th Ave. Turn right onto 7th ⅓ mile to store on left corner 7th & NW 143rd St in Santa Fe Shopping Center.

MAN'S HEALTH IS GOD'S WEALTH ✕🍃
831 N.E. 125th St. ℂ 305-899-9927 ⊘ M-F 9:30-7, Sat 10-6
· organic produce · deli · vegetarian · counter · tables · self-service · take-out
🗐 **From I-95**, take exit 10A toward N Miami/Bal Harbour east on NW 125th St (left from 95S, right from 95N) about 1¾ miles to store on left.

NORTH MIAMI BEACH

ARTICHOKE'S NATURAL CUISINE ✕
3055 N.E. 163rd St. ℂ 305-945-7576 ⊘ M-Th 5:30-10, F-Sat 5:30-10:30, Sun 5-9:30
The focus is on vegetarian, chicken and fish. Lots of vegetables and brown rice.
· vegetarian friendly · alcohol · tables · wait staff
🗐 **From I-95**, take 826E (exit 12B from 95N, 12 from 95S) toward Miami Beach (becomes NE 163rd St/Sunny Isles Blvd) about 4¾ miles (over 1st causeway) to restaurant on left (north side) in strip mall.

KONATO'S TAKE-OUT RESTAURANT & GROCERY ✕🍃
73 N.E. 167th ST. ℂ 305 652-6780 ⊘ M-Sat 11-7
Small grocery selection, plus Jamaican vegetable patties and a daily home-made combination plate of Ital vegan specialties to go.
· freshly prepared food · vegan · take-out
🗐 **From I-95**, take 826E/NW 167th (exit 12B from 95N, 12 from 95S) toward Beaches less than ¼ mile to store on left (north side) in small strip mall.

NORTH PALM BEACH

NATURE'S WAY CAFE ✕ &

11911 U.S. Hwy. 1, Ste. 103 © 561-627-3233 ⊙ M-F 9-4, Sat 11-4
Healthy lunch menu and outdoor seating in the Florida sunshine.
· juice bar · café · vegetarian friendly · tables · self-service · take-out
From I-95, take PGA Blvd (exit 79AB or B) east about 2 miles to US 1.
Turn north (left) onto US 1 to restaurant ½ mile on left.

OCALA

MOTHER EARTH MARKET 🍃

1917 E. Silver Springs Blvd. © 352-351-5224 ⊙ M-Sat 9-8, Sun 11-6
From I-75, take exit 352 onto SR 40E/Silver Springs Blvd (left from
75S, right from 75N) about 5 miles to store on left in Ocala Center.

ORANGE PARK

THE GRANARY WHOLE FOODS, INC. 🍃

1738 Kingsley Ave. © 904-269-7222 ⊙ M-Sat 9-6
From I-295, take exit 10 toward Orange Park onto US 17S about 2½
miles to Kingsley Ave. Turn right onto Kingsley (stay in left lane after
railroad tracks) 2 miles to store on left.

ORLANDO

CHAMBERLIN'S MARKET & CAFE 🍃 &

4960 E.Colonial Drive © 407-894-8452 ⊙ M-Sat 9-8:30, Sun 11-5:30
· organic produce · freshly prepared food · bakery · vegetarian friendly · chain · take-out
From I-4E, take exit 83B (Amelia St) toward US 17/92/Colonial Dr/
FL 50. Follow N Garland Ave about ¼ mile to 50. Turn right onto 50E
about 3½ miles to store on right in Herndon Village Shoppes. **From I-4W,**
take exit 84 (Ivanhoe Blvd/US 17/92/Colonial Dr/FL 50). Take left fork
on ramp, then right fork onto 50E and follow directions above.

CHAMBERLIN'S MARKET & CAFE ✕ 🍃 &

7600 Dr. Phillips Blvd. © 407-352-2130 ⊙ M-Sat 9-8:30, Sun 11-5:30
Close to Disney attractions.
· organic produce · freshly prepared food · juice bar · bakery · vegetarian friendly
· chain · tables · self-service · take-out
From I-4, take exit 74A west on Sand Lake/FL 482W 1 mile to Dr Phillips
Blvd. Turn right on Dr Phillips then left into Marketplace Center to store.

GARDEN CAFE ✕

810 W. Colonial Drive © 407-999-9799 ⊙ Tues-F 11-10, Sat-Sun 12-10
Chinese vegetarian (mostly vegan) menu featuring tofu and meat substitutes,
plus a few western choices with cheese optional. Homemade vegetable stock,
brown rice available.
· vegetarian · vegan friendly · tables · wait staff · take-out
From I-4E, take exit 83B (Amelia St) toward US 17/92/Colonial Dr/SR
50. Follow N Garland Ave about ¼ mile and turn left onto W Colonial about
½ mile to restaurant (next to Burger King). **From I-4W,** take exit 84 (Ivanhoe
Blvd/US 17/92/Colonial Dr/SR 50) and take left fork on ramp, then right fork
to W Colonial. Turn right onto W Colonial and follow directions above.

TASTE OF INDIA ✕ ㅎ
9251 S. Orange Blossom Trail ℭ 407-855-4622 ☉ Tues-Th 11-9, F-Sun 11-10
Vegetarian Indian food with buffet lunch available.
· vegetarian · vegan friendly · alcohol · tables · self-service · wait staff

🍴 **From FL 528E** (Bee Line Expwy), take exit 6 south on US 441/17 onto Consulate Dr to S Orange Blossom Trail. Turn left onto S Orange Blossom to restaurant in Bib Plaza. **From FL 528W**, take the turnpike exit on left toward 441/17 to Landstreet Rd. Turn right onto Landstreet and right onto S Orange Blossom about ½ mile to restaurant.

WOODLAND'S PURE VEGETARIAN ✕ ㅎ
6040 S. Orange Blossom Trail ℭ 407-854-3330 ☉ M-Th, Sun 11:30-9:30, F-Sat 11:30-10
South Indian vegetarian cuisine, vegan selections and weekday lunch buffet.
· vegetarian · vegan friendly · tables · self-service · wait staff · take-out

🍴 **From I-4**, take US 441S/US 17S/92W exit (80 from 4W, 80A from 4E) onto 17S (Orange Blossom Trail) about 2½ mile to restaurant (across from Lakshmi Plaza).

ORMOND BEACH

HARVEST HOUSE NATURAL FOODS 🍂
124 S. Nova Rd. ℭ 386-677-7723 ☉ M-F 9-7, Sat 9-6

🍴 **From I-95**, take exit 268 toward Ormond Beach onto SR 40E/W Granada Blvd about 2½ miles to Nova Rd. Turn right onto Nova about ¼ mile to store on right in plaza..

LOVE WHOLE FOODS ✕ 🍂
275 Williamson Blvd. ℭ 386-677-5236 ☉ M-F 10-6, Sat 9-5
· organic produce · freshly prepared food · juice bar · café · deli · vegetarian friendly · tables · self-service · take-out

🍴 **From I-95**, take exit 268 toward Ormond Beach onto SR 40E to 1st traffic light at Williamson Blvd. Turn right (south) onto Williamson about ½ mile to store (next to Regal Cinema, across from post office).

OSPREY

RICHARD'S WHOLE FOODS 🍂
1092 S. Tamiami Trail ℭ 941-966-0596 ☉ M-Sat 9:30-5:30
Large selection of bulk foods.
· chain

🍴 **From I-75N**, take exit 195 toward Nokomis/Laurel left (west) on Laurel Rd about 3 miles to Tamiami Trail. Turn right onto Tamiami/US 41N about 3½ miles to store on west side (41S). **From I-75S**, take exit 200 toward Venice/Osprey onto FL 681 about 3¼ miles to Tamiami Trail. Turn right onto Tamiami/US 41N about 2¾ miles to store on west side (41S).

OVIEDO

CHAMBERLIN'S MARKET & CAFE ✕ 🍂 ㅎ
1170 Oviedo Marketplace Blvd. ℭ 407-359-7028 ☉ M-Sat 9-9, Sun 11-7
· organic produce · freshly prepared food · juice bar · café · bakery · vegetarian friendly · chain · tables · self-service · take-out

🍴 **From I-4W**, take exit 101B toward Sanford/Intl Airports onto Hwy 417S 13½ miles to Red Bug Lake Rd (exit 41). Turn right (west) onto Red Bug about ¼ mile to Oviedo Marketplace Blvd. Turn right about ¼ mile to store on right in Oviedo Markeplace Mall. **From I-4E**, take exit 92 onto SR 436E about 4½ miles to Red Bug Lake Rd. Turn left (west) onto Red Bug 5½ miles to Oviedo Marketplace Blvd. Turn left about ⅓ mile to store on right in Oviedo Marketplace Mall.

PALM BEACH

SUNRISE HEALTH FOOD STORE 🍃
233 Royal Ponnisiana Way © 561-655-3557 ⊙ M-F 8:30-6, Sat 8:30-7
· freshly prepared food · vegetarian friendly · take-out
🍎 **From A1A** at Breakers Hotel on the beach, go north to 1st traffic light and turn left onto Royal Ponnisiana Way to store on right.

PALM HARBOR

PALM HARBOR NATURAL FOODS, INC. ✗🍃
30555 US 19 N. © 727-786-1231 ⊙ M-Sat 8:30-8, Sun 9-7
· freshly prepared food · deli · vegetarian friendly · tables · self-service · take-out
🍎 **From I-275**, take exit 39 toward Clearwater/Tampa Airport onto 60W/ Memorial Hwy 11 miles (over causeway) to 19N. Turn right onto 19N (34th St N) about 6½ miles to store on left at Curlew Rd in Seabreeze Shopping Ctr.

PENSACOLA

EVER'MAN NATURAL FOODS CO-OP 🍃
315 W. Garden St. © 850-438-0402 ⊙ M-Sat 8-7
· organic produce · freshly prepared food · deli · vegetarian friendly · co-op · take-out
🍎 **From I-10**, take exit 12 right onto I-110S about 6¼ miles to exit 1C (98Bus W/Garden St) toward Historical District. Take Garden St west about ⅔ mile to store on south side.

PINECREST

WILD OATS MARKET 🍃
11701 S. Dixie Hwy. © 305-971-0900 ⊙ Daily 7-10
· organic produce · freshly prepared food · juice bar · salad bar · deli · bakery
· vegetarian friendly · chain · take-out
🍎 **From FL 826** (Palmetto Expwy), go south to end at US 1 (South Dixie Hwy). Merge onto 1S about 1 mile (past 2 major intersections) to 117th Ave. Turn left onto 117th and immediately right into shopping center to store.

PLANTATION

WHOLE FOODS MARKET ✗🍃   ♿
7720 Peters Rd. © 954-236-0600 ⊙ Daily 8-10
· organic produce · freshly prepared food · juice bar · salad bar · café · deli · bakery
· vegetarian friendly · chain · tables · self-service · take-out
🍎 **From I-595W**, take exit 5 (SR 817/University Dr) onto 84W almost 1 mile to S University. Turn right onto University about ½ mile to Peters Rd. Turn left onto Peters to store on left in 1st shopping center. **From I-595E**, take exit 4 toward Pine Island Rd onto 84E less than ¼ mile to Pine Island. Turn left onto Pine Island about ½ mile to Peters. Turn right onto Peters about ⅔ mile to store on right in shopping center (before University).

PORT CHARLOTTE

RICHARD'S WHOLE FOODS 🍴
3012 S. Tamiami Trail ✆ 941-749-0892 ⊙ M-Sat 9-7
Large selection of bulk foods.
   • organic produce • chain
🍎 **From I-75**, take exit 191 toward US 41/Englewood/Gulf Beaches onto
N River Rd about 5½ miles to Tamiami Trail (US 41). Turn left onto
Tamiami/US 1S about 13⅓ miles to store on opposite side (41N).

PORT ORANGE

HARVEST HOUSE NATURAL FOODS 🍴🍴
4032 S. Ridgewood Ave. ✆ 386-756-3800 ⊙ M-F 7-7, Sat 7-6
   • organic produce • deli • vegetarian friendly • tables • self-service • take-out
🍎 **From I-95**, take exit 256 toward Port Orange/Daytona Beach onto SR
421E (Dunlawton Ave) about 4 miles to US 1. Turn right onto 1S (S Ridgewood
Ave) to store at corner Dunlawton & S Ridgewood in Port Orange Plaza.

SARASOTA

RICHARD'S WHOLE FOODS 🍴
3226 Clark Rd. ✆ 941-925-9726 ⊙ M-Sat 9-7
Large selection of bulk foods.
   • organic produce • chain
🍎 **From I-75**, take exit 205 toward Siesta Key/Sarasota onto 72W (Clark Rd)
about 3¾ miles to store on opposite side (U-turn at S Lockwood Ridge Rd).

RICHARD'S WHOLE FOODS 🍴
2856 Ringling Blvd. ✆ 941-316-0546 ⊙ M-Sat 9-7
Large selection of bulk foods.
   • chain
🍎 **From I-75**, take exit 210 toward Sarasota/Gulf Beaches onto FL
780W/Fruitville Rd (left from 75N, right from 75S) about 4½ miles to
Brink Ave. Turn left onto Brink 1 block to Ringling Blvd. Turn right
onto Ringling to store.

THE GRANARY 🍴🍴   ♿
1279 Beneva Rd. S. ✆ 941-365-3700 ⊙ M-Sat 9-8, Sun 10-6
   • organic produce • freshly prepared food • juice bar • salad bar • deli • vegetarian
   friendly • tables • self-service • take-out
🍎 **From I-75**, take exit 210 toward Sarasota/Gulf Beaches west on
Fruitville Rd (right from 75S, left from 75N) about 3¼ miles to Beneva Rd.
Turn left onto Beneva about 1 mile to store at Bahia Vista St.

THE GRANARY 🍴🍴   ♿
1930 Stickney Point Rd. ✆ 941-924-4754 ⊙ M-Sat 9-8, Sun 10-6
   • organic produce • freshly prepared food • juice bar • salad bar • deli • vegetarian
   friendly • tables • self-service • take-out
🍎 **From I-75**, take exit 205 toward Siesta Key/Sarasota onto 72W (Clark
Rd) about 5 miles to just past US 41/Tamiami Trail where Clark becomes
Stickney Rd. Store is on left.

SOUTH MIAMI

NATURAL FOODS MARKET-KENDALL ✘🍴
9455 S. Dixie Hwy. © 305-666-3514 ⊗ M-Sat 8:30-9:30, Sun 10-8

· organic produce · freshly prepared food · deli · vegetarian friendly · tables · self-service · take-out

🚗 **From FL 826** (Palmetto Expwy), head south to end at N Kendall Dr. Loop around right and merge east onto Kendall about 1 mile to Dadeland Blvd. Turn right onto Dadeland ¼ mile to US 1 (S Dixie Hwy). Turn right onto 1S less than ¼ mile to store on east side in Dadeland Plaza. **Or take US 1** to store from points north or south.

ST. AUGUSTINE

A NEW DAWN ✘🍴
110 Anastasia Blvd. © 904-824-1337 ⊗ M-F 9:30-7, Sat 9-5:30   ♿

· freshly prepared food · juice bar · salad bar · vegetarian friendly · tables · self-service · take-out

🚗 **From I-95**, take exit 318 toward St Augustine onto FL 16E (left from 95S, right from 95N) 5⅓ miles to US 1 (Ponce De Leon Blvd). Turn right onto 1S about 2 miles to King St. Turn left onto King across the Bridge of Lions onto Anastasia Blvd (A1A) about ¼ mile to store on left.

DIANE'S NATURAL FOOD MARKET 🍴
240 State Rd. 312 © 904-808-9978 ⊗ M-Sat 9:30-7, Sun 12-5

· freshly prepared food · juice bar · vegetarian friendly · take-out

🚗 **From I-95**, take exit 311 toward St Augustine Beach onto SR 207E (left from 95S, right from 95N) about 4 miles to SR 312. Turn right onto 312E about 1 mile to store (about ¼ mile east of US 1).

THE MANATEE CAFE ✘
525 State Rd. 16 #106 © 904-826-0210 ⊗ M-Sat 8-8, Sun 8-3
A mostly vegetarian and vegan breakfast and lunch place, emphasizing wholefoods and organic ingredients whenever possible.

· vegetarian friendly · organic focus · tables · wait staff

🚗 **From I-95**, take exit 318 toward St Augustine onto FL 16E (left from 95S, right from 95N) about 4 miles to store on left in Westgate Plaza. (To get onto 16W, turn left onto Collins Ave and make 3 right turns back onto 16W.)

ST. PETERSBURG

EVOS FRESH & HEALTHY ✘
2631 4th St. N © 727-571-EVOS ⊗ Daily 11-10
Healthy fast-food concept, featuring naturally raised beef, chicken, soyburgers, veggie patties, whole wheat tortilla wraps, salads with organic greens, vegan chili, veggie corn dogs, "airfries"™, smoothies, and such.

· vegetarian friendly · chain · tables · self-service · take-out

🚗 **From I-275**, take exit 24 east on 22nd Ave (left from 275S, right from 275N) about 1¼ miles to 4th St N. Turn left onto 4th about ¼ mile to store at 26th Ave N.

NATURE'S FINEST FOODS ✗ ✿
6651 Central Ave. © 727-347-5682 ⊘ M-Sat 8-8, Sun 10-6

• freshly prepared food • café • deli • vegetarian friendly • tables • self-service • take-out

From I-275S, take exit 23B toward Treasure Island onto 5th Ave N/US 19 AltN about 3½ miles to 58th St N. Turn left onto 58th St about ½ mile to Central Ave. Turn right onto Central about 1 mile to store on right. **From I-275N**, take exit 18 west on 26th Ave S to US 19N/34th St S. Turn right onto 19N about 2 miles to Central Ave. Turn left onto Central about 3 miles to store on right.

RICHARD'S WHOLE FOODS ✿
3455 Tyrone Blvd. © 727-343-0084 ⊘ M-Sat 9-6
Large selection of bulk foods.

• organic produce • chain

From I-275S, take exit 23B toward Treasure Island onto 5th Ave N/US 19 AltN about 3½ miles to Tyrone Blvd. Turn right onto Tyrone about 2½ miles to store. **From I-275N**, take exit 18 west on 26th Ave S to US 19N/34th St S. Turn right onto 19N about 2¼ miles to 5th Ave. Turn left onto 5th about 2 miles to Tyrone Blvd N (Alt 19N). Turn right onto Tyrone about 2½ miles to store.

ROLLIN' OATS MARKET & CAFE ✗ ✿
2842 9th St. N. © 727-821-6825 ⊘ M-F 9:30-7, Sat 9:30-6, Sun 10-4

• organic produce • freshly prepared food • salad bar • café • deli • vegetarian friendly • chain • tables • self-service • take-out

From I-275, take exit 24 east on 22nd Ave (left from 275S, right from 275N) about ¾ mile to 9th St N. Turn left onto 9th less than ½ mile to store.

STUART

NATURE'S WAY CAFE ✗   ♿
25 S.W. Osceola St. © 772-220-7306 ⊘ M-Sat 8-5
Fresh salads, soups, sandwiches, wraps, and such, with vegetarian and meat options. Healthy option for downtown employees and travelers.

• juice bar • café • vegetarian friendly • chain • tables • self-service • take-out

From I-95, take exit 101 toward Stuart onto FL 76E (right from 95N, left from 95S) about 6½ miles (across intercoastal) to SW Osceola St. Turn left onto Osceola to store. **From FL TpkeS**, take exit 142 toward Port St Lucie onto FL 716E about 4 miles (across intercoastal) to US 1. Turn right onto 1S about 5 miles (across water) to SW Joan Jefferson Way. Turn left onto Joan Jefferson 4 blocks (across tracks) to SW Osceola. Turn right onto Osceola to store.

TALLAHASSEE

HIGHER TASTE CAFE & BAKERY ✗   ♿
411 St. Francis St. © 850-894-4296 ⊘ Lunch M-F 11-2:30, Dinner W, F 5:30-9
A generous buffet of vegetarian and vegan dishes.

• vegetarian • vegan friendly • organic focus • tables • self-service • take-out

From I-10, take exit 203 toward Tallahassee onto Rt 61S 5 miles to E Gaines St. Turn right onto E Gaines 5 blocks (⅓ mile) to S Boulevard St. Turn left onto S Boulevard 1 block to end and veer right onto St Francis St ½ block to restaurant.

HONEYTREE NATURAL FOODS ✕🦴

1660 North Monroe St. © 850-681-2000 ⊙ M-F 9-7, Sat 9-6, Sun 10-6, Juice bar M-Sat 11:30-2:30

Vegan sandwiches and hot entrees available at the juice bar. After hours, sandwiches can be found in the cooler.

· freshly prepared food · juice bar · vegan · counter · tables · self-service · take-out

🗂 **From I-10,** take exit 199 south on N Monroe St/US 27S (right from 10E, left from 10W) about 2½ miles to store in shopping center at Monroe & Tharp St.

NEW LEAF MARKET ✕🦴

1235 Apalachee Pkwy. © 850-942-2557 ⊙ M-Sat 9-9, Sun 12-7, Deli M-Sat 11-4

· organic produce · freshly prepared food · deli · bakery · vegetarian friendly · tables · self-service · take-out

🗂 **From I-10,** take exit 199 onto US 27S about 3⅔ miles to Apalachee Pkwy/US 27. Turn left (in front of State Capitol) onto US 27S less than 1 mile to store on right in Parkway Shopping Center. **From I-10W,** take exit 209A toward Tallahassee left onto Magnolia Dr ¾ mile to Apalachee Pkwy/US 27N. Turn right onto Apalachee to store on left.

TAMPA

If you're interested in dinosaurs, visit Tampa's Museum of Science and Industry, which houses some of the hugest specimens on display anywhere.

ANSLEY'S NATURAL MARKETPLACE 🦴

3936 W. Kennedy Blvd. © 813-879-6625 ⊙ M-F 9-7, Sat 9-6, Sun 11-5

· organic produce · juice bar · take-out

🗂 **From I-275N,** take exit 39A toward SR 60E onto W JFK Blvd. Turn right (east) onto Kennedy about 1¼ miles to store just past Grady Ave. **From I-275S,** take exit 41B (92E/Dale Mavery Hwy) left (south) onto N Dale Mavery ¾ mile to Kennedy. Turn right onto Kennedy ¼ mile to store at Grady Ave.

ANSLEY'S NATURAL MARKETPLACE ✕🦴

402 E. Sligh Ave. © 813-239-2700 ⊙ M-F 9-7, Sat 10-6, Sun 10-5

· organic produce · freshly prepared food · juice bar · deli · vegetarian friendly · tables · self-service · take-out

🗂 **From I-275,** take exit 48 west on Sligh Ave (left from 275N, right from 275S) 1 block to store.

EVOS FRESH & HEALTHY ✕

250 E. Kennedy Blvd. © 813-258-0005 ⊙ Daily 10-9

Healthy fast-food concept featuring naturally raised beef, chicken, soyburgers, veggie patties, whole wheat tortilla wraps, salads with organic greens, vegan chili, veggie corn dogs, "airfries"[TM], smoothies, and such.

· vegetarian friendly · chain · tables · self-service · take-out

🗂 **From 1-75N,** take exit 256 toward Tampa onto Crosstown Expwy 2⅓ miles. Merge onto Crosstown Expwy S/618W almost 8 miles to exit 8 (SR 60) toward Downtown-East. Go straight onto Kennedy Blvd about ⅓ mile to restaurant in Westshore Plaza. **From I-275,** take exit 44 toward Downtown East-West. Take Ashley St ramp onto Ashley Dr south about ⅔ mile (just past Kennedy) to E Jackson St. Turn left onto Jackson, left onto N Florida and left onto Kennedy restaurant in Westshore Plaza.

EVOS FRESH & HEALTHY ✗
609 S. Howard Ave. © 813-258-EVOS ☺ Daily 11-10
See description above.

· vegetarian friendly · chain· tables · self-service · take-out

🍎 **From I-275**, take exit 42 toward Howard Ave/Armenia Ave south on Armenia (left from 275S, right from 275N) about 1 mile to Horatio St. Turn left onto Horatio 2 blocks to Howard. Turn right onto Howard to restaurant.

NATURE'S HARVEST MARKET & DELI ✗🍲
1021 N. MacDill Ave. © 813-873-7428 ☺ M-F 9-9, Sat 9-8, Sun 11-7

· freshly prepared food · deli · vegetarian friendly · tables · self-service · take-out

🍎 **From I-275**, take exit 42 toward Howard Ave/Armenia Ave south on Armenia (left from 275S, right from 275N) less than ⅓ mile to Cypress St. Turn right onto Cypress less than ¾ mile to MacDill Ave. Turn right onto MacDill to store on right.

VENICE

RICHARD'S WHOLE FOODS MARKET 🍲
105 E. Milan Ave. © 941-484-8627 ☺ M-Sat 9-6
Large selection of bulk foods.

· chain

🍎 **From I-75S**, take exit 200 toward Venice/Osprey onto FL 681S about 3¾ miles to Tamiami Trail (US 41). Merge onto 41S about 3¾ miles to store at Milan Ave. **From I-75N**, take exit 193 toward Venice. Turn left onto Jacaranda Blvd about 1 mile to Venice Ave. Turn right onto Venice about 3⅔ miles to Tamiami. Turn left onto Tamiami ½ mile to store at Milan.

RICHARD'S WHOLE FOODS MARKET 🍲
593 US 41 Bypass © 941-484-2354 ☺ M-Sat 9-6
Large selection of bulk foods.

· chain

🍎 **From I-75S**, take exit 200 toward Venice/Osprey onto FL 681S about 3¾ miles to Tamiami Trail (US 41). Merge onto 41S (becomes 41 Bypass) about 3½ miles to Substation Rd. Turn left onto Substation and left again onto 41 Bypass going north less than ½ mile to store. **From I-75N**, take exit 193 toward Venice. Turn left onto Jacaranda Blvd about 1 mile to Venice Ave. Turn right onto Venice about 3 miles to 41 Bypass. Turn right (north) onto 41 Bypass less than 1 mile to store.

WEST PALM BEACH

FRED'S ULTIMA CAFE ✗   ♿
400A Clematis St. © 561-659-9877 ☺ M-F 7-10, Sat-Sun 8-6
Healthy vegetarian and non-vegetarian options in cafe that is connected to fitness center next door. Daily passes to gym available.

· juice bar · café · vegetarian friendly · tables · self-service · take-out

🍎 **From I-95**, take exit 70 toward Downtown east on Okeechobee Blvd (left from 95S, right from 95N) about 1½ miles to S Quadrille Blvd. Turn left onto S Quadrille ½ mile to Clematis St. Turn right onto Clematis 1 block to gym on SW corner. Turn right to cafe entrance down the block.

NATURE'S WAY CAFE ✗

777 S. Flagler Drive © 561-659-1993 ⊙ M-F 8-4

A small Florida chain of health-oriented lunch shops serving fish, poultry and vegetarian fare, but no red meat.

· vegetarian friendly · chain · tables · self-service · take-out

From I-95, take exit 70 toward Downtown east on Okeechobee Blvd (left from 95S, right from 95N) about 1¾ miles to Flagler Dr (at Intercoastal). Turn left onto Flagler to restaurant in Phillips Point complex on left. (Entrance is on south side along Rt 704W).

WILD OATS MARKET ✗ ● &

7735 S. Dixie Highway © 561-585-8800 ⊙ M-Sat 8-8, Sun 10-6

· organic produce · freshly prepared food · salad bar · café · deli · bakery · vegetarian friendly · chain · tables · self-service · take-out

From I-95, take exit 66 east on Forest Hills Blvd (left from 95S, right from 95N) less than 1 mile to S Dixie Hwy. Turn right onto S Dixie (US 1S) about ½ mile to store on right.

WINTER HAVEN

Pharmacist, nutritionist, herbalist and iridologist on staff for consultations.

NATURE'S DELIGHT NATURAL FOODS & HERB SHOP ✗ ●

3015 Cypress Gardens Rd. © 863-324-1778 ⊙ M-F 9-7, Sat 9-5, Sun 9-4

· organic produce · freshly prepared food · juice bar · vegetarian · counter · self-service · take-out

Winter Haven is about 18 miles south of I-4 on US 27. **From US 27**, take SR 540W (Cypress Gardens Blvd) 4¼ miles to second Cypress Gardens Rd entrance. Turn right onto Cypress Gardens Rd (at Blockbuster Video) 1 block to store on left.

WINTER PARK

CHAMBERLIN'S MARKET & CAFE ✗ ● &

430 N. Orlando Ave. © 407-647-6661 ⊙ M-Sat 8-9:30, Sun 10-7

· organic produce · freshly prepared food · juice bar · café · bakery · vegetarian friendly · chain · tables · self-service · take-out

From I-4E, take exit 87 (Fairbanks Ave) right onto FL 426E 1 mile to Orlando Ave/US 12/92. Turn left onto 92N about ½ mile to Winter Park Village. Turn right into Winter Park Village to store on right. **From I-4W**, take exit 88 left onto FL 4423N/Lee Rd about 1⅓ miles to Orlando Ave/US 12/92. Turn right onto 92S about ⅓ mile to Winter Park Village. Turn left into Winter Park Village to store on right.

WHOLE FOODS MARKET ✗ ● &

1989 Aloma Ave. © 407-673-8788 ⊙ Daily 8-10

· organic produce · freshly prepared food · juice bar · salad bar · deli · bakery · vegetarian friendly · chain · counter · self-service · take-out

From I-4, take exit 87 (Fairbanks Ave) onto FL 426E (becomes Aloma Ave) almost 4 miles to store on left (north side) in shopping center.

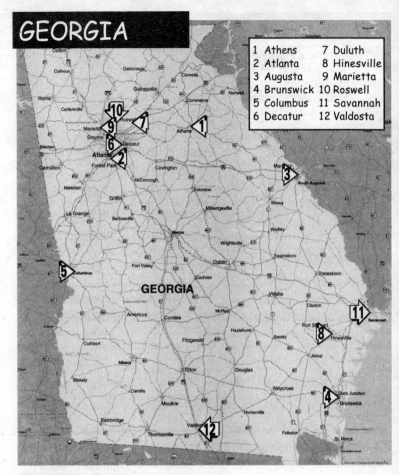

GEORGIA

1 Athens	7 Duluth
2 Atlanta	8 Hinesville
3 Augusta	9 Marietta
4 Brunswick	10 Roswell
5 Columbus	11 Savannah
6 Decatur	12 Valdosta

ATHENS

Athens is the home of the University of Georgia, bringing in a lot of music, art and culture for a fairly small town.

BLUEBIRD CAFE ✕

493 E. Clayton St. ℭ 706-549-3663 ⊙ Daily 8-3
The emphasis here is on breakfast, and lunch offers an eceletic mix of vegetarian sandwiches, quiche, mexican dishes, salads, and such.

· vegetarian · vegan friendly · tables · wait staff

🛏 **From Loop 10** around Athens, take US 78/GA 10 exit toward Downtown/Athens Airport onto 78 (Oak St) about 1½ miles to Jackson St. Turn right onto Jackson 1 block to E Clayton. Turn right onto Clayton to restaurant at N Thomas St. **From US 441S**, merge onto Commerce Rd/MLK Pkwy south 1 mile to North Ave. Turn right onto North about ½ mile to Jackson. Turn left onto Jackson 4 blocks to Clayton. Turn left onto Clayton to restaurant at N Thomas.

DAILY GROCERIES CO-OP, INC. 🌿

523 Prince Ave. ℭ 706-548-1732 ⊙ M-F 8-10, Sat-Sun 9-10

· organic produce · deli · vegetarian friendly · co-op · take-out

🛏 **From Loop 10** around Athens, take Chase St exit south less than 1 mile to Prince St. Turn left onto Prince ½ mile to store on right. **From downtown**, go west on Broad St to Pulaski St. Turn right onto Pulaski 4 blocks to Prince. Turn left onto Prince about 2 blocks to store on left (past traffic light at Finely/Barber St).

EARTH FARE ✕ 🍖 &

1689 S. Lumpkin St. © 706-227-1717 ⊘ M-Sat 8-9, Sun 9-8

· organic produce · freshly prepared food · juice bar · salad bar · café · deli · bakery · vegetarian friendly · chain · tables · self-service · take-out

🏠 **From Loop 10** around Athens, take Milledge Ave exit toward Whitehall Rd north about 1½ miles to 5 point intersection. Turn left onto Lumpkin St to store 100 yards on left.

GREEN SCENE BAKING COMPANY ✕ &

217 Hiawassee Ave. © 706-227-2881 ⊘ Tues-F 7:30-8, Sat-Sun 10-5

Housed in an historic building, the mostly vegan and organic soups, salads and sandwiches are served on antique dishes to match the decor. Fresh juices, whole grains, natural sweeteners, expeller-pressed oils.

· juice bar · bakery · vegetarian · vegan friendly · organic focus · counter · self-service · take-out

🏠 **From Loop 10** around Athens, take Chase St exit south about ½ mile (past railroad tracks) to traffic light at Boulevard. Turn right onto Boulevard 2 blocks to store right corner Hiawassee Ave & Boulevard.

PHOENIX NATURAL FOOD MARKET 🍖

296 W. Broad St. © 706-548-1780 ⊘ M-Sat 9-7

🏠 **From Loop 10** around Athens, take Commerce Rd/MLK Pkwy south about 1 mile to North St. Turn left onto North (becomes Dougherty St) ¾ mile to Pulaski St. Turn left onto Pulaski ¼ mile to store at Broad St (across from UGA campus). **Or, take 78Bus** (Broad St) toward Downtown to store at Broad & Pulaski.

THE GRIT ✕

199 Prince Ave. © 706-543-6592 ⊘ M-Th 11-9:30, F 11-10, Sat 10-3, 5-10, Sun 10-3, 5-9:30

International vegetarian classics. Smoking allowed in outdoor dining area.

· vegetarian · alcohol · tables · wait staff

🏠 **From Loop 10** around Athens, take Alt 15 (Prince Ave) toward Downtown about 1¾ miles to restaurant between N Newton & Pulaski St. **Or, take Commerce Rd/MLK Pkwy** south about 1 mile to North St. Turn left onto North (becomes Dougherty St) ¾ mile to Pulaski. Cross Pulaski onto Prince to restaurant.

ATLANTA

Among the numerous interesting things in Atlanta, are the Jimmy Carter Presidential Library and the Martin Luther King Center for Non-violent Social Change.

BROADWAY CAFÉ ✕ &

2166 Briarcliff Rd. © 404-329-0888 ⊘ M-Th 11-9, Fri 11-3, Sun 10-9

Multi-ethnic cuisine, mostly vegetarian and vegan, with the exception of a few fish dishes. Near Emory U.

· vegetarian friendly · vegan friendly · organic focus · kosher · alcohol · tables · wait staff

🏠 **From I-85**, take exit 89 east onto N Druid Hills Rd (left from 89S, right from 89N) about ½ mile to Briarcliff Rd. Turn right on Briarcliff less than 1 mile to restaurant on right.

CAFE SUNFLOWER ✕

2140 Peachtree Rd. ℂ 404-352-8859 ⊙ Lunch M-F 11:30-2:30, Sat 12-2:30, Dinner M-Th 5-9:30, F-Sat 5-10

A multi-ethnic vegetarian menu, featuring fresh vegetables, whole grains and organic ingredients when possible. Very vegan friendly (including all desserts).

· vegetarian · vegan friendly · organic focus · kosher · alcohol · tables · wait staff · take-out

🍎 **From I-75**, take exit 252A (US 41/Northside Dr) right onto Northside to Collier Rd. Turn right onto Collier less than 1 mile to Peachtree Rd. Turn left onto Peachtree less than ½ mile to restaurant on left in Brookwood Square Shopping Center.

CAFE SUNFLOWER ✕

5975 Roswell Rd. ℂ 404-256-1675 ⊙ Lunch M-F 11:30-2:30, Sat 12-2:30, Dinner M-Th 5-9:30, F-Sat 5-10

A multi-ethnic vegetarian menu, featuring fresh vegetables, whole grains and organic ingredients when possible. Very vegan friendly (including all desserts).

· vegetarian · vegan friendly · organic focus · kosher · alcohol · tables · wait staff · take-out

🍎 From I-285, take exit 25 toward Sandy Springs north onto Roswell Rd (right from 285W, left from 285E) less than ½ mile to restaurant.

CAMELI'S ✕   ♿

1263 Glenwood Ave. ℂ 404-622-9926 ⊙ M 11-10, Tues 11am-2:30am, W 11am-12:30am, Th 11am-3am, F 11am-5am, Sat noon-5am, Sun 9am-10pm

Tofu, seitan and soy "meat" in tacos, burgers, sandwiches, subs, and hearty hot entrees. Soup and salad bars and "live food." Plus, late night entertainment.

· salad bar · vegetarian · vegan friendly · alcohol · tables · wait staff · take-out

🍎 **From I-20W**, take exit 61B left on Glenwood Ave/GA 260 1 mile to restaurant. **From I-20E**, take exit 60A and bear right onto Moreland Ave SE/US 23S about ⅓ mile to Glenwood. Turn left onto Glenwood to restaurant.

ITERNAL LIFE ✕

565 Fair St. S.W. ℂ 404-942-9501 ⊙ M-W 11-8, Th-Sat 11-9

Organic raw foods to go.

· vegan · organic focus · take-out

🍎 **From I-20W**, take exit 56B (Windsor St) toward Spring St left onto Windsor about ¼ mile to Fulton St. Turn right onto Fulton about ¼ mile to McDaniel St. Turn right onto McDaniel about ⅓ mile to Northside Dr. Turn right onto Northside about ¼ mile to Fair St. Turn left onto Fair 1 block to restaurant. **From I-20E**, take exit 56A left onto McDaniel about ⅓ mile to Northside and follow directions above. **From I-75/85N**, take exit 246 toward GA Dome and take Fulton St ramp left onto Fulton Ext. Continue straight onto Fulton and follow directions above from I-20W. **From I-75/85S**, take exit 248A toward State Capitol/Stadium. Stay left at fork on ramp and veer right onto MLK Dr about 1 mile to Northside. Turn left onto Northside less than ½ mile to Fair. Turn right onto Fair 2 blocks to restaurant.

MADRAS CAFE ✕

3092 Briarcliff Rd. N.E. ℂ 404-320-7120 ⊙ Lunch M-F 11:30-3, Dinner M, W-F 5:30-9, Sat-Sun 11:30-9

All-vegetarian Indian. Daily lunch buffet or a la carte.

· vegetarian · vegan friendly · tables · self-service

🍎 **From I-85**, take exit 91 south on Clairmont Rd (right from 95N, left from 95S) about ¼ mile to Briarcliff Rd. Turn left onto Briarcliff about ½ mile to restaurant on left.

NUTS 'N BERRIES NATURAL FOODS ✗🍲
4274 Peachtree Rd. N.E. ✆ 404-237-6829 ⊙ M-F 9-8, Sat 9-7, Sun 10-6
· freshly prepared food · juice bar · café · vegetarian friendly · tables · self-service · take-out

🗓 **From I-285**, take exit 31A right onto Peachtree Industrial Rd S about 5 miles to store on right corner Peachtree & Kendrick Rd. **From I-85**, take exit 87 onto GA 400N about 2⅓ miles to exit 2. Take GA 141E ramp toward Peachtree onto GA 141E Conn about ½ mile to Peachtree. Turn left onto Peachtree about 2 miles to store on left corner at Kendrick.

RAINBOW NATURAL FOODS GROCERY & RESTAURANT ✗🍲
2118 North Decatur Rd N.E. ✆ 404-636-5553 ⊙ M-Sat 10-8, Sun 12-5, Cafe M-Sat 11-3
Lunch features soups, salads and hot entrees. Vegetarian, except for tuna salad.
· organic produce · freshly prepared food · café · deli · vegetarian friendly · tables · self-service · take-out

🗓 **From I-85**, take exit 91 south on Clairmont Rd (right from 95N, left from 95S) about 4½ miles to N Decatur Rd. Turn west onto onto N Decatur to store in North Decatur Plaza.

RETURN TO EDEN 🍲
2335 Cheshire Bridge Rd. ✆ 404-320-3336 ⊙ M-F 9-8, Sat 10-8, Sun 11-7
A totally vegetarian market.
· organic produce · freshly prepared food · deli · vegetarian · take-out

🗓 **From I-85S**, take exit 88 left onto Lennox-Cheshire Bridge Rd about ⅓ mile to store on left in Cheshire Square Shopping Center. **From I-85N**, take exit 86 onto GA 16N about 2 miles to Lennox Rd. Turn right onto Lennox (becomes Cheshire Bridge) ½ mile to store on left in Cheshire Square Shopping Center.

SEVANANDA NATURAL FOODS CO-OP MARKET 🍲   ♿
467 Moreland Ave. N.E. ✆ 404-681-2831 ⊙ Daily 9-10
An all vegetarian market with a vegan bakery, only organic produce and a purafresh water machine to refill empties. ·
· organic produce · freshly prepared food · salad bar · deli · bakery · vegetarian · vegan friendly · co-op · take-out

🗓 **From I-75/85**, take exit 248C toward Carter Center and veer right onto Freedom Pkwy NE/GA 10E 1 mile to GA 42E exit. Follow Freedom Pkwy NE/GA 42 about ¾ mile to T intersection at Moreland Ave. Turn right onto Moreland 1½ blocks to store on left. **From I-20**, take Moreland Ave (exit 60 from 20W, 60A from 20E) right (north) 1 mile to Little Five Points shopping district to store on right next to post office. (Driving time from either interstate just 5 minutes.)

SOUL VEGETARIAN ✗
652 N. Highland Ave. ✆ 404-875-4641 ⊙ M-Th 11-10, Sat 10-10, Sun 10-2, 5-10
Healthy, vegan, southern-style soul food. Soups, sandwiches, fresh vegetables, hot entrees, soy shakes, desserts. Homemade vegan soy cheese and "ice-kream."
· vegan · chain · tables · wait staff · take-out

🗓 **From I-75/85**, take exit 248C toward Carter Center and veer right onto Freedom Pkwy NE/GA 10E 1 mile to GA 42E exit. Follow Freedom Pkwy NE/GA 42 about ½ mile to N Highland. Turn left onto N Highland about ¼ mile to restaurant.

SOUL VEGETARIAN ✕

879 Ralph David Abernathy Blvd. S.W. © 404-752-5194 ◷ M 11-10, Tues-Sat 11-11, Sun 9:30-1, 5-11

See description above. Steam table with rice, beans, vegetables, and entrees.

· vegan · chain · tables · self-service · take-out

🍲 **From I-20,** take exit 55A toward Ashby St/West End south on Joseph E. Lowrey Blvd SW (right from 20E, left from 20W) about ¼ mile to Ralph David Abernathy Blvd. Turn left onto Abernathy to restaurant.

TERRA GRILLE ✕   ♿

3974-C Peachtree Rd. © 404- 841-1032 ◷ M-Sat 11-10

Soups, salads, sandwiches, and burgers. Dinner is less vegetarian-oriented, with focus on low-fat and whole grains. Claim the world's only "all animal label" wine list—Stag's Leap, Duck Pond, Ravenswood, Porcupine Ridge.

· vegetarian friendly · alcohol · tables · wait staff

🍲 **From I-85,** take exit 89 west on N Druid Hills Rd (left from 85N, right from 85S) 5 miles to Peachtree Rd. Make hard left onto Peachtree to restaurant on right in Brookhaven Shopping Center (across from MARTA station, next to Eckerd Drugs).

UNITY NATURAL FOODS 🍃   ♿

2955 Peachtree Rd. © 404-261-8776 ◷ M-Sat 10-7, Sun 12-6

· organic produce · freshly prepared food · take-out

🍲 **From I-85,** take exit 85 north on Peachtree Rd about 1 mile to store on right (after McDonalds). **From I-75,** take exit 255 toward US 41/Northside Pkwy east on W Paces Ferry Rd about 3 miles to Peachtree. Turn right onto Peachtree about ¼ mile to store on left.

WHOLE FOODS MARKET ✕🍃   ♿

650 Ponce de Leon Ave. © 404-853-1681 ◷ Daily 7-10

· organic produce · freshly prepared food · salad bar · café · deli · bakery · vegetarian friendly · chain · tables · self-service · take-out

🍲 **From I-75/85S,** take exit 248D toward US 78/Georgia Tech left onto North Ave ½ mile to Piedmont Ave. Turn left onto Piedmont and right onto Ponce de Leon Ave about 1 mile to store on left in Midtown Place Shopping Center. **From I-75/85N,** take exit 248C toward Carter Center and veer right onto Freedom Pkwy about 1¾ miles where it dead ends at Ponce de Leon. Turn left onto Ponce de Leon about ½ mile to store on right in Midtown Place Shopping Center.

WHOLE FOODS MARKET ✕🍃   ♿

5930 Roswell Rd. © 404-236-0810 ◷ Daily 8-10

· organic produce · freshly prepared food · juice bar · salad bar · café · deli · bakery · vegetarian friendly · chain · counter · tables · self-service · take-out

🍲 **From I-285,** take exit 25 toward Sandy Springs north on Roswell Rd (left from 285E, right from 285W) to store just north of exit.

WHOLE FOODS MARKET ✕🍃   ♿

2111 Briarcliff Rd. © 404-634-7800 ◷ M-Sat 8-10, Sun 8-9

· organic produce · freshly prepared food · salad bar · deli · bakery · vegetarian friendly · chain · counter · tables · self-service · take-out

🍲 **From I-85,** take exit 89 southeast on N Druid Hills Rd (left from 85S, right from 85N) about ⅓ mile to Briarcliff Rd. Turn right onto Briarcliff 1 mile to store at top of hill on right corner Briarcliff & LaVista Rd.

AUGUSTA

FOODS FOR BETTER LIVING 🍎
2606 McDowell St. © 706-738-3215 ⊗ M-F 9-5, Sat 9-1

🍎 **From I-20**, take exit 196A onto I-520E (Bobby Jones Expwy) almost 2 miles to exit 2 (Wrightsboro Rd). Turn left onto Wrightsboro 3 miles to Highland Ave. Turn left onto Highland ¼ mile (3 blocks) to McDowell St. Turn right onto McDowell 2 blocks to store on right.

BRUNSWICK

FEELING GREAT 🍎
1514 Newcastle St. © 912-265-1595 ⊗ M-Th 9:30-7, F-Sat 9:30-8, Sun 12:30-5:30

🍎 **From I-95**, take exit 36A towards Downtown right onto onto GA 25S about 5 miles to store at F St.

COLUMBUS

COUNTRY LIFE NATURAL FOOD ✗ 🍎   &
1217 Eberhart Ave. © 706-323-9194 ⊗ M-Th 10-6, F 10-3, Sun 10-5, Lunch M-F 11:30-2
Vegan groceries and weekday lunch. Run by Seventh-day Adventists.
· freshly prepared food· vegan · tables · self-service · take-out

🍎 **From I-185**, take exit 6 onto GA 22 Spur W/Macon Rd W less than 1¾ miles to store at Eberhart Ave (just past Shell station).

DECATUR

INDIAN DELIGHTS ✗
1707 Church St. © 404-296-2965 ⊗ Tues-F 11:30-8:30, Sat-Sun 12-8:30
Vegetarian Indian cooking in a basic, no frills atmosphere.
· vegetarian · vegan friendly · tables · self-service · take-out

🍎 **From I-285**, take exit 39A toward Decatur/Atlanta onto US 78W (becomes US 29) about 2½ miles to Church St. Turn left onto Church to restaurant on left in Scott Village Shopping Ctr. **From I-20W**, merge onto I-285N and follow directions above. **From I-75S/85S**, merge onto I-285E and follow directions above. **From I-20E**, merge onto I-75N/I-85N. **From I-75/85N**, take exit 248C toward Carter Center and veer right onto Freedom Pkwy about 1¾ miles where it dead ends at Ponce de Leon. Turn right onto Ponce de Leon and continue on US 29 (becomes Scott Blvd) about 4²⁄₃ miles to Church. Turn right onto Church to restaurant on left in Scott Village.

MADRAS SARAVANA BHAVAN ✗
2179 Lawrenceville Hwy. © 404-636-4400 ⊗ Daily 11:30-10 Buffet until 3:30
Vegetarian Indian buffet lunch, than full-service until closing. A big place.
· vegetarian · vegan friendly · alcohol · tables · self-service · wait staff

🍎 **From I-285**, take exit 39A toward Decatur/Atlanta onto Stone Mt Pkwy/US 78W about 1⅓ miles to N Druid Hills exit. Follow ramp right onto N Druid Hills Decatur Rd and turn right onto US 29 (Lawrenceville Hwy) to restaurant in Cub Food Shopping Center. **From I-20W**, merge onto I-285N and follow directions above. **From I-75S/85S**, merge onto I-285E and follow directions above. **From I-20E**, merge onto I-75N/85N. **From I-75/85N**, take exit 248C toward Carter Center and veer right onto Freedom Pkwy about 1¾ miles where it dead ends at Ponce de Leon. Turn right onto Ponce de Leon and continue on US 29 5¾ miles to restaurant.

RAINBOW NATURAL FOODS GROCERY & RESTAURANT ✗🍴

2118 N. Decatur Rd. © 404-633-3538 ☺ M-Sat 11-8, Sun 11-5
Vegetarian cafe and hot bar. The cafe menu Monday to Saturday only from 11 to 3, but hot bar and salad bar function during all store hours.

• organic produce • freshly prepared food • salad bar • café • deli • vegetarian • tables • self-service • take-out

🍎 **From I-285**, take exit 39A toward Decatur/Atlanta onto US 78W (becomes US 29) just over 3 miles to N Decatur Rd. Turn right (north) onto N Decatur almost 1 mile to store.

UDIPI CAFE ✗   ♿

1850 Lawrenceville Hwy. © 404-325-1933 ☺ M-Th 11:30-9:30, F-Sun 11:30-10
A casual Indian vegetarian eatery.

• vegetarian • vegan friendly • tables • wait staff

🍎 **From I-285**, take exit 39A toward Decatur/Atlanta onto US 78W (becomes US 29/Lawrenceville Hwy) about 2¼ miles to restaurant on right just past N Dekalb Mall. **From I-20W**, merge onto I-285N and follow directions above. **From I-75S/85S**, merge onto I-285E and follow directions above. **From I-20E**, merge onto I-75N/85N. **From I-75/85N**, take exit 248C toward Carter Center and veer right onto Freedom Pkwy about 1¾ miles where it dead ends at Ponce de Leon. Turn right onto Ponce de Leon and continue on US 29 about 5 miles to restaurant on left just before N Dekalb Mall.

DULUTH

HARRY'S FARMERS MARKET ✗🍲   ♿

2025 Satellite Pointe © 770-416-6900 ☺ Daily 8-8

• organic produce • freshly prepared food • salad bar • café • deli • bakery • vegetarian friendly • chain • tables • self-service • take-out

🍎 **From I-85N**, take exit 103 left onto Steve Reynolds Blvd ½ mile to Satellite Blvd. Turn left onto Satellite ¼ mile to store on left. **From I-85S**, take exit 104 right onto Pleasant Hill Rd ½ mile to Satellite. Turn left onto Satellite 1 mile to store on left.

HINESVILLE

FARMER'S NATURAL FOODS 🍲

754 Elma G. Miles Pkwy. © 912-368-7803 ☺ M-F 9-7, Sat 9-6

🍎 Hinesville is 15 miles west of I-95 exit 76 on US 84. **From US 84W**, turn right onto General Screven Way (GA 196) about ⅓ mile (across Main St) to GA 119/EG Miles Pkwy. Turn left onto Miles about 1 mile to store on left. **From 84E**, turn left onto 119/Slatten Dr almost 6 miles to store on left.

MARIETTA

HARRY'S FARMERS MARKET ✗🍲   ♿

70 Powers Ferry Rd. © 770-578-4400 ☺ M-Th 9-8, F-Sat, 9-9, Sun 10-7

• organic produce • freshly prepared food • salad bar • café • deli • bakery • vegetarian friendly • chain • tables • self-service • take-out

🍎 **From I-75**, take exit 263 (GA 120E) toward Roswell. Merge onto Loop 120/S Marietta Pkwy SE about ⅓ mile to Powers Ferry Rd. Turn left onto Powers Ferry about ¾ mile to store.

LIFE GROCERY NATURAL FOODS CO-OP & CAFE ✗ ⬤ ⅋

1453 Roswell Rd. ℂ 770-977-9583 ⊙ M-Sat 9-8, Sun 11-6

Cafe specializes in organic vegan and "living foods."

· organic produce · freshly prepared food · juice bar · salad bar · café · vegan · co-op
· counter · tables · self-service · take-out

⌂ **From I-75**, take exit 263 (GA 120E) toward Roswell. Merge onto Loop 120/S Marietta Pkwy SE ¾ mile to Lower Roswell Rd SE. Turn left onto Lower Roswell ½ mile to end at Roswell Rd. Veer left onto Roswell to store on right in Baby Super Store Plaza.

ROSWELL

HARRY'S FARMERS MARKET ✗ ⬤   ⅋

1180 Upper Hembree Rd. ℂ 770-664-6300 ⊙ M-Sat 9-8, Sun 9-7

· organic produce · freshly prepared food · salad bar · café · deli · bakery · vegetarian
friendly · chain · tables · self-service · take-out

⌂ **From GA 400N**, take exit 10 west on Old Milton Pkwy/GA 120W (left from 400N, right from 400S) about 3 miles to Harris Rd. Turn left onto Harris to store at traffic light at Upper Hambree Rd.

SPROUT CAFÉ & MARKET ✗ ⬤   ⅋

1475 Holcomb Bridge Rd, Ste. 200 ℂ 770-992-9218 ⊙ M-F 7-9, Sat 9-10, Sun 11-2:30

Specializing in raw foods (nothing heated to over 105°), using largely organic ingredients. The only animal product on the menu is honey. Even the ice cream specials are dairy-free, and desserts are wheat-free, as well. Soups, wraps, sandwiches, pizza, and changing daily self-serve food bar sold by the pound.

· organic produce · freshly prepared food · juice bar · salad bar · café · vegan · organic
focus · counter · tables · self-service · wait staff · take-out

⌂ **From GA 400N**, take exit 7A toward Norcross right onto Holcomb Bridge Rd/140E about ⅔ mile to Old Alabama Rd (2nd traffic light). Turn right onto Old Alabama to store (next to LA Fitness). **From GA 400S**, take exit 7 left onto Holcomb Bridge/140E and follow directions above.

SAVANNAH

BRIGHTER DAY NATURAL FOODS ✗ ⬤

1102 Bull St. ℂ 912-236-4703 ⊙ M-Sat 10-6, Sun 12:30-5:30, Deli M-F 11-4

· freshly prepared food · deli · vegetarian friendly · counter · tables · self-service · take-out

⌂ **From I-95**, take exit 99 toward Savannah onto I-16E/404E about 8¼ miles to exit 166 (W Gwinett St) Turn right onto Gwinett ½ mile to Whitaker St. Turn right onto Whitaker 3 blocks to Park Ave. Turn left onto W Park 1 block to store at Bull St (mural with tomatoes in sunglasses).

VALDOSTA

MA PERKINS NATURAL ⬤

2110 N. Ashley St. ℂ 229-244-5440 ⊙ M-F 9:30-6, Sat 9:30-5

⌂ **From I-75**, take exit 22 toward I-75Bus Loop/N Valdosta Rd right onto US 41S about 6 miles to store in center of town. **From US 84**, take US 41N almost 2 miles to store just pass split-off to US 221.

HAWAII

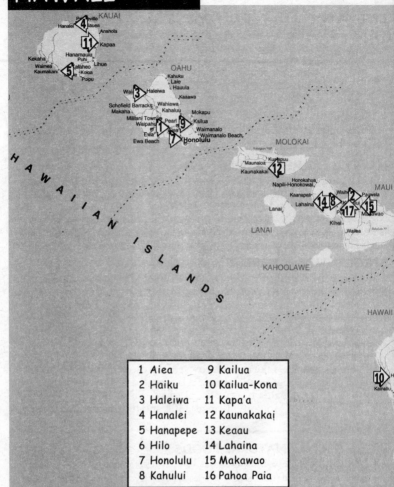

1 Aiea	9 Kailua
2 Haiku	10 Kailua-Kona
3 Haleiwa	11 Kapa'a
4 Hanalei	12 Kaunakakai
5 Hanapepe	13 Keaau
6 Hilo	14 Lahaina
7 Honolulu	15 Makawao
8 Kahului	16 Pahoa Paia

AIEA

DOWN TO EARTH NATURAL FOODS
98-131 Kaonohi St. © 808-488-1375 ⊙ Daily 8-10
All-vegetarian market.
· organic produce · freshly prepared food · deli · vegetarian · co-op · take-out
☐ On the southern coast of Oahu about 9 miles north of Honolulu. **From Kamehameha Hwy (HI-99), turn inland onto Kaonohi St.**

HAIKU

VEG-OUT
810 Kokomo Rd. © 808-575-5320 ⊙ M-F 10:30-7, Sat 11:30-6
A casual place serving sandwiches, salads, stir-fries, chili, fresh juice, and such.
· juice bar · vegetarian · vegan friendly · tables · self-service · take-out

🛏 On the northern side of Maui. **From Hana Hwy** (HI 36), turn inland onto Haiku Rd (HI 366) about 1½ miles to Kokomo Rd (HI 398). Continue straight onto Kokomo to restaurant.

HALEIWA

CELESTIAL NATURAL FOODS & PARADISE FOUND CAFE 🍴🍃

66-443 Kamehameha Hwy. ✆ 808-637-4540 ⊘ Store M-Sat 9-6, Sun 10-6, Cafe M-Sat 9-5, Sun 10-5

A 27-item vegetarian menu with sandwiches, salads, sushi, curry, and other "gourmet" items with a Thai, Japanese, Caribbean, Polynesian influence.

· vegetarian · vegan friendly · tables · wait staff · take-out

🛏 In northern Oahu. **From the south on Hwy 99**, take first exit onto Hwy 83 (Kamehameha Hwy) about ⅓ mile to store.

HANALEI

POSTCARDS CAFÉ 🍴   ♿

Kuhio Hwy ✆ 808-826-1191 ⊘ Daily 6pm-9pm

Seafood and vegetarian fare using locally grown organic produce.

· vegetarian friendly · organic focus · alcohol · tables · wait staff

🛏 On the northern coast of Kauai. **From Princeville**, heading north, cross bridge and stay right to restaurant in 1st small building on left.

HANAPEPE

HANAPEPE CAFE 🍴

3830 Hanapepe Rd. ✆ 808-335-5011 ⊘ Tues-Sat 8-2, Dinner F 6-9

Mainly a breakfast/lunch place, but on Friday night (the big night in town), there is "fine dining" at the cafe. Note, there is apt to be fish on the menu then. Be sure to make a reservation, and you may want to bring some wine.

· vegetarian · vegan friendly · tables · wait staff

🛏 On the southern coast of Kauai. **From HI 50**, turn inland onto Hanapepe Rd about ¼ mile to restaurant in the old part of town.

HILO

Visit Moku Papapa, the learning center for Hawaii's remote coral reefs, the Tsunami and Lyman Museums (world's largest seashell collection), or walk to the legendary Wailuku River or the Pacific Ocean. And that's just for starters!

ABUNDANT LIFE NATURAL FOODS & CAFE 🍴🍃

292 Kamehameha Ave. ✆ 808-935-7411 ⊘ M, Tues, Th, Fri 8:30-7, Wed, Sat 7-7, Sun 10-5

Discover exotic and local fruits like abui, dragoneyes, lychee, rollinia, rambutan, sapote, soursop, and such. The cafe features mostly vegetarian and organic soups, salads, sandwiches, plate lunches, juices, smoothies, and an espresso bar.

· organic produce · freshly prepared food · juice bar · café · deli · vegetarian friendly · counter · tables · wait staff · take-out

🛏 On the island of Hawaii on Hilo Bayfront Hwy between Mamo St & Furneaux Ln.

HONOLULU

DOWN TO EARTH NATURAL FOODS 🐑
2525 S. King St. © 808-947-7678 ⊙ Daily 7:30-10
All-vegetarian market.
- organic produce · freshly prepared food · deli · vegetarian · chain · take-out

🍎 **From I-H1**, take exit 24B onto University Ave heading toward the beach to S King St. Turn right onto S King to store.

HUCKLEBERRY FARMS 🐑
1613 Nuuanu Ave. © 808-599-7960 ⊙ M-Sat 9-8, Sun 9-6
- organic produce · freshly prepared food · take-out

🍎 **From I-H1**, exit onto HI 98 (Vineyard Blvd from H1W, Olomea St from H1E) ½-1 mile to Nuuanu Ave. Turn inland on Nuuanu about ¼ mile to store at School St in Nuuanu Shopping Center.

KOKUA COUNTRY FOOD CO-OP 🐑
2643 S. King St. © 808-941-1922 ⊙ Daily 8:30-8:30
Premade deli foods can be microwaved and eaten at the tables outside.
- organic produce · deli · vegetarian friendly · co-op · take-out

🍎 **From I-H1**, take exit 24B onto University Ave heading toward the beach to S King St. Turn left onto S King to store (makai side).

LEGEND VEGETARIAN RESTAURANT
100 N. Beretania St. © 808-532-8218 ⊙ Tues-Sun 10:30am-3pm, Seafood side 5:30-9
This restaurant has two sides. One serves a Chinese Buddhist vegan lunch. The other, open for dinner as well, has seafood (and alcohol), and vegetarian choices.
- vegan · tables · wait staff

🍎 **From I-H1E**, exit onto HI 98 (Olomea St) ½ mile to Liliha St. Turn right onto Liliha 2 blocks to King St. Turn left onto King and bear left at fork onto Beretania St about ⅓ mile to restaurant at Maunakea St (Chinese Cultural Plaza). **From I-H1W**, exit onto HI 98 (Vineyard Blvd) ½ mile to Pali Hwy (HI 61). Turn left onto Pali ¼ mile to Beretania St. Turn left onto Beretania ¼ mile to restaurant at Maunakea.

RUFFAGE NATURAL FOODS 🍴🐑
2443 Kuhio Ave. © 808-922-2042 ⊙ M-Sat 9-7
- organic produce · freshly prepared food · juice bar · café · deli · vegetarian friendly
- tables · self-service · take-out

🍎 1 block from Waikiki Beach on Kuhio Ave.

GOVINDA DINING CLUB 🍴
51 Coelho Way © 808-595-3947 ⊙ M-F 11-2
Weekday vegetarian lunch buffet run by Hari Krisha devotees.
- vegetarian · vegan friendly · tables · self-service

🍎 **From I-H1**, take exit 21A inland on Pali Hwy (HI 61) about 1¼ miles to Coelho Way. Turn left onto Coelho Way to restaurant and temple (across from Philippine consulate).

KAHULUI

DOWN TO EARTH NATURAL FOODS 🐑
305 Dairy Rd. © 808-877-2661 ⊙ M-Sat 7-9, Sun 8-8
All-vegetarian market.
- organic produce · freshly prepared food · deli · vegetarian · chain · take-out

⌂ On the northern coast of Maui. **From Hana Hwy** (HI 36), turn inland onto Dairy Rd (HI 380) ¼ mile to store.

KAILUA

DOWN TO EARTH NATURAL FOODS 🍴
201 Hamakua Dr. ℂ 808-262-3838 ☉ Daily 8-10
All-vegetarian market.

· organic produce · freshly prepared food · deli · vegetarian · chain · take-out

⌂ On the east side of Oahu. **From south**, take Pali Hwy (HI 61) inland straight onto Kailua Rd. Follow Kailua about 1 mile to Hamakua Dr. Turn right onto Hamakua ⅓ mile to store. **From Kailua beach**, take Kuulei Rd inland (becomes Kailua Rd) ⅔ mile to Hamakua. Turn left onto Hamakua ⅓ mile to store.

KAILUA-KONA

KONA NATURAL FOODS 🍴🍴
75-1027 Henry St. ℂ 808-329-2296 ☉ M-Sat 8:30-9 (deli to 6), Sun 8:30-7 (deli to 3)
Deli serves soups, salads, sandwiches, and hot dishes. After deli hours the food is packaged for "grab & go."

· organic produce · freshly prepared food · juice bar · deli · vegetarian friendly · tables
· self-service · take-out

⌂ On the island of Hawaii. **From south on HI 11,** turn inland (right) onto Henry St (just before Palani Rd/HI 190) to store. **From north along the coast on HI-19,** turn inland (left) onto Henry (just after HI 190) to store. **From northern interior on HI 190,** veer left onto Henry (nearing the coast) about ⅓ mile to store.

KAPA'A

PAPAYA'S NATURAL FOOD CAFE 🍴🍴
4-831 Kuhio Hwy. ℂ 808-823-0190 ☉ M-Sat 9-8 (Deli until 7)
The deli is mostly vegetarian, with some fish. On Friday they make a special Hawaiian plate. Outdoor tables only, but in Hawaii that's no problem.

· organic produce · freshly prepared food · salad bar · deli · vegetarian friendly · tables
· self-service · take-out

⌂ On the east coast of Kauai. Store is on HI 56 about 1 mile south of town in Kauai Village (Safeway) Shopping Ctr (under the clock tower).

KAUNAKAKAI

OUTPOST NATURAL FOODS 🍴
70 Makaena Place ℂ 808-553-3377 ☉ M-F 9-7, Sun 10-7

· deli · vegetarian friendly · take-out

⌂ Along the coast in central Molokai. **From HI 450** (Kamehameha Hwy), turn inland (right) onto Ala Malama Ave and make 1st left onto Makaena to store. **From HI 460** (Mauna Loa Hwy), turn inland (left) onto Manila Rd and make 1st right onto Makaena to store.

Please tell these businesses that you found them in Healthy Highways.

KEAAU

KEAAU NATURAL FOODS 🥬
16-586 Old Volcano Rd., Ste. 109 ℂ 808-966-8877 ⊘ M-F 8:30-8, Sat 8:30-7, Sun 9:30-5
· organic produce · deli · vegetarian friendly · take-out
▢ On the east coast of Hawaii about 7 miles south of Hilo in the Keaau Town Shopping Center at junction hwys 11 & 130.

LAHAINA

DOWN TO EARTH NATURAL FOODS 🥬
193 Lahainaluna Rd. ℂ 808-667-2855 ⊘ M-Sat 7:30-9, Sun 8:30-8
All-vegetarian market.
· vegetarian · chain
▢ On the island of Maui. **From Honoapiilani Hwy** (HI 30), turn toward the beach on Lahainaluna Rd to store.

MAKAWAO

DOWN TO EARTH NATURAL FOODS 🥬
1169 Makawao Ave. ℂ 808-572-1488 ⊘ Daily 8-8
All-vegetarian market.
· organic produce · vegetarian · chain
▢ On the northern interior of Maui. Take HI 365/400 (becomes Makawao Ave in town) to store.

PAHOA

PAHOA NATURAL GROCERIES 🍴🥬
15-1403 Nanawale Homestead Rd. ℂ 808-965-9340 ⊘ M-Sat 7:30-7:30, Sun 7:30-6
The deli is all vegetarian and provides breakfast, as well as a daily hot bar. The only tables are outside, but this is Hawaii so you can use them year-round.
· organic produce · freshly prepared food · salad bar · deli · vegetarian · tables
· self-service · take-out
▢ On the SE corner of Hawaii. **From HI 11**, go south on HI 130 (Pahoa Rd) about 11 miles to Nanawale Homestead Rd. Turn left onto Nanawale to big yellow store on left.

PAIA

FRESH MINT 🍴
115 Baldwin Avenue ℂ 808-579-9144 ⊘ Daily 11-9
Vegetarian Vietnamese cooking.
· vegan · alcohol · tables · self-service · wait staff
▢ On the north coast of Maui. **From the Hana Hwy** (HI 36), turn inland onto Baldwin Ave about 3 blocks to restaurant (across from post office).

IDAHO

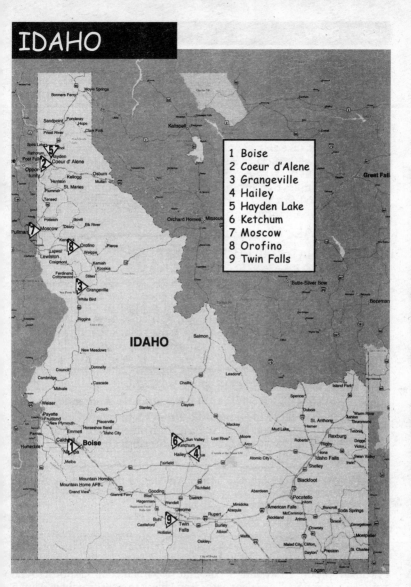

1 Boise
2 Coeur d'Alene
3 Grangeville
4 Hailey
5 Hayden Lake
6 Ketchum
7 Moscow
8 Orofino
9 Twin Falls

IDAHO

BOISE

BOISE CONSUMER CO-OP 🍃
888 W. Fort St. ⓒ 208-342-6652 ⊙ M-Sat 9-9, Sun 9-8

· organic produce · deli · vegetarian friendly · co-op · take-out

🖐 **From I-84E**, take exit 49 onto I-184E toward City Center (becomes W Myrtle St/US 20 & 26E) about 5 miles to S Capitol Blvd. Turn left onto Capitol ⅓ mile to W Bannock St. Turn left onto Bannock 1 block to N 8th St. Turn right onto 8th about ⅓ mile to W Fort St. Turn left onto W Fort to store. **From I-84W**, take exit 54 right onto S Broadway Ave (becomes N Ave B, then E Fort at hospital) about 3⅓ miles to W Fort. Veer right onto W Fort (State St is straight ahead) about ⅔ mile to store at N 8th.

KULTURE KLATSCH ✕

409 S. 8th St. © 208-345-0452 ⊘ M 7-3, Tues-Th 7-10, F 7-11, Sat 8-11, Sun 8-3
Wholefoods, vegetarian menu with hearty breakfasts and a varied selection at lunch and dinner. Fresh juices and "fountain" drinks. Plus, live free music at night and Sunday brunch.

· juice bar · café · vegetarian · vegan friendly · alcohol · tables · wait staff

🚙 **From I-84E**, take exit 49 onto I-184E (becomes W Myrtle St/US 20 & 26E) 5 miles to S 8th St. Turn left onto S 8th to restaurant in 8th St Marketplace. **From I-84W**, take exit 54 right onto S Broadway Ave (US 20 & 26W) almost 3 miles to E Front St (also 20 & 26W). Turn left onto Front about ¾ mile to S 9th St. Turn left onto S 9th, left onto Broad St and left onto S 8th to restaurant in 8th St Marketplace.

COEUR D'ALENE

PILGRIM'S NATURAL FOOD MARKET ✕ 🥘

1316 N. 4th St. © 208-676-9730 ⊘ M-Sat 9-7, Sun 11-5

· organic produce · freshly prepared food · juice bar · café · deli · bakery · vegetarian friendly · tables · self-service · take-out

🚙 **From I-90**, take exit 13 south on N 4th St (right from 90E, left from 90W) to N 3rd St. Make slight right onto N 3rd (one-way south) about ⅔ mile to Spokane Ave. Turn left onto Spokane 1 block to traffic light at N 4th. Turn left onto N 4th to store in shopping strip on right.

GRANGEVILLE

THE HEALTH FOOD STORE 🥘

709 W. North St © 208-983-1276 ⊘ M-F 9-5:30 (until 6 in summer) Sat 10-4

🚙 Take US 95 or ID 13 to Grangeville. **From 95**, turn right onto Main St (which is also ID 13). **From Main St**, turn north onto N C or N B St 1 block to North St. Store is between C & B behind Syringa Hospital.

HAILEY

Monte at Atkinsons' reports that Hailey has "one of the premier skateboard facilities in the nation."

ATKINSONS' MARKETS ✕ 🥘   ♿

93 E. Croy St. © 208-788-2294 ⊘ Daily 7:30-9

· organic produce · freshly prepared food · salad bar · deli · bakery · vegetarian friendly · counter · tables · self-service · take-out

🚙 Hailey is 65 miles north of I-84 exit 173 on ID 75. **From 75N**, pass Friedman Airport, go around "S" curve into town and continue north to 2nd traffic light (Croy St). Turn right onto Croy 1 block to store on right in Alturas Plaza. **From ID 75S**, turn left onto Croy to store on right in Alturas Plaza.

HAYDEN LAKE

FLOUR MILL NATURAL FOODS 🥘

88 W. Commerce Drive © 208-772-2911 ⊘ M-F 9-5:30, Sat 10-3

🚙 **From I-90**, take exit 12 onto US 95N (right from 90W, left from 90E) over 3½ miles to Honeysuckle Ave. Turn right onto Honeysuckle 1 block to Commerce Drive. Turn left onto Commerce to store on right.

KETCHUM

Ketchum is in view of all the Sun Valley Ski resorts.

AKASHA ✗
160 N. Main St. ℂ 208-726-4777 ⊙ M-Sat 9-9, Sun 10-9
A mostly raw foods cafe (sometimes there is cooked soup), located inside the Chapter One bookstore.

· juice bar · café · vegan · organic focus · tables · self-service · take-out

⛺ Take ID Hwy 75 to Ketchum where it becomes Main St. Restaurant is on Main between 1st & 2nd St in Chapter One bookstore.

ATKINSONS' ✗ 🍴
451 4th St. E. ℂ 208-726-5668 ⊙ Daily 7:30-9

· organic produce · freshly prepared food · salad bar · deli · bakery · vegetarian friendly
· tables · self-service · take-out

⛺ Take ID Hwy 75 to Ketchum. Go east on 4th St to store in Giacobbi Square.

MOSCOW

MOSCOW FOOD CO-OP ✗ 🍴   ♿
221 E. 3rd St. ℂ 208-882-8537 ⊙ Daily 8-8

· organic produce · freshly prepared food · deli · bakery · vegetarian friendly · co-op
· counter · tables · self-service · take-out

⛺ Take ID 95 into Moscow. Go east on 3rd St (at traffic light) ½ block to store on right.

OROFINO

CLEARWATER VALLEY NATURAL FOOD 🍴
160 Johnson Ave. ℂ 208-476-4091 ⊙ M-F 10-5:30

⛺ Take US 12 to ID 7E. Take ID 7E across river to Orofino (becomes Michigan Ave) about ¼ mile to Johnson Ave. Turn right onto Johnson to store.

TWIN FALLS

THE HEALTH FOOD PLACE 🍴
111 Blue Lakes Blvd. N. ℂ 208-733-1411 ⊙ M-F 9:30-6:30, Sat 10-5:30, Sun 12-4

⛺ **From I-84**, take exit 173 toward Twin Falls onto US 93S (right from 84E, left from 84W) about 6 miles (into Twin Falls) to store on right just past Addison Ave (where road becomes Blue Lake Blvd).

Goldbeck's "EAT IT OR NOT"
FASCINATING & FAR-OUT FACTS ABOUT FOOD

Which has more nutrition, chunky or creamy peanut butter?

Answer: Actually, it's a tie. But be sure to buy the "natural," "old-fashioned" or freshly ground kind, since regular commercial peanut butter has sugar and hydrogenated fat added.

ILLINOIS

1 Arlington Heights	8 De Kalb	15 Hinsdale	22 Palatine
2 Bloomington	9 Deerfield	16 Matteson	23 Peoria
3 Bradley	10 Dundee Township	17 Morris	24 River Forest
4 Carbondale	11 Edwardsville	18 Mount Prospect	25 Springfield
5 Charleston	12 Evanston	19 Mt. Vernon	26 Urbana
6 Chicago	13 Geneva	20 New Lenox	27 Westmont
7 Crystal Lake	14 Highland	21 Normal	28 Wheaton
			29 Willowbrook

ARLINGTON HEIGHTS

CHOWPATTI VEGETARIAN RESTAURANT ✕
1035 S. Arlington Heights Rd. © 847-640-9554 ☺ Tues-Th, Sun 11:30-3, 5-9, F-Sat 11:30-3, 5-10
The 26-page menu offers over 300 vegetarian choices. Mostly Indian, plus a smattering from all over the world.
· vegetarian · vegan friendly · tables · wait staff · take-out
From I-90, take Arlington Heights Rd exit toward Arlington Heights north on S Arlington Heights Rd 1½ miles to restaurant.

BLOOMINGTON

COMMON GROUND GROCERY 🌿
516 N. Main St. © 309-829-2621 ☺ M-Sat 9:30-5:30
· organic produce
From 1-74, take exit 160A east on W Market almost 2 miles to downtown traffic light at Main St. Turn left onto Main to store on left.

BRADLEY

KANKAKEE NATURAL FOODS 🌿
1035 Mulligan Dr. © 815-933-6236 ☺ M-Th, Sat 9-5:30, F 9-7
From I-57, take exit 315 toward Bradley south on IL 50S 1 mile to Mulligan Dr. Turn left onto Mulligan to store.

CARBONDALE

Situated within minutes of the Shawnee National Forest.

NEIGHBORHOOD CO-OP 🌿
104 E. Jackson St. © 618-529-3533 ☺ M-F 10-8, Sat 9-7, Sun 12-6
· organic produce · freshly prepared food · bakery · vegetarian friendly · co-op · take-out
Carbondale is 14½ miles west of I-57 (exit 54B) on Rt 13. **From Rt 13W**, turn right onto Washington St/US 51N (5th traffic light past "Welcome to Carbondale" sign) 1 block to Jackson St. Turn left onto Jackson to store on right (just before railroad tracks).

CHARLESTON

NATURAL FOOD & NUTRITION 🌿
422 Madison Ave. © 217-345-1130 ☺ M-F 9-5:30, Sat 9-3
From I-57, take exit 190 toward Charleston onto SR 16E about 10 miles into downtown to 4th St. Turn left onto 4th less than 1 mile to store at Madison Ave (1 block north & 1 block west of Coles County Courthouse).

CHICAGO

For something really different, *StreetWise*, the city's homeless newspaper, sponsors bus tours hosted by formerly homeless residents, providing their unique city perspective (312-554-0060 for info).

ALICE & FRIENDS VEGETARIAN CAFE ✕
5812 N. Broadway © 773-275-8797 ☺ M-F 4-10:30, Sat 12-10:30
An all-vegetarian mixture of Asian cuisines.
· vegetarian · vegan friendly · tables · wait staff
Take S Lake Shore Dr heading north from downtown Chicago to where it merges onto W Hollywood Ave (south of Sheridan Rd). Take Hollywood about ⅓ mile to N Broadway. Turn right onto N Broadway to restaurant.

AMITABUL ✗

6207 N. Milwaukee Ave. © 773-774-0276 ⊙ Tues-Th 1-9, F 12-10, Sat 10-10, Sun 10-8

Vegan Korean, based on Zen principles. Homemade organic sauces and no-oil steam stir-frying.

· vegan · tables · wait staff

🛏 **From I-90 (Kennedy Expwy)**, take exit 82A toward Nagle Ave. Turn left onto N Nagle, right onto W Huntington, and left onto N Milwaukee to restaurant.

ARYA BHAVAN ✗

2508 W. Devon Ave. © 773-274-5800 ⊙ Tues-F 11:30-3, 5-6 Sat-Sun 11:30-10

Indian vegetarian a la carte menu, plus buffet lunch weekdays and buffet dinner on the weekend.

· vegetarian · vegan friendly · tables · self-service · wait staff

🛏 **From north of Chicago on I-94S**, take exit 39B east on Trouhy Ave to IL 50 (N Cicero). Turn right (south) onto 50 about 1 mile to W Devon Ave. Turn left onto Devon about 1 mile to restaurant. **From south of Chicago on 1-94N**, take exit 47A (FullertonAve/2400N) north on Western Ave about 4¾ miles to W Devon. Turn left onto Devon to restaurant.

CHICAGO DINER ✗

3411 N. Halsted St. © 773-935-6696 ⊙ M-Th 11-10, F 11-11, Sat 10-10, Sun 10-10

Hearty diner food vegetarian style and lush vegan desserts.

· vegetarian · vegan friendly · alcohol · counter · tables · wait staff · take-out

🛏 **From I-90/94**, take exit 45C east on Belmont Ave about 3 miles to Halsted St. Turn left (north) onto Halsted 4 blocks to restaurant just past Roscoe St intersection. **From Lake Shore Dr**, go west on Belmont about ½ mile to Halsted. Turn right onto Halsted and follow directions above.

EARWAX CAFE ✗

1561 N. Milwaukee Ave. © 773-772-4019 ⊙ M-F 8am-midnight, Sat-Sun 10am-midnight

Predominantly vegetarian and vegan soups, stews and sandwiches (except for a ham, turkey and tuna option) in this combination coffee house/video store. Take note, this neighborhood place is very smoker-friendly.

· vegetarian friendly · vegan friendly · tables · wait staff

🛏 **From I-90/94**, take exit 48B west on North Ave (right from 90E, left from 90W) about ½ mile to N Honore St. Turn left onto Honore 2 blocks to N Milwaukee Ave. Turn right onto Milwaukee about 1 block to restaurant (before intersection with N Damen & W North Ave).

HEARTLAND CAFE ✗

7000 N. Glenwood Ave. © 773-465-8005 ⊙ M-Th 7am-10pm, F 7am-11pm, Sat 8am-11 pm, Sun 8am-10pm, Adjacent bar open until wee am

Come to eat, stay for the entertainment. For starters, it's mostly vegetarian (some fish, poultry, buffalo), whole grain, healthy fare. Beyond the menu, there's live music, poetry nights, political events, a radio show, performance space, the General Store, an athletic organization, the Red Line Tap bar, and more.

· vegetarian friendly · vegan friendly · alcohol · tables · wait staff

🛏 **From downtown Chicago**, take Rt 41 north, which becomes Sheridan Rd just past Rt 14. Continue 4-5 intersections to Greenleaf Ave. Turn left onto Greenleaf (or onto Estes for parking) to Glenwood Ave. Turn left onto Glenwood to restaurant complex.

KARYN'S FRESH CORNER ✕
1901 N. Halsted St. © 773-255-1590 ⊙ Daily 9-9
A "Living Foods" restaurant.
• vegan • organic focus • tables • self-service • take-out

🍴 **From I-90/94**, take exit 48B east on North Ave (right from 90W, left from 90E) almost 1 mile to Halsted St. Turn left onto Halsted to restaurant on east side.

SHERWYN'S 🍃
645 W. Diversey Pkwy. © 773-477-1934 ⊙ M-F 9-8, Sat 9-7, Sun 11-7
• organic produce

🍴 **From I-90/94**, take California St exit (46, avoid express lanes to exit). Go east on Diversey Ave (becomes Diversey Pkwy) 2²/₃ miles to store at intersection Diversey, Clark & Broadway on SW corner.

SOUL VEGETARIAN EAST ✕
203 E. 75th St. © 773-224-0104 ⊙ M-Th 8-10, F-Sat 8-11, Sun 8-9
Healthy, vegan, southern-style soul food. Soups, sandwiches, fresh vegetables, hot entrees, soy shakes, desserts. Homemade vegan soy cheese and "ice-kream."
• vegan • chain • tables • wait staff

🍴 **From I-94E**, take exit 60A toward 75th St onto S Lafayette St. Turn left onto E 75th about ¹/₃ mile (4 blocks) to restaurant at S Indiana Ave. **From I-90/94W**, take exit 60 B toward 76th St onto S State St. Turn right onto E 75th about ¼ mile (3 blocks) to restaurant at S Indiana Ave.

UDUPI PALACE RESTAURANT ✕
2543 W. Devon Ave. © 773-338-2152 ⊙ Daily 11:30-9
Indian vegetarian with daily lunch buffet.
• vegetarian • vegan friendly • tables • self-service • wait staff

🍴 **From I-94E**, take exit 39B east on Trouhy Ave to IL 50 (N Cicero). Turn right onto 50S about 1 mile to W Devon Ave. Turn left onto Devon about 2¾ miles to restaurant. **From I-90W**, take exit 47A (FullertonAve/2400N) north on Western Ave about 4¾ miles to W Devon. Turn left onto Devon about 4 blocks to restaurant.

WHOLE FOODS MARKET ✕🍃   ♿
30 W. Huron St. © 312-932-9600 ⊙ Daily 8-10
In the downtown Chicago Loop, near the major hotels and museums. Food delivery to hotels (and homes) is available.
• organic produce • freshly prepared food • juice bar • salad bar • deli • bakery
• vegetarian friendly • chain • tables • self-service • take-out

🍴 **From I-90/94**, take exit 50B east on Ohio St about ½ mile to Dearborn St. Turn left onto Dearborn past Huron St and turn right into store garage (parking is free).

WHOLE FOODS MARKET ✕🍃   ♿
3300 N. Ashland Ave. © 773-244-4200 ⊙ Daily 8-10
• organic produce • freshly prepared food • juice bar • salad bar • café • deli • bakery
• vegetarian friendly• chain • counter • tables • self-service • take-out

🍴 **From I-90/94**, take exit 45C east on Belmont Ave about 4 miles. Turn left (north) onto Ashland Ave 1 block to store on west side. **From Lake Shore Dr**, take Belmont Ave exit west on Belmont about 2 miles to Ashland. Turn right (north) onto Ashland Ave 1 block to store on west side.

WHOLE FOODS MARKET ✗ 🥗 &

1000 W. North Ave. © 312-587-0648 ☺ Daily 8-10

· organic produce · freshly prepared food · juice bar · salad bar · café · deli · bakery
· vegetarian friendly · chain · tables · self-service · take-out

From I 90/94, take exit 48B east on North Ave about ½ mile to Sheffield Ave. Turn left (north) onto Sheffield and left into store parking lot.

CRYSTAL LAKE

CRYSTAL LAKE HEALTH FOODS 🥗

25 E. Crystal Lake Ave. © 815-459-7942 ☺ M-W, F 9-6, Th 9-7, Sat 9-5

Enter Crystal Lake via Rt 176 from Rt 14 or 31. Store is in old downtown between Walkup & Main St.

DE KALB

DUCK SOUP CO-OP 🥗

129 E. Hillcrest Drive © 815-756-7044 ☺ M-F 9-8, Sat-Sun 9-5

· co-op

From I-88E (EW Tollway), take IL 23/Ann Glidden Rd/DeKalb exit onto S Annie Glidden Rd about 1⅔ miles to SR 38 (E Lincoln Hwy). Turn right onto Lincoln about 1¼ miles to IL 23. Turn left onto 23 (aka S 4th St) about 1 mile to Hillcrest Dr. Turn left onto Hillcrest to store on right. **From I-88W,** turn right onto Peace Rd about 1¾ miles to E Lincoln Hwy. Turn left onto Lincoln 1½ miles to N 4th. Turn right onto N 4th about 1 mile to Hillcrest. Turn left onto Hillcrest to store on right.

DEERFIELD

WHOLE FOODS MARKET ✗ 🥗

760 Waukegan Rd. © 847-444-1900 ☺ Daily 8-10

· organic produce · freshly prepared food · juice bar · salad bar · café · deli · bakery
· vegetarian friendly · chain · counter · tables · self-service · take-out

From I-94, take Deerfield Rd east (left from 94E, right from 94W) about 1½ miles to Waukegan Rd. Turn right onto Waukegan to store on corner Waukegan & Deerfied Rd. **From US 41,** take Lake Cook Rd west less than 2 miles to Waukegan. Turn right onto Waukegan about 1 mile to store on corner Waukegan & Deerfield.

DUNDEE TOWNSHIP

GOLDEN HARVEST HEALTH FOODS 🥗

202 Springhill Rd. © 847-551-3551 ☺ M-F 10-7, Sat 10-5

· organic produce

From I-90, take Rt 31N exit about 3 miles to Huntley Rd. Store is on corner 31 & Huntley on back side of Huntley Square Bldg.

EDWARDSVILLE

GREEN EARTH GROCERY ✗ 🥗 &

441 S. Buchanan © 618-656-3375 ☺ M-F 9-7, Sat 9-5, Sun 12-5, Deli M-F 11-5, Sat 11-4

Vegetarian soups, sandwiches and salad (except for tuna). Yeast- and gluten-free breads available.

· organic produce · freshly prepared food · juice bar · café · deli · vegetarian friendly
· counter · tables · wait staff · take-out

🚘 **From I-55 or I-70**, merge onto I-270. **From I-270**, take exit 12 toward Edwardsville north on Hwy 159 about 3½ miles to center of town. Once road becomes S Buchanan St store is 3 blocks north in Market Basket Shopping Ctr.

EVANSTON

BLIND FAITH CAFE ✗
525 Dempster St. © 847-328-6875 ◷ M-Th 9-9, F 9-10, Sat 8-10, Sun 8-9
A diverse, creative wholefoods vegetarian and vegan menu for breakfast, lunch and dinner. Self-serve counter for quick meals, table service for leisurely dining.
· café · bakery · vegetarian · vegan friendly · organic focus · alcohol · tables · self-service · wait staff · take-out

🚘 **From Chicago**, take Sheridan Ave north to Dempster St. Turn west onto Dempster 2½ blocks to restaurant on right. **From I-94**, take exit 37 east on IL 58 (becomes Dempster) about 4 miles to restaurant on left just past Chicago Ave. **From I-294N**, take Dempster St exit east to restaurant. **From I-294S**, take Golf Rd exit and make 2 lefts onto Golf. Take Golf to Waukegan Ave. Turn right onto Waukegan to Dempster. Turn left onto Dempster and continue into Evanston to restaurant on left just past Chicago Ave.

JD MILLS FOOD COMPANY INC. 🍴
635 Chicago Ave. © 847-491-0940 ◷ M-F 8-8, Sat 9-6:30, Sun 10-6
🚘 **From Chicago**, take Lake Shore Dr north to Evanston, continuing onto Ridge Ave (which becomes N Clark St, then Chicago Ave) to store on right.

PEOPLE'S MARKET ✗🍴
1111 Chicago Ave. © 847-475-9492 ◷ Daily 8-10
· organic produce · freshly prepared food · café · deli · bakery · vegetarian friendly · chain · tables · self-service · take-out

🚘 **From I-90/94**, take exit 37 east on US 58/Dempster St about 4¼ miles to Chicago Ave. Turn right onto Chicago 2 blocks to store.

WHOLE FOODS MARKET ✗🍴   ♿
1640 Chicago Ave. © 847-733-1600 ◷ Daily 8-9 fall/winter, 8-10 spring/summer
Conveniently located near Northwestern U.
· organic produce · freshly prepared food · juice bar · salad bar · café · deli · bakery · vegetarian friendly · chain · tables · self-service · take-out

🚘 **From US 41 or 1-94 (exit 37)**, go east on IL-58/Dempster St about 4 miles to Chicago Ave. Turn left (north) onto Chicago 5 blocks to store on corner Church St & Chicago. **From Sheridan Rd**, go south on Chicago 2 blocks to store at Church.

GENEVA

SOUP TO NUTS 🍴   ♿
716 W. State St. © 630-232-6646 ◷ M-F 9-7, Sat 9-6, Sun 11-5
In-house massage therapist for road-weary travelers.

🚘 **From 1-88**, take exit 4 toward Aurora/Batavia north on IL 31 about 7 miles to IL 38 (State St). Turn left (west) onto 38 about ½ mile to store on SW corner in Engstrom Plaza.

Please tell these businesses that you found them in Healthy Highways.

HIGHLAND

HIGHLAND NUTRITION

320 Walnut St. ✆ 618-654-9017 ⏲ M-F 9-7, Sat 9-5, Sun 12-4

- organic produce

From I-70E, take exit 24 toward Highland east on Rt 143 over 4 miles to Walnut St (where 143 & US 40 intersect). Turn right onto Walnut 1½ blocks to store. **From I-70W**, take exit 30 toward Highland west on US 40 about 4 miles to Walnut. Turn left onto Walnut 1½ blocks to store.

HINSDALE

Miranda at Wild Oats notes that the Brookfield Zoo ("a wonderful summertime attraction") has "all natural concessions."

WILD OATS MARKET

500 E. Ogden Ave. ✆ 630-986-8500 ⏲ M-F 7-10, Sat 7-9, Sun 7-8

- organic produce · freshly prepared food · juice bar · salad bar · café · deli · bakery · vegetarian friendly · chain · counter · tables · self-service · take-out

From I-88 (EW Tollway), merge onto I-294. **From I-294**, take Ogden Ave exit west. Make first left onto County Line Rd (pay attention, it comes up right away). Turn left into store lot (sign is visible from interstate).

MATTESON

SOUTH SUBURBAN FOOD CO-OP

21750 Main St. ✆ 708-747-2256 ⏲ M, Tues, F 11-2, Th 2-8

Although this is a members-only co-op, co-op members from other areas are welcome and travelers are given a one-time shopping allowance.

- co-op

From I-57, take Lincoln Hwy/US 30E exit (340 from 57N, 340A from 57S) east on Lincoln about 2¼ miles until Main St comes in on right. Turn right onto Main about 1 mile to store on right in Stawicki Industrial Park.

MORRIS

BODY & SOUL

216 Liberty St. ✆ 815-941-2611 ⏲ M-F 9:30-5:30, Sat 9:30-2

From I-80, take exit 112 onto Rt 47 south about 2¼ miles to 6th traffic light (Main St). Turn right onto Main 2 blocks to Liberty St. Turn left onto Liberty to store on right.

MOUNT PROSPECT

SWEETGRASS VITAMIN & HEALTH MARKET

1742 W. Golf Rd. ✆ 847-956-1939 ⏲ M-F 9-9, Sat 9-6, Sun 10-5:30

From I-90 (NW Tollway), take N Elmhurst Rd exit north about 2 miles to W Golf Rd. Turn left onto Golf 1 mile to store on NW corner Golf & S Busse Rd.

MT. VERNON

NATURE'S WAY FOOD CENTER

102 S. 4th St. ✆ 618-244-2327 ⏲ M-F 9:30-5, Sat 9:30-1

From I-57, take exit 95 onto Hwy 15E (Broadway St) about 3 miles to 4th St. Turn left onto 4th St to store on right.

NEW LENOX

NATURAL CHOICES HEALTH FOOD STORE 🍎
1340 N. Cedar Rd. © 815-485-5572 ⊙ M-F 10-6, Sat 10-2

🍎 **From I-80**, take exit 137 right onto Rt 30E/Maple Rd 1¼-1½ miles to N Cedar Rd. Turn left onto Cedar about 1 mile to store on right.

NORMAL

COFFEEHOUSE & DELI ✕   ዼ
114 E. Beaufort St. © 309-452-6774 ⊙ M-Sat 7-10, Sun 8-9
Vegetarian coffeehouse fare of soups, salads, sandwiches, and daily specials.
· vegetarian · tables · self-service · take-out

🍎 **From I-55 north of Normal**, take exit 165A toward Bloomington/ Normal onto US 51Bus S about 1¾ miles to W College Ave. Turn left onto College about ½ mile to Broadway St. Turn right onto Broadway, left onto W North St and left onto E Beaufort St to restaurant. **From I-39S or I-74E**, merge onto 1-55N and follow directions above. **From I-74W**, take exit 135 toward Bloomington left onto US 51Bus N about 4½ miles to E Beaufort. Turn right onto Beaufort about ¾ mile to restaurant.

PALATINE

WHOLE FOODS MARKET ✕🍎   ዼ
1331 N. Rand Rd. © 847-776-8080 ⊙ M-Sat 8-10, Sun 8-9
· organic produce · freshly prepared food · juice bar · salad bar · café · deli · bakery
· vegetarian friendly · chain · tables · self-service · take-out

🍎 **From I-90** (NW Tollway) **or I-290N**, take IL 53N about 6 miles to Rand Rd. Turn left onto Rand about 1 mile to store on right in Park Place Shopping Center. **From I-94 or I-294**, take Lake Cook Rd west about 5½ miles to S Arlington Rd. Turn left onto S Arlington 1 mile to W Dundee Rd. Turn right onto Dundee almost 2 miles to Rand. Make sharp left onto Rand to store on left in Park Place Shopping Center.

PEORIA

NATURALLY YOURS GROCERY ✕🍎
4700 N. University St. © 309-692-4448 ⊙ M-Sat 9-9
· freshly prepared food · deli · vegetarian friendly · tables · self-service · take-out

🍎 **From I-74**, take ext 89 onto US 150E/N War Memorial Dr 1 mile to N University St. Turn left onto University less than 1 mile to store on right in Metro Shopping Center.

RIVER FOREST

Nearby historic sites include Frank Lloyd Wright's studio, the Ernest Hemingway Museum and Pleasant Home.

WHOLE FOODS MARKET ✕🍎   ዼ
7245 W. Lake St. © 708-366-1045 ⊙ M-Sat 8-10, Sun 8-9
· organic produce · freshly prepared food · juice bar · salad bar · café · deli · bakery
· vegetarian friendly · chain · tables · self-service · take-out

🍎 **From I-290**, take 21B north on N Harlem Ave (left from 290E, right from 290W) 1 mile to Lake St. Turn left onto Lake to store on SW corner Lake & N Harlem.

SPRINGFIELD

FOOD FANTASIES 🌿
1512 W. Wabash Ave. © 217-793-8009 ⊘ M-F 9-8, Sat 9-6, Sun 12-4

⛉ **From I-72E**, take exit 93 toward Springfield left onto IL 4N (S Veteran's Pkwy) 1²/₃ miles to Wabash Ave. Turn right onto Wabash 1½ miles to store on right. **From I-72W**, take exit 92A onto I-55Bus N almost 2 miles to E Stanford Ave. Turn left onto Stanford 1 mile to end at North St. Turn left onto North, right onto MacArthur Blvd, sharp left onto Urban St and continue straight on Wasbash ½ mile to store on left just past Fillmore St. **From I-55N**, merge onto I-72W and follow directions above. **From I-55S**, take exit 96B west on S Grand Ave about 3 miles to MacArthur. Turn left onto MacArthur about 1½ miles to Urban/Wabash intersection. Follow right onto Wabash ½ mile to store on left just past Fillmore.

URBANA

The University of IL/Urbana-Champaign is the focus of the community, with a "stunning array of activities" throughout the year.

RED HERRING ✕
1209 W. Oregon S. © 217-367-2340 ⊘ M-F 11-3, F 5:30-8 Mid August-Mid May (Closed for school vacations)
All vegan, with two daily soups, sandwiches, a hot entree, and fresh baked items. Serving the U of IL community and located just 1 block from the "quad."
· vegan · organic focus · co-op · tables · self-service

⛉ **From I-74**, take exit 183 south on N Lincoln Ave (right from 74E, left from 74W) about 2 miles to W Oregon St. Turn left onto Oregon ¼ mile to restaurant at SE corner Oregon & Matthews Ave in basement of Channing Murray Foundation (Universalist Church).

STRAWBERRY FIELDS NATURAL FOOD STORE & CAFE ✕🌿 ♿
306 W. Springfield Ave. © 217-328-1655 ⊘ M-Sat 7-8, Sun 10-6
Deli and cafe offer a varied selection of vegetarian and vegan foods.
· organic produce · freshly prepared food · café · deli · bakery · vegetarian friendly
· vegan friendly · tables · self-service · take-out

⛉ **From I-74**, take exit 184 toward Cunningham Ave onto US 45S/N Cunningham Ave (right from 74E, left from 74W) over 1 mile to traffic light at US 150/University Ave. Continue straight on N Vine ¼ mile to next light at E Main St. Turn right onto E Main ¼ mile (past 2 lights) to Race St. Bear left at fork onto Springfield Ave 1 block to store on right.

WESTMONT

SHREE ✕   ♿
655 N. Cass Ave. © 630-655-1021 ⊘ Tues-F Buffet 11:30-2:30, Dinner, 5:30-9:30, Sat 12:30-3, 5:30-10:30, Sun 12-3:30, 5:30-9:30
South and North Indian vegetarian cuisine with several vegan choices.
· vegetarian · vegan friendly · tables · wait staff · take-out

⛉ **From I-55**, take exit 273B onto Rt 15N/Cass Ave almost 6 miles (just past Rt 34/Ogden Ave) to restaurant on right in Cass & Ogden Plaza.

WHEATON

WHOLE FOODS MARKET ✕🌿   ♿
151 Rice Lake Square (Butterfield Rd.) © 630-588-1500 ⊘ M-Sat 8-10, Sun 8-9

· organic produce · freshly prepared food · juice bar · salad bar · café · deli · bakery
· vegetarian friendly · chain · tables · self-service· take-out

From **I-88** (EW Tollway), take Naperville Rd north about 1½ miles to Butterfield Rd. Turn right onto Butterfield to 2nd entrance to Rice Lake Shopping Center on left. Store is next to Borders.

WILLOWBROOK

WHOLE FOODS MARKET
201 W. 63rd St. © 630-655-5000 ⊙ Daily 8-10

· organic produce · freshly prepared food · salad bar · café · deli · bakery · vegetarian
friendly · chain · tables · self-service · take-out

From **I-55**, take exit 274 onto Kingery Hwy/Rt 83N about 3 miles to W 63rd St. Turn left onto 63rd 1 block to store on left.

INDIANA

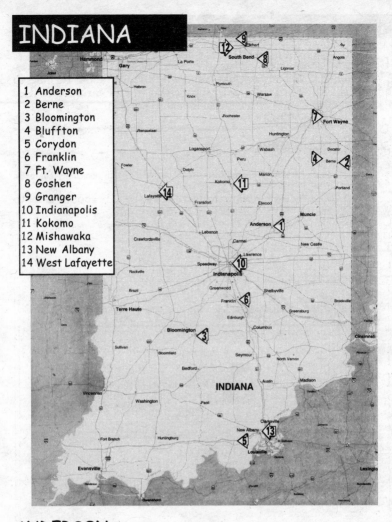

1 Anderson
2 Berne
3 Bloomington
4 Bluffton
5 Corydon
6 Franklin
7 Ft. Wayne
8 Goshen
9 Granger
10 Indianapolis
11 Kokomo
12 Mishawaka
13 New Albany
14 West Lafayette

ANDERSON

FRIST HEALTH FOOD CENTER, INC. 🍎
1203 E. 53rd St. ✆ 765-642-8992 ⊙ M-W 9-6, Th 9-7, F 9-5, Sun 1-5

🍎 From I-69, take exit 26 onto IN 9N about ½ mile to E 53rd St. Turn left onto 53rd about ⅓ mile to store on left.

BERNE

A Swiss community with a large Amish population. The "furniture capital."

EARTHEN TREASURES NATURAL FOOD MARKET ✗🍎   &
906 N. Hwy. 27 ✆ 260-589-3675 ⊙ M-Th 9-6, F 9-7, Sat 9-3

· freshly prepared food · café · deli · bakery · vegetarian friendly · tables · wait staff · take-out

🍎 Berne is about 30 miles east of I-69 exit 73 on IN 218. **From 218 in Berne**, turn north at traffic light at US 27 (left from 218E, right from 218W) about ½ mile to store on west side at Pharr Rd light.

BLOOMINGTON

BLOOMINGFOODS ✄ ☕

3220 E. Third St. ✆ 812-336-5400 ☻ Daily 8-10

· organic produce · freshly prepared food · deli · vegetarian friendly · co-op · tables
· self-service · take-out

🍎 **From Hwy 37**, take 46 Bypass east almost 4 miles to 3rd St. Turn left onto 3rd about ¼ mile to store on right.

BLOOMINGFOODS ✄ ☕

419 E. Kirkwood Ave. ✆ 812-336-5300 ☻ Daily 9-8

· organic produce · freshly prepared food · deli · vegetarian friendly · co-op · tables
· self-service · take-out

🍎 **From Hwy 37**, take 46 Bypass east about 1 mile to College Ave. Turn right onto College about 1⅓ miles to Kirkwood Ave. Turn left onto Kirkwood to store down alley on left.

LAUGHING PLANET CAFE ✄   ♿

322 E. Kirkwood Ave. ✆ 812-323-2233 ☻ Daily 11-9

"California Burritos & other Whole Foods 'in a hurry'." Ample choices for vegetarians and vegans. For fresh juice, head downstairs to the Soma Juice Bar.

· vegetarian friendly · vegan friendly · organic focus · counter · self-service · take-out

🍎 **From Hwy 37**, take 46 Bypass east about 1 mile to College Ave. Turn right onto College about 1⅓ miles to Kirkwood Ave. Turn left onto Kirkwood to restaurant.

BLUFFTON

A HARVEST OF HEALTH ☕

915 N. Main St. ✆ 260-824-1600 ☻ M-F 9-5:30, Sat 9-3

🍎 **From I-69S**, take exit 86 toward Huntington/Markle left onto US 224E (Markle Rd) about ⅓ mile to IN 116. Turn right onto 116 about 12 miles to IN 1 (aka Main St). Turn right onto Main 1 mile to store on left (east side) in Villa North Centre strip mall. **From I-69N**, take exit 78 toward Huntington/Warren. Turn left onto IN 5N/Warren Rd about 1½ miles to IN 124. Turn right (east) onto 124 about 12½ miles to W Lancaster St. Continue straight on Lancaster about 1 mile to N Bond St. Turn right onto Bond and left onto W Wabash St about ⅔ mile to IN 1/N Main St. Turn left onto Main to store on right in Villa North Centre strip mall.

CORYDON

The first capitol of Indiana, with many historical Civil War era sites. Also a state park and 3 caves within 30 minutes of town.

HARMONY & HEALTH ☕

220 E. Chestnut St. ✆ 812-738-5433 ☻ M-F 9-6, Sat 9-3

Owner remarks that "promoting natural health in rural Indiana is challenging." Self-described as "not a superstore." Organic produce seasonally, plus dairy, snacks, some natural grocery items, and chilled juices.

🍎 **From I-64**, take exit 105 toward Corydon onto 135S about 2 miles (past several traffic lights) to Hwy 62. Turn left onto 62E (Chestnut St in town). About 2 blocks into town look left for store with green awning.

FRANKLIN

FRANKLIN CORNUCOPIA
333 E. Jefferson St. © 317-736-8300 ⊙ M-F 9-7, Sat 9-5, Sun 12-5

From I-65, take exit 90 toward Franklin onto IN 44W about 1½ miles to 4-way stop sign at Forsyth St. Turn left onto Forsyth to next stop sign (Jefferson St). Turn right onto Jefferson 5-6 blocks to store on left (after railroad tracks).

FT. WAYNE

HEALTH FOOD SHOPPE
3515 N. Anthony Blvd. © 260-483-5211 ⊙ M-Sat 9-7
 · organic produce · freshly prepared food · salad bar · deli · take-out

From I-69N, take exit 111A onto US 27S about ¾ mile to Colesium Blvd. Turn left onto Colesium almost 2 miles to N Anthony Blvd. Turn right onto N Anthony about ½ mile to store. From I-69S, take exit 112A-B onto Coldwater Rd/IN 327S about 1²/₃ miles to Colesium. Turn left onto Colesium about 1 mile to N Anthony. Turn right onto N Anthony about ½ mile to store.

THREE RIVERS CO-OP NATURAL FOOD & DELI
1612 Sherman Blvd. © 219-424-8812 ⊙ M-Sat 8-8, Sun 10-6
 · organic produce · freshly prepared food · juice bar · salad bar · café · deli · vegetarian friendly · co-op · tables · self-service · take-out

From I-69, take exit 105A toward Ft Wayne east on Illinois Rd (right from 69N, left from 69S) about 2½ miles to W Main St. Veer left onto Main ½ mile to Leesburg Rd. Turn left onto Leesburg about ¾ mile to Spring St. Turn right onto Spring about 1 mile to store on corner Spring & Sherman Blvd.

GOSHEN

MAPLE CITY MARKET
314 S. Main St. © 574-534-2355 ⊙ M-W, F 9-6:30, Th 9-7:30, Sat 8-5:30
 · organic produce · freshly prepared food · deli · bakery · co-op · take-out

From I-80/90 (Indiana EW Toll Rd), take exit 101 left onto Rt 15 south about 11½ miles to store at Rt 33 & 15 intersection.

GRANGER

KOA campground up the road and Notre Dame campus nearby.

DOWN TO EARTH
14678 S.R. 23 © 574-271-1497 ⊙ M-Th 8-8, F 8-7, Sat 9-5, Sun 12-5
Fresh baked organic muffins and organic coffee bar.
 · organic produce · freshly prepared food · juice bar · vegetarian friendly · counter · tables · wait staff · take-out

From I-80/90 (Indiana EW Toll Rd), take exit 83 and follow north onto Capitol Ave (around to left from 80/90E, merge straight then right from 80/90W) to store just off hwy on SR 23.

INDIANAPOLIS

GEORGETOWN NATURAL FOODS MARKET
4375 Georgetown Rd. © 317-293-9525 ⊙ M-Sat 9-8, Sun 11-5
Many homemade vegetarian and vegan entrees with an organic focus. Eat in or pick up a meal en route to nearby Indy 500 Speedway.

· organic produce · freshly prepared food · juice bar · salad bar · deli · vegetarian friendly · organic focus · counter · tables · self-service · take-out

🚌 **From I-65**, take exit 121 south on Lafayette Rd (right from 65S, left from 65N) ½-1 mile to Georgetown Rd. Turn left onto Georgetown to store on 1st block on left. **From I-465**, take exit 17 toward Indianapolis east on 38th St about 1½ miles to Lafayette. Turn left onto Lafayette about 1 mile to Georgetown. Turn right onto Georgetown to store on 1st block on right.

GOOD EARTH NATURAL FOOD CO. 🛍️

6350 N. Guilford Ave. © 317-253-3709 ⊙ M-Sat 9-7, Sun 12-5
Located along the canal in a 100-year-old house in rustic Broad Ripple Village, with "artsy businesses," sidewalk cafes and two parks nearby.

· organic produce

🍎 **From I-465E/US 421S** (north of Indianapolis), take exit 31 onto US 31S/N Meridian St (right from 465E, left from 465/US 421S) about 3½ miles to 71st St. Turn left onto 71st about ½ mile to College Ave. Turn right onto College to 64th St. Turn left onto 64th 3 blocks to Guilford Ave. Turn right onto Guilford ½ block to store on right. **From I-65S**, merge onto I-465E and follow directions above. **From I-65N**, take exit 111 and follow Market St W ramp onto E Market St to College. Turn right onto N College 7 miles to Broad Ripple Ave. Turn right onto Broad Ripple 2 blocks to Guilford. Turn left onto Guilford to store on left.

THREE SISTERS CAFE 🍴

6360 Guilford Ave. © 317-257-5556 ⊙ Tues-Sat 8-9:30, Sun 8-4
L&JB: Laid-back restaurant in a Victorian house. Eat one of their great salads on the outside porch in summer. (Note: Smoking permitted on the porch.)

· vegetarian friendly · alcohol · tables · wait staff

🍎 **From I-465E/US 421S** (north of Indianapolis), take exit 31 onto US 31S/N Meridian St (right from 465E, left from 465/US 421S) about 3½ miles to 71st St. Turn left onto 71st about ½ mile to College Ave. Turn right onto College to 64th St. Turn left onto 64th 3 blocks to Guilford Ave. Turn right onto Guilford ½ block to restaurant on right. **From I-65S**, merge onto I-465E and follow directions above. **From I-65N**, take exit 111 and follow Market St W ramp onto E Market St to College. Turn right onto N College 7 miles to Broad Ripple Ave. Turn right onto Broad Ripple 2 blocks to Guilford. Turn left onto Guilford to restaurant.

UDUPI CAFE 🍴

4225 Lafayette Rd. © 317-299-2127 ⊙ Lunch Tues-Sun 11:30-3, Dinner Tues-Th, Sun 5:30-9, F-Sat 5:30-10
Vegetarian Indian cuisine, with buffet option at lunch.

· vegetarian · vegan friendly · alcohol · tables · self-service · wait staff · take-out

🚌 **From I-65S**, take exit 121 right onto Lafayette Rd less than 1 mile to Office Plaza Blvd (Value City sign on left). Turn left onto Office Plaza to restaurant at far end of shopping center on left (at International Bazaar). **From I-65N**, take exit 119 (38th St W) and merge left onto W 38th more than 1½ miles to Lafayette Rd. Turn right onto Lafayette about ¾ mile to Office Plaza Blvd (Value City sign on right). Turn right onto Office Plaza to restaurant. **From I-70E**, merge onto I-65N and follow directions above. **From south on I-465W**, take exit 17 right onto 38th St 1¾ miles to Georgetown Rd. Turn left onto Georgetown ⅓ mile to Lafayette. Turn left onto Lafayette about ¼ mile to Office Plaza. Turn right onto Office Plaza to restaurant. **From I-70E**, merge onto I-465N and follow directions above from 465W.

VINTAGE WHOLE FOODS 🛒
7391 N. Shadeland Ave. ℭ 317-842-1032 ⊘ M, W, F-Sat 9-7, Tues, Th 9-8
· organic produce

📇 From north of Indianapolis on I-69S or from I-465 exit 37, take Rt 37S about ¾ mile to 75th St. Turn left onto 75th about ⅔ mile to Shadeland Ave. Turn right onto Shadeland to store in Shadeland Station Shopping Center. **From I-465E** (from south of Indianapolis), take exit 40 (56th St) toward Shadeland Ave and follow I-465N/Shadeland Ave ramp, then Shadeland Ave ramp onto Shadeland. Merge onto N Shadeland Ave about 1¾ miles to store in Shadeland Station Shopping Center.

WILD OATS MARKET 🍴🛒   ♿
1300 E. 86th St. ℭ 317-706-0900 ⊘ M-Sat 8-9, Sun 9-8
· organic produce · freshly prepared food · juice bar · salad bar · café · deli · bakery
· vegetarian friendly · chain · tables · self-service · take-out

📇 From I-465E/US 421S (north of Indianapolis), take exit 31 onto US 31S/N Meridian St about 1 mile to 86th. Turn left onto 86th about 1 mile to store on left at Evergreen Ave in Nora Plaza. **From I-465W** (north of Indianapolis), take exit 33 left onto Keystone Ave N about ½ mile onto 86th St ramp toward Nora/Castleton. Turn right onto 86th about 1¼ miles to store on right at Evergreen in Nora Plaza. **From I-70E**, take exit 90 onto I-465N and follow directions above from I-465W. **From downtown Indianapolis or I-65** exit 113, take Meridian north to 86th. Turn right onto 86th and follow directions above.

KOKOMO──────────────────

SUNSPOT NATURAL FOODS 🛒
3717 S. Reed Rd. ℭ 765-453-5555 ⊘ M-Sat 9-8, Sun 11-6

📇 Kokomo is about 35 miles due north of Indianapolis on US 31. Store is on US 31(aka Reed Rd).

MISHAWAKA────────────────

GARDEN PATCH MARKET 🛒
228 W. Edison Rd. ℭ 574-255-3151 ⊘ M-Sat 10-7

📇 From I-80/90 (Indiana EW Toll Rd), take exit 83 toward Mishawaka onto Capitol Ave (left from 80/90E, right from 80/90W) to Rt 23. Turn left onto 23W about 2 miles to Main St (3rd traffic light). Turn left onto Main about 2 miles to Edison Rd. Turn right onto Edison to store on right (before Grape Rd).

NEW ALBANY────────────────

CREEKSIDE OUTPOST STORE & INTERTRIBAL CAFE 🍴🛒 ♿
614 Hausfeldt Lane ℭ 812-948-9118 ⊘ Tues-Sat 10-7
In addition to traditional "health foods," the store sells such game meats as buffalo, elk, wild boar, black bear, kangaroo, venison, and ostrich, as well as hormone-free domestic meat and fowl. One cafe menu features these meats. A second menu offers Native American and "Old West" inspired vegetarian fare, made "using separate cookware and utensils."

· organic produce · freshly prepared food · juice bar · café · vegetarian friendly · tables
· wait staff · take-out

🍽 Across the water from Louisville, KY. **From I-65**, take exit 6B onto I-265W 3½ miles to Grant Line Rd (exit 3). Turn right onto Grant Line, then left at 1st traffic light onto Hausfeldt Ln. Cross railroad tracks to restaurant in 1st driveway on left. **From I-64**, take exit 121 onto I-265E 3 miles to Grant Line (exit 3). Turn left onto Grant Line to 2nd light (Hausfefldt). Turn left onto Hausfeldt across railroad tracks to restaurant.

RICHMOND

CLEAR CREEK FOOD CO-OP ✗🛍
701 National Rd. W., Earlham College © 765-983-1547 ⊙ M-F 11-6, Sat-Sun 12-5 (may vary with school calendar, so call to check)
On the campus of Earlham College and linked to school calendar. Deli operates year-round, plus hot vegetarian lunches during the academic year, always with a vegan option. Call to see if the Sunday Pancake Breakfast is happening.

· organic produce · freshly prepared food · café · deli · vegetarian · vegan friendly · co-op · tables · self-service · take-out

🍽 **From I-70**, take exit 149A onto IN 38E almost 3 miles to National Rd W. Turn left onto National to College Ave. Turn left onto College and right onto D St to "T" intersection. Turn left at T then immediately right to store next to campus security office.

WEST LAFAYETTE

SAS HEALTH FOODS 🛍
951 Sagamore Pkwy. W. © 765-463-4827 ⊙ M-Sat 9:30-7
🍽 **From I-65**, take exit 175 toward Lafayette/Delphi onto IN 25S about 1½ miles to Sagamore Pkwy W (US 52). Turn right onto 52 about 3 miles to store on left in Osco Shopping Plaza.

Goldbeck's "EAT IT OR NOT"
FASCINATING & FAR-OUT FACTS ABOUT FOOD

POTATO CHIPS WERE INVENTED BY A NATIVE AMERICAN

An Adirondack Indian chef named George Crum invented the potato chip at a fancy resorted in upstate New York in 1853. As the story goes, Commodore Cornelius Vanderbilt, the railroad tycoon, returned his French fries to the kitchen complaining they weren't "properly thin." Angered by this insult, chef Crum shaved some potatoes paper thin and fried them up.

Today, if you laid the potato chips eaten in one year in the U.S. end to end, they would reach eight million miles long, enough to go around the earth 336 times

IOWA

1 Ames
2 Burlington
3 Cedar Falls
4 Coralville
5 Council Bluffs
6 Davenport
7 Decorah
8 Des Moines
9 Fairfield
10 Grinnell
11 Indianola
12 Iowa City
13 Waterloo

AMES

WHEATSFIELD GROCERY COOPERATIVE
413 Douglas Ave. ✆ 515-232-4094 ◷ M-Sat 9-9, Sun 12-6
· co-op

From junction I-35 & Hwy 30 (exit 111), take 30W about 2 miles to Duff Ave (exit 148). Turn north (right) onto Duff about 1½ miles (pass Lincoln Way and cross railroad tracks) to Main St. Turn left onto Main to 1st right (Douglas Ave). Turn right onto Douglas ½ block to store on left.

BURLINGTON

NATURE'S CORNER
423 Jefferson St. ✆ 319-754-8653 ◷ M-F 9:30-5:30, Sat 9:30-5

From US 34, take IA 99 exit toward Main St ((exit 263 from 34E, over bridge from 34W). Turn south onto Front St (right from 34E, left from 34W) 4 blocks to Jefferson St. Turn right onto Jefferson 4 blocks to store on SE corner N 5th St & Jefferson.

CEDAR FALLS

ROOTS MARKET   ♿
2021 Main St. ✆ 319-266-3801 ◷ M-Sat 10-6
Many locally made products, including produce, honey and Iowa beer and wine.
· organic produce

From Hwy 58, take 18th St exit west (left from 58N, right from 58S) 2 blocks to Main St. Turn left onto Main 3 blocks to store on corner Main & 21st St. From US 20, take exit 225 onto 58N about 4⅓ miles to 18th and follow directions above.

CORALVILLE

Popular tourist destinations in the area include The Herbert Hoover Museum in West Branch and the historic Amana villages.

NEW PIONEER CO-OP 🥬

1101 2nd St. ✆ 319-358-5513 ⊙ Daily 7-10, Deli 11-8, Hot entrees 11-7

Take-out deli offers soups, salads, sandwiches, hot entrees, all clearly labeled as vegetarian, vegan, seafood or meat (from "humanely raised" Niman Ranch meat). Bring it to College Green Park, 1 block east, for a picnic in the gazebo.

· organic produce · freshly prepared food · juice bar · salad bar · deli · bakery · vegetarian friendly · co-op · take-out

🚗 **From I-80E**, take exit 240 right onto Rt 965S about ¼ mile to Hwy 6. Turn left onto 6 almost 2 miles to store on left (after Appleby's) in City Center Square. **From I-80W**, take exit 242 left onto 1st Ave about 1½ miles to Hwy 6. Turn right onto 6, ¾ mile to store on left (after Hills Bank).

COUNCIL BLUFFS

GREEN ACRES NATURAL FOOD MARKET 🥬

113 W. Broadway ✆ 712-323-5799 ⊙ M-F 10-6, Sat 9-5

· organic produce

🚗 **From I-29S**, merge onto IA 192S toward Bus District/Council Bluffs about 2 miles to US 6. Turn left onto 6 (becomes W Broadway) about 1¼ miles to store. **From I-29N**, take exit 3 toward Bus District/Council Bluffs left onto 192N/S Expressway St 2 miles to W Broadway. Turn right onto Broadway about ½ mile to store. **From I-80W**, take exit 8 toward Community College/Council Bluffs right onto US6 (E Kanesville Blvd, becomes E then W Broadway) about 3¼ miles to store.

DAVENPORT

GREATEST GRAINS ✕🛒
1600 Harrison St. © 563-323-7521 ⊙ M-Sat 9-8, Sun 10-7
· organic produce · freshly prepared food · juice bar · café · deli · bakery · vegetarian friendly · tables · self-service · take-out

🍎 **From I-80**, take exit 295A onto Hwy 61S about 4½ miles to 16th St. Turn right onto 16th St to store on corner 61 (Harrison St) & 16th.

DECORAH

Numerous activities for outdoor types. If you're looking for something different, try the Vesterheim Norwegian American Museum or nearby Spillville & Postville, historic ethnic communities. There is also regular folk dancing in town.

ONEOTA COMMUNITY CO-OP ✕🛒   ♿
415 W. Water St. © 319-382-4666 ⊙ M-Th 9-8, F-Sat 9-6, Sun 12-5
The co-op is the hub of town where you can "find connections to anything you're looking for." Co-manager Liz warns: "Many visitors wind up moving to Decorah!"
· organic produce · freshly prepared food · café · deli · bakery · vegetarian friendly · co-op · chain · tables · self-service · take-out

🍎 **From US 52**, take IA 9E (right from 52N, left from 52S) to traffic light at Short St. Turn left onto Short 3 blocks and bear left onto Mechanic St. Go 2 lights to Water St and turn right to store in 2nd bldg on right. **From IA 9W**, turn right at stone "Decorah" sign onto Montgomery St to end. Turn left onto Water past 5 lights to store on left (before 6th light).

DES MOINES

NEW CITY MARKET 🛒
4721 University Ave. © 515-255-7380 ⊙ M, F 9-6:30, Tues, Th 9-8, Sat 9-6, Sun 11-5
· organic produce

🍎 **From I-235E**, take exit 4 left onto 63rd St about ½ mile to University Ave. Turn right onto University about 1 mile to store on left. **From I-35N or I-80E**, merge onto I-235E and follow directions above. **From I-235S**, take 42nd St exit north (right) about ½ mile to University. Turn left onto University about ⅓ mile to store on right. **From I-35S or I-80W**, merge onto I-235S and follow directions above.

FAIRFIELD

EVERYBODY'S MARKET ✕🛒
501 N. 2nd St. © 641-472-5199 ⊙ Daily 8:30-9:30
· freshly prepared food · café · vegetarian friendly · tables · wait staff · take-out

🍎 **From US 34**, turn north onto Rt 1/N 2nd St (right from 34W, left from 34E) about ⅓ mile to store at N 2nd & E Lowe Ave.

GRINNELL

JULI'S HEALTH & MORE FOOD STORE 🛒
931 West St. © 641-236-7376 ⊙ M-F 8-5:30, Sat 9-2
Describe themselves as the "only one-stop health food store in 60 miles."
· organic produce

🍎 **From I-80**, take exit 182 toward Grinnell onto IA 146N (left from 80E, right from 80W) almost 3½ miles to store on left 1 block past railroad tracks.

INDIANOLA

Come in August for the hot air balloon days.

HOMETOWN HEALTH FOODS 🍇

126 W. Ashland Ave. © 515-961-4874 ⊘ M-F 10-6, Sat 9-2

⛟ **From US 65/69** (aka Jefferson St) in Indianola, go west on Ashland Ave (right from 69S, left from 69N) 2 blocks to store on NW corner of square.

IOWA CITY

Jason at New Pioneer describes Iowa City as "a haven for social, intellectual and cultural progressivism."

MASALA INDIAN VEGETARIAN CUISINE ⚔

9 S. Dubuque St. © 319-338-6199 ⊘ Daily 11-10 (Buffet 11:30-2)
Indian vegetarian, with daily lunch buffet and evening specials emphasizing fresh local and organic produce from the farmers market.

· vegetarian · vegan friendly · alcohol · tables · self-service · wait staff · take-out

⛟ **From I-80,** take exit 244 toward Iowa City south on Dubuque St (right from 80E, left from 80W) about 2 miles to restaurant on right just past Iowa Ave.

NEW PIONEER CO-OP 🍇   ♿

22 S. Van Buren St. © 319-338-9441 ⊘ Daily 7-10
Take-out deli offers soups, salads, sandwiches, hot entrees, all clearly labeled as vegetarian, vegan, seafood or meat (from "humanely raised Niman Ranch" meat).

· organic produce · freshly prepared food · juice bar · salad bar · deli · bakery · vegetarian friendly · co-op · take-out

⛟ **From I-80,** take exit 244 toward Iowa City south on Dubuque St (right from 80E, left from 80W) about 2 miles to T-junction at Washington St. Turn left onto Washington 3 blocks to store on NE corner Washington & Van Buren St.

THE RED AVOCADO ⚔   ♿

521 E. Washington St. © 319-351-6088 ⊘ Tues-Sat 11-2:30, 5:30-9, Sun 12-9
Interesting selection of all-organic, vegetarian (and very vegan-friendly) dishes. Home-baked bread, homegrown specialty produce and many locally produced ingredients. No alcohol but BYOB (small corking charge).

· juice bar · café · bakery · vegetarian · vegan friendly · organic focus · tables · wait staff · take-out

⛟ **From I-80,** take exit 244 toward Iowa City south on Dubuque St (right from 80E, left from 80W) about 2 miles to T-junction at Washington St. Turn left onto Washington 3½ blocks to restaurant.

WATERLOO

GREEN FIELDS HEALTH FOOD CENTER 🍇

2920 Falls Ave. © 319-235-9990 ⊘ M-F 9:30-5:30. Sat 9:30-5

⛟ **From I-380N or I-20W,** merge onto US 218N/Washington St almost 4 miles to US 63S/Sargeant Rd. Turn left onto Sargeant and right onto University Ave about 1²/₃ miles to Falls Ave. Make sharp right onto Falls to store on left. **From I-20E,** take exit 227 right onto 63N about 2¹/₃ miles to Ansborough Ave. Turn left onto Anborough almost 1 mile to University. Turn left onto University ½ mile to Falls. Make sharp right onto Falls to store on left.

KANSAS

LAWRENCE

Lawrence boasts bike trails, hiking, nearby camping, museums, theater, and is home to the University of Kansas.

COMMUNITY MERCANTILE ✗🛒 &

901 Iowa St. ✆ 785-843-8544 🕐 Daily 7-10

· organic produce · freshly prepared food · salad bar · café · deli · bakery · vegetarian friendly · co-op · tables · self-service · take-out

🍎 **From I-70**, take exit 202 toward US 59S onto McDonald Dr about 1 mile to US 59S ramp. Merge onto 59S (aka Iowa St) about ¼ mile to store on corner Iowa & 9th St.

LENEXA

EMERALD FOREST HEALTH FOODS 🛒

12234 W. 95th St. ✆ 913-492-6336 🕐 M-Sat 10-8, Sun 12-4

· organic produce · juice bar · take-out

🍎 **From I-35**, take exit 224 east on 95th St (right from 35N, left from 35S) to 2nd traffic light. Turn left into Oak Park Commons Shopping Center to store (next to Applebee's Restaurant).

MANHATTAN

PEOPLE'S GROCERY CO-OP 🛒

517 S. 17th St. ✆ 785-539-4811 🕐 M-F 9-7, Sat 9-6

· organic produce · co-op

🍎 **From I-70**, take exit 313 onto US 177N about 8½ miles (across river) to Manhattan. Merge right off ramp onto 177S to KS 18/Ft Riley Blvd. Take

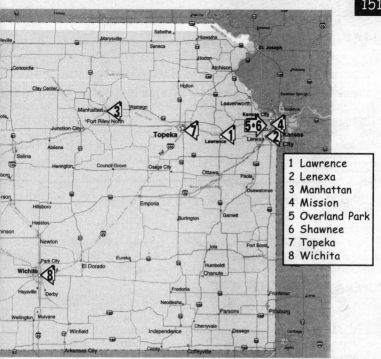

1 Lawrence
2 Lenexa
3 Manhattan
4 Mission
5 Overland Park
6 Shawnee
7 Topeka
8 Wichita

Ft Riley 1¼ miles to S 17th St. Turn right onto 17th 1 block to store at S 17th & Yuma St.

MISSION

WILD OATS MARKET ✗   ♿

5101 Johnson Dr. ✆ 913-722-4069 ⊙ Daily 8-10

· organic produce · freshly prepared food · juice bar · salad bar · café · deli · bakery · vegetarian friendly · chain · counter · tables · self-service · take-out

🥖 **From I-35,** take exit 229 left off ramp onto Johnson Dr heading east about 3 miles to store on corner Johnson & Roeland Dr.

OVERLAND PARK

WHOLE FOODS MARKET ✗   ♿

7401 W. 91st St. ✆ 913-652-9633 ⊙ Daily 9-9

· organic produce · freshly prepared food · salad bar · café · deli · bakery · vegetarian friendly · chain · tables · self-service · take-out

🥖 **From I-435,** take exit 79 north on Metcalf Ave (US 169N) about 2¼ miles to W 91st St. Turn left onto W 91st ¼ mile to store.

WILD OATS MARKET ✗   ♿

6621 W. 119th St. ✆ 913-663-2951 ⊙ Daily 7-10

· organic produce · freshly prepared food · juice bar · salad bar · café · deli · bakery · vegetarian friendly · chain · counter · tables · self-service · take-out

🥖 **From I-435,** take exit 77B south on Nall Ave (right from 435E, left from 435W) about 1¼ miles to 119th St. Turn left onto 119th to traffic light at Glenwood Ave. Turn left onto Glenwood to store in shopping center on SE corner.

SHAWNEE

THE FOOD BIN 🍎 &

12268 W. Shawnee Mission Pkwy. © 913-268-4103 ⊙ Daily 10-6

🜋 **From I-35**, take exit 228B west on Shawnee Mission Pkwy (left from 35N, right from 35S) about 1½ miles just past Quivira Rd intersection. Turn right into 10 Quivira Plaza to store at west end. **From I-435**, take exit 6A (Shawnee Mission Pkwy East) 1 mile, merging onto Shawnee Mission Pkwy about 2 miles to traffic light at Long Ave. Turn left onto Long ½ block. Turn right into 10 Quivira Plaza to store at west end.

TOPEKA

AKIN'S NATURAL FOODS MARKET 🛒 &

2913 S.W. 29th St. © 785-228-9131 ⊙ Daily 9-9

· organic produce · chain

🜋 **From I-470/Hwy 75**, take exit 4 north on Gage Bvd (right from 470W, left from 470E) less than ½ mile to 29th St. Turn right onto 29th more than ½ mile to store on right in Brookwood Shopping Center.

TOPEKA FOOD CO-OP, INC. 🍎

1195 S.W. Buchanan Ave. © 785-235-2309 ⊙ M-F 4-7, Sat 11-5, Sun 12-2

· organic produce · co-op

🜋 **From I-70**, take exit 362 west on 10th Ave about 1½ miles to Buchanan Ave. Turn left onto Buchanan 2 blocks to Buchanan Center. Store is in alley behind Buchanan Center.

WICHITA

FOOD FOR THOUGHT 🍎

2929 E. Central Ave. © 316-683-6078 ⊙ M-F 9-6, Sat 9-5:30

· organic produce · freshly prepared food · deli · bakery · vegetarian friendly · take-out

🜋 **From I-135**, take exit 7A east on Central Ave to store on right between Hillside St & Grove St.

GREEN ACRES ✕🍎

8141 E. 21st St. © 316-634-1088 ⊙ M-F 9-9, Sat 9-6, Sun 12-6

· organic produce · freshly prepared food · deli · bakery · vegetarian friendly · tables · self-service · take-out

🜋 **From I-135**, take exit 9 east on 21st St (right from 135N, left from 135S) about 4½ miles to store at Rock Rd in Bradley Fair Shopping Center.

NATURE'S MERCANTILE LTD. 🍎

2900 E. Central Ave. © 316-685-3888 ⊙ M-F 9:30-6, Sat 9:30-5:30

🜋 **From I-135S**, take exit 7A left onto Central Ave ¾ mile to store on corner Central & Erie St. **From I-135N**, take exit 6B right onto E 1st St N about ¼ mile to N Grove St. Turn left onto N Grove about ⅓ mile to Central. Turn right onto Central about ¼ mile to store on corner Central & Erie.

TANYA'S SOUP KITCHEN ✕ &

725 E. Douglas St. © 316-267-5349 ⊙ M-Sat 10-3:30, F-Sat 5:30-10

The daily lunch menu consists of homemade soups, sandwiches and salads, and there is always a vegetarian and vegan choice in each category. Weekend dinners are more upscale and less vegan-friendly.

· vegetarian friendly · alcohol · tables · wait staff · take-out

From I-135N, take exit 5B onto Hwy 54W about 1 mile to Washington Ave exit. Turn right onto Washington less than ½ mile to Douglas St. Turn left onto Douglas about 2 blocks to restaurant on left. From I-135S, take exit 7B (9th St) toward 8th St and follow exit to Murdock St. Turn right onto Murdock about ½ mile to Washington. Turn left onto Washington less than ½ mile to Douglas. Turn right onto Douglas about 2 blocks to restaurant on left.

TASTE OF HEALTH ✕ ⅙
3100 N. Hillside Ave. © 316-682-2100 ⊗ M-F 11am-1:30pm
The restaurant, which is open to the public, is part of the Center for the Improvement of Human Functioning, a holistic research and treatment center. All-you-can-eat buffet lunch emphasizes natural foods and homegrown organic produce in season. Not always a vegetarian entree, but enough soup, salad and side dishes for vegetarians to partake.

· vegetarian friendly · organic focus · tables · self-service

From I-135, take exit 10 from 135S, 10A from 135N onto KS 96 Expwy E 1-1½ miles to Hillside St. Turn right onto Hillside less than 1 mile to Center for Improvement of Human Functioning on left side (white stone entrance). Follow winding road to restaurant (inside the Center).

WHOLE FOODS ASSOCIATION ✎
6574 E. Central Ave. © 316-685-4285 ⊗ M-F 9-7, Sat 9-6, Sun 12-5

· organic produce

From I-35, take exit 50 onto US 400W/Kellog Ave 1½ miles to Woodlawn St. Turn right onto Woodlawn 1 mile to store on NE corner Central Ave & Woodlawn in Normandy Shopping Center. From I-135S, take exit 6A onto US 400E/Kellog Ave about 3¼ miles to Woodlawn. Turn left onto Woodlawn 1 mile to store on NE corner Woodlawn & Central in Normandy Shopping Center.

WHOLE FOODS ASSOCIATION ✎
2172 N. Amidon © 316-832-1227 ⊗ M-F 9-7, Sat 9-6, Sun 12-5

· organic produce

From I-235, take exit 11 onto W 25th St N (left from 235S, right from 235N) 1 mile to Amidon St. Turn right onto Amidon 4 blocks to store on SE corner Armidon & W 21st St N in Twin Lakes Shopping Center.

WHOLE FOODS ASSOCIATION ✎
10555 W. 21st St. N. © 316-729-4365 ⊗ M-F 9-7, Sat 9-6, Sun 12-5

· organic produce

From I-235, take exit 10 left (west) onto Zoo Blvd almost 1 mile until Zoo becomes W 21st St N. Continue on 21st 3 miles to store just past Maize Rd on south side.

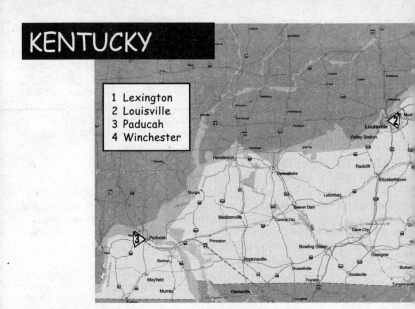

KENTUCKY

1 Lexington
2 Louisville
3 Paducah
4 Winchester

LEXINGTON

In a nation of odd attractions, the Lexington Ice and Recreation Center's Bible Theme Miniature Golf is right up there, with 18 Old Testament holes, 18 New Testament holes and 18 biblical miracle holes.

ALFALFA RESTAURANT ✕
557 S. Limestone Ave. ℂ 859-253-0014 ☺ Lunch M-F 11-2, Sat-Sun 10-2, Dinner Tues-Th 5:30-9, F-Sat 5:30-10
The menu changes seasonally, and the majority of the varied offerings are vegetarian, including the signature dish, "Hoppin' John" (black-eyed peas and brown rice). Homemade bread is whole wheat.
 · vegetarian friendly · alcohol · tables · wait staff

🛏 **From I-75N**, take exit 110 onto US 60W about 3½ miles to 60Bus (Midland Ave). Continue on Midland ½ mile to Main St. Turn right onto Main ½ mile to S Upper St. Turn left onto S Upper (becomes S Limestone Ave) less than 1 mile to restaurant. **From I-64**, take exit 113 toward Lexington onto US 68W about 3¼ miles to 60Bus E. Turn left onto 60 2 blocks to S Upper. Turn right onto S Upper (becomes S Limestone) less than 1 mile to restaurant. **From I-75S**, merge onto I-64S and follow directions above.

GOOD FOODS CO-OP ✕ 🍴
455-D Southland Drive ℂ 859-278-1813 ☺ M-Sat 9-9, Sun 11-9
 · organic produce · freshly prepared food · juice bar · café · deli · vegetarian friendly · co-op · tables · self-service · take-out

🛏 **From KY 4** (New Circle Rd) in Lexington, take exit 19 north on Nicholasville Rd about 1 mile to Southland Dr. Turn left onto Southland to store.

LOUISVILLE

AMAZING GRACE WHOLE FOODS & NUTRITION CTR ✕ 🍴 ♿
1133 Bardstown Rd. ℂ 502-485-1122 ☺ M-Sat 9-9, Sun 11-7
Store includes fresh sushi bar, video rental department, and seminar space for classes in nutrition, yoga, tai chi, and meditation.
 · organic produce · freshly prepared food · deli · bakery · vegetarian friendly · tables · self-service · take-out

 **From I-64**, take exit 8 west on Grinstead Dr (left from 64W, right from 64E) about 1½ miles to Bardstown Rd. Turn left onto Bardstown ½ block to store on left.

APPLE ANNIE'S 🌿
6515 Dixie Highway ℂ 502-995-4200 ⊘ M-F 9-6, Sat 10-5
From I-264, take exit 8A toward Ft Knox. Merge onto Dixie Hwy heading south (left from 264W, right from 264E) about 2¼ miles to store.

HEALTH & HARVEST NATURAL FOOD MARKET ✕🌿 ♿
3030 Bardstown Road ℂ 502-451-6772 ⊘ M-Sat 9-9, Sun 11-7, Cafe M-Sat 9-5
Fresh prepared dishes reflect a somewhat South American/Latin flair.
· organic produce · freshly prepared food · juice bar · café · deli · vegetarian friendly
· tables · self-service · take-out
From I-264, take exit 16 onto Bardstown Rd North (right from 264W, left from 264E) to store about 1½ blocks from hwy.

RAINBOW BLOSSOM ✕🌿 ♿
12401 Shelbyville Rd. ℂ 502-244-2022 ⊘ M-Sat 9-9, Sun 12-6
· organic produce · freshly prepared food · juice bar · deli · bakery · vegetarian friendly
· chain · tables · self-service · take-out
From I-264, take exit 20A east on US 60/Shelbyville Rd about 5⅓ miles (into Middletown) to store across from Government Ctr & library. **From I-265**, take exit 27 west on Shelbyville (left from 265N, right from 265S) about 1⅓ miles to store across from Government Ctr & library. **From I-64**, take 19B onto I-265N about 1 mile to exit 27 and follow directions above.

RAINBOW BLOSSOM BAKERY & CAFE ✕
311 Wallace Ave. ℂ 502-897-3648 ⊘ Daily 7am-9pm
Organic whole grain baked goods from flour ground on premises. Serving breakfast, soups and sandwiches.
· freshly prepared food · bakery · vegetarian friendly · organic focus · chain · counter
· tables · self-service · take-out
From I-264, take exit 20B (US 60/Shelbyville Rd) toward St Matthew's. Go west on Shelbyville 2 miles to split. Take left fork (Lexington Rd) to 1st left onto Wallace Ave to store.

RAINBOW BLOSSOM NATURAL FOODS ♿
3608 Springhurst Blvd. © 502-339-5090 ⊙ M-Sat 9-10, Sun 11-7
· organic produce · freshly prepared food · juice bar · deli · vegetarian friendly · chain · take-out

🚙 **From I-71**, take exit 9A onto I-265S. **From I-64**, take exit 19B onto I-265N. **From I-265**, take exit 32 right onto Westport/KY 1447W to first right (Towne Center Dr). Turn right onto Towne Center about ½ mile to Springhurst Blvd. Turn left onto Springhurst to store.

RAINBOW BLOSSOM NATURAL FOODS MARKET 🍴🐑
3738 Lexington Rd. © 502-896-0189 ⊙ M-Sat 9-10, Sun 11-7
· organic produce · freshly prepared food · juice bar · salad bar · café · deli · bakery · vegetarian friendly · chain · counter · tables · self-service · take-out

🚙 **From I-264**, take exit 20B (US 60/Shelbyville Rd) toward St Matthew's. Go west on Shelbyville Rd 2 miles to split. Take left fork (Lexington Rd) 2 blocks to store on left.

WILD OATS MARKET 🍴🐑   ♿
4600 Shelbyville Rd. © 502-721-7373 ⊙ Daily 7-10
· organic produce · freshly prepared food · juice bar · salad bar · café · deli · bakery · vegetarian friendly · chain · tables · self-service · take-out

🚙 **From I-264**, take exit 20B (US 60/Shelbyville Rd) toward St Matthew's west on Shelbyville Rd about ½ mile to store in Shelbyville Plaza (behind post office, next to Mall of St Matthews).

ZEN GARDEN 🍴   ♿
2240 Frankfort Ave. © 502-895-9114 ⊙ M-Th 11-10, F-Sat 11-11
An amalgam of vegetarian Asian cuisines.
· vegetarian · vegan friendly · tables · wait staff

🚙 **From I-64**, take exit 8 east on Grinstead Dr (left from 64E, right from 64W) about ¼ mile to S Peterson Ave. Turn left onto Peterson about ⅓ mile to Frankfort Ave. Turn left onto Frankfort ⅓ mile to restaurant.

PADUCAH

GOLDEN CARROT NATURAL FOODS 🐑
433 Jefferson St. © 270-760-0999 ⊙ M-Sat 9-5:30

🚙 **From I-24**, take exit 16 toward Paducah onto 24BL/60BR (right from 24W, left from 24E) almost 9 miles to Jefferson St. Turn left onto Jefferson 2 blocks to store on corner Jefferson & 5th St.

WINCHESTER

Ten minutes from Boonesboro State Park (swimming, camping, hiking). The last healthy shopping place on the way to Red River Gorge, where you'll find numerous hiking and rock-climbing venues, as well as over 80 natural rock bridges located inside Daniel Boone National Forest.

FULL CIRCLE MARKET-HEALTH FOODS 🐑   ♿
260 Redwing Drive © 859-744-3008 ⊙ M-F 10-7, Sat 10-5
· organic produce

🚙 **From I-64**, take exit 94 toward Winchester onto Bypass Rd (right from 64E, left from 64W) about 1 mile to Redwing Dr (at Speedway). Turn right onto Redwing to store in Colby Ridge Plaza.

LOUISIANA

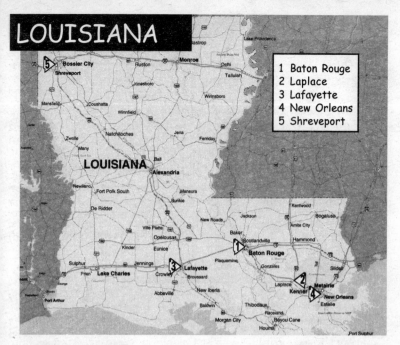

1	Baton Rouge
2	Laplace
3	Lafayette
4	New Orleans
5	Shreveport

BATON ROUGE

LIVING FOODS
3033 Perkins Rd. © 225-346-1886 ⊙ M-F 9-6:30, Sat 9-6, Sun 12-6
· organic produce · freshly prepared food · deli · vegetarian friendly · take-out
From I-10E, take exit 157A and follow ramp onto Perkins Rd to store just off hwy. **From I-10W,** take exit 157B left onto S Arcadian Thwy ¼ mile to Perkins. Turn right onto Perkins about ⅓ mile to store.

LIVING FOODS
8875-A Highland Rd. © 225-767-8222 ⊙ M-F 9-7, Sat 9-6, Sun 12-5
· organic produce
From I-10, take exit 162 south on Bluebonnet Dr (right from 10E, left from 10W) 3½ miles to Highland Rd. Turn right onto Highland about 1 mile to store in shopping center at Highland & Staring Ln.

OUR DAILY BREAD MARKET & BAKERY
9414 Florida Blvd. © 225-924-9910 ⊙ M-F 8-6, Sat 9-6, Sun 12-6, Cafe M-Sat 11-3
· organic produce · freshly prepared food · juice bar · café · deli · bakery · vegetarian friendly · tables · self-service · take-out
From I-12, take exit 2B onto US 61N (Airline Hwy) 2½ miles to Florida Blvd. Turn right onto Florida ¾ mile to store (2 blocks east of Cortana Mall).

LAPLACE

NATURALLY YOURS HEALTH FOODS
421 W. Airline Hwy. © 985-652-2975 ⊙ M-F 10-6, Sat 10-2
From I-10E, take exit 206 toward La Place onto Belle Terrace Blvd 2½ miles to W Airline Hwy (US 61) Turn left onto Airline Hwy about 1 mile to store at intersection with US 51 (in cluster of pink buildings). **From I-10W,** take exit 209 onto US 51S 3 miles to end at Airline Hwy (US 61). Turn right onto Airline Hwy to store (in cluster of pink buildings).

LAFAYETTE

OIL CENTER HEALTH FOODS ✗🍎
326 Travis St. ℂ 337-232-7774 ⊙ M-F 9-5:30, Sat 9-3

· freshly prepared food · deli · vegetarian friendly · tables · self-service · take-out

🍎 **From I-10**, take exit 103A onto US 167S (becomes 90 E) about 3½ miles to 90Bus. Turn right onto 90Bus (becomes Pinhook Rd) 1 mile (past 3 traffic lights) to Travis St. Turn right onto Travis 2 blocks to store on right. **From I-49S**, take exit 1 onto 167S and follow directions above.

NEW ORLEANS

All Natural Foods is near the Audubon Zoo and Park. Around Wholefoods Esplanade attractions include City Park, the nation's third largest urban park, and the New Orleans Fairgrounds, right behind the store, where seasonal events include horse racing (Nov-March), the Jazz & Heritage Festival (end of April-May) and more.

ALL NATURAL FOODS ✗🍎
5517 Magazine St. ℂ 504-891-2651 ⊙ M-Th 10-7, F-Sat 10-6, Sun 10-5

In addition to the mostly vegetarian deli sandwiches (tuna is the exception), daily soups and hot specials are vegan, with organic ingredients emphasized. Enjoy your meal in the lovely garden patio.

· organic produce · freshly prepared food · juice bar · café · deli · vegetarian friendly · vegan friendly · organic focus · tables · self-service · take-out

🍎 **From I-10**, take exit 232 south on Carrollton Ave to end. Turn left onto Leake Ave to Magazine St. Turn left onto Magazine (pass Audubon park & zoo) to store on left (2½ blocks past Nashville Ave). **From downtown French Quarter**, take Canal St to Magazine. Turn right onto Magazine about 3 miles to store on right (1½ blocks past traffic light at Jefferson Ave).

EVE'S MARKET 🍎   ♿
4601 Freret St. ℂ 504-891-4015 ⊙ M-Sat 9-6:30

Fresh food to go prepared by a local cafe/juice bar.

· organic produce · freshly prepared food · vegetarian friendly · take-out

🍎 **From I-10E**, take exit 234A and follow onto S Claiborne/90W about 2 miles to Napoleon Ave. Turn left onto Napoleon 5 blocks to Feret Ave. Turn right onto Feret 2 blocks to store on right corner Feret & Cadiz St. **From I-10W**, take exit 234C onto 90W and follow directions above.

OLD DOG NEW TRICK CAFE ✗
517 Frenchmen St. ℂ 504-943-6368 ⊙ Daily 11:30-10

In meat-heavy New Orleans, an almost entirely vegetarian and vegan restaurant (except for tuna). Soups, salads, sandwiches, burgers, pizza (organic whole wheat crust), all-day breakfast, and eclectic hot entrees predominate. All-vegan desserts.

· vegetarian · vegan friendly · tables · wait staff

🍎 Not too far from the French Quarter in the area known as Faubourg Marigny. **From I-10**, take exit 237 south on Elysian Fields Ave about 1 mile to Decatur St. Turn right onto Decatur and right onto Frenchman St to store between Decatur & Chartres St.

WHOLE FOODS MARKET ✗🍎   ♿
3135 Esplanade Ave. ℂ 504-943-1626 ⊙ Daily 8-9:30

In nice weather there are outside tables. Otherwise, it's strictly takeout.

· organic produce · freshly prepared food · salad bar · deli · bakery · vegetarian friendly · chain · counter · self-service · take-out

🛏 **From I-10W**, take exit 238B onto I-610W to exit 2B (90W) toward N Broad St. Follow exit south onto N Broad 1¼ miles to Esplanade Ave. Turn right onto Esplanade ½ mile to store on right. **From I-10E**, merge onto I-610E to exit 2A toward St Bernard Ave. Turn right off ramp and stay in right lane to 2nd right at Gentilly Blvd. Turn right onto Gentilly and follow curve to traffic light at Broad. Turn right onto Broad 1 light to Esplanade. Turn right onto Esplanade ½ mile to store on right.

WHOLE FOODS MARKET ✗🍴   ♿

5600 Magazine St. © 504-899-9119 ⊙ M-Sat 8-9, Sun 8-8
 · organic produce · freshly prepared food · salad bar · café · deli · bakery · vegetarian friendly · chain · counter · tables · self-service · take-out

🛏 **From I-10E**, take exit 232 onto S. Carrollton Ave more than 2 miles to St Charles Ave. Turn left onto St Charles about 1⅓ miles to Nashville Ave. Turn right onto Nashville about ½ mile to Magazine St. Turn left onto Magazine 2 blocks to store. **From I-10W**, take exit 234C toward Clairborne Ave onto 90W 2¼ miles to Jefferson Ave. Turn left onto Jefferson 1½ miles to Magazine. Turn right onto Magazine 2 blocks to store.

SHREVEPORT _____

Among the many things to do in Shreveport: The American Rose Center (lit around Christmas with millions of lights), the Huddie Ledbetter (LeadBelly) Statue, Watertown USA for summer fun, the "ultimate" paintball experience, the Fragrance Garden for the visually impaired at Barnwell Art Center, the "Once in a Millennium Moon" Mega Mural, plus plenty of nightlife and special monthly events.

EARTHEREAL RESTAURANT & BAKERY ✗   🍴♿

3309 Line Ave. © 318-865-8947 ⊙ M-F 9:30-3:30, Bakery 9:30-4
Predominantly vegetarian, except for tuna and chicken salads.
 · bakery · vegetarian friendly · tables · self-service · take-out

🛏 **From I-20**, take exit 17B and merge onto I-49S about 1 mile to exit 205. **From I-49**, take exit 205 east on Kings Hwy (left from 49S, right from 49N) about ½ mile to Line Ave. Turn right onto Line 1 block to restaurant at Line & Gladstone Ave.

GOOD LIFE HEALTH FOODS 🍴

6132 Hearne Ave. © 318-635-4753 ⊙ M-W, F 9-5, Th 9-7, Sat 10-5, Deli 11-3
 · organic produce · freshly prepared food · deli · vegetarian friendly · take-out

🛏 **From I-20**, take exit 16A onto LA 171S/Hearne Ave (left from 20W, right from 20E) about 2 miles to store on right (5 blocks past Hollywood Ave intersection) in small shopping complex.

SUNSHINE HEALTH FOODS ✗🍴   ♿

5751 Youree Dr. © 318-219-4080 ⊙ M-Sat 9-6
Cafe uses organic food when possible (and tells you when it's not), whole grain breads, nitrite-free deli meats, and offers two hot vegetarian entrees and home-made soups daily. Plus, fresh juices and dairy or vegan smoothies.
 · organic produce · freshly prepared food · juice bar · salad bar · café · deli · vegetarian friendly · organic focus · tables · wait staff · take-out

🛏 **From I-20W**, take exit 19A (Spring St) and follow LA 1S/Market St ramp. Take 1S (becomes Youree Dr) about 4½ miles to store on SE corner Youree & Southfield Rd. **From I-20W**, take exit 17B onto I-49S 3 miles to exit 203 (Pierremont Rd). **From I-49**, take exit 203 east on Pierremont (left from 49S, right from 49N) 2 miles (becomes Southfield Rd) to store on right just past Youree.

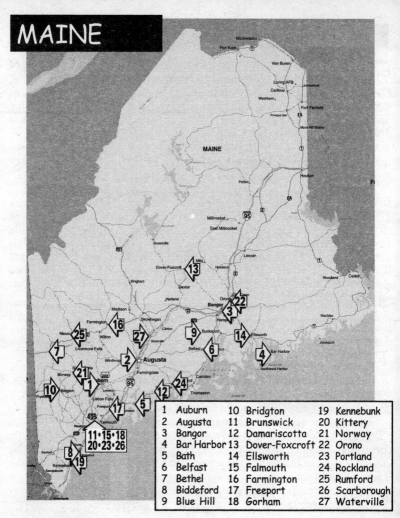

MAINE

MAINE

1	Auburn	10	Bridgton	19	Kennebunk
2	Augusta	11	Brunswick	20	Kittery
3	Bangor	12	Damariscotta	21	Norway
4	Bar Harbor	13	Dover-Foxcroft	22	Orono
5	Bath	14	Ellsworth	23	Portland
6	Belfast	15	Falmouth	24	Rockland
7	Bethel	16	Farmington	25	Rumford
8	Biddeford	17	Freeport	26	Scarborough
9	Blue Hill	18	Gorham	27	Waterville

AUBURN

AXIS NATURAL FOODS
250 Center St. © 207-782-3348 ⊙ M-F 9-8, Sat 9-6
· organic produce

From I-495 (ME Tpke), take exit 12 (Auburn/US 202) left off exit onto Washington St (Rt 202E). After about 5 miles 202 becomes Minot Ave, then Union St after traffic light at Court St. Continue on Union to Center St. Turn left onto Center about 2 miles to store in small strip mall on left (with Play it Again Sports and The Fishery).

AUGUSTA

HARVEST TIME NATURAL FOODS
110 Western Ave. © 207-623-8700 ⊙ M-Tues 9-6, W-F 9-8, Sat 9-5, Sun 10-4
· organic produce

From I-95, take 202E/Augusta exit (30 or 30A) onto Western Ave/202E about 1 mile to store on right in Capital Shopping Center (2nd strip mall).

BANGOR

NATURAL LIVING CENTER ✕🛒
670 Stillwater Ave. ℭ 207-990-2646 ☉ M-F 9-7, Sat-Sun 9-5
· freshly prepared food · deli · vegetarian friendly · tables · self-service · take-out
🍎 **From I-95**, take exit 49 (Hogan Rd) toward Bangor. Merge onto Hogan (ramp toward Bangor Mall Blvd) about ⅔ mile to Stillwater Ave. Turn left onto Stillwater about ½ mile to store behind Bangor Mall at cinema entrance.

BAR HARBOR

CAFE BLUEFISH ✕
122 Cottage St. ℭ 207-288-3696 ☉ Daily 5:30-8 or later
Although the fare is mostly seafood and fish, there is always Cajun Tempeh and Hungarian Mushroom Strudel on the menu for vegetarians.
· vegetarian friendly · alcohol · tables · wait staff
🍎 Take Rt 3 into Bar Harbor and turn left onto Cottage St to restaurant.

EDEN VEGETARIAN CAFE ✕
78 West St. ℭ 207-288-4422 ☉ April-Sept M-Sat 11-9:30, Winter 5-9
Enjoy the ocean view and the creative vegetarian and vegan dishes on the changing daily menu.
· vegetarian · vegan friendly · organic focus · alcohol · counter · tables · wait staff
🍎 Take Rt 3 into Bar Harbor and turn left onto West St (which runs along the coast) less than ½ mile to restaurant.

BATH

MORNING GLORY NATURAL FOODS 🛒
36 Centre St. ℭ 207-442-8012 ☉ M-F 9-6, Sat 9-5, Sun 12-4
· organic produce
🍎 **From I-95**, take exit 24 toward Topsham/Lisbon east on ME 196 2½ miles to US 1. Merge onto 1E toward Bath 7¼ miles to ME 209/High St exit toward Phippsburg. Turn left onto High and right onto Centre St ¼ mile to store.

BELFAST

BELFAST CO-OP ✕🛒
123 High St. ℭ 207-338-2532 ☉ Daily 7:30-8
· organic produce · freshly prepared food · café · deli · vegetarian friendly · co-op · tables · self-service · take-out
🍎 Belfast is over 40 miles east of Augusta. **From Rt 3** in Belfast, merge onto Main St to High St. Turn right onto High to store on left. **From Rt 1N**, take Northport St (becomes High) about 1 mile to store on right. **From 1S**, take ramp onto ME 137/Dowtown Belfast & Waterfront to High. Turn right onto High about ¾ mile to store on left.

BETHEL

Bethel is close to two ski resorts and numerous gem mines for "rock hounds."

CAFE DICOCOA'S MARKET/BAKERY ✕🛒   ♿
119 Main St. ℭ Store 207-824-6386 Restaurant 824-5282 ☉ Call (variable)
A family-owned business, including both a market and separate vegetarian restaurant serving globally-inspired fare with a strong Mediterranean influence.
· organic produce · freshly prepared food · juice bar · salad bar · café · deli · bakery · vegetarian · tables · self-service · wait staff · take-out

🛏 Bethel is about 50 miles NE of ME Tpke exit 11 on Rt 26 and ½ hour east of NH on Rt 2. Entering town **from west on 26**, continue straight past "Welcome" sign (26 becomes Main St). Restaurant is 7th business on left. Store is next door at corner Main & Vernon S (aka Rt 35). **From 2E**, pass "Welcome" sign and take exit for 26E. Turn right off exit and right at end of road onto Main to restaurant & store.

BIDDEFORD

NEW MORNING NATURAL FOODS ✗🛒

230 Main St. ℰ 207-282-1434 ⊘ M-Sat 9-5:30, Cafe M-F 11-2

· organic produce · freshly prepared food · café · vegetarian friendly · tables · self-service · take-out

🛏 **From I-95/195** (ME Tpke), take exit 4 (Biddeford) east on Rt 111 to "5 points" intersection. Turn left (north) onto Rt 1 to store at end of 2nd block.

BLUE HILL

Staff at the Co-op Market describe Blue Hill as "a beautiful coastal town."

BLUE HILL CO-OP COMMUNITY MARKET & CAFE ✗🛒 ♿

Green's Hill Place, Rte. 172 ℰ 207-374-2165 ⊘ M-F 8-7, Sat 8-6, Sun 10-5
Fresh local produce year-round.

· organic produce · freshly prepared food · juice bar · café · deli · bakery · vegetarian friendly · tables · self-service · take-out

🛏 Blue Hill is almost 40 miles SE of Bangor. **From Ellsworth**, take Rt 172 south about 12 miles to store on right as you come down hill into downtown.

BRIDGTON

Located in the lakes region of Maine. Ideal hiking, boating and swimming, and just ½ hour to the White Mountains of New Hampshire.

MORNING DEW NATURAL FOODS GROCERY & DELI ✗🛒 ♿

1721 Sandy Creek Rd. ℰ 207-647-4003 ⊘ M-F 9-6, Sat 9-5:30, Sun 10-5

· organic produce · freshly prepared food · café · deli · vegetarian friendly · tables · self-service · take-out

🛏 **From the only traffic light in Bridgton**, go south on Rt 302 1¼ miles to Rt 117. Turn right onto 117 to store on right (1st building).

BRUNSWICK

MORNING GLORY NATURAL FOODS 🛒

60 Main St. ℰ 207-729-0546 ⊘ M-F 9-7, Sat 9-6, Sun 11-5

· organic produce

🛏 **From I-95**, take exit 22 toward Brunswick/Bath onto US 1N just over 1 mile to Pleasant St. Stay straight onto Pleasant about ½ mile to Main St. Turn left onto Main to store.

DAMARISCOTTA

A water town, with ocean, lakes and rivers. The vibrant art community boasts a world class chamber string quartet and the Round Top Center for the Arts.

RISING TIDE COOPERATIVE MARKET ✗🛒 ♿

15 Coastal Marketplace ℰ 207-563-5556 ⊘ Daily 8-7
100% local produce.

· organic produce · freshly prepared food · café · deli · bakery · vegetarian friendly · co-op · tables · self-service · take-out

⬚ Between Bath and Rockland. **From US Rt 1**, take Rt 1Bus exit to Newcastle. Cross Damariscotta River into town and continue less than 1 mile to store on left in Coastal Marketplace.

DOVER-FOXCROFT

Off the Appalachian Trail, with Sebac and Moosehead Lakes, Borestone and Squaw Mountains, and Gulf Hagus nearby.

BOB'S FARM HOME & GARDEN 🐄
15 Lincoln St. © 207-564-2581 ⊙ M-F 8-5:30, Sat 8-5

· organic produce

⬚ **From Rt 7**, turn left at traffic light in town onto Main St 2 lights to Lincoln St. Make sharp right onto Lincoln to store.

ELLSWORTH

Southeast Maine, before crossing to Mt. Desert Island and Arcadia National Park.

JOHN EDWARD'S WHOLE FOODS MARKET 🍴🐄
158 Main St. © 207-667-9377 ⊙ M-Th, Sat 9-5:30, F 9-8, Sun 12-5

· bakery · tables · self-service · take-out

⬚ Ellsworth is about 25 miles southeast of Bangor via Rt 1A E. **From 1A**, turn right onto Main St (Rt 1) to store. **From Rt 3**, turn left onto Main to store. **From 1E**, stay straight onto Main to store.

FALMOUTH

O'NATURALS 🍴
240 Rte. 1 © 207-781-8889 ⊙ M-Th, Sun 10:30-8, F-Sat 10:30-9

A fast-food concept developed by the owners of Stonyfield Farms Yogurt, offering natural and organic soups, sandwiches, salads, and Asian noodle dishes. Meat, fish, poultry, and vegetarian choices, plus kids' menu and Sunday brunch items.

· vegetarian friendly · organic focus · alcohol · chain · tables · self-service · take-out

⬚ **From I-295N or I-95S**, take exit 10 east (toward US 1) onto Buckham Rd to Rt 1. Turn right (south) onto Rt 1 about ⅓ mile and turn right at Staples sign into Shops at Falmouth Village. Inside shopping center, turn left at 1st intersection and follow road left to restaurant facing Rt 1 (between Norway Savings & Pet Quarters).

FARMINGTON

BETTER LIVING 🐄
181 Front St. © 207-778-6018 ⊙ M-Th 7:30-6, F 7:30-3, Sun 12-4

· organic produce

⬚ Farmington is 34 miles east of I-95 exit 31 on ME 27N. **From ME 27 or 4**, turn onto Front St to store.

FREEPORT

ROYAL RIVER NATURAL FOODS 🍴🐄   ♿
443 US Route 1 © 207-865-0046 ⊙ M-F 8-8, Sat-Sun 9-7

· organic produce · freshly prepared food · café · vegetarian friendly · tables · self-service · take-out

⬚ **From I-95S**, take exit 19 right at light onto Rt 1S about 1½ miles to store on left. **From I-95N**, take exit 17 right onto Rt 1N to store on right 1½ miles north of the Big Wooden Indian.

GORHAM

THE NATURAL GROCER 🐑
104 Main St. © 207-839-6223 ⊘ M-F 8-7, Sat 9-6, Sun 11-4
Soup and sandwiches to go.
  · freshly prepared food · take-out
🍎 From I-95 (ME Tpke), take exit 8 west on Rt 25 through Westbrook (25 becomes New Gorham Rd, then New Portland Rd, then turns left onto Main St) about 6 miles to Gorham and store on right.

KENNEBUNK

NEW MORNING NATURAL FOODS 🐑
3 York St. © 207-985-6774 ⊘ M-Sat 9:30-6
  · organic produce · freshly prepared food · take-out
🍎 From I-95/195 (ME Tpke), take exit 3 (Kennebunk) and bear right at fork. Turn right (south) at traffic light onto Rt 1. Cross bridge to store on right.

KITTERY

While in Kittery you can visit "The Maine Outlets."

RISING TIDE NATURAL FOODS 🐑
165 State Rd. © 207-439-8898 ⊘ M-Sat 9-6, Sun 11-5
Vegan take-out.
  · organic produce · freshly prepared food · vegan · take-out
🍎 From I-95, take exit 2 (ME 236) toward Kittery onto 236S. At traffic circle take 1st right onto Rt 1S and next right onto State Rd. to store.

NORWAY

FARE SHARE MARKET (CO-OP) 🐑
443 Main St. © 207-743-9044 ⊘ M-F 9-6, Sat 10-4
  · freshly prepared food · deli · vegetarian friendly · co-op · take-out
🍎 Rt 117 is Main St in Norway. Store is just west of intersection with Rt 26S.

ORONO

THE STORE & AMPERSAND 🍴🐑
22 Mill St. © 207-866-4110 ⊘ M-Sat 7-7, Sun 9-4
  · café · bakery · vegetarian friendly · tables · take-out
🍎 From I-95, take exit 50 (Kelley Rd) toward Orono east on Kelley (right off ramp from 95N, left from 95S) about 1 mile to end at Rt 2. Turn left onto 2 about 1¼ miles to Mill St. Turn right onto Mill to store on left in center of town.

PORTLAND

O'NATURALS 🍴
83 Exchange St. © 207-321-2050 ⊘ M-Th, Sun 10:30-8, F-Sat 10:30-9
A fast-food concept developed by the owners of Stonyfield Farms Yogurt, offering natural and organic soups, sandwiches, salads, and Asian noodle dishes. Meat, fish, poultry, and vegetarian choices, plus kids' menu and Sunday brunch items.
  · vegetarian · organic focus· alcohol · chain · tables · self-service · take-out
🍎 From I-295, take exit 7 onto US 1A S/Franklin Arterial less than 1 mile to Congress St. Turn right onto Congress past 2nd intersection to Exchange St. Turn left onto Exchange less than 2 blocks to restaurant on left (before park).

THE WHOLE GROCER 🛒
127 Marginal Way ℂ 207-774-7711 ⊘ M-F 9-9, Sat 9-7, Sun 11-6
· organic produce · deli · vegetarian friendly · take-out

🍎 **From I-295**, take exit 7 (US 1A S/Franklin Arterial). Make 1st right off ramp onto Marginal Way 2 blocks to store on left.

WILD OATS MARKET ✗🛒 ♿
87 Marginal Way ℂ 207-699-2626 ⊘ Daily 7-10
· organic produce · freshly prepared food · juice bar · salad bar · café · deli · bakery
· vegetarian friendly · chain · tables · self-service · take-out

🍎 **From I-295**, take exit 7 (US 1A S/Franklin Arterial). Make 1st right off ramp onto Marginal Way about ¼ mile to store on left.

ROCKLAND

GOOD TERN CO-OP 🛒
216 S. Main St. ℂ 207-594-9286 ⊘ M-F 9-6, Sat 9-5
· co-op

🍎 Take Rt 1 into Rockland. At traffic light at ME 73/S Main St, turn right 2 blocks to store on right.

RUMFORD

RED HILL NATURAL FOODS 🛒
29 Hartford St. ℂ 207-369-9141 ⊘ M-W, F-Sat 9-6, Th 9-7

🍎 Enter Rumford from Rt 108, 2 or 17. **From 108**, take Canal St to store at Hartford St intersection.

SCARBOROUGH

LOIS' NATURAL MARKETPLACE ✗🛒 ♿
152 US Route 1 ℂ 207-885-0602 ⊘ M-Sat 8:30-7:30, Sun 10-6
· organic produce · freshly prepared food · café · deli · bakery · vegetarian friendly
· counter · tables · self-service · take-out

🍎 **From I-95N** (ME Tpke), take exit 6A (S Portland/Portland) onto I-295 (toward US 1/S Portland). **From I-295N or S**, take exit 2 (US 1/Scarborough) onto Scarborough Connector (becomes 1S) about 2 miles to store on left in Scarborough Marketplace.

WATERVILLE

NEW MOON RISING NATURAL FOODS 🛒
110 Pleasant St. ℂ 207-873-6244 ⊘ M-F 9-6, Sat 9-5, Sun 11-5

🍎 **From I-95**, take exit 34 (ME 104/Main St) toward Waterville. Turn south (right from 95N, left from 95S) onto Main about 1 mile to Pleasant St. Turn right onto Pleasant to store on right.

Goldbeck's "EAT IT OR NOT"
FASCINATING & FAR-OUT FACTS ABOUT FOOD

TRUE OR FALSE?
The most popular flavor in sweet baked goods is chocolate.

False It's vanilla (chocolate is # 3).

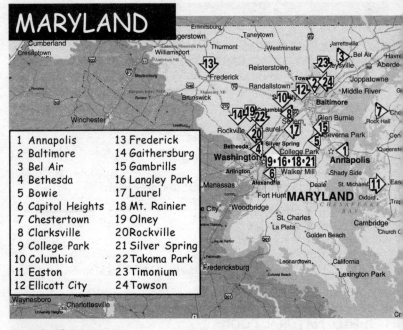

MARYLAND

1 Annapolis	13 Frederick
2 Baltimore	14 Gaithersburg
3 Bel Air	15 Gambrills
4 Bethesda	16 Langley Park
5 Bowie	17 Laurel
6 Capitol Heights	18 Mt. Rainier
7 Chestertown	19 Olney
8 Clarksville	20 Rockville
9 College Park	21 Silver Spring
10 Columbia	22 Takoma Park
11 Easton	23 Timonium
12 Ellicott City	24 Towson

ANNAPOLIS

The "Sailing Capitol of the World!" says Diana at Whole Foods.

SUN & EARTH FOODS

1933 West St. © 410-266-6862 ⊘ M-Sat 9:30-6:30, Sun 12-4
Fresh sandwiches available during the week.

From I-97, take exit 4 onto Rt 50E. From I-495/95, take exit 19A onto 50E. From 50E, take exit 23 and follow MD 450E ramp to West St. Turn left onto West almost 1 mile to store at West & Lee St. From 50W, take exit 23A toward MD 450 onto Solomon's Island Rd (MD 2S) to West. Turn left onto West ½ mile to store at West & Lee.

WHOLE FOODS MARKET ✗⬛   ♿

2504 Solomon's Island Rd. © 410-573-1800 ⊘ M-F 9-9, Sat 8-9, Sun 9-8

· organic produce · freshly prepared food · salad bar · café · deli · bakery · vegetarian friendly · chain · tables · self-service · take-out

From I-97, take exit 4 onto Rt 50E. From I-495/95, take exit 19A onto 50E. From 50 E, take exit 23 and follow 450E ramp to West St. Turn left onto West ¼ mile to Solomon's Island Rd. Turn right onto Solomon's Island about ½ mile to store on right in Harbor Center. From Rt 50 W, take exit 23A toward MD 450 onto Solomon's Island Rd (MD 2S) 1¼ miles (past 2 lights) to store on right in Harbor Center.

BALTIMORE

LIQUID EARTH ✗

1626 Aliceanna St. © 410-276-6606 ⊘ M-F 7-7, Sat 9-7, Sun 10-3
An "All Vegetarian" restaurant. To quote Liquid Earth owners, "A portabello grilled next to a steak is not vegetarian!"

· juice bar · café · vegetarian · vegan friendly · counter · tables · wait staff

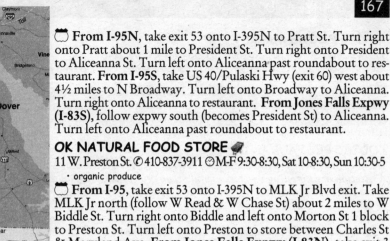

From **I-95N**, take exit 53 onto I-395N to Pratt St. Turn right onto Pratt about 1 mile to President St. Turn right onto President to Aliceanna St. Turn left onto Aliceanna past roundabout to restaurant. **From I-95S**, take US 40/Pulaski Hwy (exit 60) west about 4½ miles to N Broadway. Turn left onto Broadway to Aliceanna. Turn right onto Aliceanna to restaurant. **From Jones Falls Expwy (I-83S)**, follow expwy south (becomes President St) to Aliceanna. Turn left onto Aliceanna past roundabout to restaurant.

OK NATURAL FOOD STORE

11 W. Preston St. © 410-837-3911 ⊙ M-F 9:30-8:30, Sat 10-8:30, Sun 10:30-5

· organic produce

From **I-95**, take exit 53 onto I-395N to MLK Jr Blvd exit. Take MLK Jr north (follow W Read & W Chase St) about 2 miles to W Biddle St. Turn right onto Biddle and left onto Morton St 1 block to Preston St. Turn left onto Preston to store between Charles St & Maryland Ave. **From Jones Falls Expwy (I-83N)**, take exit 3 onto Fallsway (becomes Guilford St) to E Preston. Turn left onto Preston about ¼ mile to store. **From I-83S**, take exit 4 onto St Paul St to Preston. Turn right onto Preston 2 blocks to store.

ONE WORLD CAFE

100 W. University Blvd. © 410-235-5777 ⊙ M-Sat 8am-2am, Sun 8am-5pm
Some fish and eggs, but mostly vegetarian/vegan, with all-vegan baked goods.

· juice bar · café · vegetarian friendly · vegan friendly · counter · tables · wait staff · take-out

From **I-95**, take I-395N to Conway St. Turn right onto Conway to Light St (at harbor). Turn left onto Light and merge straight onto Calvert St to University Blvd. Turn left onto University 4 blocks to restaurant on right.

SUNSPLASH NATURAL FOODS FOR LESS

7006 Reisterstown Rd. © 410-486-0979 ⊙ M-F 9-8, Sat 9-7, Sun 10-5

From **I-695**, take exit 20 onto Reisterstown Rd/Rt 140S (left from 695W, right from 695E) about 2 miles to store on right.

THE YABBA POT

2433 St. Paul St. © 410-662-8638 ⊙ Tues-Sat 11:30-9
The menu changes daily, offering a selection of vegan plates, soups, sandwiches, wraps, patties, and more. Primarily carryout, but there are a few tables.

· vegan · tables · self-service · take-out

From **I-95**, take exit 53 onto I-395N to MLK Jr Blvd exit. Follow MLK Jr Blvd about 1¾ miles to N Howard St. Veer left onto N Howard over 1 mile to W 25th St. Turn right onto 25th 4 blocks (about ¼ mile) to St Paul St. Turn right onto St Paul to retaurant. **From Jones Falls Expwy (I-83)**, take exit 7 (7A from 83N) east on W 28th St (left from 83S, right from 83N) about ⅓ mile to Huntingdon Ave. Turn right onto Huntingdon (becomes W 25th) about ½ mile to St Paul. Turn right onto St Paul to restaurant.

WHOLE FOODS MARKET

1330 Smith Ave. © 410-532-6700 ⊙ M-Sat 8-9, Sun 8-8

· organic produce · freshly prepared food · salad bar · café · deli · bakery · vegetarian friendly · chain · tables · self-service · take-out

From **Jones Falls Expwy (I-83)**, take exit 10A onto Northern Pkwy East to 1st traffic light at Falls Rd. Turn left onto Falls to 3rd light at Smith Ave. Turn left onto Smith to store.

WHOLE FOODS MARKET ✕🥗   ♿

600 S. Exeter St. ✆ 410-528-1640 🕐 Daily 8-10, Cafe from 7

· organic produce · freshly prepared food · salad bar · café · deli · bakery · vegetarian friendly · chain · tables · self-service · take-out

🍎 In Baltimore's Inner Harbor district. **From I-95**, take I-395N to Conway St. Turn right onto Conway to Light St (at harbor). Turn left onto Light and merge to right onto Pratt St to President St. Turn right onto President, left onto Eastern Ave and right onto Exeter St to store.

ZODIAC RESTAURANT ✕   ♿

1724 N. Charles St ✆ 410-727-8815 🕐 W, Th 5-10, F 5-11, Sat-Sun 3-10

A selection of interesting vegetarian and vegan choices (all noted on the menu) in the company of fish, poultry and a sprinkling of meat. Conveniently located in the "Arts & Entertainment" district, across the street from an art house movie theater and one block from the repertory theater.

· vegetarian friendly · vegan friendly · alcohol · tables · wait staff · take-out

🍎 **From I-95**, take exit 53 onto I-395N to MLK Jr Blvd exit. Follow MLK Jr Blvd north about 1¾ miles to N Howard St. Veer left onto N Howard about ½ mile to US 1N (North Ave). Turn right onto North 1 block to Maryland Ave. Turn right onto Maryland 3 blocks to W Lanvale St. Turn left onto Lanvale 1 block to E Charles St. Turn left onto Charles ¾ block to restaurant on left (blue awning). **From Jones Falls Expwy (I-83)**, take exit 5 right onto Maryland 1 block to Lanvale St. Turn right onto Lanvale and left onto Charles ¾ block to restaurant on left.

BEL AIR_____

DAVIDS NATURAL MARKET 🥗

3 Red Pump Rd. ✆ 410-803-0784 🕐 M-F 8-8, Sat 9-7, Sun 10-5

· organic produce · juice bar · take-out

🍎 **From I-95**, take exit 77B toward Bel Air onto MD 24N 8¼ miles. Follow MD 24N ramp onto Rock Spring Rd/MD 24 to store on left at Red Pump Rd.

BETHESDA_____

WHOLE FOODS MARKET ✕🥗   ♿

5269 River Rd. ✆ 301-984-4860 🕐 M-Sat 8-9, Sun 8-8

· organic produce · freshly prepared food · salad bar · café · deli · vegetarian friendly · chain · tables · self-service · take-out

🍎 **From I-495** (Capitol Beltway), take exit 39 or 39B toward Washington onto River Rd (190E) about 4 miles to store on north side (190W).

BOWIE_____

HEALTHWAY NATURAL FOODS 🥗   ♿

6856 Race Track Rd ✆ 301- 805-8255 🕐 M-F 10-7, Sat 10-6, Sun 12-5

· organic produce · chain

🍎 **From I-495** (Capitol Beltway), take exit 19A onto US 50E about 7½ miles to exit 13A-B-C (US 301/MD 3). Merge onto MD 3N (toward Baltimore) about 2¾ miles to Annapolis Rd (MD 450). Turn left onto Annapolis a little over 1 mile to Race Track Rd. Turn right onto Race Track to store in Hilltop Plaza.

CAPITOL HEIGHTS

EVERLASTING LIFE ✕🍴
9185 Central Ave. ✆ 301-342-6900 ⊙ M-Sat 9-9, Sun 11-9
*Source of Life Juice Bar & Deli serves healthy, vegan, southern-style food from
the Soul Vegetarian chain.*

· organic produce · freshly prepared food · juice bar · vegan · co-op · self-service · take-out

🍎 **From I-495** (Capitol Beltway), take exit 15B west on Central Ave
(214W) to store in Hampton Mall.

CHESTERTOWN

Founded in 1706, this is a good place to see classic American architecture.

CHESTERTOWN NATURAL FOODS 🍴   ♿
214 Cannon St. ✆ 410-778-1677 ⊙ M-F 10-6, Sat 9-5, Sun 12-4

· organic produce

🍎 On the Delmarva Peninsula. Take MD Rt 213 to Chestertown. Turn
onto Cross St (right coming south, left going north) 2 blocks to Cannon St.
Turn left onto Cannon ½ block to store on the right set back about 100 feet.

COLLEGE PARK

BERWYN CAFE ✕
5010 Berwyn Rd. ✆ 301-345-9898 ⊙ Tues-Sat 11-9, Sun 10-3
*Organic vegetarian and vegan fare, featuring multigrain pancakes and tofu
breakfast choices, sandwiches on wholegrain breads, salads, Mexican and Mediterranean mostly vegan platters, fresh organic juices, vegan baked goods, and
more. Local art hangs on the walls and Wednesday night is open mike.*

· juice bar · café · bakery · vegetarian · vegan friendly · organic focus · counter
· tables · wait staff · take-out

🍎 **From I-495** (Capitol Beltway), take exit 25 (25B from 495N) toward
College Park/U MD onto Rt 1S about 1½ miles to Berwyn Rd. Turn left
onto Berwyn about 2½ blocks to restaurant on left.

MD FOOD COLLECTIVE ✕🍴   ✉♿
B-0203 Stamp Student Union, UMD ✆ 301-314-8089 ⊙ M 7:30-6, Tues-Th
7:30-9, F 7:30-7, Sat 11-5, Sun 12-3
*A student operated store and eatery on the University of Maryland campus,
serving a totally vegetarian menu.*

· organic produce · freshly prepared food · café · deli · vegetarian · vegan friendly
· co-op · tables · self-service · take-out

🍎 **From I-495** (Capitol Beltway), take exit 25 (25B from 495N) toward
College Park/U MD onto Rt 1S about 3 miles to UMD. Turn right onto
Campus Drive (main entrance of UMD campus). Continue straight through
circle up hill to Stamp Student Union on right. Store is in basement on
north side entrance.

MY ORGANIC MARKET (MOM'S) 🍴
9827 Rhode Island Ave. ✆ 301-220-1100 ⊙ M-F 10-9, Sat 9-8, Sun 10-7

· organic produce

🍎 **From I-495** (Capitol Beltway), take exit 25 (25B from 495N) toward
College Park/U MD onto Rt 1S about ½ mile to Edgewood Rd. Turn left
onto Edgewood about ⅓ mile to Rhode Island Ave. Turn right onto Rhode
Island about 1 block to store.

COLUMBIA

DAVID'S NATURAL MARKET ✕🐑

5430 Lynx Lane © 410-730-2304 ⊙ M-F 8-8, Sat 9-7, Sun 10-5, Cafe M-F 11:30-4
Vegan bakery, plus vegan and dairy-free specialty items on the cafe menu.

· organic produce · freshly prepared food · juice bar · café · deli · bakery · vegetarian friendly · vegan friendly · tables · self-service · take-out

🍎 **From I-95N**, take exit 38B onto Rt 32W about 3 miles to US 29N. Merge onto 29N 1½ miles to exit 18A-B and take ramp toward Columbia Town Center onto Broken Land Pkwy. Take Broken Land past 3 traffic lights to Twin Rivers Rd. Turn left onto Twin Rivers 3 lights to Lynx Ln. Turn left onto Lynx (between KFC and Crown Gas) to store in Wild Lake Shopping Ctr. **From I-95S**, take exit 41A-B toward Columbia onto 175W (merging onto Little Patuxent Pkwy) 5½ miles to right fork onto Governor Warfield Pkwy. Take Governor Warfield to 2nd light (Twin Rivers Rd). Turn right onto Twin Rivers ½ mile to Lynx Ln (2nd light). Turn left onto Lynx to store in Wild Lake Shopping Ctr. **From I-70**, take exit 87A onto US 29S 5 miles to Columbia Town Center ramp. Merge onto Little Patuxent Pkwy ½ mile to Governor Warfield Pkwy and follow directions above.

MANGO GROVE ✕

6365 Dobbin Road © 410-884-3426 ⊙ M 11:30-3, 5-9, W-Th 11:30-3, 5-9:30, F 11:30-3, 5-10, Sat 12-10, Sun 12-9
Vegetarian Indian, with a buffet available at lunchtime.

· vegetarian · vegan friendly · alcohol · tables · self-service · wait staff

🍴 **From I-95N**, take exit 41B toward Columbia onto MD 175W about 2-2¾ miles to Dobbin Rd. Turn left onto Dobbin to restaurant on left in Dobbin Center (behind Wendy's). **From I-70**, take exit 87A onto US 29S about 5½ miles to MD 175E. Merge onto 175E almost 3 miles to Dobbin. Turn right onto Dobbin to restaurant on left in Dobbin Center.

EASTON

RAILRAY MARKET ✕🐑

108 Marlboro Rd. © 410-822-4852 ⊙ M-F 9-7, Sat 9-6, Sun 11-6

· freshly prepared food · deli · bakery · vegetarian friendly · tables · self-service · take-out

🍎 On the Delmarva Peninsula. From Rt 50, take MD 322/Easton Bypass to traffic light at Marlboro Rd. Turn east (left going south, right heading north) onto Marlboro to store in Marlboro Shopping Center (2nd strip mall).

ELLICOTT CITY

SARAH AND DESMOND'S ✕

8198 Main St. © 410-465-9700 ⊙ Tues-Sat 9-6, Sun 9-5
All-day breakfast, open-faced pita sandwiches, and assorted other vegetarian sandwiches, salads and hot dishes.

· vegetarian · vegan friendly · tables · self-service

🍎 **From I-695**, take exit 13 toward Catonsville onto MD 144 (Frederick Rd). Turn west onto 144 (right from 695S, left from 695N) about 4¼ miles to restaurant. **From I-70**, take exit 87A toward Columbia onto US 29S 1½ miles to US 40E (Baltimore National Pike). Merge onto 40E 1 mile to Rogers Ave. Turn right onto Rogers about ½ mile to Court House Dr. Veer right onto Court House less than ¼ mile to Ellicott Mills Dr. Turn right onto Ellicott Mills ½ mile to Main St. Turn left onto Main to restaurant.

FREDERICK

COMMON MARKET CO-OP 🐑
5813 Buckeystown Pike ℰ 301-663-3416 ☺ M-Sat 9-9, Sun 11-7
· organic produce · freshly prepared food · deli · co-op · take-out

🍎 **From I-70**, take exit 54 onto Rt 85. Veer right to stay on 85 to traffic light at Guilford Dr. Turn left into Pointe Plaza Shopping Center to store.

GAITHERSBURG

WHOLE FOODS MARKET ⚔️🐑   ♿
316 Kentlands Blvd. ℰ 301-258-9500 ☺ M-Sat 8-9, Sun 8-8
· organic produce · freshly prepared food · salad bar · café · deli · bakery · vegetarian friendly · chain · tables · self-service · take-out

🍎 **From I-270**, take exit 9 onto Sam Eig Hwy west to 3rd traffic light. Bear right onto Great Seneca Hwy to 3rd light (Kentlands Blvd). Turn left onto Kentlands through traffic circle to store on left.

GAMBRILLS

DAVID'S NATURAL MARKET 🐑
871 Annapolis Rd. ℰ 410-987-1533 ☺ M-F 8-8, Sat 8-7, Sun 9-5
· organic produce · freshly prepared food · juice bar · deli · take-out

🍎 **From I-97**, take exit 12 toward MD 3Bus/Glen Burnie onto New Cut Rd 1¾ miles to Gambrills Rd. Veer left onto Gambrills about 2¾ miles to Annapolis Rd. Turn right onto Annapolis to store at Dairy Farm Rd.

LANGLEY PARK

WOODLANDS ⚔️
8046 New Hampshire Ave. ℰ 301-434-4202 ☺ M-Th, Sun 11:30-9:30, F-Sat 11:30-10 Buffet Daily 11:30-3
Vegetarian Indian, with a buffet lunch option daily.
· vegetarian friendly · vegan friendly · tables · self-service · wait staff

🍎 **From I-495** (Capitol Beltway), take exit 28B toward Tacoma Park right onto New Hampshire Ave (MD 650S) over 2 miles to restaurant at University Blvd.

LAUREL

LAUREL HEALTH FOOD ⚔️🐑
131 Bowie Rd. ℰ 301-498-7191 ☺ M-F 10-8, Sat 10-6
· organic produce · freshly prepared food · deli · vegetarian friendly · tables · self-service · take-out

🍎 **From I-95**, take exit 33 (Gorman Ave/Rt 198) east just past Rt 1 to store near intersection 198 & Bowie Rd (look for Office Depot).

MT. RAINIER

GLUT FOOD CO-OP 🐑
4005 34th St. ℰ 301-779-1978 ☺ M, Sat, Sun 10-7, Tues, Th 10-8,
· co-op

🍎 **From I-495** (Capitol Beltway), take exit 25 onto Rt 1S to Mt Ranier. Turn right onto 34th St to store on right. **From Washington, DC**, take Rhode Island Ave (1N) to Mt Ranier and turn left onto 34th to store on right.

OLNEY

OLNEY ALE HOUSE ✕
2000 Olney Sandy Spring Rd. © 301-774-6708 ⊙ Tues-Th, Sun 11:30-10, F-Sat 11-10:30
*Not vegetarian, but more than the usual number of meatless choices, including a
veggie BLT, a tofu sandwich (on homemade molasses-sweetened bread) and wraps.*
· vegetarian friendly · alcohol· tables · wait staff
🍎 **From I-95**, take exit 33B toward Burtonville onto MD 198W (right
from 95S, loop around right from 95N) about 6¼ miles to New Hampshire
Ave. Turn right onto New Hampshire about 2½ miles to Olney Sandy
Spring Rd. Turn left onto Olney Sandy Spring about 1¾ miles to restaurant.

ROCKVILLE

MY ORGANIC MARKET (MOM'S) 🥬
11711 Parklawn Drive © 301-816-4944 ⊙ M-F 10-9, Sat 9-8:30, Sun 11-7
· organic produce
🍎 **From I-495**(Capitol Beltway), take exit 34 north on Rockville Pike
(Rt 355N) 2 miles to Nicholson Ln. Turn right onto Nicholson (becomes
Parklawn Dr) ½ mile to store on right.

THE VEGETABLE GARDEN ✕
11618 Rockville Pike © 301-468-9301 ⊙ Daily 11:30-10
*Vegan- and macrobiotic-friendly. No dairy, eggs or refined sugar, and much of the
food is organically grown.*
· vegetarian · vegan friendly · organic focus · tables · wait staff · take-out
🍎 **From I-495** (Capitol Beltway), take exit 34 north on Rockville Pike
(Rt 355N) about 2½ miles (past White Flint Mall on right). Restaurant is
on left across from White Flint metro stop.

WHOLE FOODS MARKET ✕🥬   ♿
1649 Rockville Pike © 301-984-4880 ⊙ M-Sat 8-10, Sun 8-8
· organic produce · freshly prepared food · salad bar · café · deli · bakery · vegetarian
friendly · chain · tables · self-service · take-out
🍎 **From I-495** (Capitol Beltway), take exit 34 north on Rockville Pike
(Rt 355N) about 3²/₃ miles to store on left in Congressional Plaza.

YUAN FU VEGETARIAN ✕
798 Rockville Pike © 301-762-5937 ⊙ M-Th, Sun 11-10, F-Sat 11-10:30
Vegetarian Chinese. Brown rice available.
· vegetarian · vegan friendly · tables · wait staff · take-out
🍎 **From I-495** (Capitol Beltway), take exit 34 north on Rockville Pike (Rt
355N) about 4¾ miles to restaurant on right in strip mall (next to Wendy's).

SILVER SPRING

TAKOMA PARK SILVER SPRINGS CO-OP 🥬
8309 Grubb Rd. © 240-247-2667 ⊙ Daily 8-9
· organic produce · co-op
🍎 **From I-495E**, take exit 31B and merge onto Georgia Ave ½ mile to
16th St. Turn right onto 16th 1 mile to East-West Hwy (MD 410). Turn
right onto 410 to traffic light at Grubb Rd. Turn left onto Grubb a few
blocks to store on left in Rock Creek Shopping Ctr. **From I-495W**, take
exit 31 (MD 97/Georgia Ave) toward Silver Spring. Stay left at fork off
ramp, turn left onto Georgia and follow directions above.

WHOLE FOODS MARKET ✗🍴 &

833 Wayne Ave. ℂ 301-608-9373 ⊙ M-Sat 8-10, Sun 8-9

· organic produce · freshly prepared food · juice bar · salad bar · café · deli · bakery · vegetarian friendly · chain · counter · tables · self-service · take-out

🍎 From I-495 (Capitol Beltway), take exit 30B onto Colesville Rd (US 29S) about 1 mile to Spring St. Turn left onto Spring 3 blocks to Pershing Dr. Turn right onto Pershing into store lot (Silver Spring Shopping Ctr).

TAKOMA PARK

TAKOMA PARK SILVER SPRINGS CO-OP 🍴

201 Ethan Allen Ave. ℂ 301-891-2667 ⊙ Daily 9-9

· organic produce · co-op

🍎 From I-495 (Capitol Beltway), take exit 28B toward Takoma Park south on New Hampshire Ave (MD 650S) about 3½ miles to East-West Hwy (MD 410). Turn right onto 410 (aka Ethan Allen Ave) about ⅔ mile to store on left.

UDUPI PALACE ✗

1329 University Blvd. E. ℂ 301-434-1531 ⊙ Daily 11:30-9:30
Indian vegetarian, with a daily lunch buffet.

· vegetarian · vegan · tables · self-service · wait staff

🍎 From I-495 (Capitol Beltway), take exit 29B toward Langley Park onto 193E/University Blvd E about 2½ miles. After New Hampshire Ave turn right at 1st traffic light to restaurant at University & 14th St.

WASHINGTON ADVENTIST HOSPITAL ✗ &

7600 Carroll Ave. ℂ 301-891-5012 ⊙ M-F 6am-10am, 11-2, 4:30-6:30, Sat-Sun 6:30-9:30, 11:30-2, 5-6:30 (7 on Sat)
A vegetarian cafeteria in the Seventh-day Adventist tradition.

· vegetarian · tables · self-service

🍎 From I-495 (Capitol Beltway), take exit 28B toward Takoma Park south on New Hampshire Ave (MD 650S) about 1½ miles to Piney Branch Rd. Turn right onto Piney Branch ½ mile to Carroll Ave. Veer left onto Carroll about 1¼ miles to cafeteria in hospital basement (LL2).

TIMONIUM

THE NATURAL ✗🍴

2150 York Rd. ℂ 410-628-1262 ⊙ M-F 9-8, Sat 10-6, Sun 11-6

· organic produce · freshly prepared food · juice bar · café · deli · vegetarian friendly · tables · self-service · take-out

🍎 From I-695 (Baltimore Beltway), take exit 24 onto I-83N to 1st exit onto Timonium Rd E. At 3rd traffic light turn left onto York Rd. At next light turn right into Timonium Shopping Ctr to store (across from fairgrounds).

TOWSON

HEALTH CONCERN 🍴 &

28 W. Susquehanna Ave. ℂ 410-828-4015 ⊙ M-F 9:30-8, Sat 9:30-6, Sun 11-5
All the produce is organic and on weekdays there's a salad bar.

· organic produce · freshly prepared food · salad bar · take-out

🍎 From I-695 (Baltimore Beltway), take York Rd exit (26A from 695W, 26B from 695E) south on York about 1 mile to Washington Ave. Turn right onto Washington 3 blocks to Susquehana Ave. Turn left onto Susquehanna to store on left (with green window shades).

MASSACHUSETTS

1	Acton	21	Gloucester
2	Allston	22	Great Barrington
3	Amherst	23	Greenfield
4	Andover	24	Hadley
5	Ashland	25	Harwich Port
6	Bedford	26	Jamaica Plain
7	Bellingham	27	Lee
8	Beverly	28	Lenox
9	Boston	29	Leverett
10	Brighton	30	Mansfield
11	Brookline	31	Medford
12	Cambridge	32	Melrose
13	Centerville	33	Newton
14	Charlton	34	Northhampton
15	Chatham	35	Orleans
16	Dennisport	36	Pittsfield
17	Dorchester	37	Plymouth
18	Falmouth	38	Provincetown
19	Framingham	39	Saugus
20	Gardner	40	Seekonk

41	Springfield	45	Westborough
42	Sturbridge	46	Woburn
43	Wayland	47	Worcester
44	Wellesley		

ACTON

O'NATURALS ✕
149 Great Rd. © 978-266-0222 ☺ M-Th, Sun 10:30-8, F-Sat 10:30-9
A fast-food concept developed by the owners of Stonyfield Farms Yogurt, offering natural and organic soups, sandwiches, salads, and Asian noodle dishes. Meat, fish, poultry, and vegetarian choices, plus kids' menu and Sunday brunch items.

· vegetarian friendly · organic focus · alcohol · chain · tables · self-service · take-out

From I-495N, take exit 29A onto Rt 2A E (toward Boston) 7¼ miles to Concord rotary. Take 4th St exit off rotary west onto Rt 2A (Great Rd) over 1½ miles to restaurant on right in Brookside Shops. **From I-495S**, take exit 31 onto Rt 119E (Great Rd, becomes 119/2A) toward Little Common almost 6 miles to restaurant on left in Brookside Shops. **From I-95S**, take I-495S and follow directions above. **From I-95N/128**, take exit 29B onto 2W about 3½ miles. Bear left and continue on 2/2A about 4½ miles to Concord rotary. Take 2nd exit off rotary and continue on 2A/Great Rd 1½ miles to restaurant.

ALLSTON

GRASSHOPPER VEGETARIAN RESTAURANT ✕
1 N. Beacon St. © 617-254-8883 ☺ M-Th 11-10, F-Sat 11-11, Sun 12-10
Pan-Asian vegan selection.

· vegan · tables · wait staff

From Mass Pike (I-90), take exit 20 toward Allston/Brighton onto Cambridge St 1 mile to restaurant at N Beacon St.

AMHERST

PEOPLE'S MARKET 🛒
U Mass Student Union © 413-545-2060 ☺ M, F 8:45-4, Tues-Th 8:45-5
A student-run whole foods store.

· co-op

From I-91, take exit 19 in Northampton east on Rt 9 about 4½ miles to Rt 116N. Turn left onto 116 1 mile to U Mass exit to campus. The store is in the rear of Student Union Bldg located on the campus pond, next to "The Beach."

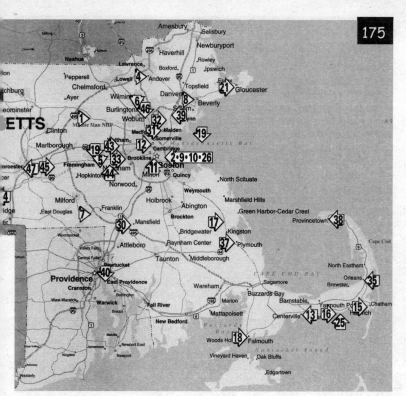

ANDOVER

WILD OATS MARKET
40 Railroad St. © 978-749-6664 ⊙ M-Sat 7:30-10, Sun 8-9

· organic produce · freshly prepared food · juice bar · salad bar · café · deli · bakery · vegetarian friendly · chain · tables · self-service · take-out

From I-93, take exit 44 east on Rt 133 about 2 miles to Rt 28 (4-way traffic light). Turn right onto 28S (N Main St) 3 lights to store on right. **From I-495,** take exit 41 toward Andover onto 28S 4 lights to store on right.

ASHLAND

UDUPII BHAVAN
59 Pond St. © 508-820-0230 ⊙ Tues-Sun 12-9:30
South Indian vegetarian.

· vegetarian · vegan friendly · tables · wait staff

From I-90E (Mass Pike), take exit 12 onto Rt 9E 3-4 miles to Rt 126. Turn right onto 126S (becomes Pond Ave) 3⅓ miles to restaurant in Pond Plaza. **From I-90W,** take exit 13 onto Rt 30W almost 2 miles to 126. Turn left onto 126S 3⅓ miles to restaurant in Pond Plaza

BEDFORD

WHOLE FOODS MARKET
170 Great Rd. © 781-275-1570 ⊙ Daily 8-9

· organic produce · freshly prepared food · salad bar · café · deli · bakery · vegetarian friendly · chain · tables · self-service · take-out

From I-95/Rt 128, take exit 31B toward Bedford onto Rts 4 & 225 (aka The Great Road) 2 miles to store on right in shopping plaza with Marshall's.

BELLINGHAM

The gateway to the Blackstone River Valley National Heritage Corridor, with nearby state parks, hiking and camping.

WHOLE FOODS MARKET ✗ ♿ &

255 Hartford Ave. © 508-966-3331 ☉ Daily 8:30-9
Store will pack your perishables on ice if you're traveling.

· organic produce · freshly prepared food · salad bar · café · deli · bakery · vegetarian friendly · chain · tables · self-service · take-out

🍎 **From I-495**, take exit 18 to store just off exit on Rt 126N (Hartford Ave).

BEVERLY

See what's happening at the Cabot Theater (near the Organic Garden Restaurant). Chef Robert at the restaurant says that in additon to movies, they have the "world's most spectacular magic show."

A NEW LEAF ♿

261 Cabot St. © 978-927-5955 ☉ M-W, F-Sat 9:30-6, Th 9:30-8

🍎 **From I-95N/Rt 128N**, follow 128N to the right (north to Gloucester) when it splits off of 95. **From Rt 128**, take exit 20B toward Beverly south on Rt 1A (becomes Cabot St) about 1¾ miles to store on left.

ORGANIC GARDEN RESTAURANT & JUICE BAR ✗ &

294 Cabot St. © 978-922-0004 ☉ M-Th, Sun 11-9, F-Sat 11-10
Gourmet raw foods. "Cooking" is done in special dehydrators "to maintain vital nutrients." No processed ingredients, wheat, dairy or sweeteners of any kind. The all-organic menu is made from plants, nuts, seeds, herbs, spices, and dried fruit. The beer and wine are organic, as well.

· juice bar · café · vegan · organic focus · alcohol · counter · tables · self-service · wait staff · take-out

🍎 **From I-95N/Rt 128N**, follow 128N to the right (north to Gloucester) when it splits off 95. **From Rt 128N**, take exit 22E toward Beverly right onto Rt 62 about 5 miles to Cabot St. Turn right onto Cabot 2 blocks to restaurant on right (before Cabot Cinema). **From 128S**, take exit 20B toward Beverly onto Rt 1AS (becomes Cabot St) about 1¾ miles to restaurant on right.

BOSTON

BUDDHA'S DELIGHT ✗

5 Beach St. © 617-451-2395 ☉ M-Th, Sun 11-10, F-Sat 11-11
Pan-Asian vegetarian.

· vegetarian · vegan friendly · tables · wait staff · take-out

🍎 **From I-93N**, take exit 20 toward I-90/Logan Airport/South Station and follow ramp for Kneeland St toward Downtown/South Station. Turn left onto Kneeland less than ¼ mile to Tyler St. Turn right onto Tyler 1 block to Beach St. Turn left onto Beach a few blocks to restaurant (in Chinatown). **From I-93S** (becomes Fitzgerald Pkwy), take exit 22 toward South Station/Chinatown and follow Surface Rd to Kneeland. Turn right onto Kneeland and follow directions above. **From I-90E** (Mass Pike), take exit 24A toward South Station, turn left onto Kneeland and follow directions above.

COUNTRY LIFE VEGETARIAN RESTAURANT ✗ &

200 High St © 617-951-2462 ☉ Lunch M-F 11:30-3, Sun 10:30-3, Dinner Tues-Th, Sun 5-8
All-vegan lunch and dinner buffets run by Seventh-day Adventists. Easy walk

to many attractions, including the aquarium, Boston Children's Museum and Quincy Market. Or, hop on a whale watching ship from the pier across the street.

· vegan friendly · tables · self-service

From I-93N/MA 3N, take exit 22 and stay left on Atlantic to 2nd left at High St (after 1st traffic light). Turn left onto High to restaurant in 1st building on right. **From I-93S** (becomes Central Artery/Fitzgerald Pkwy), take High St exit to 3rd intersection at Milk St. Turn right onto Milk to 2nd right at Broad St. Turn right onto Broad to restaurant in last building on right at end of street.

FRESH CITY ✕

201 Brookline Ave. © 617-424-7907 ⊙ M-F 6:30-5

A fast-food alternative featuring fresh food prepared in customer viewing area. Wraps, stir-fries, noodles, soups, salads, smoothies, and such. Vegetarian possibilities noted and the option to add tofu, poultry, steak or shrimp to most dishes.

· juice bar · café · vegetarian friendly · chain · tables · self-service · take-out

From I-93, take exit 18 and follow onto Mass Ave Connector (becomes Melnea Cass Blvd) over 1 mile to end at Tremont St. Turn left onto Tremont to 2nd right (at Police Station). Turn right onto Ruggles St (which runs into Louis Prang St, then bears right and becomes Fenway, then Park Dr) 1 mile to Brookline Ave. Turn right onto Brookline to restaurant at corner Park & Brookline in Landmark Center.

FRESH CITY ✕

2 Seaport Lane © 617-443-0963 ⊙ M-F 6:30-4

See Fresh City description above.

· juice bar · café · vegetarian friendly · chain · tables · self-service · take-out

From I-93, take exit 22 (South Station). At top of exit ramp turn left at 2nd traffic light onto Summer St which merges onto Congress St. After merge, move left to turn left onto B St to Northern Ave. Turn right onto Northern and follow signs to Seaport Hotel. Turn right onto Seaport Lane to restaurant on left.

WHOLE FOODS MARKET ✕🛒   ♿

15 Westland Ave. © 617-375-1010 ⊙ Daily 9-10

· organic produce · freshly prepared food · salad bar · café · deli · bakery · vegetarian friendly · chain · tables · self-service · take-out

From I-93, take exit 18 (Mass Ave/Roxbury). Follow exit onto New Frontage Rd and Mass Ave Connector to Mass Ave. Turn right onto Mass Ave about 1 mile to Huntington Ave (Symphony Hall on left). Take a "diagonal left" onto Westland to store on right on bottom floor of parking garage.

BRIGHTON

WHOLE FOODS MARKET ✕🛒   ♿

15 Washington St. © 617-738-8187 ⊙ Daily 9-9

· organic produce · freshly prepared food · salad bar · café · deli · bakery · vegetarian friendly · chain · counter · self-service · take-out

From I-90 (Mass Pike), take Prudential Ctr exit onto Rt 9W about 2 miles to store at Washington Ave. **From Coolidge Corner in Brookline,** follow Beacon St outbound to Washington Square. Turn right onto Washington St 4-5 blocks to store on right at Commonwealth Ave. **From Cleveland Circle,** follow Beacon St inbound to Washington Square. Turn left onto Washington St 4-5 blocks to store on right at Commonwealth Ave.

BROOKLINE

BUDDHA'S DELIGHT 2 ✗
404 Harvard St. © 617-739-8830 ☉ M-Th, Sun 11-10, F-Sat 11-11
Pan-Asian vegetarian.
• vegetarian • vegan • tables • wait staff • take-out
🏠 From I-90E (Mass Pike), take exit 18 (on left) toward Allston/Brighton onto Cambridge St (goes east and loops around back west) to Harvard Ave. Turn left onto Harvard (Ave becomes St) about ¾ mile to restaurant. **From I-90W**, take exit 20 onto Commonwealth Ave/MA 2W and follow 2W about 1 mile to Beacon St. Merge straight onto Beacon less than 1 mile to Harvard St. Turn right onto Harvard ⅓ mile to restaurant.

NATURAL FRONTIER 🍎
1028 Beacon St. © 617-232-3286 ☉ M-F 8-10, Sat 9-11, Sun 9-10
• organic produce • freshly prepared food • juice bar • salad bar • deli • vegetarian friendly • take-out
🏠 From I-90 (Mass Pike), take exit 18 toward Cambridge/Sommerville and follow signs to Rt 2E toward Brookline/Kenmore Square. Take 2E about ¾ mile to Beacon St. Turn right onto Beacon 2 blocks to store.

CAMBRIDGE

HARVEST CO-OP MARKETS ✗🍎
581 Massachusetts Ave. © 617-661-1580 ☉ Daily 8-10, Cafe M-Sat 8-9, Sun 9-7
• organic produce • freshly prepared food • café • vegetarian friendly • tables • self-service • take-out
🏠 From I-90 (Mass Tpke), take exit 18 (from I-90E) or 20 (from I-90W) toward Cambridge/Sommerville onto Cambridge St over River St bridge onto River St. Go 12 blocks and turn right onto Bishop Allen Dr (1 block past Massachusetts Ave) to public parking.

VEGGIE PLANET ✗
47 Palmer St. © 617-661-1513 ☉ Daily 11:30-10:30
Vegetarian restaurant by day, restaurant/folk music Club Passim by night. Specializing in organic-crust pizza or the toppings over (brown) rice.
• vegetarian • vegan friendly • tables • wait staff • take-out
🏠 From I-90 (Mass Pike), take exit 18 (from I-90E) or 20 (I-90W) toward Cambridge/Sommerville onto Cambridge St to Soldiers Field Rd. Turn left onto Soldiers Field to ramp for Cambridge/Harvard Square. Veer right onto N Harvard St over bridge onto JF Kennedy St. Take Kennedy about ¼ mile to Brattle St. Follow Brattle onto Church St onto Palmer St to restaurant on Harvard Sq inside Club Passim.

WHOLE FOODS MARKET ✗🍎   ♿
200 Alewife Brook Pkwy. © 617-491-0040 ☉ Daily 8-9:30
• organic produce • freshly prepared food • salad bar • café • deli • bakery • vegetarian friendly • chain • tables • self-service • take-out
🏠 From I-95, take exit 29A onto MA 2E 7 miles to store. **From I-90E** (Mass Pike), take exit 14 onto I-95N and follow directions above. **From I-90W**, take exit 20 toward Cambridge onto Soldier Field Rd about 1 mile to Elliot Bridge. After crossing bridge, take Rt 2/US 3 ramp toward Arlington/Fresh Pond Pkwy onto 2W (Fresh Pond Pkwy) about 1¼ miles to roundabout onto Alewife Brook Pkwy to store.

WHOLE FOODS MARKET 🛒
115 Prospect St. ✆ 617-492-0070 ⊙ M-Sat 9-10, Sun 9-9
  · organic produce · freshly prepared food · salad bar · deli · bakery · vegetarian friendly
  · chain · counter · take-out
🛏 **From I-90** (Mass Pike), take exit 18 (from I-90E) or 20 (I-90W) toward Cambridge/Sommerville onto Cambridge St across River St Bridge and onto River St about ⅔ mile to Western Ave. Merge onto Western, then onto Prospect St ¼ mile to store.

WHOLE FOODS MARKET 🍴🛒   ♿
340 River St. ✆ 617-876-6990 ⊙ Daily 9-9:30
  · organic produce · freshly prepared food · salad bar · café · deli · bakery · vegetarian
  friendly · chain · tables · self-service · take-out
🛏 **From I-90** (Mass Pike), take exit 18 (from I-90E) or 20 (I-90W) toward Cambridge/Sommerville onto Cambridge St. Cross River St Bridge and continue on River St to store.

CENTERVILLE

CAPE COD NATURAL FOODS 🛒
1600 Falmouth Rd. ✆ 508-771-8394 ⊙ M-Sat 9-7, Sun 12-5:30
  · organic produce
🛏 **From Rt 6** (Mid Cape Hwy), take exit 6 south on Rt 132 1 mile to 1st traffic light. Turn right onto Phinney's Lane 2 miles to next light. Turn right onto Rt 28 ¼ mile to store on right in Bell Tower Mall.

CHARLTON

FRESH CITY 🍴   ♿
Mass Tpke East, Mile 81 ✆ Hdqtrs: 781-453-0200 ⊙ Daily 10-9
A fast-food alternative for highway travelers featuring fresh food. Wraps, soups, salads, smoothies and such, with vegetarian possibilities noted on the menu. S&DG: Truly an oasis amidst the burgers and donuts on the interstate! We nominate the Mass Pike for the first Healthy Highways (Highway) Award.
  · vegetarian friendly · chain · self-service · take-out
🛏 On I-90E (Mass Pike) at milepost 81.

FRESH CITY 🍴   ♿
Mass Tpke West, Mile 89 ✆ Hdqtrs: 781-453-0200 ⊙ Daily 10-9
See Fresh City description above.
  · vegetarian friendly · chain · self-service · take-out
🛏 On I-90W (Mass Pike) at milepost 89.

CHATHAM

CHATHAM NATURAL FOODS 🛒
1218 Main St. ✆ 508-945-4139 ⊙ M-Sat 9-6, Sun 10-5
🛏 **From Rt 6**, take exit 11 onto Rt 137S over 2 miles to end. Turn left (east) onto Rt 28 (Main St) about 2½ miles into Chatham to store on left.

DENNISPORT

DENNISPORT NATURAL MARKET 🛒
640 Main St. ✆ 508-760-3043 ⊙ M-Sat 9-6, Sun 10-5
🛏 **From Rt 6**, take exit 9 onto Rt 134S about 2 miles to end. Turn left (east) onto Rt 28 1⅓ miles into Dennisport to store.

DORCHESTER

COMMON GROUND CAFE ✕ 🛒
2243-47 Dorchester Ave. ✆ 617-298-1020 ⊙ M-Th 10-10, F 10-3, Sun (store only) 10-5
Store and cafe are part of the Twelve Tribes Community.
· organic produce · freshly prepared food · juice bar · café · vegetarian friendly · tables
· wait staff · take-out

⬠ **From I-93**, take exit 11 (from I-93N) or 11B (I-90S) onto Granite Ave ½ mile to Milton St. Turn left onto Milton about ¼ mile to Adams St. Turn left onto Adams ⅓ mile to Richmond St. Turn right onto Richmond ⅓ mile to Dorchester Ave. Turn right onto Dorchester to store just off corner.

FALMOUTH

AMBER WAVES NATURAL FOODS 🛒
445 Main St. ✆ 508-540-3538 ⊙ M-Sat 10-6, Sun 12-5
· organic produce

⬠ Take Rt 28 into Falmouth (becomes Main St) to store in center of town.

FRAMINGHAM

FRESH CITY ✕   ♿
Mass Tpke West, Mile 115 ✆ Hdqtrs: 781-453-0200 ⊙ Daily 10-9
See Charlton location for description.
· vegetarian friendly · chain · self-service · take-out

⬠ On I-90W (Mass Pike) at milepost 115.

WHOLE FOODS MARKET ✕ 🛒
575 Worchester Rd. (Rte. 9) ✆ 508-628-9525 ⊙ Daily 8-9
· organic produce · freshly prepared food · salad bar · café · deli · bakery · vegetarian
friendly · chain · tables · self-service · take-out

⬠ **From I-90E** (Mass Pike), take exit 12 onto Rt 9E about 3½ miles to store at Prospect St on westbound side. **From I-90W**, take exit 13 onto Rt 30W toward Framingham about 2¾ miles to store on right at Prospect.

GARDNER

HAPPY TRAILS 🛒
24 Main St. ✆ 978-632-4076 ⊙ M-W, F-Sat 9:30-5:30, Th 9:30-7

⬠ **From Rt 2**, take exit 22 (3rd St) onto Rt 68N (becomes Main St) about 1 mile to store on right.

GLOUCESTER

CAPE ANN FOOD CO-OP 🛒
26 Emerson St. ✆ 978-281-0592 ⊙ M-Sat 8-8, Sun 11-6

⬠ **From I-95N/Rt 128N**, follow 128N to the right (north to Gloucester) when it splits off 95. **From Rt 128N**, at first rotary in Gloucester take first exit onto Washington St about ⅓ mile to Centennial Ave. Turn right onto Centennial ¼ mile to to Emerson Ave. Turn right onto Emerson 1 block to store on left.

GREAT BARRINGTON

Nestled in the Berkshires, home to Tanglewood, Jacob's Pillow Dance Company, the Norman Rockwell Museum, Mass MoCa, and several ski areas.

BERKSHIRE CO-OP MARKET 🐑

37 Rosseter St. © 413-528-9697 ⊙ M-F 9-7:30, Sat 9-6, Sun 11-5

· organic produce · freshly prepared food · vegetarian friendly · co-op · take-out

🍎 From I-90 (Mass Pike), take exit 2 (US 20/Lee) toward Great Barrington onto Rt 102W about 4½ miles to Rt 7. Turn left onto 7S about 7 miles to Rosseter St. Turn right onto Rosseter to store.

GUIDO'S FRESH MARKETPLACE 🐑   ᬗ

760 S. Main St. © 413-528-9255 ⊙ M-F 9-6, Sat 9-7, Sun 10-6

· organic produce · freshly prepared food · bakery · take-out

🍎 From I-90 (Mass Pike), take exit 2 (US 20/Lee) toward Great Barrington onto Rt 102W about 4½ miles to Rt 7. Turn left onto 7S about 8 miles to store on right after Big Y.

LOCKE STOCK & BARREL 🐑

265 Stockbridge Rd. © 413-528-0800 ⊙ M-Sat 9-5

🍎 From I-90 (Mass Pike), take exit 2 (US 20/Lee) west on Rt 102 about 4½ miles to Rt 7. Turn left onto 7S about 5½ miles to store on right (across from McDonalds).

GREENFIELD

GREENFIELDS MARKET FOOD CO-OP ✗🐑   ᬗ

144 Main St. © 413-773-9567 ⊙ M-F 8-8, Sat 9-6, Sun 10-5

Deli food is 80% organic.

· organic produce · freshly prepared food · salad bar · café · deli · bakery · vegetarian friendly · organic focus · co-op · tables · self-service · take-out

🍎 From I-91, take exit 26 toward Greenfield onto Rt 2A E 1 mile to store on left (look for green awning).

HADLEY

WHOLE FOODS MARKET ✗🐑   ᬗ

Rte. 9 Russell St. © 413-586-9932 ⊙ Daily 9-9

· organic produce · freshly prepared food · juice bar · salad bar · café · deli · bakery · vegetarian friendly · chain · tables · self-service · take-out

🍎 From I-91N, take exit 19 onto Rt 9E across bridge about 4 miles to store on right. From I-91S, take exit 20 and turn left at traffic light after ramp and left at next light onto 9E about 4 miles to store on right.

HARWICH PORT

WILD OATS NATURAL FOODS 🐑

509 Rte. 28 © 508-430-2507 ⊙ M-Sat 9-6, Sun 11-5

· juice bar · take-out

🍎 Take Rt 28 into Harwich Port to store on south side. From Harwich or north shore Cape Cod, take Rt 124 south to Main St in town. Turn left onto Main and right onto Bank St to Rt 28. Turn right onto 28 to store on left.

JAMAICA PLAIN

HARVEST CO-OP MARKETS ✗🐑
57 South St. © 617-524-1667 ☉ Daily 8-10, Cafe M-Sat 8-9, Sun 9-7

· organic produce · freshly prepared food · café · vegetarian friendly · co-op · tables
· self-service · take-out

🍎 **From I-95**, take exit 20A onto Rt 9E about 7 miles to Riverway. Turn right onto Riverway (becomes Jamaicaway) about 1⅓ miles to Pond St. Turn right onto Pond a few blocks to Centre St. Turn right onto Centre about ⅓ mile to South St (at monument). Stay left of monument onto South to store on right just before traffic light at Custer St. **From I-93**, take exit 18 and follow onto Mass Ave Connector (becomes Melnea Cass Blvd) over 1 mile to end at Tremont St. Turn left onto Tremont (Rt 28S) and follow 28S about 1⅔ miles to Washington St. Turn right onto Washington less than 1 mile to Williams St. Turn right onto Williams (becomes Carolina St, then Custer) less than ½ mile to store at corner Custer & South.

LEE

FRESH CITY ✗   ♿
Mass Tpke East © Hdqtrs: 781-453-0200 ☉ Daily 10-9
See Charlton location for description.

· vegetarian friendly · chain · self-service · take-out

🍎 On I-90E (Mass Pike) at Lee.

SUNFLOWER'S NATURAL FOOD MARKET 🐑
42 Park St. © 413-243-1775 ☉ M-Sat 9:30-6, Sun 12-5

· organic produce

🍎 From I-90 (Mass Pike), take exit 2 (Lee) onto US 20W 1 mile to store on right.

LENOX

Home of Tanglewood, Shakespeare & Co. and the Kripalu vegetarian yoga retreat.

CLEARWATER NATURAL FOODS 🐑   ♿
11 Housatonic St. © 413-637-2721 ☉ M-Sat 9:15 -6, Sun 11-3

· organic produce

🍎 From I-90 (Mass Pike), take exit 2 (Lee) onto US 20W about 4½ miles (into Lenox) to Walker St. Turn left onto Walker 1 mile to Main St. Turn right onto Main, then first right onto Housatonic St to store on left.

LEVERETT

VILLAGE CO-OP ✗🐑
180 Rattlesnake Gutter Rd. © 413-367-9794 ☉ Daily 7-7

· organic produce · freshly prepared food · vegetarian friendly · co-op · tables · self-service · take-out

🍎 From I-91, take exit 24 (Deerfield) onto US 5N to Rt 116. Turn right onto 116 almost 4 miles to Bull Hill Rd. Turn left onto Bull Hill about 1⅓ miles and veer left onto Long Plain Rd (Rt 63), then right onto Depot Rd another 1½ miles to Montague St. Veer left onto Montague almost 2 miles to Rattlesnack Gutter Rd. Turn left onto Rattlesnake Gutter to store on left.

MANSFIELD

GREEN EARTH GROCERY 🐑
310 N. Main St. © 508-261-1400 ☉ M-W 10-6, Th 10-7, F-Sat 10-9

From **I-95**, take exit 7A onto Rt 140S about 1 mile to traffic light at Rt 106 (Chauncy St). Turn left onto 106 less than 1 mile to 2nd set of lights (down hill, under railway) at Main St. Make sharp right onto Main and pull into parking lot on left. Double glass doors in back lead to store.

MEDFORD

WILD OATS MARKET
2151 Mystic Valley Pkwy. © 781-395-4998 ⊘ M-Sat 7-10, Sun 8-9
· organic produce · freshly prepared food · juice bar · salad bar · café · deli · bakery
· vegetarian friendly · chain · tables · self-service · take-out

From **I-93N**, take exit 31 toward Arlington onto Mystic Valley Pkwy/ MA 16W about 1²/₃ miles to store. **From I-93S**, take exit 32 onto Rt 60W/ Salem St toward Medford about ¹/₃ mile (across water) to Main St. Turn left onto Main and merge onto Mystic Valley Pkwy/16W 1 mile to store.

MELROSE

GREEN STREET NATURAL FOODS
164 Green St. © 781-662-7741 ⊘ M-W, F 9-6, Th 9-7, Sat 9-5, Sun 12-5
All items are vegetarian and egg-free in this 2nd-generation, family-owned store.
· organic produce · freshly prepared food · vegetarian · take-out

From **I 95**, take exit 39 onto North Ave (left off ramp from 95S, right from 95N) to 4th traffic light (Main St). Turn right onto Main to 3rd light at Green St (before going down large hill). Turn left onto Green to store on right.

NEWTON

FRESH CITY
241 Needham St. © 617-244-7071 ⊘ M-F 6:30am-9pm, Sat-Sun 10-9
A fast-food alternative featuring fresh food prepared in customer viewing area. Wraps, stir-fries, noodles, soups, salads, smoothies, and such. Vegetarian possibilities noted and the option to add tofu, poultry, steak or shrimp to most dishes.
· vegetarian friendly · chain · tables · self-service · take-out

From **I-95/128**, take exit 19A toward Newton Highlands onto Highland Ave (becomes Needham St) less than 1 mile to restaurant on left in Marshall's Plaza. **From Rt 9W** (Boston area), veer left onto Boylston St to Winchester St. Turn left onto Winchester to Needham and right onto Needham about ½ mile to restaurant on right in Marshall's Plaza.

WHOLE FOODS MARKET
647 Washington St © 617-965-2070 ⊘ Daily 8-9
· organic produce · freshly prepared food · salad bar · café · deli · bakery · vegetarian
friendly · chain tables · self-service · take-out

From **I-90** (Mass Pike), take exit 17 toward Newton/Watertown. **From I-90W**, go straight onto Washington St less than 1 mile to store. **From I-90E**, veer right onto Center St, right onto Richardson St, right onto Church St and left onto Washington ½ mile to store.

WHOLE FOODS MARKET
916 Walnut St. © 617-969-1141 ⊘ Daily 8-9
· organic produce · freshly prepared food · salad bar · deli · bakery · vegetarian friendly
· chain · take-out

From **I-95/128**, take Rt 16/Waban exit (21 from 95/128N, 21A from 95/128S) and follow to right onto Beacon St 2-3 miles to store parking lot on right just past traffic light at Walnut St (Mobile station on right).

NORTHAMPTON

BELA VEGETARIAN RESTAURANT ✕
68 Masonic St. ✆ 413-586-8011 ☺ Tues-Sat 12-8:45
Casual vegetarian dining. Soups, salads and sandwiches, plus four tofu/tempeh and four pasta specials. Local produce in season. If you want alcohol, BYOB.
• vegetarian • vegan friendly • tables • self-service
🍎 **From I-91N**, take exit 18 (1st Northampton exit) left off ramp onto Rt 5N a little more than 1 mile to traffic light at Main St. Turn left onto Main to Masonic St. Turn right onto Masonic to restaurant. **From I-91S**, take exit 20 onto Rt 5S almost 1½ miles to Main. Turn right onto Main to Masonic. Turn right onto Masonic to restaurant.

HAYMARKET CAFE ✕
185 Main S. ✆ 413-586-9969 ☺ Daily 11:30-9, Juice bar M-Th 7am-10pm, F-Sat 7am-11pm, Sun 8am-10pm
Downstairs dine on sandwiches, salads and vegetarian choices with an "Indian influence." Go upstairs to the juice bar for fresh juice, smoothies and hot drinks.
• juice bar • café • vegetarian friendly • vegan friendly • tables • self-service
🍎 **From I-91N**, take exit 18 (1st Northampton exit) left off ramp onto Rt 5N a little more than 1 mile to traffic light at Main St. Turn left onto Main to restaurant. **From I-91S**, take exit 20 onto Rt 5S almost 1½ miles to Main. Turn right onto Main to restaurant.

PAUL AND ELIZABETH'S ✕
150 Main St. ✆ 413-584-4832 ☺ M-W 11:30-9:15, Th 11:30-9:30, F-Sat 11:30-9:45, Sun 11:30-9
Vegetarian and seafood offerings.
• vegetarian friendly • vegan friendly • alcohol • tables • wait staff
🍎 **From I-91N**, take exit 18 (1st Northampton exit) left off ramp onto Rt 5N almost 1½ miles to Armory St. Turn left onto Armory to parking garage and lots. Restaurant is on Main St level in Thornes Market (attached to garage). **From I-91S**, take exit 20 onto Rt 5S almost 1½ miles (past traffic light on Main) to Armory. Turn right onto Armory and proceed as above.

CORNUCOPIA FOODS 🥕
150 Main St. ✆ 413-586-3800 ☺ M-W 9:30-7, Th-Sat 9:30-9, Sun 12-6
Cornucopia supports local organic farmers and claims "no non-organic produce touches our shelves."
• organic produce
🍎 **From I-91N**, take exit 18 (1st Northampton exit) left off ramp onto Rt 5N almost 1½ miles to Armory St. Turn left onto Armory to parking garage and lots. Store is in Thornes Market (attached to garage). **From I-91S**, take exit 20 onto Rt 5S almost 1½ miles (past traffic light on Main) to Armory. Turn right onto Armory and proceed as above.

ORLEANS

ORLEANS WHOLE FOOD STORE 🥕
46 Main St. ✆ 508-255-6540 ☺ M-Sat 8:30-6, Sun 9-6 (closes 9pm in summer)
• organic produce • freshly prepared food • deli • bakery • vegetarian friendly • take-out
🍎 **From Rt 6W**, take 6A west off rotary almost 1 mile to Main St (2nd traffic light.) Turn left onto Main to store on left. **From Rt 6E**, take exit 12 right onto 6A east almost 1 mile to Main (2nd light). Turn right onto Main to store on left.

PITTSFIELD

GUIDO'S FRESH MARKETPLACE 🛒 &

1020 South St. ✆ 413-442-9912 ⊘ M-F 9-6, Sat 9-7, Sun 9-5

· organic produce · freshly prepared food · bakery · take-out

🛍 **From I-90** (Mass Pike), take exit 2 (Lee/US 20) onto 20W about 8½ miles until it merges with Rt 7N. Continue on 7N about 4¾ miles to store on left.

PITTSFIELD HEALTH FOOD CENTER 🛒

407 North St. ✆ 413-442-5662 ⊘ M-F 9:30-5:30, Sat 9:30-3:30

🛍 **From I-90** (Mass Pike), take exit 2 (Lee/US 20) onto 20W about 8½ miles until it merges with Rt 7N. Continue on 7N about 1 mile and after rotary bear right onto North St past 2 traffic lights to store on left (across from church).

PLYMOUTH

Home to historic Plymouth Rock, Leyden St (the "first" street in America), and right next to the store you can see a 225+ year-old tree.

COMMON SENSE WHOLESOME FOOD MARKET 🛒 &

53 Main St. ✆ 508-732-0427 ⊘ M-Th 9-7, Sun 10-5

Fresh bakery products, a small selection of organic foods and Common Sense soaps, salves, beeswax candles, and "earth friendly" furniture from recycled wood.

· organic produce · bakery

🛍 **From Rt 3**, take US 44E (exit 6 from 3N, 6A from 3S) about ¾ mile to traffic light at Court St (Rt 3A). Turn right onto Court (becomes Main St at North St) about ⅓ mile to store on left (next to Sam Diego's Restaurant).

PROVINCETOWN

The famous Provincetown where you can head for the sand dunes, go on a whale watch, or just stroll the streets where there's always "a show."

LEMBAS HEALTH FOODS 🛒

141 Bradford St. ✆ 508-487-9784 ⊘ Daily 8-7 June-Labor Day, 10-6 off-season

· organic produce

🛍 Take Rt 6 into Provincetown. Turn left at traffic lights (not blinkers) onto Conwell St to Bradford St. Turn right onto Bradford 2½ blocks to store (red building across from florist).

TOFU A GO-GO! ✗

336 Commercial St. ✆ 508-487-6237 ⊘ Daily 11-3 June-Labor Day, 11-10 off-season (but best to call as hours are subject to change)

Place your order to go or eat on the year-round outdoor deck.

· vegetarian · vegan friendly · tables · self-service · take-out

🛍 Take Rt 6 into Provincetown. Turn left at traffic lights (not blinkers) onto Conwell S to Commercial St. Turn right onto Commercial to restaurant.

SAUGUS

WILD OATS MARKET ✗ 🛒 &

357 Broadway ✆ 781-233-5341 ⊘ M-Sat 8-10, Sun 8-9

· organic produce · freshly prepared food · juice bar · salad bar · café · deli · bakery
· vegetarian friendly · chain · tables · self-service · take-out

🛍 **From I-95N**, take exit 44A toward Boston right onto Broadway/US 1S about 2½ miles to turn-around at Lynn Fells Pkwy. Follow back onto US 1N about ⅔ mile to store on right. **From I-95S or MA128S**, take exit 44 onto US 1S about 4¼ miles and follow directions above.

SEEKONK

THE GOOD SEED 🍎
138 Central Ave. © 508-399-7333 ⊙ M-Tues, F-Sat, 10-6, W-Th 10-8, Sun 12-5
🛒 **From I-95**, take exit 2A right onto Newport Ave/Rt 1AS about ¾ mile to Benefit St. Turn left onto Benefit (becomes Central Ave) about 1 mile to store on left at corner Central & Rt 152.

SPRINGFIELD

Springfield is the home of the Dr. Seuss National Memorial (at the Quadrangle) and the Basketball Hall of Fame.

BETTER LIFE WHOLE FOODS 🍎
1514 Allen St. © 413-783-9424 ⊙ M-W, F 9-30-6, Th 9:30-7, Sat 9:30-5
🛒 **From I-91N**, take exit 2 (Rt 83) toward Forest Park/E Longmeadow to 2nd traffic light (Rt 83). Turn right onto 83E/Sumner Ave 3 miles and bear right after Wendy's to store in Bicentennial Plaza. **From I-91S**, take exit 4 (Main St). Turn left at light (do not bear left before light!) and right onto Longhill St to Sumner. Turn left onto Sumner 3 miles and bear right after Wendy's to store in Bicentennial Plaza.

STURBRIDGE

CEDAR STREET RESTAURANT ✗
12 Cedar St. © 508-347-5800 ⊙ M-Sat from 5
Three different menus: one all vegetarian, with half vegan; one local fish and seafood; one meat and game. Each has its own appetizers, salads and entrees.
· vegetarian friendly · alcohol · tables · wait staff
🛒 **From the north end of I-84** (exit 3B) or from **I-90** (Mass Pike) exit 9, take Rt 20W to 4th set of traffic lights at Cedar St. Turn right onto Cedar to restaurant in 3rd building on right. (Total distance from hwy 1½ miles.)

WAYLAND

WHOLE FOODS MARKET ✗ 🍎
317 Boston Post Rd. © 508-358-7770 ⊙ Daily 8-8
· organic produce · freshly prepared food · salad bar · bakery · vegetarian friendly
· chain · counter · self-service · take-out
🛒 **From I-95/128**, take exit 26 west on Rt 20 (aka Boston Post Rd) about 5 miles to store just past Rt 27.

WELLESLEY

A 3-college town and home of the Map and Globe Museum.

WHOLE FOODS MARKET 🍎
278 Washington St. © 781-235-7262 ⊙ Daily 8-9
One of the oldest (and smallest) stores in the Whole Foods chain.
· organic produce · freshly prepared food · deli · bakery · vegetarian friendly · chain
· take-out
🛒 **From I-95S**, take exit 22-21B and take ramp for Rt 16W/Wellesley to Washington St. Turn right onto Washington (Rt 16W) about 1½ miles to store just past Rt 9 junction (across from Clocktower Park). **From I-95N**, take exit 20B onto Rt 9W about 2 miles to Rt 16 ramp. Veer left onto Washington to store.

WESTBOROUGH

FRESH CITY ✗

Mass Tpke West © Hdqtrs: 781-453-0200 ⊙ Daily 10-9
See Charlton location for description.

· vegetarian friendly · chain · self-service · take-out

🍎 On I-90W (Mass Pike) at Westborough.

WOBURN

FRESH CITY ✗

385 Washington St. © 781-932-1120 ⊙ M-F 6:30am-8pm, Sat 10-8
A fast-food alternative featuring fresh food prepared in customer viewing area. Wraps, stir-fries, noodle dishes, soups, salads, smoothies, and such, with vegetarian possibilities noted and the option to add tofu, poultry, steak or shrimp to most dishes.

· juice bar · vegetarian friendly · chain · tables · self-service · take-out

🍎 **From I-95N**, take exit 36 and bear right onto Washington St ⅓ mile to restaurant on left. **From I-95S**, take exit 36 and make 2 rights onto Washington St. Follow directions from 95N. **From I-93S**, take exit 37 onto I-95S ¼ mile to exit 36. Make 2 rights onto Washington St and follow directions from 95N. **From I-93N**, take exit 36 (Montvale Ave). Turn right at bottom of ramp (pass under I-93) 2 blocks to traffic light at Washington St. Turn right onto Washington 1 mile (past 2 lights) to restaurant on right.

WORCESTER

LILY PAD VEGETARIAN RESTAURANT ✗

755 Grafton St. © 508-890-8899 ⊙ Tues-F, 4-10, Sat 12-10, Sun 12-9
Chinese and Japanese vegetarian (actually vegan), with simulated meat dishes.

· vegan · tables · wait staff

🍎 From I-290, take exit 14 (Rt 122) toward Barre. Turn right at 1st traffic lights onto Grafton St. Pass 2 sets of lights and bear right at rotary, following Grafton/Rt 122S. Bear left at light and continue on Grafton/Rt 122S another ¾ mile (about 1½ miles total) to restaurant on left.

LIVING EARTH ✗ 🥪

232 Chandler St. © 508-753-1896 ⊙ M-F 9-9, Sat 9-7, Sun 11-6, Cafe M-F 11-8, Sat 11-6, Sun 11-5
Vegetarian meals, as well as seafood, organic meat and additive-free chicken.

· organic produce · freshly prepared food · café · deli · bakery · vegetarian friendly · tables · wait staff · take-out

🍎 From I-290, take exit 13 onto Rt 122N about 1½ miles (becomes Madison St, then Chandler St) to store on left just before Rt 9 (Park Ave).

QUAN YIN ✗

56 Hamilton St. © 508-831-1322 ⊙ M-F 11-9, Sat 11-4, Sun 12-9
Vegan Chinese and Vietnamese, using "faux" meat. Small place, mostly takeout.

· vegan · tables · self-service · take-out

🍎 From I-290, take exit 14 toward Barre/Uxbridge onto Grafton St (right from 290N, follow Rt 122S ramp and right from 290S) less than ½ mile to Hamilton St. Turn right onto Hamilton a few blocks to restaurant.

MICHIGAN

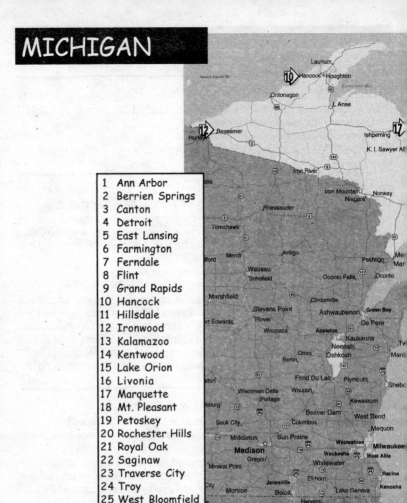

1 Ann Arbor
2 Berrien Springs
3 Canton
4 Detroit
5 East Lansing
6 Farmington
7 Ferndale
8 Flint
9 Grand Rapids
10 Hancock
11 Hillsdale
12 Ironwood
13 Kalamazoo
14 Kentwood
15 Lake Orion
16 Livonia
17 Marquette
18 Mt. Pleasant
19 Petoskey
20 Rochester Hills
21 Royal Oak
22 Saginaw
23 Traverse City
24 Troy
25 West Bloomfield
26 Woodland
27 Ypsilanti

ANN ARBOR

ARBOR FARMS NATURAL FOODS MARKET
2215 W. Stadium Rd. ☏ 734-996-8111 ⊙ M-Sat 9-9, Sun 10-6
· organic produce · freshly prepared food · deli · vegetarian friendly · take-out
⊟ **From I-94**, take exit 172 onto 94Bus E (Jackson Rd) ⅔ mile to W Stadium Blvd. Turn right onto W Stadium about ½ mile to store (near Liberty St).

EARTHEN JAR ✄
311 S. Fifth Ave. ☏ 734-327-9464 ⊙ M-Th, Sat 11-9, F 11-9
Indian vegetarian served buffet-style and charged by the pound.
· vegetarian · vegan friendly · tables · self-service · take-out

🍽 **From I-94,** take exit 172 onto 94Bus E (Jackson Rd) about 2¼ miles to Main St. Turn right onto Main 2 blocks to Liberty St. Turn left onto Liberty 2 blocks to 5th. Turn right onto 5th to restaurant.

INN SEASON CAFE ✗

211 E. Washington St. ℰ 734-302-7701 ⊙ Tues-Th 11:30-9, F-Sat 11:30-9:30
Vegetarian menu draws from all over the world, but the common denominator is unrefined foods, whole grains and organic when possible. L&JB: Romantic and charming ambience, with a range of simple fare to elegant dishes.

· vegetarian · vegan friendly · organic focus · alcohol · tables · wait staff

🍽 **From I-94,** take exit 177 north on State St about 2¼ miles to Packard St. Turn left onto Packard ½ mile to 4th Ave. Turn right onto 4th 3 blocks to restaurant on SW corner E Washington St & 4th.

PEOPLE'S FOOD CO-OP & CAFE VERDE ✗ ● &

216 N. Fourth Ave. ✆ 734-994-9174 ⊘ Store M-Sun 9-10, Cafe M-Sat 7am-9:30pm, Sun 9-8, Soup/Salad bar M-Sat 9-9, Hot bar M-F 11-2, 5-8, Sat 11-3, Sun 10-1, 3-7
Near Ann Arbor Hands-On Museum, Kerrytown shops and U of MI campus.
· organic produce · freshly prepared food · salad bar · café · vegetarian friendly · co-op
· tables · self-service · take-out

🍎 **From I-94**, take exit 177 north on State St about 2¼ miles to Packard St. Turn left onto Packard ½ mile to 4th Ave. Turn right onto 4th less than ½ mile (2 blocks past Huron) to store at 4th & Catherine St.

SEVA RESTAURANT ✗ &

314 E Liberty St. ✆ 734-662-1111 ⊘ M-Th 11-9, F 11-10, Sat 10-10, Sun 10-9
Multi-ethnic vegetarian cuisine. An Ann Arbor institution since 1973.
· vegetarian · vegan friendly · alcohol · tables · wait staff · take-out

🍎 From I-94, take exit 177 north on State St 2¼ miles to Packard St. Turn left onto Packard ⅓ mile to Division St. Turn right onto Division ⅓ mile to Liberty St. Turn left onto Liberty to store between Division & 5th Ave.

WHOLE FOODS MARKET ✗ ● &

3235 Washtenaw Ave. ✆ 734-971-3366 ⊘ Daily 9-10
· organic produce · freshly prepared food · salad bar · café · deli · bakery · vegetarian
friendly · chain · counter · tables · self-service · take-out

🍎 **From US 23**, take exit 37B west on Washtenaw Ave (toward downtown Ann Arbor) about 1 mile to store on right just past Huron Pkwy (in shopping plaza with Barnes & Noble).

BERRIEN SPRINGS

ANDREWS UNIVERSITY CAFETERIA ✗

US 31N ✆ 269-471-3161 ⊘ Daily 6am-6:30 pm (may vary with school calendar)
Vegetarian food in the Seventh-day Adventist tradition. No cash transactions on Saturdays.
· salad bar · vegetarian · vegan friendly · tables · self-service

🍎 Berrien Springs is about 8 miles south of I-94 exit 28 or about 15 miles north of South Bend, IN on US 31. Restaurant is on 31 at Andrews University, upstairs in the Campus Center.

CANTON

GOOD FOOD COMPANY WEST ✗ ●

42615 Ford Rd. ✆ 734-981-8100 ⊘ M-Sat 8-9, Sun 10-6
· organic produce · freshly prepared food · deli · vegetarian friendly · tables · self-
service · take-out

🍎 **From I-275**, take exit 25 (MI 153/Ford Rd) toward Westland/Garden City west on Ford Rd ¾ mile to store on left in Canton Corners Shopping Ctr.

DETROIT

CASS CORRIDOR FOOD CO-OP ●

456 Charlotte St. ✆ 313-831-7452 ⊘ M-F 9-7, Sat 9-6, Sun 10-5
· organic produce · co-op

🍎 **From I-75**, take exit 52 west on Mack Ave (becomes MLK Jr Blvd/Myrtle St) about ¾ mile to Cass Ave. Turn left onto Cass and right onto Charlotte St to store between Cass & 2nd St (behind Masonic Temple).

SPROUT HOUSE 🌱
15233 Kercheval St. ℂ 313-331-3200 ⊗ M-Sat 10-6
In the Grosse Point Park section of Detroit.
 · organic produce · juice bar · take-out
🛏 **From I-94,** take exit 222A onto Outer Dr E (left from 94W, onto Edsel Ford Fwy then right from 94E) about ¼ mile to Alter Rd. Merge straight onto Alter 1²/₃ miles to Kercheval St. Turn left onto Kercheval about ¼ mile to store.

THE TRAFFIC JAM & SNUG RESTAURANT ✕   &
511 W. Canfield St. ℂ 313-831-9470 ⊗ M-Th 11-10:30, F 11-12, Sat 12-12
Ample vegetarian choices, along with meat, in a traditionally meat-oriented city. Home brewed beer and live entertainment.
 · vegetarian friendly · alcohol · tables · self-service · wait staff
🛏 **From I-94,** take exit 215A south on John Lodge Fwy (MI 10) to Forest Ave. Turn left (east) onto Forest Ave to 3rd St. Turn right onto 3rd to Canfield St. Turn left onto Canfield to restaurant. **From I-75,** take exit 53A west on E Warren St to Woodward Ave. Turn left (south) onto Woodward to Hancock St. Turn right onto Hancock to Cass Ave. Turn left onto Cass to Canfield. Turn right onto Canfield to restaurant.

EAST LANSING
EAST LANSING FOOD CO-OP 🌱
4960 Northwind Drive ℂ 517-337-1266 ⊗ M-Sat 9-8, Sun 11-7
 · co-op
🛏 **From Hwy 127** (easily accessible from I-96, I-69 & I-496), take Michigan Ave east (merges into Sagamore St) about 3 miles (past MSU) to Northwind Dr. Turn right onto Northwind to store on right.

FARMINGTON
THE TREE HOUSE ✕ 🌱
22906 Mooney St. ℂ 248-473-0624 ⊗ M-F, Sun 11-9, Sat 10-9, Deli 12-7
All the deli offerings are vegetarian.
 · organic produce · freshly prepared food · deli · vegetarian · tables · self-service · take-out
🛏 **From I-275,** take exit 167 east on 8 Mile Rd about 4 miles to Orchard Lake Rd. Turn left onto Orchard Lake 1 mile to Grand River Ave. Turn left onto Grand River about ¼ mile to Mooney St. Turn right onto Mooney to store.

FERNDALE
NATURAL FOOD PATCH 🌱
221 W. 9 Mile Rd. ℂ 248-546-5908 ⊗ M-Th, Sat 9:30-7, F 9:30-9, Sun 10-6
 · organic produce
🛏 **From I-696,** take exit 16 toward Woodward Ave/Detroit Zoo onto W 10 Mile Rd to Woodward Ave. Turn south onto Woodward (right from 696E, left from 696W) over 1 mile to W 9 Mile Rd. Turn right onto W 9 Mile to store. **From I-75S,** take exit 61 onto I-696W about 1½ miles to exit 16 and follow directions above. **From I-75N,** take exit 60 toward John R St/9 Mile Rd onto N Chrysler Dr about ¼ mile to 9 Mile Rd. Turn left (west) onto W 9 Mile 1½ miles to store.

OM CAFE ✗
23136 Woodward Ave. ℂ 248-548-1941 ⊙ M-Sat 11-2:30, 4-9
Macrobiotic, vegetarian orientation. L&JB: Make sure to try the cake. Have them hold it at the beginning of the meal...they often run out.
· vegan · tables · wait staff

🍴 **From I-696**, take exit 16 toward Woodward Ave/Detroit Zoo onto W 10 Mile Rd to Woodward Ave. Turn south onto Woodward (right from 696E, left from 696W) just over 1 mile to restaurant on east side. **From I-75S**, take exit 61 onto I-696W about 1½ miles to exit 16 and follow directions above. **From I-75N**, take exit 60 toward John R Rd/9 Mile Rd onto N Chrysler Dr about ¼ mile to 9 Mile Rd. Turn left (west) onto W 9 Mile almost 1½ miles to Woodward. Turn right onto Woodward about ¼ mile to restaurant on east side.

FLINT

THE GRAINERY NATURAL GROCERY 🥬
809 Church St. ℂ 810-235-4621 ⊙ M-F 10-7
· organic produce · freshly prepared food · juice bar · vegetarian friendly · take-out

🍴 **From I-475**, take exit 7 (Court St/MI 21) toward Downtown. Go west on Court less than ½ mile to Church St. Turn right onto Church to store in 2nd bldg. **From I-69**, take exit 136 (Saginaw St/Downtown) onto service road to Church St. Turn north onto Church (left from 69N, right from 69S) less than ½ mile to store in 2nd bldg past Court St.

GRAND RAPIDS

GAIA CAFE ✗
209 Diamond Ave. S.E. ℂ 616-454-6233 ⊙ Tues-F 8-8, Sat 8-3
A simple menu with healthy vegetarian and vegan breakfast fare, plus a selection of classics featuring beans, rice and veggies.
· vegetarian · vegan friendly · tables · wait staff · take-out

🍴 **From I-96W**, take I-196W to exit 79. Turn left (south) onto Fuller Ave NE almost 1 mile to Hermitage St SE. Turn right onto Hermitage ¼ mile to Diamond Ave SE. Turn left onto Diamond to restaurant. **From I-96E or US 131S**, take I-196E to exit 78. Turn right onto College Ave NE about ½ mile to Fulton St E. Turn left onto Fulton to Lake Dr SE. Veer right onto Lake ½ mile to Diamond. Turn right onto Diamond to restaurant. **From US 131N**, take exit 84B (131Bus) toward Downtown. Head north (left) on Iona Ave SW to Fulton. Turn right onto Fulton less than 1 mile to Lake. Veer right onto Lake ½ mile to Diamond. Turn right onto Diamond to restaurant.

HARVEST HEALTH FOODS 🥬
1944 Eastern Ave S.E. ℂ 616-245-6268 ⊙ M, F 9-8, Tues-Th, Sat 9-6
· organic produce

🍴 **From I-96W**, take exit 43A toward Kent Co Airport west on 28th St SE about 5⅔ miles to Eastern Ave SE. Turn right onto Eastern 1 mile to store. **From I-96E**, take exit 31A onto US 131S about 6¾ miles to exit 82A. **From US 131**, take exit 82A onto Burton St SW (loop around right from 131S, right from 131N) about 1¾ miles to Eastern. Turn left onto Eastern to store.

HARVEST HEALTH FOODS 🌿
6807 Cascade Rd. S.E. ℰ 616-975-7555 ⊘ M-Sat 9-8
· organic produce

⛫ **From I-96,** take exit 46B east on 28th St (loop around right from 96E, right from 96W) about 1¾ miles to Cascade Rd SE. Turn right onto Cascade to store.

HANCOCK

The northern tip of Michigan on Lake Superior.

KEWEENAW CO-OP 🌿
1035 Ethel Ave. ℰ 906-482-2030 ⊘ M-Sat 10-8, Sun 10-5
· organic produce · deli · vegetarian friendly · co-op · take-out

⛫ Entering Hancock **from Rt 41N,** turn left onto N Lincoln Dr (just before 41 veers right) and immediately right onto Ethel Ave less than ¼ mile (about 2 blocks) to store on right. **From north of town on Rt 41,** turn left onto Summit St (just before 41 turns left) 1 block to Hill St. Turn left onto Hill 1 block to Ethel. Turn right onto Ethel to store.

HILLSDALE

HILLSDALE NATURAL GROCERY 🌿
31 N. Broad St. ℰ 517-439-1397 ⊘ M-F 9-6, Sat 9-5

⛫ Rt 34 & 99 meet in Hillsdale to become Broad St. Store is on east side.

IRONWOOD

"Big Snow Country" with an average of 200 inches a year. Five downhill ski areas within 10 miles, plus groomed wilderness trails for cross-country skiers. Other seasons there's fly fishing and swimming in Lake Superior.

NORTHWIND NATURAL FOODS CO-OP 🌿   ♿
116 S. Suffolk St. ℰ 906-932-3547 ⊘ M-F 9-6, Sat 9-5
· organic produce · co-op

⛫ Just over the MN border. **From US 2,** turn south onto 2Bus (Douglas St, then Suffolk St) less than ¾ mile to store just before Aurora St.

KALAMAZOO

KALAMAZOO PEOPLE'S FOOD CO-OP 🌿
436 S. Burdick St. ℰ 269-342-5686 ⊘ M-Sat 9-7, Sun 12-6
All vegetarian, mostly organic, take-out deli.
· organic produce · freshly prepared food · deli · vegetarian · organic focus · co-op · take-out

⛫ **From I-94,** take exit 76B north on Westnedge Ave a few miles to Cedar Ct. Turn right onto Cedar to store at corner Cedar & S Burdick St. **From Hwy 131/94Bus,** take exit 36A toward Kalamazoo onto 94Bus E (Stadium Dr, then Michigan Ave) about 4 miles to Burdick. Turn right onto Burdick about ¼ mile to store at Cedar.

SAWALL HEALTH FOODS 🌿
2965 Oakland Drive ℰ 269-343-3619 ⊘ M-Sat 9-8, Sun 12-5
· organic produce

⛫ **From I-94,** take exit 75 north on Oakland Dr 1 mile to store on right.

KENTWOOD

APPLE VALLEY NATURAL FOODS 🍎
6070 Kalamazoo Ave. S.E. © 616-554-3205 ⊘ M-Th 9-8, F 9-4 (until 6 in summer), Sun 11-5
A *"vegetarian health food store."*
 · vegetarian

From Hwy 131, take exit 77 toward Cutlerville east on 68th St about 2¾ miles to Kalamazoo Ave. Turn left onto Kalamazoo less than 1 mile to store on corner 60th St & Kalamazoo.

LAKE ORION

Area lakes offer canoeing, fishing, and swimming. Also, hiking and cross country skiing on state land. For non-sporting activity, the Upland Hills Farm School and Ecological Awareness Center is close by.

LUCKY'S NATURAL FOODS 🍎
101 S. Broadway St. © 248-693-1209 ⊘ M-Th 9:30-7, F 9:30-6, Sat 10-6
 · organic produce

From I-75, take exit 81 onto MI 24N (Lapeer Rd) about 6 miles. After McDonald's, veer right at historic business district onto Broadway St to store on right at Broadway & Front St (1st corner).

LIVONIA

ZERBO'S HEALTH FOODS 🍎
34164 Plymouth Rd. © 734-427-3144 ⊘ M-F 9:30-8, Sat 9:30-7, Sun 11-5
 · organic produce

From I-96 (Jeffers Fwy), take exit 174 south on Framington Rd 1 mile to Plymouth Rd. Turn right onto Plymouth less than ½ mile to store.

MARQUETTE

On Lake Superior and home to Northern Michigan U.

MARQUETTE ORGANIC FOOD CO-OP 🍎
C © 906-225-0671 ⊘ M-Sat 10-7
 · organic produce · co-op · chain

Take Rt 41 to Marquette. Turn left onto 41Bus/Washington St to store between 4th & 5th St.

MT. PLEASANT

Twenty minutes west of town is the Whispering Brook Biblical Garden and Nature Trail (look for the giant flat-wood dinosaur on M 20).

GREEN TREE CO-OP 🍎
214 N. Franklin © 989-772-3221 ⊘ M-F 9-7, Sat 10-7
 · organic produce · co-op

From US 27N, take 1st Mt Pleasant exit (US 27Bus) about 3½ miles to Mosher St. Turn left onto Mosher ⅓ mile (5 blocks) to Franklin St. Turn right onto Franklin to store on right. **From US 27S**, take take 1st Mt Pleasant exit (US 27Bus/Mission St) about 1½ miles to Mosher. Turn right onto Mosher and follow directions above.

PETOSKEY

THE GRAIN TRAIN NATURAL FOODS CO-OP ✗ 🍖 &

220 E. Mitchell St. © 231-347-2381 ⊙ M-Sat 7:30-8:30, Sun 10-6

· organic produce · freshly prepared food · café · bakery · vegetarian friendly · alcohol
· co-op · tables · self-service · take-out

🍎 **From juncture of US 31 & 131**, take 31N (becomes W Mitchell, then E Mitchell) to store.

ROCHESTER HILLS

HEALTH FOODS OF ROCHESTER 🍖

2952 S. Rochester Rd. © 248-852-0336 ⊙ M, Sat 9:30-6, Tues-F 9:30-7, Sun 11-3

🍎 **From I-75**, take exit 77A toward Utica onto MI 59E (Veteran's Memorial Fwy) 5½ miles to MI 150 exit toward Rochester/Troy. Turn left onto 150 (S Rochester Rd) ¾ mile to store on NW corner Rochester & Auburn Rd.

WHOLE FOODS MARKET ✗ 🍖

1404 Walton Blvd. © 248-652-2100 ⊙ Daily 9-9

· organic produce · freshly prepared food · salad bar · café · deli · bakery · vegetarian
friendly · chain · tables · self-service · take-out

🍎 **From I-75**, take exit 79 onto University Dr (left from 75S, right from 75N). Follow University left onto Squirrel Rd to E Walton Dr. Turn right onto Walton (becomes Walton Blvd) about 2²/₃ miles to store on north side in Rochester Hills Plaza.

ROYAL OAK

INN SEASON CAFE ✗

500 E. 4th St. © 248-547-7916 ⊙ Tues-Th 11:30-9, F 11:30-9:30, Sat 12-9:30, Sun 11-3
Menu draws from all over the world, but the common theme is vegetarian whole foods and organic when possible. Sunday brunch at this location. L&JB: Romantic and charming, with a range of simple fare to elegant dishes.

· vegetarian · vegan friendly · organic focus · tables · wait staff

🍎 **From I-696**, take exit 16 toward Woodward Ave/Main St onto W 10 Mile Rd to Main St. Turn north onto Main (left from 696E, right from 696W) about 1 mile to 4th St. Turn right onto 4th 3 blocks to restaurant on right (across from Aco Hardware). **From I-75,** take exit 62 toward 11 Mile Rd/W 10 Mile Rd west on 11 Mile (right from 75S, left from 75N) about 1 mile to Phillips Pl. Turn left onto Phillips 2 blocks to 4th. Turn right onto 4th 1 block to restaurant on left.

SAGINAW

GRAINS & GREENS 🍖

3641 Bay Rd. © 989-799-8171 ⊙ M-F 9-8, Sat 9-6, Sun 12-5

🍎 From I-75, merge onto I-675 toward Downtown (exit 150 from 75N, 155 from 75S) to exit 6 (Tittawbawsee Rd) toward Zilwaukee. Go west on Tittabawsee 1 mile to Bay Rd. Turn left onto Bay 1¹/₃ miles to store on left.

HERITAGE NATURAL FOODS 🍖

717 Gratiot Ave. © 989-793-5805 ⊙ M-Sat 9:30-5:30

🍎 **From I-75**, take exit 149B onto Rt 46W (Holland , then Sheridan, Rust & Gratiot Ave) about 2½ miles (across water). When 46 becomes Gratiot turn right 1 block to store.

TRAVERSE CITY

ORYANA FOOD CO-OP 🍎
260 East 10th St. ℰ 231-947-0191 ⏰ M-F 8-8, Sat 8-6, Sun 11-5

· organic produce · freshly prepared food · deli · vegetarian friendly · co-op · take-out

🍎 **From south,** take MI 37N to Traverse City. Turn right onto 14th St about ²/₃ mile to Cass Rd. Turn left onto Cass about ¹/₃ mile to 10th St. Turn right onto 10th to store at end (Lake Ave). **From north on US 31S or MI 37S,** turn left onto Cass about ½ mile to 10th. Turn left onto 10th to store at end.

TROY

GOOD FOOD COMPANY EAST ⚔️🍎
74 W. Maple Rd. ℰ 248-362-0886 ⏰ M-Sat 8-9, Sun 8-8

· freshly prepared food · deli · vegetarian friendly · tables · self-service · take-out

🍎 **From I-75,** take exit 65B west on 14 Mile Rd to Main St. Turn right onto Main (becomes Livernois Rd at Maple Rd) to store on left corner Livernois & W Maple.

WHOLE FOODS MARKET 🍎   ♿
2880 W. Maple Rd. ℰ 248-649-9600 ⏰ M-Sat 9-10, Sun 9-9

· organic produce · freshly prepared food · juice bar · salad bar · deli · bakery
· vegetarian friendly · chain · take-out

🍎 **From I-75,** take exit 69 west on Big Beaver Rd about 2 miles to Coolidge Hwy. Turn south onto Coolidge 1 mile to store on NE corner Coolidge & Maple Rd.

WEST BLOOMFIELD

WHOLE FOODS MARKET ⚔️🍎   ♿
7350 W. Orchard Lake Rd. ℰ 248-538-4600 ⏰ M-Sat 9-10, Sun 9-9

· organic produce · freshly prepared food · juice bar · salad bar · café · deli · bakery
· vegetarian friendly · chain · counter · tables · self-service · take-out

🍎 **From I-696,** take exit 5 north on Orchard Lake Rd 2 miles to 14 Mile Rd. Turn left onto 14 Mile and immediately right to store in Gateway Shopping Plaza.

WOODLAND

WOODLAND CO-OP 🍎
116 N. Main St. ℰ 616-367-4188 ⏰ M, F 12-5, W 12-7
Packaged foods only.

· co-op

🍎 Take Rt 43 into Woodland. At blinking light turn north onto Main St to 3rd store on left (in old bank).

YPSILANTI

YPSILANTI FOOD CO-OP 🍎
312 N. River St. ℰ 734-483-1520 ⏰ M-Tues, Th-F 10-8, W 10-9, Sat 9-8, Sun 12-5
Next door is the Depot Town Sourdough Bakery, a community-owned bakery with a wood-fired brick oven.

· organic produce · freshly prepared food · vegetarian friendly · co-op · take-out

🍎 **From I-94,** take exit 183 north on Huron St to Michigan Ave. Turn right onto Michigan ¼ mile to River St. Turn left onto River to store on right (just before railroad tracks).

Goldbeck's "EAT IT OR NOT"
FASCINATING & FAR-OUT FACTS ABOUT FOOD

AMERICANS eat more bananas than any other fresh fruit.

Annual consumption is about 25 pounds per person, with apples a distant second place. Virtually none of the bananas are grown in the U.S. Almost all are imported from Central America. This banana bonanza is particularly remarkable given that in the 1920s, Americans were so ignorant of bananas that importers had to advise consumers to peel them before eating.

MARACHINO CHERRIES are naturally the reddest of all cherries.

Actually this is not so. To make them, cherries are first bleached and then dyed. Two formerly used dyes were banned as health hazards.

BLEACH

RED DYE #?

TONI BERNHARD

MINNESOTA

ALBERT LEA

Two big lakes and a state park for camping. Check out the Doll & Toy Museum.

WINTERGREEN NATURAL FOODS 🛒 &
1442 W. Main St. © 507-373-0386 ⏰ M-F 10-5:30, Sat 9-5

· organic produce · co-op

🏕 **From I-90E**, take exit exit 154 toward Albert Lea onto MN 13S about 3¼ miles to W Main St. Turn left onto W Main to store. **From I-90W**, take exit 159A onto I-35S. **From I-35**, take exit 12 onto E Main St heading west about 4 miles. After Broadway Ave and 2 viaducts make 1st right to store.

ANOKA

ANOKA FOOD CO-OP 🍴🛒
1917 2nd Ave. S. © 763-427-4340 ⏰ M-F 8-7, Sat 10-6, Sun 12-4, Deli M-F 11-2

· freshly prepared food · deli · vegetarian friendly · co-op · tables · self-service · take-out

 **From I-94/694,** take US 169N (exit 29B) more than 8½ miles (across bridge) to Main St. Turn right onto E Main 2 blocks to S 2nd Ave. Turn right onto 2nd to store.

BAXTER

LIFE PRESERVER
875 Edgewood Drive ✆ 218-829-7925 ⏱ M-F 9-6, Sat 9-5

· organic produce

 Baxter is in the middle of MN at Hwy 210 & 371. **From 371N** (past 210 intersection), turn left onto Excelsior Rd and immediately right onto Edgewood Dr over ½ mile to store (1 mile north of Paul Bunyan Amusement Center). **From 371S,** turn right onto Woida Rd and immediately left onto Edgewood under ½ mile to store.

BEMIDJI

HARMONY NATURAL FOODS CO-OP
117 3rd St., N.W. ✆ 218-751-2009 ⏱ M-F 9-7, Sat 9-6, Sun 12-5

· organic produce · freshly prepared food · deli · co-op · take-out

 Take US 71 or US 2 to Bemidji and take MN 197 into town. Turn west onto 3rd St ½ block to store.

BLAINE

CAFE ORGANICA ✖
4000 Pheasant Ridge Drive N.E. ✆ 763-783-4069 ⏱ M-F 8-2

At the Aveda Headquarters. Come for a treatment or just to eat. Soups, salads, sandwiches, fresh pizza, plus hot entrees with a daily theme—Asian, Pasta, South of the Border, "Home Cooking," and "Anarchy Day" when anything goes.

· salad bar · café · vegetarian friendly · organic focus · tables · self-service

 **From I-35W,** take exit 33 (CR 17/Lexington Ave) north on Lexington about ¼ mile to Pheasant Ridge Dr. Turn left onto Pheasant Ridge to restaurant in Aveda Headquarters.

1 Albert Lea
2 Anoka
3 Baxter
4 Bemidji
5 Blaine
6 Blue Earth
7 Brainerd
8 Burnsville
9 Cambridge
10 Duluth
11 Edina
12 Fergus Falls
13 Grand Marais
14 Hastings
15 Lake City
16 Litchfield
17 Long Prairie
18 Minneapolis
19 Minnetonka
20 Morris
21 Owatonna
22 Rochester
23 Roseville
24 St. Cloud
25 St. Paul
26 St. Peter
27 Stillwater
28 Virginia
29 Wadena
30 Willmar
31 Windom
32 Winona

BLUE EARTH

RAINBOW FOOD CO-OP
103 South Main St. ✆ 507-526-3603 ⏱ M-F 10-5:30, Sat 10-3

· co-op

 **From I-90,** take exit 119 south on US 169 to 7th St. Turn right onto 7th to Main St. Turn right onto Main to store on right.

BRAINERD

CROW WING FOOD CO-OP
823 Washington St. ✆ 218-828-4600 ⏱ M-F 9:30-6, Sat 10-4

· organic produce · co-op

 Baxter is in the middle of MN at Hwy 210 & 371. Take 210 into town (becomes Washington St) to store at Washington & N 9th St.

BURNSVILLE

VALLEY NATURAL FOODS ✗🍲 &
13750 County Rd. 11 ☎ 952-891-1212 ⏰ M-Th 8-9, F-Sat 8-8, Sun 10-8, Drive-thru M-Sat 6:30am-8pm, Sun 9-8
Lots of vegetarian food and 80% organic. Drive-thru window for early birds.
· organic produce · freshly prepared food · juice bar · salad bar · deli · bakery
· vegetarian friendly · organic focus · co-op · counter · tables · self-service · take-out
🍎 **From I-35E**, take exit 90 (CR 11) south to store just off hwy on right corner McAndrews Rd & 11.

CAMBRIDGE

MOMS FOOD CO-OP 🍲
1709 E. Hwy 95 ☎ 763-689-4640 ⏰ M-F 9-8, Sat 9-6, Sun 12-5
· organic produce · co-op
🍎 Store is on MN 95 in Cambridge (12 miles west of I-35 exit 147, ¼ mile east of MN 65).

DULUTH

Duluth is at the point of Lake Superior, where the scenic trip up the North Shore to the Boundary Waters begins. The drive from downtown Duluth along the North Shore Scenic Drive has been designated a National Scenic By-way.

NEW SCENIC CAFE ✗ &
5461 North Shore Drive ☎ 218-525-6274 ⏰ Daily 11-10
Chef Scott Graden strives for "fresh, contemporary vegetarian and vegan foods," which make up at least half the menu, in addition to poultry, red meat and fish. Fine dining overlooking Lake Superior. Reservations suggested.
· vegetarian friendly · vegan friendly · alcohol · tables · wait staff
🍎 Take I-35 north to end onto Hwy 61 (North Shore Scenic Dr). Follow N Scenic Shore to restaurant (7½ miles past Lester River).

WHOLE FOODS CO-OP 🍲
1332 E. 4th St. ☎ 218-728-0490 ⏰ M-F 7-9, Sat-Sun 8-8
Produce is almost all organic, there are over 500 bulk items, breads are locally baked, and the vegetarian/vegan take-out deli is mostly organic, as well.
· organic produce · freshly prepared food · vegetarian · vegan friendly · organic focus
· co-op · take-out
🍎 **From I-35**, take exit 256 (Mesabe Ave/MN 23E) toward Superior St onto MN 23E (aka 2nd St) about 1¾ miles to 14th Ave. Turn left onto 14th to store on corner 14th & 4th St.

EDINA

GOOD EARTH RESTAURANT & BAKERY ✗ &
3460 W. 70th St. ☎ 612-925-1001 ⏰ M-Sat 8-10, Sun 8-9
A "natural foods" restaurant with poultry, fish and vegetarian choices. Soups, salads, sandwiches, burgers, hot entrees, wholegrains, fresh juices, and shakes.
· juice bar · bakery · vegetarian friendly · alcohol · chain · tables · wait staff
🍎 **From I-494**, take exit 6B onto France Ave S/Rte 17N about 1⅓ miles to W 70th St. Turn right onto 70th to restaurant in Galleria Shopping Center.

FERGUS FALLS

Over 1,000 lakes in the county and "more maple trees than the state of VT."

MEADOW FARM FOODS

23064 County Hwy. 1 © 218-739-4585 ⊙ M-Sat 9-6 (5:30 in winter)

· organic produce

From I-94, take exit 54 (Perkins Wal-Mart) toward Downtown (left from 94E, right from 94W) onto Lincoln Ave to traffic light at Union Ave. Turn left onto Union 2 blocks to Summit Ave. Turn right onto Summit to 4-way stop. Turn left onto Friberg Ave (CR 1) 3 miles to store on right.

GRAND MARAIS

Grand Marais is a gateway into the Boundary Waters canoe area wilderness, with miles of pristine lakes and boreal forest. The rocky coastline is dramatic, with crashing waves from the inland sea. Excellent camping and hiking along the shores of Lake Superior.

ANGRY TROUT CAFE

408 W. Hwy. 61 © 218-387-1265 ⊙ Daily 11-8

The emphasis is on organic produce and the fish is caught by the fisherman next door. Free-range chickens and something for vegetarians, as well. Outdoor dining at the edge of Lake Superior. A Certified Green Restaurant.

· vegetarian friendly · organic focus · tables · wait staff

Enter town on Hwy 61. Restaurant is on the harbor.

COOK COUNTY WHOLE FOODS CO-OP

20 E. 1st St. © 218-387-2503 ⊙ M-F 9-6:30, Sat 10-5

The only natural food store in a 100-mile radius.

· organic produce · freshly prepared food · co-op

Take Hwy 61 into Grand Marais and turn south at the only traffic light in town onto 1st Ave E. Take 1st Ave E 1 block to 1st St E. Turn left onto 1st St to store directly ahead.

HASTINGS

On the Mississippi River. A good place to see historic architecture.

SPIRAL NATURAL FOODS

307 2nd St. E. © 651-437-2667 ⊙ M-Th 10-7, F-Sat 9-5, Sun 11-5

· organic produce · freshly prepared food · deli · vegetarian friendly · co-op · tables · self-service · take-out

From Hwy 61S (Minneapolis-St Paul area), cross the Mississippi bridge and immediately turn right onto 3rd St. Turn right and right again (going under bridge) onto 2nd St. Go 3 blocks to store on left (across from post office).

LAKE CITY

OAK CENTER GENERAL FOOD STORE CO-OP

Hwy. 63 © 507-753-2080 ⊙ M-Sat 9-6

· co-op

On Hwy 63, about 25 miles north of Rochester or 10 miles south of intersection Hwy 61 & 63.

LITCHFIELD

NATURAL FOODS MARKET

230 N. Sibley St. © 320-693-7539 ⊙ M-F 10-6, Sat 10-5

· organic produce · co-op

About 40 miles west of Minneapolis on Hwy 12 (N Silbey St in town).

LONG PRAIRIE

EVERYBODY'S MARKET FOOD CO-OP 🥬
11 1st St. N. © 320-732-3900 ⊙ M-F 9-5:30, Sat 9-1

· co-op

📖 Long Prairie is about 20 miles north of I-94 exit 127 on US 71. **From US 71**, go east on Central Ave 1 block to store on left corner Central & 1st St. **From MN 27**, turn left onto 71 and follow directions above.

MINNEAPOLIS

BIRCHWOOD CAFE ✕
3311 E. 25th St. © 612-722-4474 ⊙ Tues-F 7-9, Sat 8-9, Sun 9-2
Mostly vegetarian, with exceptions (including free-range chicken).

· vegetarian friendly · vegan friendly · organic focus · alcohol · tables · wait staff

📖 **From I-94**, take exit 235A south on Riverside Ave (right from 94E, sharp left from 94W) 1 block to Franklin Ave. Turn left onto Franklin 2 blocks to 31st Ave. Turn right onto 31st 4 blocks to 25th St. Turn left onto 25th 2 blocks to restaurant on right.

CAFE BRENDA ✕
300 1st Ave. N. © 612-342-9230 ⊙ Lunch M-F 11:30-2, Dinner M-Th 5:30-9, F-Sat 5:30-10
A "Gourmet Vegetarian and Fresh Seafood" restaurant. Free-range turkey also on the menu.

· vegetarian friendly · alcohol · tables · wait staff

📖 **From I-94E**, take exit 230 onto N 4th St to free parking on left between 2nd & 1st Ave. To walk from parking, turn left onto 1st Ave. (To drive to restaurant, turn left onto 2nd Ave, right onto Washington St and right onto 1st Ave). **From I-94W**, take 5th St exit past Metrodome through the loop to Hennepin Ave. Turn right onto Hennepin 2 blocks to 3rd St. Turn left onto 3rd 1 block to restaurant on SW corner 3rd & 1st Ave. **From I-35W heading south**, take exit 17C west (right) onto Washington about 1 mile to 1st Ave N. Turn left onto 1st 1 block to restaurant. **From I-35W heading north**, take 5th Ave (last downtown exit) north (5th turns into Washington) to 3rd St. Turn left onto 3rd to restaurant on SW corner at 1st Ave.

CAFE ORGANICA ✕   ⊜ ᚦ
400 Central Ave. S.E. © 612-378-7413 ⊙ Tues-Sat 7:30-3
At the Aveda Institute. Come for a treatment or just to eat. Soups, salads, sandwiches, fresh pizza, plus daily specials. Small menu but always something for vegetarians.

· vegetarian friendly · organic focus · tables · self-service

📖 From I-94E, take exit 230 onto N 4th St almost 1 mile to Hennepin Ave E. Turn left onto Hennepin almost 1 mile (across river) to SE University Ave. Turn right onto Unversity 2 blocks to Central Ave. Turn left onto Central 1 block to restaurant at 4th & Central in Aveda Institute. **From I-94W**, take exit 235B onto Huron Blvd (becomes SE 4th St) about 1¼ miles to restaurant on right at 4th & Central (Aveda Institute) . **From I-35W**, take exit 18 (4th St/University) onto 4th (right heading south, left heading north) about 9 blocks to restaurant on right at 4th & Central (Aveda Institute).

CAYOL'S NATURAL FOODS 🥬
811 Lasalle Ave. © 612-339-2828 ⊙ M-F 8:30-6, Sat 10-4:30

🛏 **From I-94E**, take exit 230 onto N 4th St about ¾ mile to 1st Ave N. Turn left onto 1st 4 blocks to 8th Ave N. Turn left onto 8th 2 blocks to Lasalle Ave. Turn right onto Lasalle to store. **From I-94W**, take exit 233A north onto 11th St about ½ mile to Lasalle. Turn right onto Lasalle 3 blocks to store on right.

ECOPOLITAN ✕   ᕦ
2409 Lyndale Ave. S. ℂ 612-874-7336 ⊙ Tues-Th, Sun 9-10, F-Sat 9-11
100% organic, vegan, raw foods menu, as well as organic, vegan, sulfite-free wines. Store also carries a range of "green" products and holds free weekly educational seminars, recipe demos, and monthly "uncooking classes." They recycle and compost, as well. A Certified Green Restaurant.

· juice bar · vegan · organic focus · counter · tables · wait staff

🛏 **From I-94**, take exit 231 (Hennepin/Lyndale) south on Lyndale Ave 4 blocks to 24th St. Restaurant is on left. (For free parking, turn left onto 24th and make immediate right into alleyway.)

FRENCH MEADOW BAKERY ✕
2610 Lyndale Ave. S. ℂ 612-870-7855 ⊙ M-Th, Sun 6:30am-9pm, F-Sat 6:30am-11pm
Homemade organic yeast- and dairy-free breads. Vegetarian, fish, free-range poultry, local and organic ingredients. From wholesome hearty breakfasts to inventive dinners. A Certified Green Restaurant.

· café · bakery · vegetarian friendly · organic focus · alcohol · tables · self-service
· wait staff · take-out

🛏 **From I-94**, take exit 231 (Hennepin/Lyndale) south on Lyndale Ave 6 blocks to restaurant at 26th St.

LINDEN HILLS CO-OP ✕🖫🛒
2813 W. 43rd St. ℂ 612-922-1159 ⊙ Daily 8-9
Jeanne at the Co-op recommends stopping in at the old firehouse for a copy of the neighborhood walking tour. If you come in summer, enjoy free concerts at the Lake Harriet Bandshell.

· organic produce · freshly prepared food · juice bar · salad bar · deli · bakery
· vegetarian friendly · co-op · tables · self-service · take-out

🛏 **From I-35W**, take Diamond Lake Rd exit (12B) west on Diamond Lake (aka 54th St) to Xerxes Ave. Turn right (north) onto Xerxes to 43rd St. Turn right onto W 43rd to store on right between Vincent & Upton Ave.

NORTH COUNTRY COOPERATIVE GROCERY 🛒
1929 S. 5th St. ℂ 612-338-3110 ⊙ Daily 8-9

· co-op

🛏 **From I-94**, take exit 235A north on Riverside Ave (slight right from 94W, left from 94E) about ½ mile to store on corner Riverside & 20th Ave S. **From I-35W**, take exit 17C (3rd St) toward UMN and follow ramp to Washintgon Ave S. Turn right onto Washington to Riverside. Turn left onto Riverside 2 blocks to store.

SEWARD COMMUNITY CAFE ✕   ᕦ
2129 Franklin Ave. E. ℂ 612-332-1011 ⊙ M-F 7-3, Sat-Sun 8-4
Wholefoods, almost entirely vegetarian and vegan breakfasts and lunches, run collectively with an eye toward affordability. A good place to hang out.

· vegetarian friendly · vegan friendly · organic focus · co-op · counter · tables · self-service

🛏 **From I-94**, take exit 235A (Riverside Ave) straight off exit to 25th Ave S. Turn south onto 25th (right from 94E, left from 94W) 1-2 blocks to Franklin Ave. Turn right onto Franklin 5 blocks to restaurant on SW corner 22nd Ave & Franklin.

SEWARD COMMUNITY CO-OP 🍎
2111 Franklin Ave. E. © 612-338-2465 ⊙ Daily 9-9
· organic produce · juice bar · deli · co-op · take-out

📷 **From I-94**, take exit 235A (Riverside Ave) straight off exit to 25th Ave S. Turn south onto 25th (right from 94E, left from 94W) 1-2 blocks to Franklin Ave. Turn right onto Franklin 4½ blocks to store on left. **From I-35W**, take exit 17A (Hiawatha Ave) and stay right onto Cedar Ave to traffic light at Franklin. Turn left onto Franklin 2 blocks to store on right.

ST. MARTIN'S TABLE ✕   ふ
2001 Riverside Ave. © 612-339-3920 ⊙ M-F 11-2:30, Sat (winter only) 8-2:30
This bookstore/restaurant is run by the Community of St. Martin's, an ecumenical center for peacemaking and justice. The intentionally simple vegetarian menu reflects their "solidarity with our neighbors around the world who have limited choices for their own daily menu." Each day's offering includes two soups (one vegan), spreads, salads, whole grain bread, yogurt, granola, and desserts. Ingredients are organic and local whenever possible. The volunteer waitstaff donates the tips to programs that alleviate world hunger.
· vegetarian · vegan friendly · organic focus · tables · wait staff · take-out

📷 **From I-94**, take exit 235A north on Riverside Ave (slight right from 94W, left from 94E) about ½ mile to store/restaurant at Riverside & 20th Ave S.

TAO NATURAL FOODS & BOOKS 🍎
2200 Hennepin Ave. S. © 612-377-4630 ⊙ M-Th 9-8, F-Sat 9-6, Sun 11-6
· juice bar

📷 **From I-94**, take exit 231 (Hennepin/Lyndale) south on Hennepin Ave to store 1 block south of Franklin Ave.

WEDGE COMMUNITY CO-OP 🍎
2105 Lyndale Ave. S. © 612-874-7275 ⊙ M-F 9-10, Sat-Sun 9-9
· organic produce · co-op

📷 **From I-94**, take exit 231 (Lyndale/Hennepin) south on Lyndale Ave ½ block past traffic light at Franklin Ave to store on left.

WHOLE FOODS MARKET ✕🍎   ふ
3060 Excelsior Blvd. © 612-927-8141 ⊙ Daily 8-10
· organic produce · freshly prepared food · juice bar · salad bar · café · deli · bakery
· vegetarian friendly · chain · tables · wait staff · take-out

📷 **From I-94**, take exit 231 (Hennepin/Lyndale) south on Hennepin Ave about 1 mile to Lagoon Ave. Turn right onto Lagoon and continue on Rt 3W about 1¼ miles (across water, becomes W Lake Ave, then Excelsior Blvd) to store.

MINNETONKA

LAKEWINDS NATURAL FOODS 🍎
17523 Minnetonka Blvd. © 952-473-0292 ⊙ M-Sat 8-8, Sun 9-8
In addition to food, there is a "Natural Home" store with earth-friendly products.
· organic produce · freshly prepared food · deli · vegetarian friendly · co-op · take-out

📷 **From 1-494**, take exit 17 west on Minnetonka Blvd about 2 miles to store at Minnetonka & Hwy 101.

MORRIS

POMME DE TERRE FOOD CO-OP 🛒
613 Atlantic Ave. © 320-589-4332 ⏰ M-W, F 10-6, Th 10-8, Sat 10-4

· co-op

🏬 Rt 28, 9 & US 59 all converge in Morris. Store is on Rt 9 (aka Atlantic Ave) at about 6th St.

OWATONNA

HARVEST FOOD CO-OP 🛒
137 E. Front St. © 507-451-0340 ⏰ M-F 9:30-5:30, Sat 9-1

· co-op

🏬 **From I-35**, take exit 42 (14W/CR 45) onto Hoffman Dr (aka 14Bus) about 1 mile to W Rose St. Turn left onto W Rose, left onto Cedar Ave and right onto E Front St to store (across from big grain elevator).

ROCHESTER

THE GOOD FOOD STORE 🍴🛒
1001 6th St. N.W. © 507-289-9061 ⏰ M-F 9-9, Sat 9-8, Sun 10-7

· organic produce · freshly prepared food · deli · vegetarian friendly · tables · self-service · take-out

🏬 **From I-90**, take exit 218 north on Hwy 52 about 10 miles to Civic Center Dr NW exit. Merge onto Civic Center (heading east) about ½ mile to 11th Ave. Turn left onto 11th 1 block to 6th St NW. Turn right onto 6th to store in 1st building on left.

ROSEVILLE

GOOD EARTH RESTAURANT & BAKERY 🍴   ♿
1901 W. Hwy 36 © 651-636-0956 ⏰ M-Sat 7-10, Sun 7-9

A "natural food" restaurant with poultry, fish and vegetarian choices. Soups, salads, sandwiches, burgers, hot entrees, wholegrains, fresh juices, and shakes.

· juice bar · bakery · vegetarian friendly · alcohol · chain · tables · wait staff

🏬 **From I-35W**, take exit 23B onto MN 36E almost 1 mile to Fairview Ave N exit. Merge onto Fairview and back onto 36W to restaurant on NW side of 36 (2 blocks west of Fairview) in gray building with blue roof. **From I-35E**, take exit 111B onto MN 36W about 4½ miles to restaurant.

ST. CLOUD

GOOD EARTH FOOD CO-OP 🍴🛒
2010 8th St. N. © 320-253-9290 ⏰ M-Sat 8:30-8, Sun 10-6

· organic produce · freshly prepared food · deli · vegetarian friendly · co-op · tables · self-service · take-out

🏬 **From I-94**, take exit 167B (St Cloud/Kimbell) onto MN 15N about 5¼ miles to 8th St N. Turn right onto 8th about 1 mile to store on right in shopping plaza.

INEZ NATUREWAY FOODS 🛒
3715 3rd St. N. © 320-259-0514 ⏰ M-F 9-7, Sat 9-3

Limited stock of packaged natural foods.

🏬 **From I-94**, take exit 167B (St Cloud/Kimbell) onto MN 15N about 4¾ miles to 3rd St N. Turn right onto 3rd to store on left.

ST. PAUL

HAMPDEN PARK FOOD CO-OP 🐑
28 Raymond Ave. ✆ 651-646-6686 ⏰ M-F 9-9, Sat 9-7, Sun 10-7
· organic produce · freshly prepared food · deli · bakery · co-op · take-out
🍴 From I-94, merge onto 280N about 1 mile to Kasota Ave/Energy Park Dr. Turn right onto Energy Park about ⅓ mile to Raymond Ave. Turn right onto Raymond about ¼ mile to store.

MISSISSIPPI MARKET NATURAL FOODS CO-OP 🐑 ⅚
622 Selby Ave. ✆ 651-310-9499 ⏰ Daily 8:30-9:30
· organic produce · freshly prepared food · juice bar · deli · co-op · take-out
🍴 From I-94, take exit 240 south on Dale St about ⅓ mile to store on SW corner Dale & Selby Ave.

MISSISSIPPI MARKET NATURAL FOODS CO-OP 🐑 ⅚
1810 Randolph Ave. ✆ 651-690-0507 ⏰ Daily 8:30-9
· organic produce · freshly prepared food · co-op · take-out
🍴 From I-94, take exit 238 south on Snelling Ave (MN 51S) about 1⅔ miles to Randolph Ave. Turn right onto Randolph 4 blocks store on SE corner Randolph & Fairview Ave. **From I-35E**, take exit 104A west on Randoph Ave over 1½ miles to store on SE corner Randolf & Fairview.

WHOLE FOODS MARKET 🍴🐑
30 S. Fairview Ave. ✆ 651-690-0197 ⏰ Daily 9-10
· organic produce · freshly prepared food · deli · bakery · vegetarian friendly · chain · tables · self-service · take-out
🍴 From I-94, take exit 238 south on Snelling Ave (MN 51S) ¾ mile to Grand Ave. Turn right onto Grand ½ mile to store on corner Grand & Fairview Ave.

ST. PETER

ST. PETER FOOD CO-OP 🍴🐑
119 W. Broadway Ave. ✆ 507-934-4880 ⏰ M-Sat 8-8, Sun 9-7
· organic produce · freshly prepared food · deli · vegetarian friendly · co-op · tables · self-service · take-out
🍴 From US 169, go east on W Broadway Ave to store just off hwy.

STILLWATER

RIVER MARKET COMMUNITY CO-OP 🍴🐑
221 Main St. ✆ 651-439-0366 ⏰ M-F 8-9, Sat 8-8, Sun 10-7
· freshly prepared food · deli · vegetarian friendly · co-op · tables · self-service · take-out
🍴 From I-694, take exit 52B east on MN 36 about 10 miles to Stillwater. Store is on 36/95 (aka Main St) at Commercial Ave.

VIRGINIA

NATURAL HARVEST WHOLE FOOD CO-OP 🍴🐑
505 3rd St. N. ✆ 218-741-4663 ⏰ M-F 8-8, Sat 10-5, Sun 10-3
· freshly prepared food · deli · vegetarian friendly · co-op · tables · self-service · take-out
🍴 From intersection Hwy 169 & 53, take 53N (ramp on left) to 1st traffic light at 9th St. Turn right onto 9th (past hospital) 2 lights to 6th Ave. Turn right onto 6th to 2nd St N. Turn left onto 2nd and drive around onto N 3rd St to store (big log cabin on Bailey Lake). **From north on 53S**, turn left

onto 9th St and follow directions above. **From south on 53N**, take 2nd Ave exit almost 1 mile to Chestnut St. Turn left onto Chestnut to 5th Ave. Turn right onto 5th to end. Turn left onto N 3rd to store.

WADENA

Wadena isn't near any major highway, but it's on the route to Minnesota lakes from all directions.

DOWN HOME FOODS

636 N. Jefferson ℂ 218-631-2323 ⊘ M-F 9-5:30, Sat 9-2:30
This health food store has no produce, but specializes in cheese.
· freshly prepared food · deli · take-out

🍎 In the middle of MN, where Hwy 10 & 71 meet. Store is on east side of Hwy 71N (aka N Jefferson) after KFC.

WILLMAR

KANDI CUPBOARD FOOD CO-OP

412 Litchfield Ave. S.W. ℂ 320-235-9477 ⊘ M-F 9-6, Sat 9-3 (until 5 Nov & Dec)
· organic produce · co-op

🍎 **From intersection Hwy 12, 23 & 71** (all converge in Wilmar), take Hwy 12 west to 4th St NW. Turn south (left) onto 4th, then right onto Litchfield to store just off corner on right.

WINDOM

PLUM CREEK FOOD CO-OP

910 4th Ave. ℂ 507-831-1882 ⊘ M 9:30-8, Tues-F 9:30-5, Sat 9:30-3
· co-op

🍎 Take Hwy 60 or 71 to Windom. Turn west onto 10th St 2 blocks to 4th Ave. Turn left onto 4th 1 block to store on west side.

WINONA

BLUFF COUNTRY CO-OP

121 W. Second St. ℂ 507-452-1815 ⊘ M-W, Sat 8:30-7, Th-F 8:30-8, Sun 11-5
· organic produce · deli · vegetarian friendly · co-op · tables · self-service · take-out

🍎 **From I-90**, take exit 252 onto MN 43N toward Winona almost 9½ miles (43N becomes Sarnia St at almost 7½ miles, then Main St after about another mile) to 2nd St. Turn left onto 2nd to store just off Main. **From US 61**, turn north onto Huff St toward Mississippi River (left from 61S, right from 61N) to traffic light at 2nd St. Turn right onto 2nd 3 blocks to store.

Goldbeck's "EAT IT OR NOT"
FASCINATING & FAR-OUT FACTS ABOUT FOOD

Iceberg lettuce, frozen potatoes (mainly French fries) and potato chips account for more than one-third of the daily vegetables eaten in the U.S.

MISSISSIPPI

1 Gulfport
2 Jackson
3 Long Beach
4 Ocean Springs
5 Pass Christian

GULFPORT

RENAISSANCE NATURAL FOODS 🍎
1702 West Pass Rd. © 228-864-4898 ⊘ M-F 10-5:30, Sat 10-4

🛒 **From I-10,** take exit 34A (toward Gulfport) onto US 49S almost 4 miles to Pass Rd. Turn left onto Pass (aka 25th St) 8 blocks to store (just past 17th Ave).

JACKSON

Home of MS Agriculture Museum, Sports Hall of Fame and the historic Fondren district shopping area.

BEST OF HEALTH ✕🍎
235 Highland Village © 601-981-2838 ⊘ M-Sat 10-6

· organic produce · freshly prepared food · deli · tables · self-service · take-out

🛒 **From I-55,** take exit 100 (Northside Dr) east (left from 55S, right from 55N) to 1st entrance on right into Highland Village shopping center (corner I-55 & Northside). Store is on 2nd level in south end of shopping center.

RAINBOW WHOLEFOODS COOPERATIVE GROCERY ✕🍎 ♿
2807 Old Canton Rd. © 601-366-1602 ⊘ M-Sat 8-8, Sun 12-6

Food is primarily vegan, with vegetarian options and organic when available.

· organic produce · freshly prepared food · juice bar · salad bar · café · deli · bakery
· vegetarian · vegan · organic focus · coop · counter · tables · self-service · take-out

🛒 **From I-55,** take exit 98B west on Lakeland Dr about ½ mile until it dead-ends at Old Canton Rd. Store is right there.

LONG BEACH

RENAISSANCE NATURAL FOODS 🍎
104 W. Railroad © 228-865-9911 ⊘ M-F 10-6, Sat 10-5

🛒 **From I-10,** take exit 31 south on Canal Rd about 3 miles to 28th St. Turn right onto 28th about 1 mile to Klondyke Rd. Turn left onto Klondyke about 2⅓ miles to Railroad St. Turn left onto Railroad 1 block to store at Railroad & Jeff Davis Ave. **From Hwy 90,** go north on Jeff Davis about 5 blocks (less than ½ mile) to store at Jeff Davis & Railroad.

OCEAN SPRINGS

FIVE SEASONS WHOLE FOODS MARKET 🍎
601 Washington Ave. © 228-875-8882 ⊘ M-Sat 9:30-5:30, Sat 9:30-5

🛒 **From I-10,** take exit 50 south on Washington Ave more than 3 miles (past Hwy 90) to store on right.

PASS CHRISTIAN

MORNING MARKET 🍎
101 E. Scenic © 228-452-7593 ⊘ M-Sat 9:30-5:30

· organic produce

🛒 **From I-10,** take exit 28 toward Pass Christian south on County Farm Rd (right from 10E, left from 10W) over 1 mile to Red Creek Rd. Veer right onto Red Creek 3¼ miles to Menge Ave. Veer left onto Menge 2¾ miles to I-90. Turn right onto 90W almost 2 miles to Market St. Turn left onto Market 1 short block to store at E Scenic Dr.

MISSOURI

COLUMBIA

A college town with lots of independently owned businesses, funky eateries, galleries, and "midwest kindness."

CLOVERS NATURAL FOOD 🍀

802 Business Loop 70E ☎ 573-449-1650 ⏰ M-Sat 9-7, Sun 12-5

· organic produce

🛒 **From I-70,** take exit 126 toward Downtown south on Providence Rd 1 block to 70 Bus Loop. Turn left onto 70Bus about ⅓ mile to store on right.

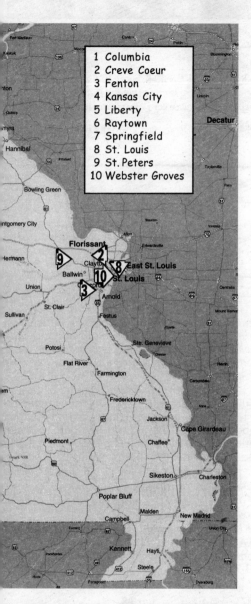

1 Columbia
2 Creve Coeur
3 Fenton
4 Kansas City
5 Liberty
6 Raytown
7 Springfield
8 St. Louis
9 St. Peters
10 Webster Groves

MAIN SQUEEZE NATURAL FOODS CAFE & JUICE BAR ✕ ♿

28 S. Ninth St. ✆ 573-817-5616 ⏲ M-Sat 10-3

Mostly organic, vegetarian and vegan menu featuring soups, salads, wraps, daily specials, vegan baked goods, plus fresh juice and smoothies.

· juice bar · café · vegetarian · vegetarian friendly · organic focus · tables · self-service

🖸 **From Hwy 70**, take exit 128A toward Downtown onto Hwy 63S, then immediately exit at Broadway. Go west (right) about 1½ miles on Broadway into downtown to 9th St. Turn left onto 9th 1 block to store on left (just before Cherry St).

CREVE COEUR

THE NATURAL WAY ✖🍃   ♿
12345 Olive Blvd. ℂ 314-878-3001 ⊙ M-F 9:30-8, Sat 9:30-6:30, Sun 12-5
The juice bar food is vegetarian and there is one table for indoor eating.
- organic produce · freshly prepared food · juice bar · vegetarian · tables · self-service · take-out

🍎 **From I-270**, take exit 14 west on Olive Ave 2 blocks to store on right (with blue awning).

FENTON

THE NATURAL WAY 🍃   ♿
468 Dierberg's Fenton Plaza ℂ 636-343-4343 ⊙ M-F 9-9, Sat 9-7, Sun 10-6
- organic produce

🍎 **From I-44**, take exit 272 onto Rt 141S about 3½ miles to Rt 30. Store is on SW corner 141 & 30. **From I-270**, take exit 3 west on Rt 30 about 2¾ miles to Rt 141. Store is on SW corner 141 & 30.

KANSAS CITY

EDEN ALLEY ✖   🍽♿
707 W. 47th St. ℂ 816-561-5415 ⊙ M-Sat 11-9, 1st & 3rd Sun 9-1
A primarily vegetarian menu, but fish appears among the daily specials. On the 1st and 3rd Sundays of the month, Unity Temple (home to the restaurant) hosts an indoor vendors' market with organic produce, baked goods, local crafts, and more. On these Sundays, Eden Alley is open for brunch.
- vegetarian · tables · wait staff · take-out

🍎 **From I-35S**, take exit 1A onto Southwest Tfwy (becomes Belleview Ave) about 2½ miles to 47th St. Turn left onto 47th 3 blocks to restaurant on plaza at corner 47th & Jefferson St in Unity Temple. **From I-70**, take 35S and follow directions above. **From I-35N**, take exit 228B onto Shawnee Mission Pkwy/56E 6¼ miles (across MO/KS state line) to 47th St. Turn right onto 47th 2 blocks to restaurant at 47th & Jefferson in Unity Temple.

NUTTY GIRL CAFE & JUICE BAR ✖
1621 W. 39th St. ℂ 816-756-5650 ⊙ M-Sat 10-9, Sun 10-4
Sandwiches, fresh juices and smoothies. Mostly vegetarian and vegan, with one tuna and one free-range turkey offering.
- juice bar · café · vegetarian friendly · vegan friendly · tables · self-service

🍎 **From I-35S**, take exit 1A onto Southwest Tfwy 1⅓ miles to W 38th St. Turn right onto 38th, left onto Summit St and right onto 39th St less than ½ mile to restaurant. **From I-70**, take I-35S and follow directions above.

WILD OATS MARKET 🍃
4301 Main St. ℂ 816-931-1873 ⊙ M-F 8-9, Sat-Sun 9-8
- organic produce · chain

🍎 **From I-35S**, take Broadway exit (1B) south about 2 miles to 43rd St. Turn left onto 43rd 1 block to store on corner 43rd & Main St. **From I-70**, take I-35S and follow directions above.

LIBERTY

Jesse James' birthplace and the Homestead Museum. Plenty of state parks for camping and hiking.

MOTHER NATURE'S HEALTH MARKET 🍇

344 S. 291 Hwy. ✆ 816-415-4638 ⊙ M-Sat 9-8

· organic produce

🍎 **From I-35**, take exit 16 onto Hwy 152E into Liberty about ½ mile to 4th traffic light at Hwy 291. Turn right (south) onto 291 to store on right in Crossroads Shopping Center.

RAYTOWN

Check out Worlds of Fun amusement park and the Nelson Art Gallery.

THE PUMPKIN SEED HEALTH FOOD STORE 🍇

9055 E. 350 Hwy. ✆ 816-358-1700 ⊙ M-Th 10-5:30, F-Sat 10-5

🍎 **From I-435**, take exit 66 onto 350E (Blue Pkwy) about 2⅓ miles. At first traffic light turn right to store. **From I-70**, take I-435S and follow directions above.

SPRINGFIELD

AKIN'S NATURAL FOODS MARKET 🍇   ♿

1330 E. Battlefield Rd. ✆ 417-887-5985 ⊙ Daily 8-8

· organic produce · chain

🍎 **From I-44,** take exit 72 east on Chestnut Expwy about 3½ miles to Rt 13/Kansas Expwy. Turn right (south) onto 13 about 3½ miles to Battlefield Rd. Turn left onto Battlefield about 2⅓ miles to store in Fremont Shopping Ctr.

SPRING VALLEY HERBS & NATURAL FOODS 🍇

1738 S. Glenstone Ave. ✆ 417-882-1033 ⊙ M-F 10-10, Sat 10-6, Sun 12-6

🍎 **From I-44E**, take exit 80A south on N Gladstone Ave about 4½ miles to store on left at Sunshine St (next to Park Inn). **From I-44W**, take exit 82A onto 65S almost 5 miles to Sunshine St exit. Turn west (right) onto Sunshine 2 miles to S Gladstone. Turn right onto Gladstone to store on right.

WELLSPRING CAFE ✗   ♿

300 W. McDaniel St. ✆ 417-865-1818 ⊙ M-F 10-3

Vegetarian and vegan soups, salads, hot and cold sandwiches and wraps (on whole grain bread or tortillas), Tex-Mex plates, plus daily specials. Local organic produce in season. A homey place where you can browse the healthy lifestyle reading matter and check the bulletin board for local events and services.

· vegetarian · vegan friendly · organic focus · counter · tables · self-service · take-out

🍎 **From I-44,** take exit 80A south on Glenstone Ave (Loop 44) about 2 miles to Walnut St. Turn right (west) onto Walnut about 1¾ miles to S Campbell St. Turn right onto Campbell to McDaniel St. Turn right to restaurant on corner McDaniel & Patton St (across from free parking lot). **From US 60**, go north on Glenstone Ave (65Bus) to Walnut, turn left onto Walnut, and follow directions above.

ST. LOUIS

ETERNITY VEGETARIAN DELI & JUICE BAR ✕
11 S. Euclid Ave. ✆ 314-454-1851 ⊙ M-Th 10-9, F-Sat 10-11
Cooked and raw vegan sandwiches, salads, soups, fresh juice, smoothies, plus a "soul food" buffet from the Atlanta, GA-based Soul Vegetarian chain.
· juice bar · vegan · tables · self-service · take-out

🍎 From I-70, take exit 344 south on N Kingshwy Blvd about 3⅓ miles to Laclede Ave. Turn left onto Laclede 2 blocks to Euclid. Turn right onto Euclid to restaurant. **From I-44**, take exit 287A north on S Kingshwy Blvd 1½ miles to Forest Park Ave. Turn right onto Forest Park 1 block to Euclid. Turn left onto Euclid to restaurant. **From I-64 (US 40)**, take exit 36B north on S Kingshwy Blvd to Forest Park and follow directions above.

GOLDEN GROCER ✕ 🍖
335 N. Euclid Ave. ✆ 314-367-0405 ⊙ M-Sat 10-7, Sun 12-5
· organic produce · freshly prepared food · deli · vegetarian · tables · self-service · take-out

🍎 From I-70, take exit 244 south on N Kingshwy Blvd almost 3 miles to Maryland Ave. Turn left onto Maryland 1 block to Euclid Ave. Turn left onto Euclid to store on left (set back from road). **From I-44**, take exit 287A north on S Kingshwy Blvd over 1½ miles to Maryland. Turn right onto Maryland and left onto Euclid to store on left. **From I-64 (US 40)**, take exit 36B north on S Kingshwy Blvd to Maryland and follow directions above.

GOVINDA'S VEGETARIAN RESTAURANT ✕
3926 Lindell Blvd. ✆ 314-535-8085 ⊙ M-F 11:30-2:30, 5-8:30, Sun 6pm-8:30pm
A vegetarian all-you-can-eat buffet in the Hare Krishna temple.
· vegetarian · vegan friendly · tables · self-service

🍎 From I-64E (US 40), take exit 36D left onto Vandeventer about ¾ mile to Lindell. Turn right onto Lindell to restaurant in Hare Krishna temple (next to St Louis U). **From I-64W**, take exit 38A onto Forest Park Blvd ¼ mile to S Grand Blvd. Turn right onto Grand about ¼ mile to Lindell. Turn left onto Lindell about ½ mile to restaurant.

KALDI'S COFFEE HOUSE & MARKET BAKERY ✕
700 De Mun Ave. ✆ 314-727-9955 ⊙ Daily 7am-11pm
Vegetarian menu and homemade pastries.
· café · bakery · vegetarian · tables · self-service · take-out

🍎 From I-64E (US 40E), take exit 33D north on Skinker Blvd about ¼ mile to traffic light at Rosebury Ave. Turn left onto Rosebury to end at De Mun Ave. Turn right onto De Mun to restaurant at end. **From I-64W (US 40W)**, take exit 34B right onto Skinker and follow directions above.

TANGERINE ✕
1405 Washington Ave. ✆ 314-621-7335 ⊙ M-Th 5:30-10, F-Sat 5-10:30
· vegetarian · alcohol · tables · wait staff · take-out

🍎 From I-70E, take exit 249A south on 10th St about ¾ mile to Washington Ave. Turn right onto Washington to restaurant on right at 14th St. **From I-64E (US 40)**, take exit 39B left (north) onto 14th St ⅔ mile to Washington. Turn left onto Washington to restaurant on right. **From I-64W**, take exit 40A left onto Clark Ave about ¼ mile to Tucker Blvd. Turn right onto Tucker ½ mile to Washington. Turn left onto Washington 2 blocks to restaurant on right.

WHOLE FOODS MARKET ✗ 🍇 &

1601 S. Brentwood Blvd. ✆ 314-968-7744 ☺ Daily 9-10

· organic produce · freshly prepared food · juice bar · salad bar · café · deli · bakery · vegetarian friendly · chain · tables · self-service · take-out

From I-64 (US 40), take exit 31 (31A from 64W) right on Brentwood Blvd to store on right in Brentwood Square shopping center (just south of hwy).

WILD OATS MARKET ✗ 🍇 &

8823 Ladue Rd. ✆ 314-721-8004 ☺ Daily 7-10

· organic produce · freshly prepared food · juice bar · salad bar · café · deli · bakery · vegetarian friendly · chain · tables · self-service · take-out

From I-170, take exit 1F east on Ladue Rd past 2 traffic lights to store on right.

ST. PETERS

NUTRITION STOP INC. 🍇 s

4101 Mexico Rd. ✆ 636-928-7550 ☺ M-F 9-8, Sat 9-5

Kids can enjoy the play area while you shop.

· organic produce

From I-70, take exit 225 south (left from 70W, right from 70E) onto Cave Springs Rd about ¼ mile to Mexico Rd. Turn right onto Mexico about ⅓ mile (1st traffic light) to store on left corner Mexico & Cave Springs Blvd.

WEBSTER GROVES

THE NATURAL FACT DELI ✗

7919 Big Bend Blvd. ✆ 314-961-2442 ☺ M-F 11-7:30 (6:30 winter), Sat 11-4

More than half vegetarian, but there is also a generous amount of chicken.

· vegetarian friendly · tables · self-service · take-out

From I-44E, take exit 282 right onto Laclede Station Rd 1 block to Murdock Ave. Turn right onto Murdock to 1st main intersection at Big Bend Blvd. Turn right onto Big Bend to store on left. **From I-44W**, take exit 283 left off ramp onto Shrewsbury Ave to Big Bend. Turn left onto Big Bend to store on right.

THE NATURAL WAY 🍇 &

8110 Big Bend Blvd. ✆ 314-961-3541 ☺ M-F 9-9, Sat 9-7, Sun 10-6

· organic produce

From I-44E, take exit 282 right onto Laclede Station Rd 1 block to Murdock Ave. Turn right onto Murdock to 1st main intersection at Big Bend Blvd. Turn left onto Big Bend 1 block to store on left (large tomato sign on building). **From I-44W**, take exit 283 left off ramp onto Shrewsbury Ave to Big Bend. Turn left onto Big Bend 4 blocks to store on left.

MONTANA

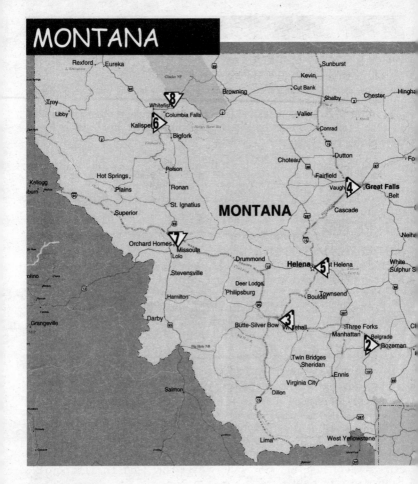

BILLINGS

GOOD EARTH MARKET 🍖
3115 10th Ave. N. ✆ 406-259-2622 ⏰ M-Sat 8-8, Sun 10-5, Deli M-F 8-2
Deli offers sandwiches, soups, salads, and daily specials to go. Menu stresses local products, including locally-raised beef and turkey.
· organic produce · freshly prepared food · deli · vegetarian friendly · co-op · take-out
🛏 From I-90/94, take exit 450 (MT 3) towards City Center onto 27th St (right from 90W, left from 90E) about 2 miles to 10th Ave N. Turn left onto 10th 4½ blocks to store between 31st & 32nd St.

BOZEMAN

COMMUNITY FOOD CO-OP ✗🍖   ♿
908 W. Main St. ✆ 406-586-4039 ⏰ Daily 8:30-9, Cafe 7am-8pm
· organic produce · freshly prepared food · juice bar · salad bar · café · deli · bakery
· vegetarian friendly · co-op · counter · tables · self-service · take-out
🛏 From 1-90, take exit 306 south on N 7th Ave (right from 90E, right then immediately left from 90W) about 1⅓ miles to Main St. Turn right onto Main 2 blocks to store at 9th Ave (big, funky barn).

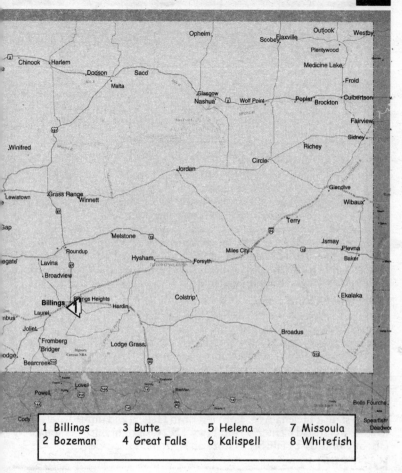

| 1 Billings | 3 Butte | 5 Helena | 7 Missoula |
| 2 Bozeman | 4 Great Falls | 6 Kalispell | 8 Whitefish |

BUTTE

A local reports that this historic mining community is home to the "largest (toxic) open pit mine in the nation."

DANCING RAINBOW NATURAL GROCERY

9 S. Montana St. ℂ 406-723-8811 ⊙ M-F 10-5:30, Sat 10-5
• organic produce

🗂 **From I-15/90,** take exit 126 north (uphill) on Montana St about 1½ miles to store on left between Galena & Park St.

NATURAL HEALING

1875 Harrison Ave. ℂ 406-782-8314 ⊙ M-F 10-6, Sat 10-5
• organic produce

🗂 **From I-90,** take Harrison Ave N exit (127B from 90E, 127 from 90W) north on Harrison (aka 15Bus S/90W) about 1 mile to store.

GREAT FALLS

2-J'S PRODUCE INC. 🍖
105 Smelter Ave., N.E. © 406-761-0134 ⊙ M-Sat 9-7
· organic produce

🍎 **From I-15**, take exit 280 east on Central Ave W (right from I-15E, left from I-15W) about 1¼ miles to 3rd St NW. Turn left onto 3rd about 1 mile to Division St. Turn left onto Division ⅓ mile to store at Smelter Ave.

HELENA

NO SWEAT CAFE ✗
427 N. Last Chance Gulch © 406-442-6954 ⊙ Tues-F 7-2, Sat-Sun 8-2
The emphasis is on breakfast, and while there is plenty of meat, there are also innovative egg dishes, oatmeal, yogurt, and whole grain pancakes and French toast. They strive to use naturally-raised meat, organic grains and local produce.
· vegetarian friendly · organic focus · counter · tables · wait staff · take-out

🍎 **From I-15**, take exit 192 west on Prospect Ave about 1½ miles to Montana Ave. Turn left onto Montana to 11th Ave. Turn right onto 11th almost 1 mile to downtown. When 11th ends, turn left onto Last Chance Gulch 2 blocks to restaurant on left.

REAL MARKET & DELI ✗🍖
1096 Helena Ave. © 406-443-5150 ⊙ M-F 8-8, Sat-Sun 9-6, Lunch 11:30-1:45, Dinner 5-7:30
Homemade soups, sandwiches, quiche, deli salads, plus organic salad bar and hot food bar selections by the pound.
· organic produce · freshly prepared food · salad bar · deli · vegetarian friendly · tables · self-service · take-out

🍎 **From I-15**, take US 12W exit (192 or 192B) towards Capitol Area onto Hwy 12W almost 2 miles to Boulder Ave. Turn left onto Boulder 1 block to stop sign at Helena Ave. Turn left onto Helena and immediately right to store in Hustad Center. **From Hwy 12E**, turn right onto National Ave (about 1 mile past Main St) to store on right in Hustad Center.

KALISPELL

MOUNTAIN VALLEY FOODS 🍖
404 1st Ave. E. © 406-756-1422 ⊙ M-Sat 9-5:30
· organic produce

🍎 **From Rt 93**, take 4th St E (½ mile south of Rt 2 intersection) to 1st Ave E. Turn right onto 1st Ave E to store on right.

MISSOULA

In addition to the University of Montana, there is hiking, mountain biking, skiing, and whitewater rafting nearby.

GOOD FOOD STORE ✗🍖
920 Kensington Ave. © 406-541-3663 ⊙ Daily 7-10
· organic produce · freshly prepared food · deli · vegetarian friendly · tables · self-service · take-out

🍎 **From I-90**, take exit 104 south on Orange St (becomes Stephens Ave) about 2 miles to store on left corner Stephens & Kensington Ave.

TIPU'S INDIAN CAFE ✕ ♿

115½ S. 4th West ✆ 406-542-0622 ⊕ Sun-Th 11:30-9 (9:30 in summer), F-Sat 11:30-9:30

This Buddhist-run cafe serves vegetarian/mostly vegan Indian and Mexican food. At lunch there is an all-you-can-eat buffet. At night you will be waited on.

• vegetarian • vegan friendly • counter • tables • self-service • wait staff

🍎 **From I-90**, take exit 104 south on Orange St 2 traffic lights to Broadway. Turn left onto Broadway 2 lights to Higgins Ave. Turn right onto Higgins, across bridge, to light at S 4th St W. Turn right onto S 4th W to cafe in first alley on left (next to Holiday Station).

WHITEFISH

THIRD STREET MARKET 🥬

244 Spokane Ave. ✆ 406-862-5054 ⊕ M-Sat 9-6

• organic produce

🍎 Take Hwy 93 to Whitefish. Store is on corner 93 & 3rd St.

Goldbeck's "EAT IT OR NOT"

FASCINATING & FAR-OUT FACTS ABOUT FOOD

TRUE OR FALSE?

You can get drunk on water.

True You should drink plenty of water, but you can go overboard. You don't really get "drunk," but people who have consumed large quantities of water to purify their body or while competing in sports events have become "water intoxicated." Symptoms include confusions, lethargy, stupor, loss of consciousness, and seizures. They are caused by an over dilution of essential body elements known as electrolytes.

NEBRASKA

1 Lincoln
2 North Platte
3 Omaha
4 Ralston
5 Scottsbluff
6 Winnetoon

LINCOLN

Prairie Peace Park, situated 7 miles west of Lincoln, is a multifaceted site dedicated to promoting peace and ending violence and exploitation. For something completely different, visit the Museum of the Odd, a residence chock full of the curator's life-long collection of just about everything.

AKIN'S NATURAL FOODS MARKET 🥬   ♿

6900 "O" St., Ste. 100 ℂ 402-466-5713 ☺ Daily 9-9

· organic produce · chain

🗓 **From I-80**, take exit 409 west on Cornhusker Hwy/Hwy 6W about 2½ miles to N 84th St. Turn left (south) onto 84th about 4¼ miles to O St. Turn right onto O 1 mile to store on right in Meridian Park Shopping Center.

MAGGIE'S 🍴   🥗♿

3111 N. 8th St. ℂ 402-277-3959 ☺ M-F 8-3

Vegetarian soups, wraps, daily specials, fresh juices, and homemade vegan baked goods made with organic flour.

· juice bar · vegetarian · vegan friendly · tables · self-service · take-out

🗓 **From I-80W**, take exit 401 toward Downtown/9th St and follow ramp onto US 34E about 3½ miles. Continue straight onto 9th St to Q St. Turn right onto Q 1 block to 8th St. Turn right onto 8th to restaurant. **From I-80E**, take exit 397 onto US 77S (Salt Valley Rd) 1⅓ miles to Capitol Pkwy. Turn left onto Capitol (becomes K St) 2 miles to 10th St. Turn left onto 10th ½ mile to Q. Turn left onto Q 2 blocks to 8th. Turn right onto 8th to restaurant.

OPEN HARVEST NATURAL FOODS ✂🍎

1618 South St. ℂ 402-475-9069 ⊙ Daily 9-9, Deli 9-8

· organic produce · freshly prepared food · deli · vegetarian friendly · co-op · tables
· self-service · take-out

🍎 **From I-80W**, take exit 401 toward Downtown/9th St and follow ramp onto US 34E about 3½ miles. Continue straight onto 9th St about 1½ miles (through downtown) to South St (next major intersection after A St). Turn left onto South 8 blocks to 17th St. Turn left onto 17th and left just before Burger King to store in South St Mall. **From I-80E**, take exit 397 onto US 77S (Salt Valley Rd) 2½ miles to NE 2E (Van Dorn Rd). Take 2E to 10th St. Turn left onto 10th St about 5 blocks to South. Turn right onto South 6 blocks to store on left in South St Mall.

NORTH PLATTE——————

HAPPY HEART SPECIALTY FOODS 🍎

301 S. Jeffers ℂ 308-532-1505 ⊙ M-F 9-5:30, Sat 9-5

· organic produce

🍎 **From I-80**, take exit 177 toward North Platte onto US 83N (Dewey St) 1¼ miles to C St. Turn left onto C 1 block to store on corner C & Jeffers St.

NATURAL NUTRITION HOUSE 🍎

203 W. 6th St. ℂ 308-532-9433 ⊙ M-Sat 9-5:30

🍎 **From I-80**, take exit 177 toward North Platte onto US 83N (Dewey St) 1¾ miles to 6th St. Turn left onto 6th 1 block to store at corner Vine St & 6th.

OMAHA

For baseball fans, Omaha hosts the College Baseball World Series.

MCFOSTER'S NATURAL KIND CAFE ✂ &

302 S. 38th St. © 402-345-7477 ☺ M-Th 11-10, F-Sat 11-11, Sun 10-3
*Natural foods with many vegetarian and vegan selections, free-range chicken
and fish. All vegetarian Sunday brunch. No refined flours or sugars, emphasis
on organic ingredients and locally grown produce. Dine inside the historic
"Jacobethian structure" or on the patio with a view of the spectacular "Gold
Coast neighborhood." Bring in a container for takeout and get a 10% discount.*

 · juice bar · café · vegetarian friendly · vegan friendly · organic focus · alcohol · tables · wait staff · take-out

🍎 **From I-80**, go north on I-480 to exit 2A. Stay in left lane to 2nd traffic
light (Farnam St). Turn left onto Farnam 10 blocks to restaurant on SW
corner 38th St & Farnam.

WILD OATS MARKET ✂🍲 &

7831 Dodge St. © 402-397-5047 ☺ M-Sat 8-10, Sun 8-9

 · organic produce · freshly prepared food · juice bar · salad bar · café · deli · bakery · vegetarian friendly · chain · counter · tables · self-service · take-out

🍎 **From I-80**, take exit 449 north on 72nd St (left from 80E, right from
80W) 2½ miles to Dodge St (Hwy 6). Turn left onto Dodge about ½ mile to
78th St. Turn left onto 78th to 1st right into store lot.

RALSTON

GRAINERY WHOLE FOODS MARKET & RESTAURANT ✂🍲

7409 Main St. © 402-593-7186 ☺ M-F 10-6:30, Sat 10-6, Sun 1-4:30
Totally vegan sandwiches, soups, hot entrees, and fresh baked goods.

 · organic produce · freshly prepared food · café · deli · bakery · vegan · tables · self-service · wait staff · take-out

🍎 **From I-80**, take exit 449 south on 72nd St (right from 80E, left from
80W) about 1⅓ miles to 3rd traffic light at Main St. Turn right onto Main
1 block to store on left (just past Neon Bucking Bronco).

SCOTTSBLUFF

In the scenic North Platte Valley, surrounded by Scottsbluff National Monument,
Agate Fossil Beds, Chimney Rock, the Wildcat Hills, and the historic Oregon Trail.

TAMARAK'S WELLNESS CENTER 🍲 &

1613 1st Ave. © 308-635-1514 ☺ M-F 10-5:30

 · organic produce · bakery · take-out

🍎 **From Hwy 71**, go east on S Beltline 1 mile to Broadway. Turn left (north)
onto Broadway 10 blocks to 16th St. Turn right onto 16th 1 block to 1st Ave.
Turn left onto 1st ½ block to store on east side (across from Elks Lodge).

WINNETOON

TOWN & COUNTRY NATURAL FOODS STORE 🍲

312 Main St. © 402-847-3368 ☺ M-Sat 8-4 (closes Sat 10 am after summer)
*Located in the Winnetoon Mall, a "Boardwalk Back in Time," including an
1871 trading post, 1888 schoolhouse, and working 1890s post office.*

🍎 Winnetoon is 3 miles west of Hwy 13 or 4 miles east of Hwy 14 on SR
59. Store is on 59 (Main St in town).

NEVADA

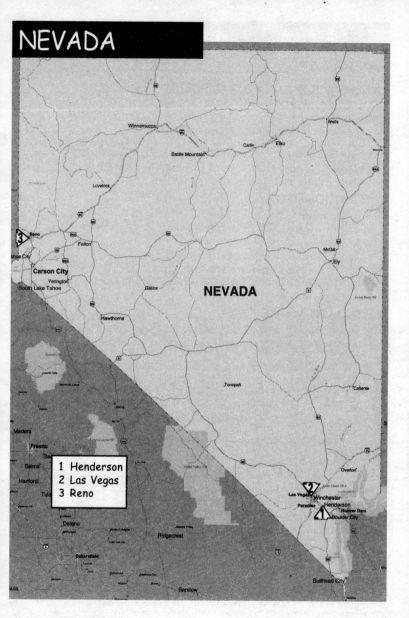

1 Henderson
2 Las Vegas
3 Reno

HENDERSON

WILDS OATS MARKET ✕ 🦪 &

517 N. Stephanie St. © 702-458-9427 ⊘ Daily 7-11

· organic produce · freshly prepared food · juice bar · salad bar · café · deli · bakery
· vegetarian friendly · chain · tables · self-service · take-out

🍴 **From I-515,** take exit 70 toward Henderson/Phoenix south on Boulder Hwy (left from 515S, right from 515N) 2 miles to E Flamingo Rd. Turn left onto Flamingo less than 1 mile to Jimmy Durante Blvd. Turn right onto Jimmy Durante ¾ mile to Stephanie St. Turn left onto Stephanie to store.

LAS VEGAS

RAINBOW'S END NATURAL FOODS ✗🍴

1100 E. Sahara Ave. © 702-737-7282 ⊙ M-Sat 9-8, Sun 11-6, Cafe M-Sat 10-4:30, Sun 11-4

Cafe is vegetarian, except for the tuna sandwich.

· freshly prepared food · juice bar · salad bar · café · vegetarian friendly · tables · self-service · take-out

🍎 **From I-15**, take exit 40 toward Convention Ctr/Las Vegas Strip east on Sahara Aveabout 1¾ miles to store on left.

THE RAW TRUTH ✗   ♿

2381 E. Windmill Lane © 702-450-9007 ⊙ M-Sat 10-6

Primarily raw foods, with the exception of steamed veggies and a cooked soup.

· vegan · organic focus · tables · self-service

🍎 **From I-215E**, take exit 6 onto Windmill Ln E ramp. Turn left onto E Windmill less than 1 mile to restaurant. **From I-215W**, take exit 5 right onto S Eastern Ave almost 1¼ mile to E Windmill. Turn left onto Windmill to restaurant.

WILD OATS MARKET ✗🍴   ♿

7250 W. Lake Mead Blvd. © 702-942-1500 ⊙ Daily 7-11

· organic produce · freshly prepared food · juice bar · salad bar · café · deli · bakery · vegetarian friendly · chain · tables · self-service · wait staff · take-out

🍎 **From US 95S**, take exit 82 toward Lake Mead Blvd onto Rock Springs Dr to W Lake Mead Blvd. Turn right onto W Lake Mead to store. **From US 95N**, take exit 82B (Rainbow North) toward W Lake Mead. Follow ramp right onto W Lake Mead less than ½ mile to store. **From I-515 or I-15**, merge onto 95N and follow directions above.

RENO

PNEUMATICS ✗   ♿

501 W. 1st St. © 775-786-8888x106 ⊙ M-F 11-11, Sat 9am-11pm, Sun 7am-11pm

An eclectic mix of vegetarian dishes. Located in the Truckee River Lodge.

· vegetarian · vegan friendly · alcohol · tables · wait staff

🍎 **From I-80**, take exit 12 south on Keystone Ave (left from 80W, right from 80E) about ½ mile to 2nd St. Turn left onto 2nd ⅓ mile to Ralston St. Turn right onto Ralston 1 block to 1st St. Restaurant is upstairs in Truckee River Lodge.

WILD OATS MARKET ✗🍴   ♿

5695 S. Virginia St. © 775-829-8666 ⊙ Daily 7-11

· organic produce · freshly prepared food · juice bar · salad bar · café · deli · bakery · vegetarian friendly · chain · tables · self-service · take-out

🍎 **From I-80**, take exit 15 onto US 395S about 4⅓ miles to exit 63 (S Virginia St). Take S Virginia ramp left onto S Virginia/395Bus less than ½ mile to store.

NEW HAMPSHIRE

1 Amherst
2 Concord
3 Dover
4 Durham
5 Exeter
6 Hampton
7 Keene
8 Littleton
9 Manchester
10 Nashua
11 New London
12 Northwood
13 Peterborough
14 Plaistow
15 Plymouth
16 Portsmouth
17 Salem
18 Tilton
19 Wolfeboro

NEW HAMPSHIRE

Maine

AMHERST

EARTHWARD 🛒
42 Rte. 101A ℰ 603-673-4322 ⊘ M-Sat 99-6, Sun 9-5

· organic produce

🛏 Amherst is about 14 miles SW of Manchester on Rt 101W, then 1 mile east on Rt 101A E, or 8½ miles NW of Nashua on 101A W. Store is in town on north side of 101A (aka Amherst St).

CONCORD

CONCORD FOOD CO-OP 🌿
24½ S. Main St. © 603-225-6840 ⊙ M-F 9-7, Sat 9-6, Sun 9-5
· organic produce · co-op
🍎 From I-93, take exit 13 toward Downtown Concord onto Rt 3N less than 1 mile to store (south of Pleasant St).

GRANITE STATE NATURAL FOODS 🌿
164 N. State St. © 603-224-9341 ⊙ M-F 9-6:30, Sat 9-5
🍎 From I-93, take exit 15W onto US 202W toward US 3/N Main St about ⅔ mile to Rt 3. Turn right onto 3 (Bouton St, becomes N State) about ½ mile to store at Penacook St (across from City Park).

DOVER

DOVER NATURAL FOODS & CAFE ✕ 🌿   ♿
24 Chestnut St. © 603-749-9999 ⊙ M-Sat 9-6, Sun 11-5
freshly prepared food · café · vegetarian friendly · tables · self-service · take-out
🍎 From I-95, take exit 4 or 5 from Portsmouth onto Rt 16N (Spaulding Tpke) toward Dover almost 10 miles. Take Silver St exit (8A) to 2nd traffic light at Locust St. Turn left onto Locust past police station to fork in road. Bear left onto Chestnut St to store on right (past light & over bridge).

DURHAM

GREEN BAY FOOD CO-OP 🌿
12 Pettee Brook Lane © 603-868-3166 ⊙ M, W 4-7, Sat 11-2 (may vary with school calendar)
A student-run natural food store near the University of NH campus.
· organic produce · co-op
🍎 From Rt 4W, turn left onto Rt 108 toward Durham/Newmarket about ⅔ mile to Main St. Merge straight onto Main about ¼ mile to Madbury Rd. Turn right onto Madbury 2 blocks to Pettee Brook Ln. Turn left onto Pettee Brook to store. **From Rt 4E**, turn right onto Rt 155A/Concord Rd toward Durham/UNH (becomes Northwood Durham Rd, then Main) about 1¾ miles to Madbury. Turn left onto Madbury 2 blocks to Pettee Brook. Turn left onto Pettee Brook to store.

EXETER

THE BLUE MOON MARKET ✕ 🌿
8 Clifford St. © 603-778-6850 ⊙ M-F 9-6, Sat 9-4, Sun 12-4
· organic produce · freshly prepared food · café · deli · vegetarian friendly · tables
· self-service · take-out
🍎 From I-95, take exit 2 west on Rt 101 about 4 miles to exit 11 (Rt 108S) toward Exeter. Go south on 108 about 1½ miles to Pleasant St. Turn right onto Pleasant, left onto String Bridge, left onto Water St (108E), and right onto Clifford St to store on left.

Please tell these businesses that you found them in Healthy Highways.

HAMPTON

HAMPTON NATURAL FOODS 🛒   ♿
321 Lafayette Rd. ℰ 603-926-5950 ☉ M-Sat 9-6, Sun 12-4
Take out soup and salad bar.
  • organic produce • freshly prepared food • salad bar • vegetarian friendly • take-out
📷 From I-95, take exit 2 toward Exeter/Hampton Beach onto Rt 101E
about 2½ miles to Rt 1N (exit on left). Take 1N about ⅓ mile to store in
Hampton Cinema Bldg (next to Galley Hatch restaurant).

KEENE

BLUEBERRY FIELDS 🛒   ♿
49 Emerald St. ℰ 603-358-5207 ☉ M-F 9-7, Sat 9-6, Sun 10-5
  • organic produce
📷 From Rt 101, turn north onto Main St (left from 101E, right from 101W)
about ⅔ mile to Emerald St (2nd left). Turn left onto Emerald 1 block to
store on left.

COUNTRY LIFE NATURAL FOOD 🍴🛒   ⊜
15 Roxbury St. ℰ 603-357-3975 ☉ Store M-F 9-5, Restaurant M-F 11:30-3
*Daily changing vegan lunch buffet including soup, entree and vegetable. Run
by lay members of the Seventh-day Adventist church.*
  • freshly prepared food • salad bar • bakery • vegan • tables • self-service • take-out
📷 From Rt 101, turn north onto Main St (left from 101E, right from
101W) less than 1 mile to traffic light at circle. Turn right onto Roxbury St
to 4th store on right.

LITTLETON

HEALTHY RHINO 🛒
106 Main St. ℰ 603-444-2177 ☉ M-Th, Sat 9-6, F 9-8, Sun 11-5
📷 From I-93, take exit 41 toward Littleton north on Cottage St (right from
93N, left from 93S) about ⅔ mile (past hospital) to traffic light at Main St.
Turn left onto Main St 2 blocks to store on right in Parker's Marketplace.

MANCHESTER

A MARKET NATURAL FOODS 🛒
125 Loring St. ℰ 603-668-8445 ☉ M-Sat 9-7, Sun 10-6
  • organic produce • freshly prepared food • take-out
📷 From I-293, take exit 1 north on S Willow St about 1 mile to Loring St.
Turn left onto Loring (at Manchester Commons Shopping Center sign) to
store on left.

NASHUA

EARTH ENERGIES NATURAL FOODS 🛒
295 Daniel Webster Hwy. ℰ 603-888-2900 ☉ M-F 10-9, Sat 10-7, Sun 12-6
📷 **Coming from NH on Rt 3S**, take exit 2 and take S Daniel Webster
Hwy ramp toward S Nashua. Turn right onto DW Hwy 1¼ miles to store
on right (across from Pheasant Lane Mall). **Coming from MA on Rt 3N**,
take exit 36 toward S Nashua left onto Middlesex Rd (becomes DW Hwy)
¼ mile to store on left.

NEW LONDON

14 CARROTS NATURAL FOODS CO-OP 🍎
Newport Rd., New London Shopping Center © 603-526-2323 ⊘ M-W 9-5:30, Th-F 9-6, Sat 10-5, Sun 10-3

- · organic produce · freshly prepared food · juice bar · salad bar · vegetarian friendly
- · co-op · take-out

🍎 **From I-89**, take exit 12 toward New London/Sunapee east on Newport Rd (right from 89N, left from 89S) about 1 mile (into town) to store on right in New London Plaza.

NORTHWOOD

SUSTY'S CAFE ✕
159 1st NH Tpke © 603-942-5862 ⊘ M-Th, Sun 11-3, F-Sat 11-9

"Sustainable Sustenance," ergo Susty's, consisting of vegan soups, salads, sandwiches, and hot entrees.

- · vegan · organic focus · tables · wait staff

🍎 On Rt 4 (aka 1st NH Tpke), 30 minutes west of I-95 in Portsmouth and 30 minutes east of I-93 in Concord. Restaurant is on north side just before traffic lights at juncture Rt 43, 9 & 202.

PETERBOROUGH

MAGGIE'S MARKETPLACE 🍎
14 Main St. © 603-924-7671 ⊘ M-F 9-6, Sat 9-5

- · organic produce

🍎 **From Rt 101**, turn north at traffic light at Grove St (left from 101E, right from 101W) about ½ mile to Main St. Turn right onto Main 1½ blocks to store on right.

PLAISTOW

BREAD & HONEY 🍎
18 Plaistow Rd., Plaza 125 © 603-382-6432 ⊘ M-F 9-5:30, Sat 9-5

🍎 **From I-495**, take exit 51B onto Rt 125N about 1½ miles (veer right on 125 when it becomes Plaistow Rd) across MA/NH border to store on left.

PLYMOUTH

Gateway to the beautiful White Mts. Skiing, hiking, canoeing, biking, and camping.

PEPPERCORN NATURAL FOODS 🍎
43 Main St. © 603-536-3395 ⊘ M-Th 9-6, F 9-7, Sat 9-5

- · organic produce

🍎 **From I-93**, take exit 25 towards Plymouth west (right) onto Bridge St about ½ mile (over bridge) to stop sign at Main St. Turn left onto Main (Rt 3 & 25). Go around the common and follow Main/3S about 2 blocks to store on left (next to movie theater).

PORTSMOUTH

O'NATURALS ✕
100 Market St. ✆ 603-319-0101 ⊙ M-Th, Sun 10:30-8, F-Sat 10:30-9
A fast-food concept developed by the owners of Stonyfield Farms Yogurt, offering natural and organic soups, sandwiches, salads, and Asian noodle dishes. Meat, fish, poultry, and vegetarian choices, plus kids' menu and Sunday brunch items.
· vegetarian friendly · organic focus · alcohol · chain · tables · self-service · take-out
🍎 **From I-95,** take exit 7 towards Portsmouth east on Market St (right from 95N, left from 95S) about 1 mile to intersection with US 1 (stop sign). Store is on right corner (in bldg with Banana Republic & Springer's Jewelers).

PORTSMOUTH HEALTH FOODS 🍠
151 Congress St. ✆ 603-436-1722 ⊙ M-F 9-7, Sat 9-6, Sun 11-5
· organic produce
🍎 **From I-95,** take exit 7 toward Portsmouth east on Market St (right from 95N, left from 95S) about 1 mile to US 1S. Turn left onto 1S (becomes Congress St) less than ¼ mile to store on corner Congress & Maplewood Ave.

SALEM

NATURAL MARKETPLACE 🍠
419 S. Broadway ✆ 603-893-2893 ⊙ M-W 10-6, Th-F 10-8, Sat 10-5:30
🍎 **From I-93,** take exit 1 toward Rt 28 onto Rockingham Park Blvd about 1/3 mile to S Broadway/28S. Turn right onto Broadway about 1²/3 miles to store on left.

TILTON

SWAN LAKE NATURAL FOODS 🍠
266 Main St. ✆ 603-286-4405 ⊙ M-Th, Sat 9-6, F 9-8
· organic produce
🍎 **From I-93,** take exit 20 toward Tilton onto Rt 3/Daniel Webster Hwy about 1½ miles to store on left

WOLFEBORO

On Lake Winnipesawkee.

EVERGRAIN NATURAL FOODS 🍠
45 N. Main St. ✆ 603-569-4002 ⊙ M-Sat 9:30-5:30, Sun 11-4 from May 31-Dec 31
Off the beaten track in every way. According to store manager, "the only natural food store for hours," and a chance to stock up on bulk foods and staples for both people and pets.
· organic produce
🍎 **From Rt 28/109 intersection,** go south on 28/109 into town to blinking light at top of hill at 109S/Main St. Turn right onto Main 5 blocks to store on right set back from road and below ground (look for store sign).

NEW JERSEY

1 Bayonne
2 Belmar
3 Butler
4 Cedar Grove
5 Cherry Hill
6 Chester
7 Denville
8 East Rutherford
9 Edgewater
10 Egg Harbor Township
11 Emerson
12 Flemington
13 Freehold
14 Hainesport
15 Hightstown
16 Hoboken
17 Ho-ho-kus
18 Howell
19 Little Silver
20 Madison
21 Manahawkin
22 Manalapan
23 Marlton
24 Milford
25 Millburn
26 Montclair
27 Montvale
28 Morristown
29 New Brunswick
30 Newton
31 North Arlington
32 Ocean Township
33 Parsippany
34 Piscataway
35 Princeton
36 Rahway
37 Red Bank
38 Ridgewood
39 River Edge
40 Scotch Plains
41 Skillman
42 Somerville
43 Spring Lake
44 Stone Harbor
45 Teaneck
46 Toms River
47 Trenton
48 Union
49 Voorhees

BAYONNE

JOHN'S NATURAL FOODS 🛒
486 Broadway © 201-858-0088 ⊙ M, Th-F 9:30-8, Tues-W, Sat 9:30-6, Sun 10-5
· organic produce
🍎 **From NJ Tpke**, take exit 14A toward Bayonne south on Ave E about 1¾ miles to 22nd St. Turn right onto 22nd and right onto Broadway ½ block to store on right.

BELMAR

VEGGIE WORKS ✗
817 Belmar Plaza © 732-280-1141 ⊙ Tues-F 12-10, Sat 5-10, Sun 5-9
All vegan menu features tofu and seitan in All-American, Eastern European, Jamaican, Mexican, Italian, and Asian preparations. Option to add cheese (prepared using separate utensils). Daily specials and all-you-can-eat salad bar.
· organic produce · salad bar · vegetarian · vegan friendly · tables · self-service · wait staff
🍎 **From Garden State Pkwy**, take exit 98 toward Belmar onto Rt 138E almost 4 miles to Rt 35. Merge onto 35N (becomes River Rd) about 1⅓ miles to 8th St. Turn right onto 8th over railroad tracks to store on right in Belmar Plaza. **From I-195E**, merge onto 138E and follow directions above.

BUTLER

TASTE OF DAWN NATURAL FOODS 🛒
192 Main St. © 973-838-0287 ⊙ M-F 10-8, Sat 10-6
· freshly prepared food · juice bar · take-out
🍎 **From Rt 287**, take Rt 23N exit (52A from 287S, 52B from 287N) to Boonton Ave. Turn right onto Boonton to downtown Butler. Turn left at railroad tracks onto Main St to store.

CEDAR GROVE

NUTRITION WAY 🛒
479 Pompton Ave. © 973-857-4741 ⊙ M-Sat 9-9, Sun 12-5
🍎 **From I-80**, take Rt 23S (exit 53) about 3½ miles to restaurant on right. **From I-280**, take exit 8B toward Cedar Grove north onto Prospect Ave about 2⅓ miles to end at Pompton Ave/Rt 23N. Merge left onto Pompton about 1¾ miles to restaurant on left.

CHERRY HILL

SINGAPORE KOSHER VEGETARIAN RESTAURANT ✗ ♿
219-H Berlin Rd. © 856-795-0188 ⊙ M, W-Sun 11:30-10
Southeast Asian all vegan, certified kosher food. Brown rice available.
· vegan · kosher · tables · wait staff
🍎 **From Rt 295**, take exit 32 towards Haddonfield west on Haddonfield-Berlin Rd (Rt 561) about 1 mile to to restaurant on right in Centrum Shoppes.

CHESTER

THE HEALTH SHOPPE 🛒
201 Rte. 206 S. © 908-879-7555 ⊕ M-F 9-9, Sat 9:30-6, Sun 10-5
· organic produce · freshly prepared food · deli · take-out

🚌 **From I-80**, take Rt 206S toward Sommerville (exit 27A from 80W, 27 from 80E) over 8 miles to store in Chester Springs Shopping Center. **From I-78**, merge onto I-287N (exit 29) about 2 miles to 206N (exit 22B). Merge onto 206N about 8 miles to store in Chester Springs Shopping Center.

DENVILLE

MRS. ERB'S GOOD FOOD MARKET ✂🛒   ♿
20 First Ave. © 973-627-5440 ⊕ M-F 9-8, Sat 9-7, Sun 10-5
· organic produce · freshly prepared food · juice bar · salad bar · café · deli · bakery
· vegetarian friendly · counter · self-service · take-out

🚌 **From I-80E**, take exit 38 onto Rt 46E toward Rt 53/Denville about 1 mile. Take Rt 53 ramp and bear right onto E Main St to Broadway. Turn right onto Broadway to 1st left onto 1st Ave. **From I-80W**, take exit 39 onto 46E and follow directions above. **From Rt 46W**, bear right onto Bloomfield Ave where 46 forks into Denville (at Banzai restaurant) about ¼ mile to fork onto Broadway. Bear right onto Broadway to 2nd right onto 1st Ave.

EAST RUTHERFORD

THE THIRD DAY 🛒
220 Park Ave. © 201-935-4045 ⊕ M-Tues, Sat 10-6, W-Th 10-8
· organic produce · freshly prepared food · deli · take-out

🚌 **From NJ Tpke**, take exit 16W toward Rutherford onto 17W almost 1 mile to Meadow Rd ramp. Turn right onto Highland Cross and right onto Meadow about ½ mile to Park Ave. Turn right onto Park across railroad tracks to store on right. **From Garden State Pkwy**, take Rt 3E towards Meadowlands (exit 153 from Pkwy S, 153A from Pkwy N) about 3½ miles to Riverside/Park Ave exit. Turn left onto Rutherford and left onto Park about 1 mile to traffic circle. Exit onto Park across railroad tracks to store on right.

EDGEWATER

WHOLE FOODS MARKET ✂🛒
905 River Rd. © 201-941-4000 ⊕ Daily 8-10
Dine in and enjoy the river view across the Hudson to Manhattan.
· organic produce · freshly prepared food · juice bar · salad bar · café · deli · bakery
· vegetarian friendly · chain · tables · self-service · take-out

🚌 **From west or south**, take I-95 or Rt 4 toward George Washington Bridge to Palisades Pkwy/Fort Lee exit. Follow exit onto service road to end (T intersection). Turn right to next stop sign at River Rd. Turn left onto River Rd into Edgewater and store at Hilliard St (turn left at traffic light into parking lot). **From north or east**, take George Washington Bridge/Upper Level to NJ. Follow Fort Lee signs and take Hudson Terrace exit. Turn right at light off ramp to 1st stop sign. Turn left onto River Rd and follow directions above.

EGG HARBOR TOWNSHIP

BONTERRA MARKET 🛒
3112 Fire Rd. © 609-484-1550 ⊕ M-F 9-7:30, Sat 9-5, Sun 11-4

· organic produce · freshly prepared food · deli · take-out

🍎 **From Garden State Pkwy**, take exit 36 onto Rt 563E (Tilton Rd) and make 1st right onto Fire Rd to store.

EMERSON

OLD HOOK FARM 🥬
650 Old Hook Rd. ℂ 201-265-4835 ⊙ Tues-Sat 9-6, Sun 10-6

· organic produce

🍎 **From Garden State PkwyN**, take exit 168 toward Washington/Hohokus right (east) onto Washington Ave/Rt 502 (becomes Old Hook Rd) about 4¼ miles to store on left.

FLEMINGTON

BASIL BANDWAGON ✕🥬
276 Hwy. 202/31 ℂ 908-788-5737 ⊙ M-Th 10-8, F 9-8, Sat 9-6, Sun 10-5

· organic produce · freshly prepared food · juice bar · vegetarian · counter · take-out

🍎 Flemington is about 14 miles SW of I-287 and 11 miles NE of New Hope, PA on US 202. Store is on west side of hwy just south of Main St intersection in shopping complex (between supermarket & Blockbuster Video).

FREEHOLD

PAULINE'S HEALTH FOODS 🥬
3585 Rte. 9 N. ℂ 732-303-0854 ⊙ M-Th 9:30-8, F 9:30-7, Sat 9:30-6, Sun 11-5

🍎 **From NJ Tpke**, take exit 8 onto Rt 33E about 12½ miles to Rt 9S. Turn right onto 9S about ¼ mile to Schanck Rd ramp. Turn left onto Schanck and left onto Rt 9N about ½ mile to store. **From I-195**, take exit 28B onto Rt 9N about 6¼ miles to store.

HAINESPORT

HAINESPORT HEALTH HAVEN ✕🥬
1443 Rte. 38 ℂ 609-267-7744 ⊙ M-F 10-6, Sat 10-5

· freshly prepared food · vegetarian · vegan friendly · counter · tables · self-service · take-out

🍎 **From I-295**, take exit 47A toward Mt Holly onto Rt 541S/Burlington Mt Holly Rd (right from 295N, loop around right from 295S) about 5¼ miles to Rt 38. Turn right onto 38W to store on right at Lumberton Rd (behind Auto Connection).

HIGHTSTOWN

BLACK FOREST ACRES 🥬
553 Rte. 130 ℂ 609-448-4885 ⊙ M-F 9:30-7:30, Sat 9-6, Sun 12-4

This branch of Black Forest doesn't have a deli, but carries sandwiches and salads made at the Hamilton Square store.

· organic produce

🍎 **From NJ Tpke**, take exit 8 toward Freehold/Hightstown and go right at 1st fork in ramp and left at next fork in ramp onto Rt 33 (Franklin St) ½ mile to Stockton St. Turn right onto Stockton over ½ mile to Dutch Neck Rd. Turn left onto Dutch Neck about ½ mile to Rt 130N. Turn right onto 130N to store on right (between Dairy Queen & SleepEase Mattress).

HOBOKEN

BASIC FOOD 🍴
204 Washington St. ✆ 201-610-1100 ⊘ Daily 8-10
· organic produce · juice bar · take-out

🛏 **From US 1 & 9**, follow 1/9N toward Holland Tunnel (becomes 12th St) to Luis Munoz Marin Blvd (before Holland Tunnel). Turn left onto Marin to Observer Hwy. Turn right onto Observer Hwy about ⅓ mile to Washington St. Turn left onto Washington about ¼ mile to store on left just past 2nd St.

HOBOKEN FARM BOY 🍴🍴
229 Washington St. ✆ 201-656-0581 ⊘ Daily 8-10
· freshly prepared food · deli · counter · self-service · take-out

🛏 **From US 1 & 9**, follow 1/9N toward Holland Tunnel (becomes 12th St) to Luis Munoz Marin Blvd (before Holland Tunnel). Turn left onto Marin to Observer Hwy. Turn right onto Observer about ⅓ mile to Washington St. Turn left onto Washington ¼ mile to store on right between 2nd & 3rd St.

HO-HO-KUS

GREEN MARKET CAFE 🍴   ♿
195 E. Franklin Tpke. ✆ 201-652-7733 ⊘ M-W 11-8, Th-Sat 11-9, Sun 12-2:30
A *"mostly vegetarian"* venue.
· juice bar · café · deli · vegetarian friendly · tables · wait staff

🛏 **From Rt 17**, take Hollywood Ave exit onto Rt 502E less than ½ mile to Elmwood Ave. Turn left onto Elmwood less than ½ mile to E Franklin Tpke. Turn left onto Franklin to restaurant.

HOWELL

UDUPI SRI KRISHNA VEGETARIAN RESTAURANT 🍴   ♿
2450 Rte. 9 S. ✆ 732-409-3500 ⊘ Tues-Sun 11:30-9:30
Kosher Indian vegetarian with a low-fat orientation (steamed vegetables, low-fat milk). Buffet and a la carte at lunch and dinner.
· vegetarian · vegan friendly · kosher · tables · self-service · wait staff · take-out

🛏 **From Garden State Pkwy**, take exit 98 west on I-195 about 7 miles to exit 28B toward Freehold. Merge onto Rt 9N less than 1 mile to restaurant.

LITTLE SILVER

HEALTHFAIR 🍴
625 Branch Ave. ✆ 732-747-3140 ⊘ M-F 9-8, Sat 9-6, Sun 10-5
Take-out offerings include homemade soups, organic salad bar, sandwiches, and vegetarian hot entrees. Plenty of vegan choices, with tuna the only "meat."
· organic produce · freshly prepared food · juice bar · salad bar · vegetarian friendly · take-out

🛏 **From Garden State Pkwy**, take exit 109 east on Newman Springs Rd about 2 miles to end at Rt 35. Turn right onto 35, then make immediate left onto White Rd almost 1 mile to end at Branch Ave. Turn right onto Branch over ½ mile to store.

MADISON

WHOLE FOODS MARKET 🍴🍴   ♿
222 Main St. ✆ 973-822-8444 ⊘ Daily 8-9
· organic produce · freshly prepared food · café · deli · bakery · vegetarian friendly

· chain · tables · self-service · take-out

🛒 **From I-24** (easily accessed from I-287 or I-78), take Rt 124W (exit 7B-A from 24W, 7 from 24E) toward Chatham onto Main St about 2 miles to store. **From I-287N**, take exit 35 onto South St and turn left onto Woodland Ave about 1⅓ miles to Kitchell Ave. Turn left onto Kitchell ⅔ mile to Madison Ave/Rt 124. Turn right onto Madison (becomes Main) about 2½ miles to store.

MANAHAWKIN

EARTH GOODS NATURAL FOOD MARKET 🍲
777 E. Bay Ave. © 609-597-7744 ☺ M-F 10-7, Sat 10-6, Sun 11-4

· organic produce

🛒 **From Garden State Pkwy**, take exit 63 toward Manahawkin/Long Beach onto Rt 72E 2 miles to Rt 9N ramp (Bus Dist). Turn right onto 9N and right onto Bay Ave about 1⅔ miles to store on right.

MANALAPAN

PAULINE'S HEALTH FOODS 🍲
303 Rte. 9 S. © 732-308-0449 ☺ M-Th 9:30-8:30, F 9:30-8, Sat 9:30-6, Sun 11-5

🛒 **From Garden State Pkwy**, take exit 123 toward Sayreville/Old Bridge onto Rt 9S about 11 miles to store.

MARLTON

WHOLE FOODS MARKET 🍴🍲   ♿
940 Rte. 73 N. © 856-985-3292 ☺ M-Sat 8-10, Sun 8-9

· organic produce · freshly prepared food · salad bar · café · deli · bakery · vegetarian friendly · chain · counter · tables · self-service · take-out

🛒 **From NJ Tpke**, take exit 4 onto Rt 73S towards Marlton/Berlin about 3 miles to Greentree Rd. Take jughandle across 73 onto Greentree to store on corner Greentree & 73 in Greentree Shopping Center.

ZAGARA'S 🍴🍲
501 Brick Rd. © 856-983-5700 ☺ M-Sat 8-8, Sun 8-7

· organic produce · freshly prepared food · deli · vegetarian friendly · tables · self-service · take-out

🛒 **From NJ Tpke**, take exit 4 onto Rt 73S towards Marlton/Berlin almost 4 miles to Brick Rd. Turn right onto Brick to store.

MILFORD

THE HEALTHY HABIT 🍲
57 Bridge St. © 908-995-7653 ☺ M-W, F 9:30-6, Th 9:30-7, Sat 9:30-5, Sun 1-2

· organic produce· juice bar · take-out

🛒 Milford sits on the NJ/PA border about 8 miles south of I-78. **From I-78W**, take exit 7 and loop around right onto Rt 173W to Church St. Turn right onto Church 1 block to Willow St. Turn right onto Willow ½ mile to Milford Rd. Turn left onto Milford and merge left at end onto Statts Rd. Continue on Statts (becomes Myler Rd) about 1⅓ miles total to Hawks Schoolhouse Rd. Turn right onto Hawks Schoolhouse 1⅔ miles to Rt 519 (Milford Warren Glen Rd). Turn left onto 519 4 miles to Bridge St. Turn right onto Bridge to store. **From I-78E**, take exit 6 right onto Bloomsbury Rd, merge onto 173W and follow directions above.

MILLBURN

WHOLE FOODS MARKET ✂️🛒 ♿
187 Millburn Ave. © 973-376-4668 ⊙ Daily 7:30-9
· organic produce · freshly prepared food · salad bar · café · deli · bakery · vegetarian friendly · chain · counter · tables · self-service · take-out

🍎 **From I-78W**, take exit 50B toward Millburn. Turn right onto Vauxhall Rd about ¾ mile to Millburn Ave. Turn left onto Millburn 2½ blocks to store on right. **From I-78E**, take exit 49B toward Maplewood onto Rt 124/Springfield Ave continuing onto Valley Rd about ¾ mile total to Vauxhall. Turn left onto Vauxhall 2 blocks to Millburn. Turn left onto Millburn 2½ blocks to store on right.

MONTCLAIR

THE HEALTH SHOPPE 🛒
539 Bloomfield Ave. © 973-746-3555 ⊙ M-F 9-9, Sat 9-6, Sun 11-5

🍎 **From Garden State Pkwy**, take exit 148 (Bloomfield Ave). From Pkwy S, stay straight off exit on Spruce St to Montgomery St. Turn right onto Montgomery, right onto Franklin St, left onto Washington St and right onto Bloomfield Ave. **From PkwyN**, stay straight on JFK Dr N, turn left onto JFK S, and left onto Bloomfield. **Once on Bloomfield Ave**, go almost 2 miles to store on right.

WHOLE FOODS MARKET 🛒
701 Bloomfield Ave. © 973-746-5110 ⊙ Daily 7:30-9
One of the smaller Whole Foods, with no salad bar or seating. Located just across from the Montclair Art Museum.
· organic produce · freshly prepared food · deli · bakery · vegetarian friendly · chain · take-out

🍎 **From Garden State Pkwy**, take exit 148 (Bloomfield Ave). From PkwyS, stay straight off exit on Spruce St to Montgomery St. Turn right onto Montgomery, right onto Franklin St, left onto Washington St and right onto Bloomfield Ave. **From PkwyN**, stay straight on JFK Dr N, turn left onto JFK S, and left onto Bloomfield. **Once on Bloomfield Ave**, go almost 2½ miles to store on right.

MONTVALE

CHESTNUT RIDGE HEALTH FOOD 🛒 ♿
22 Chestnut Ridge Rd. © 201-391-6173 ⊙ M-Sat 10-6, Sun 10-5

🍎 **From Garden State PkwyN**, take exit 171 toward Chestnut Ridge Rd/Woodcliff Lakes. Turn left off exit to first traffic light. Turn right onto Chestnut Ridge almost 1 mile to store on left. **From PkwyS**, take Chestnut Ridge exit left to first light. Turn right then left at next light onto Chestnut Ridge Rd about 1 mile to store on right.

MORRISTOWN

THE HEALTH SHOPPE 🛒
66 Morris St. © 973-538-9131 ⊙ M-F 9-9, Sat 9-7, Sun 9-6
· organic produce · freshly prepared food · salad bar· deli · take-out

🍎 **From I-287S**, take exit 36 toward Morris Ave straight onto Lafayette Ave to 2nd traffic light at Morris St. Turn right onto Morris to store on right. **From 287N**, take exit 36B right onto Lafayette and follow directions above.

NEW BRUNSWICK

Among the surprising number of cultural venues in New Brunswick: Rutgers University's Mason Gross School of the Arts, with live performances most nights; the Rutgers Film Co-op/NJ Media Arts Center, featuring non-commercial films and speakers; and, the African-American Crossroads Theater Company.

GEORGE STREET CO-OP 🌰

89 Morris St. © 732-247-8280 ⊙ M-F 10-8, Sat 10-6, Sun 11-6

· organic produce · co-op

🚪 **From NJ Tpke or Rt 1**, take Rt 18N (exit 9 on Tpke). Stay right after Commercial Ave and exit at New St. Follow New St to 3rd traffic light at Livingston Ave. Turn left onto Livingston and make next left onto Morris to store in 1st building on left.

ZAFRA VEGETARIAN RESTAURANT ✗

46 Paterson St. © 732-214-1005 ⊙ M-F 11-10, Sat 5-10

While many vegetarian restaurants will adapt a dish for vegans, at Zafra they will make a vegan dish vegetarian by using regular cheese in place of soy. The eclectic, international menu ranges from vegan comfort foods like "meat" loaf and "chicken" parmigiana, to more exotic choices with a Caribbean flair, such as tofu croquettes and Creole seitan.

· vegan · vegetarian friendly · tables · wait staff

🚪 **From NJ Tpke**, take exit 9 onto Rt 18N (immediately after tollbooth). Pass both Rt 1 exits (about 2 miles) and get in right lane 1 mile to New St exit. Take New St to 1st light at Neilson Ave. Turn right onto Neilson 3 blocks to Church St. Turn left onto Church 2 blocks to Spring St. Turn left onto Spring 1 block to Paterson St. Turn left onto Paterson to restaurant on right (across from public parking) on 2nd fl (neon signs visible from street).

NEWTON

SUSSEX COUNTY FOOD CO-OP 🌰

30 Moran St. © 973-579-1882 ⊙ M-Th, Sat 9:30-5:30, F 9-9, Sun 1:15-5

Weekly delivery of premade sandwiches and salads.

· organic produce · co-op

🚪 Take Rt 206 into downtown Newton. Store is 1 block east of 206 between Trinity & E Clinton St.

OCEAN TOWNSHIP

DEAN'S NATURAL FOOD MARKET 🌰

1119 Hwy. 35N © 732-517-1515 ⊙ M-F 9-8, Sat 9-6, Sun 10-6

· organic produce · juice bar · salad bar · take-out

🚪 **From Garden State PkwyN**, take exit 100A onto Rt 66E about 3⅓ miles. Continue straight onto Asbury Ave/NJ 35 and stay left onto 35 past Seaview Square Mall to store on right between Sunset & Allaire Ave. **From PkwyS**, take exit 102 onto Asbury Ave about 3 miles just past Seaview Square Mall (where NJ 35 turns left) and follow directions above.

PARSIPPANY

CHAND PALACE ✗

257 Littleton Rd. © 973-334-5444 ⊙ Lunch M-F 11:30-2:30, Sat-Sun 12-3, Dinner M-Th, Sun 5-10, F-Sat 5-10:30

Indian vegetarian a la carte, plus daily lunch and 12-course dinner buffet.

· vegetarian · vegan friendly · tables · self-service · wait staff

🛏 **From I-80W**, take exit 43B (I-287N) toward Rt 46. Turn right onto Smith Rd to stop sign at Littleton Rd. Turn left onto Littleton about ½ mile to restaurant on left in shopping mall (just before traffic light). **From I-287N**, take exit 41A (I-80E) toward Rt 46. Turn left onto Smith to Littleton and follow directions above. **From I-80E** (west of 287), take exit 42A-C (Rt 202N) left at 1st fork in ramp and right at 2nd fork onto Littleton Rd. Take Littleton about ¾ mile (past 1st traffic light) to restaurant on right. **From I-287S**, take exit 42 (Rt 202S) toward Rt 46. Turn left onto Parsipanny Blvd about ⅔ mile to Littleton. Turn left onto Littleton to restaurant on left.

THE HEALTH SHOPPE 🍎
1123 Rte. 46 E. ✆ 973-263-8348 ⊕ M-F 9-9, Sat-Sun 9-6

🛏 **From I-80E** (west of 287), take exit 42A-C (Rt 202N) left at first fork in ramp and right at second fork onto Littleton Rd. Take Littleton about 1¼ miles to Rt 46E. Veer left and curve right onto 46E about 1½ miles to store on right in Whippany Shopping Center. **From I-80W**, take exit 47 onto 46W about 1½ miles to Baldwin Rd. Turn around at Baldwin back onto 46E over ½ mile to store on right in Whippany Shopping Center.

VEGGIE HEAVEN ✗
1119 Rte. 46 E. #8A ✆ 973-335-9876 ⊕ M-Th 11-10, F-Sat 11:30-10:30, Sun 11:30-9:30
Chinese vegetarian with mock meat dishes.
· vegetarian · vegan friendly · tables · wait staff

🛏 **From I-80E** (west of 287), take exit 42A-C (Rt 202N) left at first fork in ramp and right at second fork onto Littleton Rd. Take Littleton about 1¼ miles to Rt 46E. Veer left and curve right onto 46E about 1½ miles to restaurant. **From I-80W**, take exit 47 onto 46W about 1½ miles to Baldwin Rd. Turn around at Baldwin back onto 46E over ½ mile to restaurant on right.

PISCATAWAY

MALABAR HOUSE ✗
1665 Stelton Rd. ✆ 732-819-0400 ⊕ M-F 12-3, 5:30-9:30, Sat-Sun 12-9:30
Vegetarian Indian fare.
· vegetarian · vegan friendly · tables · wait staff

🛏 **From I-287**, take exit 5 toward Dunellen/Edison south on Stelton Rd (right from 287S, left from 287N) 1¾-2 miles to restaurant.

SUKH SAGAR ✗
1347 Stelton Rd. ✆ 732-777-9595 ⊕ Daily 11:30-9:30
Vegetarian Indian fare, with a buffet until 3 and sit-down service afterward.

🛏 **From I-287**, take exit 5 toward Dunellen/Edison south on Stelton Rd (right from 287S, left from 287N) 1¼-1½ miles to restaurant.

PRINCETON

WHOLE EARTH CENTER ✗🍎   ♿
360 Nassau St. ✆ 609-924-7429 ⊕ M-W, Sat 9-7, Th-F 9-9, Sun 10-5
· organic produce · freshly prepared food · juice bar · café · deli · bakery · vegetarian friendly · tables · self-service · take-out

🛏 Coming into Princeton **from Rt 206**, merge onto Nassau St (Rt 27) to store near Harrison St on east side (behind Jody's flower shop). **From Rt 1**, take Harrison St exit north to 3rd traffic light at Nassau. Turn right onto Nassau and make 1st left into driveway to store.

WILD OATS MARKET ✂️🛒 ♿

225 Nassau St. © 609-924-4993 ⊘ M-Sat 7:30-9:30, Sun 8-9

· organic produce · freshly prepared food · juice bar · salad bar · café · deli · bakery · vegetarian friendly · chain · counter · tables · self-service · take-out

🍴 Coming into Princeton **from Rt 206**, merge onto Nassau St (Rt 27) to store about ¼ mile past Washington St. **From Rt 1**, turn right onto Washington St (take jughandle left, then right across 1 from 1N) almost 1²⁄₃ miles to Nassau. Turn right onto Nassau about ¼ mile to store on right.

RAHWAY

EAT TO THE BEAT COFFEEHOUSE ✂️

1465 Irving St. © 721-381-0505 ⊘ Tues-Th 11-9, F 11-midnight, Sat 4-midnight
Vegetarian sandwiches, wraps, patties, (brown) rice dishes, salads, and such. On-site bakery makes traditional pastries.

· vegetarian · vegan friendly · tables · wait staff

🍴 **From US 1 & 9S**, turn right onto E Grand Ave ½ mile to Bridge St. Turn left onto Bridge (becomes Poplar St) about ¹⁄₃ mile to Irving St. Turn left onto Irving 1 block to restaurant at Irving & Broad St. **From NJ Tpke (I-95S)**, take exit 13 onto Rt 278W 2²⁄₃ miles to US 1 & 9. Continue on 1/9 almost 2½ miles to E Grand and follow directions above. **From NJ Tpke (I-95N)**, take exit 12 toward Rahway onto Rt 602 (Roosevelt Ave, becomes Randolf Ave) 2 miles to Woodbridge Rd. Turn right onto Woodbridge more than ½ mile to E Milton Ave. Turn left onto E Milton almost ½ mile to Broad. Turn right onto Broad 2 blocks to restaurant. **From US 1 & 9N**, turn left onto E Hazelwood Ave ¼ mile to Main St. Turn right onto Main ¹⁄₃ mile to next intersection at E Milton. Turn left onto Milton 3 blocks to Broad. Turn right onto Broad 2 blocks to restaurant.

RED BANK

Nearby are Sandy Hook Beach, and Hartshroun and Huber woods for hiking and mountain biking.

DOWN TO EARTH ✂️

7 Broad St. © 732-747-4542 ⊘ Lunch M, W-Sat 12-3, Dinner M, W-Th, Sun 5-9, F-Sat 5-10
Soups, salads, and a nice selection of prepared dishes featuring tofu, tempeh, seitan, and such, prepared Italian-, Mexican-, French-, Japanese-, Thai-, Indonesian-, Indian-, and Southern-style. Organic emphasis. No alcohol, but BYOB.

· vegan · organic focus · tables · wait staff

🍴 **From Garden State Pkwy**, take exit 109 (CR 520) toward Red Bank onto Half Mile Rd about ½ mile to W Front St. Turn right onto W Front (becomes CR 10) almost 2 miles to Broad St. Turn right onto Broad to restaurant.

SECOND NATURE NATURAL FOODS 🛒

65 Broad St. © 732-747-6448 ⊘ M-F 10-8, Sat 10-6, Sun 10-5
An all-vegetarian store.

· organic produce · freshly prepared food · juice bar · salad bar · vegetarian · take-out

🍴 **From Garden State Pkwy**, take exit 109 onto CR 520E about 2 miles to "T". Turn left onto Broad St about ²⁄₃ mile to store on right.

RIDGEWOOD

NATURE'S MARKETPLACE 🛒
1 W. Ridgewood Ave. ℅ 201-445-9210 ⊘ M-W, F-Sat 10-6, Th 10-8

🍎 Access Rt 17 from north off NY Thwy or from south off Garden State Pkwy. **From Rt 17**, take Linwood Ave exit toward Ridgewood (west) about 1½ miles to Maple Ave. Turn left onto Maple about ¼ mile to Franklin Ave. Turn right onto Franklin, go under railroad and turn left when Franklin ends onto Garber Sq to store at Ridgewood Ave. **From I-287**, take exit 59 south on 208 (toward Franklin Lakes) about 5½ miles to Goffle Rd/Ridgewood exit. Turn right onto Douglas Ave, then right onto Goffle 1⅓ miles to Lake Ave. Turn right onto Lake (becomes Godwin Ave, then Wilsey Sq) a little more than 1 mile to store at Ridgewood Ave.

WHOLE FOODS MARKET 🍴🛒   ৬
44 Godwin Place ℅ 201-670-0383 ⊘ Daily 8-9

· organic produce · freshly prepared food · salad bar · café · deli · bakery · vegetarian friendly · chain · tables · self-service · take-out

🍎 Access Rt 17 from north off NY Thwy, from south off Garden State Pkwy. **From Rt 17**, take Linwood Ave exit toward Ridgewood (west) about 1½ miles to Maple Ave. Turn left onto Maple about ¼ mile to Franklin Ave. Turn right onto Franklin (becomes Garber Sq, then Wisley Sq then Godwin Ave) about ⅔ mile to store in Ridgewood Plaza (on west side of railroad station, next to American Red Cross).

RIVER EDGE

HAPPY CARROT 🛒
636 Kinderkamack Rd. ℅ 201-986-0818 ⊘ M-F 9:30-7:30, Sat 9:30-6, Sun 11-4

· organic produce · juice bar · take-out

🍎 **From Rt 4W**, turn right onto Grand Ave and make 2nd left onto Kinderkamack about 1¼ miles to store. **From Rt 4E**, turn right onto Johnson Ave, left onto Jefferson and left onto Kinderkamack (across hwy) about 1½ miles to store. **From Rt 17N**, merge onto Rt 4E and follow directions above. **From Rt 17S**, take Midland Ave ramp toward River Edge left onto Midland almost 2½ miles to Kinderkamack. Turn right onto Kinderkamack ¾ mile to store at Madison Ave.

SCOTCH PLAINS

AUTUMN HARVEST NATURAL FOODS 🛒
1625 E. 2nd St. ℅ 908-322-2130 ⊘ M, F 9:30-7, Tues-Th 9-8, Sat 9-5:30, Sun 10:30-3:30

· organic produce

🍎 **From I-78**, take exit 41 toward Berkeley Hts/Scotch Plains. Turn right off exit onto Drift Rd and right onto Plainfield Ave. Follow Plainfield (becomes Bonnie Burn Rd) about 2 miles to Park Ave. Turn right onto Park about ⅔ mile to 2nd St. Turn right onto 2nd about ⅓ mile to store on right.

SKILLMAN

PRINCETON HEALTH FOOD 🛒
1273 Rt. 206 ℅ 609-279-1636 ⊘ M-W, F 10-6:30, Th 10-7:30, Sat 10-5, Sun 11-3

· organic produce · juice bar · take-out

🍎 Store is at intersection Rt 206 & Rt 518.

SOMERVILLE

NATURE'S HOLADAY ✗🍴
194 W. Main St. © 908-725-7716 ⊙ M-F 10-7, Sat 10-5
In addition to fresh juice, juice bar serves soup, salad, sandwiches, and hot dishes.
· freshly prepared food · juice bar · vegetarian friendly · counter · take-out
🍴 **From US 206,** go east on Somerset St (left from 206S, right from 206N) about ⅓ mile to W Main St. Turn right onto Main to store.

SPRING LAKE

NATURE'S CORNER ✗🍴
2407 Hwy. 71 © 908-725-7716 ⊙ M-Th 9-8, F 9-7, Sat-Sun 10-6
· organic produce · freshly prepared food · juice bar · salad bar · vegetarian friendly
· tables · self-service · take-out
🍴 **From I-195E,** continue on Rt 138E and merge onto Hwy 35N toward Belmar/Asbury Park about ⅓ mile to 16th Ave. Turn right onto 16th about ½ mile to H St (Hwy 71). Turn right onto 71 less than 1 mile to store. **From Garden State Pkwy,** take exit 98 onto 138E and follow directions above.

STONE HARBOR

GREEN CUISINE ✗   🌐
302 96th St. © 609-368-1616 ⊙ Mother's Day-Mid Sept Daily 11-8:30 (some-what flexible, especially at the beginning & end of season)
A varied selection of hot and cold sandwiches to satisfy most palates, from meat-eaters to the tempeh crowd. Plus, a wide choice of salads, fruit plates, and smoothies and juices made to order.
· juice bar · café · vegetarian friendly · alcohol · tables · wait staff
🍴 **From Garden State Pkwy,** turn east onto Stone Harbor Blvd (left from PkwyS, right from PkwyN) across the water (becomes 96th St) about 3⅔ miles to restaurant at 96th & 3rd Ave.

TEANECK

AQUARIUS 🍴
408 Cedar Lane © 201-836-0601 ⊙ M-F 10-2, Sat 10-6, Sun 10-2
· organic produce
🍴 **From Rt 4W,** take Teaneck Rd ramp toward Ridgefield Park right onto Teaneck Rd (across hwy) ½ mile to Cedar Lane. Turn right onto Cedar about ¾ mile to store. **From Rt 4E,** turn right onto Belle Ave ¼ mile to Claremont Ave. Turn left onto Claremont 1 block to Garrison Ave. Turn left onto Garrison 3 blocks to Cedar. Turn left onto Cedar past 1st block to store.

VEGGIE HEAVEN ✗
473 Cedar Lane © 201-836-0887 ⊙ M-Th, Sun 11-10, F-Sat 11-11
Extensive Vegetarian Chinese, kosher menu.
· vegetarian · vegan friendly · kosher · tables · wait staff
🍴 **From Rt 4W,** take Teaneck Rd ramp toward Ridgefield Park right onto Teaneck Rd (across hwy) ½ mile to Cedar Lane. Turn right onto Cedar about 1 mile (past Garrison Ave) to restaurant. **From Rt 4E,** turn right onto Belle Ave ¼ mile to Claremont Ave. Turn left onto Claremont 1 block to Garrison. Turn left onto Garrison 3 blocks to Cedar. Turn right onto Cedar to restaurant.

TOMS RIVER

NATURAL FOODS ✗🍴
679 Batchelor St.. © 732-240-0024 ☺ M-Tues, Th-F 10-6, W 10-8, Sat 10-5, Sun 12-5, Cafe M-F 10-2
   · organic produce · freshly prepared food · juice bar · café · vegetarian friendly · tables · self-service · take-out

🍎 **From Garden State Pkwy,** take exit 82 onto Rt 37E 2 miles to Peter Ave. Turn right onto Peter and immediately right onto Batchelor St to store.

TRENTON

BLACK FOREST ACRES ✗🍴
1100 Rte. 33 © 609-586-6187 ☺ M-F 9:30-7:30, Deli 10-6, Sat 9:30-6, Deli 10-4, Sun 11-4 (Deli & Juice bar closed)
Four to six hot dishes prepared daily, except Sunday.
   · organic produce · freshly prepared food · juice bar · deli · vegetarian friendly · tables · self-service · take-out

🍎 **From I-195,** take exit 3B toward Hamilton Sq north on Hamilton Yardville Rd (right from 195W, loop around right from 195E) about 1¾ miles to Rt 33. Turn left onto 33, ⅓ mile to store on corner 33 & Paxson Ave (across from Wendy's).

GOLDEN TEAPOT ✗
1750 Whitehorse Mercerville Rd. © 609-890-4881 ☺ Tues-Th 11-9:30, F-Sat 11-10:30, Sun 12-9
Vegetarian Asian menu, featuring mock meat dishes. No alcohol, but BYOB.
   · vegetarian · vegan friendly · tables · wait staff

🍎 **From I-295S,** take exit 64 toward Mercerville/Rt 33E right onto E State Ext (Rt 535). Follow 535 less than 1 mile to Whitehorse Mercerville Rd. Turn right onto Whitehorse (Rt 533S) over 1 mile to restaurant. **From I-295N,** take exit 61A toward White Horse Ave right onto Arena Dr ½ mile to White Horse. Turn left onto White Horse (becomes Whitehorse Mercerville Rd) almost 2 miles to restaurant.

UNION

HEALTH BEST ✗🍴 s
1350 Galloping Hill Rd. © 908-687-4575 ☺ M-F 10-8, Sat 10-6, Sun 12-5
Note, cafe does not take credit cards.
   · freshly prepared food · café · vegetarian friendly · tables · self-service · take-out

🍎 **From Garden State Pkwy,** take exit 138 onto Galloping Hill Rd (follow ramp toward Union right from Pkwy N, follow ramp toward Roselle Park/Elizabeth from Pwky S) ½ mile to store (shortly before Union Hospital).

VOORHEES

GOOD & NATURAL 🍴
28 Eagle Plaza © 856-627-5151 ☺ M-F 10-8, Sat 10-5, Sun 12-5
   · deli · take-out

🍎 **From Rt 295,** take exit 32 onto Rt 541E about 2½ miles (just past White Horse Rd) to store on right in Eagle Plaza Shopping Center.

NEW MEXICO

1	Albuquerque	5	Las Vegas
2	Farmington	6	Santa Fe
3	Gallup	7	Silver City
4	Las Cruces	8	Taos

ALBUQUERQUE

ANNAPURNA ✎ &

513 San Mateo Blvd. N.E. ✆ 505-254-2424 ☉ M-Sat 8-5
Vegetarian aryuvedic Indian food.

· vegetarian · vegan friendly · tables · self-service

🏠 **From I-40,** take exit 161 (161A from 40E) south on San Mateo Blvd (right from 40E, left from 40W) about 1½ miles to restaurant.

ANNAPURNA ✕   ♿
2201 Silver Ave. N.E. ✆ 505-262-2424 ⏰ M-Sat 7am-9pm, Sun 10-2
Vegetarian aryuvedic Indian food.
· vegetarian · vegan friendly · tables · self-service
📕 **From I-25N**, take exit 223 right onto Ave Cesar Chavez 1 mile to Yale
Blvd. Turn left onto Yale about ⅔ mile to restaurant at Silver Ave (a few
blocks south of UNM campus). **From I-25S**, take exit 224A onto Locust
St to Central Ave. Turn left onto Central less than 1 mile to Yale. Turn
right onto Yale 2 blocks to restaurant.

LA MONTANITA CO-OP NATURAL FOODS MARKET 🍎
2400 Rio Grande Blvd. ✆ 505-242-8800 ⏰ M-Sat 8-9, Sun 8-8
· organic produce · co-op
📕 **From I-40**, take exit 157A onto 194N (Rio Grande Blvd) almost 1 mile
to store.

LA MONTANITA CO-OP NATURAL FOODS MARKET 🍎
3500 Central Ave. S.E. ✆ 505-265-4631 ⏰ M-Sat 7-9, Sun 8-8
· organic produce · co-op
📕 **From I-40**, take exit 160 south on Carlisle Blvd (right from 40E, left
from 40W) about 2 miles to store on right at corner Carlisle & Central
Ave in Nob Hill Shopping Center.

WHOLE FOODS MARKET ✕🍎   ♿
5815 Wyoming Blvd. N.E. ✆ 505-856-0474 ⏰ Daily 7:30-9
Beer and wine sold in the store can be enjoyed on the premises with your meal.
· organic produce · freshly prepared food · salad bar · café · deli · bakery · vegetarian
friendly · alcohol · chain · counter · tables · self-service · wait staff · take-out
📕 **From I-25**, take exit 231 (San Antonio Ave/Ellison Rd) east on San
Antonio 1½ miles to Wyoming Blvd. Turn south onto Wyoming 1 mile to
store on west side in North Towne Plaza.

WILD OATS MARKET ✕🍎
2103 Carlisle Blvd. N.E. ✆ 505-260-1366 ⏰ Daily 7-11
· organic produce · freshly prepared food · juice bar · salad bar · café · deli · vegetarian
friendly · chain · tables · self-service · take-out
📕 **From I-40**, take exit 160 south on Carlisle Blvd (right from 40E, left
from 40W) to store just off hwy.

WILD OATS MARKET ✕🍎   ♿
11015 Menaul Blvd. N.E. ✆ 505-275-6660 ⏰ Daily 7-11
· organic produce · freshly prepared food · juice bar · salad bar · café · deli · bakery
· vegetarian friendly · chain · tables · self-service · take-out
📕 **From I-40**, take exit 166 north on Juan Tabo Blvd NE (left from 40E,
right from 40W) about 2¼ miles to Menaul Blvd NE. Turn left onto Menaul
about ¼ mile to store.

WILD OATS MARKET ✕🍎   ♿
6300 San Mateo Blvd. N.E. ✆ 505-823-1933 ⏰ Daily 7-11
· organic produce · freshly prepared food · juice bar · salad bar · café · deli · bakery
· vegetarian friendly · chain · tables · self-service · take-out
📕 **From I-25**, take exit 230 south on San Mateo Blvd to store just off exit
in Far North Shopping Center.

FARMINGTON

WILDLY NATURAL FOODS 🍎
2501 E. 20th St. ② 505-326-6243 ⊙ M-F 9-6:30, Sat 9-6, Sun 11-4
· organic produce · juice bar · take-out

🏠 Take Rt 64 to Farmington. **From 64**, turn north onto Scott Ave (left from 64W, right from 64E) ½ mile to E Main St. Turn right onto E Main 1 mile to Hutton Ave. Turn left onto Hutton ½ mile to 20th St. Turn left onto 20th to store on left.

GALLUP

WILD SAGE NATURAL FOODS 🍎
610½ E. Pershing Ave. ② 505-863-5383 ⊙ Tues-F 1-7:30, Sat 10-6
· organic produce · co-op

🏠 **From I-40**, take exit 22 (Miyamura Dr/Montoya Blvd) north on Ford Rd (right from 40W, left off Miyamura ramp from 40E) and follow west on Montoya to Marguerite de Franco Dr (immediately after rec center). Turn right onto M de Franco to 2nd left at Pershing Ave to store on SW corner.

LAS CRUCES

MOUNTAIN VIEW MARKET ✗🍎   ♿
1300 El Paseo St. ② 505-523-0436 ⊙ M-Sat 8-8, Sun11-5
Featuring local product, southwestern products and gifts.
· organic produce · juice bar · co-op · tables · self-service · take-out

🏠 **From I-10**, take exit 140 onto NM 28N/Avenida de Mesilla. Head east on 28N (becomes Idaho Ave) about 1¼ miles to El Paseo. Turn right onto El Paseo to store (near Walgreens). **From I-25**, take exit 6 toward Las Cruces onto 70W (becomes Main St) 2½ miles. Merge onto N Water St (478S) almost 1 mile to El Paseo. Turn left onto El Paseo ½ mile to store (just past Idaho).

LAS VEGAS

Free hot springs 5 miles from town.

SEMILLA NATURAL FOODS 🍎   ♿
510 University Ave. ② 505-425-8139 ⊙ M-F 10-6, Sat 10-5
· organic produce

🏠 **From I-25**, take exit 345 (NM 65W) onto University Ave towards town (left from 25N, right from 25S). Go 1½ blocks past traffic light to store on right.

SANTA FE

History buffs might be interested to know that Santa Fe is the oldest capitol in the U.S., founded in 1610.

CAFE OASIS ✗🍎
526 Galisto St. ② 505-983-9599 ⊙ M-Th 9:30am-midnight, F-Sat 9am-2am, Sun 9am-midnight
Most of the varied fare is vegetarian, there is all-day breakfast, the chicken is free-roaming, and the vegetables are often organic, depending on the season.
· vegetarian friendly · alcohol · tables · self-service · wait staff

🏠 **From 1-25**, take exit 282 onto US 84N/St Francis Dr (left from 25N, right from 25S) about 2²∕₃ miles to Cerrillos Rd. Turn right onto Cerrillos ½ mile to Paseo de Peralta. Turn right onto Peralta 2 blocks to Galisteo St. Turn left onto Galisteo to restaurant.

CLOUD CLIFF BAKERY & CAFE ✕

1805 2nd St. © 505-983-6254 ⊙ M-F 7:30am-2:30pm, Sat-Sun 8-2:30

Southwestern Cuisine, including vegetarian, as well as free-range meat and poultry. Baked goods made on site with organic flour.

· café · bakery · vegetarian friendly · organic focus · tables · wait staff

🚾 **From I-25**, take exit 282 onto US 84N/St Francis Dr (left from 25N, right from 25S) 1 mile to St Michael's Dr ramp. Turn left onto St Michael's ½ mile to Calle Lorca. Turn right onto Lorca 1 block to W San Mateo Rd. Turn left onto San Mateo (becomes 2nd St) to restaurant.

LONGEVITY CAFÉ ✕

112 W. San Francisco St. © 505-986-0403 ⊙ M-Sat 11am-midnight, Sun 11-7

Zen orientation, mostly organic and vegetarian, except for free-range chicken. Extensive tea selections.

· vegetarian friendly · vegan friendly · organic focus · counter · tables · self-service

🚾 In downtown historic Sante Fe, 1 block east of Plaza, corner Water & Galisteo St.

THE MARKET PLACE NATURAL GROCERY ✕🥬   ♿

913 W. Alameda © 505-984-8863 ⊙ M-Sat 7:30-9, Sun 9-8

· organic produce · freshly prepared food · juice bar · salad bar · café · deli · vegetarian friendly · tables · self-service · take-out

🚾 **From I-25**, take exit 282 onto US 84N/St Francis Dr (left from 25N, right from 25S) about 3½ miles to Alameda Ave. Turn left onto Alameda 1½ blocks to store on right in New Solana Center.

WHOLE FOODS MARKET ✕🥬   ♿

753 Cerrillos Rd. © 505-992-1700 ⊙ Daily 7:30-10

Beer and wine sold in the store can be enjoyed on the premises with your meal.

· organic produce · freshly prepared food · juice bar · salad bar · café · deli · bakery · vegetarian friendly · alcohol · chain · tables · self-service · take-out

🚾 **From I-25**, take exit 282 onto US 84N/St Francis Dr (left from 25N, right from 25S) about 2⅔ miles to Cerrillos Rd. Turn right onto Cerrillos about ¼ mile to store on right.

WILD OATS MARKET ✕🥬   ♿

1090 St. Francis Drive © 505-983-5333 ⊙ Daily 7-11

· organic produce · freshly prepared food · juice bar · salad bar · café · deli · bakery · vegetarian friendly · chain · tables · self-service · take-out

🚾 **From I-25**, take exit 282 onto US 84N/St Francis Dr (left from 25N, right from 25S) about 2½ miles to store on left.

SILVER CITY ─────────────

Gateway to the Gila Wilderness.

SILVER CITY FOOD CO-OP 🥬

520 N. Bullard St. © 505-388-2343 ⊙ M-F 9-6, Sat 9-5

· organic produce · co-op

🚾 **From Rt 180**, go south on Hudson St about ½ mile to College Ave. Turn right onto College 2 blocks to Bullard St. Turn left onto Bullard about 4 blocks to store on left.

TAOS

CID'S FOOD MARKET   ♿
623 Paseo del Pueblo Norte ℭ 505-758-1148 ⊘ M-Sat 7:30-7

· organic produce · freshly prepared food · deli · bakery · vegetarian friendly · take-out

Store is on Hwy 64/68 (aka Paseo de Pueblo Norte) about 1 mile north of Taos Plaza (2 blocks past 2nd traffic light) on right.

THE APPLETREE RESTAURANT ✗   ♿
123 Bent St. ℭ 505-758-1900 ⊘ Lunch M-Sat 11:30-3, Sun 11-3 Dinner Daily 5-9
The salad greens are mostly organic, and there are always vegetarian appetizers and entrees. RG: Best bet for vegetarians looking for a nice night out.

· vegetarian friendly · alcohol · tables · wait staff

From Hwy 64/68 (aka Paseo de Pueblo Norte), turn west onto Bent St (opposite Taos Plaza) to restaurant.

THE SHEVA CAFE ✗   ♿
812 Paseo del Pueblo Norte ℭ 505-737-9290 ⊘ M-F 8-9, Sun 9-9
The Israeli/Mediterranean food is mostly organic and vegetarian, with the exception of tuna, smoked salmon and lamb from a local, organic source. There's also a chess board, some instruments, and regular music events. RG: An unpretentious, New Age environment, with excellent food.

· vegetarian friendly · vegan friendly · organic focus · tables · wait staff

Restaurant is on Hwy 64/68 (aka Paseo de Pueblo Norte) about 2 miles north of Taos Plaza.

Goldbeck's "EAT IT OR NOT"
FASCINATING & FAR-OUT FACTS ABOUT FOOD

SALT is actually an edible rock

NEW YORK

1 Albany
2 Allentown
3 Amagansett
4 Amherst
5 Babylon Village
6 Binghamton
7 Boiceville
8 Brooklyn
9 Buffalo
10 Cambridge
11 Canton
12 Catskill
13 Chestnut Ridge
14 Clifton Park
15 Commack
16 Cornwall
17 Cross River
18 Delhi
19 East Hampton
20 East Setauket
21 Endicott
22 Flushing
23 Fresh Meadows
24 Garden City
25 Ghent
26 Glen Cove
27 Great Neck
28 Hamburg
29 Hamilton
30 Hankins
31 Hicksville
32 High Falls
33 Highland
34 Hudson
35 Huntington
36 Hyde Park
37 Ithaca
38 Jamaica
39 Jeffersonville
40 Johnson City

41 Katonah
42 Kingston
43 Larchmont
44 Liberty
45 Little Falls
46 Little Neck
47 Mahopac
48 Manhasset
49 Massapequa
50 Montauk
51 Mt. Kisco

52 New City
53 New Hartford
54 New Paltz
55 New York
56 Northport
57 Nyack
58 Oceanside
59 Oliverea
60 Oneonta
61 Phoenicia
62 Plainview

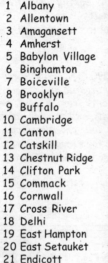

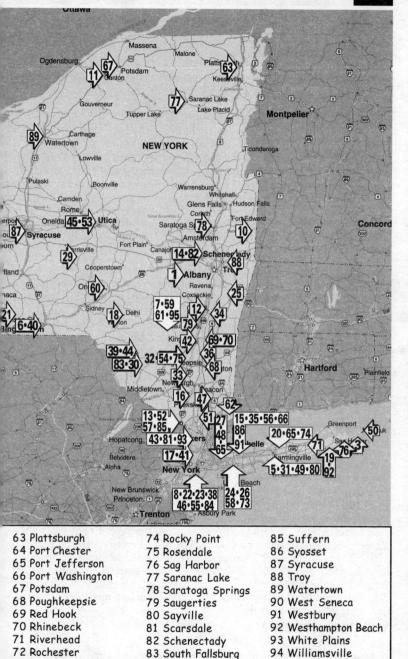

63 Plattsburgh
64 Port Chester
65 Port Jefferson
66 Port Washington
67 Potsdam
68 Poughkeepsie
69 Red Hook
70 Rhinebeck
71 Riverhead
72 Rochester
73 Rockville Centre

74 Rocky Point
75 Rosendale
76 Sag Harbor
77 Saranac Lake
78 Saratoga Springs
79 Saugerties
80 Sayville
81 Scarsdale
82 Schenectady
83 South Fallsburg
84 Staten Island

85 Suffern
86 Syosset
87 Syracuse
88 Troy
89 Watertown
90 West Seneca
91 Westbury
92 Westhampton Beach
93 White Plains
94 Williamsville
93 Woodstock

ALBANY

A TASTE OF GREECE ✕
193 Lark St. © 518-426-9000 ⏰ M-Th 11-9, F 11-10, Sat 2-10

Greek restaurants usually have some vegetarian options. This one offers more than most, including dishes you rarely see unless you are invited home by a Greek friend for dinner.

· vegetarian friendly · alcohol · tables · wait staff · take-out

🍎 **From I-90**, take exit 6 toward Arbor Hill onto US 9S almost 1 mile to US 9/Clinton Ave. Turn left onto Clinton and right onto Lark St about ⅓ mile to restaurant on right at Lark & Spring St. **From I-87S** (NY Thwy), merge onto I-90E via exit 1 and follow directions above. **From I-87N** (NY Thwy), take exit 23 onto I-787 N (toward Downtown Albany) 1¾ miles to exit 3 (US 9S/20E). Take Empire Plaza ramp straight onto S Mall Arterial ½ mile to S Swan St. Turn right onto Swan ¼ mile to Washington Ave. Turn left onto Washington ¼ mile to Lark. Turn left onto Lark 1 block to restaurant on right corner Lark & Spring.

HONEST WEIGHT FOOD CO-OP 🛍
484 Central Ave. © 518-482-2667 ⏰ M-F 7-8, Sat 7-6, Sun 10-6

· organic produce · freshly prepared food · deli · bakery · vegetarian · co-op · take-out

🍎 **From I-90**, take exit 5 south on Everett Rd (right from 5E, left from 5W) about ⅓ mile to end at Central Ave/NY 5. Turn left onto Central Ave ¾ mile to store on right (behind Family Dollar store). **From I-87S** (NY Thwy), merge onto I-90E via exit 1 and follow directions above. **From I-87N** (NY Thwy), take exit 23 onto I-787N 1¾ miles to exit 3 (US 9S/20E) toward Empire Plaza. Take Empire Plaza ramp onto S Mall Arterial to S Swan St. Turn right onto Swan ¼ mile to Washington Ave. Turn left onto Washington to Central. Turn right onto Central about 1 mile to store on left (behind Family Dollar store).

SHADES OF GREEN ✕   ♿
187 Lark St. © 518-434-1830 ⏰ M-Sat 11-9

An eclectic vegetarian menu of soups, salads, hot and cold sandwiches, burritos, and quesadillas at lunchtime. Dinner features organic pastas, and tofu and tempeh specialities (with brown rice). Fresh juices and smoothies available.

· juice bar · café · vegetarian · vegan friendly · organic focus · tables · self-service · take-out

🍎 **From I-90**, take exit 6 toward Arbor Hill onto US 9S almost 1 mile to US 9/Clinton Ave. Turn left onto Clinton and right onto Lark St about ⅓ mile to restaurant on right just past Washington Ave. **From I-87S** (NY Thwy), merge onto I-90E via exit 1 and follow directions above. **From I-87S** (NY Thwy), take exit 23 onto I-787 N (toward Downtown Albany) 1¾ miles to exit 3 (US 9S/20E). Take Empire Plaza ramp straight onto S Mall Arterial ½ mile to S Swan St. Turn right onto Swan ¼ mile to Washington. Turn left onto Washington ¼ mile to Lark. Turn left onto Lark to restaurant on right just off corner.

THE ORGANIC CAFE ✕
64 Colvin Ave. © 518-482-3749 ⏰ M-F 7-3

Natural food cafe serving breakfast and lunch. Vegetarian, free-range poultry, natural beef, whole wheat, organic cheese pizza, and more. Inside an 85,000 square foot entertainment complex.

· vegetarian friendly

From I-90, take exit 5 south on Everett Rd (right from 5E, left from 5W) about ⅓ mile to end at Central Ave/NY 5. Turn right onto Central Ave ⅓ mile to Colvin Ave. Turn left onto Colvin to restaurant in Armory Center. **From I-87S** (NY Thwy), merge onto I-90E via exit 1 and follow directions above. **From I-87N** (NY Thwy), take exit 23 onto I-787N (toward Downtown Albany) about 3½ miles to exit 5 toward Buffalo. Merge onto I-90W about 3⅓ miles to exit 5 (Everett Rd) and follow directions above.

ALLENTOWN

FEEL-RITE NATURAL FOOD SHOP 🍎
720 Elmwood Ave. ℂ 716-885-7889 ⊙ M-Sat 9-9, Sun 12-6
  · chain

From I-190 (NY Thwy), take exit 9 toward Peace Bridge/Fort Erie. Take Niagara St ramp onto Massachusetts Ave about 1 mile to W Ferry St. Veer right onto Ferry ¼ mile to Elmwood Ave. Turn left onto Elmwood to store.

AMAGANSETT

HAMPTON CHUTNEY CO. ✕
Main St., Amagansett Square ℂ 631-267-3131 ⊙ Daily 10-7
Menu features dosas–Indian sourdough crepes made from rice batter, with a selection of vegetarian fillings, as well as chicken, turkey and tuna. Also, sandwiches (whole grain bread available) and a daily vegetarian thali. Seating is outdoors at picnic tables on the lawn.
  · vegetarian friendly · take-out

Take Rt 27 (Montauk Hwy) into Amagansett. Turn onto Hedges Ln (right from Hamptons, left from Montauk) 1 block and left into parking lot for Amagansett Square. Restaurant is on right entering from lot.

AMHERST

FEEL-RITE FRESH MARKET ✕🍎
3912 Maple Rd. ℂ 716-834-3385 ⊙ M-Sat 9-9, Sun 11-7
  · organic produce · freshly prepared food · juice bar · deli · vegetarian friendly · chain
  · tables · self-service · take-out

From I-290, take exit 3 south on Niagara Falls Blvd to Maple Rd. Turn left onto Maple to store within 1 block on left.

BABYLON VILLAGE

A gateway town to Long Island beaches, Fire Island and the Hamptons.

SHERRY'S THE HEALTHY GOURMET 🍎   ♿
89 Deer Park Ave. ℂ 631-615-5832 ⊙ M-F 9-7, Sat-Sun 9-5
  · organic produce · freshly prepared food · take-out

Take Montauk Hwy (27A) to Deer Park Ave in the heart of Babylon. Turn north onto Deer Park ½ block to store on right.

BINGHAMTON

SUNRISE HEALTH FOODS 🍎
200 Main St. ℂ 607-798-6231 ⊙ M-F 9-8, Sat 11-4

From Rt 17, take exit 72 south on Mygatt St ½ mile to Clinton St. Turn right onto Clinton, left onto Jarvis, right onto Charlotte, left onto Florence, and right onto Main St to store. **From I-81**, merge onto 17W and follow directions above.

SUNY BINGHAMTON CO-OP 🛒
Student Union, SUNY Binghamton ☎ 607-777-4258 ☺ M-F 11-5
· co-op

🏠 **From I-81**, take exit 6 toward Rt 12/Chenango Bridge onto Rt 11S ⅓ mile to Front St (Rt 12). Turn left onto Front almost 1⅓ miles (follow signs to SUNY Binghamton) to store in student union. **From I-88**, take exit 2 toward Chenango Bridge onto Rt 12A (Chenango Bridge Rd) 1 mile to Front St. Turn left onto Front to SUNY Binghamton and store in student union.

WHOLE IN THE WALL RESTAURANT ✗   &
43 S. Washington St. ☎ 607-722-0006 ☺ Tues-Sat 11:30-9
Natural foods restaurant offering vegetarian, vegan, chicken and fish. Fresh whole wheat breads and bagels, specialty homemade pestos, BYOB. Live music weekends and other times during the week.
· vegetarian friendly · vegan friendly · tables · wait staff · take-out

🏠 **From Rt 17 & I-81**, take exit 4S (Rt 7S) onto Rt 363W about 1¾ miles to Rt 434W toward Vestal. Merge onto 434W, cross bridge and stay to left. Make 1st left onto S Washington St ½ block to restaurant on left.

BOICEVILLE———————————

BREAD ALONE ✗
Rte. 28 ☎ 845-657-3328 ☺ M-Th, Sat-Sun 7-7, F 7-11
Organic breads and baked goods, plus a daily selection of wholesome soups, salads and sandwiches, with vegetarian options.
· bakery · vegetarian friendly · tables · self-service · take-out

🏠 **From I-87** (NY Thwy), take exit 19 (Kingston). Take 1st exit off rotary onto Rt 28W toward Pine Hill about 16 miles to bakery on right (set back slightly on access road).

RESEVOIR NATURAL FOODS 🛒
Singer-Denman Plaza, Rt 28 ☎ 845-657-7302 ☺ M-Th, Sat-Sun 9-7, F 9-8
· organic produce

🏠 **From I-87** (NY Thwy), take exit 19 (Kingston). Take 1st exit off rotary onto Rt 28W toward Pine Hill 18 miles to store on left (across from school).

BROOKLYN———————————

BACK TO THE LAND NATURAL FOODS 🛒
142 Seventh Ave. ☎ 718-768-5654 ☺ Daily 9-9
A short walk from the Brooklyn Museum, Botanical Gardens and Prospect Park.
· organic produce · freshly prepared food · deli · take-out

🏠 In Park Slope business district. **From Manhattan**, take Manhattan Bridge onto Flatbush Ave Ext (continuing onto Flatbush Ave) less than 1 mile to 7th Ave. Turn right onto 7th less then ½ mile to store between Carroll St & Garfield Pl (a few blocks west of Prospect Park).

BLISS CAFE ✗   ⊜
191 Bedford Ave. ☎ 718-599-2547 ☺ M-F 9am-11pm, Sat-Sun 10am-11pm
In addition to the all-vegetarian menu that features tofu and tempeh, the baked goods are homemade, all vegan and include wheat-free options.
· vegetarian · vegan friendly · tables · wait staff

🏠 **From Williamsburg Bridge in Manhattan**, after crossing river continue on 5th Ave to 5th Place. Make 2 lefts back onto 5th 2 blocks to Bedford

Ave. Turn right onto Bedford ½ mile to restaurant. **From Brooklyn Queens Expwy (BQE) westbound**, take exit 32B toward Metropolitan Ave left onto Meeker Ave to N 6th St. Turn left onto 6th 4 blocks to Bedford. Turn right onto Bedford to restaurant. **From BQE eastbound**, take exit 32 toward Metropolitan onto Rodney St to Union Ave. Turn right onto Union, right onto Metropolitan, right onto 6th and follow directions above.

EVERYTHING NATURAL 🥬

1661 Ralph Ave. © 718-531-9192 ⊙ M, W 10-7:30, Tues, Th, F 10-6, Sat 10-4

· organic produce

🗓 Take Belt Pkwy to Rockaway PkwyN to Flatlands Ave. Turn left onto Flatlands 1¼ miles to Ralph Ave. Turn right onto Ralph 2 blocks to store on right between Glenwood & Farragut Rd.

FLATBUSH FOOD CO-OP 🥬

1318 Cortelyou Rd. © 718-284-9717 ⊙ Daily 7-10

· organic produce · co-op

🗓 **From Manhattan**, take Manhattan Bridge onto Flatbush Ave Ext (continuing onto Flatbush Ave) about 1 mile to Grand Army Plaza. Go halfway around plaza and veer right onto Flatbush Ave (alongside Prospect Park) ¾ mile to Ocean Ave. Turn right onto Ocean about 1⅓ miles to Cortelyou Rd. Turn right onto Cortelyou about ⅓ mile to store on right between Rugby & Argyle Rd. **From Brooklyn Queens Expwy**, take Prospect Expwy (1st exit past Brooklyn Battery Tunnel on left), which becomes Ocean Pkwy once traffic lights begin. At 2nd light, turn left onto Beverly Rd to 4th light at Rugby. Turn right onto Rugby and right at next light onto Cortelyou to store on left between Rugby & Argyle.

GOGA VEGETARIAN CAFE & LOUNGE ✕

521 Court St. © 718-260-8618 ⊙ Tues-Th, Sun 11-10, F-Sat 11-midnight
Soups, salads, sandwiches, and an interesting mixed bag of healthy meatless entrees. Plus, juice bar and homemade vegan desserts. Weekend brunch includes vegan pancakes, tempeh bacon, and live music on Sunday afternoon.

· juice bar · café · vegetarian · vegan friendly · alcohol · tables · wait staff

🗓 In Carroll Gardens. **From Manhattan**, take the Brooklyn Battery Tunnel onto Gowanus Expwy toward Hamilton Ave. Take Hamilton exit left onto Hamilton to Clinton St. Turn left onto Clinton, right onto Huntington St and right onto Court St to restaurant between 9th & Garnet St.

GREEN PARADISE ✕

609 Vanderbilt Ave. © 718-230-5177 ⊙ Tues-Th, Sun 12-9:30, F-Sat 12-11
Mostly organic, vegan, raw foods with a Caribbean slant.

· juice bar · vegan · organic focus · counter · self-service · take-out

🗓 **From Manhattan**, take Manhattan Bridge onto Flatbush Ave Ext (continuing onto Flatbush Ave) about 1¼ miles to Dean St. Turn left onto Dean less than ½ mile to Vanderbilt Ave. Turn right onto Vanderbilt past 1st block to restaurant between Bergen & St Marks St.

THE GREENS ✕

128 Montague St. © 718-246-1288 ⊙ M-Th 11-10:30, F 11-11, Sat 12-11, Sun 1-10:30
Vegetarian Chinese food.

· vegetarian · vegan friendly · tables · wait staff

🗓 **From Booklyn Bridge**, take Cadman Plaza W ramp left onto Henry St about ⅓ mile to Montague St. Turn right onto Montague to restaurant.

VEGGIE CASTLE ✕
2242 Church Ave. © 718-703-1275 ⊙ M-Th 10am-11pm, F-Sat 10am-midnight, Sun 10-10
A vegan menu inside a former White Castle hamburger joint.
· juice bar · bakery · vegan · tables · self-service · take-out
📖 **From Manhattan**, take Manhattan Bridge onto Flatbush Ave Ext (continuing onto Flatbush Ave) about 1 mile to Grand Army Plaza. Go halfway around plaza and veer right onto Flatbush Ave (alongside Prospect Park) about 1⅔ miles to Church Ave. Turn right onto Church to restaurant.

WENDY'S PLATE ✕
434 Ave. U © 718-376-3125 ⊙ M-Th 11-10, F 11-3, Sat 1 hour after sundown-10
A kosher dairy restaurant—no meat, but fish is served.
· vegetarian friendly · kosher · tables · wait staff
📖 **From Brooklyn Queens Expwy**, take Prospect Expwy (exit past Brooklyn Battery Tunnel on left) 5 miles (becomes Ocean Pkwy) to Ave U. Turn right onto U to restaurant between E 3rd & 4th St. **From Belt Pkwy**, take exit 7N onto Ocean PkwyN (loop around right eastbound, onto Shore Pkwy and right westbound) about 1 mile to Ave U. Turn left onto U to restaurant.

BUFFALO

FEEL-RITE NATURAL FOOD SHOP 🛒
1451 Hertel Ave. © 716-837-7661 ⊙ M-Sat 10-9, Sun 12-5
· chain
📖 **From Squajaquada Expwy** (NY 198), take Delaware Ave exit north to Nottingham Terrace. Turn right onto Nottingham about ½ mile to Amherst St. Turn right onto Amherst ¼ mile to Colvin Ave. Turn left onto Colvin ⅓ mile to Saranac Ave. Turn right onto Saranac and left onto Hertel Ave to store at corner Hertal & Norwalk Ave (across from Fleet Bank).

LEXINGTON REAL FOODS COMMUNITY CO-OP 🛒
230 Lexington Ave. © 716-884-8828 ⊙ Daily 9-9
· organic produce · co-op
📖 **From I-90** (NY Thwy), take exit 51W toward Buffalo onto Rt 33W about 4⅔ miles. Follow Humboldt Pkwy exit and turn right onto Ferry St 1⅔ miles to Elmwood Ave. Turn left onto Elmwood and right onto Lexington Ave to store on left.

CAMBRIDGE

VILLAGE STORE CO-OP 🛒
25 E. Main St. © 518-677-5731 ⊙ M, W, F-Sat 10-5, Tues, Th 10-8
· organic produce · co-op
📖 **From Rt 22**, go west on E Main St (left from 22N, right from 22S) to store in town.

CANTON
The northern hinterlands of New York, with 4 colleges in the area.

NATURE'S STOREHOUSE 🛒
21 Main St. © 315-386-3740 ⊙ M-Tues 9-5, W-F 9-6, Sat 10-5
· organic produce · freshly prepared food · take-out
📖 Canton is about 50 miles north of I-81 exit 49 on US 11. Turn right at 1st traffic light in town onto Main St to store on left (across from Mobil station).

CATSKILL

CATSKILL NATURAL PRODUCTS 🍵
254 W. Bridge St. ✆ 518-943-2830 ⊙ M, Tues, Th, Sat 9-5:30, W 9-6, F 9-7

🏠 **From I-87** (NY Thwy), take exit 21 (Catskill) onto 23E about 1 mile to Rt 9W south toward Catskill. Turn right onto 9W (becomes Bridge St) about 1¼ miles to store next to Trustco Bank.

KAATERSKILL FARM NATURAL STOREHOUSE 🍵
115 W. Bridge St. ✆ 518-943-1919 ⊙ M-F 9:30-6, Sat 9-6

· organic produce

🏠 **From I-87** (NY Thwy), take exit 21 (Catskill) onto 23E about 1 mile to Rt 9W south toward Catskill. Turn right onto 9W about 1 mile to Grandview Ave. Store is on right in Grandview Plaza (next to Dunkin' Donuts).

CHESTNUT RIDGE

HUNGRY HOLLOW CO-OP 🍵
841 Chestnut Ridge Rd. ✆ 845-356-3319 ⊙ M-Th 10-7, F-Sat 10-6
Featuring local organic and biodynamic produce.

· organic produce · freshly prepared food · co-op · take-out

🏠 **From Garden State Pkwy N**, take exit 172 (Grand Ave). Turn left at traffic light at end of ramp. Turn right at first light onto Chestnut Ridge Rd (becomes Rt 45) 2½ miles (across NY border and past 3 lights) to store on left at Hungry Hollow Rd. **From NY Thwy**, take exit 14A (Garden State Pkwy S). Take first exit (Red Schoolhouse Rd) right at stop sign. Turn left at first light onto Chestnut Ridge (Rt 45) to store on left at Hungry Hollow.

CLIFTON PARK

THE GREEN GROCER 🍵
1505 Rte. 9 ✆ 518-383-1613 ⊙ M-F 10-8, Sat 10-6, Sun 12-5

· organic produce

🏠 **From 1-87** (NY Thwy), take exit 8A east onto Grooms Rd (right from 87N, left from 87S) 1½ miles to Rt 9. Turn left onto Rt 9 to 1st right into Half Moon Plaza to store.

COMMACK

THE MUNG BEAN 🍵
6522 Jericho Tpke. ✆ 631-499-2362 ⊙ M-Sat 9-6

· organic produce · juice bar · take-out

🏠 **From LIE (I-495)**, take exit 52 toward CR 4/Commack north on CR 4N (Commack Rd) about 2¾ miles to Jericho Tpke. Turn right onto Jericho to store in Commack Corners Shopping Ctr. **From Northern State Pkwy**, take exit 43 toward CR 4/Commack onto CR 4N almost 2 miles to Jericho. Turn right onto Jericho to store in Commack Corners Shopping Ctr.

Please tell these businesses that you found them in Healthy Highways.

CORNWALL

Don't miss the Storm King Art Center and Sculpture Park.

HEALTHY HABITS 🛒
321 Main St. ☎ 845-534-4021 ⏰ Tues-F 10-7, Sat 10-5

· freshly prepared food · take-out

🍎 **From Rt 32,** go east on Quaker Ave (CR 107) 1 mile to roundabout. Take 3rd exit onto Rt 9N/Main St to store. **From 9W,** go east on Quaker about ½ mile to roundabout and follow directions above.

CROSS RIVER

NATURE'S TEMPTATIONS ⚔🛒
890 Rte. 35 ☎ 914-763-5643 ⏰ M-F 9:30-7, Sat 9-5, Sun 10-3

· organic produce · freshly prepared food · deli · vegetarian friendly · tables · self-service · take-out

🍎 **From I-684,** take exit 6 east on Rt 35 (Cross River Rd) about 3¾ miles to Rt 121. Store is at intersection in Cross River Plaza.

DELHI

GOOD CHEAP FOOD 🛒
53 Main St. ☎ 607-746-6562 ⏰ M-Sat 10-6

· organic produce

🍎 **From I-87** (NY Thwy), take exit 19 (Kingston). Take first exit off traffic circle onto Rt 28W 70 miles to Delhi. Turn left onto Main St to store 150 yds on left. **From I-88,** take exit 14 (Oneonta) onto Rt 28E 20 miles to Delhi. Turn right onto Main St 1 mile to store on left.

EAST HAMPTON

BABETTE'S ⚔   ♿
66 Newton Lane ☎ 631-329-5377 ⏰ M, Th 9-3, F 9-10, Sat 8-10, Sun 8-4

About half the menu is vegetarian and most ingredients are organic. Outdoor dining in nice weather. BR: Great fresh food and innovative combinations.

· vegetarian friendly · organic focus · alcohol · counter · tables · wait staff · take-out

🍎 Rt 27 becomes Main St in East Hampton. **From 27E,** turn left onto Main about 1 mile to Newton Ln. Turn left onto Newton 1½ blocks to restaurant on right. **From tip of LI on Rt 27W** (Montauk Hwy), turn right onto Newton 1½ blocks to restaurant on right.

EAST SETAUKET

WILD BY NATURE ⚔🛒
198 Main St. ☎ 631-246-5500 ⏰ M-Sat 9-9, Sun 9-8

Fresh wok cookery at the cafe-in-the-round at the center of the store.

· organic produce · freshly prepared food · salad bar · café · deli · vegetarian friendly · counter · self-service · take-out

🍎 **From LIE (I-495),** take exit 62 (97N/Nicolls Rd) onto 97N almost 10 miles to Rt 25A. Turn right onto 25A about 1½ miles to store on right at Gnarled Hollow Rd.

ENDICOTT

DOWN TO EARTH WHOLE FOODS CO. 🛒
305 Grant Ave. ☎ 607-785-2338 ⏰ M-F 9-9, Sat 10-6, Sun 12-6

· organic produce · freshly prepared food · juice bar · deli · vegetarian friendly · take-out

🍎 **From Rt 17**, take exit 67N toward Endicott and follow Rt 26N ramp onto Rt 26/E Main St which loops around to Grant Ave. Turn right onto Grant to store.

FLUSHING

HAPPY BUDDHA VEGETARIAN RESTAURANT ✕

135-37 37th Ave. © 718-358-0079 ⊙ Daily 11-10

Huge Asian vegetarian menu with faux meats and brown rice available.

· vegetarian · vegan friendly · tables · wait staff

🍎 **From Van Wyck Expwy, Grand Central Pkwy or BQE**, exit at Rt 25A (Northern Blvd) and go east to Main St. Turn right onto Main 1 block to 37th Ave. Turn right onto 37th 2 blocks to restaurant. **From Eastern LI or Clearview Expwy**, go west on Northern to Main. Turn left onto Main and right onto 37th 2 blocks to restaurant.

FRESH MEADOWS

QUANTUM LEAP ✕🍴

65-60 Fresh Meadows Lane © 718-762-3572 ⊙ M-Th, Sun 10-10, F-Sat 10-11

Store and full-service natural foods restaurant with vegetarian, vegan and fish choices. RS: The food is fresh and consistently good, with a strong macrobiotic bent. Relaxed atmosphere, designed for basic dining, not elegance.

· organic produce · freshly prepared food · café · vegetarian friendly · tables · wait staff

🍎 **From LIE (I-495)**, take exit 25 toward Utopia Pkwy/164th St onto Utopia Pkwy about 1/3 mile to 67th Ave. Turn right onto 67th 2 blocks to Fresh Meadows Lane. Turn right onto Fresh Meadows to store.

QUEENS HEALTH EMPORIUM ✕🍴

15901 Horace Harding Expwy. © 718-358-6500 ⊙ M-Sat 9:30-8, Sun 10-6

· freshly prepared food · deli · vegetarian friendly · tables · self-service · take-out

🍎 **From LIE (I-495) westbound**, take exit 24 toward Kissena Blvd onto Horace Harding Expwy N to store on corner at 159th St. **From LIE eastbound**, take exit 24 toward Kissena onto Harding Expwy S to 164th St. Turn left onto 164th and left onto Harding Expwy N to store at 159th St.

GARDEN CITY

FOOD FOR THOUGHT ✕🍴

154 7th St. © 516-747-5811 ⊙ M-F 9-6:30, Sat 9:30-5:45

· freshly prepared food · juice bar · deli · vegetarian friendly · tables · self-service · take-out

🍎 **From Northern State Pkwy**, take exit 31 and follow Glen Cove Rd ramp toward Hempstead onto Glen Cove Rd (becomes Clinton St) about 1¾ miles to Stewart Ave. Turn right onto Stewart about ¾ mile to Franklin Ave. Turn left onto Franklin 1 block to 7th St. Turn left onto 7th to store. **From Meadowbrook Pkwy**, take exit M3W onto Merchants Concourse to Stewart Ave. Turn right onto Stewart 2¼ miles to Franklin Ave. Turn left onto Franklin and left onto 7th to store.

GLEN COVE

RISING TIDE NATURAL MARKET ✗🛒
42 Forest Ave. © 516-676-7895 ⊙ M-F 9-8, Sat 9-7, Sun 10-6

· organic produce · freshly prepared food · deli · vegetarian friendly · tables · self-service · take-out

🛒 **From LIE (I-495)**, take exit 39 north on Glen Cove Rd over 6 miles to end (fire station). Turn right onto Brewster St (becomes Forest Ave) about ¾ mile (past 5 traffic lights) to store on right.

GREAT NECK

THE HEALTH NUTS ✗🛒   &
45 Northern Blvd. © 516-829-8414 ☺ M, Sat, 9:30-7, Tues-F 9:30-8, Sun 10:30-5
The deli offerings are always vegetarian. Note, the juice bar is closed Sunday.

· organic produce · freshly prepared food · juice bar · vegetarian · tables · self-service · take-out

🛒 **From LIE (I-495)**, take exit 32 onto Horace Harding Expwy and turn north onto Little Neck Pkwy (left from 495E, left from 495W) ¾ mile to Northern Blvd. Turn right onto Northern ¼ mile to store.

GHENT

HAWTHORNE VALLEY FARM STORE 🛒
327 Rte. 21C © 518-672-7500 ⊙ M-Th 8-7, F 8-8, Sat 8-6, Sun 10-5
On-site biodynamic farm, dairy and bakery where grains are freshly milled.

· organic produce · deli · bakery · vegetarian friendly · take-out

🛒 **From Taconic State Pkwy**, take Rt 217/Philmont/Harlemville exit right at end of ramp onto Rt 21C and go east 1½ miles to store on left.

HAMBURG

FEEL-RITE FRESH MARKET 🛒
6000 S. Park Ave. © 716-649-6694 ⊙ M-Sat 9-9, Sun 9-5

· organic produce · chain

🛒 **From I-90 (NY Thwy)**, take exit 57 and follow road off exit onto Rt 75S. Take 75S more than 1 mile to Legion Dr. Turn left onto Legion over ½ mile to Rt 62. Turn left onto 62 (aka S Park Ave) almost ½ mile to store.

HAMILTON

HAMILTON WHOLE FOODS ✗🛒
28 Broad St. © 315-824-2930 ⊙ M-Sat 10-5:30

· freshly prepared food · deli · vegetarian friendly · tables · self-service · take-out

🛒 **From US 20**, take Rt 46 south about 4 miles (becomes 12B, then Broad St in town). Turn right onto Broad to store across from village green.

HANKINS

EAST RIDGE COUNTRY STORE & DINER ✗🛒
10770 State Rt. 97 © 845-887-5751 ⊙ Daily 7-9
The food is typical American diner—with one big difference. It's all organic!
No vegetarian dishes on the menu, but they will customize something for
vegetarians or vegans. Run by the owners of East Ridge organic bakery.

· organic produce · freshly prepared food · bakery · organic focus · counter · tables · wait staff · take-out

From Rt 17N, take exit 104 (in Monticello) onto 17B almost 7 miles to Callicoon. Merge onto Rt 97N 4½-5 miles to Hankins and store. **From Rt 17S**, take exit 87 (in Hancock) onto Rt 97S almost 19 miles to store.

HICKSVILLE

HOUSE OF DOSAS ✖
416 S. Broadway ✆ 516-938-7517 ☺ Daily 11-10
South Indian vegetarian cuisine.

· vegetarian · vegan friendly · tables · wait staff

From LIE (I-495), take exit 41S toward Hicksville onto N Broadway/ NY 106S/107S. Take Broadway/107S (keep left after about 1 mile) about 2 miles to restaurant on right (across from Motor Vehicle Dept). **From Northern State Pkwy**, take exit 35S onto Broadway and follow directions above.

HIGH FALLS

HIGH FALLS FOOD CO-OP 🛒
1398 Rte. 213 ✆ 845-687-7262 ☺ M-Sat 9-7, Sun 9-6
RW: Lovingly cooked soups and great vegan desserts.

· organic produce · co-op

From north (Kingston), take Rt 209 south 10 miles to Rt 213. Turn left onto 213 about 1¾ miles to store on right. **From south** (New Paltz), take Main St west to Springtown Rd. Turn right onto Springtown ½ mile to Mohonk Mt Rd. Veer left onto Mohonk Mt about 8 miles (twists and turns, climbs and decends) to Rt 213. Turn right onto 213 to store on right. **From Rt 32**, take 213 west to store on left.

HIGHLAND

HIGHLAND NATURAL FOOD CENTER 🛒
73 Tillson Ave. ✆ 845-691-8105 ☺ M-F 9:30-7, Sat 9:30-3:30

· freshly prepared food · take-out

On Rt 9W in strip mall on west side of Hudson River, just before entrance to Mid-Hudson Bridge.

HUDSON

A small, bustling town with antique stores, artists' studios and many restaurants offering something for vegetarians. Be sure to take in the gorgeous views of the Hudson River at the bottom of town.

EARTH FOODS ✖
523 Warren St. ✆ 518-822-1396 ☺ M, W-Th 9-4, F-Sun 9-5
The menu runs from tofu to beef, with plenty of selections in every category. Soups, salads, sandwiches, wraps, homemade pizzas, pasta, hot entrees, and more. Bread is homemade from organic white and whole wheat flour, juice is fresh-pressed using organic produce, milk is organic, but hot chocolate comes from a supermarket mix. ME: Friendly, family-run restaurant. Special recommendation for Bombay Vegetable Soup.

· juice bar · café · vegetarian friendly · alcohol · counter · tables · wait staff

From Rt 23, take Rt 23B/9G (left from 23E right from 23W) almost 3 miles to Warren St. Turn right onto Warren about ⅓ mile to store on left between 5th & 6th St.

KAATERSKILL FARM NATURAL STOREHOUSE 🐑
173 Healy Blvd. © 518-822-0790 ⊘ M-F 9:30-7, Sat 9-6, Sun 12-5
· organic produce
🍎 **From Rt 23**, take Rt 23B/9G (left from 23E right from 23W) almost 3 miles into Hudson. Continue right on 23B (Columbia St) through town about 1 mile to Rt 66 (Union Tpke). Turn left onto 66 ¾ mile to store on corner at Healy Blvd in Corner Plaza.

HUNTINGTON

WILD BY NATURE ✂🐑
369 W. Main St. © 631-424-6480 ⊘ M-Sat 9-9, Sun 9-8
Sister store to East Setauket, with hopes of more to come.
· organic produce · freshly prepared food · salad bar · café · deli · vegetarian friendly
· counter · self-service · take-out
🍎 **From LIE (I-495)**, take exit 49N onto Rt 110N (becomes NY Ave) about 7 miles to W Main St (Rt 25A). Turn left onto Main about ¼ mile to store on right.

HYDE PARK

MOTHER EARTH'S STOREHOUSE 🐑   ♿
3949 Albany Post Rd. © 845-229-8593 ⊘ M-F 9-9, Sat 1-8, Sun 12-6
· organic produce
🍎 On Rt 9 in Hyde Park on west side in Colonial Plaza.

ITHACA

A 2-college town with numerous attractions. Among the less publicized is The Labyrinth, open 24 hours for a walking meditation. A nice way for road-weary travelers to "reharmonize body and mind."

ABC CAFE ✂
308 Stewart Ave. © 607-277-4770 ⊘ Tues-Th 11am-midnight, F 11am-1am, Sat-Sun 9:30am-11pm
Extensive all-vegetarian menu of soups, salads, burgers, sandwiches, and hot entrees, with a different ethnic cuisine featured nightly. About half organic.
· bakery · vegetarian · vegan friendly · organic focus · alcohol · tables · wait staff
🍎 **From Rt 13**, go east on Buffalo St through town and up hill (toward Collegetown) to blinking light at Stewart Ave. Turn left onto Stewart to restaurant on left.

GREENSTAR COOPERATIVE MARKET 🐑
701 W. Buffalo St. © 607-273-9392 ⊘ Daily 7-11
· organic produce · freshly prepared food · deli · bakery · vegetarian friendly · co-op · take-out
🍎 **From Rt 13**, turn west onto Seneca St (right from 13S, left from 13N). Turn right into store parking lot. **From Rt 96**, 96 becomes Buffalo St in town. Follow to parking lot on right before Fulton St.

LUDGATE FARMS 🐑
1552 Hanshaw Rd. © 607-257-1765 ⊘ Daily 9-9
· organic produce
🍎 **Coming from Ithaca**, take Rt 13 north to Warren Rd. Turn right onto Warren about ½ mile to 4-way stop sign. Turn left onto Hanshaw Rd to store about ½ mile uphill on left (just past Sapsucker Woods Rd on left & Freese Rd on right).

MOOSEWOOD RESTAURANT ✕

215 N.Cayuga St. ℂ 607-273-9610 ⏰ Lunch Daily 11:30-3, Dinner (Summer) M-Th, Sun 5:30-9, F-Sat 6-9:30 (Winter)M-Th, Sun 5:30-8:30, F-Sat 5:30-9, Bar/Cafe M-Th, Sun 11-11, F-Sat 11-midnight

This famous natural foods restaurant has a vegetarian outlook, but also serves fresh fish and seafood. Menu changes daily.

· vegetarian friendly · organic focus · alcohol · co-op · tables · wait staff

🍴 **From Rt 13**, go east on Buffalo St to Cayuga St. Restaurant is on right in DeWitt Mall.

OASIS NATURAL GROCERY 🍃

215 N. Cayuga St. ℂ 607-273-8213 ⏰ M-F 9-7, Sat 9:30-6, Sun 11-5

· organic produce · freshly prepared food· deli· vegetarian friendly · take-out

🍴 See directions above to Moosewood Restaurant.

JAMAICA

GURU'S HEALTH FOOD 🍃

86-18 Parsons Blvd. ℂ 718-291-7406 ⏰ M-F 9:30-7:30, Sat 10:30-7, Sun 12-6

🍴 **From Grand Central Pkwy E**, take Parsons Blvd exit (16) straight onto E access road to Parsons. Turn right onto Parsons about ½ mile to store between 86th & 87th Ave. **From Grand Central W**, take 168th St exit (17) onto access road almost 1 mile to Parsons. Turn left onto Parsons about ½ mile to store between 86th & 87th.

JEFFERSONVILLE

THE GOOD EARTH 🍃

4887 Main St. ℂ 845-482-3131 ⏰ M-F 10-6, Sat 9-5, Sun 10-2

· organic produce

🍴 **From Rt 17**, take exit 100 (Liberty) onto Rt 52W about 11 miles to Jeffersonville. Store is in center of town on right across from post office.

JOHNSON CITY

HEALTH BEAT NATURAL FOODS ✕🍃   ♿

214 Main St. ℂ 607-797-1001 ⏰ M-F 9-8, Sat 10-6, Sun 12-5, Deli M-F 11:30-6:30, Sat 11-5

Mostly organic, vegetarian menu (except for tuna) of soups, sandwiches and salads, with daily hot vegan specials.

· organic produce · deli · vegetarian friendly · vegan friendly · organic focus · tables · self-service · take-out

🍴 **From I-81**, merge onto Rt 17W about 2 miles to exit 71S toward Johnson City. Follow exit around onto Rt 69S to CFJ Blvd. Turn right onto CFJ and left onto Lester Ave about ¼ mile to Main St (17C). Turn right onto Main to store just past Ave B. **From Rt 17**, take exit 71S and follow directions above.

KATONAH

MRS. GREEN'S NATURAL MARKET 🍃

202 Katonah Ave. ℂ 914-232-7574 ⏰ M-W, F 8:30-6:30, Th 8:30-7, Sat 8:30-6, Sun 10-5

· organic produce · juice bar · chain· take-out

🍴 **From I-684**, take exit 6 toward Rt 35/Katonah. Follow Saw Mill Pkwy ramp toward I-684S to Jay St. Turn right onto Jay and left onto Katonah Ave to store.

KINGSTON

BREAD ALONE ✗
385 Wall St. ℂ 845-339-1295 ⊘ M-Sat 8-6, Sun 9-4
Organic breads and baked goods, plus a daily selection of wholesome soups, salads and sandwiches with vegetarian options.
 · bakery · vegetarian friendly · tables · self-service · take-out
 From I-87 (NY Thwy), take exit 19 (Kingston). Follow traffic circle all the way around and turn right onto Colonial Dr to end. Turn right onto Albany Ave to Wall St (3rd traffic light). Turn right onto Wall 3 blocks to restaurant on left corner where Wall ends at N Front St.

DOWN TO EARTH CAFE ✗
906 Rte. 28 ℂ 845-334-8455 ⊘ M-F 7:30-5, Sat-Sun 10-4
 · vegetarian · tables · self-service · take-out
 From I-87 (NY Thwy), take exit 19 (Kingston). Take 1st exit off rotary onto Rt 28W about 4 miles to restaurant on right in shopping plaza (sign also says Catskill Mt Coffee House).

JANE'S ✗
305 Wall St. ℂ 845-338-8315 ⊘ M-F 9-6, Sat 11-4
Sandwiches, wraps, soups, salads, and lots of daily specials for all appetites.
 · vegetarian friendly · tables · self-service · take-out
 From I-87 (NY Thwy), take exit 19 (Kingston). Follow traffic circle all the way around and turn right onto Colonial Dr to end. Turn right onto Albany Ave to Wall St (3rd traffic light). Turn right onto Wall past 2nd block to restaurant on left.

MOTHER EARTH'S STOREHOUSE ✗ 🥄   ♿
1200 Ulster Ave. ℂ 845-336-5541 ⊘ M-F 9-9, Sat 9-7, Sun 12-5
Vegetarian and vegan deli and salad bar.
 · organic produce · freshly prepared food · salad bar · deli · vegetarian · vegan friendly · tables · self-service · take-out
 From I-87 (NY Thwy), take exit 19 (Kingston). Take 1st exit off rotary onto Rt 28W. Take 1st exit on right onto Rt 209N to US 9WS. Exit onto 9WS (Ulster Ave) to store on left in Kings Mall.

LARCHMONT

MRS. GREEN'S NATURAL MARKET ✗ 🥄
2460 Boston Post Rd. ℂ 914-834-6667 ⊘ M, W, F 9-8, Tues, Th 9-9, Sat 9-7, Sun 10-6
 · organic produce · freshly prepared food · vegetarian friendly · chain · tables · self-service · take-out
 From I-95 (NE Thwy), take exit 16 toward Cedar St onto Cross Westchester Ave (becomes Cedar) to Ramada Plaza. Turn left onto Ramada Plaza and right onto River St (becomes Echo Ave) less than ¼ mile to Main St/Rt 1N. Turn left onto 1 (becomes Boston Post Rd) less than 1 mile to store.

LIBERTY

THE SUNFLOWER HEALTH FOOD STORE 🥄
71 N. Main St. ℂ 845-292-3535 ⊘ M-Sat 10-6
 From Rt 17W, take exit 100 left at traffic light off ramp onto Sullivan Ave and left at next light onto Rt 52W. Follow 52 onto Main St past 3 lights (1⅓ miles) to store on right (2nd store after School St). **From Rt 17E**, take

exit 99 toward Liberty and follow exit to N Main. Turn left onto Main almost 1 mile to store on left.

LITTLE FALLS

COMMUNITY CO-OP 🦬   ♿
589 Albany St. ✆ 315-823-0686 ⊙ Tues, W, F 9:30-5, Th 9:30-8, Sat 9:30-1
· organic produce · co-op

🍎 **From Rt 5**, at traffic light at Ann St turn north (left from 5E, right from 5W) 1 block to Albany St. Turn right onto Albany 2 blocks to store on right. **From I-90 (NY Thwy)**, take exit 29A or 30 to Rt 5E or W and follow directions above.

LITTLE NECK

ZEN PAVILION ✗   ♿
251-15 Northern Blvd. ✆ 718-281-1500 ⊙ Daily 11-10
Huge Asian vegetarian menu featuring seitan and tofu. Brown rice available.
· vegan · kosher · tables · wait staff · take-out

🍎 **From Cross Island Pkwy (exit 31E) or Clearview Expwy (exit 5)**, take Northern Blvd exit (Rt 25A) east 1¼ miles (a little more from Clearview) to restaurant on left. **From LIE (I-495)**, take exit 32 north onto Little Neck Pwy (right from 495W, left from 495E) ¾ mile to Northern. Turn left onto Northern to restaurant on right.

MAHOPAC

MRS. GREEN'S NATURAL MARKET 🦬
Lake Plaza Shopping Center, Rte. 6 ✆ 845-628-0533 ⊙ M-Sat 9-7, Sun 10-5
· organic produce · juice bar · chain · take-out

🍎 **From I-84**, take exit 19 onto Rt 312 toward Carmel. Turn right at 1st traffic light to Rt 6. Turn left onto Rt 6 about 5 miles to store on left in Lake Plaza Shopping Center.

MANHASSET

WHOLE FOODS MARKET 🦬   ♿
2101 Northern Blvd. ✆ 516-869-8900 ⊙ Daily 8-9
· organic produce · freshly prepared food · salad bar · deli · bakery · vegetarian friendly
· chain · take-out

🍎 **From LIE (I-495)**, take exit 36 north on Searingtown Rd (right from 495W, left from 495E) 1¼ miles to Northern Blvd. Store is on NW corner across from Americana Shopping Center.

MASSAPEQUA

EDEN'S WAY NATURAL FOODS 🦬
37 Broadway ✆ 516-798-5670 ⊙ M-W, F-Sat 10-6:30, Th 10-8
· organic produce · juice bar · take-out

🍎 **From Southern State Pkwy**, take exit onto Seaford Oyster Bay Expwy about 2 miles to exit 2E (Sunrise Hwy). Merge onto Sunrise Hwy (NY 27E) about 1⅓ miles to Broadway. Turn left onto Broadway 2 blocks to store.

MONTAUK

JONI'S ✕
9 S. Edison Plaza © 631-668-3663 ☺ M-Tues, Th-F 9-3, Sat-Sun 8-3 (Closed mid Dec-Feb, open weekends only March-May)
Vegetarian, fish and free-range poultry. Hours are seasonal.
· vegetarian friendly · tables · self-service
🍲 Take Montauk Hwy (27E) all the way to the tip of LI. **From Montauk Hwy**, take The Plaza toward the sound (left from 27E, right from 27W) onto Edgemere St 2 blocks and continue right onto Edison Ext to restaurant.

NATURALLY GOOD FOODS & CAFE ✕ 🍽   ♿
38 S. Etna Ave. © 631-668-9030 ☺ M-Sat 7-5:30 (kitchen to 4), Sun 7-4:30 (kitchen to 3)
· organic produce · freshly prepared food · juice bar · deli · bakery · vegetarian friendly · tables · self-service · take-out
🍲 Take Montauk Hwy (27E) all the way to the tip of LI. **From Montauk Hwy**, turn toward the ocean on S Essex St (right from 27E, left from 27W) 1 block to store at S Etna Ave.

MT. KISCO

MRS. GREEN'S NATURAL MARKET ✕ 🍽
666 Lexington Ave. © 914-242-9292 ☺ M, W, F 9-8, Tues, Th 9-9, Sat 9-7, Sun 10-6
· organic produce · freshly prepared food · vegetarian friendly · chain · tables · self-service · take-out
🍲 **From I-684**, take exit 4 west on NY 172/S Bedford Rd 2 miles to Main St. Turn left onto Main about ⅔ mile to Lexington Ave. Turn left onto Lexington to store in shopping plaza.

NEW CITY

BACK TO THE EARTH NATURAL FOODS 🍽
306A S. Main St. © 845-634-3511 ☺ M-F 9-7:30, Sat-Sun 10-6
· freshly prepared food · deli · take-out
🍲 **From Palisades Pkwy**, take exit 10 toward New City east on Germonds Rd (right from Pkwy N, left from Pkwy S) about ¾ mile to S Main (Rt 304). Turn left onto Main about 1½ miles to store on right just past Collyer Ave.

NEW HARTFORD

PETER'S CORNUCOPIA 🍽
52 Genessee St. © 315-724-4998 ☺ M-F 9:30-8, Sat 9:30-6, Sun 12-5
· organic produce · juice bar · take-out
🍲 **From I-90**, take exit 31 (Genessee St N) toward Rt 5/Rt 8 and follow exit onto NY 5W. Take 5W/8S about 4¼ miles and merge onto 8S (toward New Hartford) about ½ mile to Campion Rd exit. Take Campion about ¼ mile to Genessee St. Turn right onto Genessee to store at Pearl St.

NEW PALTZ

EARTHGOODS 🍽
71 Main St. © 845-255-5858 ☺ M-Sat 10-9, Sun 10-8
🍲 **From I-87** (NY Thwy), take exit 18 (New Paltz) left onto Rt 299 (becomes Main St) about 1½ miles into town to store on right.

HEALTH AND NUTRITION CENTER 🍴

15 New Paltz Plaza ✆ 845-256-0256 ⊙ M-F 10-8, Sat 10-7, Sun 10-6
· organic produce · juice bar · take-out

📅 From I-87 (NY Thwy), take exit 18 (New Paltz) left onto Rt 299 less than ½ mile to store on right in New Paltz Plaza.

NEW YORK

4TH STREET FOOD CO-OP 🍴

58 E. 4th St. ✆ 212-674-3623 ⊙ M 12-9, Tues-Th 1-9, W, F-Sun 11-9
· organic produce · co-op

📅 On Manhattan's Lower East Side on 4th St between Bowery & 2nd Ave.

ANGELICA KITCHEN ✗   🍃

300 E. 12th St. ✆ 212-228-2909 ⊙ Daily 11:30-10:30
JF: The Dragon Bowl at Angelica's is probably the best lunch in the East Village.
· vegan · organic focus · tables · wait staff

📅 On Manhattan's Lower East Side on south side of 12th St midway between 1st & 2nd Ave.

ARUVEYDA CAFE ✗

706 Amsterdam Ave. ✆ 212-932-2400 ⊙ Daily 11:30-11:30
A price-fixed vegetarian/mostly vegan meal that changes daily.
· vegetarian · vegan friendly · tables · wait staff

📅 On Manhattan's Upper East Side on west side of Amsterdam Ave between 94th & 95th St.

BACHUE ✗

36 W. 21st St. ✆ 212-229-0870 ⊙ M-F 8am-9:30pm, Sat 11-9:30, Sun 11-6
· vegan · tables · wait staff

📅 On north side of W 21st St between 5th & 6th Ave.

BELL BATES NATURAL FOODS 🍴

97 Reade St. ✆ 212-267-4300 ⊙ M-F 9-7, Sat 10-6
· organic produce · freshly prepared food · juice bar · deli · vegetarian friendly · take-out

📅 In lower Manhattan (Tribeca) on Reade St between Church St & W Bdwy.

CAFE VIVA ✗

2578 Broadway ✆ 212-663-8482 ⊙ Daily 11-11:30
A lot of pasta dishes and antipasto-type salads, all vegetarian. Largely takeout.
· vegetarian · tables · self-service · take-out

📅 On Manhattan's Upper West Side on Broadway between 97th & 97th St.

CAFE VIVA ✗🍴

179 2nd Ave. ✆ 212-420-8801 ⊙ M-Th, Sun 11-11:30, F-Sat 11-12:30
Vegetarian pasta, pizza and antipasto-type salads. Largely takeout.
· vegetarian · tables · self-service · take-out

📅 On Manhattan's Lower East Side on 2nd Ave at 11th St.

CANDLE CAFE ✗   ♿

1307 3rd Ave. ✆ 212-472-0970 ⊙ M-Sat 11:30-10:30, Sun 11:30-9
Health-conscious, vegan, organic restaurant and networking center for animal rights people, environmentalists and like-minded folks. A Certified Green Restaurant.
· vegan · organic focus · alcohol · counter · tables · wait staff · take-out

📅 On Manhattan's Upper East Side on east side of 3rd Ave at 75th St.

CANDLE 79 ✗
154 E. 79th St. © 212-537-7179 ⊘ M-Sat 5:30-10:30
Health-conscious, vegan, organic restaurant. A more upscale vibe than the original Candle Cafe.
· vegan · organic focus · alcohol · tables · wait staff
🍎 On Manhattan's Upper East Side on south side 79th St 2 stores east of Lexington Ave.

CARAVAN OF DREAMS ✗
405 E. 6th St. © 212-254-1613 ⊘ Daily 11-11
Mediterranean vegan menu with an emphasis on raw foods. LA: Warm atmosphere with live music and a neighborhood clientele.
· juice bar · café · vegan · organic focus · kosher · alcohol · counter · tables · wait staff · take-out
🍎 In the East Village on 6th St between 1st Ave and Ave A.

COMMODITIES NATURAL MARKET 🍖
165 1st Ave. © 212-260-2600 ⊘ M-Sat 9-9, Sun 10-9
Over 400 bulk items and exclusively organic produce.
· organic produce
🍎 On Manhattan's Lower East Side on 1st Ave between 10th & 11th St.

COUNTER ✗
105 1st Ave. © 212-982-5870 ⊘ M-Th 4pm-midnight, F 4pm-1am, Sat 11am-1am, Sun 11am-midnight
A classy vegetarian restaurant and wine bar. Tantalizing, unique dishes, including some raw food items, as well as gourmet burgers and panini. Over 50 organic wines, homemade sorbets and ice creams, and more.
· vegetarian · vegan friendly · organic focus · alcohol · counter · tables · wait staff
🍎 On Manhattan's Lower East Side on 1st Ave between 6th & 7th St.

DIMPLE ✗
11 W. 30th St. © 212-643-9464 ⊘ M-F 10-8:30, Sat-Sun 10-7:30
Vegetarian Indian menu with a buffet available at lunch.
· vegetarian · vegan friendly · tables · self-service · wait staff
🍎 On W 30th St just west of 5th Ave.

GOOD EARTH FOODS ✗🍖
1330 1st Ave. © 212-472-9055 ⊘ M-F 9-7:30, Sat 9-6, Sun 12-6
· freshly prepared food · deli · tables · self-service · take-out
🍎 On Manhattan's Upper East Side on 1st Ave between 71st & 72nd St.

HANGAWI ✗
12 E. 32nd St. © 212-213-0077 ⊘ Daily Lunch 12-3, Dinner 5-10:30
An elegant vegan Korean meal in an idyllic, serene, zen-like atmosphere. M&BC: Toward the high end, but worth it for body and soul.
· vegan · alcohol · tables · wait staff · take-out
🍎 On south side 32nd St between 5th & Madison Ave.

HEALTH FOR YOU 🍖
432 Park Ave. S. © 212-532-2644 ⊘ M-F 8-8, Sat 10-7
Salad bar on weekdays only.
· salad bar · take-out
🍎 On Park Ave between 29th & 30th St.

HEALTHY PLEASURES 🍷
93 University Place © 212-353-3553 ⊘ Daily 7:30-11:30
· juice bar · take-out
In the West Village on University Place between 11th & 12th St.

HEALTHY PLEASURES 🍴🍷
2493 Broadway © 212-787-6465 ⊘ Daily 7am-midnight
· freshly prepared food · deli · vegetarian friendly · tables · self-service · take-out
On Manhattan's Upper West Side on Broadway between 92nd & 93rd St.

HEALTHY PLEASURES 🍷
489 Broome St. © 212-431-7434 ⊘ Daily 7:30-10:30
· freshly prepared food · deli · vegetarian friendly · take-out
In SoHo on Broome St between W Bdwy & Wooster St.

HERBAN KITCHEN 🍴
290 Hudson St. © 212-627-2257 ⊘ Lunch M-F 11-4, Dinner M-Sat 5-11
All organic restaurant offering inventive vegetarian, vegan, fresh fish, free-range poultry, and farm-raised meat dishes.
· vegetarian friendly · vegan friendly · organic focus · alcohol · tables · wait staff
In lower Manhattan on Hudson St between Dominick & Spring St (go north on Hudson from Holland Tunnel).

HIGH VIBE HEALTH & HEALING 🍷
83 E. 3rd St. © 888-554-6645 ⊘ M-F 11-7, Sat 12-6, Sun 1-5
Store is entirely devoted to "healing with living foods."
· freshly prepared food · vegan friendly · take-out
In the East Village on north side of 3rd St between 1st & 2nd Ave in residential building (ring buzzer to enter and proceed to garden in back).

INTEGRAL YOGA NATURAL FOODS 🍷
229 W. 13th St. © 212-243-2642 ⊘ M-F 9-9:30, Sat 9-8:30, Sun 9-8:30
Nice hot and cold vegetarian food bar. Yoga center next door holds open classes.
· organic produce · freshly prepared food · salad bar · deli · vegetarian · vegan friendly · take-out
In the West Village on north side W 13th St between 7th & 8th Ave.

JOSIE'S RESTAURANT & JUICE BAR 🍴
300 Amsterdam Ave. © 212-769-1212 ⊘ M-W 12-11, Th-F 12-12, Sat-Sun 11:30-12
The emphasis is on organics, and although meat, poultry, fish, and eggs are served, all items are dairy-free. Good options for vegetarians and vegans.
· juice bar · café · vegetarian friendly · vegan friendly · organic focus · alcohol · counter · tables · wait staff
On Manhattan's Upper West Side on Amsterdam Ave at 74th St.

JOSIE'S RESTAURANT & JUICE BAR 🍴
565 3rd Ave. © 212-490-1558 ⊘ M-W 12-11, Th-F 12-12, Sat-Sun 11:30-12
See description above.
· juice bar · café · vegetarian friendly · vegan friendly · organic focus · alcohol · counter · tables · wait staff
On Manhattan's East Side on 3rd Ave at 37th St.

KATE'S JOINT ✗
58 Ave. B © 212-777-7059 ☉ M-Th, Sun 9am-midnight, F-Sat 9am-2am
A very varied array of soups, salads, sandwiches, pasta, and hot entrees, with many vegan options. JB: Don't miss the Faux Turkey Club.
   • vegetarian • vegan friendly • alcohol • tables • wait staff
🍴 On Manhattan's Lower East Side corner Ave B & 4th St.

LIFE THYME NATURAL ✗🐑
410 6th Ave. © 212-420-9099 ☉ M-F 8-10, Sat-Sun 9-10
The salad bar items are all organic.
   • organic produce • freshly prepared food • juice bar • salad bar • bakery • vegetarian friendly • tables • self-service • take-out
🍴 In the West Village on 6th Ave between 8th & 9th St.

MADRAS MAHAL ✗
104 Lexington Ave. © 212-684-4010 ☉ M-F Lunch 11:30-3, Dinner 5-10, Sat-Sun 12-10
Kosher Indian vegetarian food on a street with several kosher Indian vegetarian restaurants. Daily lunch buffet. Somewhat austere interior.
   • vegetarian • vegan friendly • kosher • tables • self-service • take-out
🍴 On west side of Lexington Ave between 27th & 28th St.

MANA RESTAURANT ✗   ♿
646 Amsterdam Ave. © 212-787-1110 ☉ M-F 11:30-11, Sat 11-11, Sun 11-10
Macrobiotic fare.
   • vegan • tables • wait staff • take-out
🍴 Manhattan's Upper West Side on Amsterdam Ave beween 91st & 92nd St.

NATURAL FRONTIER MARKET 🐑
1424 3rd Ave. © 212-794-0922 ☉ Daily 9-10
   • organic produce • freshly prepared food • juice bar • deli • vegetarian friendly • take-out
🍴 On Manhattan's Upper East Side on 3rd Ave at 84th St.

NATURAL FRONTIER MARKET 🐑
266 3rd Ave © 212-228-9133 ☉ M-F 8-10, Sat-Sun 9-10
   • organic produce • freshly prepared food • juice bar • salad bar • deli • vegetarian friendly • take-out
🍴 On 3rd Ave at 21st St.

ORGANIC MARKET 🐑
275 7th Ave. © 212-243-9927 ☉ M-F 8-9, Sat 10-7, Sun 12-7
   • organic produce
🍴 On corner 7th Ave & 26th St.

PONGAL ✗
110 Lexington Ave. © 212-696-9458 ☉ M-F 12-3, Sat-Sun 12-10
Kosher Indian vegetarian on a street with several similar restaurants.
   • vegetarian • vegan friendly • tables • wait staff
🍴 On west side of Lexington Ave between 27th & 28th St.

PRANA FOODS 🐑
125 1st Ave. © 212-982-7306 ☉ M-Sat 9-9, Sun 9-7
🍴 In the East Village on corner 1st Ave & St Marks Place.

QUANTUM LEAP ✕
88 W. 3rd St. ✆ 212-677-8050 ☺ M-Sat 11:30-10, Sun 10-11
An eclectic mix of tofu, seitan, veggie burgers, Mexican dishes, and more.
  · vegetarian · vegan friendly · tables · wait staff
🍲 In the West Village, on 3rd St between Sullivan & Thompson St (1 block east of Washington Square Park).

QUINTESSENCE ✕ &
263 East 10th St. ✆ 646-654-1823 ☺ Daily 11:30-11
One of three locations serving a creative and diverse gourmet raw foods menu.
  · vegan · organic focus · tables · wait staff · take-out
🍎 On Manhattan's Lower East Side on 10th St between Ave A & 1st Ave.

QUINTESSENCE ✕ &
566 Amsterdam Ave. ✆ 212-501-9700 ☺ Daily 11:30-11
One of three locations serving a creative and diverse gourmet raw foods menu.
  · vegan · organic focus · tables · wait staff · take-out
🍲 Manhattan's Upper West Side on Amsterdam Ave between 87th & 88th St.

QUINTESSENCE ✕ &
353 E. 78th St. ✆ 212-734-0888 ☺ Daily 11:30-11
One of three locations serving a creative and diverse gourmet raw foods menu.
  · vegan · organic focus · tables · wait staff · take-out
🍲 On Manhattan's Upper East Side on 78th St between 1st & 2nd Ave.

RED BAMBOO ✕
140 W. 4th St. ✆ 212-260-1212 ☺ M-Th 4-12, F-Sun 12-12
Vegetarian "Soul Cafe" featuring soy and gluten in dishes reflecting Creole, Caribbean and Thai influences. Non-vegan items clearly noted.
  · vegetarian · vegan friendly · tables · wait staff
🍲 In the West Village on 4th St between 6th Ave & Macdougal St.

SACRED CHOW ✕
522 Hudson St. ✆ 212-337-0863 ☺ M-F 7:30-9:30, Sat-Sun 8:30-9:30
Creative vegan sandwiches, hot entrees, daily soups and stews, vegan desserts, fresh organic juice, smoothies, and more.
  · juice bar · deli · vegan · organic focus · tables · self-service · take-out
🍲 In the West Village on Hudson St between 10th & Charles St.

SOUEN ✕
28 E. 13th St. ✆ 212-627-7150 ☺ M-Sat 10-11, Sun 10-10
Organic vegan and fish options. GS: Macrobiotics can eat here, as can others who crave fresh, tasty food that won't harm your body but can fill you up.
  · vegan friendly · organic focus · alcohol · tables · wait staff
🍲 In the West Village on 13th St between University Place & 5th Ave.

SOUEN ✕
210 6th Ave. ✆ 212-807-7421 ☺ M-F, Sun 12-10:30, Sat 11-10:30
See description above.
  · vegan friendly · organic focus · alcohol · tables · wait staff
🍲 In SoHo on 6th Ave at Prince St.

SPRING STREET NATURAL RESTAURANT ✕ &
62 Spring St. © 212-966-0290 ☺ Daily 12-12, F-Sat until 1am
Gourmet-style healthy food. Plenty for vegetarians and vegans, plus organic chicken and fish.
　· vegetarian friendly · vegan friendly · organic focus · alcohol · tables · wait staff · take-out
◖ In SoHo on SW corner Spring & Lafayette St.

STRICTLY ROOTS ✕
2058 Adam Clayton Powell Blvd. © 212-864-8699 ☺ M-F 11-9:30, Sat 12-9, Sun 12-7
"Nothing that crawls, walks, swims or flies." Afro-Caribe menu of barbecued gluten, tofu, curry, brown rice & peas, greens, fresh juice, and more.
　· juice bar · café · vegan · tables · self-service · take-out
◖ In Harlem on Adam Clayton Powell Blvd & W 123rd St on west side.

THALI ✕
28 Greenwich Ave. © 212-367-7411 ☺ Daily 12-4, 5-10:30
Vegetarian Indian fare.
　· organic produce · vegetarian friendly · tables · wait staff
◖ In the West Village on Greenwich Ave between Charles & 10th St.

THE ENERGY KITCHEN ✕
307 W. 17th St. © 212-645-5200 ☺ Daily 8am-10pm
A small (for now) chain focusing on high protein, low fat options: 5-egg white breakfasts, all kinds of burgers—from soy protein to ostrich, a variety of wraps featuring tofu, poultry or more exotic meats like bison, bean sides, brown rice, and "body builder" design-your-own shakes and meal replacement drinks.
　· vegetarian friendly · chain · counter · self-service · take-out
◖ In Manhattan's Chelsea district on 17th St just north of 8th Ave.

THE ENERGY KITCHEN ✕
1089 2nd Ave. © 212-888-9300 ☺ Daily 8am-10pm
See description above.
　· vegetarian friendly · chain · counter · self-service · take-out
◖ On 2nd Ave between 57th & 58th St.

THE HEALTH NUTS 🥬
2141 Broadway © 212-724-2972 ☺ M-Sat 9-9, Sun 11-7
　· chain
◖ On Manhattan's Upper West Side on Broadway between 75th & 76th St.

THE HEALTH NUTS ✕🥬
2611 Broadway © 212-678-0054 ☺ M-Sat 9-9, Sun 11-7
　· freshly prepared food · deli · vegetarian friendly · chain · tables · self-service · take-out
◖ On Manhattan's Upper West Side on Broadway between 98th & 99th St.

THE HEALTH NUTS ✕🥬
1208 2nd Ave. © 212-593-0116 ☺ M-F 9-9, Sat-Sun 10-8
　· freshly prepared food · deli · vegetarian friendly · chain · tables · self-service · take-out
◖ On Manhattan's Upper West Side on 2nd Ave between 63rd & 64th St.

THE HEALTH NUTS 🥬
835 2nd Ave. © 212-490-2979 ☺ M-F 8:30-8:30, Sat 10-7
　· deli · vegetarian friendly · chain · take-out
◖ On 2nd Ave between 45th & 46th St.

THE NATURAL GOURMET COOKERY SCHOOL ✕
48 W. 21st St. ✆ 212-645-5170 ⏱ Friday 6:30
Friday 4-course, prix fixe, vegetarian wholefoods dinner prepared by instructors and students in the Chef's Training Program. BYOB. Reservations required.
  · vegetarian · organic focus· tables · wait staff
⏏ On north side of W 21st St between 5th & 6th Ave (on 2nd floor).

THE ORGANIC GRILL ✕
123 1st Ave. ✆ 212-477-7177 ⏱ Daily 10-10
Sandwiches, salads, soups, and hot entrees featuring tofu, tempeh, seitan, and whole grains. Commited to sustainable agriculture and artisanal food producers.
  · juice bar · café · vegetarian · vegan friendly · alcohol · tables · wait staff
⏏ In the East Village on 1st Ave between 7th St & St Marks Place.

THE PUMP ENERGY FOOD RESTAURANT ✕
40 W. 55th St. ✆ 212-246-6844 ⏱ M-F 8:30-8:30, Sat 11-6
Low fat, high protein slant, offering tofu, legumes, veggie burgers, chicken, turkey, tuna, and lean beef. Whole grains, no processed flour, no added fats or salt.
  · juice bar · vegetarian friendly · tables · self-service
⏏ On W 55th St between 5th & 6th Ave.

THE PUMP ENERGY FOOD RESTAURANT ✕
113 E. 31st St. ✆ 212-213-5733 ⏱ M-Th 9:30-9:30, F 9:30-8, Sat 11-6:30
See description above.
  · juice bar · vegetarian friendly · tables · self-service
⏏ On E 31st St between Park & Lexington Ave.

UPTOWN WHOLE FOODS ⬤   ♿
2421 Broadway ✆ 212-874-4000 ⏱ Daily 8-11
Part of the Wild Oats chain (despite the name).
  · organic produce · freshly prepared food · juice bar · salad bar · deli · bakery
  · vegetarian friendly · chain · take-out
⏏ On Manhattan's Upper West Side on Broadway at 89th St.

VATAN ✕   ♿
409 3rd Ave. ✆ 212-689-5666 ⏱ Tues-Th, Sun 5:30-9, F-Sat 5:30-10:30
One price-fixed menu with an incredible array of vegetarian Indian Gujarati dishes (many vegan) and all the refills you want. A personal favorite of the editors.
  · juice bar · vegetarian · vegan friendly · alcohol · tables · wait staff · take-out
⏏ On SE corner 3rd Ave & 29th St.

VEG-CITY DINER ✕
55 W. 14th St. ✆ 212-490-6266 ⏱ M-Th 11am-1am, F 11am-4am, Sat 9am-4am, Sun 9am-1am (in summer 24/7)
American diner food, including soda fountain favorites, and it's all vegetarian! Breakfast all day (organic eggs). Many vegan choices.
  · vegetarian · vegan friendly · alcohol · tables · wait staff · take-out
⏏ On north side of 14th St just east of 6th Ave.

VEGE VEGE ✕   ♿
544 3rd Ave. ✆ 212-679-4702 ⏱ M-F 11-11, Sat-Sun 12-11
Chinese vegetarian menu with lots of tofu and mock meat dishes. Brown rice available. Plus, a couple of veggie deli-style sandwiches.
  · vegetarian · vegan friendly · alcohol · tables · self-service · take-out
⏏ On 3rd Ave between 36th & 37th St.

VEGETARIAN DIM SUM HOUSE ✕ 🚇
24 Pell St. ✆ 212-577-7176 ⊘ Daily 10:30-10:30
Chinese vegetarian.
- vegetarian · vegan friendly · tables · wait staff · take-out

🍎 In Chinatown. **From Canal St**, turn south onto Bowery (just before Manhattan Bridge) and make 2nd left onto Pell to restaurant.

VEGETARIAN PARADISE 3 ✕
33 Mott St. ✆ 212-406-6988 ⊘ M-Th, Sun 11-10, F-Sat 11-11
Chinese vegetarian fare with lots of mock meat dishes.
- vegetarian · vegan friendly · tables · wait staff · take-out

🍎 In Chinatown, on Mott St 2 blocks south of Canal St on left side.

VEGETARIAN'S PARADISE 2 ✕
144 W. Fourth St. ✆ 212-260-7130 ⊘ M-Th, Sun 12-11, F-Sat 12-12
Chinese vegetarian fare with lots of mock meat dishes.
- vegetarian · vegan friendly · tables · wait staff · take-out

🍎 In the West Village on W 4th St just south of 6th Ave (1 block west of Washington Square Park).

VILLAGE NATURAL ✕
46 Greenwich Ave. ✆ 212-727-0968 ⊘ M-F 11-11, Sat 10-11, Sun 10-10
International vegetarian dishes with an emphasis on organic ingredients.
- vegetarian · organic focus · counter · tables · wait staff · take-out

🍎 In the West Village on Greenwich Ave between 6th & 7th Ave (entrance down a short flight of stairs).

WESTERLY HEALTH FOODS 🛒
911- 913 8th Ave. ✆ 212-586-5262 ⊘ M-F 8-10, Sat-Sun 9-10
- organic produce

🍎 On 8th Ave between W 54th & W 55th St.

WHOLE FOODS MARKET 🛒   ♿
250 7th Ave. ✆ 212-924-5969 ⊘ Daily 8-10
- organic produce · freshly prepared food · salad bar · deli · bakery · vegetarian friendly · chain · take-out

🍎 In Manhattan's Chelsea area on 7th Ave at 24th St. Drivers note: Imperial Parking at 25th St between 7th & 8th Ave has free validated 2-hour parking if you spend $50 at Whole Foods (or Whole Body).

ZEN PALATE ✕
34 E. Union Square ✆ 212-614-9345 ⊘ Lunch M-Sat 11:30-3, Dinner Daily 5:30-10:45
Vegan Zen menu featuring soy and gluten faux meats.
- vegan · chain · tables · wait staff · take-out

🍎 On Park Ave side of Union Square between 15th & 16th St.

ZEN PALATE ✕
663 9th Ave. ✆ 212- 582-1669 ⊘ M-Sat 11:30-10:30, Sun 11:30-10:45
Vegan Zen menu featuring soy and gluten faux meats.
- vegan · chain · tables · wait staff · take-out

🍎 On 9th Ave at W 46th St.

ZEN PALATE ✕
2170 Broadway ✆ 212-501-7768 ⊘ M-Th, Sun 12-10:45, Sat 12-11:45
Vegan Zen menu featuring soy and gluten faux meats.
- vegan · chain · tables · wait staff · take-out

⬚ Manhattan's Upper West Side on Broadway between W 75th & W 76th St.

ZENITH ✖

888 8th Ave. © 212-262-8080 ⊙ M-F 12-10:30, Sat-Sun 12-10
Vegetarian Asian menu.

• vegetarian • vegan friendly • alcohol • tables • self-service • wait staff

⬚ On 48th St between 8th & 9th Ave.

NORTHPORT

ORGANICALLY YOURS 🍃

114 Main St. © 631-754-2150 ⊙ M-Th, Sat 10-6, F 10-7, Sun 12-5

• organic produce • freshly prepared food • juice bar • deli • vegetarian friendly • take-out

🍎 **From Northern State Pkwy**, take exit 42N toward Northport onto Deer Park Rd (CR 66N, becomes E Jericho Tpke) about 1 mile to Elwood Rd. Turn left onto Ellwood (becomes Reservoir Ave) about 4¼ miles to Scudder Ave. Turn left onto Scudder about ½ mile to Union Pl. Turn right onto Union 1 block to Main St. Turn left onto Main to store.

NYACK

BACK TO EARTH 🍃

1 S. Broadway © 845-353-3311 ⊙ M-F 10-7, Sat 9-6, Sun 10-6

• freshly prepared food • deli • vegetarian friendly • take-out

🍎 **From I-287/87** (NY Thwy), take exit 11 onto 9W towards Nyack to Rt 59. Turn left (east) onto 59 (becomes Main St) about 1 mile into town to store at corner Main & Broadway.

OCEANSIDE

Just 2 miles from the Long Beach boardwalk and beach.

JANDI'S ✖🍃   ♿

3000 Long Beach Rd. © 516-536-5555 ⊙ M-W, F 10-7, Th 10-9, Sat 10-6, Sat 11-5
Eat-in/take-out 98% organic vegetarian deli. No wheat, yeast or refined sugar.

• organic produce • freshly prepared food • juice bar • deli • vegetarian • vegan friendly
• tables • self-service • take-out

⬚ **From Merrick Rd**, go south on Long Beach Rd about 1 mile to store on right just past Atlantic Ave. **From Southern State Pkwy**, take exit 17 (Ocean Ave) south. Go 1 block and stay left of fork over train tracks about 7 miles then over more train tracks to next traffic light at Atlantic Ave. Turn right onto Atlantic ½ block to store on right.

OLIVEREA

Surrounded by hiking trails and 7 miles from the Belleayre ski center.

SHANGRI-LA ✖

212 McKinley Hollow Rd. © 845-254-6000 ⊙ Daily 8:30am-9:30am, 11:30am-1:30pm, 4:30pm-9:30pm
A 16-room lodge serving Indian vegetarian food prepared in a vegetarian, kosher kitchen in the (non-vegetarian) Mountain Gate Indian restaurant. Dining is open to the public, as are the spa services and free hiking trails. Note, staff will feed hikers who occasionally show up at odd times.

• vegetarian • vegan friendly • kosher • alcohol • tables • wait staff • take-out

🍎 Oliveria is about 35 miles west of I-87 exit 19 (Kingston) on Rt 28. **From Rt 28**, turn onto Rt 47 (left from 28W, right from 28E) 3 miles to McKinley Hollow Rd. Turn right onto McKinley Hollow 1 mile to resort.

ONEONTA

AUTUMN CAFE ✗

244 Main St. © 607-432-6845 ⊙ M-Sat 11-9, Sun 10:30-2:30

Tofu, tempeh and brown rice among the turkey, chicken, tuna, ham, and pastrami. Soups, salads, omelettes, hot and cold sandwiches, and specialty items. Homemade whole wheat bread.

· vegetarian friendly · alcohol · co-op · tables · wait staff · take-out

From I-88E, take exit 14 towards Oneonta. Turn left onto Main St about ⅔ mile to restaurant. **From I-88W**, take exit 15 toward Oneonta Colleges onto NY 23W about ½ mile to traffic light at Main (NY 7). Turn left onto Main to restaurant.

GREEN EARTH NATURAL FOODS 🍃 &

7 Elm St. © 607-432-7160 ⊙ M-W, F 10-6, Th 10-8, Sat 10-5

· organic produce · juice bar · take-out

From I-88E, take exit 14 towards Oneonta. Turn left onto Main St about ¾ mile to Elm St. Turn left onto Elm to store. **From I-88W**, take exit 15 toward Oneonta Colleges onto NY 23W about ½ mile to traffic light at Main. Turn left onto Main to first left at Elm. Turn left onto Elm to store.

PHOENICIA

SWEET SUE'S ✗

49 Main St. © 845-688-7852 ⊙ M, Th-Sun 7-3

A favorite local breakfast and lunch place, offering five types of whole grain pancakes, eggs, vegetarian breakfast "meats," at least half a dozen vegetarian lunch choices, as well as fish, poultry and meat options. Homemade soups, salads and sandwiches on fresh baked whole wheat bread.

· vegetarian friendly · counter · tables · wait staff · take-out

From I-87 (NY Thwy) take exit 19 (Kingston). Take 1st exit off rotary onto Rt 28W toward Pine Hill about 22 miles to Rt 214. Turn right onto 214 (Main St in town) to restaurant in first block of stores on left.

PLAINVIEW

DR. B. WELL NATURALLY ✗🍃 &

8 Washington Ave. © 516-932-9355 ⊙ M-F 8-8, Sat 9-7, Sun 11-6

Prepared food choices include vegetarian, vegan, fish, poultry, and raw foods.

· organic produce · freshly prepared food · juice bar · deli · vegetarian friendly · tables · self-service · take-out

From LIE (I-495) heading east, take exit 45 onto Manetto Hill Rd south to Washington Ave. Turn left onto Washington to store on left. **From LIE heading west**, take exit 48. Turn left onto Round Swamp Rd and merge right onto Old Country Rd about 1½ miles to Manetto Hill. Turn right onto Manetto Hill and right onto Washington to store on right.

PLATTSBURGH

NORTH COUNTRY CO-OP 🍃

25 Bridge St. © 518-561-5904 ⊙ M-F 10-7, Sat 10-4, Sun 12-5

· co-op

From I-87, take exit 38A toward Plattsburgh onto Rt 22S about 1¼ miles to Rt 3. Turn left onto 3 about ¼ mile to Rt 9 (historic district). Turn right onto 9 (Margaret St) and follow to left (becomes Bridge St) to store across from city parking lot.

PORT CHESTER

GREEN SYMPHONY ✕
427 Boston Post Rd. © 914-937-6537 ⊙ M-Th, Sun 11:30-10, F-Sat 11:30-11
Vegan Chinese, kosher cuisine.

· vegan · kosher · tables · self-service · wait staff

From I-287E (Cross Westchester Expwy), take exit 11 toward Portchester/ Rye. Make sharp left onto US 1 (Boston Post Rd) about ¼ mile to restaurant in Kohl's Shopping Center. **From I-95N**, take exit 21 toward Port Chester right onto 1N to restaurant. **From I-95S**, take exit 2 toward Byram and follow ramp to Delvan Ave. Turn right onto Delvan (becomes Mill St) ½ mile to N Main St (US 1). Turn left onto Main ½ mile to Boston Post Rd (also US 1). Turn right onto Boston Post ½ mile to restaurant.

PORT JEFFERSON

TIGER LILY CAFE ✕
156 E. Main St. © 631-476-7080 ⊙ M-Sat 9-6, Sun 9-5
A casual "funky" cafe, where people hang out and enjoy "healthy" vegetarian and non-vegetarian food, along with local art work and live performances.

· juice bar · café · vegetarian friendly · organic focus · counter · tables · self-service · take-out

Take Northern State Pkwy until it becomes NY 347E (between Commack & Hauppauge). Follow 347E 14 miles to NY 112/Port Jefferson Rd. Turn left onto 112 (becomes Main St) about 1¾ miles to E Main. Turn right onto E Main and follow around to left to restaurant.

PORT WASHINGTON

TWIN PINES CO-OP 🥬
382 Main St. © 516-883-9777 ⊙ Tues 12-5, W, F, Sat 10-5, Th 10-6

· organic produce · co-op

From LIE (I-495), take exit 36 north on Searingtown Rd about 4½ miles into Port Washington. Turn left onto Main St (post office on far right corner) about 1½ miles to store at corner Main & Prospect St in Mertz Community Center (across from town dock).

POTSDAM

POTSDAM FOOD CO-OP 🥬
24 Elm St. © 315-265-4630 ⊙ M-F 9-7, Sat 9-6, Sun 12-4

· organic produce · co-op

Take Rt 11 into Potsdam. Turn left onto Union St and right onto Elm St to store on left.

POUGHKEEPSIE

MOTHER EARTH'S STOREHOUSE ✕🥬
804 South Road Square © 845-296-1069 ⊙ M-F 9-8, Sat 10-6, Sun 12-5
All vegetarian and vegan deli and salad bar.

· organic produce · freshly prepared food · juice bar · salad bar · deli · vegetarian · vegan friendly · tables · self-service · take-out

On Rt 9, west side at Galleria Mall entrance.

RED HOOK

LUNA 61 ✕

61 E. Market St. © 845-758-0061 ☉ W, Th, Sun 5-9, F-Sat 5-10

Eclectic, mostly vegan and organic menu featuring appetizers, salads, sandwiches, hot meals, plus organic wine and beer. L&JB: This little-known gem offers a relaxed atmosphere and absolutely scrumptious food.

· vegetarian · vegan friendly · organic focus · alcohol · counter · tables · wait staff · take-out

🕮 **From Taconic Pkwy**, take Rt 199W about 8 miles (into Red Hook) to restaurant on left. **From I-87** (NY Thwy), take exit 19 (Kingston) and make first right off rotary onto Rt 28W toward Pine Hill. Make first right onto Rt 209 N (becomes Rt 199E) about 8 miles (across the Rhinecliff Bridge) to Rt 9G. Turn right onto 9G about 1⅓ miles to Rt 9. Turn left onto Rt 9 about 3 miles to E Market St (Rt 199). Turn right onto Market about ¼ mile to restaurant on right.

RHINEBECK

Check out the movies at Upstate Films and the Rhinebeck Aerodrome.

BREAD ALONE ✕

45 E. Market St. © 845-876-3108 ☉ M-Th, Sun 7-5, F-Sat 7-6

Organic breads and baked goods, plus a daily selection of wholesome soups, salads and sandwiches with vegetarian options.

· bakery · vegetarian friendly · tables · self-service · take-out

🕮 **From Rt 9** in Rhinebeck, turn east onto Market St (main traffic light in town) ½ block to store on left.

RHINEBECK HEALTH FOODS & GARDEN ST. CAFE ✕ 🍽

24 Garden St. © 845-876-2555 ☉ M-Sat 9:30-6, Sun 10-3, Cafe M-Sat 10-5

Cafe is vegetarian (except for tuna salad) and 75% organic.

· organic produce · freshly prepared food · juice bar · café · vegetarian friendly · vegan friendly · organic focus · tables · self-service · take-out

🕮 **From Rt 9** in Rhinebeck, turn west onto Market St (main traffic light in town). Make first right onto Garden St to end. Turn left into parking lot to store on right.

RIVERHEAD

GREEN EARTH NATURAL FOODS MARKET ✕ 🍽

50 E. Main St. © 631-369-2233 ☉ M-F 9:30-6, Sat 10-6, Sun 11-5

· organic produce · freshly prepared food · juice bar · salad bar · café · deli · bakery · vegetarian friendly · tables · self-service · take-out

🕮 **From LIE (I-495)**, take exit 72 onto Rt 25E (becomes W Main, then E Main) about 5 miles into Riverhead to store on north side (left), 1 block past main traffic light in downtown business district.

ROCHESTER

ABUNDANCE COOPERATIVE MARKET ✕ 🍽

62 Marshall St. © 585-454-2667 ☉ M-F 8-8, Sat 9-7, Sun 10-7

· organic produce · freshly prepared food · deli · vegetarian friendly · co-op · tables · self-service · take-out

🕮 **From I-490E**, take exit 15 (Inner Loop/South Ave) toward Rt 15. Take Inner Loop ramp and follow ramp toward Monroe Ave onto Howell St to Broadway. Turn right onto Broadway to Marshall St (store parking lot is just before Marshall). Turn left onto Marshall to store on left. **From I-490W**, take exit 17 (Goodman St) straight onto Broadway ½ mile to where road forks. Take right fork onto Union St to Monroe. Turn left onto Monroe and left onto Marshall to store on right just before Broadway.

ATOMIC EGGPLANT ✕

75 Marshall St. ℂ 585-325-6750 ☺ Tues-W 11-10, Th-Sat 11-11, Sun 12-7
Vegetarian food with a Middle Eastern/Tex-Mex flavor and a vegan emphasis. Locally grown and organic ingredients used when possible.
 · vegetarian · vegan friendly · organic focus · counter · tables · wait staff · take-out
🍴 **From I-490**, take exit 18 north on Monroe Ave (right from 490W, left from 490E) to Marshall St. Turn left onto Marshall to restaurant on left (just before Kinko's). Or follow directions above to the Abundance Co-op which is a few doors away across the street.

INDIAN HOUSE VEGETARIAN CAFÉ ✕

1009 S. Clinton Ave. ℂ 716-271-0242 ☺ Tues-Sun 11:30-2:30, 5-9:30
Vegetarian Indian menu, plus daily lunch buffet. Note, there are two restaurants here, one vegetarian and one not.
 · vegetarian · vegan friendly · alcohol · tables · self-service · wait staff
🍴 **From I-390**, take exit 16 right onto Rt 15A (E Henrietta Rd) about ½ mile to Westfall Rd. Turn right onto Westfall 1 mile to Clinton. Turn left onto Clinton 1¼ miles to restaurant (before Caroline St). **From I-490E**, take exit 17 right onto Goodman St 4 short blocks to Clinton. Turn left onto Clinton 2 blocks to restaurant (past Caroline).

LORI'S NATURAL FOODS CENTER 🍴   ६

900 Jefferson Rd. ℂ 585-424-2323 ☺ M-Sat 8-9, Sun 12-6
The homemade takeout options are mostly vegan and there is a microwave available for frozen entrees.
 · organic produce · freshly prepared food · vegetarian · vegan friendly · take-out
🍴 **From I-390N**, take exit 14 and turn left onto Rt 15AN ½ mile to Rt 252. Turn left (west) onto 252 ½ mile to store on right in Genessee Valley Regional Market Complex. **From I-390S**, take exit 14 and turn right (west) onto Rt 252 1 mile to store in Genessee Valley Regional Market Complex.

ROCKVILLE CENTRE

IT'S ONLY NATURAL 🍴

4 S. Village Ave. ℂ 516-766-4449 ☺ M-F 9-7:30, Sat 9-7, Sun 10-5
An opportunity to get fresh juice, but otherwise more supplements than food.
 · organic produce · juice bar · take-out
🍴 **From Merrick Rd**, go south on Village Ave ½ block to store on west side. **From Southern State Pkwy eastbound**, take exit 18 (Eagle Ave). Turn right off exit to end. Turn right onto Penninsula Blvd to traffic light at Lakeview Ave. Turn left onto Lakeview to Village Ave. Turn right onto Village to store ½ block past Merrick Rd on right.

ROCKY POINT

BACK TO BASICS NATURAL FOOD 🍴

632 Rte. 25A ℂ 631-821-0444 ☺ M-Th, Sat 10-6:30, F 10-7:30, Sun 11-5
 · organic produce
🍴 **From Northern State Pkwy heading east**, continue on NY 347E about 15 miles, where it becomes NY 25A E. Continue almost 6 miles to store.

ROSENDALE

ROSENDALE CAFE ✂ &
435 Main St. ✆ 845-658-9048 ⏰ M-Th 11-10, F-Sat 11-11:30, Sun 10-10
Healthy vegetarian and vegan menu, with internationally acclaimed musicians appearing on weekends.

· vegetarian · vegan friendly · alcohol · tables · wait staff · take-out

🍴 **From I-87N** (NY Thruway), take exit 18 (New Paltz). Turn left at traffic light onto Rt 299 through town to Rt 32. Turn right onto 32N almost 7½ miles to Rt 213 (immediately after Rondout Bridge). Turn left onto 213 less than ½ mile (almost to end of town) to restaurant on right. **From I-87S**, take exit 19 (Kingston). Enter traffic circle and take 2nd right onto Washington Ave to end. Turn right onto 32S about 6½ miles to Rt 213 (just before Rondout Bridge). Turn right onto 213 to restaurant on right.

SAG HARBOR

PROVISIONS ✂ 🐑
Bay & Division Sts. ✆ 631-725-3636 ⏰ Daily 8:30-6 (until 7 June-Sept)

· organic produce · freshly prepared food · juice bar · café · vegetarian friendly · tables · self-service · take-out

🍴 **From Rt 27** (Montauk Hwy), turn north onto Rt 79/Sag Harbor Tpke (left from 27E, right from 27W) about 4½ miles to Bay St. Turn right (east) onto Bay to store at Bay & Division St.

SARANAC LAKE

NORI'S WHOLE FOODS ✂ 🐑
65 Main St. ✆ 518-891-6079 ⏰ M-F 9-8, Sat 9-5, Sun 10-4

· deli · vegetarian friendly · tables · self-service · take-out

🍴 **From I-87**, take exit 30 onto Rt 73N about 30 miles (through Lake Placid) to Rt 86. Take 86W (becomes Main St in Saranac Lake) about 7 miles to store.

SARATOGA SPRINGS

During the summer, check the schedule for the Saratoga Performing Arts Center and the race track. Hot springs and mineral baths year-round.

FOUR SEASONS NATURAL FOODS STORE & CAFE ✂ 🐑
33 Phila St. ✆ 518-584-4670 ⏰ Daily 9-8, Cafe 11:30-8
The soup, salad and hot vegetarian/mostly vegan lunch and dinner buffets change daily. Take what you want, pay by the pound.

· organic produce · freshly prepared food · juice bar · salad bar · café · deli · bakery · vegetarian · vegan friendly · counter · tables · self-service · take-out

🍴 **From I-87**, take exit 13N onto Rt 9N toward Saratoga Springs about 4½ miles to Phila St. Turn right onto Phila 1 block to store on left corner Phila & Putnam St.

SAUGERTIES

MOTHER EARTH'S STOREHOUSE 🐑
249 Main St. ✆ 845-246-9614 ⏰ M-F 9-6, Sat 10-6, Sun 12-5

· organic produce

🍴 **From I-87N** (NY Thwy), take exit 20 right onto Ulster Ave almost 1 mile to end at Market St traffic light. Turn right onto Market to 1st left at Main St. Turn left onto Main to store on left. **From I-87S**, take exit 20 left onto Rt 32 to "T" at Rt 212. Turn left onto Ulster Ave and follow directions above.

NEW WORLD HOME COOKING ✂

1411 Rte. 212 © 845-246-0900 ☺ Lunch M, F-Sun 12-3, Dinner M-Sat 5-11, Sun 4-10
The motto is "clean food" and athough there is plenty of meat, there are several thoughtful vegetarian and vegan options. Local, sustainable and organic products in many dishes, brown rice, hormone- and antibiotic-free beef and chicken. The fare is eclectic, but the specialty is spicy (adjustable to taste).
· vegetarian friendly · vegan friendly · alcohol · tables · wait staff
From I-87N (NY Thwy) take exit 20 left onto Rt 212 less than 2 miles to restaurant on left. From I-87S, take exit 20 left onto Rt 32 to "T" at Rt 212. Turn right onto 212 towards Woodstock about 1½ miles to restaurant on left.

SAYVILLE

CORNUCOPIA NATURAL FOODS 🍎

39 N. Main St. © 631-589-9579 ☺ M-F 9-7, Sat 10-6, Sun 12-5
If you're heading to Fire Island, this is a good place for a snack or supplies.
· organic produce · freshly prepared food · juice bar · deli · vegetarian friendly · tables · self-service · take-out
From Sunrise Hwy going east (NY 27E), go right onto Broadway Ave less than 1½ miles to Montauk Hwy (Main St in Sayville). Turn left onto Main to store. From Montauk Hwy, store is in town.

SCARSDALE

MRS. GREEN'S NATURAL MARKET ✂🍎

365 Central Park Ave. © 914-472-9675 ☺ M-Sat 9-7, Sun 10-6
· organic produce · freshly prepared food · vegetarian friendly · chain · counter · self-service · take-out
From I-287, take exit 4 south on Rt 100A (toward Hartsdale) about 2¼ miles to Central Park Ave (Rt 100). Turn right onto Central Park less than 1 mile to store.

MRS. GREEN'S NATURAL MARKET ✂🍎

780 White Plains Rd. © 914-472-0111 ☺ M,W,F 8:30-8, Tues,Th 8:30-9, Sat-Sun 9-7
· organic produce · freshly prepared food · vegetarian friendly · chain · tables · self-service · take-out
Take Bronx River Pkwy to exit 10. Go east on Strathmore Rd (becomes Harney Rd, then Brook St) about ¾ mile to White Plains Rd (aka Rt 22). Turn right onto White Plains 1½ blocks to store on left.

SCHENECTADY

EARTHLY DELIGHTS NATURAL FOOD ✂🍎

162 Jay St. © 518-372-7580 ☺ M-W, F 9-6, Th 9-8, Sat 9-4
· freshly prepared food · salad bar · deli · vegetarian friendly · tables · self-service · take-out
From I-87N/I-90 (NY Thwy), take exit 25 onto I-890W about 4 miles to exit 5 (Broadway). Turn right (north) onto Broadway to 2nd traffic light at Clinton St. Turn right onto Clinton past 2 lights to (2-hr free) parking lot on left. Walk down brick walkway on left 4 stores to store on right.

SOUTH FALLSBURG

PRATT'S FARMER'S HARVEST 🛍️
325 Main St © 845-436-8581 ⊕ M-F 9-6, Sat-Sun 10-6

🛏️ **From Rt 17**, take exit 105 onto Rt 42N about 5 miles to South Fallsburg to store on left. **From Rt 209S** (north of Ellenville), take Rt 52W almost 12 miles to Rt 42. Turn left onto 42N about 3½ miles to store on left.

STATEN ISLAND

TASTEBUDS NATURAL FOOD ✕🛍️
1807 Hylan Blvd. © 718-351-8693 ⊕ M-Sat 9-8, Sun 10-7

· freshly prepared food · deli · vegetarian friendly · counter · self-service · take-out

🛏️ **From I-287**, take exit 13 (Clove Rd/Richmond Blvd/Hylan Blvd) straight off exit to Richmond Rd. Turn south onto Richmond (right from 287W, left from 287E) almost 1 mile to Old Town Rd. Turn left onto Old Town less than ½ mile to Hylan. Turn right onto Hylan less than 1 mile to store on right.

SUFFERN

MRS. GREEN'S NATURAL MARKET 🛍️
26 Indian Rock Shopping Ctr. © 845-369-6699 ⊕ M-W, F-Sat, 9-7, Th 9-8, Sun 10-6

· organic produce · chain

🛏️ **From I-287W**, take exit 14B south on Airmont Rd about ⅓ mile to Rt 59. Turn left (west) onto 59 a few miles to store in Indian Rock Shopping Center.

SYOSSET

LONG ISLAND HEALTH CONNECTION 🛍️
520 Jericho Tpke. © 516-496-2528 ⊕ M-F 9-8, Sat 9-7, Sun 10-6

· organic produce · juice bar · take-out

🛏️ **From LIE (I-495), Northern State or Southern State Pkwy**, take Seaford Oyster Bay Expwy north to exit 14W. Merge onto Jericho Tpke ½ mile to store.

SYRACUSE

SYRACUSE REAL FOOD COOPERATIVE ✕
618 Kensington Rd. © 315-472-1385 ⊕ Daily 9-9

· organic produce · freshly prepared food · juice bar · co-op · take-out

🛏️ **From I-690**, take exit 14 south on Teall Ave (left from 690W, right from 690E) about ½ mile to Genesee St. Turn left onto Genesee 1 block to Westcott St. Turn right onto Westcott 1 mile to Kensington Rd. Turn left onto Kensington to store on right.

TROY

UNCLE SAM'S GOOD NATURAL PRODUCTS 🛍️
77 4th St. © 518-271-7299 ⊕ M-F 10-6, Sat 10-4

· organic produce

🛏️ **From I-87N** (NY Thwy), take exit 23 onto I-787N to exit 8 (23rd St toward Watervliet/Green Island). Turn left onto 23rd and left onto Broadway about ¼ mile to Rt 2E. Turn left onto 2E ½ mile to 4th St. Turn left onto 4th to store on right. **From I-87S**, take exit 7 onto 7E toward Troy. Take Downtown Troy exit onto 6th St and head south over ½ mile to Congress St (2E). Turn right onto Congress 2 blocks to 4th St. Turn right onto 4th to store on left.

WATERTOWN

THE MUSTARD SEED 🌱

1304 Washington St. ✆ 315-788-2463 🕒 M-F 9-7, Sat 9-5, Sun 10-5

· organic produce

🍎 **From I-81N**, take exit 44 toward Rt 232/Watertown Ctr. Turn right onto 232 about 2 miles to US 11 (Washington St). Turn left onto Washington 2½ miles to store across from high school (behind Pizza Hut). **From I-81S**, take exit 45 left onto Rt 3E to Washington. Turn right onto Washington about 1 mile to store.

WEST SENECA

FEEL-RITE NATURAL FOOD SHOP 🌱

3521 Seneca St. ✆ 716-675-6620 🕒 M-Sat 9-9, Sun 11-7

· organic produce · chain

🍎 **From I-90 (NY Thwy)**, take exit 55 onto Ridge Rd E ramp toward W. Seneca. Follow Ridge almost 2 miles (turns right, then becomes Seneca St) to store in Seneca Ridge Plaza.

WESTBURY

ZEN PALATE ✕

477 Old Country Rd. ✆ 516-333-8686 🕒 M-Sat 11:30-10:30, Sun 11:30-10:45

Vegan Zen menu featuring (soy and gluten) faux meats.

· vegan · chain · tables · wait staff · take-out

🍎 **From Meadowbrook Pkwy**, take exit M1E onto Old Country Rd east just under 2 miles to restaurant. **From Wantaugh State Pkwy**, take exit W2W onto Old Country Rd west 1½ miles to restaurant.

WESTHAMPTON BEACH

WESTHAMPTON NATURAL FOODS 🌱

96 Old Riverhead Rd. ✆ 631-288-8947 🕒 M-Sat 10-6, Sun 11-4

Although open year-round, the hours may be shorter out of beach season.

· organic produce · juice bar · take-out

🍎 **From Sunrise Hwy (NY 27)**, take exit 63S toward Westhampton Beach onto CR 31S (Old Riverhead Rd) more than 2½ miles to store.

WHITE PLAINS

MANNA FOODS, INC. ✕🌱

171 Mamaroneck Ave. ✆ 914-946-2233 🕒 M-F 9-6, Sat 9-5, Lunch M-F 11:30-2:30

· freshly prepared food · juice bar · vegetarian · tables · self-service · take-out

🍎 **From Hutchinson River Pkwy**, take exit 23 north on Mamaroneck Ave about 3½ miles to store on right.

WILLIAMSVILLE

FEEL-RITE FRESH MARKET ✕🌱

5425 Transit Rd. ✆ 716-363-1000 🕒 M-Sat 9-9, Sun 9-5

· organic produce · freshly prepared food · juice bar · deli · vegetarian friendly · chain · tables · self-service · take-out

🍎 **From I-90 (NY Thwy)**, take exit 49 toward Depew/Lockport onto Rt 78N (aka Transit Rd) ¾ mile to store.

WOODSTOCK

Of course we think Woodstock is great—we live there. Art galleries, music venues, a wonderful independent bookstore, and on top of Overlook Mt, a beautiful Tibetan Stupa and hiking trail.

BREAD ALONE ✖

22 Mill Hill Rd. ☎ 845-679-2108 ⊙ M-Th, Sat-Sun 7-7, F 7-11
Organic breads and baked goods, plus a daily selection of wholesome soups, salads and sandwiches with vegetarian options.

· bakery · vegetarian friendly · counter · tables · self-service · take-out

📅 **From I-87S**, take exit 20 (Saugerties) left onto Rt 32 to "T" at Rt 212. Turn right onto 212 about 10 miles to center of Woodstock. Restaurant is at top of hill on left corner Mill Hill Rd & Maple Ln. **From I-87N**, take exit 19 (Kingston). Take 1st exit off rotary onto Rt 28W toward Pine Hill about 8 miles to traffic light at Rt 375. Turn right onto 375 to end. Turn left onto Tinker St (aka Mill Hill) to restaurant at top of hill at Mill Hill & Maple.

JOSHUA'S ✖ &

51 Tinker St. ☎ 845-679-5533 ⊙ M-F 11-10, Sat 10-10, Sun 10-9 (closed W in winter)
In addition to the vegetarian fare in keeping with the largely Israeli menu, there are nontraditional vegetarian and vegan options, brown rice is the norm and whole wheat pita is usually available on request.

· vegetarian friendly · vegan friendly · alcohol · tables · wait staff

📅 **From I-87S**, take exit 20 (Saugerties) left onto Rt 32 to "T" at Rt 212. Turn right onto 212 about 10 miles to center of Woodstock to restaurant on left corner Tinker St & Tannery Brook Rd. **From I-87N**, take exit 19 (Kingston). Take 1st exit off rotary onto Rt 28W toward Pine Hill about 8 miles to traffic light at Rt 375. Turn right onto 375 to end. Turn left onto Tinker St (aka Mill Hill Rd) about 1 mile to restaurant on left.

SUNFLOWER NATURAL FOODS 🍃 &

75 Mill Hill Rd. ☎ 845-679-5361 ⊙ M-Sat 9-9, Sun 10-7
Our hometown health food store. Well stocked with organic produce and ready-to-eat prepared food.

· organic produce

📅 **From I-87S**, take exit 20 (Saugerties) left onto Rt 32 to "T" at Rt 212. Turn right onto 212 about 9½ miles. As you enter Woodstock store is in plaza on right at far end. **From I-87N**, take exit 19 (Kingston). Take 1st exit off rotary onto Rt 28W toward Pine Hill about 8 miles to traffic light at Rt 375. Turn right onto 375 to end. Turn left onto Tinker St (aka Mill Hill Rd) to store in plaza on right.

SUNFROST FARMS ✖ 🍃

217 Tinker St. ☎ 845-679-6690 ⊙ Daily 9-6
Combination produce market, healthy "convenience" store, juice bar, and seasonal plants. Outdoor tables when weather permits.

· organic produce · freshly prepared food · juice bar · deli · vegetarian friendly · counter
· self-service · take-out

📅 **From I-87S**, take exit 20 (Saugerties) left onto Rt 32 to "T" at Rt 212. Turn right onto 212 almost 11 miles (through Woodstock) to store on left. **From I-87N**, take exit 19 (Kingston). Take 1st exit off rotary onto Rt 28W toward Pine Hill about 8 miles to traffic light at Rt 375. Turn right onto 375 to end. Turn left onto Tinker St (aka Rt 212) 1½ miles (through town) to store on left.

TACO JUAN'S ✕
31 Tinker St. ℰ 845-679-9673 ☺ Daily 12-8
The beans, tofu chili and Mexican (brown) rice are all vegan. Tacos, burritos and chili can be made for vegetarians, as well as meat- or chicken-eaters. The fast-food choice for locals and tourists.

· vegetarian friendly · vegan friendly · tables · self-service · take-out

🥡 **From I-87S**, take exit 20 (Saugerties) left onto Rt 32 to "T" at Rt 212. Turn right onto 212 about 10 miles to center of Woodstock to restaurant on left. **From I-87N**, take exit 19 (Kingston). Take 1st exit off rotary onto Rt 28W toward Pine Hill about 8 miles to traffic light at Rt 375. Turn right onto 375 to end. Turn left onto Tinker St (aka Mill Hill Rd) about 1 mile to restaurant on left.

Goldbeck's "EAT IT OR NOT"
FASCINATING & FAR-OUT FACTS ABOUT FOOD

Which of these foods are good sources of calcium?
Almonds, cheese, kale, roasted soy nuts, navy beans, yogurt

Answer: All

Which of these foods are good sources of iron?
Dried apricots, dried beans, cheese, prune juice, rice, watermelon, wheat germ

Answer: All but the cheese and rice

Which of these foods is not a good source of protein?
Cream cheese, eggs, lentils, peanut butter, tofu, yogurt

Answer: Cream cheese

NORTH CAROLINA

1 Asheville	11 Greensboro
2 Black Mountain	12 Hendersonville
3 Boone	13 Hickory
4 Brevard	14 Kill Devil Hills
5 Carrboro	15 Morrisville
6 Cary	16 Mount Airy
7 Chapel Hill	17 Raleigh
8 Charlotte	18 Wilmington
9 Durham	19 Winston-Salem
10 Gastonia	

ASHEVILLE

Marcia at Earth Fare reports that most local restaurants offer vegetarian entrees.

CAFÉ MAX & ROSIE'S ✕

52 N. Lexington Ave. ✆ 828-254-5342 ⊙ M-Sat 11-5, Sun (summer only) 12-4
Everything is vegetarian, with vegan choices. Creative sandwiches on whole grain bread, Middle Eastern and Mexican hot entrees, hormone-free yogurt, cheese made by the Amish, extensive juice bar. Psychic Fair every Saturday afternoon.

· juice bar · vegetarian · vegan friendly · organic focus · kosher · counter · tables · wait staff · take-out

🕮 From I-40, I-26 or US 23/70, merge onto I-240. From I-240W, take exit 5A (Merriman Ave) left onto Broadway (becomes Lexington Ave) about ¼ mile to store on right corner Lexington & Walnut St. From I-240E, take exit 4C left onto Haywood St about ¼ mile to Walnut. Turn left onto Walnut to store on left corner Walnut & Lexington.

EARTH FARE ✕🍎   ♿

66 Westgate Pkwy. ✆ 828-253-7656 ⊙ Daily 7-10

· organic produce · freshly prepared food · juice bar · salad bar · café · deli · bakery · vegetarian friendly · chain · counter · tables · self-service · take-out

🕮 From 1-40, I-26 or US 23/70, merge onto I-240 to exit 3B onto Westgate Pkwy to store on right just past exit.

FRENCH BROAD CO-OP 🍎

90 Biltmore Ave. ✆ 828-255-7650 ⊙ M-Sat 9-9, Sun 12-8

· organic produce · co-op

🕮 From 1-40, I-26 or US 23/70, merge onto I-240 to exit 5A (Merrimon Ave). Go south on US 25 (Merriman, becomes Biltmore Ave) about ½ mile to store on left.

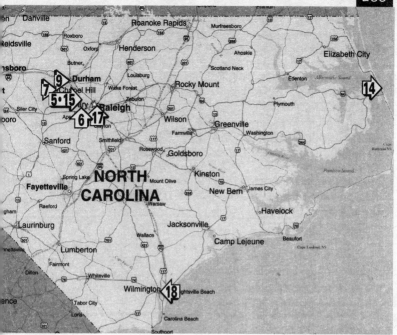

LAUGHING SEED CAFE ✄

40 Wall St. © 828-252-3445 ⊙ M, W-Th 11:30-9, Sat 10:30-10, Sun 10-9
*Enormous, diverse selection of vegetarian and vegan offerings, baking on site
and kids' menu. L&JB: Thursday is international day, with menu changing
weekly from around the globe. Get there early to avoid a long wait.*

· organic produce · bakery · vegetarian · vegan friendly · alcohol · tables · wait staff

🍲 From I-40, I-26 or US 23/70, merge onto I-240 to exit 4B (Patton
Ave) toward Downtown about ⅓ mile to Otis St. Turn left onto Otis and
right onto Wall St to restaurant.

BLACK MOUNTAIN

BLACK MOUNTAIN NATURAL FOODS 🥬

115 Black Mountain Ave. © 828-669-9813 ⊙ M-Sat 10-6

· freshly prepared food · take-out

🍲 From I-40, take exit 64 (NC 9) toward Black Mtn north on Broadway
St (left from 40E, right from 40 W). At 1st traffic light turn left onto Vance Ave
1 block to store on right corner Vance & Black Mtn Ave (old frame house).

GREENLIGHT CAFE ✄

205 W. State St. © 828-669-2444 ⊙ M-Th 11-8, F-Sat 11-9, Sun 10-3
Soups, salads, sandwiches, and hot vegetarian dishes. Beer is the only alcohol.

· vegetarian · vegan friendly · alcohol · tables · wait staff

🍲 From I-40, take exit 64 (NC 9) toward Black Mtn north on Broadway
St (left from 40E, right from 40 W) about ½ mile to Main St. Turn left onto
Main (US 70) a few blocks to restaurant.

BOONE

In the Blue Ridge Mountains.

ANGELICA ✗

506 W. King St. © 828-265-0809 ⊙M-Th 11-9, F-Sat 11-9:30
· vegetarian · alcohol · tables · wait staff

⛉ US 421/221 & 321 merge in Boone and become King St in town. Store is less than ½ mile west of intersection.

RAZZBERRY'S NATURAL MARKET, INC. 🥗

2194 Blowing Rock Rd. © 828-265-2700 ⊙M, Th, F 9-8, Tues, W, Sat 9-7, Sun 12-7
· organic produce

⛉ Store is on US 321 south of town center (about 1 mile south of Hwy 105) at intersection Blowing Rock Rd (aka 321) & Deerfield Rd.

BREVARD

HEALTHY HARVEST 🥗   ♿

410 N. Broad St. © 828-885-2599 ⊙M-F 9-8, Sat 9-4

⛉ **From I-26,** take exit 18 onto Hwy 64W toward Hendersonville about 17 miles to 64W/276S. Turn left on 64W/276S about 2 miles to store on right in College Plaza (across from Brevard College).

CARRBORO

PANZELLA ✗

101 E. Weaver St. © 919-929-6626 ⊙Lunch Tues-Sat 11:30-2, Dinner Tues-Th, Sun 5:30-9, F-Sat 5:30-10
Italian orientation, with vegetarian and vegan (highlighted on menu), along with hormone- and antibiotic-free meats and poultry.
· vegetarian friendly · vegan friendly · tables · wait staff

⛉ **From I-40,** take exit 266 south on Rt 86 about 2⅓ miles to Estes Dr exit. Turn right onto Estes (toward Carrboro) to end. Turn left onto Greensboro St to 1st traffic light (Weaver St). Turn left onto Weaver to restaurant at west end of Carr Mill Mall (facing Greensboro).

WEAVER STREET MARKET 🥗

101 E. Weaver St. © 919-929-0010 ⊙Daily 8-9
For a sit-down meal, visit Panzanella, the co-op restaurant next door.
· organic produce · bakery · co-op

⛉ See directions above to Panzella.

CARY

ONCE IN A BLUE MOON BAKERY & CAFÉ ✗

115-G W. Chatham St. © 919-319-6554 ⊙M-F 7-6, Sat 7:30-5
Casual vegetarian eatery. Note: bakery is neither whole grain or health-oriented.
· café · bakery · vegetarian · tables · self-service · take-out

⛉ **From I-40E,** take exit 287 toward Cary right onto N Harrison Ave about 3½ mile to W Chatham St. Turn left onto Chatham to restaurant in Ashworth Village. **From I-40W,** take exit 291 toward Cary right onto Farm Gate Rd 1 mile (becomes Cary Towne Blvd) to end at Walnut St. Turn right onto Walnut 1 mile to Kildaire Farm Rd. Turn right onto Kildaire Farm and take next right onto S Academy St about ¼ mile to W Chatham. Turn left onto Chatham to restaurant in Ashworth Village.

UDIPI CAFE ✗

590 E. Chatham St. © 919-465-0898 ⊘ M-Th, Sun 11:30-9:30, F-Sat 11:30-10
*Vegetarian Indian cuisine, with a lunch buffet. CF: In a brick business strip,
but the owners have done a credible job of making a boxy room into a lovely
place to dine. Most of the diners are Indian—that says it all.*

· vegetarian · vegan friendly · tables · self-service · wait staff

🚘 From I-40, take exit 290 toward Cary west on Chapel Hill Rd (right from
40E, left from 40W) about 1 mile to NE Maynard Rd. Turn left onto Maynard
¼ mile to E Chatham Rd. Turn right onto Chatham ¼ mile to restaurant.

WHOLE FOODS MARKET ✗ 🍃   ♿

102B New Waverly Place © 919-816-8830 ⊘ Daily 7:30-9, Bakery & Breakfast bar from 7:30

· organic produce · freshly prepared food · juice bar · salad bar · café · deli · bakery
· vegetarian friendly · chain · tables · self-service · take-out

🚘 From I-40/440, take exit 293 toward Sanford onto US 64W/1S about 1
mile to Cary Pkwy exit. Follow left fork and turn left onto SE Cary Pkwy
about ¾ mile to Tryon Rd. Turn right onto Tryon about ¾ mile to store
on corner Tryon & Kildaire Farm Rd in Waverly Place Shopping Center
(across from WalMart).

CHAPEL HILL

SAGE VEGETARIAN CAFE ✗   ♿

1129 Weaver Dairy Rd. © 919-968-9266 ⊘ M-Th 11:30-3, 5-9, F-Sat 12-10
Vegetarian soups, salads, sandwiches, and specials.

· vegetarian · alcohol · tables · wait staff

🚘 From I-40, take exit 266 toward Chapel Hill/Carrborro south on NC 86
(right from 40E, left from 40W) ½-⅔ mile to Weaver Dairy Rd. Turn left onto
Weaver Dairy about ¼ mile to restaurant in Timberlyne Shoppping Ctr.

WEAVER STREET MARKET 🍃

716 Market St. © 919-929-2009 ⊘ Daily 7-9

· organic produce

🚘 From I-40, take exit 270 onto Rt 15S/501S (becomes Fordham Blvd) about
7 miles to Main St. Turn right onto Main and right onto Market St to store.

WHOLE FOODS MARKET/WELLSPRING CAFE ✗ 🍃   ♿

81 S. Elliott Rd. © 919-968-1983 ⊘ Daily 8-9

· organic produce · freshly prepared food · salad bar · café · deli · bakery · vegetarian
friendly · chain · tables · self-service · take-out

🚘 From I-40, take exit 270 onto Rt 15S/501S 1½ miles to fork at E Franklin
St. Go straight onto Franklin ½ mile to S Elliot Rd. Turn left onto Elliot to
store on left.

CHARLOTTE

BERRYBROOK FARM NATURAL FOODS PANTRY 🍃

1257 East Blvd. © 704-334-6528 ⊘ M-F 9-7, Sat 9-6, Juice bar/Deli M-Th
9-5, F 9-4, Sat 10-4, Hot food M-Sat 11-3:30
*Daily menu of vegetarian soups, salads, sandwiches, and hot items. No indoor
seating (the store is small) but a couple of swings on the porch.*

· organic produce · freshly prepared food · juice bar · deli · vegetarian · take-out

🚘 From I-77, take I-277 (Brookshire Fwy) to exit 2A. Go south on Kenilworth
Ave 1 mile to East Blvd. Turn right onto East to store on corner.

HOME ECONOMIST NATURAL GOURMET MARKET 🍎 &
5410 E. Independence Blvd. © 704-536-4663 ⊙ M-F 9-9, Sat 9-8, Sun 10-6
· organic produce
🏠 **From I-77**, take I-277 (Brookshire Fwy) to exit 2B onto US 74E (Independence Blvd) about 5 miles to store (before Idlewild Rd).

TALLEY'S GREEN GROCERY ✗🍎
1408-C East Blvd. © 704-334-9200 ⊙ M-Sat 8:30-9, Sun 10-7
In addition to salad, soup and sandwiches, the Cafe Verde serves five daily entrees. Three are vegetarian. The others are either fish or natural meat.
· organic produce · freshly prepared food · salad bar · café · deli · vegetarian friendly
· tables · self-service · take-out
🏠 **From I-77**, take I-277 (Brookshire Fwy) to exit 2A. Go south on Kenilworth Ave 1 mile to East Blvd. Turn left onto East to store on right in Dilworth Garden Shopping Center.

THE PEACEFUL DRAGON ✗
12610 Steele Creek Rd. © 704-504-8866 ⊙ M-Sat 11-2:30, 5-9, Sun 11-3
Asian cultural center and restaurant serving vegetarian "Asian fusion" food.
· vegetarian · vegan friendly · organic focus · alcohol · tables · wait staff · take-out
🏠 **From I-77**, take exit 9A onto SC 160W just over 7 miles (becomes Steele Creek Rd) to restaurant on left. **From I-485W**, take exit 3 left onto Arrowood Rd (becomes Brown Greer Rd) 1 mile to traffic light at Steele Creek. Turn left onto Steele Creek 2 miles to restaurant on right (past Sam Neely Rd).

WOODLAND'S PURE VEGETARIAN ✗ &
7128-A Albemarle Rd. © 704-569-9193 ⊙ M-Th, Sun 11:30-9:30, F-Sat 11:30-10
South Indian vegetarian cuisine with lots of vegan selections.
· vegetarian · vegan friendly · tables · wait staff · take-out
🏠 **From I-77**, take I-277 (Brookshire Fwy) to exit 2B onto US 74E (Independence Blvd) about 4 miles to Albemarle Rd. Turn left onto Albemarle about 3 miles to restaurant.

DURHAM

DURHAM CO-OP 🍎 &
1101 W. Chapel Hill St. © 919-490-0929 ⊙ M-Sat 10-8, Sun 11-8
· organic produce · co-op
🏠 **From I-40**, take exit 279B toward Durham onto Durham Fwy (NC 147N) about 8⅓ miles to exit 13. Turn right onto Chapel Hill St 3 blocks to store on left corner Chapel Hill & Carroll St.

GEORGE'S GARAGE ✗ &
737 9th St. © 919-286-4131 ⊙ Market Daily 9-9
The main attraction is the market, with salad bar, sandwich station, hot and cold stations, and more. Dine in or get it to go. LP: Very fresh and attractively presented, with a Mediterranean flair. The self-serve salad bar has 20-30 vegetarian options, in. Hot favorites include grilled veggies, garlic mashed potatoes, specialty pizzas, and eggplant parmesan. Plus, near the Duke campus on hip and happening 9th St.
· salad bar · vegetarian friendly · alcohol · counter · tables · self-service · take-out
🏠 **From I-40**, take exit 279B toward Durham onto Durham Fwy (NC 147N) 9 miles to Swift Ave exit. Turn right onto Swift to traffic light at Main St. Turn left onto Main 2 blocks to 9th St. Turn right onto 9th to restaurant on left

corner 9th & Hillsborough Rd (in bldg with Kerr Drugs). **From I-85**, take exit 175 south on Guess Rd (right from 85N, left from 85S) to Broad St. Turn right onto Broad about 1 mile to Hillsborough. Turn right onto Hillsborough 2 blocks to 9th. Turn right onto 9th to restaurant on right.

WHOLE FOODS MARKET/WELLSPRING CAFE ✖🥄　　ㅎ
621 Broad St. ℰ 919-286-0371 ⊙ Daily 9-9, Cafe from 7:30
LP: Adjacent to the Duke campus and just 1 block from 9th St, the most hip and happening part of Durham. Also, close to the interstate.
· organic produce · freshly prepared food · salad bar · café · deli · bakery · vegetarian friendly · chain · counter · tables · self-service · take-out

🍎 **From I-40**, take exit 279B toward Durham onto Durham Fwy (NC 147N) 9 miles to Swift Ave exit. Turn right onto Swift across tracks and past Main St (becomes Broad St) to store on left. **From I-85**, take exit 175 south on Guess Rd to Broad. Turn right onto Broad about 1 mile to store on right.

GASTONIA

Tourist stops in the area include the Daniel Stowe Botanical Gardens, Crowers Mt. State Park, Kings Mt. National Military Park, and Christmastown, U.S.A.

ORGANIC MARKETPLACE 🥄
904 S. New Hope Rd. ℰ 704- 864-0605 ⊙ M-F 9:30-6, Sat 9:30-5
· juice bar · take-out

🍎 **From I-85**, take exit 20 south on New Hope Rd (left from 85E, right from 85W) about 1½ miles to Milano's Center. Turn left into parking lot to store in back.

GREENSBORO

A&S NATURAL HEALTH 🥄　　ㅎ
435C Dolley Madison Rd. ℰ 336-855-6500 ⊙ M-F 10-9, Sat 10-8, Sun 1-6
· organic produce

🍎 **From I-40**, take exit 213 north on Guilford College Rd (left from 40E, right from 40W) about 2 miles (becomes College Rd after 1 mile) to Tomahawk Dr. Turn right onto Tomahawk and left to store in Guilford Village Shopping Center (behind Pizza Hut, next to GrapeVine Cafe & Juice Bar).

A&S NATURAL HEALTH 🥄　　ㅎ
5710 High Point Rd. ℰ 336-547-0608 ⊙ M-F 10-9, Sat 10-8, Sun 1-6
· juice bar · take-out

🍎 **From I-40W**, take exit 217 toward Coliseum area left onto High Point Rd 4 miles to store. **From I-40E**, take exit 213 toward Jamestown right onto Guilford College Rd 1¾ miles to Hilltop Rd. Turn left onto Hilltop ¾ mile to Adams Farm Pkwy. Turn right onto Adams Farm over 1½ miles to Mackay Rd. Turn left onto Mackay ½ mile to High Point. Turn left onto High Point to store.

DEEP ROOTS MARKET NATURAL FOODS CO-OP 🥄　　ㅎ
3728 Spring Garden St. ℰ 336-292-9216 ⊙ M-Sat 9-8, Sun 12-7
· organic produce · co-op

🍎 **From I-40**, take Wendover Ave exit (214 from 40E, 214B from 40W) right (east) onto Wendover about 2 miles to Spring Garden St exit. Turn left off ramp to store on left.

EARTH FARE ✗🍴 ⬧
2965 Battleground Ave. © 336-369-0190 ⏱ Daily 7-10, Deli 10-8

· organic produce · freshly prepared food · juice bar · salad bar · café · deli · bakery
· vegetarian friendly · chain · tables · self-service · take-out

🏠 **From I-40,** take Wendover Ave exit (214 from 40E, 214B from 40W) right (east) onto Wendover about 5 miles to Westover Terrace. Turn left (north) onto Westover and merge onto Battleground Ave about 2 miles (past Cornwallis Ave & Cone Blvd) to store on left in Battleground Village Shopping Center.

THE GRAPEVINE CAFE & JUICE BAR ✗
435B Dolley Madison Rd. © 336-856-0070 ⏱ M-Th, Sat 11-8, Sat 11-8:30
Menu changes daily, but it's always vegetarian and predominantly vegan, including soups, salads, burgers, sandwiches, three or four hot entrees, and all-vegan desserts. Full ingredient list available for everything. Friday night there's free music, poetry and local talent from 8 to 11 (after kitchen hours).

· juice bar · café · vegetarian · vegan friendly · organic focus · alcohol · counter
· tables · self-service · take-out

🏠 **From I-40,** take exit 213 north on Gilford College Rd (left from 40E, right from 40W) about 2 miles (becomes College Rd after 1 mile) to Tomahawk Dr. Turn right onto Tomahawk and left to store in Guilford Village Shopping Center (behind Pizza Hut, next to health food store).

HENDERSONVILLE

This part of western NC is full of national forests, good hiking and kayaking.

HENDERSONVILLE CO-OP & BLUE MOUNTAIN CAFE ✗🍴 ⬧
715 Old Spartanburg Hwy. © 828-693-0505 ⏱ M-F 9-7, Sat 9-6, Sun 12-5
Cafe is mostly vegetarian, using local and organic ingredients when possible.

· organic produce · freshly prepared food · juice bar · café · vegetarian friendly
· organic focus · alcohol · co-op · tables · self-service · take-out

🏠 **From I-26,** take exit 22 west on Upward Rd 4-5 traffic lights to Hwy 176/Spartanburg Hwy. Turn right onto Spartanburg 4 lights to Old Spartanburg Hwy. Turn right onto Old Spartanburg to store on left.

HICKORY

NATURE'S SUPERMARKET 🍴
1155 Hwy 70 S.W. © 828-327-8517 ⏱ M-Sat 9-9

· organic produce

🏠 **From I-40,** take exit 123 toward US 70/Hickory and follow long exit ramp onto 321N (right from 40W, loop around right from 40E) to Hwy 70 (1st exit). Turn left onto 70W across bridge to store on left. **From 321S,** turn right onto 70W to store immediately on left.

KILL DEVIL HILLS

The outer banks of NC, with pristine beaches, safe swimming and a wild life refuge.

DAILY MENU HEALTH A RAMA 🍴
2200H N. Croatan Hwy. © 252-480-6368 ⏱ M-Sat 9-7

· organic produce · juice bar · take-out

🏠 **Coming from north,** take Hwy 158E onto 158S across water about 30 miles to Kill Devil Hills and store at mile marker 6. **Coming from south,** take 64E across water to 158W. Turn left onto 158 about 9 miles to store.

MOUNT AIRY

A&S NATURAL HEALTH 🍃
192 N. Main St. ✆ 336-786-4260 ⊙ M-F 10-9, Sat 10-8, Sun 1-6

⌚ Mount Airy is near the VA border and US 52 runs into town. **From 52S,** merge onto 52Bus (Main St in town) to store just south of Franklin St. **From 52N,** merge onto 52Bus to Moore Ave. Turn left onto Moore 1 block to Main. Turn left onto Main past Franklin to store. **From I-77N,** take exit 100 onto NC 89E about 8¼ miles to Dixie St. Turn left onto Dixie 1 block to Franklin. Turn left onto Franklin 1 block to Main. Turn right onto Main to store.

MORRISVILLE

TOWER RESTAURANT ✕
144 Morrisville Square Way ✆ 919-465-2326 ⊙ M-Th 11-2:30, 5:30-9:30, F-Sun 11-3, 5-9:30
Vegetarian Indian food.
 · vegetarian · vegan friendly · tables · wait staff

⌚ **From I-40,** take exit 285 toward Morrisville/Airport south on Aviation Pkwy (right from 40E, left from 40W) 2½-2¾ miles where it becomes Morrisville Carpenter Rd. Continue less than ¼ mile to Morrisville Sq Way and turn left to restaurant.

RALEIGH

HARMONY FARMS 🍃
5653 Creedmoor Rd. ✆ 919-782-0064 ⊙ M-F 10-7, Sat 10-6, Sun 1-6

⌚ **From I-40E,** take exit 283 onto I-540 (Wake Expwy) to exit 9 (NC 50). Go south on Creedmoor Rd (aka 50) almost 4 miles to store in Creedmoor Cross Shopping Center. **From I-40W,** merge onto I-440E via exit 301 about 10 miles to exit 7B (Glenwood Ave). Merge onto Glenwood/70W about 1 mile (past Crabtree Valley Mall) to Creedmoor. Turn right onto Creedmoor about 1 mile to store in Creedmoor Crossing Shopping Center.

THIRD PLACE COFFEEHOUSE ✕
1811 Glenwood Ave. ✆ 919-834-6566 ⊙ M-F 6am-midnight, Sat-Sun 7am-midnight
A casual place to hang out, serving vegetarian soups, salads and sandwiches.
 · vegetarian · vegan friendly · tables · self-service

⌚ **From I-40E,** merge onto I-440N to exit 7. **From I-440,** take exit 7 onto US 70E (Glenwood Ave) about 2¾ miles to restaurant (at 5 Points intersection). **From I-40W,** take exit 298B toward Raleigh/Downtown onto US 401N/NC 50N less than 3 miles to US 70W. **From US 70W** (Wade Ave), take Glenwood Ave N ramp onto Glenwood less than ½ mile to restaurant.

WHOLE FOODS MARKET/WELLSPRING CAFE ✕🍃
3540 Wade Ave. ✆ 919-828-5805 ⊙ Daily 9-9, Cafe from 7:30
A friend in Raleigh raves about this store and the Wellspring Cafe.
 · organic produce · freshly prepared food · salad bar · café · deli · bakery · vegetarian friendly · chain · counter · tables · self-service · take-out

⌚ **From I-440,** take exit 4A (off outer loop from north, inner loop from south) onto Wade Ave. Store is just ahead on left corner Wade & Ridge Rd in Ridge Wood Shopping Center. **From I-40E,** take exit 289 (Wade Ave) about 3 miles east to store on left in Ridge Wood Shopping Center.

WILMINGTON

Hope at Tidal Creek claims that the barrier island beaches (just 4 miles east) have "clear, almost Caribbean water." She also sites best camping on uninhabited Masonboro Island, best hiking at Carolina Beach State Park and, in general, makes this sound like a cool place to spend time.

TIDAL CREEK COOPERATIVE FOOD MARKET ✗ 🍴 &

5329 Oleander Drive ✆ 910-799-2667 ⏰ M-Sat 8-8, Sun 10-6

A community hub with a bulletin board to plug into local happenings. Also, check out the Great Harvest Bakery next door and yoga center upstairs.

- organic produce · freshly prepared food · juice bar · salad bar · café · deli · bakery · vegetarian friendly · co-op · tables · self-service · take-out

🍎 **From I-40E** where hwy ends, continue on Hwy 132S (N College Rd) about 4½ miles to Oleander Dr (Hwy 76). Turn left onto Oleander about 1⅓ miles to store on left.

WINSTON-SALEM

FRIENDS OF THE EARTH 🍴

114 Reynolda Village ✆ 336-725-6781 ⏰ M-F 10-7, Sat 10-5

🍎 **From I-40W**, merge onto I-40Bus via exit 206. **From I-40E**, merge onto US 421E via exit 188. Take 40Bus/421E to Stratford Rd N exit (3B). Go north on Stratford about 1½ miles to Reynolda Rd. Turn left onto Reynolda about 1 mile to Reynolda Village. Turn right into Reynolda Village to store (in barn).

WHOLE FOODS MARKET ✗ 🍴 &

41 Miller St. ✆ 336-722-9233 ⏰ Daily 9-9, Cafe from 7am

- organic produce · freshly prepared food · salad bar · café · deli · bakery · vegetarian friendly · chain · counter · tables · self-service · take-out

🍎 **From I-40W**, merge onto I-40Bus via exit 206. **From I-40E**, merge onto US 421E via exit 188. Take 40 Bus/421E to Stratford Rd N exit (3B). Go north on Stratford to 1st traffic light at Miller Rd. Turn right onto Miller 1 block to store on left.

Please tell these businesses that you found them in Healthy Highways.

Goldbeck's "EAT IT OR NOT"
FASCINATING & FAR-OUT FACTS ABOUT FOOD

- The word restaurant comes from the French word for restorative.
- Kids and teens eat about twice as much at a restaurant meal as they do at home.
- When McDonalds first opened, a typical meal of burger, fries and Coke totaled about 600 calories. Today, a Super Size Value Meal (including a Quarter Pounder with Cheese, Super Size Fries and a Super Size Coke) adds up to 1,550 calories.
- You'd have to play touch football for 1½ hours to burn off the 530 calories in a Quarter Pounder with Cheese. Add a Super Size Coke and Super Size French Fries, and you'd have to play for more than 4½ hours.
- On average, Americans spend a total of six years eating. If half of these meals are in restaurants, you can add another 2 years.

NORTH DAKOTA

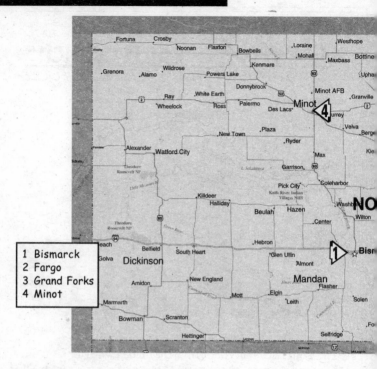

1 Bismarck
2 Fargo
3 Grand Forks
4 Minot

BISMARCK

TERRY'S HEALTH PRODUCTS
801 E. Main Ave. © 701-223-1026 ⊘ M-F 9-6, Sat 9-3

🏠 **From I-94**, take exit 159 onto Hwy 83S/1804S 2 miles (turns left onto N 7th St) to Main Ave. Turn left onto Main to store on right.

FARGO

SWANSON HEALTH PRODUCTS
109 N. Broadway © 701-293-9842 ⊘ M-W, F 9-6, Th 9-8, Sat 9-5, Sun 12-5
· organic produce

🏠 **From I-94**, take exit 351 toward Downtown Fargo onto 81Bus N (University Dr). Follow 81Bus N (turns right onto 13th Ave and left onto 10th St S) 2 miles to NP Ave. Turn right onto NP to Broadway. Turn left onto Broadway to store on left. **From I-29**, take exit 65 (US 10) toward Downtown Fargo. Turn east onto Main Ave (left from 29S, right from 29N) about 2½ mile to Broadway. Turn left onto Broadway to store on left.

TOCHI PRODUCTS
1111 2nd Ave. N. © 701-232-7700 ⊘ M-W, F-Sat 10-6, Th 10-8
Organic produce seasonally.

🏠 **From I-94**, take exit 351 toward Downtown Fargo onto 81Bus N (University Dr). Follow 81Bus N (turns right onto 13th Ave and left onto 10th St S) about 2⅔ miles to 2nd Ave N. Turn left onto 2nd 1 block to store on

right. **From I-29**, take exit 65 (US 10) toward Downtown Fargo. Turn east onto Main Ave (left from 29S, right from 29N) less than 1 mile to 25th St NW. Turn left onto 25th and right onto 1st Ave less than 1 mile to 14th St N. Turn left onto 14th and right onto 2nd Ave 3 blocks to store on right.

GRAND FORKS

AMAZING GRAINS NATURAL FOOD MARKET 🍎
214 Demers Ave. © 701-775-4542 ⊘ M-F 9-8, Sat-Sun 9-6
Sandwiches and soups to go.
· organic produce · freshly prepared food · deli · bakery · vegetarian friendly · take-out
🗂 **From I-29**, take exit 141 onto US 2E about 2¼ miles to 2Bus. Veer right onto 2Bus (N 5th St) 1 mile to Demers Ave. Turn left onto Demers almost 3 blocks to store.

MINOT

THE MAGIC MILL 🍎
115 S. Main St. © 701-852-4818 ⊘ M-F 10-5:30, Sat 10-2
🗂 **From Hwy 83**, turn east onto 1st Ave SE 2 blocks to Main St. Turn right onto Main to store.

Please tell these businesses that you found them in Healthy Highways.

OHIO

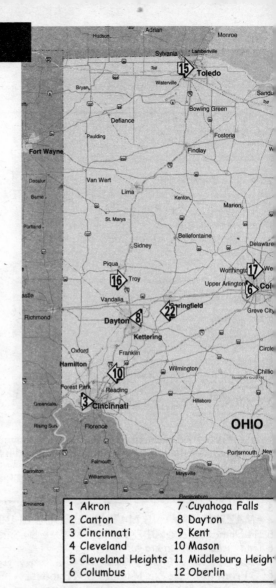

1 Akron	7 Cuyahoga Falls
2 Canton	8 Dayton
3 Cincinnati	9 Kent
4 Cleveland	10 Mason
5 Cleveland Heights	11 Middleburg Heigh‧
6 Columbus	12 Oberlin

AKRON

MUSTARD SEED MARKET & CAFE ✕ 🗐 &

3885 W. Market St. ℂ 330-666-7333 ⊘ M-Th 9-9, F-Sat 9-10, Sun 10-6 , Cafe M-Th 11-8, F-Sat 11-9, Sun 10:30-2:30

At the cafe, you can get everything from wheat grass and carrot juice to champagne and scotch! L&JB: It's a pleasure to relax in the dining area, situated next to a spa-like bar with wonderfully eclectic decor.

· organic produce · freshly prepared food · juice bar · salad bar · café · deli · bakery
· vegetarian friendly · alcohol · counter · tables · self-service · wait staff · take-out

🗂 **From I-77**, take exit 137A toward Fairlawn onto Rt 18E about ⅓ mile to store on left in West Market Plaza (next to Old Navy).

3 Stow	19 Willoughby
4 Tallmadge	20 Woodmere
5 Toledo	21 Wooster
6 Troy	22 Yellow Springs
7 Westerville	23 Youngstown
8 Westlake	

CANTON

RAISIN RACK 🛍️
4629 Cleveland Ave. N.W. ℰ 330-966-1515 ⊗ M-F 9-8, Sat 9-6
· organic produce

🏠 **From I-77S**, take exit 109 toward Whipple Ave left onto Everhard Rd about 1¾ miles to S Main St. Turn right onto Main (becomes Cleveland Ave) about ⅔ mile to store between 47th & 46th St. **From I-77N**, take exit 107B toward Alliance onto US 62E less than 1 mile to Cleveland Ave exit. Follow exit around to right (north) onto Cleveland about 1½ miles to store between 46th & 47th St.

CINCINNATI

CINCINNATI NATURAL FOODS 🍴
9268 Colerain Ave. ☏ 513-385-7000 ⊙ M-F 10-8, Sat 10-6, Sun 12-5
· organic produce

🛒 **From I-275**, take exit 33 south on Colerain Ave (left from 275W, right from 275E) almost 1½ miles (past Northgate Mall) to store on left at Round Top Rd.

CINCINNATI NATURAL FOODS 🍴
6911 Miami Ave. ☏ 513-271-7777 ⊙ M-F 10-8, Sat 10-6, Sun 12-5
· organic produce

🛒 **From I-71**, take exit 12 east on Montgomery Rd (left from 71S, right from 71N) to Hosbrook Rd. Turn right onto Hosbrook to Euclid Ave. Turn left onto Euclid to Miami Ave. Turn right onto Miami across railroad tracks to store on right.

CLIFTON NATURAL FOODS 🍴
169 W. McMillan St. ☏ 513-961-6111 ⊙ M-Sat 9-8, Sun 11-5
Located near the University of Cincinnati.
· organic produce

🛒 **From I-71S**, take exit 3 right onto Taft St (becomes Calhoun St) over 1 mile to end at Clifton Ave. Turn left onto Clifton 1 block to McMillan St. Turn left onto McMillan 2 blocks to store on right corner. **From I-75**, take exit 3 left onto Hopple St and veer left onto ML King Dr W about 1 mile (past traffic light at Dixmyth) to Clifton. Turn right onto Clifton ½ mile to McMillan. Turn left onto McMillan 2 blocks to store on right corner.

MULLANE'S PARKSIDE CAFE 🍴
723 Race St ☏ 513-381-1331 ⊙ M-Th 11:30-11, F 11:30-midnight, Sat 5-midnight
Although meat is served, the lacto-vegetarian choices are in the majority and many dishes can be modified to include tofu or tempeh.
· vegetarian friendly · vegan friendly · alcohol · tables · wait staff

🛒 **From I-71S**, take exit 2 south on Reading Rd less than 1 mile to Liberty St. Turn right onto Liberty about ½ mile to Race St. Turn left onto Race 7 blocks to restaurant on right. **From I-71N or I-75N**, take exit 1G right onto 5th St about ¼ mile to Elm St. Turn left onto Elm about ¼ mile to Garfield Pl. Turn right onto Garfield and right onto Race to restaurant on right. **From I-75S**, take exit 1F left onto 7th St less than ½ mile to Elm. Turn left onto Elm and follow directions above.

MYRA'S DIONYSUS RESTAURANT 🍴
121 Calhoun St ☏ 513-961-1578 ⊙ M-Th 11-10, F-Sat 11-11, Sun 5-10
Big vegetarian selection and a few choices for confirmed carnivores. Brown rice, whole wheat pita, lots of ethnic variety. A healthy option near the University.
· vegetarian friendly · alcohol · tables · wait staff · take-out

🛒 **From I-71S**, take exit 3 right onto Taft Rd (becomes Calhoun St) less than 1 mile to restaurant on left. **From I-71N**, take exit 2 north on Reading St less than 1 mile to Taft. Turn left onto Taft (becomes Calhoun) about ¾ mile to restaurant on left. **From I-75**, take exit 3 left onto Hopple St and veer left onto ML King Dr W about 1 mile to Clifton Ave. Turn right onto Clifton ½ mile to McMillan St. Turn left onto McMillan about ½ mile to Vine St. Turn left onto Vine and left onto Calhoun to restaurant on left.

SPATZ NATURAL LIFE HEALTH FOOD 🥔
607 Main St. © 513-621-0347 ⊙ M-F 9-5

🍎 **From I-71S**, take exit 2 and follow Gilbert Ave ramp onto US 22W (continues left onto 8th St) over ½ mile to Sycamore St. Turn left onto Sycamore to 1st right (6th St). Turn right onto 6th 2 blocks to store at 6th & Main St. **From I-75N**, take exit 1G right onto 5th St ½ mile to Main. Turn left onto Main 2 blocks to store.

WHAT'S FOR DINNER? ✕   ♿
3009 O'Bryon St. © 513-321-4404 ⊙ Deli M-F 10-8, Sat 10-4, Restaurant M-Th 11-9, F-Sat 11-11

A dual set up. Deli offers eat-in or carry-out entrees, sides and salads, about half vegetarian or vegan. The restaurant (and smoke-free bar) is about one-third vegetarian.

· deli · vegetarian friendly · alcohol · tables · self-service · wait staff · take-out

🍎 **From I-71S**, take exit 5 left (south) on Dana Ave about ½ mile to Madison Rd. Turn right onto Madison about ½ mile to store at corner Madison & O'Bryon St (look for dancing eggplant). **From I-71N**, take exit 1A ontoUS 50E about 3 miles to Torrence Pkwy. Turn left onto Torrence ½ mile (almost to end) to Grandin Rd. Turn left onto Grandin 1 block to restaurant at O'Bryon & Madison.

WILD OATS MARKET ✕🥔   ♿
2693 Edmondson Rd. © 513-531-8015 ⊙ M-Sat 8-10, Sun 9-9

· organic produce · freshly prepared food · juice bar · salad bar · café · deli · bakery
· vegetarian friendly · chain · counter · tables · self-service · take-out

🍎 **From I-71**, take exit 6 (Smith Rd/Edwards Rd). **From 71S**, turn right off exit and left at 1st traffic light onto Edmonston, crossing back over highway. Turn right at light to store in Rockwood Commons. **From 71N**, turn right off exit and right at light to store in Rockwood Commons.

CLEVELAND

CO-OP CAFE ✕
2130 Adelbert Rd. © 216-368-3095 ⊙ M-F 7:30-7:30, Sat 10-3

Run by the Food Co-op nearby on Euclid.

· vegetarian friendly · tables · self-service · take-out

🍎 **From I-90**, take exit 173B onto Chester Ave/322E about 3 miles to Euclid Ave. Turn left onto Euclid about ¼ mile to Adelbert Rd. Turn right onto Adelbert ¼ mile to restaurant in fitness center across from hospital. **From I-77 or I-71**, merge onto I-90 and follow directions above.

FOOD CO-OP 🥔
11702 Euclid Ave. © 216-791-3890 ⊙ M-Sat 9-8, Sun 10-6

· organic produce · co-op

🍎 **From I-90**, take exit 173B onto Chester Ave/322E about 3 miles to Euclid Ave. Turn left onto Euclid about ¾ mile to store. **From I-77 or I-71**, merge onto I-90 and follow directions above.

NATURE'S BIN 🍴   ♿

18120 Sloane Ave. ℂ 216-521-4600 ⊙ M-F 9-8, Sat 9-7, Sun 10-6

Nature's Bin was founded in the 1970s by an organization that gives support and employment to people with disabilities. The (two) stores continue to uphold that ideal. This one is strictly takeout, except in summer when there is seating outside.

· organic produce · freshly prepared food · deli · bakery · vegetarian friendly · take-out

🚌 **From I-90**, take exit 164 toward McKinley Ave. **From 90E**, turn right onto Niagara Dr, right onto Lakewood Hts Blvd and right onto Riverside Dr about ¾ mile to W Clifton Blvd. Turn right onto Clifton less than ½ mile to Sloane Ave. Turn left onto Sloane to store. **From 90W**, go straight onto Marginal Dr, left onto Hilliard Rd, right onto Riverside, and follow directions above.

SHTICK'S VEGETARIAN KITCHEN ✗   🍽♿

11075 East Blvd., Gund Law School ℂ 216-231-0922 ⊙ M-Th 7:30-4, F 7:30-2, Summer M-F 8:30-2:30 (hours may vary with school calendar)

In Gund Law School at Case Western Reserve. Soups, falafels, wraps, potato pancakes, and similar offerings with an Israeli/Arab leaning. Mostly vegetarian, except for tuna and a few poultry items.

· vegetarian friendly · tables · self-service · take-out

🚌 **From I-90**, take exit 173B onto Chester Ave/322E about 3 miles to Euclid Ave. Turn left onto Euclid and veer left onto East Blvd about ⅓ mile to restaurant in Gund Law School at Case Western Reserve.

SHTICK'S VEGETARIAN KITCHEN ✗   🍽♿

1948 W. 25th St. ℂ 216-589-8344 ⊙ W-Th 11-7, F 11-8, Sat 10-8, Sun 12-5

Falafels, wraps, "pitzas," potato pancakes, and similar items with an Israeli/Arab leaning. Mostly vegetarian, except for tuna and a few poultry items.

· vegetarian friendly · tables · self-service · take-out

🚌 **From I-90**, take exit 171 (W 14th St/Abbey Ave) east on Abbey about ½ mile to Lorain Ave. Veer left onto Lorain and turn right onto W 25th St to restaurant in Market 25.

WILD OATS MARKET ✗🍴   ♿

27249 Chagrin Blvd. ℂ 216-464-9403 ⊙ M-Sat 8-9, Sun 9-8

· organic produce · freshly prepared food · salad bar · café · deli · bakery · vegetarian friendly · chain · tables · self-service · take-out

🚌 **From I-271**, take exit 29 (US 422W/Chagrin Blvd) and follow exit about ⅓ mile to Chagrin Blvd. **From 271N** turn right onto Chagrin and **from 271S** turn left onto Chagrin to store. **From I-480**, merge onto I-271 and follow directions above.

CLEVELAND HEIGHTS

NATURE'S BIN ✗🍴   ♿

2255 Lee Rd. ℂ 216-932-2462 ⊙ M-F 9-8, Sat 9-6, Sun 12-6

See description of Cleveland location. Here there are tables so you can sit and eat.

· organic produce · freshly prepared food · deli · bakery · vegetarian friendly · tables · self-service · take-out

🚌 **From I-271**, take exit 32 west on Cedar Rd (loop around right from 271N, from 271S turn left onto Brainard Rd and right onto Cedar) about 4½ miles to Edgewood Rd. Turn left onto Edgewood 1 block to Meadowbrook Blvd. Turn left onto Meadowbrook 1 block to Lee Rd. Turn right onto Lee 1 block to store.

TOMMY'S ✕🍴 ⊜&
1824 Coventry Rd. © 216-321-7757 ⊙ M-Th 7:30am-10pm, F-Sat 7:30am-11pm, Sun 9am-10pm

Huge menu ranges from standard American fatty meat and white bread fare, to a surprising selection of vegetarian offerings, including tempeh, tofu, seitan, a dozen variations of falafel, over a dozen savory vegetable pies, 11 kinds of toasted cheese sandwiches (including a soy cheese option), and more.

· vegetarian friendly · vegan friendly · tables · wait staff · take-out

🗓 **From I-90**, take exit 173B on 322E (Chester Ave, becomes Mayfield Rd) about 5 miles to Coventry Rd. Turn right onto Coventry to restaurant. **From I-271**, take exit 35 onto Mayfield Rd (322W) about 5 miles to Coventry. Turn left onto Coventry to restaurant.

COLUMBUS_____

Columbus has a big music scene. If you're in the area the last week in June, head for Goodale Park and 3 days of music.

BEECHWOLD NATURAL FOODS 🍱
4185 N. High St. © 614-262-0192 ⊙ M-F 9:30-7, Sat 9:30-5

· organic produce

🗓 **From I-71**, take exit 115 west on Cooke Rd (right from 71S, left from 71N) to Indianola Ave. Turn right onto Indianola 1-2 blocks back to Cooke. Turn left onto Cooke about 1 mile to end at High St. Turn left onto High 3 blocks to store on right (in blue house).

BENEVOLENCE ✕
41 W. Swan St. © 614-221-9330 ⊙ Tues-F 11-3, Sat 11-4

Vegetarian lunch menu of fresh soups, salads and homemade bread changes daily. Also, cookbooks, gardening and other "new age" books, cards and gifts.

· vegetarian · tables · self-service

🗓 **From I-71S**, take exit 109A onto I-670W about 1²⁄₃ miles to US 33W/ Goodale St exit toward Neil Ave. Take 4th St ramp and turn right onto W Goodale, right onto N Park St and left onto W Swan St to restaurant. **From I-71N**, merge onto Rt 315N about 2 miles to Grandview Heights exit toward Goodale. Turn left off exit onto Goodale Neil Connector (becomes Vine St) ¾ mile to N Park. Turn left onto Park and right onto Swan to restaurant.

BEXLEY NATURAL MARKET 🍱
508 N. Cassady Ave. © 614-252-3951 ⊙ M-F 10-8, Sat 10-6, Sun 11-5

· organic produce · co-op

🗓 **From I-71**, take exit 109 toward Airport onto I-670E about 3 miles to exit 7 (5th Ave) toward 62W. Turn right onto 5th about ⅓ mile to traffic light at Cassady Ave. Turn right onto Cassady to store.

CLINTONVILLE COMMUNITY MARKET ✕🍱 ⊜&
200 Crestview Rd. © 614-261-3663 ⊙ M-Sat 7-10, Sun 9-10

· organic produce · freshly prepared food · deli · vegetarian friendly · co-op · take-out

🗓 **From I-71**, take exit 113 onto Silver Rd to Weber Rd. Turn west onto Weber (left from 71N, right from 71S) and cross railroad tracks. At 2nd traffic light (about ²⁄₃ mile) turn left onto Calumet St 3 blocks to store on right corner Calumet & Crestview Rd.

DRAGONFLY ✕

247 King Ave. ℂ 614-298-9986 ☺ Tues-Th 11:30-10, F-Sat 11:30-11, Sun 10-3, 5-9
"95% certified organic ingredients" in vegetarian and fish preparations. Live music, poetry and art on display.
· vegetarian friendly · organic focus · tables · wait staff

From I-71, take exit 110A west on 5th Ave about 1⅓ miles to Forsythe Ave. Turn right onto Forsythe to King Ave. Turn right onto King 1 block to restaurant at King & Neil Ave. **From I-70**, take I-670 to Grandview Heights exit north onto Olentangy River Rd. Go north about 1¼ miles to King. Turn right onto King less than ¾ mile to restaurant at King & Neil.

WHOLE WORLD PIZZA ✕

3269 N. High St. ℂ 614-268-5751 ☺ Tues-Th 11-9, F-Sat 11-10, Sun 10-9
In addition to whole wheat pizza topped with fresh vegetables, the all-vegetarian menu includes homemade burgers, Sloppy Joes and other tofu dishes, quesadillas, quiche, weekly specials, and more.
· vegetarian · vegan friendly · tables · wait staff · take-out

From I-71, take exit 114 west on E Broadway St (right from 71S, left from 71N) about ⅔ mile to Clinton Heights Rd. Turn left onto Clinton Heights less than ½ mile High St. Turn left onto High about 2 blocks to restaurant.

WILD OATS MARKET ✕🥗   ♿

1555 W. Lane Ave. ℂ 614-481-3400 ☺ M-Sat 8-9, Sun 8-8
· organic produce · freshly prepared food · juice bar · salad bar · café · deli · bakery
· vegetarian friendly · chain · counter · tables · self-service · take-out

From north of Columbus on I-270 or south of Columbus on I-670, I-70 or I-71N, take Rt 315 to Lane Ave exit toward Ohio State U. Turn west onto Lane (right from 315S, left from 315N) to store on left at 3rd traffic light.

WOODLANDS ✕

816 Bethel Rd. ℂ 614-459-4101 ☺ Lunch M-F 11:30-2:30, Sat 11:30-3:30, Dinner M-Th 5-9, F-Sun 5-9:30
Vegetarian Indian menu, plus a buffet lunch option.
· vegetarian · vegan friendly · tables · wait staff

From north of Columbus on I-270 or south of Columbus on I-670, I-70 or I-71N, take Rt 315 to Bethel Rd exit. Turn west onto Bethel (right from 315S, left from 315N) ⅓-½ mile to restaurant in Olentangy Sq Plaza.

CUYAHOGA FALLS

NEW EARTH NATURAL FOODS 🥗

1605 State Rd. ℂ 330-929-2415 ☺ M-F 9-8, Sat 10-6
Juice bar serves only fresh carrot and wheat grass juices.
· juice bar

From I-77N, take exit 125A onto OH 8N 3 miles to exit toward Talmadge Ave. Go straight onto Gorge Blvd and left onto Tallmadge ½ mile to N Main St. Turn right onto Main (becomes State Rd) less than 1¾ miles to store. **From OH 8S**, turn right onto Broad Blvd about 1⅓ miles to State. Turn left onto State about ½ mile to store.

Please tell these businesses that you found them in Healthy Highways.

DAYTON

CHRISTOPHER'S RESTAURANT ✗ &

2318 E. Dorothy Lane © 937-299-0089 ⊘ M-Sat 7:30am-9pm

In an area where vegetarian/whole foods eateries are uncommon, this all-American menu offers some options tucked in among the standard burgers, deli sandwiches, chops, and stews. For example, biscuits with gravy, veggie breakfast patties, multi-grain pancakes, falafel, chili, mushroom stroganoff, meatless lasagna. But you won't find whole grains, tofu or organic produce.

· vegetarian friendly · tables · wait staff · take-out

🍎 In Dayton's Kettering suburb. **From I-675**, take exit 10 (Indian Ripple Rd) toward Dorothy Ln. Turn west (left from 675N, right from 675S) onto Indian Ripple (becomes E Dorothy) about 1½ miles to restaurant on left in Woodlane Plaza Ctr. **From I-70W**, merge onto I-675 and follow directions above. **From I-75**, take exit 52B toward Xenia onto Rt 35E over 4½ miles to Woodman·Dr exit. Turn right onto Woodman about 3 miles to Dorothy. Turn left onto Dorothy to restaurant on right in Woodlane Plaza Ctr. **From I-70E**, merge onto I-75S and follow directions above.

HEALTHY ALTERNATIVES 🍲

8258 N. Main St. © 937-890-8000 ⊘ M-F 10-8, Sat 10-6, Sun 12-5

· freshly prepared food · juice bar · deli · take-out

🍎 **From I-70**, take exit 29 (Englewood) south on Main St (left from 70W, right from 70E) about 1½ miles to store.

HEALTHY ALTERNATIVES 🍲

6204 Wilmington Pike © 937-848-8881 ⊘ M-F 10-8, Sat 10-6, Sun 12-5

🍎 **From I-675**, take exit 7 south on Wilmington Pike about ⅓ mile to store on left.

WORLD OF NATURAL FOODS 🍲

2314 Far Hills Ave. © 937-293-8978 ⊘ M-Sat 10-6

🍎 **From, I-75N**, take exit 47 toward Kettering onto S Dixie Hwy about 2⅓ miles to Dorothy Ln. Turn right onto Dorothy about 1⅔ miles to Far Hills Ave. Turn left onto Far Hills to store on left in Oakwood Plaza. **From I-75S**, take exit 52A onto Campbell St to Stewart St. Turn left onto Stewart about 1 mile to S Main St (Rt 48). Turn right onto Main (becomes Far Hills) over 2½ miles to store on right in Oakwood Plaza.

KENT

While in Kent, take in the Cuyahoga River waterfall, the historic P&O Canal locks and the Breakneck Creek Conservation Area. For evening entertainment, see what's happening at the Kent Folk Stage. If you're here in early June, there's also the National Women's Music Festival.

KENT NATURAL FOODS CO-OP 🍲

151 E. Main St. © 330-673-2878 ⊘ M-Tues, Th-Sat 10-6:30, W 10-7

· organic produce · freshly prepared food · co-op

🍎 **From south, west or east of Akron**, take I-76 to exit 33 toward Kent. Turn north onto Rt 43 (left from 76E, right from 76W) less than 3½ miles to Main St. Turn right onto Main across bridge to store on left as you go up hill (dark green awning). **From north**, take I-80 to Streetsboro exit and go east ½ mile to Rt 43. Turn right (south) onto 43 about 4 miles to Main. Turn left onto Main across bridge to store on left as you go up hill.

MASON

AMY'S NATURAL NUTRITION 🍎
9370 Mason Montgomery Rd. © 513-229-3666 ⊘ M-F 10-8, Sat 10-5, Sun 12-5
  • organic produce

From I-71, take exit 19 north on Mason Montgomery Rd (right from 71S, left from 71N) about ¾ mile to store at Parkway Dr (in front of Lowe's).

MIDDLEBURG HEIGHTS

AMERICAN HARVEST ✕🍎
13387 Smith Rd. © 440-888-7727 ⊘ M-Sat 9-9, Sun 12-6
  • organic produce • freshly prepared food • deli • vegetarian friendly • tables • self-service • take-out

From I-71S, take exit 235 toward Middleburg Hts. Turn left onto Bagley Rd 1 mile to Pearl Rd. Turn left onto Pearl less than 1 mile to Smith Rd. Turn right onto Smith to store on right in Southland Shopping Center. **From I-71N**, take exit 234 toward Parma Hts. Turn right onto Pearl about 2 miles to Smith. Turn right onto Smith to store on right in Southland Shopping Center.

OBERLIN

GOOD FOOD CO-OP 🍎
West College St., Oberlin College © 216-775-6533 ⊘ M, W 6:30pm-8:30pm, Tues 4:30pm-6:30pm, Sat 10:30am-1pm, Sun 1-3 (may vary with school term)
Run by Oberlin College students and community volunteers.
  • co-op

On the Oberlin College Campus. **From east**, take I-480W onto OH 10W (becomes 20W) about 12 miles to OH 511 toward Oberlin. Turn left onto 511 about 1½ miles to Professor St. Turn left onto Professor 1 block to College St. Turn right onto College to store in basement of Harkness (2nd building, south side). **From I-80/I-90**, take OH 58 south about 6 miles to W Lorain St (aka 511). Turn right onto Lorain 1 block to Professor. Turn left onto Professor and follow directions above.

SOLON

MUSTARD SEED MARKET & CAFE
6025 Kruse Drive © 440-519-3663 ⊘ M-Sat 9-9, Sun 10-7, Cafe M 11-3, Tues-Th 11-8, F-Sat 11-9, Sun 10:30-3
At the cafe, you can get everything from wheat grass and carrot juice to champagne and scotch!
  • organic produce • freshly prepared food • juice bar • salad bar • café • deli • bakery • vegetarian friendly • alcohol • tables • self-service • wait staff • take-out

From west of Solon, take I-480E to Rt 422E. Take 422E to 2nd exit (Rt 91/Solon). Turn right off exit ramp to traffic light at Solon Rd. Turn right onto Solon and make 1st right onto Kruse Dr to store on right in Uptown Solon Shopping Center (at far west end). **From I-90 north of Solon, or I-77 or I-71 south of Solon**, take I-271 to 422E and follow directions above. **From 422W**, take Rt 91/Solon exit left off exit and under fwy to 2nd light at Solon Rd. Turn right onto Solon and make 1st right onto Kruse to store on right in Uptown Solon Shopping Center.

STOW

CAPPABIANCA'S NATURAL FOODS 🐑
4946 Darrow Rd. ✆ 330-650-1588 ⊙ M-Th 10-8, F-Sat 10-6

🍲 **From I-77N**, take exit 125A toward Cuyahoga Falls onto OH 8N 9 miles to Steel Corner Rd exit. Turn right onto E Steel Corner (becomes Hudson Dr) 2 miles to Norton Rd. Turn right onto Norton ¾ mile to Darrow Rd. Turn right onto Darrow about ¼ mile to store. **From I-271S**, take exit 18 onto OH 8S about 5 miles to OH 303 exit toward Hudson. Turn left onto 303 to Terex Rd. Turn right onto Terex 3 miles to Darrow. Turn right onto Darrow 1¼ miles to store.

TALLMADGE

SEVEN GRAINS NATURAL MARKET 🐑
92 West Ave. ✆ 330-633-9999 ⊙ M-Sat 9-8, Sun 10-6

· organic produce · freshly prepared food · deli · vegetarian friendly · take-out

🍲 **From Akron or further south on I-77N**, take exit 125A on left onto OH 8N 3 miles to Tallmadge Ave exit. Stay straight onto Gorge Blvd to E Tallmadge Ave. Turn right (east) onto Tallmadge almost 3 miles to store. **From OH 8S**, take Broad Blvd ramp left onto Broad Blvd (becomes Broad Ave, then Talmadge) about 1¼ miles onto Northwest Ave. Continue about 1¾ miles to roundabout. Take 1st exit onto West Ave about ¼ mile to store.

TOLEDO

BASSETT'S HEALTH FOODS 🐑
3301 W. Central St. ✆ 419-531-0334 ⊙ M-F 9:30-9, Sat 9:30-7:30, Sun 11:30-5:30

· organic produce

🍲 **From I-475**, take exit 17 south on Secor Rd (left from 475W, right from 475E) about ⅔ mile to Central Ave. Store is on right in West Gate Shopping Center.

BASSETT'S HEALTH FOODS 🐑
4315 Heatherdowns ✆ 419-382-4142 ⊙ M-Sat 9:30-8, Sun 11:30-5:30

🍲 **From I-80/90**, take exit 59/4 toward I-475 onto Reynolds Rd/US 20N 1⅓ miles to Heatherdowns. Turn right onto Heatherdowns 1 mile to store on right.

PHOENIX EARTH FOOD CO-OP 🐑
1447 W. Sylvania Ave. ✆ 419-476-3211 ⊙ M-F 9-8, Sat 9-7, Sun 11-5

· organic produce · co-op

🍲 **From I-75**, take exit 205A (Willys Pkwy) onto Jeep Pkwy to Willys Pkwy. Turn north onto Willys (right from 75S, left from 75N) about ⅔ mile to W Sylvania Ave. Turn left onto W Sylvania about ¼ mile to store.

TROY

CORNERSTONE NATURAL FOODS 🐑
110 E. Main St. ✆ 937-339-8693 ⊙ M-F 9-7, Sat 9-5

🍲 **From I-75**, take exit 74A toward Troy onto Rt 41S (becomes Main St) about 2 miles onto roundabout in town center. Take 2nd exit onto E Main 2 blocks to store on right. **From I-75N**, take exit 73 onto OH 55E about 1¾ miles to roundabout. Take 1st exit onto E Main 2 blocks to store on right.

WESTERVILLE

RAISIN RACK 🛒
618 W. Schrock Rd. ☎ 614-882-5886 ⏰ M-F 9-8, Sat 9-6, Sun 12-5

· organic produce

🛒 From I-270, take exit 27 toward OH 710/Schrock Rd onto Cleveland Ave N less than ½ mile to W Schrock. Turn right onto Schrock to store.

WESTLAKE

THE WEB OF LIFE NATURAL FOODS MARKET ✂🛒   ♿
25923 Detroit Rd. ☎ 440-899-2882 ⏰ M-Sat 9-9, Sun 10-6
Deli is all vegan, cafe is vegetarian and vegan, and most of the fare is organic.

· organic produce · freshly prepared food · juice bar · café · deli · vegetarian · vegan friendly · organic focus · tables · wait staff · take-out

🛒 From I-90, take exit 159 south on Columbia St (right from 90E, left from 90W) to Detroit Rd. Turn right onto Detroit about 1 mile to store in Williamsburg Square.

WILLOUGHBY

JUST NATURAL HEALTH FOODS ✂🛒
38669 Mentor Ave. ☎ 440-954-8638 ⏰ M-Th 9:30-7, F 9:30-5, Sat 10-5, Eatery until 4:30, Juice bar until 6:30
Healthy vegan breakfast and lunch items.

· freshly prepared food · juice bar · vegan · counter · tables · self-service · take-out

🛒 From I-90, take exit 193 north on OH 306 (right from 90W, left from 90E) about 1 mile to Mentor Ave. Turn left onto Mentor about 1 mile to store across from Willoughby School of Fine Arts & Andrews School for Girls.

WOODMERE

WILD OATS MARKET ✂🛒   ♿
27249 Chagrin Blvd. ☎ 216-464-9403 ⏰ M-Sat 8-10, Sun 9-9

· organic produce · freshly prepared food · juice bar · salad bar · café · deli · bakery · vegetarian friendly · chain · counter · tables · self-service · take-out

🛒 From I-271, take Chagrin Blvd exit. From 271N go east directly to store on left. From 217S, go west over interstate overpass to store on left.

WOOSTER

WOOSTER NATURAL FOODS 🛒
138 E. Liberty St. ☎ 330-264-9797 ⏰ M-F 10-6, Sat 10-5

· organic produce

🛒 From I-71, take exit 204 onto Rt 83S about 14 miles. Turn right onto W Milltown Rd about ½ mile to Oak Hill Rd. Turn left onto Oak Hill almost 3 miles to W Liberty. Turn left onto W Liberty about 1 mile (past Market St) to store on E Liberty. From the east, US 30W goes into Wooster and becomes E Liberty St in town.

YELLOW SPRINGS

Excellent hiking, camping and a bike path that runs all the way to Cincinnati.

ORGANIC GROCERY 🥬

230 Keith's Alley © 937-767-7215 ⊘ M-Sat 9-7, Sun 11-6

· organic produce · freshly prepared food · juice bar · deli · vegetarian friendly · take-out

🏠 **From I-675**, take exit 20 east on Dayton-Yellow Springs Rd more than 5½ miles to Limestone St. Turn right onto Limestone about ½ mile to US 68 (Xenia Ave). Turn left onto 68 1 block to Glen St. Turn right onto Glen 1 block to Keith's Alley. Turn left onto Keith's to store. **From I-70**, take exit 52A toward Xenia onto US 68S about 7⅓ miles to Glen. Turn left onto Glen 1 block to Keith's Alley. Turn left onto Keith's to store.

SUNRISE CAFE ✗ &

259 Xenia Ave. © 937-767-7211 ⊘ M-Sat 8-2, 5:30-9, Sun 9-2, 5:50-8:30

Always options for vegetarians and vegans, including a daily vegan special. Organic eggs, equal exchange coffee, homemade bread, pies made with local fruit.

· vegetarian friendly · vegan friendly · tables · wait staff · take-out

🏠 **From I-675**, take exit 20 east on Dayton-Yellow Springs Rd more than 5½ miles to Limestone St. Turn right onto Limestone about ½ mile to US 68 (Xenia Ave). Turn left onto 68 to restaurant (across from US Bank). **From I-70**, take exit 52A toward Xenia onto Rt 68S (becomes Xenia Ave) over 7 miles into Yellow Springs to restaurant (across from US Bank).

YOUNGSTOWN

GOOD FOOD CO-OP 🥬

62 Pyatt St. © 330-747-9368 ⊘ M-Th, Sat 10-6, F 10-8

· organic produce

🏠 **From I-680S**, take exit 6A toward OH 62W/7S. Turn right onto Market St less than ¼ mile to Pyatt St. Turn left onto Pyatt to store on left (across from Pyatt St Market). **From I-680N**, take exit 7 toward OH 62W/7S. Turn right onto South St ¼ mile to Williamson Ave (OH 62/7). Turn left onto Williamson ½ mile to Market. Turn right onto Market 2 blocks to Pyatt. Turn right onto Pyatt to store on right.

Goldbeck's "EAT IT OR NOT"

FASCINATING & FAR-OUT FACTS ABOUT FOOD

TRUE OR FALSE?

Organically grown foods are higher in cancer-fighting chemicals than conventionally grown foods.

True The total antioxidants are significantly higher in foods grown organically (using no synthetic herbicides, pesticides or fertilizers) and sustainably (artificial fertilizers but not herbicides or pesticides), compared to foods grown conventionally (using synthetic chemicals to protect the plants and increase yield.

OKLAHOMA

PEARSON'S NATURAL FOOD CENTER 🦽

131 W. Garriott ✆ 580-234-5000 ⏰ M-F 9-5:30, Sat 9-1
Organic produce seasonally.

🛍 **From US-81**, take Hwy 412W (Garriot Rd) over ½ mile to store on right at Independence St. **From I-35** (exit 194), take 412W about 30 miles.

NORMAN

EARTH NATURAL FOODS ✗🦽   🦽

309 S. Flood Ave. ✆ 405-364-3551 ⏰ M-Sat 9-6
Organic juice bar with smoothies and homemade soup.

· organic produce · freshly prepared food · juice bar · café · deli · vegetarian friendly
· counter · tables · self-service · take-out

🛍 **From I-35**, take exit 109 toward Downtown east on W Main St (follow loop off exit from 109S, right from 109N) about 2 miles to 4-way traffic light. Turn right onto S Flood Ave to store on left (in little cottage).

OKLAHOMA CITY

AKIN'S NATURAL FOODS MARKET ✗🦽   🦽

2924 N.W. 63rd St. ✆ 405-843-3033 ⏰ Daily 9-9

· organic produce · freshly prepared food · deli · vegetarian friendly · chain · tables
· self-service · take-out

🛍 **From I-44E**, merge onto OK 3W/74N about 8½ miles to NW 50th St exit. Turn right onto 50th about ½ mile to May Ave. Turn left onto May about 1 mile to store on left in Mayfair Place Shopping Ctr. **From I-44W**, take exit 125C (on left) onto Northwest Expwy over 1½ miles to northbound May Ave ramp. Merge onto May about ⅔ mile to store on left in Mayfair Place.

HEALTH FOOD CENTER ✗🦽

2219 S.W. 74th St. ✆ 405-681-6060 ⏰ M-Sat 9-8, Sun 12-6

· organic produce · juice bar · counter · take-out

🛍 **From I-44E**, take exit 115 onto I-240E. Take exit 1B (May Ave) and continue straight on 240/OK3 (becomes SW 74th St) less than 1 mile to store. **From I-44W**, merge onto I-35S. **From I-35S**, take exit 1C toward S Pennsylvania Ave onto SW 74th about ¼ mile to Pennsylvania. Turn left onto Pennsylvania 1 block to 76th St. Turn right onto 76th 1 block to Youngs Blvd. Turn right onto Youngs 1 block to 74th. Turn right onto 74th to store.

HEALTH WAY 🦽

6207 N. Meridian Ave. ✆ 405-721-2121 ⏰ M-W 9-6, Th 9-8, F 9-4

🛍 **From I-44E**, merge onto OK 3W/74N about 9 miles to OK3 W exit toward NW 63rd St. Turn left onto Northwest Expwy (aka 3W) about ¾ mile to 63rd St. Turn left onto 63rd about ⅔ mile to Meridian Ave. Turn left onto Meridian to store. **From I-44W**, take exit 125C (on left) onto Northwest Expwy about 3¼ miles to NW 63rd and follow directions above.

NUTRITIONAL FOOD CENTER 🦽

1022-32 Classen Blvd. ✆ 405-232-8404 ⏰ M-Sat 8-6
JM: A grocery store plus a lot more. Like a Ma & Pa "HEALTHY" Target.

· organic produce · juice bar · take-out

🛍 **From I-40E**, take exit 149A (Reno Ave) toward Western Ave and follow ramp left for Sheridan Ave. Veer right onto Sheridan 2 blocks to

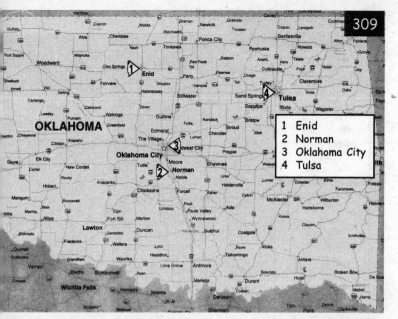

Claussen Blvd. Turn left onto Claussen to store at 10th St. **From I-40W,** take exit 149B and follow ramp onto Claussen Blvd N about 10 blocks to store at Claussen & 10th. **From I-35 or I-44,** merge onto I-40E or W as appropriate and follow directions above.

TULSA

AKIN'S NATURAL FOODS MARKET
7807 E. 51st St. ℂ 918-663-4137 ⊙ Daily 8-9

· organic produce · juice bar · chain · take-out

🍽 **From I-44,** take exit 231 toward Muskeegee/Broken Arrow onto US 64E/OK 51E about ⅔ mile to Memorial Dr exit. Turn right (south) onto Memorial about 1¼ miles to E 51st St. Turn right onto E 51st to store on NW corner in Fontana Shopping Ctr. **From Hwy 169,** exit at E 51st and go west about 1½ miles to store just past Memorial (in Fontana Shopping Ctr).

AKIN'S NATURAL FOODS MARKET
3321 E. 31st St. ℂ 918-742-6630 ⊙ Daily 8-9

· organic produce · chain

🍽 **From I-44E,** take exit 228 toward Harvard Ave. Take E 51st ramp and turn left (north) onto Harvard about 2 miles to store at 31st St on NE corner in Newport Square Shopping Ctr. **From I-44W,** take exit 231 toward Sand Spring onto US 64W/OK 51W almost 1½ miles to 31st St exit toward Fairgrounds/Drillers Stadium. Turn left (west) onto E 31st about 1 mile to store at Harvard (NE corner in Newport Square Shopping Ctr).

WILD OATS MARKET
1401 E. 41st St. ℂ 918-712-7555 ⊙ Daily 7-11

· organic produce · freshly prepared food · juice bar · salad bar · café · deli · bakery
· vegetarian friendly · chain · tables · self-service · take-out

🍽 **From I-44,** take exit 226B toward Peoria Ave. Turn north onto Peoria (right from 44E, left from 44W) about 1 mile to E 41st St. Turn right onto 41st to store.

OREGON

1	Ashland
2	Astoria
3	Bandon
4	Beaverton
5	Bend
6	Brookings
7	Canyonville
8	Coquille
9	Corvallis
10	Cottage Grove
11	Eugene
12	Gold Beach
13	Grants Pass
14	Gresham
15	Hillsboro
16	Jacksonville
17	Lake Oswego
18	Lincoln City
19	Milwaukie
20	Newport
21	North Bend
22	Port Orford
23	Portland
24	Rogue River
25	Salem
26	Waldport

ASHLAND

Home of the Oregon Shakespeare Festival. Nearby skiing, white water rafting and Southern Oregon U. While in Ashland, Annie at the Co-op suggests a wine or farm tour by trolley, or "exciting river rafting" on the Rogue River.

ASHLAND FOOD CO-OP ✕ 🍷   ♿

237 N. 1st St. © 541-482-2237 ⊙ M-Sat 8-9, Sun 9-9

· organic produce · freshly prepared food · juice bar · salad bar · deli · bakery
· vegetarian friendly · co-op · tables · self-service · take-out

🍴 **From I-5S**, take exit 19 toward Ashland right onto Valley View Rd to end at OR 99. Turn left onto 99 about 2½ miles (into town) to 1st St. Turn left onto 1st to store on left just past B St. **From I-5N**, take exit 14 left at stop sign onto Hwy 66, 1⅓ miles to end at Siskiyou Blvd (OR 99). Turn right onto Siskiyou 1⅓ miles to 1st. Turn right onto 1st to store on left.

PILAF RESTAURANT ✕   ♿

18 Calle Guanajuato © 541-488-7898 ⊙ Tues-Sat 11-9, Sun 11-4

Polyethnic vegetarian menu with a Greek, Israeli, Turkish, Egyptian, Indian, and Mediterranean influence. Many vegan options and about half organic.

· vegetarian · vegan friendly · alcohol · tables · wait staff

🍴 **From I-5S**, take exit 19 toward Ashland right onto Valley View Rd to end at OR 99. Turn left onto 99, 2-2½ miles to Calle Guanajuato. Turn right onto Guanajuato to restaurant on back side of plaza. (Enter via Masonic Walkway through tallest building). **From I-5N**, take exit 14 left at stop sign onto Hwy 66, 1⅓ miles to end at Siskiyou Blvd (OR 99). Turn right onto Siskiyou 1½ miles to Water St. Turn left onto Water (becomes Guanajuato) to restaurant.

ASTORIA

THE COLUMBIAN CAFE ✕ 🍴

1114 Marine Dr. ✆ 503-325-2233 🕐 Days
M-F 8-2, Sat-Sun 9-2, Dinner W-Sat 5-9
The fare is mostly vegetarian, along with fish and seafood. The evening menu changes regularly and the chef uses local produce whenever possible.

· vegetarian friendly · alcohol · tables · wait staff

🗂 Hwy 101 (from north or south) and Hwy 30 (from east) converge in Astoria (which is just south of the WA border). **From Hwy 30W** (Marine Dr in town), store is at 11th St. **From Hw 30E**, turn right onto 8th St 1 block to Commercial St (aka 30E). Turn left onto Commercial to 16th St and turn left back onto 30W (Marine) to store at 11th.

THE COMMUNITY STORE 🍴

1389 Duane St. ✆ 503-325-0027 🕐 M-Sat 9-6, Sun 10-3
The co-op is moving to a new home at 10th & Commercial St. Call for updates.

· organic produce · co-op

🗂 Hwy 101 (from north or south) and Hwy 30 (from east) converge in Astoria (which is just south of the WA border). **From Hw 30**, turn south (away from river) onto 15th St 2 blocks to Duane St. Turn right onto Duane 1 block to store at 14th St.

BANDON

MOTHER'S NATURAL GROCERY & DELI ✕ 🍴

975 2nd St. S.E. ✆ 541-347-4086 🕐 M-Sat 10-6
Styled like a traditional country grocery, with natural foods and a vegetarian deli.

· organic produce · freshly prepared food · juice bar · deli · vegetarian · vegan friendly · tables · self-service · take-out

🗂 Bandon is along the OR coast and store is on Hwy 101 (2nd St in town) just before Rt 42 intersection.

BEAVERTON

NATURE'S-A WILD OATS MARKET ✕ 🍴 ♿

4000 S.W. 117th St. ✆ 503-646-3824 🕐 Daily 8-9

· organic produce · freshly prepared food · deli · vegetarian friendly · chain · tables · self-service · take-out

🗂 **From I-5**, take exit 292 (292B from I-5N) toward Beaverton onto Rt 217N about 5½ miles to Canyon Rd (exit 2A). Follow exit ramp ⅓ mile and turn left onto Canyon ⅓ mile to SW 117th Ave. Turn right on 117th to store on right.

BEND

Bend is known as an "outdoor mecca," with "high dessert eastern Cascade sunshine." For indoor fun, try the World Famous Fantastic Museum, en route to Redmond, which houses more than a million unrelated collectibles, assembled by a man who reportedly "can afford to buy just about anything that strikes his fancy."

COLORS-A FULL SPECTRUM EATERY ✗

1110 N.W. Newport Ave. ☎ 541-330-8181 ☉ Daily 8-2, Dinner Tues-Sat 5-9
Self-described as "A Place for all Tastes." About half vegetarian or easily made so (as noted on the menu). Some organic ingredients, but not much whole grain. In a converted 1930s craftsman's home decorated with local grassroots art.

· vegetarian friendly · alcohol · tables · wait staff

⬭ **From Hwy 97**, turn west onto Greenwood Rd about 1 mile (through downtown Bend and across river where Greenwood becomes Newport Ave) to restaurant at NW 11th St.

DEVORE'S GOOD FOOD STORE 🌿

1124 N.W. Newport Ave. ☎ 541-389-6588 ☉ M-Sat 8-7, Sun 10-6
· organic produce · freshly prepared food · deli · vegetarian friendly · take-out

⬭ **From Hwy 97**, turn west onto Greenwood Rd about 1 mile (through downtown Bend and across river where Greenwood becomes Newport Ave) to store between NW 11th & 12th St.

NATURE'S GENERAL STORE ✗🌿

1950 N.E. 3rd St. ☎ 541-382-6732 ☉ M-F 9-9, Sat-Sun 9-8
· organic produce · freshly prepared food · juice bar · deli · vegetarian friendly · tables · self-service · take-out

⬭ **From Hwy 97N**, take exit 137 onto Division St and turn right (east) onto NE Revere Ave 3 blocks to NE 3rd St. Turn left onto NE 3rd to store on right in Wagner Payless Mall. **From 97S**, take exit 135A toward Business District onto US 20E about 2 miles to store on left in Wagner Payless Mall.

WILD OATS MARKET ✗🌿   ♿

2610 N.E. Hwy. 20 ☎ 541-389-0151 ☉ Daily 7-11
· organic produce · freshly prepared food · salad bar · café · deli · bakery · vegetarian friendly · chain · tables · self-service · take-out

⬭ **From Hwy 97N**, take Knott Rd ramp toward Baker Rd. Turn right onto Knott about 7½ miles (becomes SE 27th St) to US 20. Turn left onto 20 to store. **From Hwy 97S**, take exit 135A toward Business District onto 20E through downtown, past Pilot Butte Park to store at SE 27th St.

CANYONVILLE

Umpqua National Forest up the road offers hiking, camping and swimming in the South Umpqua River.

PROMISE NATURAL FOODS & BAKERY 🌿

503 S. Main ☎ 541-839-4167 ☉ M-F 9:30-6, Sat 10-5
On-site organic bakery makes whole grain breads, rolls, pastries, and cookies. On Friday, there is homemade pizza.

· organic produce · bakery

⬭ **From I-5N**, take exit 98 toward Canyonville right onto SW 5th St 2 blocks to store at corner 5th & Main St. **From I-5S**, take exit 98 left onto Canyonville Riddle Rd 2 blocks to Main. Turn right onto Main 4 blocks to store at 5th. (Look for big peace symbol on top of building.)

COQUILLE

EDEN VALLEY 🌱
99 E. 1st St. ℂ 541-396-4823 ⏰ M-F 10-6, Sat 12-5

· organic produce · freshly prepared food · vegetarian friendly · take-out

🍎 Take Rt 42 to Coquille. Turn onto N Adams (right from 42N, left from 42S) 1 block to store at 1st St (across from Safeway).

CORVALLIS

On the Willamette River, with lots of hiking (nearby Mary's Peak is the largest mountain in the Oregon coast range), wineries and blueberry picking. Corvallis is a smoke-free town!

FIRST ALTERNATIVE NATURAL FOODS CO-OP ✗ 🌱   ♿
1007 S.E. 3rd St. ℂ 541-753-3115 ⏰ Daily 9-9
Store motto is: "Fresh, Local, Organic, Good-For-You Food." Deli is mostly organic, with vegan, vegetarian, non-vegetarian, wheat- and dairy-free dishes.

· organic produce · freshly prepared food · deli · bakery · vegetarian friendly · organic focus · co-op · tables · self-service · take-out

🍎 **From I-5**, take exit 228 onto Hwy 34W about 11 miles (bypass Corvallis) to exit 99W on right. Store is on left on Chapman Pl (across from Papa's Pizza). **From downtown Corvallis**, go south on 3rd St, pass under Hwy 34 and over Mary's River to store on left in Chapman Pl.

INTABA'S KITCHEN ✗
1115 S.E. 3rd St. ℂ 541-754-6958 ⏰ Daily 11-9, Espresso service M-F 7-10am
"Inspired by a tradition of sustainable culinary, agricultural and economic practices." Innovative, mostly organic, vegan world cuisine, with limited dairy and local northwest seafood. Plus, gourmet pizza from a wood-fired earthen oven. Early morning organic espresso and pastries weekdays. Live music Saturday nights.

· juice bar · café · vegetarian friendly · vegan friendly · organic focus · tables · wait staff · take-out

🍎 **From I-5**, take exit 228 onto Hwy 34W about 11 miles (bypass Corvallis) to exit 99W on right. Restaurant is on left on Chapman Pl (next to First Alternative Co-op). **From downtown Corvallis**, go south on 3rd St, pass under Hwy 34 and over Mary's River to restaurant on left in Chapman Pl.

INTERZONE ✗   ♿
1653 Monroe St. ℂ 541-754-5965 ⏰ M-F 7am-midnight, Sat-Sun 8am-midnight
A vegetarian coffeehouse serving sandwiches, burritos, lasagna, and such.

· vegetarian · vegan friendly · tables · wait staff

🍎 **From I-5**, take exit 228 onto Hwy 34W about 10 miles. Continue straight onto NW Harrison Blvd about ⅔ mile to NW 16th St. Turn left onto NW 16th 3 blocks to Monroe St. Turn right onto Monroe to restaurant (across from College Cleaners).

NEARLY NORMALS ✗   ♿
109 N.W. 15th St. ℂ 541-753-0791 ⏰ M-Sat 8-9
Vegetarian and vegan "world cuisine," with plenty of Mexican fare and pasta, hearty breakfast items, and whole grains. All sauces and many condiments are homemade. Seating indoors and out.

· vegetarian · vegan friendly · organic focus · alcohol · tables · self-service

🍎 **From I-5**, take exit 228 onto Hwy 34W about 10 miles. Continue straight onto NW Harrison Blvd about ½ mile to NW 15th St. Turn left onto NW 15th ¼ mile to restaurant.

COTTAGE GROVE

SUNSHINE GENERAL STORE 🌿
824 W. Main St. ✆ 541-942-8836 ⊘ M-Sat 10-7

· organic produce

🛏 **From I-5**, take exit 174 toward Cottage Grove west (right) on E Cottage Grove Conn (becomes Hwy 99) about 1 mile to Main St. Turn right onto Main about ⅓ mile to store on right.

EUGENE

CAFE YUMM! ✕   ♿
130 Oakway Center ✆ 541-225-0121 ⊘ M-Th 8-7, F 8-8, Sat 10-6, Sun 10-5
The signature dish in this 3-venue chain is rice, beans and various add-ons, topped with wheat-free vegan Yumm! sauce. Other items include fresh soups, salads and sandwiches. Mostly vegetarian, with options for poultry- and fish-eaters. At this site, order at the counter and the food is delivered to your table.

· vegetarian friendly · vegan friendly · alcohol · chain · tables · self-service

🛏 **From I-5**, take exit 194B onto I-105W about 1⅓ miles to exit 2 (OR 99S/Coburg Rd) toward Downtown. Take Coburg Rd ramp onto Oakway Rd to restaurant in Oakway Center.

CAFE YUMM! ✕   ♿
1801 Willamette St. #140 ✆ 541-431-0204 ⊘ M-F 8-6 (food from 10), Sat 10-6, Sun 10-5
See description of Cafe Yumm! above. This site opens early weekdays for coffee and pastry, but you'll have to wait until 10 am for Yumm Bowls.

· vegetarian friendly · vegan friendly · alcohol · chain · tables · self-service

🛏 **From I-5S**, take exit 194B onto I-105W 3½ miles to exit 1 (Jefferson St) toward Fairgrounds. Turn left onto Jefferson about 1 mile to W 18th Ave. Turn left onto 18th almost ½ mile to Willamette St. Turn right onto Willamette to restaurant on SE corner. **From I-5N**, take exit 189 west on 30th Ave (becomes Amazon Pkwy) 4½ miles to E 19th Ave. Turn left onto E 19th, right onto Oak St, left onto E 18th and left onto Willamette to store on SE corner 18th & Willamette.

CAFE YUMM! ✕   ♿
296 E. 5th Ave. #108 ✆ 541-484-7302 ⊘ Daily 10-6
See description of Cafe Yumm! above.

· vegetarian friendly · vegan friendly · alcohol · chain · tables · self-service

🛏 **From I-5S**, take exit 194B onto I-105W about 1⅓ miles to exit 2 (OR 99S/Coburg Rd) toward Downtown. Take Coburg ramp onto Coburg almost 1 mile to High St. Turn right onto High 1 block to 5th Ave to restaurant in 5th St Public Market (historic bldg). **From I-5N**, take exit 192 toward Eugene onto OR 99N/126Bus W almost 2½ miles until it becomes E 6th Ave. Follow 6th left 1 block to High. Turn right onto High to restaurant in 5th St Public Market.

FRIENDLY FOODS & DELI ✕🌿
2757 Friendly St. ✆ 541-683-2079 ⊘ M-Sat 8-10, Sun 9-10

· organic produce · freshly prepared food · deli · vegetarian · vegan friendly · tables · self-service · take-out

🛏 **From I-5**, take exit 189 toward S Eugene west on E 30th Ave (left from 5N, straight onto McVay Hwy then right from 5S). Continue on E 30th about 3¼ miles until it becomes Amazon Pkwy and zig zag onto 29th Ave over ½ mile to Lincoln St. Turn right onto Lincoln and immediately left onto 28th Ave less than ½ mile to Friendly St. Turn right onto Friendly to store on right.

HOLY COW CAFE ✕

EMU Student Union/U OR ✆ 541-345-2562 ⏰ M-Th 10-7, F 10-3 (11-3 in summer) Call for current schedule

An organic vegetarian (mostly vegan) cafeteria in the U OR student union.

· salad bar · vegetarian · vegan friendly · tables · self-service · take-out

🚌 **From I-5S**, take exit 194B onto I-105W about 1⅓ miles to exit 2 (OR 99S/Coburg Rd). Take 99S and merge onto E Broadway heading east (becomes Franklin Blvd) to Agate St. Turn right onto Agate to 15th Ave (at Hayward Field). Turn right onto 15th and take 1st or 2nd entrance on right (before street dead ends at University St) to parking behind Student Union. Restaurant is on main floor of Student Union in food court. **From I-5N**, take exit 192 toward Eugene/Hwy 99 onto Franklin about 1⅓ miles to Agate. Turn left onto Agate to 15th Ave and follow directions above.

KIVA 🍐

125 West 11th Ave. ✆ 541-342-8666 ⏰ M-Sat 9-8, Sun 10-5

· organic produce · freshly prepared food · deli · vegetarian friendly · take-out

🚌 **From I-5S**, take exit 194B onto I-105W about 3½ miles to Jefferson St/OR 99S exit. Take 99S ramp toward City Center/Mall left onto W 7th Ave. Take 7th east (left) about ⅓ mile to Olive St. Turn right onto Olive about ⅓ mile to store at W 11th Ave. **From I-5N**, take exit 192 toward Eugene onto OR 99N/126Bus W about 1⅔ miles to 11th. Turn left onto 11th about 1 mile to store at Olive.

LOTUS GARDEN ✕

810 Charnelton St. ✆ 541-344-1928 ⏰ M, W-Sat 11:30-3, 4:30-8:30

Vegetarian Chinese featuring faux meat dishes.

· vegetarian · vegan friendly · tables · wait staff · take-out

🚌 **From I-5S**, take exit 194B onto I-105W about 3½ miles to Jefferson St/OR 99S exit. Take 99S ramp toward City Center/Mall left onto W 7th Ave. Take 7th east (left) about ¼ mile to Charnelton St. Turn right onto Charnelton 1 block to restaurant at W 8th Ave. **From I-5N**, take exit 192 toward Eugene onto OR 99N/126Bus W (becomes E Broadway) about 2½ miles to Olive St. Turn right onto Olive 1 block to 8th Ave. Turn left onto 8th 1 block to restaurant at Charnelton.

MORNING GLORY ✕   ⬛♿

450 Willamette Street ✆ 541-687-0709 ⏰ Daily 7:30-3:30

Vegetarian and vegan breakfast, lunch, fresh juice, and all-vegan baked goods.

· juice bar · café · bakery · vegetarian · vegan friendly · organic focus · tables · wait staff

🚌 **From I-5S**, take exit 194B onto I-105W about 1⅓ miles to exit 2 (OR 99S/Coburg Rd) toward Downtown. Take Coburg ramp onto Coburg almost 1 mile to High St. Turn right onto High 1 block to 5th Ave. Turn left onto 5th (past 5th St Market) 3 blocks to Willamette St. Turn right onto Willamette to restaurant at end on left. **From I-5N**, take exit 192 toward Eugene onto OR 99N/126Bus W almost 2½ miles until it becomes E 6th Ave. Follow 6th left 1 block to High. Turn right onto High and follow directions above.

NEW FRONTIER MARKET WEST

1101 W. 8th Ave. ℃ 541-345-7401 ⊙ M-Sat 7am-midnight, Sun 7am-11pm
· organic produce

📷 **From I-5**, take exit 194B onto I-105W about 3½ miles to Jefferson St/
OR 99S exit. Merge onto Jefferson to W 8th Ave. Turn right onto 8th about
⅓ mile to store on corner 8th & Van Buren St.

PLANET GOLOKA

679 Lincoln St. ℃ 541-465-4555 ⊙ M-Th 2-8, F 12-9, Sat 10-4
Tofu, tempeh, veggie burgers, sandwiches on organic bread, stir-fries, salads,
fresh juice, smoothies, and a shop with spiritual and alternative books and incense.
· juice bar · vegetarian · vegan friendly · organic focus · tables · self-service · take-out

📷 **From I-5**, take exit 194B onto I-105W about 3½ miles to Jefferson St/OR
99S exit. Take 99S ramp toward City Center/Mall left onto W 7th Ave. Take
7th east (left) 3 blocks to Lincoln St. Turn left onto Lincoln to restaurant.

RED BARN

357 Van Buren St. ℃ 541-342-7503 ⊙ M-Sat 9-8, Sun 10-9
· organic produce · freshly prepared food · café · deli · vegetarian friendly · alcohol
· tables · wait staff · take-out

📷 **From I-5**, take exit 194B toward Eugene onto I-105W about 3½ miles
to OR 99N/OR 126 exit. Turn right onto W 6th Ave about 4 blocks to
Blair Blvd. Turn right onto Blair about ¼ mile to Van Buren St. Turn right
onto Van Buren to store.

SAM BOND'S GARAGE

407 Blair Blvd. ℃ 541-431-6603 ⊙ Daily 4pm-1am or beyond
A no-smoking bar (except outside in the courtyard), with a vegetarian, organic
menu, lots of local beers and live music.
· vegetarian · vegan friendly · organic focus · alcohol · tables · self-service

📷 **From I-5**, take exit 194B toward Eugene onto I-105W about 3½ miles
to OR 99N/OR 126 exit. Turn right onto W 6th Ave about 4 blocks to
Blair Blvd. Turn right onto Blair Blvd about ¼ mile to restaurant at Blair
& 4th Ave.

SUNDANCE NATURAL FOODS

748 E. 24th Ave. ℃ 541-343-9142 ⊙ Daily 7-11
Vegetarian hot food bar, extensive wine cellars and an annex specializing in
organic clothing, tools and gifts.
· organic produce · freshly prepared food · salad bar · vegetarian friendly · tables · self-
service · take-out

📷 **From I-5**, take exit 189 toward S Eugene west on E 30th Ave (left from
5N, straight onto McVay Hwy then right from 5S) about 3¼ miles to
traffic light at Hilyard St. Turn right onto Hilyard about ⅔ mile (park will
be on left) to light at 24th Ave. Turn right onto 24th to store just off corner.

THE LOCOMOTIVE

291 E. 5th Ave. ℃ 541-465-4754 ⊙ W-Sat from 5pm
Weekly menu of upscale, international vegetarian dishes featuring organic
ingredients. Breads, desserts, even the ice creams are made on the premises.
· vegetarian · vegan friendly · organic focus · alcohol · tables · wait staff · take-out

📷 **From I-5**, take exit 192 toward Eugene onto OR 99N/126Bus W almost
2½ miles until it becomes E 6th Ave. Follow 6th left 1 block to High St.
Turn right onto High 1 block to E 5th Ave. Turn left onto 5th to restaurant.

WILD OATS MARKET ✕🥘 &

2580 Willakenzie Rd. © 541-334-6382 ⏱ Daily 7-11

· organic produce · freshly prepared food · juice bar · salad bar · café · deli · bakery
· vegetarian friendly· chain · tables · self-service · take-out

From I-5, take exit 195 toward Florence/Airport west on Beltline Hwy W about 1 mile to Coburg Rd. Turn left onto Coburg about ½ mile to store on right at Willkenzie Rd.

WILD OATS MARKET ✕🥘 &

2489 Willamette St. © 541-345-1014 ⏱ Daily 7-11
Outdoor seating only.

· organic produce · freshly prepared food · juice bar · salad bar · café · deli · bakery
· vegetarian friendly · chain · tables · self-service · take-out

From I-5, take exit 189 toward S Eugene west on E 30th Ave (left from 5N, straight onto McVay Hwy then right from 5S). Continue on E 30th about 3¼ miles (becomes Amazon Pkwy). Turn right onto Amazon about ½ mile to Willamette St. Turn right onto Willamette to store on right.

GOLD BEACH

SAVORY NATURAL FOODS 🥘

29441 Ellenburg Ave. © 541-247-0297 ⏱ M-F 10-6, Sat 11-4

· organic produce · freshly prepared food · juice bar · deli · vegetarian friendly · tables
· self-service · take-out

Hwy 101 runs through Gold Beach (about 35 miles north of CA and 78 miles south of Coos Bay). Store is on 101 set back in L-shaped complex.

GRANTS PASS

FARMER'S MARKET 🥘

603 Rogue River Hwy. © 541-474-0252 ⏱ M-Sat 8:30-6:30, Sun 10-5

· organic produce

From I-5, take exit 55 (US 199/Redwood Hwy) toward Crescent City. Merge onto Grants Pass Pkwy about 1⅔ miles to Parkdale Dr. Turn left onto Parkdale about ¼ mile to Rogue River Hwy. Turn right onto Rogue River to store.

SUNSHINE NATURAL FOOD MARKET ✕🥘

128 S.W. H St. © 541-474-5044 ⏱ M-F 9-6, Sat 9-5
Salad bar week days only.

· organic produce · freshly prepared food · juice bar · salad bar · vegetarian friendly
· tables · self-service · take-out

From I-5, take exit 55 (US 199/Redwood Hwy) toward Crescent City. Take Redwood Hwy/199 Spur about 2 miles to NW 6th St. Turn left onto 6th to H St. Turn right onto H to store.

GRESHAM

NATURE'S-A WILD OATS MARKET ✕🥘 &

2077 N.E. Burnside Rd. © 503-674-2827 ⏱ Daily 7-11

· organic produce · freshly prepared food · juice bar · salad bar · café · deli · bakery
· vegetarian friendly · chain · tables · self-service · take-out

From I-84, take exit 16 toward Wood Village south on NE 238th Dr (left from 84W, right from 84E) over 3 miles (becomes NE 242nd Dr, NE 242nd Ave, then NE Hogan Dr) to NE Burnside Rd. Turn left onto Burnside past 1st traffic light to store. (Heading east on Burnside store is 1 light past Hogan.)

HILLSBORO

NEW SEASONS MARKET/ORENCO STATION 🌱　　　　&

1453 N.E. 61st Ave. © 503-648-6968 ⊘ Daily 8-10
In-store organic bakery and take-out deli. Special events every weekend.
- · organic produce · freshly prepared food · salad bar · deli · bakery · vegetarian friendly
- · chain · take-out

🍎 **From Hwy 26,** take exit 64 south onto NW 185th (left from 26W, right from 26E) ½ mile to NW Cornell Rd. Turn right onto Cornell about 2½ miles to store at NE 61st Ave.

JACKSONVILLE

RUCH NATURAL FOODS ✕🌱

181 Upper Applegate Rd. © 541-899-1519 ⊘ M-F 7-7, Sat-Sun 7-5
- · freshly prepared food · deli · vegetarian friendly · tables · self-service · take-out

🍎 **From I-5,** take exit 30 (Medford) onto Hwy 238 (Jacksonville Hwy) about 13 miles through Jacksonville to Ruch. Turn left onto Upper Applegate Rd about ¼ mile to store on left.

LAKE OSWEGO

NATURE'S-A WILD OATS MARKET ✕🌱　　　　&

17711 Jean Way © 503-635-8950 ⊘ Daily 7-11
- · organic produce · freshly prepared food · juice bar · salad bar · café · deli · bakery
- · vegetarian friendly · chain · tables · self-service · take-out

🍎 **From I-5S,** take exit 290 toward Lake Oswego/Durham east on Lower Boones Ferry Rd (right from 5N, left from 5S) about ½ mile to Jean Way. Turn right onto Jean to store.

LINCOLN CITY

TRILLIUM NATURAL FOODS 🌱　　　　&

1026 S.E. Jetty Ave. © 541-994-5665 ⊘ M-Sat 9:30-7, Sun 11-6
- · organic produce

🍎 **From Hwy 101 in Lincoln City,** turn east onto 9th St (right from 101N, left from 101S) 1 block to SE Jetty Ave. Turn right onto Jetty to store (across from factory outlet stores).

MILWAUKIE

BOB'S RED MILL NATURAL FOODS MILL OUTLET & BAKERY ✕

5000 S.E. International Way © 503-654-3215 ⊘ M-Sat 8-5
Bob's Red Mill is a manufacturer/distributor of stone-ground whole grain flours, hot cereals, flaxseed, specialty flours (many gluten-free), beans, and more. These are sold at the store, along with coffee and baked goods.
- · café · bakery · counter · tables · self-service · take-out

🍎 **From I-205,** take exit 13 (Hwy 224/Milwaukie) onto 224W about 2⅓ miles to SE Freeman Way. Turn right onto Freeman 1 block to International Way. Turn right onto International to first left onto Mallard Way. Enter 1st driveway on left to store.

NEWPORT

OCEANA NATURAL FOODS CO-OP ✕ 🍎 ♿
159 S.E. 2nd St. ✆ 541-265-3893 🕐 M-F 8-7, Sat 8-6, Sun 10-6
*Daily vegetarian, mostly vegan menu (except for the occasional tuna sandwich
and tuna/salmon in sushi rolls). The salad bar sometimes offers tuna in a
separate covered container. Most items are made with organic ingredients.*
 · organic produce · freshly prepared food · salad bar · café · deli · vegetarian · vegan
 friendly · organic focus · co-op · tables · self-service · take-out
🗀 **From Hwy 101 in Newport,** turn east onto Hwy 20 (right from 101N,
left from 101S) 2 blocks to Benton St. Turn right onto Benton 2 blocks store
on corner Benton & SE 2nd St.

SARANG VEGETARIAN RESTAURANT ✕
706 S.W. Hurbert St. ✆ 541-265-5803 🕐 M, W-Sun 11-8
Korean vegetarian fare, curries and a few western dishes.
 · vegetarian · vegan friendly · tables · wait staff
🗀 **From Hwy 101 in Newport,** turn west onto NW Hurbert St (left
from 101N, right from 101S) 1 block to restaurant just before 7th St.

NORTH BEND

On the southern OR coast: Ocean, bay, lakes, streams, great parks, and camping.

COOS HEAD FOOD STORE 🍎
1960 Sherman Ave. ✆ 541-756-7264 🕐 M-F 9-7, Sat 10-6, Sun 12-5
 · organic produce · juice bar · co-op · take-out
🗀 In North Bend, Hwy 101S is Sherman Ave. Store is 1 block south of
North Bend Library.

PORT ORFORD

SEAWEED NATURAL GROCERY & CAFE ✕ 🍎
832 Hwy. 101 ✆ 541-332-3640 🕐 M-Sat 10-6, Cafe 10-3
 · organic produce · freshly prepared food · café · bakery · vegetarian friendly · tables
 · self-service · take-out
🗀 On the southern OR coast on Hwy 101 at mile post 301.

PORTLAND

DOG DIGS ✕
212 N.W. Davis St. ✆ 503-223-3362 🕐 M-F 9-5
Vegetarian, mostly vegan take-out. Soup, salad, sandwiches, vegan baked goods.
 · vegetarian · vegan friendly · take-out
🍎 **From I-5S,** take exit 302A toward City Center onto N Broadway
about ¼ mile and take Broadway Bridge across water to NW Broadway.
Turn left onto NW Broadway ⅓ mile to NW Davis St. Turn left onto
Davis 5 blocks to store at 2nd Ave. **From I-5N,** take exit 299B on left onto
I-405N. **From I-405N,** take exit 1A on left toward Naito Pkwy/Historic
District straight onto SW Harbor Dr over ½ mile to SW Front Ave/Naito
Pkwy. Turn right onto Front almost ¾ mile to SW Ash St. Turn left onto
Ash 2 blocks to SW 2nd. Turn right onto 2nd 4 blocks to NW Davis. Turn
left onto Davis to store. **From I-405S,** take exit 2B onto NW 16th Ave to
NW Everett St. Turn left onto Everett ⅔ mile to NW 3rd Ave. Turn right
onto 3rd 1 block to NW Davis. Turn left onto Davis 1 block to store.

FOOD FRONT CO-OP 🍎
2375 N.W. Thurman St. © 503-222-5658 ☺ Daily 8-9
· freshly prepared food · deli · vegetarian friendly · co-op · take-out
🍎 From I-405, take exit 3 onto Rt 30W to Vaughn St exit (comes up quickly). Turn left onto NW 23rd Ave 1 block to store on right at NW Thurman St.

GARDEN CAFE ✖   ♿
10123 S.E. Market St. © 503-251-6125 ☺ M-F 6:30-6:30
Vegetarian cafe in the Seventh-day Adventist Medical Center.
· vegetarian · vegan friendly · tables · self-service
🍎 From I-205, take exit 19 east on SE Division St (left from 205S, right from 205N) about ⅓ mile to SE 101st Ave. Turn left onto 101st ½ mile to SE Market St. Turn right onto Market to restaurant on ground floor in Adventist Medical Center.

KALGA KAFE ✖
4147 S.E. Division St. © 503-236-4770 ☺ M-Tues, Th-Sun 12-12
The food is largely Indian vegetarian, but there are other meatless items as well. At night there is often live music and a late scene.
· vegetarian · vegan friendly · alcohol · tables · wait staff
🍎 From I-205, take exit 19 (Powell Ave/Division St) straight off exit to Division. Turn west onto Division (left from 205N, right from 205S) about 2½ miles to restaurant between 42nd & 41st St. From I-84W, take exit 9 onto I-205S and follow directions above. From I-84E, take exit 2 right onto NE 39th St almost 2 miles to Division. Turn left onto Division about 2½ blocks to restaurant. From I-5S, merge onto I-84E via exit 300B and follow directions above.

LAUGHING PLANET CAFE ✖   ♿
3320 S.E. Belmont St. © 503-235-6472 ☺ M-Sat 11-10, Sun 11-9
The restaurant's mission is to use whole foods, support local and sustainable businesses, serve delicious, healthful food at moderate prices, and "increase the world's supply of mirth, humor, and beans." Daily vegan soups, organic rice and beans, veggie burgers. House specialty is (veg and non-veg) burritos.
· juice bar · café · vegetarian friendly · vegan friendly · organic focus · counter · tables · self-service · take-out
🍎 From I-84, take exit 2 to 39th Ave (straight from 84E, left onto Halsey St from 84W). Go south on 39th (right from 84E, left from 84W) about 1¼ miles (through 1st roundabout) to Belmont St. Turn right onto Belmont 5 blocks to restaurant at 33rd Ave. From I-5N, follow exit 300 onto SE Yamhill St to 3rd Ave. Turn left onto 3rd 1 block to Belmont. Turn right onto Belmont 1½ miles to restaurant at 33rd. From I-5S, take exit 300B and take ramp toward OR City left at fork onto Belmont about 1½ miles to restaurant. From downtown Portland, cross Morrison Bridge onto Belmont about 2 miles to restaurant at 33rd.

NATURE'S-A WILD OATS MARKET 🍎   ♿
6344 S.W. Capitol Hwy. © 503-244-3110 ☺ Daily 7-11
· organic produce · freshly prepared food · salad bar · deli · bakery · vegetarian friendly · chain · take-out
🍎 From I-5, take exit 297 (Terwilliger Blvd) onto SW Bertha Blvd (2 lefts off exit from 5N, straight from 5S). Take Bertha about ¾ mile to SW Capitol Hwy. Turn right onto Capitol to store.

NATURE'S-A WILD OATS MARKET ✕🍽 &

2825 E. Burnside St. ☎ 503-232-6601 ☉ Daily 7-11
Outdoor patio seating only.

· organic produce · freshly prepared food · salad bar · café · deli · bakery · vegetarian friendly · chain · tables · self-service · take-out

🍎 **From I-84**, take exit 2 to 39th Ave (straight from 84E, left onto Halsey St from 84W). Go south on 39th (right from 84E, left from 84W) about ¾ mile (through 1st roundabout) to E Burnside St. Turn right onto Burnside about ⅔ mile to store at 28th Ave. **From I-5N**, follow exit 300 to Water St. Turn right onto Water 1 block to SE Taylor St. Turn right onto Taylor about ¼ mile to SE Grand Ave. Turn left onto Grand ½ mile to E Burnside. Turn right onto Burnside about 1 mile to store at 28th. **From downtown Portland**, cross Burnside Bridge onto E Burnside about 1¼ miles to store at 28th.

NATURE'S-A WILD OATS MARKET ✕🍽 &

3016 S.E. Division St. ☎ 503-233-7374 ☉ Daily 8-10

· organic produce · freshly prepared food · deli · vegetarian friendly · chain · tables · self-service · take-out

🍎 **From I-205**, take exit 19 (Powell Ave/Division St) straight off exit to Division. Turn west onto Division (left from 205N, right from 205S) about 3½ miles to store on left. **From I-5N**, take exit 299A across Ross Island Bridge onto SE Powell Ave to SE 21th Ave. Turn left onto 21th ⅓ mile to Division. Turn right onto Division ½ mile to store on right just past 30th Ave. **From I-5S**, take exit 300B and take ramp toward OR City left at fork onto SE Belmont St about ¼ mile to SE 11th Ave. Turn right onto 11th about ⅓ mile to Hawthorne Blvd. Turn left onto Hawthorne 1 block and veer right onto SE Ladd Ave (through roundabout) ⅔ mile to Division. Turn left onto Division ½ mile to store on right.

NATURE'S-A WILD OATS MARKET ✕🍽 &

3535 N.E.15th Ave. ☎ 503-288-3414 ☉ Daily 7-11
Outdoor seating only.

· organic produce · freshly prepared food · juice bar · salad bar · café · deli · bakery · vegetarian friendly · chain · tables · self-service · take-out

🍎 **From I-405**, turn left onto N Cook St ¼ mile to NE Rodney Ave. Turn left onto Rodney 2 blocks to NE Fremont St. Turn right onto Fremont about ⅔ mile to store at NE 15th Ave. **From I-5N**, take exit 302A toward Rose Quarter/Broadway right onto NE Weidler St about ¾ mile to NE 15th. Turn left onto 15th about 1 mile to store at Fremont. **From I-5S**, take exit 302B left onto Fremont less than 1½ miles to store at 15th.

NEW SEASONS MARKET/CONCORDIA ✕🍽 &

5320 N.E. 33rd Ave. ☎ 503-288-3838 ☉ Daily 8-10
In-store certified organic bakery and deli. Special events on weekends..

· organic produce · freshly prepared food · salad bar · deli · bakery · vegetarian friendly · chain · tables · self-service · take-out

🍎 **From I-84E**, take exit 1 north (left) onto 33rd Ave about 2 miles to store. **From I-84W**, merge onto I-205N via exit 9. **From I-205**, take exit 23 (B from 205N, A from 205S) west on US 30 Bypass about 3⅓ miles to NE 33rd Ave. Turn left onto 33rd about ¾ miles to store.

Please tell these businesses that you found them in Healthy Highways.

NEW SEASONS MARKET/RALEIGH HILLS ✗🍎 &

7300 S.W. Beaverton Hillsdale Hwy. ℂ 503-230-6838 ☺ Daily 8-10
In-store certified organic bakery and deli. Special events on weekends..
  · organic produce · freshly prepared food · salad bar · deli · bakery · vegetarian friendly
  · chain · tables · self-service · take-out

🍎 **From Hwy 26W** (I-405 exit 1D), take exit 71B (Sylvan) left onto Skyline Blvd (becomes SW Scholls Ferry Rd) about 2 miles to Beaverton Hillsdale Hwy. Make slight right onto Beaverton Hillsdale to store.

NEW SEASONS MARKET/SELLWOOD ✗🍎 &

1214 S.E. Tacoma St. ℂ 503-230-4949 ☺ Daily 8-10
In-store certified organic bakery and deli. Special events on weekends..
  · organic produce · freshly prepared food · salad bar · deli · bakery · vegetarian friendly
  · chain · tables · self-service · take-out   2/3

🍎 **From I-5N,** take exit 297 right onto SW Terwilliger Blvd about ½ mile to SW Taylors Ferry Rd. Turn left onto Taylors Ferry 1 mile to Macadam Ave. Turn right onto Macadam ½ mile to Sellwood Bridge. Turn left onto Sellwood Bridge (becomes SE Tacoma St) to store ⅓ mile past bridge. **From I-5S,** take exit 299A toward Lake Oswego right onto on SW Hood Ave (becomes Macadam) about 2 miles to Sellwood Bridge and follow directions above.

OLD WIVES' TALES ✗ &

1300 E. Burnside St. ℂ 503-238-0470 ☺ M-Th, Sun 8-9, F-Sat 8-10
An extensive breakfast menu, a lot of vegan choices and very kid friendly.
  · vegetarian · vegan friendly · alcohol · tables · wait staff

🍎 **From I-5N,** follow exit 300 to Water St. Turn right onto Water 1 block to SE Taylor St. Turn right onto Taylor about ¼ mile to SE Grand Ave. Turn left onto Grand ½ mile to E Burnside St. Turn right onto Burnside about ⅓ mile to restaurant between 12th & 14th Ave. **From I-5S,** take exit 300B and take ramp toward OR City left at fork onto SE Belmont St to SE Grand. Turn left onto Grand less than ½ mile to E Burnside. Turn right onto Burnside about ⅓ mile to restaurant. **From I-84W,** take exit 1 and follow ramp toward Grand Ave left onto 12th Ave almost ½ mile to Burnside. Turn left onto Burnside to restaurant.

OMEGA GARDENS ✗

4036 S.E. Hawthorne Blvd. ℂ 503-235-2551 ☺ M-Sat 11-7
A vegetarian salad bar, hot deck, sandwiches, and such, with many vegan choices and mainly organic ingredients. In the same locale as The Daily Grind.
  · salad bar · vegetarian · vegan friendly · organic focus · tables · self-service · take-out

🍎 **From I-405N,** take exit 1A on left toward Naito Pkwy/Historic District straight onto SW Harbor Dr over ½ mile to SW Front Ave/Naito Pkwy. Turn right onto Front across Hawthorne Bridge and follow ramp onto SE Hawthorne Blvd almost 2 miles to restaurant on right (past 39th Ave). **From I-5N,** take exit 299B on left onto I-405N and follow directions above. **From I-84,** take exit 2 to 39th Ave (straight from 84E, left onto Halsey St from 84W). Go south on 39th (right from 84E, left from 84W) about 1½ miles (through 1st roundabout) to Hawthorne. Turn left onto Hawthorne to restaurant on right. **From I-5S,** take exit 301 onto I-84E and follow directions above.

PARADOX PALACE CAFE ✗ 🝛

3439 S.E. Belmont St. ℂ 503-232-7508 ☺ M, Sun 8-9, Tues-W 9-9, Th-Sat 8-10
Except for a beef burger and chicken sausage, the menu is vegetarian.
  · vegetarian friendly · vegan friendly · alcohol · tables · wait staff

🛏 **From I-84**, take exit 2 to 39th Ave (straight from 84E, left onto Halsey St from 84W). Go south on 39th (right from 84E, left from 84W) about 1¼ miles (through 1st roundabout) to Belmont St. Turn right onto Belmont 3 blocks to store between 35th & 34th Ave. **From I-5N**, follow exit 300 onto SE Yamhill St to 3rd Ave. Turn left onto 3rd 1 block to Belmont. Turn right onto Belmont 1½ miles to restaurant between 34th & 35th Ave. **From I-5S**, take exit 300B and take ramp toward OR City left at fork onto SE Belmont about 1½ miles to restaurant. **From downtown Portland**, cross Morrison Bridge onto Belmont about 2 miles to restaurant at 34th.

PEOPLE'S FOOD STORE 🌱   ⚐

3029 S.E. 21st Ave.. © 503-232-9051 ⊙ Daily 9-9
Recent store expansion incorporated many green building principles, including cob wall infill and passive heating and cooling systems. The community room holds events, classes and meetings. And every Wednesday, the co-op hosts a farmers' market.
  · organic produce · freshly prepared food · vegetarian friendly · co-op · take-out

🛏 **From I-5**, take exit 299A (OR 43/Macadam Ave) toward US 26E/Ross Island Bridge onto SW Hood Ave (slight right from 5N, straight from 5S) 2 blocks to Whittaker St. Turn right onto Whittaker, left onto Kelly Ave and slight left onto ramp toward US 26E/Ross Island Bridge. Turn right onto 26 about 1½ miles (across bridge) to SE 21st Ave. Turn left onto SE 21st 1 block to store on corner 21st & SE Tibbets St.

THE DAILY GRIND NATURAL FOODS 🌱

4026 S.E. Hawthorne Blvd. © 503-233-5521 ⊙ M-Sat 9:30-9, Sun 10-8
A totally vegetarian grocery, with vegetarian and vegan takeout.
  · organic produce · freshly prepared food · salad bar · bakery · vegetarian · vegan friendly · take-out

🛏 **From I-405N**, take exit 1A on left toward Naito Pkwy/Historic District straight onto SW Harbor Dr over ½ mile to SW Front Ave/Naito Pkwy. Turn right onto Front across Hawthorne Bridge and follow ramp onto SE Hawthorne Blvd almost 2 miles to store on right (past 39th Ave). **From I-5N**, take exit 299B on left onto I-405N and follow directions above. **From I-84**, take exit 2 to 39th Ave (straight from 84E, left onto Halsey St from 84W). Go south on 39th (right from 84E, left from 84W) about 1½ miles (through 1st roundabout) to Hawthorne. Turn left onto Hawthorne to store on right. **From I-5S**, take exit 301 onto I-84E and follow directions above.

THE PURPLE PARLOR ✗

3560 N. Mississippi Ave. © 503-281-3560 ⊙ Tues-F 7:30am-2:30pm, Sat-Sun 8-3
A vegetarian breakfast and lunch cafe and neighborhood gathering place. Features local, sustainably farmed, organic produce, organic coffee, and home-made vegan, low-fat desserts.
  · vegetarian · vegan friendly · organic focus · counter · tables · wait staff

🛏 **From I-5S**, take exit 303 left onto Alberta St to 1st traffic light at N Albina Ave. Turn right onto Albina (becomes Mississippi Ave at Skidmore St) to restaurant 4 blocks past Skidmore on left between Failing & Beech St. **From I-405**, take Kerby Ave exit off Fremont Bridge to Williams Ave. Turn left onto Williams to 1st light at Fremont St. Turn left onto Fremont 2 lights to Mississippi. Turn right onto Mississippi 1 block to restaurant on right.

VITA CAFE ✕ &

3024 N.E. Alberta St. © 503-335-8233 ⊙ M-W 10-10, Th-F 10-11, Sat 8-11, Sun 8-10

Most of the fare is vegetarian or vegan, as well as organic. The menu is divided into four sections: Italian, Asian (with brown rice), Mexican, and American. The latter offers vegetarian versions of traditional comfort foods, like tempeh "steak" and mashed potatoes, tofu "fish" and chips, grilled cheese, and such.

· vegetarian friendly · vegan friendly · organic focus · alcohol · tables · wait staff

 From I-84E, take exit 1 north (left) on 33rd Ave about 1¾ miles to NE Alberta St. Turn left onto Alberta about 5 blocks to restaurant (before 30th Ave). **From I-84W**, merge onto I-205N via exit 9. **From I-205**, take exit 23 (B from 205N, A from 205S) west on US 30 Bypass about 3⅓ miles to 33rd. Turn left onto 33rd less than 1 mile to Alberta. Turn right onto Alberta about 4 blocks to restaurant.

WHOLE FOODS MARKET ✕ 🍃 &

1210 N.W. Couch St. © 503-525-4343 ⊙ Daily 8-10

· organic produce · freshly prepared food · juice bar · salad bar · deli · bakery
· vegetarian friendly · chain · tables · self-service · take-out

 From I-405S, take exit 2A left onto NW Couch St 3 blocks to store at NW 12th Ave. **From I-405N**, take exit 2B toward Everett St left onto NW 14th Ave, right onto NW Everett and right onto NW 13th Ave 2 blocks to NW Couch. Turn left onto Couch 1 block to store. **From east side of river**, take Morrison Bridge onto SW Washington St to SW 12th Ave. Turn right onto 12th 3 blocks to Couch. Turn left onto Couch to store.

ROGUE RIVER

ROGUE RIVER NATURAL FOODS 🍃

510 E. Main St., Ste. 4 © 541-582-3075 ⊙ M-F 9:30-5:30, Sat 10-4

 From I-5, take exit 48 toward City of Rogue River/Savage Rapid Dam. Turn right onto Depot St, then right onto Main St about ¼ mile to store.

Goldbeck's "EAT IT OR NOT"
FASCINATING & FAR-OUT FACTS ABOUT FOOD

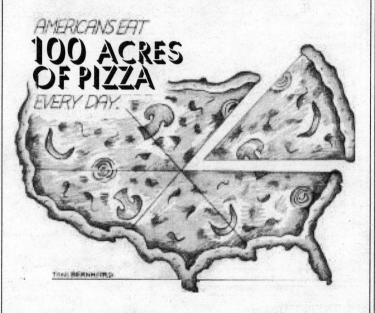

AMERICANS EAT
100 ACRES OF PIZZA
EVERY DAY.

THE PIZZA BOX

- Americans eat about 350 slices of pizza per second or almost 3 billion pizzas per year.
- Top 10 Most Popular Pizza Toppings (by country)
  - Squid (Japan)
  - Tuna and corn (England)
  - Black bean sauce (Guatemala)
  - Mussels and clams (Chile)
  - Barbecued chicken (Bahamas)
  - Eggs (Australia)
  - Pickled ginger (India)
  - Fresh cream (France)
  - Green peas (Brazil)
  - Guava (Colombia)

PENNSYLVANIA

1 Allentown
2 Annville
3 Ardmore
4 Bethlehem
5 Brodheadsville
6 Bryn Mawr
7 Clarks Summit
8 Dallas
9 Easton
10 Erie
11 Hanover
12 Harrisburg
13 Honesdale
14 Jenkintown
15 Kimberton
16 Lancaster
17 Lansdale
18 Luzerne
19 Malvern
20 Marshall's Creek
21 Media
22 Morrisville
23 Mt. Lebanon
24 New Cumberland
25 New Holland
26 New Hope
27 North Wales
28 Paoli
29 Penndel
30 Philadelphia
31 Pittsburgh
32 Plumsteadville
33 Reading
34 Sharpsburg
35 Southampton
36 Spring Grove
37 Stahlstown
38 State College
39 Stroudsburg
40 Tannersville
41 Trexlertown
42 Wayne
43 Williamsport
44 Willow Grove
45 Wynnewood
46 York

ALLENTOWN

GARDEN GATE NATURAL FOODS 🍃

17 S. 9th St. ℄ 610-433-8891 ⏰ M, Tues, Th-F 8:30-9, W 8:30-6:30, Sat 9-6:30, Sun 11-5

· organic produce · deli · vegetarian friendly · take-out

🍂 **From Rt 22**, merge onto PA 145S toward 7th St (right from 22E, left from 22W) about 1¾ miles to Linden St. Turn right onto Linden 2 traffic lights to N 9th St. Turn left onto 9th 1½ blocks to store on right.

SIGN OF THE BEAR NATURAL FOODS 🍃

514 N. Saint Cloud St. ℄ 610-439-8575 ⏰ M-F 9:30-7, Sat 9:30-5

· organic produce · deli · vegetarian friendly · take-out

🍂 **From Rt 22**, take 15th St exit toward Allentown onto Mauch Chunk Rd (right from 22E, left from 22W) to 15th St. Bear right onto 15th ¾ mile to Tilghman St. Turn right onto Tilghman about ¼ mile to Saint Cloud St. Turn left onto Saint Cloud to store.

SYB'S WEST END DELI 🍴

2151 Liberty St. ℄ 610-434-3882 ⏰ M-F 8-5:30, Sat 8-3, Sun 8-1

Lots of deli meat, but vegetarians and vegans can be satisfied, as well. There are always two vegetarian soups, plus salads, Middle Eastern dishes, black bean burritos, meatless quiche, vegetable lasagna, and more.

· vegetarian friendly · tables · wait staff · take-out

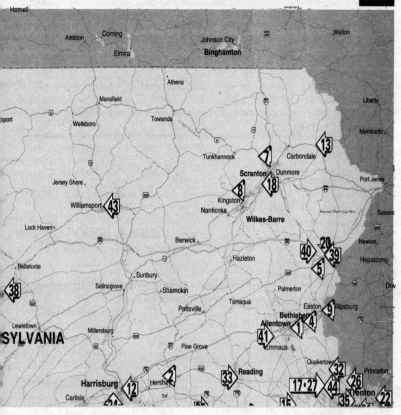

From Rt 22E, take PA 309S towards Quakertown 1 mile to Tilghman St E ramp. Merge onto W Tilghman 2⅔ miles to St Lucas St. Turn right onto St Lucas less than ¼ mile to Liberty. Turn right onto Liberty past 1st block to restaurant (before 22nd St). **From Rt 22W**, take 15th St exit toward Scherersville/Ballietsville onto Mauch Chunk Rd to Stanley St. Turn left onto Stanley 4 blocks to 19th St. Turn right onto 19th 1 mile Tilghman. Turn right onto Tilghman about ¼ mile to Albright Ave. Turn left onto Albright about ¼ mile to Liberty. Turn right onto Liberty past 2nd block to restaurant.

ANNVILLE

ANNVILLE NATURAL FOOD MARKET 🌳
37 W. Main St. ✆ 717-867-2773 ⊕ M-F 9:30-6, Sun 9-4
· organic produce

US 422 runs through Annville (Main St in town). Store is on W Main 1 block west of PA 934 & Valley Lebanon College.

ARDMORE

ALL NATURAL MARKET ✗ 🌳
30 E. Lancaster Ave. ✆ 610-896-7717 ⊕ M-Sat 9-9, Sun 10-6, Kitchen M-F 11-8, Sat 11-5:30, Sun 12-5
The kitchen is almost completely organic and vegan (except for tuna salad).

· organic produce · freshly prepared food · juice bar · deli · vegan · organic focus · tables · self-service · take-out

From I-76W, take exit 342 onto US 30W (Girard Ave, then Lancaster Ave) 5¾ miles to store. From I-76E, take exit 330 onto PA 320S less than 2 miles to Montgomery Ave. Stay straight on Montgomery less than 1½ miles to N Merion Ave. Turn right onto Merion 2 blocks (across tracks) to E Lancaster. Turn left onto Lancaster (US 30E) 2 miles to store. From I-476, take exit 13 right onto E Lancaster about 4 miles to store.

BETHLEHEM

THE GREEN CAFE ✕
22 W. 4th St. ℃ 610-694-0192 ⊘ M, Sun 11-3, Tues-Sat 11-9
Practically everything is vegan or can be made so at this worker-owned restaurant. Monday is soup-and-salad lunch only. Sunday is all-you-can eat brunch. Evening menu is full waitstaff service. If you want alcohol, BYOB.

· vegetarian · vegan friendly · organic focus · co-op · tables · self-service · wait staff

From Rt 22, take PA 378S exit toward Bethlehem about 4 miles to W 4th St. Turn left onto W 4th about ⅓ mile to restaurant (1 block from Lehigh Campus).

BRODHEADSVILLE

EARTHLIGHT NATURAL FOODS 🍎
Rte. 209, Ames Plaza ℃ 610-681-8396 ⊘ M-Sat 9:30-6, Sun 10-2
· organic produce

Rt 209 runs through Brodheadsville (about 14 miles SW of I-80/Stroudsburg & 17 miles NE of I-476 exit 74/Leghighton). Store is on 209 in Ames Plaza.

BRYN MAWR

ARROWROOT NATURAL MARKET ✕🍎
834 W. Lancaster Ave. ℃ 610-527-3393 ⊘ M-F 9-9, Sat 9:30-6, Sun 10-5:30
· organic produce · freshly prepared food · deli · vegetarian friendly · tables · self-service · take-out

From I-476, take exit 13 onto Rt 30E almost 2½ miles to Bryn Mawr. Store is in center of town near movie theater.

CLARKS SUMMIT

EVERYTHING NATURAL ✕🍎   ᵬ
426 S. State St. ℃ 570-586-9684 ⊘ M-Sat 9-8
· organic produce · freshly prepared food · vegetarian friendly · tables · self-service · take-out

From I-476N (PA Tpke Ext), take US 6W/US 11N exit toward Clarks Summit. Turn right at fork in ramp onto 6W/11N about 1¼ miles (past 6 traffic lights) to store on left. From I-81, take exit 194 (PA Tpke) toward Clarks Summit onto I-476N and follow directions above.

DALLAS

HOUSE OF NUTRITION 🍎   ᵬ
RR1 Box 128A ℃ 570-675-1413 ⊘ M-Sat 10-6, Sun 12-5
· organic produce

Dallas is about 11 miles from I-81 (exit 170) on PA 309N. Store is ½ mile past Commonweath Telephone Buildings on left.

EASTON

A tour of the Crayola Factory or a visit to the Easton Museum of PEZ offers some offbeat entertainment while in Easton.

NATURE'S WAY MARKET �

143 Northhampton St. © 610-253-0940 ⊙ M-W, Th 9-6, Tues, F 9-8, Sat 9-5, Sun 12-4

🍎 **From Rt 22E**, take 4th St exit onto PA 248 past traffic light and forced right (becomes PA 611/Larry Holmes Dr) to light at bridge. Turn right onto Northhamptom St ½ block to store on right. **From Rt 22W**, take first exit after Delaware River Toll Bridge (Rt 611). Follow exit and stay right under bridge, then left to stop sign. Turn left onto 611 1 block to light at Northampton. Turn right onto Northampton ½ block to store on right.

ERIE

WHOLE FOODS CO-OP ✕�   ♿

1341 W. 26th St. © 814-456-0282 ⊙ M-Sat 9-8, Sun 12-6

· organic produce · freshly prepared food · juice bar · café · vegetarian friendly · co-op
· counter · tables · self-service · take-out

🍎 **From I-79**, take exit 182 onto US 20E/W 26th St (right from 79N, left from 79S) about 1½ miles (4th traffic light) to store on right at 26th & Brown Ave. **From I-90**, take exit 22B onto I-79N and follow directions above.

HANOVER

ALLEN'S NATURAL FOODS �

398 York St. © 717-637-7230 ⊙ M-F 9-6, Sat 9-4

· organic produce

🍎 Hanover is between Gettysburg and York on Rt 30. **From Rt 30**, take Rt 94 south about 5½ miles to Broadway (PA 116). Turn left onto Broadway to traffic light at York St. Turn right onto York to store at 3rd light (in front of mini-mall).

HARRISBURG

GENESSEE NATURAL FOODS �   ♿

5405 Locust Lane © 717-545-3712 ⊙ M, Tues, Sat 10-6, W-F 10-7

· organic produce · co-op · chain · counter · tables · self-service · wait staff · take-out

🍎 **From I-83**, take exit 48 east on Union Deposit Rd (right from 83N, left from 83S) about 1 mile to Rutherford Rd (look for Turkeyhill and school bus garage). Turn left onto Rutherford less than 1 mile to 1st traffic light at Locust Ln. Turn right onto Locust ½ mile to store on right (past bowling alley).

HONESDALE

Home of the Stourbridge Lion, the first train in the U.S.

NATURE'S GRACE HEALTH FOOD & DELI �   ♿

947 Main St. © 570-253-3469 ⊙ M-Th 10-6, F 10-7, Sat 10-5

· organic produce · freshly prepared food · juice bar · deli · bakery · vegetarian friendly
· take-out

🍎 **From I-81 in Scranton**, take exit 187 toward Carbondale onto Rt 6E 28 miles to Main St in Honesdale. **From Rt 6**, turn south onto Main (right from 6E, left from 6W) to store on left just past 10th St (3rd intersection).

JENKINTOWN

WHOLE FOODS MARKET ✗ 🍏

1575 The Fairway ✆ 215-481-0800 ⊙ M-Sat 8-9, Sun 8-8

· organic produce · freshly prepared food · salad bar · café · deli · bakery · vegetarian friendly · chain · tables · self-service · take-out

🍎 **From I-276** (PA Tpke), take exit 343 toward Willow Grove onto PA 611S about 4½ miles to The Fairway. Turn left onto The Fairway to store on left in Baederwood Shopping Center.

KIMBERTON

About 15 minutes from Valley Forge National Park. Yogurt fans note, this is the home of Seven Stars biodynamic farm.

KIMBERTON WHOLE FOODS ✗ 🍏

2140 Kimberton Rd. ✆ 610-935-1444 ⊙ M-F 8-8, Sat 9-6, Sun 10-6

· organic produce · freshly prepared food · café · vegetarian friendly · tables · self-service · take-out

🍎 **From I-76** (PA Tpke), take exit 327 (King of Prussia) toward Valley Forge onto PA 363 (N Gulph Rd) about 1⅔ miles to PA 23 (Port Kennedy Rd). Turn left onto 23W about 7 miles (through Phoenixville) to PA 113. Turn left onto 113/Kimberton Rd about 1¼ miles and bear right to stay on Kimberton about 1 mile to store on left.

LANCASTER

RHUBARB'S MARKET 🍏

1342 Columbus Ave. ✆ 717-392-0333 ⊙ M-F 9-8, Sat 9-6

🍎 **From Rt 30**, take Rohrerstown Rd/Rt 741 exit south on 741 about 1½ miles to Columbia Ave (Rt 462). Turn left onto Columbia about 1 mile to store on right in Stone Mill Plaza.

RHUBARB'S MARKET 🍏

1521 Lititz Pike ✆ 717-390-3001 ⊙ M-F 9-8, Sat 9-6

🍎 **From Rt 30**, take Lititz Pike (Rt 501) south about ⅓ mile to store on left.

LANSDALE

ARNOLD'S WAY ✗ 🍏

319 W. Main St. ✆ 215-361-0116 ⊙ Daily 10-6, Cafe M-Th, Sun 10-4:30, F-Sat 10-5:30
Vegan raw foods deli.

· organic produce · freshly prepared food · juice bar · deli · vegan · tables · self-service · take-out

🍎 **From I-476**, take exit 31 toward Landsdale onto Rt 63 (left from 476S, right from 476N). Follow 63 (Sumneytown Pike) as turns left onto Forty Foot Rd after about ¼ mile, right onto Welsh Rd after another 1⅔ miles and continue on 63 (becomes Main St) another 2 miles (about 4 miles total) to store.

NORTH PENN HEALTH FOOD CENTER 🍏

1313 N. Penn St. ✆ 215-855-1044 ⊙ M-Sat 9-6

· bakery

🍎 **From I-476**, take exit 31 (Landsdale) onto Sumneytown Pike (left from 476S, right from 476N) 2 miles to Broad St. Turn left onto Broad about 2 miles to Main St. Turn right onto Main 4 blocks to Woodland Dr. Turn right onto Woodland 1 block to Penn St. Turn left onto Penn to store.

LUZERNE

HOUSE OF NUTRITION
140 Main St. © 570-714-0436 ⊙ M, Th 8-8, Tues, W-Sat 10-6, Sun 12-5
· organic produce

From I-81, take exit 170 onto Rt 309N about 4¾ miles to exit 6 toward Luzerne. Turn right at traffic light onto Union St, right at next light onto Buckingham St and left onto Tenner St to stop sign at Main St. Turn left onto Main to store on left.

MALVERN

SU TAO CAFÉ
81 Lancaster Avenue © 610-651-8886 ⊙ M-Sat 11:30-9:30, Sun 12-8:30
Cafe features a vegan lunch buffet, sandwiches, wraps and "gourmet express items." Full service restaurant is mostly Asian, with many mock meat dishes.
· vegan · tables · self-service · wait staff · take-out

From Rt 202, take Rt 29 south about 2½ miles to Lancaster Pike. Turn right onto Lancaser Pike to restaurant in Great Valley Shopping Center.

MARSHALL'S CREEK

NATURALLY RITE NATURAL FOODS MARKET
Rte. 209 © 570-223-1133 ⊙ M, F-Sat 9-5, Tues-Th 9-7, Sun 12-5
In a complex along with a medical center and The Bistro cafe.
· organic produce

From I-80, take exit 309 onto Rt 209N (left from 80E, right from 80W) to store on east side in Healthplex Medical Center.

THE BISTRO AT MARSHALLS CREEK
Rte. 209 © 570-223-1133 ⊙ M, W-Th, Sun 11-9, F-Sat 11-10
· vegetarian friendly · tables · wait staff · take-out

See directions above to Naturally Rite.

MEDIA

SELENE WHOLE FOODS CO-OP
305 W. State St. © 610-566-1137 ⊙ M-Tues 10-6, W-F 10-7, Sat 10-5
· organic produce · freshly prepared food · vegetarian friendly · co-op · take-out

From I-476, take exit 3 toward Media west onto E Baltimore Pike (left from 467N, right from 476S) about 1 mile to Rt 252 (N Providence Rd). Turn right onto 252 to 1st traffic light at State St. Turn left onto State past 4 lights to store on right at Orange St. **From I-95**, take exit 7 onto I-476N almost 3 miles to exit 3 and follow directions above.

MORRISVILLE

BIG BEAR NATURAL FOOD
332 W. Trenton Ave. © 215-736-0553 ⊙ M-F 9-8, Sat 10-7, Sun 12-5
· organic produce · juice bar · deli · vegetarian friendly · take-out

From US 1N, take US 13S exit toward Bristol to Lower Morrisville Rd exit . Follow exit back around onto 13N over 1 mile to W Trenton Ave. Turn right onto Trenton about ½ mile to store a few blocks past Pennsbury Shopping Ctr. **From US 1S**, take N Pennsylvania Ave exit right onto S Pennsylvania about ¾ mile to W Trenton. Turn left onto Trenton about ¼ mile to store (a few blocks before Pennsbury Shopping Ctr).

MT. LEBANON

THE GOOD LIFE MARKET ✖️🍎
1121 Bower Hill Rd. © 412-279-8499 ⊙ M-F 10-7, Sat 10-5 (Cafe closes 1 hour earlier)
*Juice and smoothies only, but store carries vegetarian food to go from Maggie's
Mercantile (Stahlstown, PA), that you can eat at the juice bar or (one) table.*
  · organic produce · juice bar · deli · counter · tables · take-out
🍎 **From I-79,** take exit 54 onto Rt 50 about ½ mile to Bower Hill Rd.
Turn right onto Bower Hill 3 miles to store on right just before St Clair
Hospital. **From Pittsburgh,** take W Liberty Ave south through Dormont
to Bower Hill Rd in Mt Lebanon. Turn right on Bower Hill to store on left
just past hospital.

NEW CUMBERLAND

AVATAR'S NATURAL GROCERY & CAFE ✖️🍎   �ػ
321 Bridge St. © 717-774-7215 ⊙ M-Th 9-7, F-Sat 9-9, Cafe F-Sat 5-9
*The cafe above the store serves a vegetarian dinner on Friday and Saturday
nights, with many vegan options*
  · organic produce · freshly prepared food · juice bar · café · vegetarian · vegan friendly
  · tables · wait staff · take-out
🍎 On the outskirts of Harrisburg. **From I-83,** take exit 40B (New Cumberland)
east on Simson Ferry Rd (curves around and becomes Brandt Ave, then
Reno Ave) to 3rd St. Turn left onto 3rd 1 block to traffic light at Bridge St.
Turn left onto Bridge ½ block to store on right (next to movie theater).

NEW HOLLAND

COMMUNITY NATURAL FOODS STORE 🍎
12 S. Railroad Ave. © 717-355-0921 ⊙ M-W 9-6:30, Th 9-8, F 9-8, Sat 9-4
  · organic produce
🍎 **From US 322 eastbound,** turn right onto Railroad Ave about 3⅓
miles to store. **From 322 westbound,** turn left onto Main St 1⅓ miles to
Railroad. Turn left onto Railroad to store.

NEW HOPE

NEW HOPE NATURAL MARKET 🍎
415B Old York Rd. © 215-862-3441 ⊙ M-F 10-7, Sat 10-6, Sun 11-5
  · organic produce · freshly prepared food · take-out
🍎 At intersection Rt 202 & Rt 179 (Old York Rd) about 1 mile west of
town. **From I-95,** take exit 51 toward New Hope north on Taylorsville
Rd (left from 95N, right from 95S) about 5 miles to River Rd. Turn left
onto River about 4⅔ miles to W Bridge St (aka Rt 179). Turn left onto W
Bridge (becomes Old York) about 1 mile to store at Rt 202 intersection.

NORTH WALES

WHOLE FOODS MARKET ✖️🍎   ⅽ
1210 Bethlehem Pike © 215-646-6300 ⊙ M-Sat 8-9, Sun 8-8
  · organic produce · freshly prepared food · salad bar · deli · bakery · vegetarian friendly
  · chain · tables · self-service · take-out
🍎 **From I-76 (PA Tpke),** take exit 339 (Fort Washington) onto Rt 309N
about 6½ miles to Rt 63. Turn west (left) onto 63 to store on corner in
Gwynedd Crossing Shopping Ctr (across from 309 AMC Movie Theater).

PAOLI

ARROWROOT NATURAL MARKET 🍃
83 E. Lancaster Ave. © 610-640-2720 ⊘ M-Sat 9-6, Sun 10-4
Huge homeopathic pharmacy on site.
  · organic produce
📖 **From I-76**, take exit 328 toward W Chester onto Rt 202S about 3¼ miles to Rt 252. Merge onto 252S (toward Paoli) about 2½ miles to E Lancaster Ave/US 30. Turn right onto Lancaster to store on right (past Goodyear Tire, across from Pier Imports). **From I-476**, take exit 13 (St Davids) onto US 30W about 7 miles (just past Rt 252 intersection) to store on right.

PENNDEL

THE NATURAL FOODS STORE 🍃
131 Hulmeville Rd. © 215-752-7268 ⊘ M-F 10-6:30, Sat 10-5:50, Sun 11-4
  · freshly prepared food · deli · vegetarian friendly · take-out
📖 **From I-95N**, take exit 44 toward Penndel/Levittown onto Rt 1Bus/E Lincoln Hwy. Follow exit left onto S Flowers Mill Rd almost 1 mile to Old Lincoln Hwy/E Maple Ave. Turn left onto E Maple and continue almost 1½ miles until Old Lincoln turns off to left. Veer left onto Old Lincoln to Hulmeville Rd. Veer left onto Hulmeville to store on right. **From Rt 1S** (Roosevelt Blvd), take PA 213 exit toward Maple Ave onto 213S ramp toward Langhorne. Turn west (left) off ramp onto E Maple and follow directions above. **From Rt 1N**, take Langhorne exits and follow right onto Park Ave and right onto Highland Ave to Old Lincoln Hwy. Turn right onto Old Lincoln about 1⅓ miles to Hulmeville. Turn right onto Hulmeville to store on left.

PHILADELPHIA

BASIC FOUR VEGETARIAN SNACK ✕
136 Arch St. © 215-440-0991 ⊘ M-Sat 10:30-5
Vegetarian sandwiches and light fare at a stand in the Reading Terminal Market.
  · vegetarian · vegan friendly · tables · self-service · take-out
📖 At 12th St & Arch in the Reading Terminal Market.

CHARLES PLAZA ✕   ♿
234 N. 10th St. © 215-829-4383 ⊘ M-Th 11:30-10, F 11:30-12, Sat 3-12, Sun 3-10:30
This "natural health" Chinese restaurant has an extensive vegetarian menu, uses mostly organic vegetables, brown rice, filtered water, no msg, no beef or pork, but does serve chicken and seafood.
  · vegetarian friendly · vegan friendly · organic focus · tables · wait staff · take-out
📖 In Philadelphia's Chinatown on corner Vine & N 10th St.

CHERRY STREET CHINESE RESTAURANT ✕
1010 Cherry St. © 215-922-8957 ⊘ M-Sat 11-11, Sun 12-11
All vegetarian Chinese.
  · vegetarian · vegan friendly · tables · wait staff · take-out
📖 In Philadelphia's Chinatown on Cherry St at N 10th St.

ESSENE MARKET & CAFE ✕ 🍃
719 S. 4th St. © 215-922-1146 ⊘ M-Tues, Th, Sat 9-8, W, F 9-9
Cafe fare is vegan, with no refined sweeteners and organic when possible. RTW: A delicious vegetarian restaurant in a terrific natural food store, with terrific lunches.

· organic produce · freshly prepared food · café · deli · bakery · vegan · organic focus
· counter · tables · self-service · take-out

⭐ **From I-95N**, take exit 16 (Columbus Blvd/Washington Ave) left onto Columbus to 1st traffic light at Washington Ave. Turn left onto Washington to 3rd light at 3rd St. Turn right onto 3rd to Monroe St. Turn left onto Monroe 1 block to store at 4th & Monroe. **From I-95S**, take exit 16 right onto Columbus to 1st light at Christian St. Turn right onto Christian 3 blocks to 3rd St and follow directions above.

GIANNA'S GRILLE ✕
507 S. 6th St. ℂ 215- 829-4448 ☺ Tues-Th 12-8, F-Sat 12-9
Caters to both steak eaters and vegans. For the latter, the soy cheese, vegetarian "meats," and 100% vegan desserts are all homemade. Fare includes sandwiches, salads, pizza, and vegan lasagna.

· vegetarian friendly · vegan friendly · tables · self-service · take-out

🍎 **From I-676**, take Independence Mall/6th St exit south on 6th to store between Lombard & South St.

GOVINDA'S CAFE ✕
1408 South St. ℂ 215-985-9303 ☺ M-Th 11-11, F-Sat 11-12, Sun 11-9
Daytime and Monday to Wednesday evenings is vegetarian take-out and tables for eating in. After 5 pm Thursday to Sunday is all-you-can-eat dinner buffet, as well as table service, with an eclectic menu of vegetarian "continental" food.

· vegetarian · vegan friendly · tables · self-service · take-out

⭐ **From I-95**, take exit 20 to Washington Ave. Turn west onto Washington about 1 mile to Broad St. Turn right onto Broad about ½ mile to South St. Restaurant is to the left but street goes one-way in the opposite direction. (To access by car continue 1 block to Lombard St, turn left onto Lombard, left onto 15th St and left onto South to restaurant.) **From I-76** take exit 346A onto South St across the water (right from 76W, left from 76E) about 1¼ miles to restaurant between 15th & Broad.

HARMONY VEGETARIAN RESTAURANT ✕
135 N. 9th St. ℂ 215-627-4520 ☺ M-Th, Sun 11:30-10:30, F-Sat 11:30-11:30
Chinese vegetarian. RTW: Carefully prepared and all the veggies beautifully cut

· vegetarian · vegan friendly · tables · wait staff · take-out

🍎 In Philadelphia's Chinatown on 9th St at Cherry St.

KINGDOM OF VEGETARIANS RESTAURANT ✕
129 N. 11th St. ℂ 215-413-2290 ☺ Daily 11-11
Chinese vegetarian.

· vegetarian · vegan friendly · tables · wait staff · take-out

🍎 In Philadelphia's Chinatown on 11th St at Cherry St.

SAMOSA INDIAN VEGETARIAN ✕
1214 Walnut St. ℂ 215-545-7776 ☺ Lunch M-F 11-3, Sat-Sun 12-3, Dinner Daily 5:30-9:30
RTW: An inexpensive, big vegetarian Indian buffet and rice pudding for dessert. Note: Alcohol is not permitted in the restaurant.

· vegetarian · vegan friendly · tables · self-service

🍎 Downtown on south side of Walnut St between 12th & 13th St.

SINGAPORE KOSHER VEGETARIAN RESTAURANT ✕
1006 Race St. ℂ 215-922-3288 ☺ Daily 11-11
Southeast Asian all vegan, certified kosher food. Brown rice available. RTW

The owner has a very strong vision. Lots of soy and wheat products shaped and flavored to taste like various meats, served with various nice veggies.

· vegan · kosher · tables · wait staff · take-out

In Philadelphia's Chinatown on Race St at N 10th St.

WEAVER'S WAY CO-OP
559 Carpenter Lane © 215-843-2350 ⊘ M-Th 10-8, F 9-8, Sat-Sun 9-6
In addition to food, you can send or receive a fax, get film developed, buy stamps, or pick up pet supplies at the annex two doors away.

· organic produce · freshly prepared food · deli · vegetarian friendly · co-op · take-out

From I-76, take exit 340A toward Lincoln Dr onto City Ave to Lincoln. Turn left onto Lincoln about 3 miles to Green St. Turn left onto Green 2 blocks to Carpenter Ln. Turn right onto Carpenter to store on right.

WHITE DOG CAFE
3420 Sansom St. © 215-386-9224 ⊘ M-Th 11:30am-midnight, F 11:30am-1am, Sat 11am-1am, Sun 11am-midnight
The menu is heavily weighted towards non-vegetarians, but there are several vegetarian choices at this politically active cafe. A Certified Green Restaurant, buying food from local sustainable farmers. Live music and community events.

· vegetarian friendly · alcohol · tables · wait staff

From I-95N or I-76, take 76W (Schuylkill Expwy) to exit 346A (South St). Turn left onto South to 1st right onto 33rd St. Take 33rd to 3rd left onto Market St, then left onto 34th St 1½ blocks to Sansom St (sign says Sansom Row). Turn right onto Sansom ½ block to restaurant. **From I-95S or I-676**, take 676W to 76E (Schuylkill Expwy) toward airport. Take exit 345 (30th St Station) around station to 2nd light at Market. Turn right onto Market 4 blocks to 34th. Turn left onto 34th 1½ blocks to Sansom St (sign says Sansom Row). Turn right onto Sansom ½ block to restaurant.

WHOLE FOODS MARKET   ⅌
2001 Pennsylvania Ave. © 215-557-0015 ⊘ Daily 8-10

· organic produce · freshly prepared food · salad bar · café · deli · bakery · vegetarian friendly · chain · tables · self-service · take-out

From I-95, take I-676W to Museum exit (exit past Broad St). Take ramp toward Ben Franklin Pkwy/Art Museum. Make 1st left onto N 22nd St, cross over Ben Franklin Pkwy and turn right onto Hamilton St (traffic light with Best Western on far corner). At 1st stop sign turn right onto N 21st St ½ block to Pennsylvania Ave. Turn left onto Pennsylvania to store parking on left. **From I-76**, take exit 344 onto Vine St Expwy/I-676E/US 30E. Take 676E to 23rd St exit toward Ben Franklin Pkwy and follow directions above from Ben Franklin Pkwy.

WHOLE FOODS MARKET   ⅌
929 South St. © 215-733-9788 ⊘ Daily 8-10

· organic produce · freshly prepared food · juice bar · salad bar · café · deli · bakery · vegetarian friendly · chain · counter · tables · self-service · take-out

From I-95, take exit 20 (Washington Ave). Turn west onto Washington about ¾ mile to 11th St. Turn right onto 11th less than ½ mile to South St. Turn right onto South about 4 blocks to store at 9th St. **From I-76**, take exit 349 onto PA 611N/Broad St (from 76E circle around and left across hwy, from 76W exit onto Pollack St and turn right) about 2 miles to South St. Turn right onto South less than ½ mile to store at 9th.

PITTSBURGH

SREE'S LUNCH ✕
Tech St. © 800-390-SREE ☺ M-F 11-2
Indian vegan and chicken lunches from a street trailer at Carnegie Mellon U.
· vegan friendly · take-out

🍴 **From I-376W or US 30E**, take exit 5 ramp toward Squirrel Hill/Homestead to Forward Ave. Turn left onto Forward about ¼ mile to Murray Ave. Make slight left onto Murray about ½ mile to Forbes Ave. Turn left onto Forbes about 1 mile to Margaret Morrison St. Turn left onto Margaret Morrison (Carnegie Mellon campus) about ¼ mile to Tech Ave. Turn left onto Tech to red takeout trailer.

JENS JUICE JOINT & CAFE ✕
733 Copeland St. © 412-683-7374 ☺ M-Sat 10-6:30, Sun 10-5
Mostly vegetarian (but also poultry and tuna) sandwiches, salads and wraps.
· juice bar · salad bar · café · vegetarian friendly · tables · self-service · take-out

🍴 **From I-376W**, take exit 5 ramp toward Squirrel Hill/Homestead to Forward Ave. Turn left onto Forward about ¼ mile to Murray Ave. Make slight left onto Murray 1 mile to Wilkins Ave. Turn left onto Wilkins ¾ mile to 5th Ave. Make sharp right onto 5th 2 blocks to Aiken Ave. Turn left onto Aiken ¼ mile to Elmer. Turn right onto Elmer 2 blocks to Copeland St. Turn right onto Copeland to restaurant. **From US 30E**, take exit 2A toward Oakland onto Forbes Ave 1½ miles to Moorewood Ave. Turn left onto Moorewood to 1st right onto 5th. Take 5th almost ½ mile to Aiken and follow directions above.

SARI'S ✕
2109 Murray Ave. © 412-421-7208 ☺ M-Th 11-8, F 11-2, Sat 1 hour after sundown-midnight, Sun 11-8
Kosher dairy fare, which includes fish (in this case mostly fried).
· vegetarian friendly · kosher · tables · wait staff

🍴 **From I-376W or US 30E**, take exit 5 ramp toward Squirrel Hill/Homestead to Forward Ave. Turn left onto Forward about ¼ mile to Murray Ave. Make slight left onto Murray about ¼ mile to restaurant at about Hobart St.

SREE'S VEGGIE CAFE ✕
2107 Murray Ave. © 800-390-SREE ☺ M-F 5-9
One-price, daily-changing, boxed vegan Indian dinner to go.
· vegan · take-out

🍴 **From I-376W or US 30E**, take exit 5 ramp toward Squirrel Hill/Homestead to Forward Ave. Turn left onto Forward about ¼ mile to Murray Ave. Make slight left onto Murray about ¼ mile to restaurant at about Hobart St.

THE EAST END FOOD CO-OP ✕
7516 Meade St. © 412-242-3598 ☺ Daily 9-9
· freshly prepared food · juice bar · salad bar · café · deli · vegetarian · co-op · tables · self-service · take-out

🍴 **From I-376**, take exit 8B onto PA 8N about 2¼ miles to Braddock Ave. Turn right onto Braddock 1 block to Meade St. Turn left onto Meade to store in "The Factory" (on lower level).

WHOLE FOODS MARKET ✕
5880 Centre Ave. © 412-441-7960 ☺ Daily 8-10

· organic produce · freshly prepared food · salad bar · café · deli · bakery · vegetarian friendly · chain · counter · tables · self-service · take-out

🍎 **From downtown Pittsburgh**, take PA 380E (Baum Blvd) about ¾ mile to Liberty Ave. Turn right onto Liberty 1 block to Centre Ave. Turn left onto Centre about ½ mile to store. **From I-376**, take exit 8B onto PA 8N about 3¾ miles to Penn Ave (PA 380). Stay straight onto Penn almost 1 mile to S Highland Mall. Turn left onto S Highland and right onto 380 (Penn Cir S, becomes Centre) about ¼ mile to store.

ZENITH TEA ROOM ✕ &

86 S. 26th St. ℂ 412-481-4833 ☺ Th-Sat 11:30-9, Sun 11:30-3

Vegetarian and vegan soups, salads, sandwiches, and hot entrees on the weekly menu. In a large industrial space along with an antique store and art gallery.

· vegetarian · vegan friendly · tables · wait staff · take-out

🍎 In Pittsburgh's Southside. **From I-376W**, take exit 3A and cross bridge on Hot Metal St to E Carson St. Turn right onto E Carson about ¼ mile to 26th St. Turn left onto 26th to restaurant. **From downtown**, take Birmingham Bridge across and turn left onto E Carson over ½ mile to 26th. Turn right onto 26th to restaurant.

PLUMSTEADVILLE

PLUMSTEADVILLE NATURAL FOODS 🍖

Rte. 611 ℂ 215-766-8666 ☺ M-F 9-6:30, Sat 9:30-5

· organic produce

🍎 **From I-276** (PA Tpke), take exit 343 and follow PA 611 ramp toward Doylestown/Willow Grove Naval Air station onto 611N about 13 miles to store in Plumstead Shopping Center.

READING

NATURE'S GARDEN NATURAL FOODS 🍖

4290 Perkiomen Ave. ℂ 610-779-3000 ☺ M-F 9-8, Sat 10-7, Sun 11-5

No cooking on the premises, but they get a weekly delivery (on Thursday) of fresh prepared vegetarian food to go.

· organic produce

🍎 **From US 422E**, take exit toward Mt Penn left onto E Neversink Rd over ½ mile to Perkiomen Ave. Turn right onto Perkiomen (422Bus E) ⅓ mile to store in Reading Mall. **From US 422W**, take 422Bus exit toward Mt Penn. Follow 422Bus W and make 1st left onto 422Bus E to store.

SHARPSBURG

SREE'S FOODS ✕

606 Main St. ℂ 412-781-4765 ☺ F-Sat 5:30pm-8:30pm

Sree's has three venues in the Pittsburgh area. Although there is chicken at this site, the rest of the (dinner only) thali menu that is brought family-style to the table, is completely vegan. Food is based on hyderabadi principles, blending traditional South Indian vegetarian and court cooking.

· vegan friendly · tables · wait staff

🍎 **From Rt 28N**, take exit 5A straight through 4-way intersection onto Main St to restaurant on left (between Tappin' Bar and Allegheny Health Products, across from high-rise). **From Rt 28S**, take exit 6 onto Highland Park Bridge to Sharpsburg exit (before crossing). Turn right off ramp onto Main past 3 traffic lights (about 1¼ miles) to restaurant on right.

SOUTHAMPTON

BLUE SAGE VEGETARIAN GRILL ✗ &

772 Second Street Pike ℂ 215-942-8888 ☉ Lunch Tues-F 11:30-3, Sat 11:30-4, Dinner Tues-Th 4:30-9, F-Sat 4:30-10

Intriguing vegetarian and vegan soups, appetizers, salads, pressed sandwiches, and hot entrees that you probably haven't encountered elsewhere. Even the quesadillas, falafel and other seemingly familiar items have an interesting twist. If you want alcohol, BYOB.

· vegetarian · vegan friendly · organic focus · tables · wait staff · take-out

🍎 **From I-276** (PA Tpke), take exit 351 and follow onto US 1S/Lincoln Hwy to E Street Rd/PA 132N exit. Take E Street (132N) about 5 miles (through Feasterville to Southampton) to 2nd St Pike (PA 232, Walgreens on left). Turn right onto 2nd St Pike less than ¼ mile to restaurant on left in 2-store shopping center (next to Bucks County Beauty Supply). **From Rt 202**, take Bristol Rd south about 10 miles to 2nd St Pike. Turn right onto 2nd St Pike about 1 mile to restaurant on right (in shopping center).

SPRING GROVE

Bikers can enjoy the PA rail trail.

SONNEWALD NATURAL FOODS 🍃 &

4796 Lehman Rd. ℂ 717-225-3825 ☉ Tues-Th 10-6, F 10-9, Sat 8-5

Most of the produce is grown on their 60-acre organic farm and in their two greenhouses. On-site flour mill and refrigerated bulk food room.

· organic produce

🍎 **From Rt 30** (west of York), go south on Rt 616, 2½ miles to traffic light in New Salem. Turn right onto New Salem Rd (becomes Stoverstown Rd) 2⅓ miles to Lehman Rd (church on corner). Turn right onto Lehman to store in 1st building on left.

STAHLSTOWN

MAGGIE'S MERCANTILE ✗ 🍃 &

RD 1 Box 162-C Rt 711 ℂ 724-593-5056 ☉ W 10-6, Th-Sat 10-8, Sun 10-6

Totally vegan menu using primarily organic ingredients. Portion of profits goes to an animal sanctuary.

· organic produce · freshly prepared food · juice bar · café · deli · bakery · vegan
· organic focus · tables · self-service · take-out

🍎 **From I-76** (PA Tpke), take exit 91 (Donegal) and follow onto Rt 31E to Rt 711N. Turn left onto 711N 2½ miles to store on right.

STATE COLLEGE

THE GRANARY 🍃 &

2766 W. College Ave. ℂ 814-228-4844 ☉ M-Sat 10-6

🍎 **From I-80**, take exit 161 (Bellefont) onto Rt 26S (left from 80W, right from 80E) about 17 miles to State College where Rt 26 is W College Ave. (Store is about 3 miles past intersection with Rt 322.)

STROUDSBURG

EARTHLIGHT NATURAL FOODS 🍃

829 Ann St. ℂ 570-424-6760 ☉ M-Sat 9:30-6, Sun 12-4

· organic produce

🍎 **From I-80W**, take exit 307 right onto PA 191N to 1st left (Ann St.) Turn left onto Ann ⅓ mile to store. **From I-80E**, take exit 307 left onto Park Ave ¼ mile to Ann. Turn left onto Ann about 1 block to store.

EVERYBODY'S CAFE ✕

905 Main St. ℰ 570-424-0896 ⊕ M-Th, Sun 11-9:30, F-Sat 11-10 (closes ½ hour earlier in winter)

The enormous dinner menu includes meat, fish, poultry, and about 30 vegetarian entrees (10 of them vegan). Plus, soups, 15 salads, 50-60 tapas items, and specials. At lunch the fare is more "burgers," including non-meat versions, as well as mock meatloaf. Situated in a renovated mansion with 5 dining rooms.

· vegetarian friendly · vegan friendly · alcohol · tables · wait staff

🍎 **From I-80W**, take exit 307 right onto PA 191N. Make 2nd left onto US 209Bus (W Main St) less than ½ mile to restaurant. **From I-80E**, take exit 305 and follow ramp toward Rt 209Bus right onto W Main less than 1 mile to restaurant.

TANNERSVILLE

EARTHLIGHT NATURAL FOODS 🥬

1632 Fountain Springs E. ℰ 570-619-6592 ⊕ M-Sat 10-6

This branch of Earthlight does not carry produce.

🍎 **From I-80W**, take exit 299 toward Tannersville onto Rt 715 about ¼ mile to Rt 611. Turn right (south) onto 611 about 2 miles to store on left (across hwy from Friendly's). **From I-80E**, take exit 299 right onto 715 more than ½ mile, merge south onto 611 and follow directions above.

TREXLERTOWN

HEALTHY ALTERNATIVES 🥬

7150 Hamilton Blvd. ℰ 610-366-9866 ⊕ M-W 9:30-6, Th 9:30-7, F 9:30-8, Sat 10-5

The take-out offerings include soups, sandwiches, salads, and a steam table with hot entrees, all prepared with organic ingredients.

· organic produce · freshly prepared food · vegetarian friendly · organic focus · take-out

🍎 **From I-78**, take exit 49A toward Trexlertown onto PA 100S about 2½ miles to US 222 (Hamilton Blvd). Turn left onto Hamilton ½ mile to store. (**From US 222**, store is on hwy.)

WAYNE

WHOLE FOODS MARKET ✕🥬

821 Lancaster Ave. ℰ 610-688-9400 ⊕ M-Sat 8-9, Sun 9-9

· organic produce · freshly prepared food · salad bar · café · deli · bakery · vegetarian friendly · chain · tables · self-service · take-out

🍎 **From I-476**, take exit 13 toward St Davids left off ramp onto Rt 30W (E Lancaster Ave) about 2½ miles (through town) to traffic light at Berkley Rd. Turn right onto Berkley to store in Devon Square. **From Rt 202**, take Devon exit south on Valley Forge Rd (left past light and left at fork from 202S, right at light and left at fork from 202N) about 1½ miles to Conestoga Rd. Turn left onto Conestoga ½ mile (to bend) and bear right onto Old Conestoga Rd, under overpass and immediately right into store lot.

Please tell these businesses that you found them in Healthy Highways.

WILLIAMSPORT

FRESHLIFE WHOLE FOOD MARKET & CAFE ✕ ⬥ &
2300 E. 3rd St. © 570-322-8280 ⊙ M-F 9-8, Sat 9-5

· organic produce · freshly prepared food · café · deli · bakery · vegetarian friendly
· counter · tables · self-service · take-out

🍎 Get to I-180/Williamsport via I-80, Rt 15 or Rt 220, depending on point of departure. **From I-180**, take exit 23B and merge onto E 3rd St about ¼ mile to store on left. **From 220N/I-180E**, take exit 25 (Faxon) onto Northway Rd to E 3rd. Turn right onto E 3rd less than 1 mile to store on right.

WILLOW GROVE

HORIZONS CAFE ✕ &
101 E. Moreland Rd. © 215-657-2100 ⊙ Lunch Th-F 12-2:30, Dinner Tues-Th 4:30-9, F-Sat 4:30-10

South American/Caribbean-inspired fine meatless dining. Very vegan friendly (including all desserts). L&JB: We were wowed by the Philly sandwich made with sauteed onions and local, home-made seitan.

· vegetarian · vegan friendly · organic focus · tables · wait staff

🍎 **From I-276 (PA Tpke)**, take exit 343 toward Willow Grove onto Rt 611S almost 2 miles to restaurant at intersection 611 & Rt 63 in Moreland Plaza.

NATURE'S HARVEST ⬥ &
101 E. Moreland Rd. © 215-659-7705 ⊙ M-10-8, Tues-Sat 10-9, Sun 11-6

· organic produce

🍎 **From I-276 (PA Tpke)**, take exit 343 toward Willow Grove onto Rt 611S almost 2 miles to store at intersection 611 & Rt 63 in Moreland Plaza.

WYNNEWOOD

WHOLE FOODS MARKET ⬥ &
339 E. Lancaster Ave. © 610-896-3737 ⊙ M-Sat 8-9, Sun 8-8

A smaller Whole Foods than most. Lots of food demo tastings.

· organic produce · freshly prepared food · salad bar · deli · bakery · vegetarian friendly
· chain · take-out

🍎 **From I-76**, take exit 339 (City Line Ave) onto Rt 1S (right from 76E, left from 76W) about 2¾ miles to Rt 30/E Lancaster Ave. Turn right onto Lancaster less than 2 miles to Wynnewood Rd (Amoco Gas on right). At next traffic light turn right into store parking lot.

YORK

ALLEN'S NATURAL FOODS ⬥
350 S. Richland Ave. © 717-845-8085 ⊙ M-F 9-6, Sat 9-4

· organic produce

🍎 **From US 30**, take PA 74 (Carlisle Rd) toward W York (merge straight from 30E, left off ramp from 30W) over 1 mile to Linden Ave. Turn right onto Linden 1 block to Richland Ave. Turn left onto Richland ½ mile to store. **From I-83S**, merge onto 30W via exit 22 and follow directions above. **From I-83N**, take exit 15 toward S George St onto 83Bus N 2 miles to Country Club Rd. Turn left onto Country Club 1 mile to Richland. Turn right onto Richland ¾ mile to store.

RHODE ISLAND

1	East Greenwich
2	Narragansett
3	Newport
4	Pawtucket
5	Providence
6	Smithfield
7	Wakefield
8	Warwick
9	Westerly

EAST GREENWICH

BACK TO BASICS NATURAL FOOD GROCERY
500 Main St. ✆ 401-885-2679 ⏰ M-F 9-7, Sat 9-6, Sun 12-5

· organic produce

🏠 From I-95S, take exit 9 onto Rt 4S less than ½ mile to exit 8 (Rt 401). Follow Division St ramp onto 401E about 2½ miles to Main St. Turn left onto Main to store on right. From I-95N, take exit 8A (Rt 2S) onto 401E and follow directions from 401E above.

NARRAGANSETT

FOOD FOR THOUGHT
140 Point Judith Rd. #32 ✆ 401-789-2445 ⏰ M-Th, Sat 10-6, F 10-7, Sun 12-5

🏠 At the SE tip of RI. From Rt 1, take Rt 108S (toward Point Judith) over ½ mile to store on left in Mariner Square Mall (across from Stop & Shop).

NEWPORT

HARVEST NATURAL FOODS 🍎
1 Casino Terrace ✆ 401-846-8137 ⏲ M-Sat 9-7, Sun 11-5

· organic produce

🍎 Take Rt 138 into Newport. Turn south onto Rt 138S/238S (bends left and becomes Memorial Blvd) about 1½ miles to Bellevue Ave. Turn right onto Bellevue to store on left in Bellevue Shopping Center (just past Tennis Hall of Fame).

PAWTUCKET

GARDEN GRILLE ✗
727 East Ave. ✆ 401-726-2826 ⏲ M-Sat 10-10, Sun 9-9

Vegetarian salads, sandwiches, burgers, wraps, homemade pizza, quesadillas, and a variety of hot entrees featuring vegetables and soyfoods. Many vegan options, including all soups and desserts. If you want alcohol, BYOB.

· vegetarian · vegan friendly · organic focus · tables · wait staff

🍎 From I-95N, take exit 25 (N Main St) right off ramp to traffic light at N Main (US 1N). Turn left onto N Main about ½ mile to Lafayette St. Turn right onto Lafayette about 3 blocks to end. Restaurant is on left in Blackstone Plaza. From I-95S, take exit 27 (downtown Pawtucket) toward US 1. Turn left at light onto George St about ⅓ mile to light at East Ave. Bear left onto East Ave less than 1 mile to restaurant on right in Blackstone Plaza.

PROVIDENCE

WHOLE FOODS MARKET ✗🍎   ♿
601 N. Main St. ✆ 401-621-5990 ⏲ Daily 8-9

· organic produce · freshly prepared food · salad bar · café · deli · bakery · vegetarian friendly · chain · tables · self-service · take-out

🍎 From I-195, take exit 24 onto Branch Ave (left from 195S, right from 195N) to 1st traffic light at N Main St. Bear right onto N Main about 3 blocks to store on left.

WHOLE FOODS MARKET 🍎   ♿
261 Waterman St. ✆ 401-272-1690 ⏲ Daily 8-9

· organic produce · freshly prepared food · salad bar · deli · bakery · vegetarian friendly · chain · take-out

🍎 From I-195, take exit 3 and turn right (north) onto Gano St to 3rd traffic light at Waterman St. Turn right onto Waterman 3 blocks to store on right. From I-95N, take exit 20 onto I-195E and follow directions above. From I-95S, take exit 22C-B-A toward Downtown and make two lefts off ramp onto US 6E/Memorial Dr about ¼ mile to Washington Pl. Turn left onto Washington (becomes Waterman) about 1¼ miles to store on right.

SMITHFIELD

Birdlovers will enjoy the nearby Audobon Society, with walking trails and lectures.

FOODWORKS 🍎
9 Cedar Swamp Rd. ✆ 401-232-2410 ⏲ M-F 9-7, Sat 10-6

· organic produce

🍎 From I-295, take exit 7B toward Greenville onto RI 44W/Putnam Pike about 1¼ miles to Cedar Swamp Rd (3rd traffic light). Turn right onto Cedar Swamp to store on right in Apple Valley Plaza.

WAKEFIELD

ALTERNATIVE FOOD COOPERATIVE 🍎
357 Main St. © 401-789-2240 ⊙ M-F 8-8, Sat-Sun 9-6
· organic produce · freshly prepared food · vegetarian · co-op · take-out

🍎 **From Rt 1S**, take 1st Wakefield exit right onto Old Tower Hill Rd (becomes Main St) about 1 mile (past 3 trafffic lights, then ⅓ mile) to store on right in brick building across from Kenyon Ave. **From Rt 1N** (Post Rd), take Pond St exit left off ramp onto Pond about ¾ mile to Main. Turn right onto Main ⅓ mile to store on left.

WARWICK

THE VILLAGE NATURAL 🍎
18 Post Rd. © 401-941-8028 ⊙ M-Sat 10-6, Sun 12-5

🍎 **From I-95**, take exit 14 toward Warwick onto Rt 37E about ⅔ mile to exit 5B on left. Merge onto Post Rd about 3⅓ miles to end at Narragansett Pkwy. Turn left onto Narragansett and left onto Post Rd to store..

WESTERLY

ALLEN'S HEALTH FOOD 🍎
62 Franklin St. © 401-596-5569 ⊙ M-Th 9:30-5:30, F 9:30-6, Sat 9:30-5

🍎 **From I-95N** (CT), take exit 92 onto Rt 2S 1¼ miles to Rt 78. Merge onto 78E 4½ miles to Rt 1S. Turn right onto 1S (Franklin St) about ½ mile to store on right in Ocean Plaza. **From I-95S**, take exit 1 onto Rt 3S about 4 miles to 78E. Merge onto 78E 2½ miles to 1S and follow directions above.

Goldbeck's "EAT IT OR NOT"
FASCINATING & FAR-OUT FACTS ABOUT FOOD

DONUTS WERE INVENTED BY A TEENAGER

In 1847, Hanson Gregory of Rockport, Maine, came up with the donut as a way of improving pancakes that were soggy in the middle. He removed the center and asked his mother to cook them.

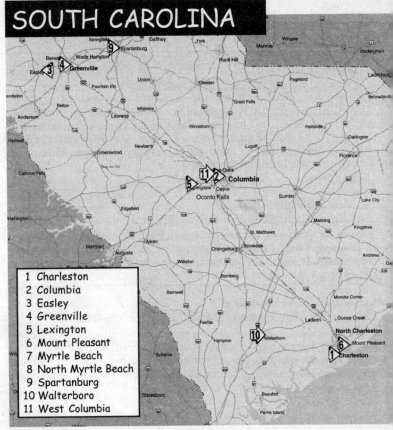

SOUTH CAROLINA

1 Charleston
2 Columbia
3 Easley
4 Greenville
5 Lexington
6 Mount Pleasant
7 Myrtle Beach
8 North Myrtle Beach
9 Spartanburg
10 Walterboro
11 West Columbia

CHARLESTON

BOOKS, HERBS & SPICES
1409 Ste. B Folly Rd. ℂ 843-762-3025 ⊙M-F 10-6, Sat 9:30-6

🛏 Take US 17 onto SC 30W toward James Island/Folly Beach about 2½ miles to exit 3 (SC 171/Folly Rd). Merge onto Folly Rd 2½ miles to store.

EARTH FARE
74 Folly Rd. Blvd. ℂ 843-769-4800 ⊙M-Sat 8-10, Sun 9-9
· organic produce · freshly prepared food · juice bar · salad bar · café · deli · bakery · vegetarian friendly · chain · tables · self-service · wait staff take-out

🛏 **From Rt 30**, take exit 1 west on Rt 61 about 1 mile to Folly Rd Blvd. Turn left onto Folly about ½ mile to store in S Windermere Shopping Ctr.

RASPBERRY'S NATURAL FOOD STORE
1331 Ashley River Rd. ℂ 843-556-0076 ⊙M-F 9:30-6:30, Sat 9:30-5:30, Sun 1-6
Vegetarian takeout deli with vegans in mind.
· organic produce · freshly prepared food · deli · bakery · vegetarian · vegan friendly · take-out

🛏 **From I-26**, take exit 216A onto SC 7S about 2 miles to SC 171S. Merge onto 171S about 1½ miles (curves right to Hwy 61/Ashley River Rd) to store on right.

SOUL VEGETARIAN SOUTH
3225-A Rivers Ave. N. ℂ 843-744-1155 ⊙M-Th 11-8, F-Sat 11-9:30, Sun 9-1, 4-8

Healthy, vegan, southern-style soul food. Soups, sandwiches, fresh vegetables, hot entrees, soy shakes, desserts. Homemade vegan soy cheese and "ice-kream."

· vegan · chain · tables · wait staff · take-out

🍎 From I-26, take exit 215 toward US 78/52 east on Dorchester Rd (left from 26E, right from 26W) about ¾ mile to Rivers Ave (US 72/52). Turn right onto Rivers ½ mile to restaurant.

COLUMBIA———————————————

Take in the Riverbanks Zoo and Botanical Gardens, the Congaree National Swamp, or see what's happening at the University of SC.

BLUE CACTUS CAFE ✗

2002 Greene St. ℂ 803-929-0782 ☺ Tues-F 11-3, 5-9, Sat 12-9

The mainstay is Korean, but there are also burritos, variously spiced "beans & rice," sandwiches, and other surprises. Although there's plenty of meat, a dancing carrot marks the many vegan possibilities.

· vegetarian friendly · vegan friendly · tables · wait staff

🍎 2 blocks from USC on Greene St near Harden St. Hidden on 1st floor of apartment building across from Claussen's Inn.

EARTH FARE ✗ 🍃   ♿

3312 B Devine St. ℂ 803-799-0048 ☺ M-Sat 8-9, Sun 9-8

· organic produce · freshly prepared food · juice bar · salad bar · café · deli · bakery
· vegetarian friendly · chain · tables · self-service · take-out

🍎 From I-77, take exit 10 onto SC 760W/Fort Jackson Blvd (left from 77N, right from 77S) 1 mile to end at Devine St (US 76). Turn right onto Devine about 2 blocks to store on left.

ROSEWOOD MARKET & DELI ✗ 🍃   ♿

2803 Rosewood Dr. ℂ 803-765-1083 ☺ M-Sat 9-9, Sun 10-6

Deli menu features vegetarian, vegan and macrobiotic selections.

· organic produce · freshly prepared food · café · deli · vegetarian friendly · vegan friendly
· counter · tables · self-service · take-out

🍎 From I-77N, take exit 5 onto SC 48W ramp toward Columbia. Take SC 48N/Bluff Rd about 2¾ miles to Rosewood Dr. Turn right onto Rosewood almost 1½ miles to store on left at S Maple St. From I-26W, take exit 116 onto I-77N about 4¼ miles to exit 5 and follow directions above. From I-26E, merge onto I-126S about 3 miles then straight onto Elmwood Ave about ½ mile to Assembly St (US 76). Turn right onto Assembly about 2 miles (through downtown, past Coliseum and several railroad tracks) to Rosewood Dr. Turn left onto Rosewood 1 mile to store on left corner Rosewood & S Maple.

THE BASIL POT ✗   🍴♿

928 Main St. ℂ 803-799-0928 ☺ M-F 8-2:30, 6-9, Sat 9-2:30, 5:30-8:30, Sun 9-2:30

"Mostly vegetarian," plenty of vegan and a smattering of chicken and fish.

· vegetarian friendly · vegan friendly · alcohol · tables · wait staff · take-out

🍎 From I-26W, take exit 115 toward Cayce/Columbia. Merge right onto 176W/21N about 5¾ miles (across river, becomes S Blossom St) to Assembly St. Turn left onto Assembly ¼ mile to College St. Turn right onto College 1 block to Main St. Turn left onto Main to restaurant (across from Nickelodeon theater & 1 block south of Capitol Bldg). From I-26E, merge onto I-126S/76E about 3⅓ miles to Huger St exit. Merge onto 176E/21S about ¾ miles to Gervais St. Turn left onto Gervais about ½ mile to Assembly. Turn right onto Assembly 2 blocks to Pendleton St. Turn left onto Pendleton 1 block to Main. Turn right onto Main 1 block to restaurant.

EASLEY

NATURE'S HEALTH SHOP 🍎
109 W. Main St. © 864-855-3773 ⏰ M-F 10-6, Sat 10-5

🍎 **From I-85**, take exit 40 toward Easley onto SC 153N almost 5½ miles to US 123S. Merge left onto 123S about 2½ miles to E Main St. Veer right onto Main about 2¼ miles to store.

GREENVILLE

EARTH FARE ✗🍎   ♿
6 S. Lewis Plaza © 864-250-1020 ⏰ M-Sat 8-8, Sun 11-6
   · organic produce · freshly prepared food · juice bar · salad bar · café · deli · bakery
   · vegetarian friendly · chain · counter · tables · self-service · take-out

🍎 **From I-85S**, take exit 46 toward SC 291N right onto Mauldin Rd (becomes Augusta St) almost 2 miles to store on left in back of Lewis Plaza. **From I-85N**, take exit 42 toward Greenville left onto I-185N/US 29N about 3¾ miles to Augusta. Turn right onto Augusta less than ½ mile to store on right (back of Lewis Plaza). **From I-385** in downtown Greenville, turn left onto Church St (29S) about 2 miles to Augusta. Turn left onto Augusta less than ½ mile to store on right (back of Lewis Plaza).

GARNER'S NATURAL MARKET & CAFE ✗🍎
60 E. Antrim Dr. © 864-233-9258 ⏰M-Sat 9-9, Sun 1-6, Lunch bar M-Sat 11-3:30
   · organic produce · freshly prepared food · café · deli · bakery · vegetarian friendly
   · tables · self-service · take-out

🍎 **From I-85S**, take exit 48B right onto Lauren's Rd about 1½ miles to Antrim. Turn left onto Antrim to store (next to McAlister U Center, behind Chic Filet). **From I-85N**, take exit 46C left onto Mauldin Rd less than ½ mile to S Pleasantburg Dr. Turn right onto Pleasantburg (SC 291N) about 3 miles to E Antrim. Turn right on Atrim to store.

SWAD ✗
1421A Laurens Rd. © 864-233-2089 ⏰ M-Sat 11-8:30
Vegetarian Indian fare.
   · vegetarian · vegan · tables · wait staff · take-out

🍎 **From I-85**, take exit 48B toward Greenville onto Laurens Rd (right from 85S, loop around right from 85N) about 2½ miles to restaurant.

LEXINGTON

14 CARROT WHOLE FOODS 🍎
5300 Sunset Blvd. © 864-233-2089 ⏰ M-Sat 9-7, Sun 1-6
   · organic produce

🍎 **From I-20W**, take exit 61 toward Lexington/Lake Murray Dam onto US 378W (Sunset Blvd) less than 3 miles to store. **From I-20E**, take exit 55 toward Lexington/Lake Murray Dam left onto SC 6, 2⅔ miles to US 378. Continue straight onto 378E about 1½ miles to store.

MOUNT PLEASANT

THE GOOD NEIGHBOR ✗🍎
423 Coleman Blvd. © 843-881-3274 ⏰ M-F 10-6, Sat 10-5
Soup, muffins, carrot juice, and smoothies.
   · freshly prepared food · juice bar · vegetarian friendly · tables · self-service · take-out

From I-26, take exit 221B toward Mt Pleasant onto 17N about 2½ miles (across bridge). Bear right onto Coleman Blvd (17Bus) about 1½ miles (past 3 traffic lights) to store on right in Peach Orchard Plaza.

MYRTLE BEACH

NEW LIFE NATURAL FOODS ✕ 🍲
1209 38th Ave. N. © 843-448-0011 ⊘ M-Sat 9-8, Sun 11-6
· organic produce · freshly prepared food · juice bar · deli · vegetarian friendly · tables · self-service · take-out

From Hwy 501, take 17N/Byp 17N toward N Myrtle Beach about 3 miles to 38th Ave N. Turn right onto 38th to store.

NORTH MYRTLE BEACH

NEW LIFE NATURAL FOODS 🍲
3320 Hwy. 17 S. © 843-272-4436 ⊘ M-Sat 9-6
A limited sporadic supply of organic produce.

From Hwy 501, take 17N/Byp 17N toward N Myrtle Beach about 13 miles to store on left at 33rd Ave S. From Rt 22E, take US 17S exit on left toward Myrtle Beach. Go left at fork onto 17 (N Kings Hwy) almost 3 miles to store on left at 33rd Ave S.

SPARTANBURG

GARNER'S NATURAL FOODS ✕ 🍲
1855 E. Main St. © 864-585-1021 ⊘ M-Sat 10-6
· freshly prepared food · café · vegetarian friendly · tables · self-service · take-out

From I-26N, take exit 21B onto US 29N (E Main St) about 7 miles to store on right in Hillcrest Specialty Row. From I-85N, take exit 72 toward Spartanburg onto US 176E about 3⅓ miles (becomes N Pine St). Follow N Pine almost 2 miles to E St John St (US 29). Turn left onto 29 (E Main) about 2¼ miles to store on right in Hillcrest Specialty Row. From I-85S, take exit 83 toward SC 110/Cowpens. Follow exit right onto Horry Rd, left onto Dewberry Rd and left onto SC 110/Battleground Rd 2 miles to US 29. Turn right onto 29 (N Main) 6 miles to store on left in Hillcrest Specialty Row.

WALTERBORO

NO JUNK JULIE'S 🍲
281 Cooler's Dairy Rd. © 843-538-8809 ⊘ M-Sat 10-6

From I-95, take exit 57 onto SC 64 toward Waterboro about 2 miles to Alt 17. Continue on Alt 17 about 2 miles (past airport) to fork. Bear right (continuing on Alt 17) to Circle M Ranch. Turn left after Circle M and take next left onto Cooler's Dairy Rd to store.

WEST COLUMBIA

14 CARROT WHOLE FOODS 🍲
2250 Sunset Blvd. W. © 803-791-1568 ⊘ M-Sat 9-7, Sun 1-6
· organic produce

From I-26, take exit 110 toward Lexington/W Columbia onto US 378E (left from 26E, right from 26W) about ½ mile to store on left in Westland Sq. From I-20W, take exit 64A onto I-26E toward Charleston about 2½ miles to exit 110 and follow directions above. From I-20E, take exit 61 toward W Columbia onto 378E (Sunset Blvd) 3 miles to store on left in Westland Sq.

SOUTH DAKOTA

SOUTH DAKOTA

1 Aberdeen
2 Brookings
3 Mitchell
4 Rapid City
5 Sioux Falls
6 Spearfish

ABERDEEN

NATURAL ABUNDANCE FOOD STORE
125 S. Main St. © 605-229-4947 ⊙ M-F 9-6, Sat 9-5
· organic produce · co-op

From Hwy 12, go north on Main St 4 blocks to store on corner 2nd Ave & Main.

BROOKINGS

NATURE'S PARADISE
1455 6th St. © 605-697-7404 ⊙ M-Sat 10-5:30
· organic produce

From I-29, take exit 132 onto Hwy 14W (right from 29S, left from 29N) 1 mile (past 3 traffic lights) to store (across from swimming pool).

MITCHELL

Home of the world's only Corn Palace, a castle-shaped structure decorated with 3,000 bushels of corn, grain and grass that is redesigned every year.

WAYNE & MARY'S
1313 W. Havens © 605-996-9868 ⊙ M-F 9-7, Sat 9-5

From I-90, take exit 330 north on 90Bus (right from 90W, left from 90E) about ⅔ mile to 1st traffic light at W Havens Ave. Turn right onto W Havens to store on right at west end of mall.

RAPID CITY

Rapid City is en route to Mt. Rushmore, but perhaps less known is the Black Hills Maze, 3 miles south on Hwy 16, with its 37,000 square-foot, two-story labyrinth.

BREADROOT NATURAL FOOD CO-OP
807 Columbus St. © 605-348-3331 ⊙ M-F 10-7, Sat 12-6
· organic produce · deli · vegetarian friendly · co-op · take-out

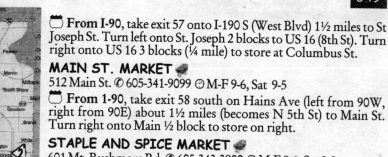

🏠 **From I-90,** take exit 57 onto I-190 S (West Blvd) 1½ miles to St Joseph St. Turn left onto St. Joseph 2 blocks to US 16 (8th St). Turn right onto US 16 3 blocks (¼ mile) to store at Columbus St.

MAIN ST. MARKET 🌿

512 Main St. ☏ 605-341-9099 ⊙ M-F 9-6, Sat 9-5

🏠 **From 1-90,** take exit 58 south on Hains Ave (left from 90W, right from 90E) about 1½ miles (becomes N 5th St) to Main St. Turn right onto Main ½ block to store on right.

STAPLE AND SPICE MARKET 🌿

601 Mt. Rushmore Rd. ☏ 605-343-3900 ⊙ M-F 9-6, Sat 9-5
· organic produce

🏠 **From 1-90,** take exit 57 onto I-190S (West Blvd) 1½ miles to St Joseph St. Turn left onto St Joseph 2 blocks to store on corner St Joseph & Mt Rushmore Rd.

VEGGIES NUTRITION CENTER ✗ 🌿 ♿

2050 W. Main St. ☏ 605-348-5019 ⊙ Store M-Th 8-8 (6 in winter), F 8-4, Sun 10-3, Restaurant M-Th 11-7 (4 in winter), F, Sun 11-2
Owned by a registered dietitian. All the bakery products and dishes on the (vegan) menu are made from scratch, with about half organic. The bulk foods are housed in a climate controlled room.
· organic produce · freshly prepared food · vegan · tables · wait staff

🏠 **From I-90,** take exit 57 onto I-190S (West Blvd) less than 1½ miles to Main St. Turn right onto Main about 2 miles to store on right.

SIOUX FALLS

EAST DAKOTAH FOOD COOP 🌿

420 1st Ave. S. ☏ 605-339-9506 ⊙ M-F 9-7, Sat 9-6, Sun 9-5
· co-op

🏠 **From I-29,** take exit 79 east on 12th St (right from 29N, left from 29S) 2¾ miles to 1st Ave. Turn right onto 1st to store on left.

SPEARFISH

BAY LEAF CAFE ✗

126 W. Hudson St. ☏ 605-642-5462 ⊙ Daily 11-9 (closed Sundays Labor Day-Memorial Day)
The varied offerings include a selection of vegetarian dishes (including home-made black bean burgers), as well as seafood, poultry, buffalo, elk—and beef.
· vegetarian friendly· alcohol · tables · wait staff

🏠 **From I-90,** take exit 12 toward Spearfish/Black Hills State U west on Jackson Blvd (left from 90W, right from 90E) less than ⅓ mile to Main St. Turn left onto Main 2 blocks to W Hudson St. Turn right onto Hudson ½ block to restaurant.

GOOD EARTH NATURAL FOODS 🌿

138 E. Hudson St. ☏ 605-642-7639 ⊙ M-Sat 9-5:30

🏠 **From I-90,** take exit 12 toward Spearfish/Black Hills State U west on Jackson Blvd (left from 90W, right from 90E) about ½ mile to 7th St. Turn left onto 7th 2 blocks to Hudson St. Turn right onto Hudson to store.

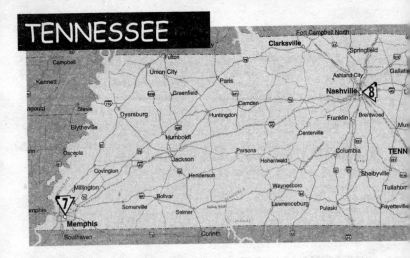

CHATTANOOGA

COUNTRY LIFE NATURAL FOODS & RESTAURANT ✕ 🍴
3748 Ringgold Rd. ✆ 423-622-2451 ⏰ M-Th 9:30-5, Sun 11-5, Lunch M-Th, Sun 11:30-3:30

Vegan groceries and weekday lunch. Run by laymen from the Seventh-day Adventist church and part of the Wildwood Lifestyle Center and Hospital.

· freshly prepared food · vegan · tables · self-service

🚗 From I-24E, take exit 181A toward East Ridge onto US 41S (Westside Dr, then veers right as Ringgold Rd) about 1½ miles to store. From I-24W, take exit 183A toward Belvoir Ave/Germantown Rd. Merge onto N Terrace Rd ¾ mile to Germantown. Turn left onto Germantown about 1 mile to Ringgold. Turn left onto Ringgold ¼ mile to store.

GREENLIFE GROCERY ✕ 🍴   ♿
1100 Hixon Pike ✆ 423-267-1960 ⏰ M-Sat 9-9, Sun 12-8

· organic produce · freshly prepared food · juice bar · salad bar · café · deli · vegetarian friendly · co-op · tables · self-service · take-out

🚗 From I-24, take exit 178 toward Downtown onto US 27N about 1⅔ miles to exit 1C (4th St). Turn right onto 4th about ½ mile to Georgia Ave. Turn left onto Georgia (across bridge, becomes Barton Ave) less than 1½ miles to Hixon Pike. Bear right onto Hixon 1 block to store on right at traffic light after bridge. From I-75, take I-24W and follow directions above.

COLLEGEDALE

VILLAGE MARKET ✕ 🍴
5002 University Dr. ✆ 423-238-3286 ⏰ M-Th 8-8, F 8-4, Sun 9-8, Soup/Salad/Sandwiches M-Th 10:30-6, F 10:30-3, Deli/Hot bar M-F 10:30-2:30

· organic produce · freshly prepared food · salad bar · deli · vegetarian · tables · self-service · take-out

🚗 From I-75N, take exit 7A onto Old Lee Hwy (TN 317E) about 2⅓ miles to Apison Pike (TN 317). Turn right onto Apison about 3¼ miles (past McKee Baking on right) to 4-way stop at University Dr. Turn right onto University through Southern Adventist U 1 block to store on left in shopping plaza. From I-75S, take exit 11 toward Ooltewah right onto Lee Hwy and U-turn at Snow Hill Rd back onto Lee to Little Debbie Pkwy.

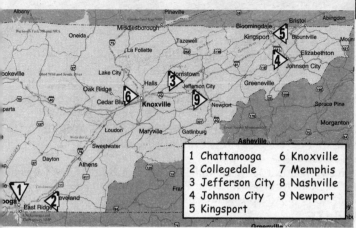

1 Chattanooga	6 Knoxville
2 Collegedale	7 Memphis
3 Jefferson City	8 Nashville
4 Johnson City	9 Newport
5 Kingsport	

Turn right onto pkwy 1¾ miles to Apison. Turn left onto Apison about 1½ miles (past McKee Baking) to University and follow directions above.

JEFFERSON CITY

HILL'S HEALTH HUT
107 E. Old Ajay Hwy. © 865-475-2993 ⊙ M-Th 9:30-5:30, F 9:30-6, Sat 10-5

🛏 **From I-40**, take exit 417 onto TN 92N (right from 40W, left from 40E) over 7 miles (at over 6 miles 92 turns right onto George Ave, right onto College St, and left onto S Banner Ave) to Old Andrew Johnson (Ajay) Hwy. Turn left onto Ajay Hwy to store.

JOHNSON CITY

NATURAL FOOD MARKET
3211 People's St. © 423-610-1000 ⊙ M-Sat 10-9, Sun 1-5
· freshly prepared food · take-out

🛏 **From I-81**, take exit 57A onto I-181S about 10 miles to exit 36 (State of Franklin Rd). Turn right onto State of Franklin (left from 181N) to Davis St. Turn left onto Davis to store at People's St.

KINGSPORT

GOOD FOOD GROCERY
1425 E. Center St. © 423-246-3663 ⊙ M-F 8-7, Sat 8-6, Sun 1-5

🛏 **From I-81**, take exit 59 onto TN 36N (Center St in Kingsport) about 5½ miles to store.

KNOXVILLE

KNOXVILLE COMMUNITY FOOD CO-OP
937 N. Broadway © 865-525-2069 ⊙ Daily 9-9
· organic produce · co-op

🛏 **From I-40W**, take exit 389A and at Broadway turn around to head south about 1 mile to store on right between Glenwood & Gill Ave (across from Broadway Carpet). **From I-40E**, take exit 388 (Henley St) toward Downtown and follow exit ramp toward TN 62 for Western Ave. Turn left onto Western to Broadway. Turn left onto Broadway 1 mile to store on left between Gill & Glenwood Ave.

NATURAL & ORGANIC 🌱

7025 Kingston Pike ℂ 865-584-8422 ⊙ M 10-8, Tues-Th 10-6, F 10-4

🏠 **From I-75/40E**, take exit 380 left (east) onto Kingston Pike 1 mile to store on left in West Hill Shopping Center. **From I-40W**, take exit 383 left onto Papermill Dr 1¼ miles to Kingston Pike. Turn right onto Kingston Pike about ⅓ mile to store on right in West Hill Shopping Center.

NATURE'S PANTRY GOURMET & WHOLE FOODS MARKET 🍴🌱

6600 KingstonPike ℂ 865-584-4714 ⊙ M-Sat 9-9, Sun 12-7

· organic produce

🏠 **From I-40**, take exit 383 (Papermill Dr) onto Northshore Drive (straight from I-40E, 2 lefts from I-40W) about ½ mile to Kingston Pike. Turn right onto Kingston Pike to store about 1 mile up hill on left.

MEMPHIS

LA MONTAGNE 🍴

3550 Park Ave. ℂ 901-458-1060 ⊙ Lunch Tues-Sun 11:30-2:30, Dinner M-Th, Sun 5:30-10, F-Sat 5:30-11

Food for vegetarians, chicken- and fish-eaters. Fresh bread from organic whole grains, no lard or hydrogenated fats, and vegetarian specials "combine grains, legumes, nuts, seeds and dairy products to ensure meals rich in complete proteins." A different ethnic cuisine (drawing from about 30 countries) featured daily.

· vegetarian friendly · alcohol · tables · wait staff

🏠 **From I-40**, merge onto Sam Cooper Blvd (straight from 40W, via exit 12B from 40E) about 3¼ miles to exit 7 (Highland St). Turn left onto Highland about 2¾ miles to restaurant at Park Ave (just south of U Memphis). **From I-55**, merge onto I-240E to exit 21 (US 78/Lamar Ave). Follow exit as it loops around and turns right onto Lamar to S Prescott Rd. Turn right onto S Prescott about 2 miles as it veers right into Ratford Rd then merges into Highland to restaurant at Park.

MIDTOWN FOOD CO-OP 🍴🌱   ♿

2158 Central Ave. ℂ 901-276-2250 ⊙ M-F 8-8, Sat 9-8, Sun 10-8, Cafe M-Sat 11-8, Sun 11-4

Check out the all-vegan One Love Juice Bar and Cafe inside the co-op.

· organic produce · freshly prepared food · juice bar · salad bar · café · vegan · co-op
· tables · self-service · take-out

🏠 **From I-40W**, merge onto Sam Cooper Blvd about 4 miles to Broad Ave. Merge onto Broad 1½ miles to E Pkwy N. Turn left onto E Pkwy 1½ miles to Central Ave. Turn right onto Central ⅓ mile to store on right (before traffic light at Cooper St). **From I-55N**, merge onto I-240N. **From I-40E**, merge onto I-240S. **From I-240**, take exit 29 onto Lamar Ave (right from 240N, left from 240S) ⅓ -½ mile to Central Ave. Turn left onto Central about 1½ miles to store on left (just past Cooper).

WILD OATS MARKET 🍴🌱   ♿

5022 Poplar Ave. ℂ 901-685-2293 ⊙ M-Sat 8-10, Sun 9-9

· organic produce · freshly prepared food · juice bar · salad bar · café · deli · bakery
· vegetarian friendly · chain · counter · self-service · take-out

🏠 **From I-240**, take Poplar Ave exit (15 from 240W, 15B from 240E) onto US 78W/Poplar Ave (right from 240W, left from 240E) about 1⅓ miles to store on right at intersection Poplar & Mendenhall/Mt Moriah Rd (next to Office Depot, big bowl of fruit on top).

NASHVILLE

GRINS VEGETARIAN RESTAURANT ✗ ♿
2421 Vanderbilt Place © 615-322-8571 ◷ M-W 8-3, Th 8-8, F 8-2
Kosher, vegetarian, all-homemade, changing menu of soups, salads, sandwiches, and hot and cold entrees. On the Vanderbilt U campus, but open to all. Verify hours—they can vary with the semester and dinner may be expanded.

· vegetarian · kosher · tables · self-service

🍎 **From I-40W**, take exit 209A straight onto 13th Ave N to Broadway. Turn left onto Broadway about 1 mile (stay right at fork onto West End Ave) to traffic light at 25th Ave. Turn left onto 25th 2 blocks to restaurant on corner at Vanderbilt Pl (in Schulman Center). **From I-40E**, merge onto I-440E. **From I-440E**, take exit 1 toward West End Ave/US70S E. Turn left onto Murphy Rd and left onto West End about 1 mile to light at 25th. Turn right onto 25th 2 blocks to restaurant at Vanderbilt.

PRODUCE PLACE 🍎
4000 Murphy Rd. © 615-383-2664 ◷ M-F 9-6:30, Sat 8-6

· organic produce

🍎 **From I-440**, take exit 1 toward West End Ave onto Murphy Rd. Turn west onto Murphy (right turn from 440E, left turn from 440W) about ½ mile to store at Murphy & 40th St.

WILD OATS MARKET ✗ 🍎
3909 Hillsboro Pike © 615-463-0164 ◷ Daily 8-10
Massage therapists on site most days.

· organic produce · freshly prepared food · juice bar · salad bar · café · deli · bakery
· vegetarian friendly · chain · tables · self-service · take-out

🍎 **From I-440**, take exit 3 south on Hillsboro Pike (right from 440E, loop around right from 440W) about 1½ miles to store on left 1 block past Green Hills Mall (next to Walgreens).

WILD OATS MARKET 🍎
3201 Belmont Blvd. © 615-297-5100 ◷ M-Sat 8-10, Sun 10-8

· organic produce · freshly prepared food · juice bar · deli · bakery · vegetarian friendly
· chain · take-out

🍎 **From I-440**, take exit 3 south on Hillsboro Pike (right from 440E, loop round right from 440W) about ¼ mile to Lombardy Ave. Turn left onto Lombardy almost ½ mile to Brightwood Ave. Turn left onto Brightwood, right onto Gale Lane and right onto Belmont Blvd to store.

NEWPORT

Located in the Smoky Mountains, with lots of hiking and camping in the area.

THE MUSTARD SEED HEALTH FOOD STORE & DELI ✗ 🍎
331 Cosby Hwy. © 423-623-4091 ◷ M-Th 10-6, F 10-4, Sun 11:30-2:30
Vegan soups, sandwiches and salads.

· organic produce · freshly prepared food · juice bar · salad bar · café · vegan · tables
· wait staff · take-out

🍎 **From I-40**, take exit 435 toward Newport onto Hwy 321N (left from 40E, right from 40W) over 1 mile (past 3 traffic lights) to store on left in The Village Shopping Center. **From I-81**, merge onto I-40E and follow directions above.

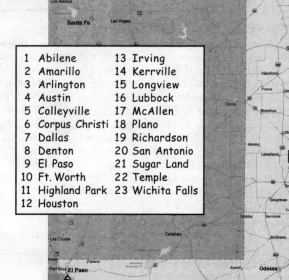

1   Abilene   13 Irving
2   Amarillo   14 Kerrville
3   Arlington   15 Longview
4   Austin   16 Lubbock
5   Colleyville   17 McAllen
6   Corpus Christi   18 Plano
7   Dallas   19 Richardson
8   Denton   20 San Antonio
9   El Paso   21 Sugar Land
10 Ft. Worth   22 Temple
11 Highland Park   23 Wichita Falls
12 Houston

ABILENE_____

NATURAL FOOD CENTER ✖️🛒
2534 S. 7th St. © 915-673-2726 ⊙ M-Sat 10-6 Lunch counter 11-2
· freshly prepared food · vegetarian friendly · counter · take-out
🍴 **From I-20**, take exit 283A onto US 83S almost 4 miles to 7th St. Turn left onto 7th about 2 miles to store on left.

AMARILLO_____

While here you can visit Palo Duro Canyon State Park and Cadillac Ranch.

EAT-RITE HEALTH PROMOTION CENTER ✖️🛒   ♿
2425 I-40W © 806-353-7476 ⊙ M-Sat 9-6
Focus is on fresh, whole foods. Whole grain bread, organic greens and salt-free soups. Weighted toward animal products, with vegetarian options.
· organic produce · freshly prepared food · juice bar · salad bar · deli · bakery
· vegetarian friendly · counter · tables · self-service · take-out
🍴 **From I-40**, take exit 68B toward Georgia St to store just off hwy on SE corner at Georgia.

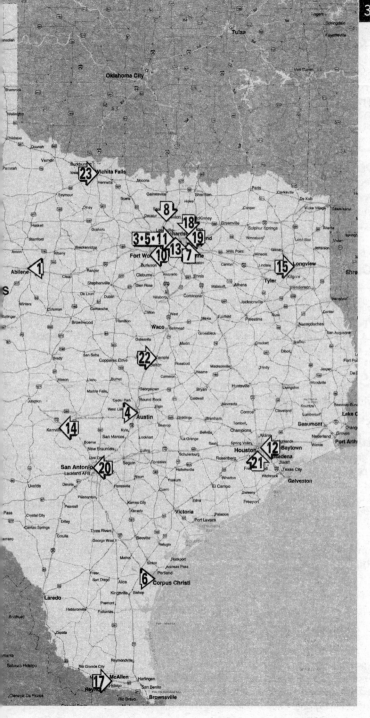

NUTRITION HOUSE 🛒
839 Martin Rd. © 806-374-9587 ⊙ M-Sat 9-6
 · organic produce
 From **I-27N**, merge onto I-287N/US 60E about 2 miles to Hwy 66. Turn right onto 66 1 mile to Martin Rd. Turn left on Martin 1 block to store. **From I-40**, take exit 70 toward Downtown onto 287N/60E (left from 40E, right from 40W) about 2½ miles to 66 and follow directions above.

ARLINGTON

GOOD HEALTH PLACE 🛒
860 Secretary Dr. © 817-265-5261 ⊙ M-W, F-Sat 9:30-6:30, Th 9:30-8
 From **I-30**, take exit 27 south on Cooper St (right from 30W, loop around right and turn right from 30E) about 3½ miles to store on east side in Pecan Plaza. **From I-20**, take exit 450 north on Matlock Rd (left from 20E, right from 20W) less than 2 miles to Cooper. Turn left onto Cooper to store on east side in Pecan Plaza.

WHOLE FOODS MARKET ✕🛒   ♿
801 East Lamar Blvd. © 817-461-9362 ⊙ Daily 8-9
 · organic produce · freshly prepared food · juice bar · salad bar · café · deli · bakery
 · vegetarian friendly · chain · tables · self-service · take-out
 From **I-30W**, take exit 28 (FM 157/Collins St). Follow 157N ramp onto Collins less than ¼ mile to Lamar Blvd. Turn left onto Lamar to store. **From I-30E**, take exit 27 left onto Cooper St and right onto Lamar about 1 mile to store.

AUSTIN

BOULDIN CREEK COFFEEHOUSE ✕
1501 S. 1st St. © 512-416-1601 ⊙ M-F 7am-midnight, Sat-Sun 9am-midnight
All-day breakfast, salads, sandwiches, and combo plates featuring fresh vegetables, beans and brown rice.
 · vegetarian · vegan friendly · alcohol · counter · self-service
 From **I-35N**, take exit 232A (Oltorf St/Live Oak) and follow S I-35 about ½ mile to Oltorf. Turn left onto Oltorf 1¼ miles to S 1st St. Turn right onto 1st over ½ mile to restaurant on corner S 1st & Elizabeth St. **From I-35S**, take exit 234A right onto Caesar Chavez St/E 1st St less than ½ mile to Barzos St. Turn right onto Barzos, left onto 2nd St and left onto Congress Ave ⅓ mile (across river) to Barton Springs Rd. Turn right onto Barton Springs ¼ mile to S 1st. Turn left onto 1st about ⅔ mile to restaurant on corner S 1st & Elizabeth.

CASA DE LUZ ✕   ♿
1701 Toomey Rd. © 512-476-2535 ⊙ Daily 11:30-2, 6-8
Community restaurant and meeting place, serving a set vegan/macrobiotic plate that changes twice daily. Includes soup, whole grain, beans, steamed greens with sauce, cooked vegetable, salad, and macrobiotic pickle. Fresh organic local produce, home baked spelt and rye breads, and wheat-free, sugar-free desserts.
 · vegan · organic focus · tables · self-service
 From **I-35**, take exit 233 west on Riverside Dr (left from 35N, right from 35S) about 2 miles to Lamar St. Turn left onto Lamar and make next right onto Toomey Rd 2 blocks to restaurant on left.

MADRAS PAVILION ✕

9025 Research Blvd. © 512-719-5575 ⊘ M-F 11:30-3, 6-10, Sat-Sun 11:30-10
Vegetarian Indian food, offering a daily lunch buffet.

· vegetarian · vegan friendly · alcohol · tables · wait staff

🍴 **From I-35N**, take exit 240B onto US 183N to FM 1325 exit toward Burnet Rd. Bear left onto Research Blvd ⅓ mile to restaurant. **From I-35S**, take exit 241 toward Rundberg Ln and follow exit almost 1 mile to Rundberg. Turn right onto Rundberg about 2¼ miles to Metric Blvd. Turn left onto Metric ⅓ mile to Research. Turn right onto Research to restaurant.

MOTHER'S CAFE & GARDEN ✕

4215 Duval St. © 512-451-3994 ⊘ M-F 11:15-10, Sat-Sun 10-10

· vegetarian · vegan friendly · alcohol · tables · wait staff

🍴 **From I-35**, take exit 237A (Airport Blvd). Follow Airport Blvd ramp onto E 45th St about ½ mile to Duval St. Turn left onto Duval almost 2 blocks to restaurant (just before Park Blvd).

SUN HARVEST FARMS ✕🍴

4006 S. Lamar Blvd. © 512-444-3079 ⊘ Daily 8-10

· organic produce · freshly prepared food · juice bar · café · deli · vegetarian friendly · chain · tables · self-service · take-out

🍴 **From I-35**, take exit 230 (230B from 35S) left onto US 290W/TX 71W/ W Ben White Blvd 2 ½ miles to Lamar Blvd exit. Turn right onto Lamar about ⅓ mile to store.

SUN HARVEST FARMS 🍴

2917 W. Anderson Lane © 512-451-0660 ⊘ Daily 8-9

· organic produce · freshly prepared food · deli · vegetarian friendly · chain· take-out

🍴 **From I-35N**, take exit 240B toward Research Blvd onto 183N (W Anderson Ln) about 1 mile to exit toward Ohlen Rd/Peton Gin Rd. Follow onto Research Blvd and turn right onto W Anderson again (continuing west) about 1⅓ miles to store. **From I-35S in Austin**, take exit 240A to 183N and follow directions above. **From north of Austin on I-35S**, take exit 250 onto N Mo Pac Expwy about 10 miles to W Anderson. Turn left onto W Anderson less than ½ mile to store.

VEGGIE HEAVEN ✕

1914A Guadalupe St © 512-457-1013 ⊘ Tues-F 11-9:30, Sat-Sun 12-9:30
Asian vegetarian with lots of tofu. Mostly (but not all) vegan.

· vegetarian · vegan friendly · tables · wait staff · take-out

🍴 **From I-35**, take exit 235A toward 15th St/MLK Blvd/State Capitol. Turn west onto MLK (right from 35S, left from 35N) about 1 mile to Guadalupe St. Turn right onto Guadalupe 1 block to restaurant on left (across from Dobie Mall).

WEST LYNN CAFE ✕

1110 W. Lynn St. © 512-482-0950 ⊘ Tues-Th 11:30-10, F 11:30-10:30, Sat 11-10:30, Sun 11-9:30
Upscale vegetarian menu featuring southwestern cuisine and pasta.

· vegetarian · alcohol · tables · wait staff

🍴 **From I-35**, take exit 235A toward 15th St/MLK Blvd/State Capitol. Turn west onto E 15th St (right from 35S, left from 35N) about 1¾ miles (becomes Enfield Rd) to W Lynn St. Turn left onto W Lynn ¼ mile to restaurant at 11th St.

WHEATSVILLE CO-OP ✗🛒   Ⅳ
3101 Guadalupe St. ✆ 512-478-2667 ☼ Daily 9-11

· organic produce · freshly prepared food · deli · bakery · vegetarian friendly · coop
· tables · self-service · take-out

🍎 **From I-35**, take 38½ St exit west (becomes 38th St) under 2 miles to Guadalupe St. Turn left onto Guadalupe 7 blocks to store on left at 31st St.

WHOLE FOODS MARKET ✗🛒   Ⅳ
601 N. Lamar Blvd. ✆ 512-476-1206 ☼ Daily 8-10

· organic produce · freshly prepared food · salad bar · café · deli · bakery · vegetarian
friendly · chain · tables · self-service · take-out

🍎 **From I-35N**, take exit 234C toward 6th-12th St to 8th St. Turn left onto 8th across hwy 2 blocks to 6th St. Turn right onto 6th about 1¼ miles to store on NE corner 6th & Lamar Blvd. **From I-35S**, take exit 234B toward 8th-3rd St to 6th. Turn right onto 6th and follow directions above.

WHOLE FOODS MARKET ✗🛒   Ⅳ
9607 Research Blvd.# 300 ✆ 512-345-5003 ☼ Daily 8-10

· organic produce · freshly prepared food · salad bar · café · deli · bakery · vegetarian
friendly · chain · tables · self-service · take-out

🍎 **From I-35N**, take exit 240B onto 183N about 4 miles to Gateway Loop 360 exit. Stay straight onto Research Blvd about ¼ mile to store on west side in Gateway Market (next to Old Navy & REI). **From I-35S north of Austin**, take exit 250 onto Mo Pac Expwy about 7½ miles to 183N ramp to Research Blvd. Turn right onto Research to store on west side in Gateway Market.

COLLEYVILLE————————————

THE HEALTHY APPROACH MARKET 🛒
5100 Hwy. 121 ✆ 817-399-9100 ☼ M-Sat 9-9, Sun 12-6

🍎 **From I-820**, take exit 22 B (Airport Fwy) onto 183E/121N (stay left on 121N at split) about 8½ miles to Hall Johnson Rd exit. U-turn under 121S to store on right on service road (next to Blockbuster Video).

CORPUS CHRISTI————————

SUN HARVEST FARM 🛒
1440 Airline Rd. ✆ 361-993-2850 ☼ Daily 9-9

· organic produce · freshly prepared food · deli · vegetarian friendly · chain · take-out

🍎 **From I-37**, take exit 4A toward Padre Island Airport onto TX 358E about 10 miles to Airline Rd exit. Store is on corner Airline & S Padre Island Dr (aka TX 358).

DALLAS—————————————

KALACHANDJI'S RESTAURANT & PALACE ✗
5430 Gurley Ave. ✆ 214-821-1048 ☼ Lunch Tues-F 11:30-2, Sat 12-3, Dinner Tues-Sun 5:30-9

The all-vegetarian buffet changes daily, but there is always dahl, rice, vegetetable curry, steamed vegetables, pakoras, a hot international entree, and salad bar. The adjacent serene and lavish spiritual palace is open to the public.

· salad bar · vegetarian · vegan friendly· tables · self-service

🍎 **From I-30E**, take exit 48B (E Grand Ave/Munger Blvd) and follow service road to 2nd traffic light at E Grand. Turn left onto Grand (under hwy) and left onto westbound service road 2 blocks to Gurley Ave. Turn right onto Gurley (after Comerica Bank) to restaurant/palace on right (before Graham Ave). **From I-30W**, take exit 49A and follow service road past 2 lights to Gurley (2 blocks past Grand). Turn right onto Gurley to restaurant/palace on right.

WHOLE FOODS MARKET ✖🛒 &

2218 Greenville Ave. © 214-824-1744 ⊙ Daily 8-10

· organic produce · freshly prepared food · juice bar · salad bar · café · deli · bakery
· vegetarian friendly · chain · tables · self-service · take-out

From I-30, take exit 48A and follow ramp to S Munger Blvd. Turn north onto S Munger (right from 30W, left from 30E) about 1⅔ miles until N Munger ends at Greenville Ave. Turn right onto Greenville about ⅓ mile to store on SE corner Belmont Ave & Greenville. **From US 75** (Central Expwy), take exit 3 east on Mockingbird Lane (right from 75N, left from 75S) to Greenville. Turn right onto Greenville about 1½ miles to store on SE corner Belmont & Greenville.

WHOLE FOODS MARKET ✖🛒 &

11661 Preston Rd. © 214-361-8887 ⊙ Daily 8-10

· organic produce · freshly prepared food · juice bar · salad bar · café · deli · bakery
· vegetarian friendly · chain · tables · self-service · take-out

From US-75S (Central Expwy), take exit 8 right (west) on Forest Ln 2 miles to Preston Rd. Turn left onto Preston to store in Preston Forest Village. **From I-35E N**, take exit 429D onto Dallas North Tollway about 7⅓ miles to Forest Ln exit. Turn right onto Forest about ½ mile to Preston. Turn right onto Preston to store in Preston Forest Village. **From I-635**, take exit 21 onto LBJ Fwy to Preston. Turn south on Preston (right from 635E, left from 635W) over 1 mile to store just past Forest in Preston Forest Village.

DENTON

CUPBOARD NATURAL FOODS

200 W. Congress St. © 940-387-5386 ⊙ M-Sat 8-9, Sun 11-6

· freshly prepared food · juice bar · café · vegetarian friendly · tables · self-service · take-out

From I-35, take exit 469 onto US 380E/W University Dr (right from 35N, left from 35S) less than 3 miles to N Elm St (US 77). Turn right onto Elm (77S) about ¾ mile to Congress St. Turn right onto Congress to store on corner.

TARA PHERMA ✖

1306 W. Hickory St. © 940-387-9222 ⊙ M-Sat 12-6

Mostly vegan and raw cuisine. Dine at a table or zen-style on floor pads. A good place to find out about community events, drum jams, get a massage, or take a dance or yoga class.

· vegetarian · vegan friendly · tables · wait staff

From I-35S, take exit 468 toward Airport Rd left onto W Oak St (becomes W Hickory St) about 1⅓ miles to restaurant at Fry St (behind Voyager's Dream). **From I-35E N**, take exit 466B toward Ave D right onto Kendolf St 2 blocks to Eagle Dr. Turn right onto Eagle 1 block to Ave C. Turn left onto C ½ mile (through U N TX campus) to Hickory. Turn right onto Hickory ¼ mile to restaurant. **From I-35W N**, take exit 84 left onto Bonnie Brae St ½ mile to Hickory. Turn right onto Hickory less than ½ mile to restaurant.

EL PASO

SUN HARVEST FARM 🛒
6100 N. Mesa St. ℂ 915-833-3380 ⊘ Daily 7-9
· organic produce · freshly prepared food · deli · vegetarian friendly · chain · take-out
🍎 **From I-10**, take exit 13 to Sunland Park Dr. Turn north onto Sunland Park (right from 10W, left from 10E) to N Mesa St. Turn left onto Mesa to 1st traffic light at Balboa Rd. Turn right onto Balboa to store on left in shopping plaza.

FT. WORTH

Check out Tandy Hills Park, a primitive prairie land with seasonally changing native wildflowers. Especially stunning in spring.

HERB 'N HEALTH NATURAL FOODS & NURSERY 🛒   ♿
3539 E. Lancaster Ave. ℂ 817-535-1152 ⊘ Tues-Th 9:30-6, F-Sat 9:30-5
A wild-scaped, solar-powered, rainwater-catching, health-conscious store housed in a renovated 1926 craftsman-style home.
· organic produce · freshly prepared food · take-out
🍎 **From I-30**, take exit 18 south on Oakland Blvd (right from 30E, left from 30W) about ½ mile to Lancaster Ave. Turn right onto Lancaster 8 blocks to Perkins St. Turn right onto Perkins, then make immediate left onto circular one-way drive and park between the cobblestone markers.

SPIRAL DINER 🍴
1401 Jones St. ℂ 817-332-8834 ⊘ M-Sat 10-7, Sun 11-5
Focus is on organic (when possible) vegan fare, featuring burgers, sandwiches, salads, hot plates, and smoothies. A Certified Green Restaurant.
· bakery · vegan · organic focus · counter · tables · self-service · take-out
🍎 **From I-30E**, take exit 15 to Main St. Turn left onto Main and pass in front of Water Gardens to 15th St. Turn right onto 15th 2 blocks to Jones St. Turn left onto Jones. Restaurant is in Ft Worth Rail Market. **From I-30W or I-35W N**, take Lancaster Ave exit west to Jones. Turn right onto Jones to restaurant. **From I-35W S**, exit onto 280 Spur W (toward Downtown) to 6th St exit to Calhoun St. Turn left onto Calhoun to 14th St. Turn left onto 14th 1 block to Jones. Turn left onto Jones to restaurant.

SUNFLOWER SHOPPE 🍴🛒
5817 Curzon Ave. ℂ 817-738-9051 ⊘ M-Sat 9-9, Sun 12-6
· organic produce · freshly prepared food · café · deli · vegetarian friendly · tables · self-service · take-out
🍎 **From I-30W**, take exit 9B onto Camp Bowie Blvd about 1 mile to Curzon Ave. Turn left onto Curzon to store on right corner. **From I-30E**, take exit 9B and follow onto Calmont Ave, right onto Horne St and left onto Camp Bowie 2 blocks to Curzon. Turn left onto Curzon to store on right corner.

HIGHLAND PARK

WHOLE FOODS MARKET 🍴🛒   ♿
4100 Lomo Alto Drive ℂ 214-520-7993 ⊘ Daily 8-10
· organic produce · freshly prepared food · juice bar · salad bar · café · deli · bakery · vegetarian friendly · chain · counter · tables · self-service · take-out
🍎 **From I-35E N**, take exit 420A right onto Oak Lawn Ave about 1¼ miles to Lemmon Ave. Turn left onto Lemmon about 1 mile to store on right at Lomo Alto Dr. **From I-35E S**, take exit 432A left onto Inwood Rd about 2 miles to Lemmon. Turn right onto Lemmon about 1 mile to store

on left at Lomo Alto. **From Dallas North Tollway**, take Lemmon Ave exit to store just east of tollway.

HOUSTON

A MOVEABLE FEAST ✗🛒

9341 Katy Fwy. ✆ 713-365-0368 🕒 M-Sat 9-9 , Cafe M-Sat 11-9

· freshly prepared food · café · vegetarian friendly · tables · self-service · take-out

🍎 **From I-10E**, take exit 758B toward Blalock Rd/Campbell Rd straight onto Katy Fwy to store. **From I-10W**, take exit 758A toward Bunker Hill Rd onto Katy Fwy and make U-turn onto Katy Fwy heading east to store.

BABA YEGA ✗

2607 Grant St. ✆ 713-522-0042 🕒 M-Th 11-10, F-Sat 11-11, Sun 10:30-10

The menu ranges from hamburgers, steak, chicken and fish to a Veggie Club and black bean burgers. The bread is whole wheat and the rice brown.

· vegetarian friendly · alcohol · tables · wait staff

🍎 **From I-10E**, take exit 767A toward Studemont St onto Katy Fwy to Studemont. Turn right onto Studemont 1 mile to Montrose Blvd. Continue straight on Montrose 1 mile to Missouri St. Turn left onto Missouri 1 block to Grant St. Turn right onto Grant to restaurant. **From I-45N**, take exit 47A onto Allen Pkwy about 1 mile to Studemont. Turn left onto Studemont (immediately becomes Montrose) and follow directions from Montrose above. **From I-10W**, merge onto I-45S. **From I-45S**, take exit 47D toward Dallas St/Fort Pierce St onto Heiner St ½ mile to Bagby St. Veer right onto Bagby ¾ mile to Westheimer Rd. Turn right onto Westheimer about ½ mile to Grant. Turn right onto Grant to restaurant.

MADRAS PAVILION ✗

3910 Kirby Dr. Ste. 130 ✆ 713-521-2617 🕒 M-F 11:30-3, 6-10, Sat-Sun 11:30-10

Vegetarian Indian food, offering a daily lunch buffet.

· vegetarian · vegetarian friendly · alcohol · tables · self-service · wait staff

🍎 **From I-610**, take exit 8A onto US 59N toward Downtown (left from 610S, right from 610N) about 2¼ miles to Kirby Dr exit. Follow exit onto SW Fwy to Kirby. Turn left onto Kirby to restaurant. **From I-45**, take exit 46B onto US 59S toward Victoria about 3½ miles to Kirby Dr exit. Follow exit to Lomitas St. Turn right onto Lomitas 1 block to Algerian Way. Turn left onto Algerian 1 block to restaurant at Kirby.

WHOLE FOODS ✗🛒   ♿

2955 Kirby Drive ✆ 713-520-1937 🕒 Daily 8-10

· organic produce · freshly prepared food · juice bar · salad bar · café · deli · bakery · vegetarian friendly · chain · tables · self-service · take-out

🍎 **From I-610**, take exit 8A onto US 59 toward Downtown (left from 610S, right from 610N) about 2¼ miles to Kirby Dr exit. Follow exit onto SW Fwy to Kirby. Turn left onto Kirby about ½ mile to store. **From I-45**, take exit 47A onto Allen Pkwy about 2⅓ miles where Allen becomes Kirby. Continue on Kirby about 1¾ miles to store.

WHOLE FOODS ✗🛒   ♿

11145 Westheimer Rd. ✆ 713-784-7776 🕒 Daily 9-10

· organic produce · freshly prepared food · juice bar · salad bar · café · deli · bakery · vegetarian friendly · chain · tables · wait staff · take-out

🍎 **From Beltway 8** (Sam Houston Tollway), take Westheimer Rd west less than 1 mile to store at Wilcrest Dr (behind Houstons Restaurant).

WHOLE FOODS MARKET ✗ 🍴   ⅋
4004 Bellaire Blvd. ✆ 713-667-4090 ⏱ Daily 8:30-10
  · organic produce · freshly prepared food · juice bar · salad bar · café · deli · bakery
  · vegetarian friendly · chain · tables · self-service · take-out

🗂 **From I-610** take exit 6 east on Bellaire Blvd about 1 mile to store at corner Bellaire & Weslayan St. **From Rt 59**, go south on Weslayan to store at Bellaire.

WHOLE FOODS MARKET ✗ 🍴   ⅋
6401 Woodway #149 ✆ 713-789-4477 ⏱ Daily 8-9
  · organic produce · freshly prepared food · juice bar · salad bar · café · deli · bakery
  · vegetarian friendly · chain · tables · self-service · take-out

🗂 **From I-610**, take exit 10 onto W Loop Fwy to Woodway Dr. Turn right from 610S, left from 610N onto Woodway almost 3 miles to store. **From I-10E**, take exit 760 onto Katy Fwy to Voss Rd. Turn right onto Voss 2 miles to Woodway. Turn left onto Woodway about ¼ mile to store.

IRVING

SAI KRISHNA ✗
2836 O'Connor Rd. ✆ 972-257-9726 ⏱ Daily 11-3, 6-10
Vegetarian Indian menu, offering daily lunch buffet.
  · vegetarian · vegan friendly · tables · self-service · wait staff

🗂 **From I-35E N**, take exit 433A (on left) onto Hwy 183W 5 miles to O'Connor Rd exit. Turn left onto W Airport Fwy ¼ mile to O'Connor. Turn right onto O'Connor ½ mile to restaurant. **From I-35S E**, take exit 436 onto TX 12 Loop S 2¼ miles to Hwy 183W toward Fort Worth. Merge onto 183W less than 2 miles to O'Connor exit and follow directions above.

KERRVILLE

KERRVILLE HEALTH FOODS 🍴   ⅋
130 W. Main St. ✆ 830-896-7383 ⏱ M-F 9-6, Sat 9:30-5:30

🗂 **From I-10**, take exit 508 toward Kerrville onto TX 16S/Frederickburg Rd (left from 10W, right from 10E) almost 2½ miles to Main St. Turn right onto Main about ½ mile to store.

LONGVIEW

JACK'S NATURAL FOOD STORE ✗ 🍴
1614 Judson Rd. ✆ 903-753-4800 ⏱ M-F 9-5 Deli 9-3
  · freshly prepared food · juice bar · deli · vegetarian friendly · tables · self-service · take-out

🗂 **From I-20E**, take exit 595A north on Estes Pkwy (becomes High St, then Judson Rd) about 7 miles to store on right. **From I-20W**, take exit 595 and follow access road to Estes Pkwy. Turn right onto Estes and follow directions above.

JACK'S NATURAL FOOD STORE ✗ 🍴
400 E. Loop 281 ✆ 903-758-9777 ⏱ M-F 9-6, Sat 9-5 Deli M-F 9-4, Sat 9-3
  · freshly prepared food · deli · vegetarian friendly · tables · self-service · take-out

🗂 **From I-20**, take exit 599 north on TX 281 Loop (right from 20W, left from 20E) about 8 miles to store at Airline Rd.

JACK'S NATURAL FOOD STORE ✗ 🍴
2199 Gilmer Rd. ✆ 903-759-4262 ⏱ M-F 9-6, Sat 9-5 Deli M-F 9-4, Sat 9-3
  · freshly prepared food · deli · vegetarian friendly · tables · self-service · take-out

🗂 **From I-20E**, take exit 589B toward Downtown Longview onto TX 31E about 6½ miles to US 80 (Marshall Ave). Turn left onto 80 about 1 mile to Gilmer Rd/Hwy 300. Turn right onto Gilmer about 2 miles to store. **From I-20W**, take exit 595 and follow access road to Estes Pkwy. Turn right onto Estes (becomes High St) about 5 miles to US 80. Turn left onto 80 about 2 miles to Gilmer. Turn right onto Gilmer about 2 miles to store.

LUBBOCK

Home of National Ranching Heritage Center, Lubbock Lake Landmark natural history preserve, the Buddy Holly Center, and the American Wind Power Center.

NATURAL HEALTH MARKET 🥬
3833 50th St. © 806-796-1230 ⊙ M-Sat 9-6
· organic produce

🍎 **From I-27**, take exit 1C east on 50th St (right from 27S, left from 27N) about 3 miles to store on left. **From Loop 289**, take Quaker Ave north (right) coming from south or south (left) coming from north to 50th St. Turn east onto 50th to store on right.

THE ALTERNATIVE FOOD COMPANY 🥬
2611 Boston Ave. © 806-747-8740 ⊙ M-Sat 9-6
· organic produce

🍎 **From I-27S**, take exit 3 right onto US 62W/19th St about 1²/₃ miles to University Ave. Turn left onto University about ½ mile (7 blocks) to 26th St. Turn right onto 26th 2 blocks to Boston Ave. Turn right onto Boston to store on right. **From I-27N**, take exit 2 left onto 34th St about 1¾ miles to Boston. Turn right onto Boston about ½ mile (8 blocks) to store on right.

MCALLEN

SUN HARVEST FARMS 🥬
2008 N. 10th St. © 956-618-5388 ⊙ Daily 8-9
· organic produce · chain

🍎 **From US 281** (about ⅓ mile north of US 83), turn west onto W Ferguson St (becomes Pecan Blvd) about 3 miles to 10th St. Turn right onto 10th a few blocks to store.

PLANO

WHOLE FOODS MARKET ✕🥬   ♿
2201 Preston Rd., Ste. C © 972-612-6729 ⊙ Daily 8-10
· organic produce · freshly prepared food · juice bar · salad bar · café · deli · bakery
· vegetarian friendly · chain · tables · self-service · take-out

🍎 **From Pres George Bush Tpke** (TX 190), take Preston Rd/TX 289N (left from 190E, right from 190W) about 1¼ miles to store on NW corner Preston & Park Blvd (across from WalMart).

RICHARDSON

Devotees of vegetarian Indian or Chinese food will be well-served in Richardson.

GOPAL ✕
758 S. Central Expwy © 972-437-0155 ⊙ Lunch M-Sun 11:30-2:30, Dinner M-F 5:30-9:30, Sat 6-10, Sun 6-9:30
A vegetarian buffet for lunch and dinner, as well as the regular menu.
· vegetarian · vegan friendly · tables · self-service · wait staff

🍎 On US 75S (aka S Central Expwy) about ¾ mile south of Main St in the Continental Inn Motel.

MADRAS PAVILION ✗🍴
101 S. Coit Rd. ✆ 972-671-3672 ⏰ M-F 11:30-3, 6-10, Sat-Sun 11:30-10
Vegetarian Indian food, offering a daily lunch buffet.
  · vegetarian · vegan friendly · alcohol · tables · self-service · wait staff
🛏 **From I-635**, take exit 19 (B from 635W, C from 635E)and follow Coit Rd ramp onto LBJ Expwy about ¼ mile to Coit. Turn north onto Coit (right from 635W, left from 635E) less than 2 miles to restaurant on left at Belt Line Rd in Dallas Metroplex. **From US 75S**, take exit 24 toward Belt Line and follow N Central Expwy to Belt Line. Turn right onto Belt Line 2 miles to Coit. Turn left onto Coit to restaurant in Dallas Metroxplex.

VEGGIE GARDEN ✗   ♿
510 W. Arapaho Rd. ✆ 972-479-0888 ⏰ M-F 11:30-2:30, 5-9, Sat-Sun 11-9
Vegan Chinese, wth a buffet available at lunchtime.
  · vegan · tables · wait staff
🛏 **From I-635**, take exit 19A onto US 75N. **From US 75**, take exit 25 toward Arapaho Rd and follow expwy to Arapaho. Turn west onto Arapho (sharp left from 75N, right from 75S) about ½ mile to restaurant (behind Arby's).

UDIPI CAFE ✗
35 Richardson Heights Village ✆ 972-437-2858 ⏰ M, W-Sun 11:30-9
Vegetarian Indian food, offering a daily lunch buffet.
  · vegetarian · vegan friendly · tables · self-service · wait staff
🛏 **From I-635**, take exit 19A onto US 75N. **From US 75**, take exit 24 and follow expwy to Belt Line Rd. Turn west onto Belt Line (left from 75N, right from 75S) and make 1st left into Richardson Heights Ctr to restaurant.

WHOLE FOODS MARKET ✗🍴
60 Dal-Rich Village ✆ 972-699-8075 ⏰ Daily 9-10
  · organic produce · freshly prepared food · juice bar · salad bar · café · deli · bakery
  · vegetarian friendly · chain · tables · self-service · take-out
🛏 **From I-635**, take exit 19 (B from 635W, C from 635E) and follow Coit Rd ramp onto LBJ Expy about ¼ mile to Coit. Turn north onto Coit (right from 635W, left from 635E) about 1¾ miles to store at SE corner Coit & Belt Line Rd. **From US 75N** (Central Expwy), take exit 8B north on Coit about 3 miles to store at SE corner Coit & Belt Line. **From US 75S**, take exit 24 to Belt Line. Turn right (west) onto Belt Line about 2½ miles to store at SE corner Belt Line & Coit.

SAN ANTONIO

SUN HARVEST FARMS 🍴
8101 Callaghan Rd. ✆ 210-979-8121 ⏰ Daily 8-10
  · organic produce · freshly prepared food · deli vegetarian friendly · chain · take-out
🛏 **From I-10E**, take exit 562 left onto WI-10/87S/McDermott Fwy to I-10E/87S ramp toward Callaghan Rd. Turn left onto Callaghan to store. **From I-140 Loop**, take exit 16B onto WI-10/US 87N/McDermott Fwy about ⅓ mile to Callaghan Rd. Turn right onto Callahan to store.

SUN HARVEST FARMS ✗🍴
17700 N. US Hwy. 281 ✆ 210-499-1446 ⏰ Daily 8-9
  · organic produce · freshly prepared food · juice bar · café · deli · vegetarian friendly
  · chain · counter · tables · self-service · take-out
🛏 **From 1604 Loop north of downtown**, turn left onto San Pedro Ave about ¾ mile to Donella Dr. Turn left onto Donella and left onto San

Pedro to store on east side. **From I-410 Loop**, take US 281N about 5¼ miles to Anderson Loop exit. Follow exit onto San Pedro to store.

SUN HARVEST FARMS 🏪

2502 Nacogdoches Rd. © 210-824-7800 ⊙ Daily 8-9

· organic produce · freshly prepared food · deli · vegetarian friendly · chain · take-out

From I-410 Loop, take exit 23 onto Nacogdoches Rd (left from 410E, right from 410W) less than ¼ mile to store.

WHOLE FOODS MARKET ✕🏪 &

255 E. Basse Rd., Ste. 130 © 210-826-4676 ⊙ Daily 8-10

· organic produce · freshly prepared food · juice bar · salad bar · café · deli · bakery · vegetarian friendly · chain · tables · self-service · take-out

From I-410E Loop, take exit 21B onto US 281S about ½ mile to Jones-Maltsberger Rd exit. Turn left at traffic light onto Jones-Maltsberger and go under hwy and over railroad tracks. Turn right into Quarry Shopping Center and follow access road on right to store at south end. **From I-410W Loop**, take exit 23 onto Nacogdoches Rd 1½ miles to E Basse Rd. Veer right onto E Basse about 1 mile to store in Quarry Shopping Center.

SUGAR LAND

MADRAS PAVILLION ✕

16260 Kensington Blvd. © 281-481-3672 ⊙ Daily 11-2:30, 5:30-9:30

Vegetarian Indian food, offering a daily lunch buffet.

· vegetarian · vegan friendly · alcohol · tables · self-service · wait staff

From US 59, take TX 6 exit onto 6N (right from 59S, left from 59N) about ½ mile to Fluor Daniel Dr. U-turn back onto 6S ¼ mile to Kensington Blvd. Turn right onto Kensington to restaurant.

TEMPLE

DISCOVER NATURAL FOODS INC. ✕🏪

1706 W. Ave. M © 254-773-7711 ⊙ M-F 9-6, Sat 9-4

From I-35N, take exit 300 toward Ave H/49th-57th St right onto 57th St to W Ave M. Turn left onto M less than 1 mile to store in Natural Medicine Resource Center. **From I-35S**, take exit 300 toward Ave H/49th-57th St left onto W Ave H about ¼ mile to S 35th St. Turn left onto S 35th about ⅓ mile to M. Turn right onto M to store in Natural Medicine Resource Center.

WICHITA FALLS

SUNSHINE NATURAL FOODS ✕🏪 &

2907 Bob Ave. © 940-767-2093 ⊙ M-F 9-6, Sat 10-5:30, Salad bar M-Sat 11-2

· organic produce · freshly prepared food · salad bar · bakery · vegetarian friendly · tables · self-service · take-out

From US 287, take US 82W over 2 miles to Kemp Blvd exit. Turn left onto Kemp to 2nd traffic light. Turn left into Parker Square shopping center to store in NW corner.

Please tell these businesses that you found them in Healthy Highways.

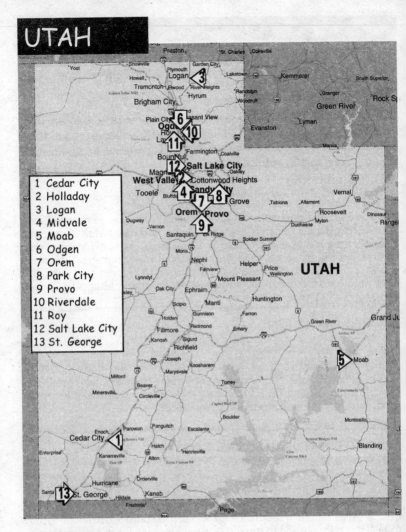

UTAH

Map legend:

1 Cedar City
2 Holladay
3 Logan
4 Midvale
5 Moab
6 Odgen
7 Orem
8 Park City
9 Provo
10 Riverdale
11 Roy
12 Salt Lake City
13 St. George

CEDAR CITY

SUNSHINE NUTRITION
111 W. 535 S. © 435-586-4889 ⊙ M-Sat 9-6
· organic produce

⌂ **From I-15**, take exit 59 east on W 200 N (loop around from 15S, left from 15N) to Main St. Turn right onto Main to W 535 S. Turn right onto W 535 S to store on left (behind Autozone).

HOLLADAY

KEEBA'S ✕
6522 Big Cottonwood Canyon Rd. © 801-272-3455 ⊙ M-Sat 10:30-9, Sun 11-7
A vegetarian fast-food concept, with five meatless burgers on whole grain bun, sandwiches, wraps, burritos, soups, chili, "fryless" fries, salads, smoothies, and such.
· vegetarian · vegan friendly · counter · tables · self-service · take-out

🛏 **From I-15**, take exit 302 onto I-215E 5-6 miles to exit 6. Follow ramp toward ski areas onto E 6200 S to S 3000 E (1st right). Turn right onto S 300 E to Big Cottonwood Canyon Rd (1st left). Turn left onto Big Cottonwood Canyon to restaurant on north side of Old Mill Village.

LOGAN

CAFFE IBIS ✗

52 Federal Ave. ✆ 435-753-4777 ⊘ M-Th 6am-9pm, F-Sat 6am-10pm, Sun 7am-5pm
The focus is organically grown, fair-trade coffee. The food is mostly sandwiches and burritos, with several vegetarian options.

· vegetarian friendly · tables · self-service · take-out

🛏 US 91, US 89 and UT 30 converge in Logan. **From US 91 (Main St in Logan)** turn east onto Federal Ave (right from 91N, left from 91S) 1 block to store at Federal & Church St (½ block north of Tabernacle Park). **From UT 30E**, continue straight on E 200 N 1 block past 91 to Church. Turn right onto Church 1 block to store at Church & Federal.

SHANGRI-LA HEALTH FOODS 🍃

438½ N. Main St. ✆ 435-752-1315 ⊘ M-Sat 9-6

🛏 US 91, US 89 and UT 30 converge in Logan. **From US 91 or 89**, store is at corner Main St & 400 N (where 91 & 89 merge) in Albertson's shopping plaza. **From UT 30E**, continue straight on E 200 N to Main. Turn left onto Main ⅓ mile to store.

MIDVALE

GOOD EARTH NATURAL FOODS 🍃

7206 S. 900 E. ✆ 801-562-2209 ⊘ M-Sat 9-8

· organic produce

🛏 **From I-15S**, merge onto I-215E (exit 302). Take 215E to exit 9 onto Union Park Ave N ramp. Turn left onto Union Park, left onto E 600S and left onto S 900 E about ¾ mile (past Ft Union Blvd) to store. **From I-15N**, take exit 301 right onto W 7200 S/UT 48 (becomes Ft Union Blvd) about 2 miles to S 900 E. Turn right onto S 900 E to store.

MOAB

MOONFLOWER MARKET 🍃

39 E. & 100 N. ✆ 435-259-5712 ⊘ M-Sat 9-6:30, Sun 10-3

· organic produce

🛏 Moab is about 30 miles south of I-70 exit 180 on Rt 191. **From 191**, turn east onto E 100 N (left from 191S, right from 191N) to store at 39 E.

ODGEN

BRIGHT DAY NATURAL FOODS 🍃

952 28th St. ✆ 801-399-0260 ⊘ M-Sat 9:30-6:30

· organic produce

🛏 **From I-15**, take exit 344A onto E 31st St (merge right from 15N, loop around right from 15S) about 1½ miles to Washington Blvd. Turn left onto Washington 2 blocks to 30th St. Turn right onto 30th about ½ mile to Monroe Blvd. Turn left onto Monroe about ¼ mile to 28th St. Turn right onto 28th 3 blocks to store at Fowler Ave.

HARVEST HEALTH FOOD 🍎
341 27th St. © 801-621-1627 ⊙ M-F 9-6:30, Sat 9-5

🍎 **From I-15,** take exit 344A onto E 31st St (merge right from 15N, loop around right from 15S) about 1 mile to Wall Ave. Turn left onto Wall ½ mile to 27th St. Turn right onto 27th ⅓ mile to store.

OREM

GOOD EARTH NATURAL FOODS 🍎
500 S. State St. © 801-765-1616 ⊙ M-Sat 9-8

· organic produce

🍎 **From I-15,** take exit 272 east on Center St (left from 15S, right from 15N) about 1½ miles to S State St. Turn right onto S State about ⅔ mile (past 400 S) to store.

PARK CITY

FAIRWEATHER NATURAL FOODS 🍎
1270 Iron Horse Drive © 435-649-4561 ⊙ M-F 9-7, Sat 10-6, Sun 12-6

· organic produce · freshly prepared food · juice bar · take-out

🍎 **From I-80E,** take exit 145 toward Kimball Jct/Park City onto UT 224S about 5½ miles to Iron Horse Dr. Turn left onto Iron Horse to store on left (last driveway). **From I-80W,** take exit 148 toward Heber/Provo left onto Silver Creek Rd (becomes US 40E) 3½ miles to exit 4 (UT 248). Turn right onto 248 about 2½ miles to Bonanza Dr. Turn left onto Bonanza about ¼ mile to Iron Horse. Turn right onto Iron Horse to store on right. **From US 40W,** take exit 4 toward Park City left onto UT 248 about 2¾ miles to Bonanza. Turn left onto Bonanza about ¼ mile to Iron Horse. Turn right onto Iron Horse to store on right.

MORNING RAY CAFE & EVENING STAR ✗
255 Main St. © 435-649-5686 ⊙ Daily 7-4ish , Dinner Thanksgiving-March 5-10
Morning Ray is open year-round for breakfast and lunch. All-day breakfast features eggs, tofu dishes, whole grain cereals, and more. Lunch includes vegan and vegetarian soups, salads, whole grain thin-crusted pizzas, and a few vegetarian sandwiches, plus fish and poultry. Thanksgiving through March, it becomes the Evening Star for dinner, with a primarily fish and chicken menu, but several choices for vegetarians, and pot roast for meat-eaters.

· vegetarian friendly · organic focus · alcohol · tables · wait staff

🍎 **From I-80E,** take exit 145 toward Kimball Jct/Park City onto UT 224S about 5¾ miles to Park Ave. Continue straight onto Park over 1 mile to 4th St. Turn left onto 4th 1 block to Main St. Turn right onto Main to restaurant in Treasure Mt Inn (mezzanine level). **From I-80W,** take exit 148 toward Heber/Provo left onto Silver Creek Rd (becomes US 40E) 3½ miles to exit 4 (UT 248). Turn right onto 248 about 2½ miles to Bonanza Dr. Turn left onto Bonanza ½ mile to Deer Valley Dr. Turn left onto Deer Valley over ½ mile to Main. Turn right onto Main over ½ mile to restaurant (mezzanine level in Treasure Mt Inn).

PROVO

GOOD EARTH NATURAL FOODS 🍎
1045 S. University Ave. © 801-375-7444 ⊘ M-Sat 9-8
· organic produce

🍎 **From I-15**, take exit 266 onto UT 189N/University Ave (staight from 15N, loop around right from 15S) ½-1 mile to store.

RIVERDALE

GOOD EARTH NATURAL FOODS 🍎
1050 W. Riverdale Rd. © 801-334-5500 ⊘ M-Sat 9-8
· organic produce

🍎 **From I-15N**, take exit 342 toward I-84E/Riverdale onto UT 26/W Riverdale Rd 1 mile to store. **From I-15S**, merge onto I-84-E. **From I-84**, take exit 81 onto UT 26 (left from 84E, right from 84W) less than ⅓ mile to store.

ROY

DOWN TO EARTH NATURAL FOODS 🍴🍎
5418 S. 1900 W. © 801-728-0234 ⊘ M-Sat 9-8
· organic produce · freshly prepared food · deli · vegetarian friendly · tables · self-service · take-out

🍎 **From I-15**, take exit 341 west on W 5600 S (left from 15N, right from 15S) to 1st right at S 1900 W. Turn right onto S 1900 W past 1st block to store.

SALT LAKE CITY

OASIS CAFE 🍴
151 S. 500 E. © 801-322-0404 ⊘ M-Th, Sun 8-9, F-Sat 8-10
Not exclusively meat-free (serves seafood and chicken), but all soups and sauces are vegetarian and there are ample vegetarian (and vegan) possibilities.
· vegetarian friendly · vegan friendly · alcohol · counter · tables · wait staff

🍎 **From I-15N**, take exit 310 right onto W 600 S less than 1 mile to Main St. Turn left onto Main over ½ mile to E 200 W. Turn right onto E 200 W ¾ mile to S 500 E. Turn left onto S 500 E ½ block to restaurant. **From I-15S**, take exit 312 left onto W 600 N ½ mile to N 300 W (US 89). Turn right and follow 89 (turns left onto N W Temple, then right onto State St) 1½ miles to E S Temple. Turn left onto E S Temple over ½ mile to S 500 E. Turn right onto S 500 E 1½ blocks to restaurant.

SAGE'S CAFE 🍴
473 E. 300 S. © 801-322-3790 ⊘ W-Th 5-9:30, F 5-10, Sat 9-10, Sun 9-9
Eclectic vegan, mostly organic menu, including a few raw food choices and a monthly "raw special night."
· vegan · organic focus · alcohol · tables · wait staff · take-out

🍎 **From I-15S**, take exit 312 onto 600 NE ramp and turn left onto W 600 N about ½ mile to N 300 W. Turn right onto N 300 W about ¾ mile to NW Temple. Turn left onto NW Temple over ½ mile to State St. Turn right onto State over ½ mile to E 300 S. Turn left onto E 300 S to restaurant on left. **From I-15N**, take exit 310 onto W 600 S to S 500 E. Turn left onto S 500 E 3 blocks to E 300 S. Turn left onto E 300 S to restaurant on right. **From I-80E**, take 600 S exit onto W 600 S and follow directions from I-15N above. **From I-80W**, take exit 125 right onto S 700 E 3 miles to E 300 S. Turn left onto E 300 S about ⅓ mile (past 500 E) to restaurant on right.

WILD OATS MARKET ✗🍴   ♿
645 E. 400 S. © 801-355-7401 ⊘ M-Sat 7-11, Sun 8-9

· organic produce · freshly prepared food · juice bar · salad bar · café · deli · bakery
· vegetarian friendly · chain · tables · self-service · take-out

🍎 **From I-80**, take exit 125 north onto 700 E (left from 80E, right from 80W) almost 3 miles to E 400 S. Turn left onto E 400 S to store. **From I-15N**, merge onto 1-80E and follow directions above. **From I-15S**, take exit 312 onto 600 NE ramp and turn left onto W 600 N about ½ mile to N 300 W. Turn right onto N 300 W about ¼ mile to W N Temple. Turn left onto W N Temple over ½ mile to State St. Turn right onto State 1 block to E S Temple. Turn left onto E S Temple almost 1 mile to S 700 E. Turn right onto S 700 E over ½ mile to E 400 S. Turn right onto E 400 S to store.

WILD OATS MARKET ✗🍴   ♿
1131 E. Wilmington Ave. © 801-359-7913 ⊘ M-Sat 7-11, Sun 8-9

· organic produce · freshly prepared food · juice bar · salad bar · café · deli · bakery
· vegetarian friendly · chain · tables · self-service · take-out

🍎 **From I-80**, take exit 126 (UT 181/13th E) north on S 1300 E (left from 80E, right from 80W) about ¼ mile to Wilmington Ave. Turn left onto Wilmington about ¼ mile to store.

ST. GEORGE

HEALTH NUT NATURAL FOODS MARKET 🍴
700 S. 100 W. © 435-652-4372 ⊘ M-F 9-7, Sat 9-6
There are two vegan sandwiches offered daily to go.

· organic produce · juice bar · vegan friendly · take-out

🍎 **From I-15S**, take exit 6 onto Bluff St/15Bus (right from 15S, left from 15N) about ¾-1 mile to W 700 S. Turn right onto 700 1 block to store at corner W 700 S & S 100 W.

Goldbeck's "EAT IT OR NOT"

FASCINATING & FAR-OUT FACTS ABOUT FOOD

TRUE OR FALSE?

Maple trees can provide syrup for 40 or more years.

False Actually a maple tree isn't worth tapping until it's about 40 years old but after that, it can provide syrup for 150 years or more. Another surprising maple syrup fact: It takes 35 to 40 gallons of sap to make one gallon of syrup.

VERMONT

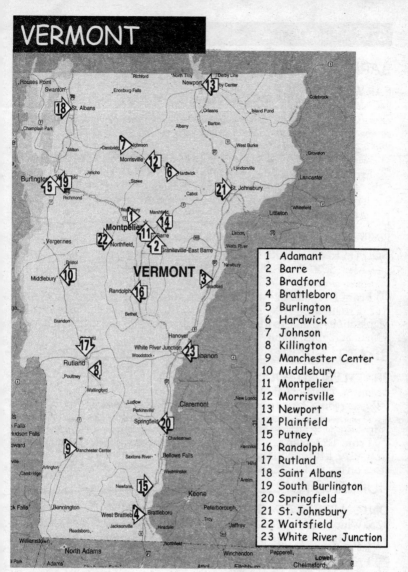

1	Adamant
2	Barre
3	Bradford
4	Brattleboro
5	Burlington
6	Hardwick
7	Johnson
8	Killington
9	Manchester Center
10	Middlebury
11	Montpelier
12	Morrisville
13	Newport
14	Plainfield
15	Putney
16	Randolph
17	Rutland
18	Saint Albans
19	South Burlington
20	Springfield
21	St. Johnsbury
22	Waitsfield
23	White River Junction

ADAMANT

ADAMANT CO-OP
1313 Haggett Rd. © 802-223-5760 ☺ M-F 9:30-6, Sat 9:30-3, Sun 10-1
· organic produce · co-op

⬭ **From I-89,** take exit 8 (Montpelier) onto Memorial Dr about 1 mile to traffic light at Main St. Turn left onto Main through town to traffic circle. Take 1st right off traffic circle to stay on Main (becomes County Rd). At fork turn right onto Center Rd about 5 miles to store at crossroad in Adamant.

BARRE

FARMERS DINER ✕ &
240 N. Main St. © 802-476-7623 ⊙ M-W, Sun 7am-3pm, Th-Sat 7am-8pm
Familiar diner fare, but distinguished by the fact that 70 percent of the food comes from farmers and small-scale producers within 70 miles of the place, and is organic whenever possible.
· vegetarian friendly · organic focus · alcohol · counter · tables · waitstaff · take-out
🍎 **From I-89**, take exit 7 toward Barre onto Rt 65E about 5 past 3 taffic lights and left at fork down long hill to 2nd light at Main St (about 5 miles). Turn right onto Main less than ¼ mile to restaurant on right.

BRADFORD

For live folk music, go to Middle Earth Music.

SOUTH END MARKET 🥬
45 S. Main St. © 802-222-5701 ⊙ M-F 9-6, Sat-Sun 10-5
· organic produce
🍎 **From I-91**, take exit 16 toward Bradford (US 5/Bradford ramp) onto Rt 25E (right from 91N, left from 91S) to 1st left at Maple St. Turn left onto Maple about ⅓ mile to Mill St. Turn right onto Mill and merge right onto S Main St (25Bus) about ⅓ mile to store on left.

BRATTLEBORO

BRATTLEBORO FOOD CO-OP ✕ 🥬
2 Main St. © 802-257-1841 ⊙ M-Sat 8-9, Sun 9-9
RW: Easygoing, casual atmosphere in their small cafe area.
· organic produce · freshly prepared food · juice bar · salad bar · café · deli · vegetarian friendly · co-op · tables · self-service · take-out
🍎 **From 1-91**, take exit 1 toward Brattleboro onto US 5/Canal St (right from 91N, left from 91S) over 1 mile (to where Canal becomes Main St) to store on left in Brookside Shopping Center.

BURLINGTON

ONION RIVER CO-OP CITY MARKET ✕ 🥬
82 S. Winooski Ave. © 802-863-3659 ⊙ Daily 7-11
· organic produce · freshly prepared food · café · deli · vegetarian friendly · co-op · tables · self-service · take-out
🍎 **From I-89**, take exit 14W toward Burlington onto US 2W (becomes Main St) about 1½ miles to Winooski Ave. Turn right onto Winooski to store. **From Rt 7N**, turn left onto Main ¼ mile to Winooski and follow directions above.

STONE SOUP ✕ 🥬&
211 College St. © 802-862-7616 ⊙ M, Sat 7-7, Tues-F 7-9
The all-vegetarian, vegan friendly hot buffet and salad bar offer a culturally mixed menu that changes daily. The set sandwich menu provides free-range poultry for those seeking a meat option.
· salad bar · vegetarian friendly · vegan friendly · alcohol · tables · self-service
🍎 **From I-89**, take exit 14W toward Burlington onto US 2W (becomes Main St) 1½ miles to Church St. Turn right onto Church 1 block to College St. Turn left onto College to restaurant. **From Rt 7N**, turn left onto Main ⅓ mile to Church and follow directions above.

HARDWICK

BUFFALO MOUNTAIN CO-OP 🍎
Main St. © 802-472-6020 ⊘ M-Th, Sat 9-6, F 9-7, Sun 10-3
· organic produce · co-op
⬛ Take Rt 15 to Hardwick. Store is in town on east side of Main St (aka Rt 15).

JOHNSON

ROO'S NATURAL FOODS 🍎
2 Lower Main St. E. © 802-635-1788 ⊘ M-F 10-5:30, Sat 11-4
· organic produce
⬛ Take Rt 15 to Johnson. Store is in town on Main St (aka Rt 15) in large yellow house.

KILLINGTON

HEMINGWAY'S RESTAURANT ✗
4988 Rte. 4 © 802-422-3886 ⊘ W-Sun 6-10
This upscale, gourmet restaurant features several price-fixed, multi-course menus, including a 4-course vegetarian choice. (Vegan can be accomodated with advance notice, as can other dietary restrictions.)
· vegetarian friendly · alcohol · tables · wait staff
⬛ On Rt 4 between junctions 100N & 100S.

MANCHESTER CENTER

NATURE'S MARKET 🍎
303 Center Hill Rd. © 802-362-0033 ⊘ M-Sat 9-6, Sun 11-5
· organic produce
⬛ **From Rt 7**, take exit 4 toward Historic VT/Rt 7A west on VT 11 (right from 7S, left at fork in ramp from 7N) less than 1 mile to Center Hill Rd. Turn right onto Center Hill to store.

NEW MORNING NATURAL FOODS 🍎
Rte. 11 & 30 © 802-362-3602 ⊘ M-Sat 9-6:30, Sun 11-5
· organic produce
⬛ **From Rt 7**, take exit 4 toward Historic VT/7A west on VT 11 (right from 7S, left at fork in ramp from 7N) to store in red barn next to VFW (across from Price Chopper Plaza).

MIDDLEBURY

MIDDLEBURY NATURAL FOODS CO-OP 🍎
1 Washington Sq. © 802-388-7276 ⊘ Daily 8-7
· organic produce · co-op
⬛ Take Rt 7 to Middlebury. At traffic circle turn onto Washington St to store on left.

MONTPELIER

EVERGREEN CAFÉ ✗
20 State St. © 802-223-0120 ⊘ M-F 11:30-6:30, Weekends seasonal (call)
All vegan and almost entirely organic hot meals and sandwiches, plus salad bar and hot buffet priced by the pound. Café also sells fresh baked goods. Located in the State Street Market.

· salad bar · café · vegan · organic focus · tables · self-service · take-out

See directions below for State Street Market.

HUNGER MOUNTAIN CO-OP

623 Stone Cutters Way © 802-223-8000 ⊙ Daily 8-8

All vegetarian salad bar, daily soups and hot entrees. Fresh deli selection also includes non-vegetarian items.

· organic produce · freshly prepared food · salad bar · café · deli · vegetarian friendly · co-op · tables · self-service · take-out

From I-89, take exit 8 toward Montpelier/US 2 onto Memorial Dr over 1 mile to traffic light at Main St (Rt 12). Turn left onto Main and make 1st right onto Stonecutter's Way to store on right.

STATE STREET MARKET

20 State St. © 802-229-9353 ⊙ M-Th 10-6:30, F 10-7, Sat 10-6, Sun 11-5

· organic produce · freshly prepared food · salad bar · café · vegan · tables · self-service · take-out

From I-89, take exit 8 toward Montpelier/US 2 onto Memorial Dr over 1 mile to traffic light at Main St (Rt 12). Turn left onto Main to 1st light at State St. Turn left onto State ½ block to store on left.

MORRISVILLE

APPLETREE NATURAL FOODS

Munson Ave. © 802-888-8481 ⊙ M-F 9-6, Sat 10-5

Take Rt 15 to Morrisville. Turn onto Munsun Ave (on south side of Rt 15 past Rt 100) to store on left in Mountainville Plaza.

NEWPORT

NEWPORT NATURAL FOODS

194 Main St. © 802-334-2626 ⊙ M-F 9-5:30, Sat 9-5, Sun 10-4

Most of the homemade offerings are vegetarian and they aim for organic. Studio on the premises for tai chi, yoga and massage. If you're looking for information, the staff "knows all about what's going on in the area."

· organic produce · freshly prepared food · café · bakery · vegetarian friendly · organic focus · tables · self-service · take-out

From I-91N, take exit 27 toward Newport/VT 105 right onto VT 191 about 2¼ miles to end at US 5/VT 105. Turn left onto 5/105 about ½ mile (across water, becomes Main St) to store on right (2 blocks past traffic light). From I-91S, take exit 28 toward Newport right onto US 5/VT 105 about 4 miles (across water) to store on right.

PLAINFIELD

PLAINFIELD CO-OP

153 Main St. © 802-454-8579 ⊙ M-F 10-7, Sat 10-5, Sun 10-4

Store promotes locally produced and organic foods. There is a children's play area, and classes, music, dances, and movies in the community center upstairs.

· organic produce · co-op

From US Rt 2E, turn right at blinking light in Plainfield down hill to village. Cross bridge and bear left onto Main St to end. Store is on left behind fire station. From Rt 2W, turn left just before blinking light, bear left, cross bridge and follow directions above.

PUTNEY

PUTNEY CO-OP ✗ 🥬
730 Main St. © 802-387-5866 ⊘ M-Sat 7:30-8, Sun 8-8
  · organic produce · freshly prepared food · deli · bakery · vegetarian friendly · co-op
  · tables · self-service · take-out

⌂ **From I-91N**, take exit 4 toward Putney/US 5 onto VT 4 (Putney State Hwy) and follow around left across hwy to Rt 5. Turn left onto 5 to store on right (west side). **From I-91S**, take exit 4 right onto Rt 5 to store on left.

RANDOLPH

WHITE RIVER CO-OP 🥬
24 Pleasant St. © 802-728-9554 ⊘ M-F 8-7, Sat 9-5, Sun 10-4, Deli M-F 8-6
  · freshly prepared food · deli · vegetarian friendly · co-op · take-out

⌂ **From I-89**, take exit 4 onto Rt 66E about 2½ miles to N Main St. Turn left onto N Main about ⅓ mile to Railroad St. Turn left onto Railroad and slight right onto Pleasant St to store.

RUTLAND

RUTLAND AREA FOOD CO-OP 🥬
77 Wales St. © 802-773-0737 ⊘ M-Sat 10-7, Sun 11-4
  · organic produce · co-op

⌂ **From Rt 7** (in Rutland), turn west onto Center St (right from 7S, left from 7N) 4 blocks to Wales St. Turn left onto Wales to store on right.

SUNSHINE NATURAL MARKET 🥬
42 Center St. © 802-775-2050 ⊘ M-Sat 9-7, Sun 10-6
  · organic produce

⌂ **From Rt 7** (in Rutland), turn west onto Center St (right from 7S, left from 7N) 4 blocks to store at Center & Wales St.

SAINT ALBANS

RAIL CITY MARKET 🥬
8 S. Main St. © 802-524-3769 ⊘ M-Sat 9-6

⌂ **From I-89**, take exit 19 (VT 104) toward US 7/St Albans and follow Access Road (St Albans S State Hwy)west (left from 89N, right from 89S) less than 1 mile to Rt 7. Turn right onto Rt 7 (S Main St) about ½ mile to store on left (opposite south end of park).

SOUTH BURLINGTON

HEALTHY LIVING NATURAL FOODS MARKET & CAFE ✗ 🥬 ♿
4 Market St. © 802-863-2569 ⊘ Daily 8-8
Choices for vegetarians, vegans and carnivores who want free-range, organic meat.
  · organic produce · freshly prepared food · juice bar · salad bar · café · deli · bakery
  · vegetarian friendly · tables · self-service · take-out

⌂ **From I-89**, take exit 14E onto US 2E (right from 89N, around to right from 89S) to 1st right at Dorset St. Turn right onto Dorset ¼ mile to 2nd traffic light at Market St. Turn left onto Market 1 block to store.

SPRINGFIELD

SPRINGFIELD FOOD CO-OP 🍲 &

76 Chester Rd. © 802-885-3363 ⊗ M-Sat 9-6, Sun 11-4

· organic produce · freshly prepared food · vegetarian friendly · co-op · take-out

🍎 **From I-91**, take exit 7 onto Rt 11W about 5 miles (through Springfield). Bear left at Rt 106 intersecton to stay on Rt 11W (Chester Rd) less than 1 mile to store on left.

ST. JOHNSBURY

KINGDOM COUNTY MARKET 🍲

490 Portland St. © 802-748-9498 ⊗ M-W, Sat 9-6, Th-F 9-7, Sun 11-4

· organic produce · freshly prepared food · vegetarian friendly · co-op · take-out

🍎 **From I-91**, take exit 20 (St Johnsbury) onto US 5N (Railroad St) about 1¼ miles to Portland St. Turn right onto Portland about ½ mile to store. **From I-93N**, take exit 1 (St Johnsbury) right onto VA 18N about ⅓ mile to Rt 2W. Turn left onto 2W (becomes Portland St) about 3 miles to store.

NATURAL PROVISIONS 🍲 &

537 Railroad St. © 802-748-3587 ⊗ M-F 8:30-6, Sat 9-5, Sun 10-4

Organic foods, wine and an extensive "bulk room." In an old church, complete with stained-glass windows and working steeple bell.

· organic produce

🍎 **From I-91**, take exit 20 (St Johnsbury) onto US 5N (Railroad St) about 1¼ miles to store in heart of town on corner Railroad & Maple St (in old green church). **From I-93N**, take exit 1 (St Johnsbury) right onto VT 18N about ⅓ mile to Rt 2W. Turn left onto 2W (becomes Portland St) 3 miles to Railroad. Turn right onto Railroad 1 block to store at Railroad & Maple.

WAITSFIELD

SWEET PEA NATURAL FOODS 🍲

Village Square, Rt. 100 © 802-496-7763 ⊗ M-Sat 8-6, Sun 11:30-5

· organic produce · freshly prepared food · deli · vegetarian friendly · take-out

🍎 **From Rt 89**, take exit 10 onto Rt 100S about 10 miles into Waitsfield. Store is in town in Village Square Shopping Center.

WHITE RIVER JUNCTION

UPPER VALLEY FOOD CO-OP ✕🍲

193 N. Main St. © 802-295-5804 ⊗ M-Sat 9-8, Sun 10-5

· organic produce · freshly prepared food · deli · vegetarian friendly · tables · self-service · take-out

🍎 **From I-91N**, take exit 11 toward White River Junction onto Rt 5N about 1 mile to Main St. Stay straight onto Main to store. **From I-91S**, take exit 12 toward White River Junction/US 5 left onto Bugbee St to Rt 5S. Turn right onto 5S (Hartford St) about 1 mile to Main. Turn sharp left onto Main to store.

Please tell these businesses that you found them in Healthy Highways.

Goldbeck's "EAT IT OR NOT"
FASCINATING & FAR-OUT FACTS ABOUT FOOD

LEMONADE WAS INVENTED IN PARIS IN 1630.

T. BERNHARD

TRUE OR FALSE

Citrus fruits like oranges, grapefruits, lemons and limes are the best sources of vitamin C.

False. Citrus fruits do furnish plenty of vitamin C and other important vitamins. However, when compared by weight, strawberries contain 60% more vitamin C than grapefruit and 8% more than oranges. Other great sources of vitamin C include kiwi, papaya, broccoli, arugula, Brussels sprouts, cabbage, cauliflower, dark leafy greens, peppers, potatoes, and vine-ripened summer tomatoes. Among the more exotic sources are cactus pads, celeriac, cherimoyas, fennel, jicama, litchi nuts, salsify, and seaweeds.

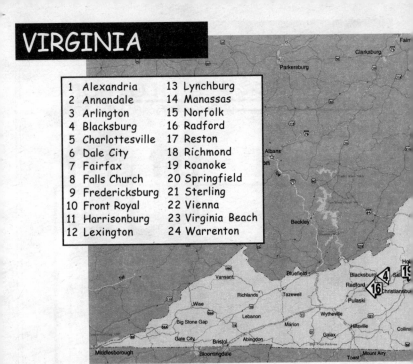

VIRGINIA

1 Alexandria	13 Lynchburg
2 Annandale	14 Manassas
3 Arlington	15 Norfolk
4 Blacksburg	16 Radford
5 Charlottesville	17 Reston
6 Dale City	18 Richmond
7 Fairfax	19 Roanoke
8 Falls Church	20 Springfield
9 Fredericksburg	21 Sterling
10 Front Royal	22 Vienna
11 Harrisonburg	23 Virginia Beach
12 Lexington	24 Warrenton

ALEXANDRIA

HEALTHWAY NATURAL FOODS 🍃
1610 Belle View Blvd. ☎ 703-660-8603 ⊙ M-W, F 10-7, Th 10-8, Sat 10-6, Sun 12-5
· organic produce · chain

📖 From I-495 (Capitol Beltway), take exit 177A south onto Richmond Hwy/US 1S about ⅔ mile to Huntington Ave. Turn left onto Huntington and right onto Fort Hunt Rd 1 mile to Belle View Blvd. Turn left onto Belle View to store.

WHOLE FOODS MARKET 🍴🍃
6548 Little River Tpke. ☎ 703-914-0040 ⊙ M-Sat 8-9, Sun 8-8
· organic produce · freshly prepared food · salad bar · café · deli · bakery · vegetarian friendly · chain · tables · self-service · take-out

📖 From I-395, take exit 1B onto Little River Tpke/Rt 236W about 1¼ miles (past 2 traffic lights) to store on right (after Jerry's Ford & Salvation Army, across from Home Depot). From I-495 (Capitol Beltway), take exit 52A-B toward Annandale onto Little River Tpke/Rt 236E almost 4 miles to store on left (U-turn back onto 236W).

ANNANDALE

HEALTHWAY NATURAL FOODS 🍃
4113 John Marr Dr. ☎ 703-354-7785 ⊙ M-W, F 10-7, Th 10-8, Sat 10-6, Sun 12-5
· organic produce · chain

📖 From I-495N (Capital Beltway), take exit 52A-B toward Annandale onto Little River Tpke/Rt 236E 1½ miles to Columbia Pike. Turn left onto Columbia (VA 244) about ⅓ mile to John Marr Dr. Turn left onto John Marr to store.

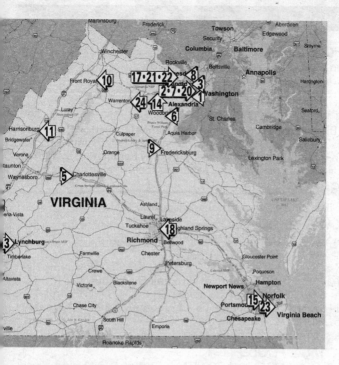

ARLINGTON——————————

SARAN FOODS ✗

5151 N. Lee Hwy. © 703-533-3600 ☺ Tues-Th 11-9:30, F-Sat 11-10, Sun 11-9
Vegetarian Indian cuisine. A la carte and lunch buffet.
· vegetarian · vegan friendly · tables · self-service · take-out
👄 **From I-66W**, take exit 71 right onto VA 120N/Glebe Rd about ¾ mile
to Lee Hwy. Turn left onto Lee less than ½ mile to restaurant in John
Mason Shopping Center (with Wendy's & Goodyear Tire). **From I-66E**,
take exit 68 (Westmoreland St) left onto Fairfax Dr about ¼ mile to Lee
Hwy/US 29N. Turn left onto Lee about 1¾ miles to restaurant on left in
John Mason Shopping Center.

THE UNCOMMON MARKET 🦞

1041 S. Edgewood St. © 703-521-2667 ☺ M-Sat 9-9, Sun 10-6
· organic produce · co-op
👄 **From I-395S**, take exit 8 toward Pentagon S Parking onto VA 27W/
Washington Blvd toward Ridge Rd. Go 1 mile to VA 244/Columbia Pike
ramp toward Bailey's Cross Rd. Veer right onto 244 ¾ mile to S Edgwood
St. Turn left onto S Edgewood (at Ski Chalet) ½ block to store. **From I-
395N**, take exit 7B toward Marymount U onto Glebe Rd 1 mile to Walter
Reed Dr. Veer right onto Walter Reed ½ mile to Columbia Pike. Turn
right onto Columbia and right onto S Edgewood ½ block to store. **From I-
66**, take exit 71 onto Glebe Rd/VA 120S (left from 66E, right from 66W) 2
miles to Columbia Pike. Turn left onto Columbia ⅓ mile to S Edgewood.
Turn right onto S Edgewod ½ block to store.

WHOLE FOODS MARKET ✗ 🍴 &

2700 Wilson Blvd. © 703-527-6596 ⊙ Daily 8-10

Food samplings every Friday, Saturday and Monday.

· organic produce · freshly prepared food · juice bar · salad bar · café · deli · bakery · vegetarian friendly · chain · tables · self-service · take-out

🍎 **From I-395**, take exit 11B and follow signs onto US 50W. Take 50W (Arlington Blvd) 1 mile and merge right onto Fairfax Dr less than ½ mile to N Danville St. Turn right onto N Danville to store on left. **From I-66E**, take exit 72 left onto Lee Hwy/US 29S and U-turn at N Kenmore St onto 29N ½ mile to N Danville. Turn right onto N Danville about ⅓ mile to store on left.

BLACKSBURG

Close to the Blue Ridge Parkway and the Appalachian Trail.

ANNIE KAY'S WHOLE FOODS 🍴

301 S. Main St. © 540-552-6870 ⊙ M-F 9-8, Sat 9-6, Sun 12-6

· organic produce

🍎 **From I-81S**, take exit 118C (US 11/US 460E) and follow ramp right onto US 460W toward Blacksburg about 5 miles to 460Bus W (S Main St). Merge right onto S Main about 2½ miles to store on right. **From I-81N**, take exit 114 toward Christianburg/Floyd left onto VA 8N/W Main about 1¼ miles to 460Bus W. Turn left onto 460Bus W (veers right at about 5 miles) almost 8 miles to store on right.

EATS NATURAL FOODS 🍴 &

1200 N. Main St. © 540-552-2279 ⊙ M-F 10-8, Sat 10-6, Sun 12-6

Large selection of bulk foods and cheeses.

· organic produce · co-op

🍎 **From I-81S**, take exit 118C (US 11/US 460E) and follow ramp right onto US 460W toward Blacksburg about 9 miles to Prices Fork Rd. Merge right onto Prices Fork almost 1½ miles to 460Bus (N Main St). Turn left onto N Main ½ mile to store on right. **From I-81N**, take exit 114 toward Christianburg/Floyd left onto VA 8N/W Main about 1¼ miles to 460Bus W. Turn left onto 460Bus W almost 5 miles. Merge onto 460W almost 3½ miles to Prices Fork and follow directions above.

CHARLOTTESVILLE

Home of Jefferson's famous Monticello and the University of VA.

INTEGRAL YOGA NATURAL FOODS ✗ 🍴 &

923H Preston Ave. © 434-293-4111 ⊙ Store/Cafe M-Sat 9:30-8, Store Sun 11-6

The Veggie Heaven Cafe features organic ingredients in the all-vegetarian deli selections, soups, sandwiches, smoothies, juice bar, and daily specials.

· organic produce · freshly prepared food · juice bar · salad bar · café · deli · bakery · vegetarian · vegan friendly · organic focus · tables · wait staff · take-out

🍎 **From I-64E**, take exit 120 left onto 5th St/VA 631N (becomes Ridge St) 2⅓ miles to Preston Ave. Turn left onto Preston about ½ mile to store in Preston Plaza. **From I-64W**, take exit 124 onto 250W almost 2 miles to 250 Bypass. Take 250 Bypass 1 mile to McIntire Rd. Turn left onto McIntire and follow onto Harris St about ⅔ mile to Preston (250Bus). Turn right onto Preston to store in Preston Plaza. **From Rt 29S**, take 29Bus S (Emmet St) almost ½ mile to Barracks Rd. Turn left onto Barracks ½ mile to Preston. Continue straight onto Preston almost ⅔ mile to store in Preston Plaza.

WHOLE FOODS MARKET ✗🍴 &

300 Shoppers World Ct. ✆ 434-973-4900 ⊘ Daily 9-9
  · organic produce · freshly prepared food · café · deli · bakery · vegetarian friendly
  · chain · tables · self-service · take-out

🛏 **From I-64E**, take 118B onto Rt 29N about 6¼ miles to store on west side (29S) in Shopper's World (across from Fashion Square Mall). **From I-64W**, take exit 124 onto Rt 250W almost 2 miles to Rt 250 Bypass. Follow 250 Bypass 2½ miles to Rt 29N (toward Washington). Turn right onto 29N (Emmet St) 1¾ miles to store on west side (29S) in Shopper's World.

DALE CITY———————————————————

THE NATURAL GROCER 🍴

14453 Potomac Mills Rd. ✆ 703-494-7287 ⊘ M-F 10-8, Sat 10-6

🛏 **From I-95S**, take exit 156 (VA 784W) and follow ramp onto Potomac Mills Rd. Stay right at fork and right onto Potomac Mills to store in Potomac Festival Shopping Ctr (behind Day's Inn). **From I-95N**, take exit 156 onto Dale Blvd/VA 784W about 1½ miles to Gideon Dr. Turn right onto Gideon about ¾ mile to Opitz Blvd. Turn right onto Opitz and right onto Potomac Mills to store in Potomac Festival Shopping Ctr (behind Day's Inn).

FAIRFAX———————————————————

HEALTHWAY NATURAL FOODS 🍴 &

10360 Lee Hwy. ✆ 703-591-1121 ⊘ M-W, F 10-7, Th 10-8, Sat 10-6, Sun 12-5
  · organic produce · chain

🛏 **From I-66**, take exit 60 toward Fairfax onto VA 123S (Chain Bridge Rd) to Lee Hwy. Turn left onto Lee 1 block to store in Fairfax Shopping Ctr.

WOODLANDS ✗

4078 Jermantown Rd. ✆ 703-385-1996 ⊘ M-Th, Sun 11:30-9:30, F-Sat 11:30-10
Vegetarian Indian food, with a buffet available at lunch.
  · vegetarian · vegan friendly · tables · self-service · wait staff

🛏 **From I-66**, take exit 57A toward Fairfax onto US 50E about 1¼ miles to Jermantown Rd. Turn right onto Jermantown to restaurant.

FALLS CHURCH———————————————

KENNEDY'S NATURAL FOODS ✗🍴

1051 W. Broad St. ✆ 703-533-8484 ⊘ M-F 9-7, Sat 10-6
  · freshly prepared food · deli · vegetarian friendly · tables · self-service · take-out

🛏 **From I-66**, take exit 66 (66A from 66W) right onto Rt 7E (Leesburg Pike) about 1 mile to store on right in West End Shopping Center. **From I-495**, take exit 47B toward Falls Church onto 7E (Leesburg Pike) about 2 miles to store on right in West End Shopping Center.

WHOLE FOODS MARKET ✗🍴 &

7511 Leesburg Pike ✆ 703-448-1600 ⊘ M-Sat 8-10, Sun 8-9
  · organic produce · freshly prepared food · salad bar · café · deli · bakery · vegetarian friendly · chain · tables · self-service · take-out

🛏 **From I-66**, take exit 66B right onto Rt 7W (Leesburg Pike) about ¼ mile to store on left.

FREDERICKSBURG

HEALTHWAY NATURAL FOODS 🍃 &
4211 Plank Rd. ℂ 540-786-4844 ⊙ M-Th 10-7, F 10-8, Sat 10-6, Sun 12-5
  · organic produce · chain
🛏 **From I-95**, take exit 130B onto Rt 3W (Plank Rd) about 2 miles to store on right (Rt 3S).

PANTRY SHELF NATURAL FOODS & GOURMET GROCERY 🍃
811 Sophia St. ℂ 540-373-2253 ⊙ M-Th, Sat 10-6, F 10-7
  · organic produce
🛏 **From I-95**, take exit 130A toward Fredericksburg onto Rt 3E about 1½ miles to Williams St (follow signs for "Historic Downtown"). Turn left onto Williams (3Bus) 1 block to Hanover St. Turn right onto Hanover about 1¼ miles to Sophia St. Turn left on Sophia to store (3rd building on right).

SAMMY T'S ✗ &
801 Caroline St. ℂ 540-371-2008 ⊙ M-Th, Sun 11-9, F-Sat 11-10, Non-smoking room hours M-F 11-3, 5-8, Sat-Sun 11-8
Well-priced eclectic menu with many vegetarian and vegan choices, including four meatless burgers (and just one with beef). Sandwiches, soups, salads, and hot entrees for every eating style. Note: the non-smoking dining room is upstairs, entered from the side street.
  · vegetarian friendly · vegan friendly · alcohol · tables · wait staff
🛏 **From I-95**, take exit 130A toward Fredericksburg onto Rt 3E about 1½ miles to Williams St (follow signs for "Historic Downtown"). Turn left onto Williams (3Bus) 1 block to Hanover St. Turn right onto Hanover 1 mile to Caroline St to store on left corner (1 block from visitor center).

FRONT ROYAL

BETTER THYMES 🍃
411-C South St. ℂ 540-636-9209 ⊙ M-W 9-6, Th-F 9-8, Sat 9-5, Sun 12-5
🛏 **From I-66**, take exit 6 toward Front Royal/VA 55 onto US 340S (becomes 340E) almost 4 miles to VA 55. Turn left onto 55E (South St) to store in 1st shopping center on right. **From I-66W**, take exit 13 (VA 79) toward Front Royal/VA 55 left onto 49 about ¼ mile to 55. Turn right onto 55E about 5¼ miles to store in shopping center on left (before 340).

HARRISONBURG

Surrounded by the natural beauty of the Shenandoah Valley.

KATE'S NATURAL PRODUCTS ✗🍃 &
451 University Blvd. ℂ 540-433-2359 ⊙ M-Sat 9-6
  · organic produce · freshly prepared food · deli · vegetarian friendly · tables · self-service
🛏 **From I-81S**, take exit 247A toward Elkton onto E Market St less than 1 mile to 2nd traffic light at University Blvd. Turn right onto University about ⅔ mile to store on right (before next light). **From I-81N**, take exit 245 right onto Port Republic Rd and immediately left onto Forest Hills Dr (becomes University) about 1⅓ miles to store on left (past light at Reservoir St).

Please tell these businesses that you found them in Healthy Highways.

THE LITTLE GRILL ✖

621 N. Main St. © 540-434-3594 ⊙ Tues-Th 7-2:30, 5-9, F 7-2:30, 5-10, Sat 7-10, Sun 9-2
The homemade wholefoods menu is largely vegetarian, there is sometimes live music or "open mic," and beer is the sole alcohol choice. Mondays the restaurant is officially closed for the free community soup kitchen.

· vegetarian friendly · alcohol · tables · wait staff

🍎 **From I-81**, take exit 247B toward Harrisonburg onto US 33W less than 2 miles to US 11N. Merge straight onto 11N (Main St) to restaurant.

LEXINGTON

Nestled between the Blue Ridge and Alleghany mountains, locals say Lexington is "a mecca for beauty." The home of Washington & Lee U, the Virginia Military Institute, the Virginia Horse Center, and an area rich in Civil War history.

BLUE HERON CAFE ✖   ⅄

4 E. Washington St. © 540-463-2800 ⊙ Lunch M-Th 11:30-2:30, F-Sat 11:30-2, Dinner F-Sat 5:30-9, Music Th 7:30-10
An all-vegetarian menu with daily specials at lunch. Dinner by candlelight on the weekend. Live music Thursday nights.

· vegetarian · vegan friendly · organic focus · alcohol · tables · wait staff

🍎 **From I-81**, take exit 188B toward Lexington onto Rt 60W almost 3 miles to downtown Lexington (60 becomes Nelson St). At 3rd traffic light turn right onto Washington St to restaurant near corner Main St & Washington.

COOL SPRING ORGANIC MARKET 🍎

800 S. Main St. © 540-463-6506 ⊙ M-Sat 8:30-7, Sun 9-5

· organic produce · freshly prepared food · juice bar · salad bar · deli · vegetarian friendly · take-out

🍎 **From I-81**, take exit 188B toward Lexington onto Rt 60W about 2¼ miles. Go under overpass and make immediate left onto Rt 11 less than 1 mile to traffic light at S Main St (Lexington Lodge on right corner). Turn right onto S Main to store in 3rd building on right (with the gas pumps).

HEALTHY FOODS MARKET ✖🍎   ⅄

110 W. Washington St. © 540-463-6954 ⊙ M-F 9-6, Sat 9-5, Cafe M-F 11-2
Heavy organic focus and a vegetarian cafe.

· organic produce · freshly prepared food · juice bar · salad bar · café · deli · vegetarian · organic focus · counter · tables · self-service · wait staff · take-out

🍎 **From I-81**, take exit 188B toward Lexington onto Rt 60W almost 3 miles to downtown Lexington (60 becomes Nelson St). At 3rd traffic light turn right onto Washington St to store on left ½ block past 2nd traffic light.

LYNCHBURG

FRESH AIR NATURAL FOODS 🍎

3225 Old Forest Rd. © 434-385-9252 ⊙ M-F 10-8, Sat 10-5

· organic produce

🍎 **US 460, 29 and 501** all come into Lynchburg. **From US 29**, take exit 4 onto Stadium Rd about ⅓ mile and veer right onto Wythe Rd about ⅓ mile until it merges into US 221. Follow 221 (Oakley Ave, becomes Lakeside Dr) 1 mile to Old Forest Rd. Turn right onto Old Forest 2 miles to store on right on Forest Plaza Shopping Center. **From US 460**, take US 501N about 5⅔ miles (becomes Old Forest). Stay on Old Forest about 1 mile to store on right in Forest Plaza Shopping Center.

MORE FRESH AIR 🍃
817½ Main St. © 434-845-7311 ⊙ M-F 9:30-5:30, Sat 11-2
· organic produce

🛒 **From US 29**, take exit 1A toward Downtown onto Main St (follow exit right and merge left onto Main from 29S, follow exit around right from 29N) about ⅔ mile to store at 8th St. Or, **from US 29S**, take 29Bus S (5th St) across river 1½ miles to Main. Turn left onto Main 3 blocks to store at 8th.

MANASSAS

HEALTHWAY NATURAL FOODS 🍃   ♿
10778 Sudley Manor Drive © 703-361-1883 ⊙ M-Th 10-7, F 10-8, Sat 10-6, Sun 12-5
· organic produce · chain

🛒 **From I-66**, take exit 47A toward Manasses onto Sudley Rd/VA 234Bus S about 1 mile to Sudley Manor Dr. Turn right onto Sudley Manor to store in Bull Run Center.

NORFOLK

HEALTH FOOD CENTER 🍃   ♿
1701 Colley Ave. © 757-625-6656 ⊙ M-F 10-7, Sat 10-6

🛒 **From I-64E**, take exit 276 toward Naval Base onto Granby St/US 460W toward Little Creek Rd almost 3 miles to W 38th St. Turn right onto W 38th about ¾ mile to Colley Ave. Turn left onto Colley about ¾ mile to store on right. **From I-64W**, take exit 276C toward 460W left onto Little Creek and right onto E Admiral Taussig Blvd about ¼ mile to Granby. Turn left onto Granby and follow directions above. **From I-264W**, take exit 10 onto E City Hall Ave to St Pauls Blvd. Turn right onto St Pauls ½ mile to Brambleton Ave. Turn left onto Brambleton about 1 mile to Colley. Turn right onto Colley less than 1 mile to store on left.

HEALTH FOOD CENTER 🍃
700 N. Military Hwy. © 757-461-2883 ⊙ M-F 10-8, Sat 10-6

🛒 **From I-64E**, take exit 281 south onto Military Hwy (US 13S) about 2 miles to store in Military Circle Shops. **From I-264**, take exit 13B north on Military Hwy (US 13N) about ½ mile to store in Military Circle Shops.

HEALTH FOOD CENTER 🍃
7639 Granby St. © 757-489-4242 ⊙ M-Sat 10-6

🛒 **From I-64E**, take exit 276 toward Naval Base onto Granby St/US 460W toward Little Creek Rd about ½ mile to store at Wards Corner. **From I-64W**, take exit 276C toward 460W left onto Little Creek and right onto E Admiral Taussig Blvd about ¼ mile to Granby. Turn left onto Granby to store at Wards Corner.

THE TAPHOUSE GRILL ✕
931 W. 21st St. © 757-627-9172 ⊙ M-F 4pm-2am
The menu includes a clearly marked selection of vegetarian items, most vegan. Weekly changing entrees and soups, plus salads, sandwiches and pizza.
· vegetarian friendly · vegan friendly · alcohol · tables · wait staff

🛒 **From I-64E**, take exit 276 south on Granby St 2½ miles to 21st St. Turn right onto 21st less than 1 mile to restaurant on left. **From I-64W**, take exit 276C toward US 460W left onto Little Creek Rd and right onto E Admiral Taussig Blvd about ¼ mile to Granby. Turn left onto Granby and follow directions above. **From I-264W**, take exit 10 onto E City Hall Ave to St Pauls Blvd. Turn right onto St Pauls ½ mile and merge onto 460W 1 mile to 21st St. Turn left onto 21st less than 1 mile to restaurant on left.

WHOLE FOODS CO-OP 🍎 &

119 W. 21st St. ✆ 757-626-1051 ⊙ M 11:30-8, Tues-Th, Sat 10-6, F 10-7

• organic produce • freshly prepared food • juice bar • vegetarian friendly • co-op • counter • self-service • take-out

🍎 **From I-64E**, take exit 276 south on Granby St 2½ miles to 21st St. Turn right onto 21st ½ block to store on left. **From I-64W**, take exit 276C toward US 460W left onto Little Creek Rd and right onto E Admiral Taussig Blvd about ¼ mile to Granby. Turn left onto Granby and follow directions above. **From I-264W**, take exit 10 onto E City Hall Ave to St Pauls Blvd. Turn right onto St Pauls ½ mile and merge onto 460W 1 mile to 21st St. Turn left onto 21st 1½ blocks to store on left.

RADFORD

ANNIE KAY'S WHOLE FOODS 🍎

601 3rd St. ✆ 540-731-9498 ⊙ M-F 9-7, Sat 9-6

• organic produce

🍎 **From I-81S**, take exit 109 onto Tyler Rd/VA 177N about 2⅓ miles to Rock Rd. Turn left onto Rock about 1¾ miles to Wadsworth St. Turn right onto Wadsworth 1¼ mile to store on left at 3rd St. **From I-81N**, take exit 105 onto VA 232N 4 miles to Wadsworth. Turn right onto Wadsworth to store on right at 3rd St.

RESTON

WHOLE FOODS MARKET ✗🍎 &

11660 Plaza America Drive ✆ 703-736-0600 ⊙ M-Sat 8-9, Sun 9-9

• organic produce • freshly prepared food • salad bar • café • deli • bakery • vegetarian friendly • chain • tables • self-service • take-out

🍎 **From Toll Rd 267**, take exit 12 north onto Reston Pkwy/VA 602N (left from 267E, right from 267W) to 1st right onto Sunset Hills Dr. Turn right onto Sunset Hills less than ½ mile (past 2 traffic lights) to store on right in Plaza America.

RICHMOND

ELLWOOD THOMPSON'S ✗🍎

4 N. Thompson St. ✆ 804-359-7525 ⊙ Daily 8-9

• organic produce • freshly prepared food • salad bar • café • deli • bakery • vegetarian friendly • tables • self-service • take-out

🍎 **From I-95S**, take exit 76 onto I-195S about 2⅓ miles to Cary St exit. Turn left onto Cary past hwy 1 block to store at N Thompson St. **From I-95N**, take exit 74A onto I-195N (Downtown Expwy) about 3½ miles to Cary. Turn right onto Cary 1 block to store at N Thompson.

GOOD FOODS GROCERY ✗🍎

1312 Gaskins Rd. ✆ 804-740-3518 ⊙ M-Sat 9-9

• organic produce • freshly prepared food • bakery • vegetarian friendly • chain • tables • self-service • take-out

🍎 **From I-64**, take exit 180 (180A from 64W) south on Gaskins Rd S about 2½ miles to store on right in Gayton Cross Shopping Center.

GOOD FOODS GROCERY ✕ 🍽

3062 Stony Point Rd. © 804-320-6767 ⊗ M-Sat 9-9

· organic produce · freshly prepared food · bakery · vegetarian friendly · chain · tables · self-service · take-out

⬤ **From I-195**, take Powhite Pkwy to Forest Hill Ave exit. Turn west onto Forest Hill (right from pkwy S, left from pkwy N) about 3 miles to store just past Huguenot Rd in Stony Point Shopping Center.

IPANEMA CAFE ✕

917 W. Grace St. © 804-213-0170 ⊗ Lunch M-F 11-3, Dinner M-Sat 5:30-11

Small daily menu features vegetarian and vegan entrees, plus a fish choice.

· vegetarian friendly · vegan friendly · alcohol · counter · tables · wait staff

⬤ **From I-95N**, take exit 74A toward 195N onto Downtown Expwy/VA 195W about 1 mile to Belvidere St exit. Follow exit onto W Canal St to Belvidere. Turn right onto Belvidere about ⅓ mile to W Grace St. Turn left onto W Grace about 3 blocks to restaurant on left. **From I-95S**, take exit 76B toward US 1/Belvidere St onto Gilmer St ¼ mile to W Broad St. Turn right onto W Broad 2 blocks to Shafer St. Turn left onto Shafer 1 block to W Grace. Turn right onto W Grace to restaurant on left.

THE NANCI RAYGUN ✕

929 W. Grace St. © 804-353-4263 ⊗ M-Th 11am-2am, F 11am-1am, Sat 2-2, Sun 2-10

Eclectic bar food with many vegetarian choices, including mock chicken nuggets, falafel, vegetable samosas, mock beef sloppy "gina," curried vegetables, jambalaya, vegetable lasagna, and create your own pasta, pizza and strombolis with chicken, ground beef, or soy-based simulations. A "divey" place, with pool table, multi-media art space and an alternative music scene happening nightly.

· vegetarian friendly · vegan friendly · alcohol · tables · wait staff · take-out

⬤ **From I-95N**, take exit 74A toward 195N onto Downtown Expwy/VA 195W about 1 mile to Belvidere St exit. Follow exit onto W Canal St to Belvidere. Turn right onto Belvidere about ⅓ mile to W Grace St. Turn left onto W Grace 4 blocks to restaurant on corner Grace & Harrison St (1 block from VA Commonwealth U). **From I-95S**, take exit 76B toward US 1/Belvidere St onto Gilmer St ¼ mile to W Broad St. Turn right onto W Broad 2 blocks to Shafer St. Turn left onto Shafer 1 block to W Grace. Turn right onto W Grace 1 block to restaurant.

ROANOKE————————————

A rich area for museum-goers, including a science museum, history museum, art museum, African-American culture museum, and more.

EDEN'S WAY VEGETARIAN GARDEN CAFE ✕　　　　♿

108 Church Ave. S.E. © 540-344-3336 ⊗ M-F 11-3, 5-8

Homemade vegan food (note, honey is used) in an indoor garden-like setting.

· juice bar · café · bakery · vegan · organic focus · tables · wait staff · take-out

⬤ **From I-81**, take exit 143 onto I-581S about 5 miles to exit 5 toward Downtown. Stay in left exit lane (Williamson Rd) past 5 traffic lights to Church Ave SE. Turn right onto Church to restaurant in 1st building on left.

ROANOKE NATURAL FOODS ✕ 🍽　　　　♿

1319 Grandin Rd. © 540-343-5652 ⊗ M-Sat 9-8, Sun 12-6

· organic produce · freshly prepared food · juice bar · café · deli · bakery · vegetarian friendly · co-op · counter · tables · self-service · take-out

⬤ **From I-81**, take exit 143 onto I-581S about 5½ miles to exit 4W. Merge onto US 11Alt W/460W about 1 mile to 10th St NW. Turn left onto 10th about 1 mile to US 11N/Campbell Ave. Turn right onto 11 (continues left on 13th and left on Grandin) about 1 mile to store on right just past Memorial Ave.

SPRINGFIELD

HEALTHWAY NATURAL FOODS 🌿 &
6402-4 Springfield Plaza © 703-569-3533 ☺ M-W, F 10-7, Th 10-8, Sat 10-6, Sun 12-5
　· organic produce · chain
　📅 **From I-95N,** take exit 169A-B toward VA 644/Springfield. Follow ramp toward Old Keene Mill Rd and merge onto 644W less than ½ mile to Bland St. Turn right onto Bland and left onto Springfield Plaza to store. **From I-395S,** continue onto I-95S about ¼ mile, merge onto Old Keene Mill/644W and follow directions above.

WHOLE FOODS MARKET ✖️🌿 &
8402 Old Keene Mill Rd. © 703-644-2500 ☺ M-Sat 8-9, Sun 8-8
　· organic produce · freshly prepared food · salad bar · café · deli · bakery · vegetarian friendly · chain · counter · tables · self-service · take-out
　📅 **From I-95N,** take exit 169A-B toward VA 644/Springfield. Follow ramp toward Old Keene Mill Rd and merge onto 644W about 3 miles to store on right just past Rolling Rd. **From I-395S,** continue onto I-95S about ¼ mile, merge onto Old Keene Mill/644W and follow directions above.

STERLING

HEALTHWAY NATURAL FOODS 🌿 &
46900 Cedar Lakes Plaza © 703-430-4430 ☺ M-W, F 10-7, Th 10-8, Sat 10-6, Sun 12-5
　· organic produce · chain
　📅 **From VA 7** (Leesburg Pike) turn south onto Cedar Lakes Plaza (right from 7W, left from 7E) to store in Shops at Cedar Lakes.

VIENNA

Vienna is alongside the W & OD trail, a multi-use recreational, environmental and historic resource. A 56-page trail guide is available at 703-729-0596.

WHOLE FOODS MARKET ✖️🌿 &
143 Maple Ave. E. © 703-319-2000 ☺ M-Sat 8-10, Sun 9-9
　· organic produce · freshly prepared food · juice bar · salad bar · café · deli · bakery · vegetarian friendly · chain · counter · tables · self-service · take-out
　📅 **From I-495,** take exit 46A toward Tyson's Corner/Vienna onto Rt 123S (Chain Bridge Rd, becomes Maple Ave E in town) about 3 miles to store on left (just past Park St). **From I-66,** take exit 62 toward Vienna north on Nutley St SW (loop around right from 66E, right from 66W) about 2 miles to Maple Ave W. Turn right onto Maple about ½ mile to store on right (just past Patrick Henry Library & W&OD Trail).

AMMA VEGETARIAN KITCHEN ✖️🌿
344-A Maple Ave. E. © 703/938-5328 ☺ M-F 11:30-2:30, 5:30-9:30, Sat-Sun 11:30-10
No-frills dining on traditional vegetarian South Indian fare.
　· vegetarian · vegan friendly · tables · self-service · take-out
　📅 **From I-495,** take exit 46A toward Tyson's Corner/Vienna onto Rt 123S (Chain Bridge Rd, becomes Maple Ave E in town) less than 3 miles to restaurant. **From I-66,** take exit 62 toward Vienna north on Nutley St SW (loop around right from 66E, right from 66W) about 2 miles to Maple Ave W. Turn right onto Maple 1 mile to restaurant.

SUNFLOWER VEGETARIAN CAFE ✗

2531 Chain Bridge Rd. ℂ 703-319-3888 ⊙ M-Sat 11:30-9:30, Sun 12-9:30
Mostly Asian vegetarian menu with American overtones.

· vegetarian · vegan friendly · tables · wait staff · take-out

⊔ **From I-66**, take exit 62 toward Vienna. Follow Nutley St SW less than 2 miles to Maple Ave. Turn left onto Maple (VA 12, becomes Chain Bridge Rd) about ⅓ mile to restaurant on other side of hwy (U-turn at Glengyle Dr).

VIRGINIA BEACH———————————

An Atlantic Ocean beach resort and home of the Edgar Cayce Foundation.

AZAR'S MARKET & CAFE ✗   ♿

108 Prescott Ave. ℂ 757-486-7778 ⊙ M-Th 11:30-8:30, F-Sat 11:30-9:30
Middle Eastern cuisine and not all vegetarian, however the many vegetarian and vegan selections are clearly marked on the menu. Owner notes, "you have to work a little to find the place."

· vegetarian friendly · alcohol · tables · wait staff · take-out

⊔ **From I-264E**, take exit 17B (Pembroke Area) onto Independence Blvd to 1st traffic light (Bonney Rd). Turn right onto Bonney (between Mc Donald's & Wendy's) about 1½ miles to restaurant on left behind Citgo gas station. **From oceanfront**, take I-264W to Rosemont Rd exit. Stay in center lane at bottom of ramp. Continue straight on Bonney about 1 mile to restaurant on right corner Bonney & Prescott Ave (behind Citgo).

FRESH FAIR CAFE ✗

700 19th St. ℂ 757-491-5383 ⊙ M-F 7-9, Sat 8-6
Although they serve deli meats, the menu is more vegetarian than non, featuring stuffed sandwiches, salads, pasta, vegetarian chili, brown rice, and fresh juices.

· juice bar · café · vegetarian friendly · tables · self-service · take-out

⊔ **From I-264E**, turn right onto Cypress St 3 blocks to restaurant at 19th St. **From oceanfront**, go inland on 19th ½ mile to restaurant at Cypress.

HEALTH FOOD CENTER 🍃

5312 Kemps River Drive #105 ℂ 757-523-8961 ⊙ M-F 10-7, Sat 10-6

⊔ **From I-64**, take exit 286B onto Indian River Rd (VA 407S) about 1 mile to Kemps River Dr. Turn left onto Kemps River about ⅓ mile to store in Kemps River Shops.

HERITAGE HEALTH FOODS & CAFE DELI ✗🍃   ♿

314 Laskin Rd. ℂ 757-428-0500 ⊙ M-Th, Sat 10-7, F 10-9, Sun 12-7
A "holistic lifestyle department store" with food, books, crystals, music, gifts, and a meeting room.

· organic produce · freshly prepared food · juice bar · café · deli · vegetarian friendly
· tables · self-service · take-out

⊔ Take I-264E to end. Turn left onto Pacific Ave about ½ mile to Laskin Rd. Turn left onto Laskin to store on right.

ORGANIC VEGETARIAN CAFÉ AT SUNRISE ✗

1340 Great Neck Village #1232 ℂ 757-496-8099 ⊙ M-Th 11-7, F-Sat 11-9
Fresh juice, sandwiches, soups, salads, and hot items with a Mediterranean flavor. Ample vegan options.

· juice bar · café · vegetarian · vegan friendly · organic focus · tables · wait staff · take-out

⊔ **From I-64**, take exit 282 toward Beaches east on Shore Dr/US 60E almost 3½ miles to Great Neck Rd/VA 279S. Turn right onto Great Neck about 3 miles to restaurant in Great Neck Village Shopping Ctr. **From I-264**, take exit 19B north on Lynnhaven Pkwy/VA 414N less than ½ mile to Virginia Beach Blvd. Turn right onto Virginia Beach less than 1 mile to Great Neck. Turn left onto Greak Neck about 2½ miles to restaurant in Great Neck Village Shopping Ctr.

TERRA NOVA NATURAL FOODS GROCER & CAFE ✕ 🍖 &

1805 Laskin Rd. ✆ 757-425-5383 ⊙ Store M-Sat 10-7, Sun 12-5, Cafe M-Sat 10-6
Healthy wholefoods menu. Carnivore-friendly (chicken and tuna).
  · organic produce · freshly prepared food · juice bar · café · vegetarian friendly
  · counter · tables · wait staff · take-out
🗓 **From I-264**, take exit 20 onto Laskin Rd/US 58E about ⅓ mile to store on right in building with Conte's Bike & Fitness Center. **From oceanfront**, take 58W about 3 miles to store on left.

WARRENTON

THE NATURAL MARKETPLACE 🍖

5 Diagonal St. ✆ 540-349-4111 ⊙ M-F 9-7, Sat 9-5
  · organic produce · freshly prepared food · juice bar · deli · vegetarian friendly · take-out
🗓 **From I-66**, take exit 43A onto 29S (Lee Hwy) about 12 miles to Rt 211 (Warrenton). Turn left onto Rt 211 about 1 mile to Diagonal St. Turn right onto Diagonal to store on left (2-story yellow house).

Goldbeck's "EAT IT OR NOT"

FASCINATING & FAR-OUT FACTS ABOUT FOOD

DISTRIBUTION OF LETTERS IN ALPHABET SOUP

A	6		N	6
B	9		O	8
C	7		P	8
D	9		Q	4
E	2		R	4
F	2		S	3
G	2		T	6
H	14		U	8
I	5		V	4
J	8		W	10
K	2		X	10
L	4		Y	10
M	6		Z	4

WASHINGTON

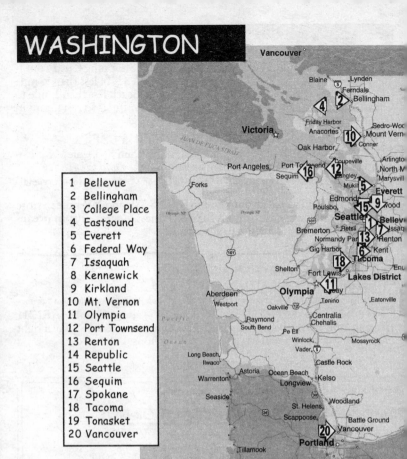

Vancouver

Blaine • Lynden
Ferndale
Bellingham

Friday Harbor
Anacortes
Sedro-Woo
Mount Vern

Victoria ☆
Oak Harbor
La Conner
Arlingto
North M
Marysvill

Port Angeles
Port Townsend
Coupeville
Langley
Mukilteo
Everett

Forks
Sequim
Edmonds
Wood

Poulsbo
Seattle
Bellev
Issaqu

Bremerton
Retsil
Normandy Par
Bellev
Renton

Gig Harbor
Kent

Shelton
Tacoma
Enu

Fort Lewis
Lakes District

Aberdeen
Olympia

Westport
Tenino
Eatonville

Oakville
Pacific
Raymond
Centralia
Chehalis

South Bend
Pe Ell
Winlock
Vader
Mossyrock

Ocean
Long Beach
Ilwaco
Castle Rock

Astoria
Ocean Beach
Kelso

Warrenton
Longview

Seaside
Woodland

St. Helens
Scappoose
Battle Ground
Vancouver

Tillamook
Portland

1 Bellevue
2 Bellingham
3 College Place
4 Eastsound
5 Everett
6 Federal Way
7 Issaquah
8 Kennewick
9 Kirkland
10 Mt. Vernon
11 Olympia
12 Port Townsend
13 Renton
14 Republic
15 Seattle
16 Sequim
17 Spokane
18 Tacoma
19 Tonasket
20 Vancouver

BELLEVUE

NATURE'S PANTRY ✕ 🍵
15600 N.E. 8th St. ✆ 425-957-0090 ⏲ M-F 9-7, Sat-Sun 9-6

· organic produce · freshly prepared food · juice bar · deli · vegetarian friendly · tables
· self-service · take-out

🛍 **From I-90W**, take exit 11 onto the 156th Ave SE ramp to SE Eastgate Way. Turn left onto Eastgate less than ¼ mile to 148th Ave SE. Turn right onto 148th 2½ miles to NE 8th St. Turn right onto NE 8th about ½ mile to store in Crossroads Shopping Center. **From I-5**, take exit 168B toward Bellevue onto WA 520E about 9 miles (across water) to 148th Ave SE exit. Merge right onto 148th about 1 mile to NE 8th. Turn left onto NE 8th about ½ mile to store in Crossroads Shopping Center.

NATURE'S PANTRY ✕ 🍵
10200 N.E. 10th St. ✆ 425-454-0170 ⏲ M-F 9-7, Sat-Sun 9-6

· organic produce · freshly prepared food · juice bar · deli · vegetarian friendly · tables
· self-service · take-out

🛍 **From I-405**, take exit 13 (A from 405S, B from 405N) and follow NE 8th St W ramp onto NE 8th St about ¾ mile to 102 Ave NE. Turn right

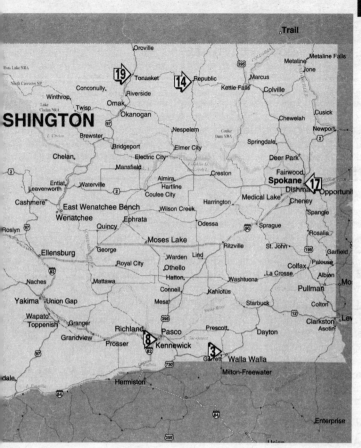

onto 102nd to store at 10th St. **From I-5**, take exit 168B toward Bellevue onto WA 520E about 6 miles (across water) to Bellevue Way NE exit. Merge right onto Bellevue Way about 1½ miles to NE 10th St. Turn right onto 10th 2 blocks to store at 102nd Ave.

BELLINGHAM

Overlooks the San Juan Islands to the west and majestic peaks of the North Cascades to the east. "A great destination for skiers, mountain bikers, hikers, climbers, kayakers, naturalists, and people who just want to relax in a beautiful environment."

COMMUNITY FOOD CO-OP ✕ 🖤

1220 N. Forest St. ℰ 360-734-8158 ☉ Daily 8-9

Staff says they have "a staggering number of fresh, local and organic products."

· organic produce · freshly prepared food · juice bar · café · deli · bakery · vegetarian friendly · co-op · tables · self-service · take-out

🚍 **From I-5**, take exit 253 onto Lakeway Dr (right from 5S, right onto King St, then right from 5N). Take Lakeway (becomes E Holly St) almost ¾ mile to N State St. Turn left onto State, left onto E Chestnut St, and left onto N Forest St to store (just over 1 mile from hwy).

TERRA ORGANICA ✗🍎   ♿

929 N. State St. © 360-715-8020 ⊘ Daily 9-9

Owner Stephan says that "every item has a reason for being on the shelf." The food and beverages in the store and cafe are over 99% organic or wild-crafted.

· organic produce · freshly prepared food · juice bar · café · bakery · vegetarian friendly · organic focus · tables · self-service · take-out

🍎 **From I-5N**, take exit 253 right onto King St, then right onto Lakeway Dr (becomes E Holly St) almost ¾ mile to N State St. Turn left onto State ½ mile to store on left. **From I-5S**, take exit 254 (State St) west on Ohio St to 2nd left (State). Turn left onto State about 1 mile to store on left.

COLLEGE PLACE

HIS GARDEN & BAKERY ✗🍎

28 S.E. 12th St. © 509-525-1040 ⊘ M-Th 7:30-7, F 7:30-5, Sun 9-2

Deli serves mostly vegan salads, sandwiches and baked goods.

· organic produce · freshly prepared food · deli · bakery · vegetarian · vegan friendly · organic focus · tables · self-service · take-out

🍎 College Place sits just above the OR border near Walla Walla. **From US 12**, turn south onto Gose St (right from 12E, left from 12W) 2 miles to SE 12th St. Turn left onto 12th to store just past corner.

WALLA WALLA COLLEGE CAFETERIA ✗

32 S.E. Ash Ave. © 509-527-2732 ⊘ M-F 7-1:15, 4:30-6:30, Sat 8:30-9:15, 12:15-1:15, 5:15-6:30, Sun 10:30-1:15, 5-6:30 during school term (call for other times)

A Seventh-day Adventist school with a vegetarian cafeteria open to all.

· vegetarian · vegan friendly · tables · self-service

🍎 **From US 12**, turn south onto Gose St (right from 12E, left from 12W) 1¼ miles (becomes N College Ave) to Whitman Dr. Turn left onto Whitman 1 block to Ash Ave. Turn right onto Ash to college.

EASTSOUND

ORCAS HOME GROWN MARKET 🍎

North Beach Rd. © 360-376-2009 ⊘ Daily 8:30-9, Deli 8:30-7

· organic produce · freshly prepared food · juice bar · deli · vegetarian friendly · take-out

🍎 **From ferry landing** in Orcas, take Horsehoe Hwy north more than 8 miles to Eastsound. Store is in town.

EVERETT

Lots of wonderful wildlife in the area—sea birds, eagles, sea lions, hawks, otters, deer, beaver, fox, coyote. And, according to Betsy at Sno-isle, home to the world's second largest building (a Boeing plant).

SNO-ISLE NATURAL FOODS CO-OP 🍎

2804 Grand Ave. © 425-259-3798 ⊘ M-Sat 8-8, Sun 12-6

· organic produce · freshly prepared food · juice bar · deli · vegetarian friendly · co-op · take-out

🍎 **From I-5N**, take exit 193 left (west) on Pacific Ave about 1 mile to Grand Ave. Turn right onto Grand 3 blocks to store on left in Everett Public Market Bldg. **From I-5S**, take exit 194 right (west) on Everett Ave about 1¼ miles to Grand. Turn left onto Grand 1 block to store on right in Everett Public Market Bldg.

FEDERAL WAY_____

MARLENE'S MARKET & DELI 🍎
31839 Gateway Center Blvd. S. ℂ 253-839-0933 ☺ M-F 9-9, Sat 9-8, Sun 10:30-6
· organic produce · freshly prepared food · juice bar · deli · vegetarian friendly · take-out
🍎 **From I-5**, take exit 143 toward Federal Way onto 320th St (right from 5S, left from 5N). Turn right onto 319th Pl and go straight onto Gateway Center Blvd to store in Gateway Center.

ISSAQUAH_____

PCC NATURAL MARKET 🍎
1810 12th Ave. N.W. ℂ 425-369-1222 ☺ Daily 7-11
· organic produce · freshly prepared food · juice bar · deli · vegetarian friendly · co-op · take-out
🍎 **From I-90E**, take exit 15 (Hwy 900/Renton) and take left exit toward Lake Sammamish State Pk to traffic light at 17th Ave NW. Turn left onto 17th 2 lights to store on right in Pickering Place shopping center (follow "S" curve to store on left). **From I-90W**, take exit 15 to the right. Turn right at light into Pickering Place and follow "S" curve to store on left.

KENNEWICK_____

HIGHLAND HEALTHFOOD SUPERSTORE 🍎
101 Vista Way ℂ 509-783-7147 ☺ M-Th 9:30-6, F 9:30-5, Sun 12-5
🍎 **From I-82E/US 12E**, take exit 5A onto WA 240E toward Kennewick about 7 miles to US 395S. Turn right onto 395S almost 1 mile to Vista Way. Turn left onto Vista to store on right. **From I-82W**, take exit 113 onto 395N about 4¼ miles to Vista Way. Turn right onto Vista to store on right.

KIRKLAND_____

PCC NATURAL MARKET 🍎
10718 N.E. 68th St. ℂ 425-828-4622 ☺ Daily 7-11
· organic produce · freshly prepared food · deli · vegetarian friendly · co-op · take-out
🍎 **From I-405**, take exit 17 left onto NE 70th Pl (2 lefts from 405N). Follow NE 70th onto NE 72nd Pl, then NE 68th St about ¾ mile to store on right in Houghton Village Shopping Center.

MT. VERNON_____

En route to the San Juan Islands, North Cascade Mountains or Vancouver, Canada.

SKAGIT VALLEY FOOD CO-OP 🍴🍎
202 S. First St. ℂ 360-336-9777 ☺ M-Sat 8-9, Sun 9-8
Deli offers vegetarian, vegan and natural meat options.
· organic produce · freshly prepared food · salad bar · café · deli · bakery · vegetarian friendly · vegan friendly · co-op · counter · tables · self-service · take-out
🍎 **From I-5**, take exit 226 west on Kincaid St/US 536 (right from 5S, left from 5N) to traffic light at 3rd St. Turn right onto 3rd 5 blocks to store at S 2nd St (after overpass).

OLYMPIA

OLYMPIA FOOD CO-OP/WESTSIDE 🍴 &

921 N. Rogers © 360-754-7666 ⊙ Daily 9-8

· organic produce · co-op

From I-5, take exit 104 onto US 101N about 1¾ miles to Black Lake Blvd exit. Take ramp toward West Olympia right onto Black Lake (becomes Division St) about 1⅔ miles to Bowman Ave. Turn right onto Bowman about ⅓ mile to store at corner Bowman & Rogers St.

OLYMPIA FOOD CO-OP/EASTSIDE 🍴🍴 &

3111 Pacific Ave. © 360-956-3870 ⊙ Daily 9-9

· organic produce · freshly prepared food · salad bar · café · deli · vegetarian friendly
· co-op · tables · self-service · take-out

From I-5, take exit 107 west on Pacific Ave (right from 5S, left from 5N) less than ¼ mile to Lansdale Rd. Turn left onto Lansdale to store on corner.

THE NEW MOON CAFE 🍴 &

113 4th Ave. W. © 360-357-3452 ⊙ M-F 7am-2:30pm

Breakfast for vegans (tofu scrambler, vegetarian sausage & biscuits), vegetarians (including meatless eggs Benedict), and the bacon-and-sausage crowd.

· vegetarian friendly · vegan friendly · tables · wait staff

From I-5S, take exit 105 toward State Capitol and follow 105B toward Port of Olympia onto Bay Dr ¼ mile to Plum St. Turn right onto Plum ½ mile to State St. Turn left onto State ½ mile to Columbia St NW. Turn left onto Columbia 1 block to 4th Ave. Turn left onto 4th to restaurant. **From I-5N**, take exit 105 toward State Capitol/City Center and swing left via Henderson St onto 14th Ave SE ½ mile to Capitol Way S. Turn right onto Capitol ⅓ mile to Talcott Ave. Turn left onto Talcott 1 block to Columbia. Turn right onto Columbia 5 blocks (¼ mile) to 4th. Turn right onto 4th to restaurant.

TRADITIONS CAFE & WORLD FOLK ART 🍴 &

300 5th Ave. SW © 360-705-2819 ⊙ M-F 9-6, Sat 10-6 (8 if live music)

Vegetarian choices include quiche, lasagna, enchiladas, sandwiches, and salads. NR: Connected with a wonderful store that sells beautiful merchandise from the Fair Trade Network.

· vegetarian friendly · tables · self-service

From I-5S, take exit 105 toward State Capitol and follow 105B toward Port of Olympia onto Bay Dr ¼ mile to Plum St. Turn right onto Plum ⅓ mile to 5th Ave. Turn left onto 5th ½ mile to restaurant. **From I-5N**, take exit 105 toward State Capitol/City Center. Swing left via Henderson St onto 14th Ave SE ½ mile to Capitol Way S. Turn right onto Capitol ⅓ mile to Talcott Ave. Turn left onto Talcott 1 block to Columbia St. Turn right onto Columbia 4 blocks (¼ mile) to 5th. Turn left onto 5th to restaurant.

URBAN ONION 🍴

116 Legion Way © 360-943-9242 ⊙ M-Th, Sun 10-9, F-Sat 10-10

· vegetarian friendly · alcohol · tables · wait staff

From I-5, take exit 105 (105A from 5S) toward State Capitol/City Center onto 14th Ave SE (straight from 5S, swing left from 5N) ⅓ -½ mile to Capitol Way S. Turn right onto Capitol ½ mile to Legion Way. Turn right onto Legion 1 block to restaurant on left corner Legion & Washington St in Hotel Olympian lobby.

VOYEUR CAFE ✖

404 E. 4th Ave. © 360-943-5710 ⊙ Daily 11:30am-midnight
Everything on the menu can be made vegan—even the steak and chicken dishes, which appear on the menu with a tempeh or tofu option. An impressive sandwich list, half a dozen hot entrees, plus salads and breakfast items.

· vegetarian friendly · vegan friendly · organic focus · alcohol · tables · wait staff · take-out

🏪 **From I-5S**, take exit 105 toward State Capitol. Follow 105B toward Port of Olympia onto Bay Dr ¼ mile to Plum St. Turn right onto Plum ⅓ mile to 5th Ave. Turn left onto 5th ¼ mile to Adams St. Turn left onto Adams 1 block to 4th Ave. Turn left onto 4th to restaurant. **From I-5N**, take exit 105 toward State Capitol/City Center. Swing left via Henderson St onto 14th Ave SE ½ mile to Capitol Way S. Turn right onto Capitol ⅔ mile to 4th. Turn right onto 4th to restaurant.

PORT TOWNSEND

Awesome natural beauty and access point to the mountains, beaches, rivers, old growth forests, and rain forest.

THE FOOD CO-OP ✖🍴   ♿

414 Kearney St. © 360-385-2883 ⊙ M-Sat 8-9, Sun 9-7

· organic produce · freshly prepared food · juice bar · deli · vegetarian friendly · co-op · tables · self-service · take-out

🏪 Take Hwy 20 to Port Townsend. Store is at the first traffic light in town at corner Sims Way (aka Hwy 20) & Kearney St.

RENTON

PABLA INDIAN CUISINE ✖

364 Renton Center Way S.W. © 425-228-4625 ⊙ Daily 11-3, 5-10
Vegetarian Indian food, with buffet available at lunch.

· vegetarian · vegan friendly · tables · self-service · wait staff

🏪 **From I-5S**, take exit 157 onto WA 900E (MLK Way, becomes SW Sunset) about 3⅓ miles to Hardie Ave SW. Turn right onto Hardie to restaurant in Fred Meyer Shopping Plaza. **From I-5N**, merge onto I-405N via exit 154. **From I-405**, take exit 2 toward Renton/Ranier Ave onto WA 167N (Valley Fwy, becomes Ranier Ave) to 7th St (1 mile from 405N, ¼ mile from 405S). Make sharp left onto 7th and 1st right onto Hardie about ¼ mile to restaurant in Fred Meyer Shopping Plaza.

REPUBLIC

FERRY COUNTY CO-OP 🥬

34 N. Clark St. © 509-775-3754 ⊙ M-F 8-5:30, Sat 10-4

· organic produce · freshly prepared food · vegetarian friendly · co-op · take-out

🏪 Republic is at the crossroads of WA 20 & 21. **From 20**, take Clark St north 1 block to store on right.

SEATTLE

ARYA'S VEGETARIAN PLACE ✖   ♿

4732 University Way N.E. © 206-524-4332 ⊙ M-Sat 11:30-9, Sun 5-9
Thai vegetarian, with a buffet option.

· vegan · tables · self-service · wait staff

🏪 **From I-5**, take exit 169 and follow ramp toward NE 50th St/Seattle Pacific U to NE 50th. Turn east onto NE 50th (right from 5N, left from 5S) ⅓ mile to University Way NE. Turn right onto University to restaurant.

BAMBOO GARDEN VEGETARIAN CUISINE �

364 Roy St. © 206-282-6616 ⊘ Daily 11-10
Chinese vegetarian.

· vegetarian · vegan friendly · kosher · tables · wait staff · take-out

📁 **From I-5**, take exit 167 and follow Fairview Ave N to Valley St. Turn left onto Valley (becomes Broad St) about ½ mile to Harrison St. Turn right onto Harrison to 5th Ave. Turn right onto 5th about ¼ mile to Roy St. Turn left onto Roy to restaurant between 4th & 3rd Ave.

CAFE AMBROSIA ✗

2501 Fairview Ave. E. © 206-325-7111 ⊘ Tues-Th 5-9, F-Sat 5-10, Sun 10-2, 5-9
Gourmet vegetarian dining emphasizing organic ingredients. Waterfront setting on Lake Union. Reservations recommended.

· vegetarian · vegan friendly · organic focus · alcohol · tables · wait staff

📁 **From I-5S**, take exit 168A. After crossing Ship Canal Bridge, turn right at traffic light onto Roanoke St down hill toward Lake Union. At bottom follow bend left to restaurant immediately on right. **From I-5N**, take exit 168A to stop sign and turn left onto Lakeview Blvd to 2nd light (Roanoke). Turn left onto Roanoke and follow directions above.

CAFE FLORA ✗   ♿

2901 E. Madison St. © 206-325-9100 ⊘ Tues-Th 11:30-9, F 11:30-10, Sat 9-2, 5-10, Sun 9-2, 5-9
Upscale vegetarian restaurant with an international menu emphasizing local foods. NR: Located close to the arboretum.

· vegetarian · vegan friendly · alcohol · tables · wait staff

📁 **From I-5S**, take exit 168 onto Hwy 520 and make first right onto Montlake Blvd exit. Stay in right lane and pass Montlake intersection straight onto Lake Washington Blvd. Follow Lake Washington (winds through arboretum) about 1 mile to traffic light at E Madison St. Turn right onto E Madison 1 long block to restaurant on left at 29th Ave E. **From I-5N**, take exit 164A (Madison St). Follow long ramp right (east) onto Madison about 2 miles to 29th. Restaurant is on SE corner. **From I-90W**, take Ranier Ave N exit to 3-way intersection with S Jackson, Boren & 14th Ave S. Turn right onto 14th to Madison. Turn right onto Madison to 29th. Restaurant is on SE corner.

CARMELITA ✗   ♿

7314 Greenwood Ave. N. © 206-706-7703 ⊘ Tues-Sun 5-10
Mediterranean-influenced, upscale vegetarian and vegan dining, using local and organic produce whenever possible.

· vegetarian · vegan friendly · organic focus · alcohol · tables · wait staff

📁 **From I-5**, take exit 172 west on 85th St (right from 5S, left from 5N) about 1⅓ miles to Greenwood Ave. Turn left onto Greenwood about 11 blocks to restaurant on left between N 74th & 73rd St.

GLOBE CAFE ✗   ⬤

1531 14th Ave. © 206-324-8815 ⊘ Tues-Sun 7am-3pm
Vegan "diner" food.

· vegan · tables · self-service · take-out

📁 **From I-5S**, take exit 166 (Stewart St) toward Denny Way left onto Eastlake Ave E (becomes Howell St) about ¼ mile to Boren Ave. Turn left onto Boren across hwy to E Pike St. Turn left onto Pike about ¾ mile to 14th Ave. Turn left onto 14th to restaurant. **From I-5N**, take exit 164A (Dearborn St/James St) and follow exit toward Madison St/Convention Pl onto 7th Ave to Madison. Turn right onto Madison less than 1 mile to E Pike. Make sharp left onto Pike and right onto 14th to restaurant.

GOOD MORNING HEALING EARTH ✗

901 N.E. 55th St. ✆ 206-523-8025 ☺ Tues-F 11-8:30, Sat 10-8:30, Sun 10-4:30
Wholefoods vegan menu with an organic slant. A neighborhood place.

· vegan · organic focus · tables · wait staff · take-out

⌂ **From I-5**, take exit 169 and follow ramp toward NE 50th St/Seattle Pacific U to NE 50th St. Turn east onto NE 50th (right from 5N, left from 5S) to 1st traffic light at 9th Ave. Turn left onto 9th 2 blocks to restaurant.

GREEN CAT CAFE ✗

1514 E. Olive Way ✆ 206-726-8756 ☺ Daily 8-4
Breakfast fare, sandwiches, salads, soups, chili, pasta, brown rice bowls, and similar casual vegetarian fare.

· vegetarian · vegan friendly · tables · self-service

⌂ **From I-5S**, take exit 166 toward Denny Way right onto Stewart St to Denny Way. Turn left onto Denny (across hwy) ¼ mile to E Olive Way. Turn right onto Olive to restaurant. **From I-5N**, take exit 166 and veer right onto Olive past 3rd block to restaurant.

HILLSIDE QUICKIE'S VEGAN SANDWICH SHOP ✗ 🌱

4106 Brooklyn Ave. N.E. ✆ 206-632-3037 ☺ M-Sat 11-9
Just what it says—vegan sandwiches, plus salads and accoutrements.

· vegan · tables · self-service · take-out

⌂ **From I-5**, take exit 169 and follow ramp toward NE 45th St/U of WA to NE 45th. Turn east onto 45th (right from 5N, left from 5S) about ⅓ mile to Brooklyn Ave NE. Turn right onto Brooklyn about ⅓ mile to restaurant.

LUCKY PALATE ✗

307 McGraw St. ✆ 206-352-2583 ☺ M 9-6, Tues 9:30-6 and various other times, so call to see if someone is around
Primarily home-delivered meals, but the storefront sells the healthy vegetarian and vegan "Grab-and-Go Meals," along with other homemade items.

· deli · vegetarian · vegan friendly · organic focus · take-out

⌂ **From I-5S**, take exit 172 toward NE 80th St onto N 85th St ramp toward Aurora Ave N. Veer right onto 85th about ⅔ mile to Aurora/WA 99S. Turn left onto Aurora about 3¼ miles to Queen Anne Dr. Turn right onto Queen Anne to 4th Ave N. Turn left onto 4th and right onto Raye St (becomes Nob Hill Ave N). Veer right on Nob Hill to store at McGraw St. **From I-5N**, take exit 167 toward Aquarium/Seattle Center. Turn right onto Fairview Ave, left onto Valley St (becomes Broad St) and right onto Roy St to Aurora/WA 99N. Turn right onto Aurora almost 1¼ miles to Halladay St. Turn right onto Halladay, left onto 6th Ave N (becomes Queen Anne), left onto 4th, and right onto Raye (becomes Nob Hill). Follow Nob Hill right to store at McGraw.

PCC NATURAL MARKET 🍃   ♿

716 N. 34th St. ✆ 206-632-6811 ⏰ Daily 7-11

· organic produce · freshly prepared food · juice bar · deli · bakery · vegetarian friendly · co-op · take-out

🛏 From I-5S, take exit 169 and follow ramp toward NE 45th St/U of WA. Turn right onto 45th almost 1 mile to Stone Way. Turn left onto Stone almost 1 mile to N 34th St. Turn right onto 34th about ¼ mile to store on right just past Fremont Ave N at Evanston St. **From I-5N**, take exit 167 on left toward Seattle Center right onto Fairview Ave, left onto Valley St and right onto Westlake Ave N about 1⅔ miles to 4th Ave N. Veer right onto 4th across water (becomes Fremont) to N 34th. Turn right onto 34th to store. **From Hwy 99** (Aurora Ave), go west 1 block to N Freemont and take Freemont to N 34th. Turn west onto 34th to store.

PCC NATURAL MARKET 🍃   ♿

7504 Aurora Ave. N. ✆ 206-525-3586 ⏰ Daily 7-11

· organic produce · freshly prepared food · deli · vegetarian friendly · co-op · take-out

🛏 From I-5, take exit 172 toward Aurora Ave N west on N 85th St (left from 5N, right from 5S) less than 1 mile to Aurora. Turn left onto Aurora (Hwy 99) ½ mile to store on right just before Winona Ave N intersection (turn left onto Winona for parking on left).

PCC NATURAL MARKET 🍃   ♿

5041 Wilson Ave. S. ✆ 206-723-2720 ⏰ Daily 7-10

· organic produce · freshly prepared food · deli · vegetarian friendly · co-op · take-out

🛏 From I-5, take W Seattle Bridge/Columbian Way exit (163A from 5S, 163 from 5N). Take fork toward Columbian and get into right lane. At 3rd traffic light ("Y" intersection) bear left onto S Columbian (becomes S Alaska St) more than 1 mile to Ranier Ave S. Turn right onto Ranier to 2nd left at S Edmunds St. Turn left onto Edmunds ¼ mile to 42nd St S. Turn right onto 42nd and immediately left onto S Ferdinand St ½ mile to 50th Ave S. Turn right onto 50th (becomes Wilson Ave S) 1½ blocks to store on right.

PCC NATURAL MARKET 🍃   ♿

6514 40th Ave. N.E. ✆ 206-526-7661 ⏰ Daily 7-11

· organic produce · freshly prepared food · deli · vegetarian friendly · co-op · take-out

🛏 From I-5S, take exit 171 (NE 71st St/NE 65th St) onto 6th Ave NE to stop sign at NE 70th St. Turn left onto 70th ¼ mile to Roosevelt Way NE. Turn right onto Roosevelt ¼ mile NE 65th. Turn left onto 65th 1½ miles to 40th Ave NE. Turn left onto 40th to store on NE corner 40th & 65th. **From I-5N**, take exit 170 (Ravenna Blvd) toward NE 65th and follow ramp (becomes 8th Ave) to 65th. Turn right onto 65th 1½ miles to store (NE corner 40th & 65th).

PCC NATURAL MARKET 🍃   ♿

2749 California Ave. S.W. ✆ 206-937-8481 ⏰ Daily 7-11

· organic produce · freshly prepared food · deli · vegetarian friendly · co-op · take-out

🛏 From I-5, take W Seattle Bridge exit (163A from 5S, 163 from 5N) onto bridge 2 miles to Admiral Way ramp. Take Admiral 1 mile to California Ave SW. Turn right onto California to store on right.

RAINBOW GROCERY 🍴🍃

417 15th Ave. E. ✆ 206-329-8440 ⏰ Daily 8-9

· organic produce · juice bar · vegetarian friendly · counter · tables · self-service · take-out

🛏 From I-5S, take exit 166 (Stewart St) toward Denny Way right onto

Stewart St and left onto Denny across hwy about ¼ mile to E Olive Way. Turn left onto Olive (becomes E John St) almost ⅔ mile to 15th Ave E. Turn left onto 15th to store on left between Harrison & Republican St. **From I-5N**, take exit 166 right onto Olive (becomes E John) less than 1 mile to 15th. Turn left onto 15th to store on left.

SILENCE-HEART-NEST ✕ &

5247 University Way N.E. ℂ 206-524-4008 ☻M, Tues, Th-Sat 11-9, Sun 10-2
In the University of WA district.

· vegetarian · tables · wait staff · take-out

🍎 **From I-5**, take exit 169 and follow ramp toward NE 50th St/Seattle Pacific U to NE 50th St. Turn east onto NE 50th (right from 5N, left from 5S) ⅓ mile to University Way NE. Turn left onto University to restaurant on left.

SUNLIGHT CAFÉ ✕

6403 Roosevelt Way N.E. ℂ 206-522-9060 ☻Daily 9-9
A varied vegetarian menu from breakfast to dinner, with light fare available between meal hours.

· vegetarian · vegan friendly · alcohol · tables · wait staff

🍎 **From I-5S**, take exit 171 toward NE 71st St/NE 65th St onto 6th Ave and follow across hwy on NE 70th St about ¼ mile (2 blocks) to Roosevelt Way. Turn right onto Roosevelt about ⅓ mile to restaurant (just past 64th St.) **From I-5N**, take exit 170 (Ravenna Blvd) toward NE 65th and follow ramp (becomes 8th Ave) to 65th. Turn right onto 65th 2 blocks to Roosevelt. Turn right onto Roosevelt past 1st block to restaurant.

TEAPOT VEGETARIAN HOUSE ✕

125 15th Ave. E. ℂ 206-325-1010 ☻Daily 11:30-10
Vegetarian Chinese menu.

· vegetarian · vegan friendly · tables · wait staff · take-out

🍎 **From I-5S**, take exit 166 (Stewart St) toward Denny Way right onto Stewart and left onto Denny across hwy about ¼ mile to E Olive Way. Turn left onto Olive (becomes E John St) almost ⅔ mile to 15th Ave E. Turn right onto 15th to restaurant. **From I-5N**, take exit 166 right onto Olive (becomes E John) less than 1 mile to 15th. Turn right onto 15th to restaurant.

WHOLE FOODS MARKET ✕🥩 &

1026 N.E. 64th St. ℂ 206-985-1500 ☻Daily 8-10

· organic produce · freshly prepared food · juice bar · salad bar · café · deli · bakery
· vegetarian friendly · chain · tables · wait staff · take-out

🍎 **From I-5S**, take exit 171 (NE 71st St/NE 65th St) onto 6th Ave NE to stop sign at NE 70th St. Turn left onto 70th about ¼ mile to Roosevelt Way NE. Turn right onto Roosevelt about ⅓ mile to NE 64th St. Turn left onto 64th to store in Roosevelt Square. **From I-5N**, take exit 170 (Ravenna Blvd) toward NE 65th St and follow ramp (becomes 8th Ave) to NE 64th. Turn right onto 64th 2 blocks to store in Roosevelt Square.

SEQUIM

Along the northern WA coast in the shadow of the majestic Olympic mountains.

SUNNY FARMS COUNTRY STORE 🐷

261461 Hwy. 101 ⓒ 360-683-8003 ☺ Daily 8-7 (until 8 after daylight savings)
· organic produce · deli · vegetarian friendly · take-out

🍎 On Hwy 101 about 1 mile west of Sequim (20 miles west of Port Townsend).

SPOKANE

LORIEN HERBS & NATURAL FOODS 🐷   ₺

414 E. Trent Ave. ⓒ 509-456-0702 ☺ M-F 10-6, Sat 10-5, Sun 12-4
· organic produce

🍎 **From I-90**, take exit 281 toward Newport-Colville onto US 2E/395N/
Division St (merge right from 90W, turn left from 90E) about ½ mile to
Trent Ave. Turn right onto Trent 4 blocks to store.

MIZUNA ✗   ₺

214 N. Howard St. ⓒ 509-747-2004 ☺ Lunch M-F 11:30-2:30, Dinner Tues-Sat 5-9
*Fine dining with varied menu of vegetarian, vegan and seafood selections.
Live music on the weekend.*

· vegetarian friendly · vegan friendly · alcohol · tables · wait staff · take-out

🍎 **From I-90W**, take exit 280B and merge right onto S Lincoln St about ⅓
mile to W Main Ave. Turn right onto Main 3 blocks to Howard St. Turn
left onto Howard to restaurant on left. **From I-90E**, take exit 280 (Maple
St) toward Lincoln. Turn left onto S Walnut St and right onto W 3rd Ave
less than ½ mile to S Lincoln. Turn left onto S Lincoln and follow directions above from Lincoln.

TOP OF THE LINE HEALTH FOOD STORE 🐷

809 W. Garland Ave. ⓒ 509-325-1580 ☺ M-F 9:30-6, Sat 10-5, Sun 12-4
· organic produce · co-op

🍎 **From I-90W**, take exit 281 toward Newport-Colville onto US 2E/
395N/Division St. Follow 2E almost 3 miles to Garland Ave. Turn left
onto Garland ½ mile to store on left (across from Milk Bottle bldg). **From
I-90E**, take exit 280 (Maple St) toward Lincoln St. Turn left onto S Walnut
St and follow across Maple St Bridge and onto Maple almost 3 miles to
Garland. Turn right onto Garland about ¾ mile to store on right.

TACOMA

ANTIQUE SANDWICH COMPANY ✗   ₺

5102 N. Pearl St. ⓒ 253-752-4069 ☺ Daily 7-7:30 (10 Tues)
*In addition to sandwiches and salads, there is always a vegetarian soup, quiche,
burrito, lasagna, and hummus plate. Tuesday is open mike night. NR: An
institution in Tacoma. A fun time and yes, there are antiques, too.*

· vegetarian friendly · tables · self-service

🍎 From I-5, take exit 132 toward Bremerton/Gig Harbor onto WA 16W
(from 5N follow 38th St W exit on left toward Tacoma Mall onto 16W).
Take 16W about 3⅓ miles to 6th Ave exit toward WA 163. Turn left onto
6th 1 block to N Pearl St. Turn right onto Pearl 3 miles to restaurant.

MARLENE'S MARKET & DELI 🐑
2951 S. 38th St. © 253-472-4080 ⊙ M-F 9-8, Sat 9-7, Sun 10:30-6
· organic produce · freshly prepared food · juice bar · deli · vegetarian friendly · take-out
📙 **From I-5**, take exit 132 toward Bremerton/Gig Harbor and take S 38th St W exit (toward Sprague Ave from 5S, toward Tacoma Mall from 5N). Veer right onto S 38th about ½ mile to store on right in Best Plaza.

WESTGATE NUTRITION CENTER 🐑
5738 N. 26th St. © 253-759-1990 ⊙ M-F 9-6, Sat 10-5, Sun 12-5
📙 **From I-5**, take exit 132 toward Bremerton/Gig Harbor onto WA 16W (from 5N follow 38th St W exit on left toward Tacoma Mall onto 16W). Take 16W about 3⅓ miles to 6th Ave exit toward WA 163. Turn left onto 6th 1 block to N Pearl St. Turn right onto Pearl 1 mile to N 26th St. Turn right onto 26th to store just off Pearl.

TONASKET_____

Great wilderness area for camping, hiking, fishing, and skiing. 16 miles below Canada.

OKANOGAN RIVER NATURAL FOODS CO-OP 🐑
21 W. 4th St. © 509-486-4188 ⊙ M-F 9-6 winter, 9-7 summer, Sat 9-5, Sun 9-4
· organic produce · freshly prepared food · deli · vegetarian friendly · take-out
📙 Take US Hwy 97 to Tonasket. Turn west (left from 97N, right from 97S) onto 4th St 1 block to store.

VANCOUVER_____

WILD OATS MARKET 🐑
8024 E. Mill Plain Blvd. © 360-695-8878 ⊙ Daily 8-9
· organic produce · freshly prepared food · deli · vegetarian friendly · chain · take-out
📙 **From I-5S**, take exit 7 onto I-205S about 9 miles to exit 28 (Mill Plain Blvd) toward Vancouver. Merge right onto Mill Plain about 1⅓ miles to store at corner Mill Plain & Garrison Rd in Garrison Square Mall. **From I-5N**, take exit 1C right onto Mill Plain about 3⅔ miles to store at corner Mill Plain & Garrison (in Garrison Square Mall).

Goldbeck's "EAT IT OR NOT"
FASCINATING & FAR-OUT FACTS ABOUT FOOD

TOP TEN U.S. PASTA MARKETS, BY CITY (POUNDS PER CAPITA)
Albany (287)
Boston (212)
New York (182)
Miami (131)
Minneapolis (92)
Denver (86)
Chicago (81)
Atlanta (77)
Seattle (76)
San Francisco (73)

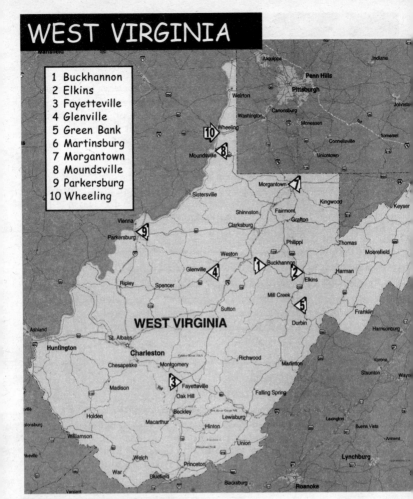

WEST VIRGINIA

1 Buckhannon
2 Elkins
3 Fayetteville
4 Glenville
5 Green Bank
6 Martinsburg
7 Morgantown
8 Moundsville
9 Parkersburg
10 Wheeling

BUCKHANNON

This small, friendly college town in the hills of West Virginia has a "micro-theatre" that features art films from all over the world.

MOLLY'S PANTRY 🍴   ♿

39 College Ave. ☏ 304-472-5099 ⊙ M-Sat 9-5
Combination food store and boutique.

🍴 **From I-79**, take exit 99 onto Rt 33E/119N about 12 miles to Buckhannon. Take Main St exit and turn right onto Main about ½ mile to traffic light at Kanawaha St (at courthouse). Turn right onto Kanawaha about ⅔ mile to light at College Ave (McDonald's). Turn left onto College 2 blocks to store on right corner College & Florida St (rainbow striped awning).

ELKINS

GOOD ENERGY FOODS 🍴

214 Third St. ☏ 304-636-5169 ⊙ M-Th, Sat 9-6, F 9-7

🍴 Elkins is about 37 miles east of I-79 exit 99. **From Rt 33E**, turn right onto Railroad Ave 4 blocks to 3rd St. Turn left onto 3rd 2½ blocks to store on right.

FAYETTEVILLE

Fayetteville attractions include the New River Gorge, Gauley River rafting, and the longest arch bridge in the world.

HEALTH HARVEST
309 N. Court St. © 304-574-1788 ☺ Daily 10-7 Memorial Day-mid Oct (call for winter hours)

· organic produce

From I-64/I-77 (WV Tpke), take exit 60 toward WV 612/Mossy/Oak Hill onto 612 (left from 64E/77S, right from 64W/77N) about 8 miles to US 19N. Turn left onto 19N about 8½ miles to Rt 16/Court St. Turn right onto Court to 2nd traffic light. Store is on corner.

GLENVILLE

COUNTRY LIFE
211 N. Lewis St. © 304-462-8157 ☺ M, W-Th 10-6, F 10-3

From I-79, take exit 79 (Burnsville) west on Rt 5 (left from 79N, right from 79S) about 15 winding miles to Glenville. Turn left at "T" onto WV 33W about ¾ mile to store on right.

GREEN BANK

Surrounded by the Monongahela National Forest. A destination iitself, not a place you'll just be passing through.

SWEET THYME INN ✕
Route 92/28 © 304-456-5535 ☺ Call for hours
A place to stay the night (or several). Organic vegan family-stye breakfast, boxed lunches and dinner. Rooms feature chemical-free, unbleached cotton linens and only chemical-free products are used in cleaning. Non-guests are welcome at dinner, but if the inn is empty, meals aren't served.

· vegan · organic focus · tables · self-service · wait staff

Green Bank is about 50 miles south of Elkins and about 55 miles north of White Sulphur Springs. **From north on US 250S,** merge onto SR 92/28 about 8 miles to Green Bank. Watch for Inn sign on right just before BP station. **From south on SR 92N,** watch for Inn sign on left (just past BP).

MARTINSBURG

HEALTHWAY NATURAL FOODS
740 Foxcroft Ave. © 304-263-7728 ☺ M-Th 10-7, F 10-8, Sat 10-6, Sun 12-5

· organic produce · chain

From I-81N, take exit 12 towards Martinsburg right onto Winchester Ave/WV 45 to 1st left at Foxcroft Ave. Turn left onto Foxcroft ½ mile to Martinsburg Circle. Turn left onto Martinsburg ¼ mile to store. **From I-81S,** take exit 13 toward Downtown left onto King St almost ⅓ mile to Foxcroft. Turn right onto Foxcroft almost ¾ mile to store.

MORGANTOWN

MAXWELL'S ✖

1 Wall St. © 304-929-0982 ⊘ M-Th 11-8:45, F-Sat 11-9:45, Sun 11-2

The all-hours menu offers salads, soups (always a vegetarian choice), vegetarian appetizers, sandwiches (on whole grain bread,) and Maxwell's own vegetarian Beantown and Mushroom Burgers. At dinner there are also stir-fry, curry and creole dishes, made with tofu, shrimp or chicken. Thursday is pasta night.

· vegetarian friendly · vegan friendly · alcohol · tables · wait staff

🛏 **From I-68W**, take exit 7 toward Airport right onto Rt 857S 1 mile to US 119. Turn left onto 119 3 miles to High St. Turn left onto High 3 blocks to Wall St. Turn right onto Wall past University Ave to restaurant (behind International Outdoors). **From I-68E**, take exit 1 toward Downtown/University Ave left onto 119 (becomes US 19/University Ave) about 4 miles to Wall. Turn left onto Wall to restaurant. **From I-79N**, take exit 148 onto I-68E and follow directions above. **From I-79S**, take exit 152 left onto 19N 2 miles. After crossing river, turn left (continuing on 19) 3 blocks to Wall. Turn left onto Wall to restaurant.

MOUNTAIN PEOPLE'S CO-OP ✖ 🌱

1400 University Ave. © 304-291-6131 ⊘ M-F 9-8, Sat 9-6, Sun 10-6, Restaurant M-Tues, Fri 8-6, W-Th 8-8, Sun 10-2

The Co-op runs a vegetarian restaurant with ample choices for vegans. The store is a "hub of Morgantown's alternative community."

· organic produce · freshly prepared food · café · vegetarian · vegan friendly · co-op · tables · self-service · take-out

🛏 **From I-68W**, take exit 7 toward Airport right onto Rt 857S 1 mile to US 119. Turn left onto 119 3 miles to Willey St. Go straight onto Willey a few blocks to end at University Ave. Turn left onto University to store. **From I-68E**, take exit 1 toward Downtown/University Ave left onto 119 (becomes US 19/University Ave) about 4 miles to store. **From I-79N**, merge onto I-68E and follow directions above. **From I-79S**, take exit 155 toward WV 7/WV University left onto Osage Rd about 2/3 mile and continue around to right on US 19 (across water) about 3 1/3 miles to store.

MOUNDSVILLE

Moundsville is about 10 miles south of Wheeling, just over the Ohio border. About 8 miles east of town is the Palace of Gold, a popular tourist attraction, with a lovely lake walk, peacocks, gardens, and an extravagant Krishna temple.

YAMUNA'S NATURAL FOODS 🌱

RD 1 Box 292 © 304-843-4811 ⊘ Tues-Sun 1:30-5:30

Near the Palace of Gold.

· freshly prepared food · take-out

🛏 **From I-70W**, take exit 5A on left onto I-470W to exit 2 (Bethlehem). Turn left off exit ramp onto E Bethlehem Blvd about 1/4 mile to WV 88. Turn right onto 88 about 8 miles to end at US 250. Turn left onto 250 1 1/2 miles to Palace Rd (aka Limestone Rd, look for Palace of Gold sign). Turn left onto Palace 4 1/2 miles (past Palace of Gold) to store in Palace Lodge building. **From I-70E**, take exit 219 onto I-470E about 8 2/3 miles (across river) to exit 2 toward Bethlehem and follow directions above.

PARKERSBURG

MOTHER EARTH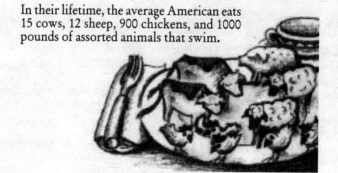
1638 19th St. ✆ 304-428-1024 ⊙ M-Sat 9-7
· organic produce

🍎 **From I-77**, take exit 176 toward 7th St/Downtown onto Rt 50W (right from 77S, left from 77N) about 2⅓ miles to Plum St. Turn right onto Plum about ½ mile to store at corner Plum & 19th St.

WHEELING

HEALTH NUTS
1908 Market St. ✆ 304-232-0105 ⊙ M-Sat 10:30-6:30

🍎 **From I-70E**, take exit 1A right onto US 40E/Main St about ½ mile to 16th St. Turn right onto 16th and immediately right onto State St 1 block to Market St. Turn right onto Market to store at north end of Center Market. **From I-70W**, take exit 5A onto I-470W about 3 miles to exit 1 (US 250N). Merge right onto 250N about 1 mile to WV 2N/18th St exit. Turn left onto 17th St and follow around to left onto Chapline St to Market. Turn right onto Market to store at north end of Center Market.

WISCONSIN

1 Ashland	12 New Richmond
2 Cumberland	13 Oshkosh
3 East Troy	14 Rice Lake
4 Gays Mills	15 Richland Center
5 Green Bay	16 River Falls
6 La Crosse	17 Spring Green
7 Luck	18 Steven's Point
8 Madison	19 Viola
9 Menomonie	20 Viroqua
10 Milwaukee	21 Wauwatosa
11 Mt. Horeb	22 Wisconsin Dells

ASHLAND

On the shores of Lake Superior, with 12 miles of national shoreline and the 21 Apostle Islands. Pristine stretches of sandy beach, sea caves, old-growth forests, bald eagles, black bears, and the most lighthouses in the National Park System.

BLACK CAT COFFEE HOUSE ✕

211 Chapple Ave. ✆ 715-682-3680 ⏰ M-F 7am-10pm, Sat 8am-10pm, Sun 8-4 (summer only)

Vegetarian sandwiches, salads, pizza, nachos, and such, using organic and local ingredients when possible. There are also used books for sale, a children's playroom and open air seating in summer.

· vegetarian · organic focus · alcohol · tables · self-service

🚗 Take US Hwy 2 to Ashland and go south on Chapple Ave 1½ blocks to restaurant on left between Main & 3rd St.

CHEQUAMEGON FOOD CO-OP

215 Chapple Ave. ✆ 715-682-8251 ⏰ M-Sat 9-8

· organic produce · freshly prepared food · vegetarian friendly · co-op · take-out

🚗 Take US Hwy 2 to Ashland and go south on Chapple Ave 1½ blocks to store on left between Main & 3rd St.

CUMBERLAND

ISLAND CITY FOOD CO-OP & CITY BAKERY ✕

1490 2nd Ave. ✆ 715-822-8233 ⏰ Store M-F 9-5:30, Sun 9-3, Bakery M-W 9-5:30, Th-Sat 7-5:30 (opens 8 am in winter)

The coffee shop serves organic coffee, along with freshly made baked goods.

· organic produce · café · bakery · co-op · tables · self-service · wait staff · take-out

🛏 **From junction US 63 & WI 48,** go north on Main St 4 blocks to store on corner Main & Water St (across from bank).

EAST TROY

NOKOMIS FARMS 🍃
W. 2463 County Trunk ES ℂ 262-642-9665 ⏲ M, W-F 10-6, Tues 10-8, Sat 9-5, Sun 10-5
An all organic market and bakery.

· organic produce · bakery · co-op

🛏 **From I-43,** take exit 38 toward East Troy onto WI 20W (right from 43S, left from 43N) to 1st traffic light at Main St (McDonald's). Turn left onto Main (aka CR-ES) almost 1 mile (through town to high school and Milkies Shopping Plaza on right and field on left). Store is on left just past field.

GAYS MILLS

Southwest Wisconsin, along the Kickapoo river. "A beautiful ridge and valley setting," according to Laura at the Co-op.

KICKAPOO EXCHANGE FOOD CO-OP 🍃
209 Main St. ℂ 608-735-4544 ⏲ M-F 11-6, Sat 9-6
Store hosts regular cultural events, including music, dance and films.

· organic produce · co-op

🛏 At intersection WI 131 & WI 171. **From US 61,** about 7 miles south on 131. **From WI 35,** 13 miles east on 171.

GREEN BAY

KAVERNA ✗
112 S. Broadway ℂ 920-430-3200 ⏲ M-Th 9am-11pm, F-Sat 11am-midnight, Sun 1-6 (kitchen stops 1 hour before closing time)
A casual place serving vegetarian soups, sandwiches, wraps, pasta, and such. Live music Friday nights.

· vegetarian · vegan friendly · alcohol · tables · self-service

🛏 **From I-43N,** take exit 180 onto WI 172W almost 4 miles to Webster Ave exit toward WI 57/Riverside Dr. Turn right onto 57N (Riverside, becomes Monroe Ave) 3 miles to E Walnut St. Turn left onto Walnut almost 2/3 mile (across river) to Broadway. Turn left onto Broadway to restaurant. **From I-43S,** take exit 189 right onto Atkinson Dr less than ½ mile to US 141S. Turn left onto 141S 1 mile to Broadway. Turn right onto Broadway over ½ mile to restauarant.

LA CROSSE

PEOPLE'S FOOD CO-OP 🍃
315 5th Ave. S. ℂ 608-784-5798 ⏲ M-F 7-8, Sat 7-7, Sun 8-6

· organic produce · deli · bakery · vegetarian friendly · co-op · take-out

🛏 **From I-90,** take exit 3 toward La Crosse (3A from 90E) onto US 53S over 4 miles to Main St. Turn left onto Main 2 blocks to 5th Ave. Turn right onto 5th to store on left.

LUCK

NATURAL ALTERNATIVES FOOD CO-OP 🐄
241 Main St. ℰ 715-472-8084 ☉ M-W 9-5, Th-F 9-6, Sat 9-4
· organic produce · co-op
🗂 Luck is 37 miles west of Hwy 53 exit 143 (Rice Lake) on Rt 48. **From Rt 48,** turn south onto Main St to store on right.

MADISON

MAGIC MILL NATURAL FOOD MARKET ✕🐄
2862 University Ave. ℰ 608-238-2630 ☉ M-F 8-9, Sat-Sun 9-8
· organic produce · freshly prepared food · juice bar · deli · vegetarian · counter · tables · self-service · take-out
🗂 **From I-90/94,** take exit 142A toward Madison onto US 12/18W 9 miles to exit 258 (Midvale Blvd/Verona Rd). Turn right onto Midvale more than 2½ miles to University Ave. Turn right onto University to store on left in University Station.

MIFFLIN STREET COMMUNITY CO-OP 🐄
32 N. Bassett St. ℰ 608-251-5899 ☉ M-F 10-9, Sat-Sun 10-8
· organic produce · co-op
🗂 **From I-90S/94E,** take exit 135A onto US 151S/E Washington St about 6 miles to N Webster St. Turn right onto Webster 2 blocks to E Dayton St. Turn left onto Dayton 4 blocks to N Fairchild St. Turn left onto Fairchild 1 block to W Mifflin St. Turn right onto Mifflin 3 blocks to N Bassett St. Turn left onto Bassett to store. **From I-39N/I-90W,** take exit 142A onto US12/18W about 5 miles to John Nolen Dr (exit 263). Take John Nolen 2 miles to S Broom St. Turn left onto Broom about ⅓ mile to W Mifflin St. Turn left onto Mifflin 1 block to N Basset. Turn left onto Bassett to store.

PEACEMEAL VEGETARIAN RESTAURANT ✕   ♿
115 State St. ℰ 608-294-0380 ☉ Daily 11-9 (open Sat 9am in summer)
Collectively owned and operated, completely vegetarian, and vegan an option on all items. Buys as much produce as possible from local community supported agriculture farms.
· vegetarian · vegan friendly · organic focus · alcohol · counter · tables · wait staff
🗂 **From I-90/94,** take exit 135 (A from 90S/94E, B from 90N/94W) toward Madison onto US 151S/E Washington St about 6 miles to capitol building. State St is on west side of Capitol Square and restaurant is on 1st block.

WHOLE FOODS MARKET ✕🐄   ♿
3313 University Ave. ℰ 608-233-9566 ☉ Daily 8-9
· organic produce · freshly prepared food · juice bar · salad bar · café · deli · bakery · vegetarian friendly · chain · counter · tables · self-service · take-out
🗂 **From I-90/94,** take exit 142A toward Madison onto US 12/18W 9 miles to exit 258 (Midvale Blvd/Verona Rd). Turn right onto Midvale more than 2½ miles to University Ave. Turn right onto University to store on right.

WILLY STREET CO-OP ✕🐄
1221 Williamson St. ℰ 608-251-6776 ☉ Daily 8-9
· organic produce · freshly prepared food · juice bar · salad bar · deli · vegetarian friendly · co-op · tables · self-service · take-out
🗂 **From I-90S/94E,** take exit 135A toward Madison onto US 151S/E Washington St about 6 miles to Baldwin St. Turn left onto Baldwin 3

blocks to Williamson. Turn right onto Williamson to store before next corner (Few St). **From I-39N/90W**, take exit 138B on left toward Madison onto WI 30W 3 miles to US 151S/E Washington. Merge onto Washington 2 miles to Baldwin and follow directions above from Baldwin.

MENOMONIE

MENOMONIE MARKET FOOD CO-OP 🍲

521 E. 2nd St. ☎ 715-235-6533 ⏰ M-F 9-7, Sat 9-5, Sun 12-5
Many locally produced items, including breads, honey, maple syrup, meats, eggs, and (organic) produce.

· organic produce · deli · co-op · take-out

🍎 **From I-94**, take exit 41 south on WI 25 (left from 94W, right from 94S) about 2 miles to WI 12/29 (on south side of Lake Menomonie). Turn left onto 12/29 1 block to store at corner 12/29 & 2nd St.

MILWAUKEE

BEANS & BARLEY 🍴🍲   ♿

1901 E. North Ave. ☎ 414-278-0234 ⏰ M-Sat 9-9, Sun 9-8
· freshly prepared food · juice bar · café · deli · bakery · vegetarian · alcohol · counter · tables · wait staff · take-out

🍎 **From I-43S**, take exit 73C onto N 8th St to North Ave. Turn left onto North almost 2 miles to store on right just past Oakland Ave. **From I-43N**, take exit 310C onto I-794E about 1 mile to exit IF on left to Lincoln Mem Dr. Take Lincoln Mem almost 1½ miles to Lafayette Hill Rd. Turn left onto Lafayette to end at E Lafayette Pl. Turn left onto Lafayette Pl to 2nd right (N Prospect Ave). Turn right onto Prospect ⅓ mile to North Ave. Turn left onto North to store on left. **From I-94E**, merge onto I-43N and follow directions above.

BOMBAY SWEETS 🍴

3401 S. 13th St. ☎ 414-383-3553 ⏰ Daily 10-10
A no-frills vegetarian Indian eatery.

· vegetarian · vegan friendly · tables · self-service · take-out

🍎 **From I-43S**, take exit 314A right onto W Holt Ave (becomes Morgan Ave) ½ mile to S 13th St. Turn right onto 13th to restaurant on left. **From I-43N**, take exit 314A-B left onto Howard Ave ¾ mile to 13th. Turn right onto 13th almost ⅔ mile (past Holt) to restaurant on left. **From I-94E**, merge onto I-43S and follow directions above from 43S.

CARINI'S LA CONCA D'ORO 🍴   ♿

3468 N. Oakland Ave. ☎ 414-963-9623 ⏰ Vegetarian buffet Tues-F 11-2
Typical Italian restaurant with a weekday vegetarian lunch buffet.

· vegetarian friendly · alcohol · tables · self-service · wait staff · take-out

🍎 **From I-43S**, take exit 76A-B toward Capitol Dr onto Green Bay Ave to Capitol. Turn left onto Capitol (WI 190E) about 1¼ miles to Oakland Ave. Turn right onto Oakland about ½ mile to restaurant on left just past Edgewood Ave. **From I-43N**, take exit 76A directly onto Capitol and follow directions above. **From I-94E**, take exit 310B on left toward Green Bay onto I-43N and follow directions above.

Please tell these businesses that you found them in Healthy Highways.

OUTPOST NATURAL FOODS ✗🍴 ♿
100 E. Capitol Drive © 414-961-2597 ⊙ Daily 8-9
· organic produce · freshly prepared food · juice bar · salad bar · café · deli · bakery
· vegetarian friendly · co-op · counter · tables · self-service · take-out

🍎 **From I-43S**, take exit 76A-B toward Capitol Dr onto Green Bay Ave to Capitol. Turn left onto Capitol (WI 190E) about 3 blocks to store on left in River Glen Market Plaza. **From I-43N**, take exit 76A directly onto Capitol and follow directions above. **From I-94E**, take exit 310B on left toward Green Bay onto I-43N and follow directions above.

MT. HOREB

For mustard-lovers, there's the Mt. Horeb Mustard Museum, with more than 3,400 different mustards from all over the world.

TRILLIUM NATURAL FOODS COMMUNITY CO-OP 🍴
517 Springdale St. © 608-437-5288 ⊙ M-W, F 10-6, Th 10-8, Sat 10-4, Sun 10-2
· organic produce · co-op

🍎 Take US 18/151 or WI 78 to Mt Horeb. Store is ½ block west of Hwy 78/92 traffic light on the "trollway" (next to Yapp's Antiques).

NEW RICHMOND

NATURE'S PANTRY CO-OP 🍴
258 S. Knowles St. © 715-246-6105 ⊙ M-F 9-5, Sat 9-1
· co-op

🍎 **From I-94**, take exit 10 toward New Richmond onto WI 65N (right from 94W, left from 94E) about 2 miles (through town of Roberts) to US 12. Turn right onto WI 12/65N 1 mile, than left back onto 65N almost 9 miles to New Richmond. Store is at 2nd intersection on right corner S Knowles & 3rd St.

OSHKOSH

VILLAGE MARKET 🍴
463 N. Main St. © 920-426-1280 ⊙ M-F 9-6, Sat 9-5
· organic produce

🍎 **From Hwy 41S**, take exit 124 south on US 45/Jackson St about 5¼ miles to Church Ave. Turn left onto Church about ⅓ mile to N Main St. Turn right onto Main to store. **From Hwy 41N**, take exit 117 east (right) on 9th Ave about 2 miles to S Main. Turn left onto Main about ½ mile to store.

RICE LAKE

MAIN STREET MARKET WHOLE FOODS COOPERATIVE ✗🍴
1 S. Main St. © 715-234-7045 ⊙ M-W, F-Sat 10-5:30, Th 10-7
Small deli specializes in simple vegan fare.
· organic produce · freshly prepared food · deli · vegan · co-op · tables · self-service · take-out

🍎 **From Hwy 53**, take exit 143 toward Rice Lake onto Hwy 48E/W Knapp St (right from 53N, left from 53S) about 1⅓ miles to Main St. Turn right onto Main ½ mile (2 traffic lights) to store at corner Main & Messenger St.

RICHLAND CENTER

PINE RIVER FOOD CO-OP 🍴
134 W. Court St. © 608-647-7299 ⊙ M-F 9-6, Sat 10-2
· co-op

🍎 Take US 14 to Richland Center (about 50 miles west of Madison) where 14 and WI 80 merge and become Main St. **From 14/80 intersection**, go west on Main about ½ mile to Court St. Turn left onto Court 1 block to store.

RIVER FALLS

WHOLE EARTH GROCERY 🍠
126 S. Main St. ℂ 715-425-7971 ⊙ M-F 9-7, Sat-Sun 10-6
· organic produce
🍎 **From I-94**, take exit 10 toward River Falls onto WI 65S (left from 94W, right from 94E) almost 8 miles onto N Main St. Continue on Main almost 1½ miles to store in town on right.

SPRING GREEN

In the area you'll find Frank Lloyd Wright's Taliesin, the Wisconsin River and, in-season, the American Players outdoor Shakespeare theater.

SPRING GREEN GENERAL STORE ✗ 🍠   ♿
137 S. Albany St. ℂ 608-588-7070 ⊙ M-F 9-6 (continental breakfast 9-11, lunch 11-5:30), Sat 8-6, Sun 8-4 (full breakfast 8-12, lunch 11:30-5:30)
Order at the counter from the mostly vegetarian menu of soups, salads, sandwiches and daily specials, and the food will be delivered to your table. While waiting, browse through the store, which along with food, sells women's apparel, jewelry, cards, candles, CDs, toys, and other gift items. Or, explore the old books in the basement or just relax on the front porch.
· freshly prepared food · café · deli · vegetarian friendly · tables · self-service · take-out
🍎 **From US 14**, take WI 23S about ½ mile into Spring Green. Turn left onto Jefferson St 1 block to Albany St. Turn left onto Albany to store in big blue building next to railroad tracks.

STEVEN'S POINT

STEVEN'S POINT AREA FOOD CO-OP 🍠
633 2nd St. ℂ 715-341-1555 ⊙ M, W-F 9-8 Tues 9-7, Sat 9-5, Sun 9-4
· organic produce · freshly prepared food · deli · bakery · vegetarian friendly · co-op · take-out
🍎 **From I-39**, take exit 161 toward Stevens Point onto US 51Bus about 1 mile to 4th Ave (3rd traffic light). Turn right onto 4th ½ mile to 2nd St. Turn right onto 2nd to store on right.

VIOLA

VIOLA NATURAL FOODS CO-OP 🍠
110 Commercial St. ℂ 608-627-1476 ⊙ M, Sat 12-4, Tues, Th 2-6, F 10-6
· co-op
🍎 **From US 14**, take WI 131 north (right from 14W, left from 14E) about 7 miles into Viola. Store is on 131 (aka Commercial St) on right.

VIROQUA

VIROQUA FOOD CO-OP 🍠
303 N. Center Ave. ℂ 608-637-7511 ⊙ M-Sat 8-8, Sun 11-5
· co-op
🍎 Viroqua is about 32 miles east of La Crosse on US 14. **From US 14**, turn east onto WI 56 (left from 14E, right from 14W) 1 block to Center Ave. Turn left onto Center 1 block to store (behind Nelson's Agri Center).

WAUWATOSA

This Milwaukee suburb is home to the Milwaukee Brewers baseball team. Hikers and basketball players will enjoy Hart Park, while in the heart of the village there are locally owned shops to browse.

MILK'N HONEY 🌶

10948 W. Capitol Dr. © 414-535-0203 ⊙ M-F 10-7, Sat 9-4, Sun 10-5

· organic produce · deli · take-out

🍎 **From I-94**, merge onto US 45N (exit 305B from 94E, 305A from 94W) about 5 miles to exit 44 (WI 190E/Capitol Dr E). Turn right onto W Capitol 3 blocks to store on left at Capitol & Mayfair Rd.

OUTPOST NATURAL FOODS CO-OP ✗ 🌶   ⅄

7000 W. State St. © 414-778-2012 ⊙ Daily 8-9

· organic produce · freshly prepared food · juice bar · salad bar · café · deli · bakery
· vegetarian friendly · co-op · tables · self-service · take-out

🍎 **From I-94**, take exit 307A toward 68th St/70th St. Follow exit to S 68th and turn north (left from 94E, right from 94W) about 1 mile to W State St. Turn left onto State 1 block to store on corner State & 70th St.

WISCONSIN DELLS

Wisconsin Dells is a "year-round playground," with skiing, indoor/outdoor water parks, camping, lakes, water-skiing, and a Native American-owned casino.

THE CHEESE FACTORY RESTAURANT ✗   ⅄

521 Wisconsin Dells Pkwy. © 608-253-6065 ⊙ M, W-Sun 9-9 summer, call for winter hours

A wide selection of international vegetarian dishes, with many vegan options. The soda fountain, decadent desserts and cappuccino bar are enticing but not health-oriented. Kids and motorcoaches welcome.

· vegetarian · vegan friendly · tables · wait staff

🍎 **From I-90/94**, take exit 92 north on US 12 (left from 90S/94E, right from 90N/94W) about 1 mile to restaurant on right.

THE SECRET GARDEN CAFE ✗   ⅄

910 River Rd. © 608-254-4724 ⊙ Summer (May 31-Sept 30) M, W-F 9-9, Sat-Sun 8-9, Winter F 11-9, Sat 8:30-9, Sun 8:30-2

Interesting "faux" meat and classic vegetarian dishes served in a century old mansion that also is home to the (vegetarian) White Rose Bed & Breakfast.

· vegetarian · vegan friendly · organic focus · kosher · tables · wait staff · take-out

🍎 **From I-90/94**, take exit 87 onto WI 131E about 1½ miles to River Rd (4th traffic light). Turn left onto River Rd 1 block to restaurant on right at corner River & Wisconsin Ave (in White Rose B&B).

Goldbeck's "EAT IT OR NOT"

FASCINATING & FAR-OUT FACTS ABOUT FOOD

Which packs more vitamins, a red pepper or a green pepper?

Answer: A red pepper has nine times more carotene, an important antioxidant, and twice the vitamin C of a green pepper.

WYOMING

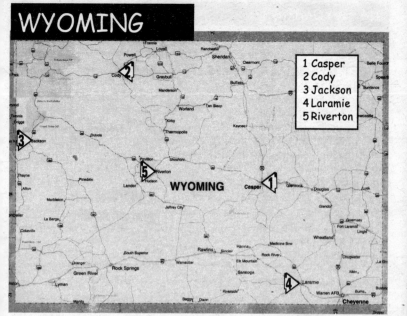

1 Casper
2 Cody
3 Jackson
4 Laramie
5 Riverton

WYOMING

CASPER

ALPENGLOW NATURAL FOODS 🍎
109 E. 2nd St. © 307-234-4196 ⊙ M-F 9:30-6, Sat 9:30-5
· organic produce
🍎 **From I-25**, take exit 188A south on N Center St (right from 25S, left from 25N) ½ mile to E 2nd St. Turn left onto 2nd to store.

CODY

Home of the Buffalo Bill Historical Center.

MOUNTAIN HIGH HEALTH FOODS 🍎   ♿
1914 17th St. © 307-587-1700 ⊙ M-Sat 9:30-6
🍎 Take US 14/16/20 into Cody. Store is in shopping area "on top of hill."

WHOLE FOODS TRADING COMPANY 🍎
1239 Rumsey Ave. © 307-587-3213 ⊙ M-Sat 9:30-5:50
🍎 **From US 14 east**, take Sheridan Ave (aka 14) to 12th St. Turn left onto 12th 1 block to Rumsey Ave. Turn right onto Rumsey to store between 12th & 13th St. **From US 14 west,** turn left onto Sheridan to 13th. Turn right onto 13th 1 block to Rumsey. Turn left onto Rumsey to store between 13th & 12th.

JACKSON

On the way to Grand Teton and Yellowstone National Park.

HARVEST NATURAL FOODS ✕🍎
130 W. Broadway © 307-733-5418 ⊙ Daily 8-6 winter, 7-8 summer
An impressive menu of organic breakfast and lunch items. Vegetarian, vegan, free-range turkey and line-caught tuna. Plus, an organic "European" bakery.
· organic produce · freshly prepared food · juice bar · salad bar · café · deli · bakery
· vegetarian friendly · vegan friendly · organic focus · counter · tables · self-service · take-out
🍎 Take US 189 or 89 into Jackson where they become Broadway. Store is 1½ blocks from town square on right.

LARAMIE

SWEET MELISSA VEGETARIAN CAFE ✗

213 S. 1st St. ℂ 307-742-9607 ☺ M-Sat 11-9

Soups, sandwiches, meat-free burgers and dogs, salads, and such hot entrees as lentil loaf, quiche, lasagna, and portobello favorites.

· vegetarian · vegan friendly · tables · wait staff

From I-80, take exit 313 (US 287/3rd St) toward Ft Collins, CO left to 3rd St. Turn right onto 3rd less than 1 mile to E Grand Ave. Turn left onto Grand 2 blocks to S 1st St. Turn right onto 1st to restaurant.

WHOLE EARTH GRAINERY

111 E. Ivinson Ave. ℂ 307-745-4268 ☺ Tues-Sat 11-6

From I-80, take exit 313 (US 287/3rd St) toward Ft Collins, CO left to 3rd St. Turn right onto 3rd about 1 mile to Ivinson Ave. Turn left onto Ivinson to store on right.

RIVERTON

WIND RIVER MERCANTILE

223 E. Main St. ℂ 307-856-0862 ☺ M-Sat 10-5:30

· organic produce

From US 26/Rte 789 intersection, go west on E Main St less than ½ mile to store just past 3rd St.

Goldbeck's "EAT IT OR NOT"
FASCINATING & FAR-OUT FACTS ABOUT FOOD

THERE WERE ORIGINALLY OVER **7,000 VARIETIES** OF APPLES. TODAY YOU'RE LUCKY TO FIND 6 VARIETIES IN THE SUPERMARKET.

EATING ON AND OFF THE HEALTHY HIGHWAY

As the *Healthy Highways* listings reveal, there are many food establishments that strive to serve healthy fare. However, no matter where you eat, it takes attention to maintain good eating habits when you aren't in charge. There is no question that is it much easier to have a better meal or snack when choosing *Healthy Highways* locations, since they provide greater choice and better and more varied ingredients. But even these establishments may serve some items you wish to forgo, such as processed grains, refined sugars, hydrogenated fats, animal products, and the like.

We want to emphasize the idea of *better and more varied ingredients*. Much is made of the benefits of avoiding "fast food," but little is said about the potential gains from eating in more health conscious places. A good diet is not about what you don't eat, but what you do. Great variety is always the key to healthful eating, as it increases your chances of obtaining a full range of nutrients.

Fast food restaurants are mostly based on just a small pool of ingredients—beef, chicken, cheese, eggs, potatoes, white bread, iceberg lettuce, tomatoes. Conversely, health-oriented eateries focus on a wide range of produce, grains of all kinds (usually in the whole form), non-animal proteins like soy products and beans, and offer more choices of fish and meat (i.e. turkey, lamb or perhaps bison). Many also incorporate local and organic ingredients.

Nonetheless, in any eating place, there can be pitfalls. If you go for the bread and butter (or olive oil), eat rich sauces and fried food, drown your salad in dressing, drink excessively (whether it's real juice, soda or a sweetened hot beverage), or indulge in dessert (always a temptation), your diet may be higher in calories, fat, sugar, and salt than you realize.

To assist you, here are some ways you can continue to enjoy the fun of dining out, without being done-in by dinner.

Dining Out Tactics

When looking for a place to eat, there are often too few or too many options. Sometimes it's easier to rationalize that one meal can't really have a big impact on our overall diet, so why make the effort to choose well. Perhaps this reasoning held up 20 years ago, when eating out was less popular. But this attitude is obviously not sensible in a society that gets more than one-third of its calories away from home.

You Are Where You Eat

To a large part, *where* you eat dictates *what* you eat. This, of course, is why we assembled *Healthy Highways* in the first place.

If there is no suitable listing in *Healthy Highways*, consult the yellow pages under "health food stores," "vegetarian" or look through the various "restaurants." Start by eliminating places that are unsuitable. Then scout around to find eating establishments that are in tune with your objectives. Another tactic is to ask locally where you might find a place with vegetarian options or real "homemade" food.

Be adventurous about trying other cuisines. Many cultures feature more vegetables and diverse ingredients than conventional American eateries. Indian, Thai, Chinese, Japanese, Ethiopian, Mexican, and Middle Eastern restaurants all present possibly healthful dining opportunities.

The Waiting Game

It's easy to consume a meal's worth of calories before your meal arrives. Do you order alcohol or a soft drink to tide you over while waiting in a restaurant, or use the bread and butter—or chips and salsa—to curb your hunger? Here are some ways you can cut down on "unintentional" eating.

- Eat a small healthy snack beforehand to keep you from becoming too hungry.
- Order mineral water or seltzer with a wedge of lemon to keep you occupied.
- Order salad right away.
- If no one at the table objects, ask to have the bread held until the food is served. Otherwise, place the breadbasket or chips out of your reach to avoid reflexive munching.

Mental Grazing

It's easy to be tempted by food you see being delivered to other tables or by the choices of your eating companions. Be confident in your decision.

Quit the "Clean-plate Club"

One of the biggest risks people who eat out face is enormous portion sizes. While a 3- to 4-ounce piece of meat or fish is sufficient for adequate protein, a 10- to 16-ounce serving is more typical restaurant fare. If you eat in places that serve large portions and lots of "free" extras, you may have to learn to hold back, share dishes with a companion or ask for a "doggie bag."

Consider wrapping up part before you dig in. If you are uncomfortable about asking for a take-home sack before the meal has even arrived, you can bring in your own container and set some food aside right away without drawing attention. If you are traveling with a cooler, it's easy to preserve leftovers for a second meal. Moreover, many motels and hotels have small refrigerators in the room, an option we always ask about on the road.

Sharing is Saving

It isn't unusual to order one dessert for the table. By extension, people are becoming increasingly comfortable sharing an entree and adding an extra salad or appetizer. Another way to cut down is to order an appetizer or soup plus salad, instead of a full dinner. The outcome of these strategies is both a healthier bank account and body.

Have It Your Way

How many times have you ordered a seemingly healthy dish, only to be surprised by what actually arrives at the table? If a menu item is unfamiliar, inquire about how it is prepared to make sure it suits your needs and taste. Ask about seasoning, sauces, if the soup is made with animal broth, and such. If anyone gives you a hard time or you feel embarrassed, just say you are on a "special diet." (You are!)

Insure your satisfaction by making reasonable requests beforehand. If they agree, you have the right to expect your request to be honored. If you are brought something other than what you ordered, be polite—but send it back.

Here are some ordering options:

- Order vegetables with care so they don't arrive swimming in a pool of butter or sauce. You can always season them with a splash of vinegar or lemon and pepper.
- Whenever appropriate, get the sauce or gravy on the side.
- When you order your salad ask for dressing on the side. Better still, request some oil and vinegar or a wedge of lemon in order to moderate the amount of fat and salt.
- Specify that your toast be brought dry. That way you can control the amount of butter that goes on it.
- Ask to substitute a baked potato, salad or other vegetable for chips, fries, white rice or pasta.
- Load up sandwiches with healthy extras like lettuce, tomato, cucumber slices, fresh pepper strips, mushrooms, and such, (And don't forget the vegetable toppings on pizza.)
- When ordering something broiled, specify no (or light on) added fat.
- If you like something on the menu that is fried, ask if it can be broiled instead.
- Always ask if there is whole wheat bread or brown rice.

The Portable Pantry

When embarking on a trip that allows for a little extra luggage (perhaps as little as a purse, briefcase or backpack), it's a good idea to pack a few staples that can greatly improve your away-from-home meals. By adding a cooler, you can extend the selection. And don't forget to include a few utensils—knife, spoon, fork, reusable mug—plus napkins or paper towels, plastic bags and twisters.

Here are some favorites:

- Bottled water
- Juice
- Cheese
- Cottage Cheese
- Yogurt
- Nuts
- Nut butters
- Hummus
- Whole grain crackers

- Whole grain bread
- Cut-up vegetables
- Fruit
- Honey/Maple Syrup
- Mustard, hot sauce, soy sauce, and other favorite condiments

Savvy Snacks

There is nothing inherently wrong with snacking. As a matter of fact, eating small meals interspersed with snacks over the course of a day is an excellent way to keep your energy up and blood sugar levels more uniform.

If you think about typical snacks, you will probably conjure up foods high in sugar, fat and/or salt. This is hardly surprising since thirty percent of the money spent on food advertising each year in the U.S. is for candy, gum, mints, nuts, chips and other salty snacks, crackers, cookies, baked goods, and soft drinks. Not only do these snack choices provide calories without any real sustenance, for carbohydrate-sensitive individuals they can trigger overeating. By choosing smarter snacks with the right balance of nutrients you can satisfy hunger and even boost your nutritional status.

- Always carry something healthy to munch on. (A traveling sister-in-law keeps her energy up by carrying soy nuts to sprinkle on salad or yogurt.)
- Most commercial trail mixes are high caloric. You can adapt them by "diluting" with a ready-to-eat whole grain cereal or create your own mix with the cereal, favorite nuts, seeds, and dried fruit.
- Bean dips like hummus are readily available. Cottage cheese is another good protein-rich snack.
- Buy vegetables along the way to use with dips instead of chips.
- Pack a box of whole grain crackers for snacks (or when restaurants have no whole grain alternative).
- Pick up bags of plain popcorn at natural foods stores rather than the "natural" chips, which are still packed with fat and calories (even many of the "baked" versions).
- Spread slices of apples or pears with natural peanut butter or other nut butters. Although nut butters are best refrigerated, they can be safely kept at room temperature for a week or two while traveling.
- A container of yogurt is a better choice than a fast food snack.

Portion Distortion

If you've bought a muffin lately, you may have noticed how they seem to be expanding. Once a typical muffin weighed about 2 ounces; nowadays muffins are simply huge, often weighing five to six ounces. Bagels have undergone a similar expansion. Since the U.S. government standard for a serving of breadstuff is one ounce, just one of these items can be the equivalent of five to six servings.

These additional government-defined serving sizes illustrate the disconnect between health recommendations and reality.

One serving: ½ cup cooked pasta (about 32 strands of spaghetti), 10 French fries, 15 grapes, ½ cup nuts (a small handful), four ounces wine (roughly half a teacup). Are they kidding!

The information below will help you to better assess what's on your plate. The number of servings listed next to each grouping is the recommended daily intake in the Dietary Guidelines for Americans. After the serving sizes are some visual aids (*in italics*).

<u>STANDARD SERVING SIZES</u>

BREADS/CEREALS/GRAINS
(6-11 servings daily)

1 serving = 1-ounce slice bread (*CD case*)
" 1 tortilla or 3-inch pancake (*compact disc*)
" ½ small muffin, English muffin or bagel
" ½ cup cooked cereal, rice, pasta (*cupcake liner*)
2 servings = 1 cup pasta (*half grapefruit*)

MEAT AND NONMEAT PROTEINS
(2-3 servings daily)

1 serving = 2 to 3 ounces meat, poultry (*cassette tape*)
" 2 to 3 ounces fish (*checkbook*)
" 1 cup cooked beans (*baseball*)
" 4 to 6 ounces tofu (*deck of cards*)
" 2 eggs
" ¼ cup roasted soybeans/soynuts (*2 ping pong balls*)
" ½ cup nuts or seeds (*modest handful*)
" 4 tablespoons nut butter(*2 ice cubes*)

MILK AND DAIRY PRODUCTS
(2-3 servings daily; 4 servings ages 9-18 or over 51)

1 serving = 1 cup milk or yogurt
" 1½ ounces hard cheese, chunk (*3 dominoes*)
" 1½ ounces hard cheese, slice (*computer disc*)

VEGETABLES
(2-5 servings daily, but more vegetables is always better)

1 serving = 1 cup raw leafy greens (*man's fist*)
" ½ cup vegetables, cooked or raw (*light bulb*)
" 1 medium potato (*computer mouse*)
" ¾ cup vegetable juice

FRUIT
(2-4 servings daily)

1 serving = 1 medium fruit (*tennis ball*)
" ½ cup cut-up fruit (*7 cotton balls*)
" ¼ cup dried fruit (*small egg*)
" ¾ cup fruit juice

SIX HEALTHY HIGHWAYS' "RULES FOR THE ROAD"

1. Choose different ethnic foods when possible. *Gained*: New foods, greater variety, new experiences.

2. Order vegetarian. Even if you aren't a vegetarian, seize every opportunity to eat like one. This will automatically improve your diet because meatless dining depends on beans, grains, vegetables, fruit, nuts, and seeds. *Gained*: More variety, more fiber, less saturated fat.

3. Go for salad and vegetables (but go light on dressing and sauce). There is no such thing as too many vegetables. *Gained*: Numerous vitamins, minerals, fiber, health-protecting phytochemicals.

4. Avoid unnecessary fats. Chefs are accustomed to using butter, oil and other fats when they cook, so don't add to this yourself. Be sparing with dressings, sauces, butter on bread (even the trendy olive oil.) Order foods poached or broiled instead of fried. *Gained*: Less fat, fewer calories.

5. Always ask if there is whole grain bread or brown rice. Even if there isn't, with enough requests they may start to stock it. *Gained*: More fiber, greater restaurant awareness.

6. Just desserts. Many of us find dessert hard to pass up. Even in health-oriented eateries, desserts are often calorie-laden. Look for lower fat options (sorbet, biscotti), something fruit-based (apple crisp, strawberry shortcake), or a treat with some nutritious ingredients (baked custard, rice pudding). If you can't resist something really indulgent, suggest sharing. *Lost*: Empty calories, fat and sugar.

Happy Trails,
Nikki & David

Better World Club: Environment-oriented automobile association. Roadside assistance for cars and bikes nationwide and in Canada and Puerto Rico. www.betterworldclub.com 866-304-7540 Discount Code: HYHY0312 (ad next page)

Disability Travel and Recreation Resources: www.makoa.org/travel.htm

State and Local Governments On The Net: All state, county and local town websites. www.statelocalgov.net/index.cfm

Recreation.gov: All kinds of information for travelers, from recreational activities to weather maps. www.recreation.gov/

Weather: Current weather or 5-day forecast for anywhere in the U.S. http://cirrus.sprl.umich.edu/wxnet

Road Closures: Information on road closures due to construction, weather, road conditions, traffic, etc. From the Federal Highway Administration. www.fhwa.dot.gov/trafficinfo/

Rail Travel: Information on railroad travel from the Association of Rail Travel in the US (RUTUS). www.ustraintravel.com 847-433-0731

Hostelling International-USA: Find hostels, educational programs and other travel advice. www.hiayh.org/localcouncils/councils1.htm 301-495-1240

"Green" Hotels Association: Find hotels with an environmental viewpoint. www.greenhotels.com 713-789-8889

Reserve America: Online camping reservations for federal, state and private campgrounds. www.reserveamerica.com

RV Travel: Information about RV campgrounds and more. www.allcampgrounds.com

National Recreation Reservations Service: Accommodations for federal campgrounds only. 877-444-6777

The National Park Service: www.nps.gov 202-208-6843
    Alaska 907-644-3510   Midwest 402-221-3471   Southeast 404-562-3100
    Northeast 215-597-7013   Capital Area 202-619-7222   Pacific West 510-817-1300
                Intermountain 303-969-2500

Traveling with Pets: Dog-friendly lodgings, restaurants, beaches, attractions, and more. www.dogfriendly.com 877-475-2275

National Public Radio: Find public radio stations for your trip. www.NPR.org

Rails-to-Trails Conservancy: National network of public recreational trails from former rail lines. www.railtrails.org 202-331-9696

Festival Fun: Online information about festivals and events throughout the US. www.fulltiming-america.com/festivals

Swimmer's Guide: International directory of full-size, year-round swimming pools open to the public. www.swimmersguide.com

Yoga Finder: Find a yoga class, retreat center or event. www.yogafinder.com

Conversation cafes: An ideal way for travelers to plug in to the local scene. www.Conversationcafe.org Hotline for Washington State only 206-781-5700.

ORGANIZATIONS OF INTEREST TO RESTAURANTS

Greening Ethnic Restaurants: Helps ethnic restaurants adopt environmental principals. www.thimmakka.org 510-655-5566

Green Restaurant Association: Encourages an ecologically sustainable restaurant industry and certifies restaurants that meet certain criteria in such areas as recycling, composting, energy and water efficiency and conservation, sustainable food, nontoxic cleaning practices, green construction, and more. www.dinegreen.com 858-452-7378

1-886101-09-4

CONTENTS:
- 275 recipes (with nutritional analysis) for every meal and in between
- Simple instructions for making YoChee
- Quick and easy recipes marked
- Creamy soups and sauces with little or NO fat
- OneLESS Egg recipes — YoChee is the natural egg extender
- Healthier (& tastier) versions of such favorites as pizza, quiche, wraps, lasagna, pesto, stuffed mushrooms, deviled eggs
- Appealing ideas for vegetables
- Rich desserts like brownies & cheese cake with less calories and fat
- Web community at www.YoChee.com

312 page illustrated paperback

HOW TO
Save Fat & Calories, Boost Calcium & Protein With Natural
YoChee® (Yogurt Cheese)

YoChee is the new name for the age-old food called yogurt cheese. YoChee can help you overcome today's most pressing dietary concerns — particularly those linked to calcium, fat and calories. Its rich taste makes it hard to believe that YoChee has zero fat and is low in calories. In fact, it has all the renowned health benefits of yogurt. But YoChee is even better than yogurt since it is spreadable, less tart and a more versatile cooking ingredient.

The Healthy Spread You Use Instead
You don't have to cook to get the benefits of YoChee. The smooth, creamy texture makes YoChee the perfect substitute for cream cheese, sour cream, mayonnaise, butter and margarine. With just 10 calories and no fat, you save 40-100 calories and 5-10 grams of fat per tablespoon by using YoChee instead.

If You Can Use a Spoon, You Can Make YoChee!
YoChee is made in minutes by spooning yogurt into a draining device.
Gravity does all the work. Fun for Kids too.

Deluxe YoChee Maker
This self-contained unit has a reservoir to hold the drained liquid and a lid to provide a clean, sealed environment. The durable stainless steel strainer is specially designed to promote quick and thorough draining. Holds about 1 quart yogurt to make 2 cups YoChee. Dishwasher safe.
Material: Plastic/Stainless steel
mesh size: 5x5x5"